The Medieval Records

of a

London City Church

(St. Mary at Hill)

A.D. 1420–1559.

edited by

Henry Littlehales

Parts I and II

EARLY ENGLISH TEXT SOCIETY

Original Series, 125 and 128

1904, 1905

Reprinted as one volume

KRAUS REPRINT
Millwood, N.Y.
1987

The paper in this book meets the guidelines for
permanence and durability of the Committee on
Production Guidelines for Book Longevity of the Council
on Library Resources.

Library of Congress Cataloging-in-Publication Data

St. Mary at Hill (Church : London, England)
   The medieval records of a London city church
(St. Mary at Hill) A.D. 1420-1559.

   (Early English Text Society. Original series ;
125, 128)
   Reprint. Originally published: London : Published
for the Early English Text Society by Kegan Paul,
Trench, Trübner, 1904-1905.
   Includes bibliographical references and index.
   1. St. Mary at Hill (Church : London, England)--
History--Sources. 2. London (England)--Church
history--Sources. 3. London (England)--History--
To 1500--Sources. I. Littlehales, Henry, 1859-
II. Title. III. Series: Early English Text Society
(Series). Original series 125, 128)
BX5195.L667S75   1987   283'.4212   87-21512
ISBN 0-527-00121-X

*Unaltered Reprint produced with the permission of the
Early English Text Society.*

KRAUS REPRINT

Manufactured in the U.S.A.

The Medieval Records
of a
London City Church.

Early English Text Society.
Original Series, No. 125.
1904

BERLIN: ASHER & CO., 13, UNTER DEN LINDEN.
NEW YORK: C. SCRIBNER & CO.; LEYPOLDT & HOLT.
PHILADELPHIA: J. B. LIPPINCOTT & CO.

The Medieval Records

of a

London City Church

(St. Mary at Hill)

A.D. 1420–1559.

TRANSCRIBED AND EDITED

With Facsimiles and an Introduction

BY

HENRY LITTLEHALES.

PART I

WITH FIVE FACSIMILES AND A TEMPORARY INTRODUCTORY NOTE.

LONDON:
PUBLISHED FOR THE EARLY ENGLISH TEXT SOCIETY
By KEGAN PAUL, TRENCH, TRÜBNER & CO., LIMITED,
DRYDEN HOUSE, 43, GERRARD STREET, SOHO, W.
1904.

"There was de*lyuer*cd also at the ende of this accompt, ij gret bokes ape*rtayn*ing to the seid Church. And in one of the saide bok*es* were co*n*tayned in, the Accompt*t*e*s* of nycolas Awsthorpe, Thomas Lvcas, Willi*am* Stewen, Edmonde Candishe and meny others."—St. Mary's Accounts, A.D. 1551-2.

"In the heart of the city . . . .
Daily the tides of life go ebbing and flowing . . . .
Thousands of aching brains, where theirs no longer are busy,
Thousands of toiling hands, where theirs have ceased from their labours.
        Longfellow's *Evangeline*.

Original Series, No. 125.

R. CLAY & SONS, LIMITED, LONDON AND BUNGAY.

To
Alderman Sir Reginald Hanson, Bart.,
M.A., LL.D., ETC.,

THE GENEROUS DONOR OF THE BUST

OF

Geoffrey Chaucer

TO THE GUILDHALL LIBRARY, LONDON,

THESE RECORDS

OF A CITY CHURCH

ARE INSCRIBED

BY

THE EDITOR AND MEMBERS

OF

THE EARLY ENGLISH TEXT SOCIETY.

I.
[WILLS.]

[*MS. B. is a book containing a series of copies and abstracts of documents, the collection of which was commenced in* 1486.]

[1] The Testament of Rose Wrytell.
[A.D. 1323, but from 1486 copy.]

In the name of God: Amen. on Saturday, in the feest of Saynt Barnabye thapostle, The yere of our lord god m^l ccc xxiij, and the xvj yere of the Reigne of Kyng Edward, the Son of Kyng Edward; I, Rose Wrytell, wydue, sumtyme the wyf of William ffayrstede, Clerk, make my testament of my tenementes & Rentes which I haue in the parissh of Saynt Mary atte hill of london in the fourme foloyng.

I gyve and bequethe to Robert hamond, Citezein and Corder of london, & to Margery his wyf, my Nece, the doughter of Piers atte lee of wrytell, all my tenement with thappurtenauntes which I haue & dwell in, in the said parissh, togider with all the vesselles & necessaryes beyng in the same tenement belongyng to bruyng, and also all my tenement with þappurtenauntes which I haue in the said parissh of the gyfte & feoffament of William of Sandwych, toward Billyngesgate of london, and xx d of yerely quyte Rent which I haue & yerely receyue of the tenement sumtyme Rauf a Beryes, Cordewaner, in the same parissh, To haue & to hold the forsaid ij tenementes with thappurtenauntes, togider with the said vesselles & necessaries, and also to receyue yerly the said xx d of quyte Rent to the forsaid Robert & Margery, & to the heires of their bodyes laufully begoten, hoolly, frely, & peasibly for euermore, Of the chief lordes of the fee by the seruice therof due & of right accustumed, And also yeldyng & paying therfore yerely vj marc of money, wherwith I charge the seid tenementes for euer. And the which yerely vj marc I bequethe to the sustentacion of an honest Preest to syng dyvyne seruice euery day & yere for euermore in the said Chirch of

[1] MS. B, leaf 2.

Saynt Mary atte hiłł at the Awter of Saynt Edmond the Kyng & martir, for my Soule & for the soule of the said William sumtyme myn husbond, & the soules of my ffader & moder William & Maude & ałł christen soules.

And yf it hap the forsaid Robert & Margery to deceasse withoute heires of their bodyes laufully begoten, than I bequethe the forsaid tenementes with thappurtenauntes togider with the said vesselles & necessaryes, & the said xx d of quyte Rent to my next heyre, To haue & to hold to hym & his heires of his body laufully begoten, & so from heyre to heyre grely in fee & in herytage for euer, Of the chief lordes of the fee by the seruice therof due & of right accustumed. And for the forsaid yerely vj marc to the sustentacion of the said Preest as is aforsaid to be paid, So that none of myn heyres shałł nat sełł, alien, nor gyve, nor with eny Rent or seruyce charge the said tenementes, Rent, vesselles, & necessaryes, nor eny part of them, This I adde to & Wołł, that they which shałł hold the said tenementes after my deceasse shall susteyn for euer the Ornamentes belongyng to the said Chauntry, & also a taper of wex of iiij ℔ weight to brenne there before the ymage of our lady.

And yf it hap [1] that they which shałł hold the said tenementes after my deceasse wołł nat susteyn and maynteyn the same tenementes with the vesselles & necessaries aforsaid; Or elles yf that they suffre the said tenementes wilfully to decay or fałł doun, Or yf that they gyve, sell, or alien the same tenementes, vesselles & necessaries, or eny part of the same, or charge the same with eny Rent or seruyce, or eny part therof, ayenst my Wille aboue expressed, wherthurgh the said yerely vj marc to the sustentacion of the said Preest in the fourme aforsaid can nat be levyed & payd; that than they shałł vtterly for euermore lakke, be put & excluded from my bequeste to them aboue made of the forsaid tenementes, Rent, vesselles, & necessaries for ceassyng the said Preestes seruice; I wołł that their estate, right & possession in the same tenementes, rent, vesselles & necessaries, by force of my bequeste aboue made, shałł ceasse for euer. And than I wołł and bequethe that the forsaid tenementes & Rent, with the said vesselles, necessaries, & other thappurtenauntes, withoute eny ageynseying or lette of eny persone, shałł hoolly remayn to the parisshens of the forsaid Chirche of Saynt Mary atte hiłł for the tyme beyng for euer, To hold by the seruice therof due to the chief lordes, and for the

[1] MS. B, leaf 2, back.

forsaid yerely vj marc to the sustentacion of the said Preest as is aforsaid to be payd, So that the said Chauntry in no wise fayle.

Item, I woll that the said Preest be chosen, & in the Ordynaryes stede be presented to the forsaid Chauntry by myn Executours while they live, and after the deceasse of myn Executours I woll that the said Preest be chosen & presented to the said Chauntry by the parisshens of the said Chirch of Saynt Mary at hill for euermore. And I woll that the same Preest be at all hours canon in the said Chirch, and yf he be necligent therof & doo it nat, or yf he evyll bere hym or behaue hym, & that by the said parisshens it be duely proeved, that than anon he be ammoved & put oute of the said Chauntry, and another honest Preest in his stede be chosen & presented to the said Chauntry in the fourme aforsaid, To the which myn executours & to the parisshens and preest aforsayd I bequethe, gyve & graunte, full power to entre in to the said tenementes with þappurtenauntes for euery defaute of payment of the said yerely vj marc for the sustentacion of the said Preest at iiij pryncipall termes of the yere & in the Citee of london vsuell to be payd, & in the same tenementes to distreyne & distresses lefully to bere awey & reteyn till the said yerely vj marc for the sustentacion of the said Preest, Ornamentes & taper be fully payd. And of this my testament I make myn executours & cetera.

[*The two following Notes are in a different hand. The final paragraph of the first commencing 'And now at Midsomer' is clearly a still later addition of 1504.*]

[1] The Rentall of Rose Wrytell.

A tenement of olde tyme callid the 'Swann on the hope,' lying in temmystrete in the parysch of Seynte marye atte hill, bytwene the tenement of my lady Astrey in the west partye, and tenement belongyng to the chyrche of Seynte [*blank*] on the Est partye. And Boundyth to the tementes of Rychard Gosslyne on the northe partye, with o yard & an Entrey durre byldyd ouer yt vnto loue lane on the Est side; and the Schopp of the saide tenement strechith vnto the kynges hye waye in temmystrete on the sowthe partye. And the saide tenement occupyeth william Miln, yremonger, paying yerelye vj li xiij s iiij d, and he to make all maner reparacyons vppon hys propre costes by yer. And now at Midsomer, anno 1504, Iohn halhed, grocer, hath a lesse of þe saide tenement for xxiiij yer.

[1] MS. B, leaf 3.

Seynte Botolphis, in temmystrete.

The parson and the parisshens of Seynte Botolphus ar bounden by the reason of A DEEDE made by Sir Thomas Snodlonde, parson of the saide Chirch of Sent Botolphus, hevyng the date of owr lorde m¹ iij° lij, Beryng ij s vj d a yer of Quyterente, payable every half yer at Ester & at Mighelmas by euyn porcyoneȝ, The which quytrente now a late daye was behynde, not payed by the space of vij yer compleate, Whervppon Mr William Wylde, parson of this chirch of Seynte Mary atte hyll, with Wylliam prewne and Iohn halhed, chirchwardeyns, Resseyued the iiij daye of nouember, the yer of owre lorde god m¹ cccc lxxxvj for the reragis of the said vij yeres, Summa xvij s vj d, by the handes of Richard odiham and Thomas Bodyley, chirchwardenȝ of the saide chirch of Seynte botolphus, Maister Iohn Neele beyng parson of the saide chirch at that tyme. They deleyed yt by cause we schewed not owre Euydence.

[1] The testament of Iohn of Causton.
[A.D. 1353, but from 1486 copy.]

In the name of god: Amen. I, Iohn of Causton, Citezein & mercer of london, beyng hole of mynde & in gode memory, the xxx^t day of the moneth of Iuly, The yere of our lord god m¹ ccc liij, make & ordeyn this my present testament conteynyng my last Will in the fourme ffolowyng:—ffirst, I bequethe & commend my Soule to god, & cetera, And my Body to be buryed in the Chirch of Saynt Pancrace, beside Soper lane of london, in the North Chapell of our lady of the same Chirch, & cetera.

Item, I gyve & bequethe to the said Thomas of langton for terme of his lyf, And after his deceasse to the Prioresse & Couent of the hous of Saynt Elyn withyn Bisshoppesgate of london, & to their Successours for euermore, all that tenement with thappurtenauntes wheryn I dwell the day of makyng herof, in the parissh of Saynt Mary atte hill of london, the which is sette betwene the tenement sumtyme the Erle of Penbrokes on the North part, and the Chircheyerd of the same Chirche on the South part, togider with iiij s of yerely Rent to the said tenement, due of the tenement which Richard of lamehithe sumtyme held in the parissh of Saynt Andrewe huberd beside Estchepe of london of the graunt of the Prioresse & Couent of the hous of Saynt Elyn. Also I gyve & graunt to the same Thomas for terme of

---
[1] MS. B, leaf 4.

his lyf and after his deceasse to the said Prioresse & Couent of the hous of Seynt Elyn those ij Shoppes with Solers aboue bielded & thappurtenauntes, which I haue at Billyngesgate, with the keye lying to & thappurtenauntes in the said parissh of Saynt Mary atte hiH. I gyve also & bequethe to the same Thomas for terme of his lyf, & after his deceasse to the said Prioresse & Couent of the said hous of Saynt Elyn, those iij Shoppes, with the gardyn therto lying, & aH other thappurtenauntes which I haue withoute Algate, in the parissh of Saynt Botolphe there, and those ij Shoppes with Solers aboue bielded & thappurtenauntes beyng in parisch of S₃ Andrew hubberd, which I late purchaced of Iohane, which was the wyf of Robert the Roper, sumtyme Citezein & Bladare of london, & the tenement sumtyme of Iohn yonn on the west part.

Moreouer, I bequethe & gyve to the said Thomas for terme of his lyf, & after his deceasse to the said Prioresse & Couent of the said hous of Saynt Elyn of london, & to their Successours, aH that tenement with shoppes & othir thappurtenauntes, which I haue in the parissh of saynt leonard of Estchepe of london, the which is sette bitwene the tenement, sumtyme Iohn of Oxenf on the North part, & the tenement of Iohane, sumtyme the wyf of Thomas of ffreestone on the South part ; To haue & to hold aH & singuler the foresaid tenementes with the shoppes, gardyn, rent, [1] & key, with other thappurtenauntes, to the same Thomas for terme of his lyf, & after his deceas to the said Prioresse & Couent of the forsaid hous of Saynt Elyn of london & to þeire Successours, wele & peasibly for euermore, Of the chief lordes of the fee by the seruice therof due & of right accustumed, So that of aH the said tenementes, shoppes, garden, rent & key, with thappurtenauntes, there be found and honest preest to syng dyuyne seruice in the said Chirch of saynt Mary atte hiH for euermore for my Soule & the soules of my fader & moder, & of BasiH & Eve sumtyme my wyfes, Symond of Abyngdon, Stephen his Son, William my Son, William of Cawston my Cosyn, & Iohn of langton, & for the soules of our Brethern, Sustern, Sonnes & Doughters & aH christen Soules. And I woH that the same Preest be euery day at hours canon, & at aH dyuyne seruice in the same Chirch of Saynt Mary atte hiH, after the laudable custumes of he said Citee, & namely, that he be euery Day in the same Chirch after evensong, at the tyme of syngyng of Salue Regina, and that he syng the same or elles help the Syngers after his cunnyng in the

[1] MS. B, leaf 4, back.

honour of our blessed lady the virgyn with*o*ute he be lette for a resonable cause.

And I wol̄ that of all the said tene*mentes* wit*h* the rent, keye, shoppes & gardyn & other thapp*ur*tena*u*ntes, there be payed xx s sterlynge*s* to iiij of the worthyest men of the said p*ar*issh̄ of Saynt Mary at hiH̄, therwith̄ to fynde & susteyn v tape*rs* to brenne at conuenient tymes in the same Chirch̄ vnder the fourme that folowetħ for eue*r*more, that is to sey, that there be ij tape*rs* brennyng vpon the Iren Beame afore the ymage of o*u*r lady atte high̄ awter on Sondayes & halydaies, and ij tape*rs* brennyng before the Aungelle*s* Salutacion of the ymage of o*u*r lady in the body of the said Chirch̄, euery evenyng at the tyme of syngyng of Salue Regina from the begynnyng to the endyng. And that there be one taper brennyng on Sondayes & halydayes at the South̄ awte*r* of the same Chirch̄ bitwene the ymage*s* of saynt Thomas the martir & seynt Nicho*l*as, to the laude & hono*ur* of the same seynte*s*. And I wol̄ that the saide Preest to syng in the said Chirch̄ of Saynt Mary, as is aforsaid, be chosen and p*r*esented to the Official of my lord the Archedeken of london, or to his co*m*myssary, by the said Thomas while he lyveth, and afterward by the p*ar*son of the saide Chirche for the tyme beyng, & also by iiij of the worthyest & myghtyest men of the said p*ar*issh̄, & therupon the same preest to be laufully inducte in the same; And that the same Preest take & haue eue*r*y yere for his sustentac*i*on & labour, of the said tene*mentes*, rent, shoppes, gardyn & key, wit*h* thapp*ur*tena*u*ntes, x marc sterlynge*s*, at iiij principall te*r*mes of the yere & in the Citee of london vsueH, by even porcions. And that the p*ar*son of the same Chirche take & [1]haue eue*r*y yere for his labour to be doon in the day of myn Anny*u*e*r*sary aboute the syngyng of the same, of the tene*mentes*, shoppes, key, gardyn & rent aforsaid, iij s iiij d; and for the chief Clerk xij d, & for the vnder Clerk vj d for eue*r*, So that the said p*ar*son & Clerk*es* for the tyme beyng hold solempnely for eue*r* the day of myn Annyue*r*sary, eue*r*y yere in the Chirch̄ aforsaid, and that they doo & syng the same Day for my Soule & the soules aforsaid, Placebo & Dirige & masse of requiem by note, & other dyuyne se*r*uice, to the same Annyue*r*sary due & accustumed for eue*r*more.

And yf it hap the said Thomas while he lyuetħ, or afte*r* his deceasse the said p*ar*son & iiij worthy men of the said p*ar*issh̄, whan the said Chauntry shaH be voyd to abide by xv daies togider and chese nat

[1] MS. B, leaf 5.

nor present an honest preest to the same Chauntry, that than I woll & ordeyn that the said Officiall or his commyssary anon, after that the said xv daies be past & ronne, admytte for that tyme an honest preest to the said Chauntry, & hym set & inducte in the same, No preiudice therby fallyng nor growyng another tyme to the said Thomas while he lyueth, nor afterward to the said parson & iiij worthy men, as is aforsaid Chosers whan they woll another tyme be therof more diligent & ware to chose in due tyme an honest Preest to the said Chauntry.

And yf it hap, as god defende, that the said Thomas while he lyueth, or afterward the said Prioresse & Couent & their Successours, or the possessours of the said tementes, shoppes, Rent, with the key & gardyn & thappurtenauntes in the payment of the said yerely x marc to be payd to the said Preest for his sustentacion at the termes aforsaid or at eny of them to defayle, Than I woll & ordeyn þat it shall be lefull as wele to the said Preest for the money to hym due & beyng behynde in that behalf, as to the said parson for hym & his Clerkes for the yerely payment of iiijs xd to them as is aforsaid due, & to the iiij worthy men of the said parissh for the said xx s for the sustentacion of the said v tapers, to entre in to the said tementes with shoppes, Rent, gardyn, key & other thappurtenauntes, & to distreyn in the same & distresses to take & reteyn till they be fully satisfied & payd of al maner money to them in that behalf due, and so to doo as often as the said yerely Rentes shall be behynde.

Item, I woll & ordeyn that the said Thomas while he lyueth & after his deceasse that the said Prioresse & Couent of the said hous of Saynt Elyn for the tyme beyng & theire Successours, or the possessours of the said tementes, shoppes, Rent, key, gardyn & thappurtenauntes whatsoeuer [1] they be, shall repair & susteyn ayenst wynde & rayne all the houses & other necessaries of the said tementes & shoppes with thappurtenauntes, & whan nede shall be, shall bielde them newe with their owne propre costes & expenses for euermore; And that anon after my deceasse the said Prioresse & Couent & their Successours hold euery yere the day of myn Annyuersary solempnely in the said Chirch for euermore. And yf it hap the said Thomas while he lyueth, or the said Prioresse & Couent or their Successours, or the possessours whatsoeuer they be of the said tementes, in eny of the charges before wreten to be done & paied as is aforsaid, to defayle by half a yere & them woll nat pay nor doo whan therto by

[1] MS. B, leaf 5, back.

the said Preest, parson & iiij worthy men of the said parissh they shall be duely requyred, that than I woll & ordeyn that they shall be from thensforth vtterly excluded & put from all maner profite that of these tenementes shall be had & receyued, and that than the same tenementes with the shops & other thappurtenauntes shall remayn to the said parson & iiij worthy men of the said parissh for euermore, therwith to fynde & susteyn the charges aforsaid. And yf it appere that the said Preest greuously trespas, than he to be put oute & ammoeved by the said Official or his commyssary, & another Preest in his stede there be inducte in the maner & fourme aforsaid; The which, yf the said Official or his commyssary doo nat, or it prolong or tary to do it by vj daies after that he be enfourmed or knowe of the said trespas, Than it shal be lefull to the said Thomas while he lyueth, or afterward to the said parson, with iiij worthy men of his parissh, by their owne auctorite to admove & put oute the said Preest so trespassyng as is aforsaid, and another Preest to chose withyn the said xv Daies, by the same Official or his commyssary to be admytted & inducte in the said Chauntry. And yf it hap the said Preest so trespassyng to appele or ageynsey his said admovyng & puttyng oute by the said Official or his commyssary & by the said Thomas & parson in the fourme aforsaid to be made, or eny his behavyng concernyng the premisses, than I woll & ordeyn that another Preest nat induct in the fourme aforsaid shall hoolly receyue & take the money for the same Preest as is aforsaid ordeyned; And that the said Preest so appelyng or ageynseying be vtterly excluded & put from all maner profite which he shuld haue & receyue by reason of this my testament.

Also, I woll & graunte that the said Thomas & parson & iiij worthy men, which shall haue besynes & labour aboute the repayryng & susteynyng of the said tenementes with the key, gardyn & shoppes, be parteners in the masses & other dyuyne seruices by the said preest to be seyd & doon for euermore, & cetera.

Item, I gyve & bequethe to god & the said Chirche of saynt Mary atte hill & to the parisshens of the same for the tyme beyng, my tenement brewhous with the houses aboue bielded, & thappurtenauntes, which I late purchaced of Iohn lucas, Clerk, & Richard de Tystor, executours of the testament of Iohn of Gildeford, sumtyme [1]Citezein and Clerk of london, lying in the parissh of Saynt Mary atte hill aforsaid, To haue & to hold the said tenement, with all thap-

[1] MS. B, leaf 6.

purtenauntes, to the forsaid Chirch & parisshens for the tyme beyng, in perpetuall almesse, & to the help of susteynyng of another Preest to syng for euermore in the said Chirch of Saynt Mary at hill, for the soule of henry Barnard & all christen soules, So that the same Preest be alwey chosen & presented to the said Chauntry whan it shall be voyd, by the parson & iiij worthy men of the said parissh, & cetera.

[1] The testament of Iohn Nasyng.
[A.D. 1361, but from 1486 copy.]

In the name of god : Amen. The yere from the Incarnacion of our lord god m¹ ccclxj, And the xxxv yere of the Reigne of kyng Edward the iij[de]; I, Iohn Nasyng, Bruer, Citezein of london, in gode & hole mynde, make my testament in this wise that foloweth. ffirst, I bequethe my Soule to all myghty god & to our lady & all seyntes, And my Body to be buried in the Chirch of Saynt Mary atte hill of london, & cetera.

Item, I bequethe the halvendele of all my godes therwith to fynde a Preest, an honest man, to syng dyuyne seruice in the said Chirch of Saynt Mary atte hill for my soule & the Soules of my ffader & moder, & of all of them that I am bound to, & all christen soules, as long as the money of the same halvendele woll strecche & endure.

Item, I bequethe to Iohane my wyf, for terme of her lyf in the name of her dower, & for all thynges the which may falle to her by reason of my Deth in eny wise, all my tenement with the shoppes therto lying, & thappurtenauntes sette & lying in the parissh of Saynt Mary atte hill aforsaid, To haue & to hold to her for terme of her lyf as is aforsaid, Of the chief lordes of the fee by the seruice therof due & of right accustumed. The which tenement with the shoppes & thappurtenauntes after the deceasse of the said Iohane my wyf, I bequethe to remayne to the parson & iiij of the worthiest men parisshens of the Sayde Chirch of Saynt Mary atte hill for the tyme beyng, & to their Successours, parsons & parisshens, for euermore, vnder this condicion, that they fynde an honest Preest to syng dyuyne seruice for euer in the said chirche of Saynt Mary atte hill for my Soule & other soules aforsaid, To haue & to hold the said tenement & shoppes with thappurtenauntes to the said parson & parisshens & to their Successours, parson & parisshens for the tyme beyng for euermore, in the fourme aforsaid, Of the chief lordes of

[1] MS. B, leaf 7.

the fee by the seruice therof due & of right accustumed. The which Preest I woll shall be chosen & presented to the Officiall of london by the said Parson & iiij parisshens & their Successours Parson & parisshens for the tyme beyng, & therupon by the said Officiall to be inducte & institute in the said Chauntry, & so to doo as often as the same Chauntry shal be void.

And yf it hap the same Preest, or eny other Preest his Successour, by eny cause to be vnable, or of other lyvyng & condicion than gode & honeste, Than I woll, incontynently, that the said Preest shall be remoeved & put oute of the said Chauntry by the said parson & parisshens & their Successours parson & parisshens for the tyme beyng And another honest Preest in his stede by them to be chosen & presented, & in the said Chauntry to be inducte & institute in the fourme aforsaid, & thus to doo as often as such caas shall hap. The Residue of all my godes, & cetera.

[1] The testament of Iohn Weston.
[A.D. 1407, but from 1486 copy.]

In the name of god: Amen. I, Iohn Weston, Citezein and merchaunt of london, beyng hole of mynde & of body the xviij day of the moneth of Iuly, the yere of our lord god mł cccc vij, and the viij[th] yere of the Reigne of Kyng henry the iiij[th], make & ordeyn this my present testament & last wille as touchyng my tenementes lying in the said Citee of london in this wise:—ffirst, I bequethe my Soule to allmyghty god, my Creatour, & to our blessed lady the virgyn, his moder, & to all seyntes, And my Body to be buryed in the Chirch of Saynt Mary atte hill, beside Billyngesgate of london. Item, where I, the said Iohn Weston & Iohane my wyf, late Ioyntly purchaced of William Neell & Alice his wyf, which was the wyf of Iohn Walworth, late Citezein & vynter of london, a tenement with thappurtenauntes sette in the said parissh of Saynt Mary atte hill, in the Strete ledyng from Seynt Margaret Patyns toward Billyngesgate, that is to sey, bitwene the tenement sumtyme Robert of Roo, Sporyour, on the North part, & the tenement sumtyme Symond of Moordon on the parties of the South & West, & the kynges high wey on the partie of the Est, To haue & to hold to vs the said Iohn Weston & Iohane my wyf, & to the heires & assigneis of me the said Iohn Weston for euermore as in a dede therof to vs made more pleynly it may appere.

[1] MS. B, leaf 8.

I gyve & bequethe, anon, after the deceasse of the said Iohane my wyf, all the forsaid tenement with thappurtenauntes, to god & to the said Chirche of Saynt Mary at hill, & to Thomas Atherston, nowe parson of the same Chirch, & to his Successours parsons of the said Chirch, for euermore, & to the Wardeyns of the Chirche werke, & other parisshens of the said Chirch, & to their Successours wardeyns & parisshens of the same Chirch, for euermore, therwith to doo & fulfille my willes vnderwreten, that is to sey, to pay of the Issues & profites of the said tenement with thappurtenauntes whan it shall comme to their handes after the deceasse of the said Iohane my wyf, yerely for euermore vj marc sterlynges, to the help of the susteynyng of a preest, an honest man, to syng dyuyne seruice in the said Chirch of Seynt Mary atte hill, at the awter of seynt Iohn Baptist there, for my Soule & for the soule of the said Iohane my wyf, & for the soules of our ffaders & moders, & of all those soules that we be bound to pray for, & for all christen soules, So, alwey, that the parisshens of the said Chirche of Saynt Mary atte hill woll fulfille the full & competent sustentacion of such an honest Preest to syng dyuyne seruice in the fourme aforsaid,

And also to take & pay therof yerely to the parson of the said Chirche of Saynt Mary atte hill for the tyme beyng, xx d, yf he be personally in the said chirch to sey euery yere placebo & Dirige by note & a solempne masse in the day of myne annyuersary for my soule & other soules aforsaid; & to pay & distribute [1] yerely, xx d to be devided evenly amonges other preestes of the same Chirche beyng at my said Annyuersary, & to pay yerely to the maister Clerk of the said Chirch iiij d & to the vnder clerk ij d for ryngyng of Belles & for doyng their Offices other weyes in due fourme as to a yerely mynde perteyneth.

And also to take & pay yerely & for euermore viij s for the sustentacion of ij torches of wexe to brenne euery Sonday & other holy daies at the high awter of the said Chirch in the masse tyme at the leuacion of the blessed Sacrament & after as it is the vse; willyng that the same Torches be renewed as often as nede shal be.

And also to take & pay yerely & for euermore to the werkes of the Body of the said Chirch iij s iiij d sterlynges. And all that shall comme ouer of the profites of the said tenement with thappurtenauntes ouer the premisses fulfilled, I woll that it shall goo & remayne, yerely to be distributed by the handes of the Wardeyns

---

[1] MS. B, leaf 8, back.

of the said Chirche of Saynt Mary atte hiH for the tyme beyng, in the Day of myn Annyuersary amonges poore people, most nedefuH, dwellyng in the said parissh of Saynt Mary atte hiH, to pray for my soule & other soules aforsaid. And I woH that the forsaid Wardeyns of the said Chirch for the tyme beyng, by the ouersight of ij other honest men of the same parissh, after the deceasse of the said Iohane my wyf, haue the disposicion of the said tenement with thappurtenauntes, & that lete to ferme & the rent therof togader to fulfille therwith my willes before wreten and also to repair & susteyn therwith the same tenement with thappurtenauntes wele & competently.

and I woH & ordeyn that the said Preest be chosen by the said Chirche Wardeyns & by ij other worthy men of the same parissh for the tyme beyng. And I woH that the same Preest be an honest man & of gode fame. And that the said Preest be in the said Chirch at matens, masse, evensong, & at the Salue with the collet & De profundis, & at aH other hours canon as it besemeth. And yf the same preest so chosen vnhonestly behave hym, than I woH that he be ammoeved & put from his seruice by the said wardeyns & parisshens and another honest preest in his stede by them to be chosen, And so to doo from tyme to tyme as often as such caas shaH hap. To haue & to hold aH the forsaid tenement with the appurtenauntes, as sone as it shaH faH after the deceasse of the said Iohane my wyf to the forsaid parson, wardeyns & other parisshens of the said Chirch & to their Successours parson, wardeyns & other parisshens of the said Chirche for the tyme beyng, for to fulfiH & pay aH the charges aforsaid accordyng to my Wille aboue rehersed, Of the chief lordes of the fee by the seruice therof due & of right accustumed for euermore.

And I woH & ordeyn that after the deceasse of the said Iohane my wyf, after that the said tenement with thappurtenauntes comme to the handes & possession [1] of the said parson, wardeyns & parisshens of the said Chirch by reason of this my testament, yf, than, the same parson, wardeyns & parisshens or their Successours wilfully defayle in doyng & fulfillyng of my willes before rehersed, or that they otherwise translate or chaunge the said tenement with thappurtenauntes, that than I woH & ordeyn that the forsaid tenement with thappurtenauntes shaH goo & remayn to the Mayre or Wardeyn & Comenaltye of the Citee of london & to their Successours, to the

[1] MS. B, leaf 9.

vse & sustentacion of the brigge of london, & to fynde an honest Preest of newe to be chosen to syng dyuyne seruice for euermore daily in the Chapell of london Brigge for my soule & other soules aforsaid, & also to hold & kepe yerely for euermore in the same Chapell myn Annyuersary in the fourme before wreten, To haue & to hold to the wardeyns of the said Brigge, in the name of the said Mayre or Warden & Comenaltye of the Citee of london, & to their Successours in the fourme aforsaid for euermore, Of the chief lordes of the fee, & cetera.

[1] The testament of Richard Gosselyn.
[A.D. 1428, but from 1486 copy.]

In the name of god: Amen. I, Richard Gosselyn, Citezein & Iremonger of london, beyng hole of mynde & in gode memory the xxvj day of the moneth of Aprill, The yere of our lord god m^t cccc xxviij .... I bequethe to Beatrice my wyf the reuersion of all those londes & tenementes .... in the parissh of Saynt leonard in ffoster lane ... Soo, alwey, that the same Beatrice duryng her lyf fynde & susteyn an honest preest to syng dyuyne seruice in saynt Kateryn's Chapell withyn the Chirch of St Mary atte hill beside Billyngesgate of london, & to be at all hours canon in the same Chirch as it besemeth, Praying for my soule & for the soules of .... And anon after the deceasse of the said Beatrice ... I bequethe to sir William Spark, nowe parson of þe said Chirche of Saynt Mary atte hill, & to Iohn Gretyng & William Gilham, nowe wardeyns .... all the forsaid londes & tenementes [2] .... [to] fynde & susteyn yerely for euermore an honest preest .... to syng dyuyne seruice daily for euermore in the said Chirch of saynt Mary atte hill and morowe masse at seynt Kateryn's awter there for my soule & other soules aforsaid ... And yf the said parsons, wardeyns & iiij parisshens of the said Chirch .... varye of their said chosyng of the same preest by the space of xl daies, & can nat accorde, than I woll & ordeyn that the said Preest be chosen for that tyme by the Mayre of the Citee of london.

[3] Item, I woll & ordeyn that the forsaid parson & wardeyns ... kepe yerely ... myn Annyuersary.

Item, I woll .... a taper of wexe of v℔ weight to stonde & brenne beside seynt Kateryn's awter euery Sonday & euery double feest, prycipall feest, & solempne feest yerely for euer.

---

[1] MS. B, leaf 13.   [2] MS. B, leaf 13, back.   [3] MS. B, leaf 14.

14   The Will of W. Cambridge, englished 1486.

Item, I woll & ordeyn that the said parson, wardeyns . . . pay yerely for euermore to ij poure men or to ij poure women, most nedefull, dwellyng in the said parish of saynt Mary atte hill for the tyme, that is to sey to either . . . . euery weke . . . vj d sterlynges perpetually to pray for my soule & other soules aforsaid; Willyng that the same ij poure men or ij poure women so to receyue & haue the said almesse as is aforsaid wekely, be named & chosen Iustely & truly of pure conscience withoute eny favoure, after the gode discrecion of the said parson, wardeyns & iiij honest parisshens . . . . .

[1] And yf the yerely Rentes . . . . extende & drawe ouer & aboue my bequestes . . . . . the same ouerplus & surplusage . . . . to the vse of the Chirch werkes . . . . Savyng, alwey, I woll that the said Chirchewardeyns of Saynt Mary at hill for the tyme beyng, shall take & haue yerely for euermore of the same ouerplus & surplusage for their labour aboute the premisses Iustly & truly to be doon, iij s iiij d betwene them evenly to be devided . . . . .

[2] The testament of William Cambrugge.
[A.D. 1431, but from 1486 copy.]

In the name of god: Amen. I, William Cambrugge, Citezein and Grocer of the cite of london, beyng hole of mynde & in gode memorye the xxvij day of the moneth of Decembre The yer of our lord god after the course & accomptyng of the Chirch of England mł cccc xxxj . . . . . my Body to be buryed in the Chapell of Saynt Stephen the martir, by me made & ordeyned on the North part of the Chirch of Saynt Mary at hille beside Billyngesgate of london. Item, I bequethe by this my present testament, to god & to the said Chirch of Saynt Mary atte hill & to maister Iohn horne, nowe parson of the said Chirche, Thomas Knolles, William Burton & to Iohn Wellys, nowe Wardeyns of the Comenaltye of the crafte of Grocers of london . . . all those my tenementes . . . . [3] in the fourme & condicion folowyng, that is to sey I woll, bequethe & ordeyn that the forsaid wardeyns . . . . shall fynde & susteyne yerely for euermore an honest Preest sufficiantly lerned in dyvynete to syng & sey dyuyne seruice in the said Chapell of Saynt Stephen by me late ordeyned & bielded withyn the said Chirch of Saynt Mary atte hill, for my Soule & for the Soules of Iohane & Anne my wyfes, luke my ffader, Alice my moder, & for all the soules that we be

[1] MS. B, leaf 14, back.   [2] MS. B, leaf 10.
[3] MS. B, leaf 10, back.

The Will of W. Cambridge, englished 1486.   15

bound to pray for & for all *chist*en soules. And also that the same Wardeyns & their Successours fynde & susteyn v tape*rs* of wexe of a ℔ apece to brenne vpon my candylstyk, by me orde*y*ned in the same Chirch, in the hono*ur* & worship of oure lord Ihe*s*u criste & of o*ur* blessed lady seynt Mary the virgyn & of all Sayntes in eue*ry* feest of o*ur* blessed lady Saynt Mary & in eue*ry* double feest at the first evensong & at the last evensong & at matens & high masse, & in eue*ry* lowe feest at the masse onely. Willyng alwey that the forsaid v tape*rs* of wexe be renewed as often as nede shall be w*ith* the old wexe lefte & with [1] newe wexe to be put therto, eue*ry* tape*r* to be of the weight aforsaid. And that the said Wardeyns . . . . kepe yerely for eue*r*more the Day of myn Annyue*r*sary in the said Chirch of Saynt Mary atte hill togide*r* w*ith* the co*m*memoracion of þe soules aforsaid, that is to sey, w*ith* placebo & Dirige, & masse of Requiem on the morowe folowyng, by note . . . . at my forsaid Annyue*r*sary ij tape*rs* of wexe to brenne, j at myn hede & j at my fete . . . . moreoue*r* that the same Preest duryng all the tyme that he shall stonde in the said se*r*uice, sey eue*ry* day placebo & Dirige, w*ith* the co*m*mendacion of Soules & the vij psalmes & the letany feriat except most double feest*es*. And also I woll & ordeyn that the said wardeyns . . . . . pay eue*ry* yere for eue*r*more afte*r* my deceasse to the Mayre or Wardeyn of the Citee of london for the tyme beyng [2] vjs viijd sterlyng*es*, and also to the Shyryffes of the same Citee for the tyme beyng, that is to sey to either of them iijs iiijd, and to the Mayres Swerd berer for the tyme beyng xxd sterlynges, to this entent that the same Mayre, Shyryf*es* & Swerd berer for the tyme beyng shall oue*r*see that the p*r*emisses in all thyng*es* be truly maynteyned . . . . And whatsoeue*r* shall come oue*r* vnspent of the issues & p*r*ofites aforsaid oue*r* & beside the said charg*es* fulfilled I woll alwey that it shall remayn & be spent to the vse of the said Chirche of Saynt Mary atte hill . . . . .

And yf the forsaid Wardeyns . . . . pay nat nor fulfill the payments & charg*es* aforsaid . . . . Than I woll & ordeyn by this my p*r*esent testament that the forsaid wardeyns of the Comenaltye of the Grocery of london or their Successou*r*s shall lese all their title & inte*r*esse therof . . . . than my forsaid bequeste . . . . to the forsaid pa*r*son & his Successou*r*s made shall stonde . . . . And yf it hap the same pa*r*son or his Successou*r*s . . . ceasse by the space of a yere of fyndyng & susteynyng of the said Preest . . . .

[1] MS. B, leaf 11.   [2] MS. B, leaf 11, back.

than I bequethe aH . . . . to the vse and sustentacion of london Brigge . . . .

[Churchwardens' Note.]

[1] Also it hathe bene acustomyd that vppon Cristmas day at the magnificat in the Evensong, be ordeyned for euerye preste, clark & childe xv smaH candelles waying aH ij ℔ di. And euery persone hauyng a surplise shaH haue one of thise smale candelles brennyng in their handes & so to go on procession to the tombe of Mr. Cambryge syngyng a Respond of Seynte Stephen with the prose therto; that done, a versicle with the colet of S₃ Stephen, And in goyng into the Queer a Antempne of owre ladye : Beryng ij candilstickes of syluer with the tapres on yt and a Sencer with a schyp.

[2] The testament of Iohn Bedham.
[A.D. 1472, but from 1486 copy.]

In the name of our lord Ihesu criste our Savyour: Amen. The Secunde day of the moneth of Nouembre, The yere of our lord god mt cccc lxxij . . . . I, Iohn Bedham, Citezein and ffishmonger, of the Citee of london, beyng hole of mynde & in gode memory, make & ordeyn this my present testament . . . . .

Item, I, the said Iohn Bedham, gyve and bequethe to maister William Wylde nowe parson of the parissh Chirch of Saynt Mary at hiH aforsaid, & to Iohn Bremonger & Iohn Dey nowe wardeyns of the godes, Rentes & werkes of the same Chirch, & to their Successours parson & wardeyns of the same Chirch for the tyme beyng & to the parisshens of the same, aH that my grete Tenement, with the houses, celers, Solers, gardyn therto adioynyng, & other thappurtenauntes sette as wele in Seynt Botophes lane beside Billyngesgate of london in the parissh of seynt George beside Estchepe of london as in love lane in the parissh of seynt Mary atte hill aforsaid, and the which forsaid grete tenement with the houses, celers, solers, gardyn & other thappurtenauntes lyeth bitwene the tenement wheryn Piers Alfold nowe dwelleth, in seynt Botolphes lane belongyng to the Chauntry of William kyngeston in the Chirch of saynt George aforsaid, and the tenement perteynyng to seynt Dunstones Chirch in the Est of london in love lane aforsaid on the North part, and the parsonage & Chirchyerd of seynt Botolphes Chirche aforsaid and the

---

[1] MS. B, leaf 12, back ; in a different hand. [2] MS. B, leaf 16.

The Will of John Bedham, englished 1486.

gardyn sumtyme Richard Gosselyns on the South pa*r*t in Brede, & it streccheth in lengthe from seynt Botolphes lane aforsaid toward the west vnto love lane aforsaid toward the Est. The which grete tenement w*ith* thappurtenauntes su*m*tyme was William Cauntbrigge, sumtyme Citezein and Iremonger of london, & afterward henry Somers . . . . [1] vnder the condicion therwith to doo, hold, obse*r*ue & fulfille all & singuler my my [2] willes & ordenau*n*ces herevnder wreten . . . .

I woll & ordeyne that the said pa*r*son & wardeyns of the said Chirch of Saynt Mary . . . shall fynde & susteyn yerely for euermore a preest, an honest man of gode fame & honest conue*r*sacion, to syng & sey dyuyne se*r*uice daily in the said Chirch of saynt Mary at the hill . . . . for the soules . . . . Willyng that the same preest shall syng his masses in the said Chirch of seynt Mary atte hill at the awter in saynt kateryns Chapell there, eue*r*y Day anon & Immediatly afte*r* the morowe masse in the said Chirch of seynt Mary, to be song yf the morowe masse in the same Chirche be contynued as heretofore it was wont to be & now is vsed, Or elles in defaute of the same morowe masse that my said Preest syng daily resonable tymely his masse in stede & tyme of the morowe masse there as sone as he may duely & resonably . . . . And ferthermore, I woll that the said preest so to be ordeyned & for me to syng, be pe*r*sonally eue*r*y day in the said Chirche of seynt Mary atte hill at all houres canon, & at all se*r*uices in the same Chirche to be seyd & song, & that he be helpyng in the same in all thynges as he best can, And namely, that the said Preest sey eue*r*y werkeday in the said Chirche of seynt Mary atte hill, his matens, pryme & ho*u*rs, evensong & complene, placebo & dirige, & all his other prayers & se*r*uices by hym self or w*ith* his ffelawes preestes of the same Chirch . . . .

[3] Item, I woll that the said wardeyns of the said Chirch . . . . shall fynde & susteyn for eue*r*more a lampe w*ith* oyle in the quere & high Chauncell of the same Chirche of seynt Mary, to brenne alwey as wele on Dayes as on nyghtes before the blessed Sacrament . . .

Item, I woll that the said wardeyns . . . . pay to iij poure people most nedefull . . . . dwellyng in the said pa*r*issh of seynt Mary atte hill, eue*r*y Sonday wekely eue*r*y yere for eue*r*more, that is to sey, to eue*r*y of the same poure people iiijd in hono*u*r of the blessed Trynyte . . . .

[1] MS. B, leaf 16, back.   [2] So in MS.   [3] MS. B, leaf 17.

[1]I woll that the same wardeyns . . . kepe yerely for euermore in the said Chirch of seynt Mary atte hill myn Annyuersary . . . .

[2]And I woll that all & euerych that which shall remayn yerely vnspent . . . . it may be spent & bestowed vpon the susteynyng & newe bieldyng of the said tenement with [3]thappurtenauntes & vpon the repayryng & renewyng of the vestymentes & Ornamentes belongyng to the awter in seynt Kateryns Chapell aforsaid . . . . .

[3]Item, I the said Iohn Bedham gvve . . . to maister William wyld, nowe parson of the said Chirche of seynt Mary . . . . for the tyme beyng, & to Iohn Bremonger & Iohn Dey, nowe wardeyns of the same Chirche of seynt Mary atte hill, & to their Successours . . . . & to the parisshens there, all that my grete Gardyn . . . . beside [4]the Tourehill in the parissh of Saynt Botolphe withoute Algate in the suburbes of london . . . . To this entent, that the same parson & wardeyns of the said Chirch of seynt Mary at hill & their Successours for the tyme beyng shall pay yerely for euermore to an honest preest . . . . to syng, daily, morowe masse in the said Chirch of seynt Mary . . . . the said preest . . . . to . . be alwey charged specially & deuoutly to pray daily at his said morowe masse . . . . [5]for the soule of the said Iohn Nasyng . . . .

[6]Ihesus.

Parte of the wyll of thomas Ryvell, grocer, Concernyng the wele of owre Chyrche ; at the begynnyng the xvij daye of the monethe of merche, the yere of owre lorde god mł cccc lxxxxvj :—

and the second egalle parte of my seyde goodes, Iuellis, Catallis and dettes I bequethe to Margery Ryvell, Alis Ryvell and Iulyan Ryvell my doughters amongest them egally to be devyded and to be delyuerd vnto them when they schall cum to ther lawfull ages or be maryed. And yf any of my seyde dougters dye before they cum to theyre lawfull ages or be maryed, than I wyll that the parte of her that so schall decesse remayne to the other of them thanne beyng on lyve, & so of euery of theym. And I wyll that my sayd chyldern togethyr with theyer parttes of my seyde goodes, Iuellis, catallis and dettis by me to theym above bequethed schal be in the guydyng and kepyng of þe seyde Iohanne my wyff, my executryx vnder named, sche fyndyng therto suffycyentt suerte afore the meyer and Aldermen of the cite of london acordyng to þe custome of the same cite.

---

[1] MS. B, leaf 17, back.   [2] MS. B, leaf 18.   [3] MS. B, leaf 19.
[4] MS. B, leaf 19, back.   [5] MS. B, leaf 20.   [6] leaf 242.

and yf aH my seyde chyldern dey byfore they cum to ther lawfuH ages or Maryages, than I wyH that aH my seyde second parte of my seyde goodes, IuelIes, Catalls & dettes be devided into ij egalle partes wherof one parte I bequethe vnto the parson and Chyrche Wardens of seyntt mary hyH besyde byllyngges gate of london, vnder condycion foloyng, that is to wete, I wyH that the seyde parson, Chyrche Wardens of the same goodes fynde or cawse to fownde an honest preste of gode name and fame to synge and prey for my sowle, þe sowles of my father and mother and aH Crysten sowles, by þe spase of as many yeres as they schalle seme best by theyr dyscrecyons, in the seyde Chyrche of seyntt Mary hyH. and the other parte of my seyde second parte of my goodes, Iuelles,. Catalles and dettes I bequethe to þe seyde Iohanne my wyff therwythe to do, ordeyn and dyspose her fre wyH yff sche thane be lyvyng. And yff sche than be deed than I bequethe her seyde parte of the seyde second parte of my seyde goodes, Iuelles, Cattallis and dettes towarde the beoyldyng and reparacion of the seyde Chyrche of seyntt Mary hyH.

Anno domini m[li] cccc lxxxxvij.

[1] The Testament of Iohn Mongeham.
[A.D. 1514.]

In dei nomine : amen. The xx[th] day of may, in the yere of our lorde god a thousande five houndrith & xiiij[th]. I, Iohn Mongeham, cite3yn and ffisshmonger of London, havyng my hole mynde and good Remembraunce, laude be to god, I make and ordeyne this my last WiH and Testament in fourme vndir wretyn. Tat is to sey,—ffirst I geve and bequeth my sowle to Ihesu criste, my redemer, and to his blessid mother our lady seint Mary, and to aH the seinttes in hevyn. And I wiH that my body shal be buryed in the southe Ile within the parissh churche of Seint Mary at hiH, directly afore the wyndowe of the vij werkes of mercy.

Item, I geve & bequeth to þe high avter in the same chirch for tithes forgoten, in dischargyng of my conscience iij[s] iiij[d].

Item, I geve & bequeth ij Torches to the Chirchwardens of the seid chirch & their successours, they to be light & Burned at þe sacryng tyme of þe high masse vppon high and doble ffestes in þe wourship of þe blessid sacrament.

[1] MS. B, leaf 78.

Item, I geve & bequeth vj Torches, that is to sey, to euery of the iij⁰ brotherodes ffounded, ordenyd & kept within þe foreseid chirch of Seint Mary at hill, to euery of the breþerhodes ij Torches, that is to say, to þe brotherhod of Seint Christofur ij, And to the brotherhod of Seint Katheryn ij, And to þe brotherhod of Seint Anne other ij.

Item, I will that myne Executrix vndir named shall geve or cause to be geven to the poure people in peny dole þe day of my buryeing the Summa of xls, except I do deale it with myne hondis or I depart this present lyeffe.

Item, I geve & bequeth xxˢ to be distributed amonge þe poure parochians of Seint Mary at hill by þe discression of myne executrix.

Item, I will þat myne executrix shall by [1]lynnen clothe and to make, or cause to be made, as many shirttes and smockes therof as shall extend or amount to the valure of xls, And she to geve the said shirttes and smockes to poure people where most neede shall appere aftir hir discression. Also I will þat my seid Executrice shall redeme and pay þe fees of xij presoners lyeng in þe kynges bench, the Merchelsee, Neugate, or Ludgate which doith lye for þer fees only off delyuery. Also I geve and bequeth to the parishe chirch of Seint Mary at hill for oon hole sute of vestymenttes, Whight or Blake, with iij Copes and all oþer thynges therto perteyning, to be bought by thaduyse of the parson and the ij Chirchwardens of the same chirch within a quarter of a yere immediatly aftir my departyng owte of this present lyffe xl. li sterling, excepte I do by the seid sute before I depart from this trauncetory worlde. Also I geve and bequeth toward the Reparacions of the body of the parissh chirch of Seint Clementtes, in Rochestur, where I was boorne, vjs viijd.

Item, I geve and bequeth to Alis my wyffe and to her ereres or assingnes My Messuage at Mepam & all my londys & Tenaunttes with thaportenaunces in Mepam and luddisdon in the counte of Kent, to geue & to sell at her owne plesure. Also I geue & bequeth to euery of the vj men of my ffelysship that shall bere my body to the chirch, xij d. Also I geue & bequeth xls to the wardens & ffeliship ffisshmongers of london, toward a banket to be kept at ther hall the day of my buryall or aftirward at ther owne plesures. Also I will that myne Executrice, her executores or administrators, shall pay for the purches of londis or Tenaunttes within þe Citie of london to the yerely value of ffyfty shillinges aboue all charges and annell reparacions resonably to be estemyd, as mych money as shal be

---

[1] MS. B, leaf 78, back.

though nesary by þe lymytacion assingment of Mr William hatclyff, doctor of Divinite, parson of þe seid chirch of Seint Mary at hill, William lawson, Clerke, and Cristofur halis, or ij Survivours of þem Iountly or þe Survivor of them only. Wherof I will þe same doctor hatclyff, William lawson and [1] Cristofur halis, and the Surviuor or Surviuors of them, by thaduyse of suche Counselours as they or eyther of them shall seme expedient, shall take astate in fe symple to þe vses and Intenttes vndir wretyn, That is to say, to thuse of Alys my wyff and her Assingnes for terme of her lyffe vndir ffourme & condicion vndir wretyn, that is to say, that the same Alys my wyff, yerely duryng her lyff, shall kepe a Solempne Obet for my Sowle and for the sowlis of my ffather & Mother, William & Ione, and all cristen sowles, and she to spend yerely at the seid Obett xs, in fourme vnder wretyn, That is to sey, ffirst I will that the parson of þe seid chirch of Seint Mary at hill shall haue viij d iff he be present at dirige or masse, and his curate shall haue for dirige & masse and þe bedrowle viij d, And to viij prestis & ij Clerkes iij s iiij d. Item, for wax viij d. And to þe clerke for dirige & Masse for Ryngyng xx d. Also I will that ther shal be bough a dosen of brede, price xij d, and a kylderkyn of ale, price ij s, And to be spent alway aftir the dirige is sonnge, amonges the prestis & clerkes and other the parisshens beyng at the seid dirige. And that aftir the decese of the seid Alis the seid londis or Tenementtes shall goo to thuse of the vj wardens of my ffeliship ffisshmongers of london, and to þe Comynalte of þe same and to their Successours wardens, vppon condicion that they shall kepe solemply, my seid Obett or Annuersary yerely for euermore þe same day of the Moneth my sowle shall depart from þe body, in þe parisshe chirche of Seint Mary at hill within london. That is to sey, dirige be note on þe Even, and Masse be note on the Morewe ffoloyng; & þat þe seid vj wardens with other of the ffelyship ffisshmongers be [2] yerly present in their lyverey at þe same Obett or Annuersary after þe good Custume of oþer obettes or Annuersaris nowe kept by þe seid feliship within þe Citie of london. Also I will þe seid vj wardens for the tyme beyng shall haue yerly at the same Annuersary, euery of theym xx d yff they be present at þe seid Annuersary. Also I will þe same wardens shall content and pay yerely x s to þe parson of Seint Mary at hill, his curate, viij prestes and ij Clerkes, for wax, for belles Ryngyng, for brede & ale as is aboue wretyn [3] ffor kepyng of the same dirige . . . .

[1] MS. B, leaf 79. [2] 'by' in MS. [3] MS. B, leaf 79, back.

II.

[LEASE OF A HOUSE IN THAMES ST. LONDON: A.D. 1507.]

[1]This ys a remembrance of a Indenture made the xiij[th] day of the monethe of Marche in y[e] yere of our lord god mł v[c] and vij, and in the xxiij[th] yere of the Reigne of kyng herry the vij[th]; betwene Maistir William hatclyff, clerk, parson of ye parishe chirche of seint Mary att hyłł beside Byllyngesgaet of london, herry Edmond, Salter, and Iołn Russełł, Skynner, Citeȝens of london, nowe wardayns of the godes, ornamentes, werkes, livelode and rentes of the same Chircħ on that one partie, And Andrewe Evyngar, Cytezen and Salter of london, Ellyn his wyff and Elysabeth ther naturałł doughter on that other partie, WITNESSYTH, that y[e] said parson and wardeyns by y[e] consent, wyłł and agrement of y[e] right worshipfułł parysshens of y[e] said paryshe haue grauntcd duuisid? and by this indentur to ferme, haue letyn and confermyd vnto y[e] said Andrewe, Ellyn and Elysabeth and to y[e] lenghest liver of them, ałł that tenement of y[e] said parson, wardeyns and parysshens, with y[e] Appurtenaunces belongyng to ye said chirch, which one Thomas hunt, draper, late dwellid in, set and lying in Thamysstret in y[e] paryshe aforsaid, yat is to witt, between y[e] tenement late in y[e] tenneur of one Robard howtyng, ffyshemongher, nowe in y[e] tenure of robard holdernes, merchaunt haberdasher, on y[e] west partie, and Iołn Collyns, ffyshemonger, on y[e] Est partie, and y[e] kynges high-way ther on y[e] northe partie; To HAUE, occipy and hold y[e] forsaid tenement with thappurtenaunces vnto y[e] said Andrewe, Ellyn and Elysabeth and to y[e] lengyst liver of them and to ther assigners tenauntes of y[e] said tenement with thappurtenaunces for y[e] tyme beyng, from y[e] ffeast of y[e] Annunciacion of our lady seint Mary y[e] virgyn next comyng aftir y[e] date hereof, vnto y[e] ende [2]and terme of .l., fyfty, hole yeris than next folowyng and fully to be compleet, yeldyng and payng therfore yerly duryng y[e] said term vnto y[e] said

---

[1] MS. B, leaf 23.   [2] MS. B, leaf 23, back.

Lease of a House in Thames St. London, A.D. 1507.

parson and wardeyns and to their Successours parson of ye said chiche and wardeyns of ye godis, ornamentes, werkes, livelode and rentes of ye same chirch or to theyr certeyn attorney or deputee, v mark sterlynges at iiij termys of ye yere, in ye Citie of london vsuell, by evyn porcions.

AND WHERE as the said tenement with thappurtenaunces ys nowe olde, febyll, ruinous, and at great decay fallyng down ye day of ye makyng hereoff, the said Andrewe Couennantith, and hym and his executours byndith to ye said parson & wardeyns and to their successurs by y^{is} presentes, that he, the sayd Andrewe, at his owne propre costes and charges, within ye first yere of ye said terme shall take down ye said tenement with ye thappurtenaunces, and vpon ye grownde of ye same shall do to be sett vpp, bildid and edified, a substaunciall newe tenement with iij stories in ye stede of ye olde, with gode and substaunciall newe tymbir, as large and as fer as ye said grownd will stretche and suffyce to be made, with shopp, Solers, dores, wyndowis, steyres, particions, hawle, chambirs, parlour, Gutturs, kechyn, and all other maner thynges necessary to such a tenement to be had, clenly and werkmanly to deuided and cast with all maner tymbre werk, Irrn werk, lede werk and stoen werk conuenient and necessary to ye same tenement, to be fownd and made at ye propre cost and charge of ye said Andrewe Evyngar. To haue hold vnto ye said Andrewe, ellyn and elyʒabeth and to ye lenger liver of them after ye said edificacion and bildyng vnto thend and complesshement of ye said terme of fyfty yeris, yff they or eny of them so long live.

AND IT YS couenauntid, and agreed betwen ye said parties, and ye said Andrewe ellyn and elysabethe grantyn and them byndyn by this presentes yat they and lenger liver of them, at their own propre costes ye said tenement with thappurtenaunces aftir it ys newe bildyd and sett vpp in ye forme above said, well and sufficiently in euery part and parcell therof, from thensforth shall kepe, repaire and mayntene, wynd tyght, water tyght, as often as shall be nedefull, and ye pament of ye kynges high way ther, afore the said tenement, competenly shall do to be pavid and made. And ye sege or prevey therof shall do to be voydid and made clene from tyme to tyme and as oftyn as nede shall require duryng ye terme and space of xx yeris than next folowyng of ye said terme of fyfty yeris.

AND AFTYR ye same terme of xx yeris fully endid and completyd ye said parson and wardeyns couenaunt, and them and their successours byndyn, by y^{is} presentes, yat they & their successours, at theyre owne propre costes & charges, ye said tenement with ye appurtenauntes in every part and parcell theroff from thensforthe well and sufficiently shall kepe, repaire and mayntene, & ayenste wynde and reyn shall make defensible, as often as nede shall require, and ye pament in ye kynges highway aforsaid afor ye said tenement, competenly shall do to be paved & made, & ye sege or prevye theroff shall do to be voided & made clene from tyme to tyme as it shall be nedefull vnto thend and accomplesshement of ye said terme of l yeris; yat is to sey, duryng ye terme and space of xxx yerys of ye same fyfty yeris aftir ye said first xx yeris fully endid & exspirid. And also yat ye said parson and wardeyns & their successours at their own propre costes well & truly shall bere, support and pay, all maner quitrentes due & goyng owt of ye said tenement with thappurtenaunces. And the said Andrew, Ellyn & elyzabeth & every of them therof shall yerly discharge duryng ye said terme of .l. yeris by this presentes.

AND IT YS ferthermore couenauntid, assentid, and fully agreed betwen ye said parties yat yff it so fortune as ye wyll of god be fullfillid yat ye said andrew, ellyn & elyzabeth & every of them passe & decease owt of this mortall lyff afore thende and complesshement of ye said terme of fyfty yeris, y^t than as moche and as many yeris of ye same terme as at ye tyme of ye last decesor of ye seid Andrew, ellyn and elyzabethe shall than be therof for to com, shall holy remayn and retorne to ye vse & behove of ye forsaid chirche of our lady; & that than, immediatly aftir ye last decessor, yt shall be lefull vnto ye said parson and wardeyns & to ther Successours, in to ye said tenement with thappurtenaunces to re-entre, and the same to resume, enioie, and possede, as in their former astat, this present lees and all thynges therin contened in eny wyse notwythstandyng. FFOR THE whiche Remaindre of ye resedu of ye said terme of .l. yeris which at ye tyme of ye last decesser of ye said Andrew, Ellyn & elyzabeth shall than be theroff for to com iff it so fortune as it ys aforesaid. And for ye possedyng ayein of ye said tenement with thappurtenauntes in ye forme aforesaid, ye said parson and wardeyns oblygien and bynden them and their Successours, by this presentes, that they their successours at their own propre costes and charges shall kepe and do to be kept and song yerly, a solempny Obite within the chirche of our lady att hyll aforesaid by ye prestes and clerkes of ye same same chirche for ye soules of ye said Andrew Evyngar, Ellyn his wyff and Elyzabeth their dowghter by naem, & generally for all christen sowles, on the day in whiche ye said last decesser shall so fortune to passe and decesse out of this mortall liff, that ys to witt, on ye evyn of ye same day with placebo and dirige by note, and on ye morowe folowyng with masse of Requiem by noet, in all thynges aftir ye vse custum and maner as it owythe to be doen for christen sowles, within the said chirche duryng ye terme and space than for to com of ye sayd .l. yeris aftir ye last decesser of ye said Andrew, ellyn & elyzabeth.

yff it so fortune yt eny of them decesse and passe out of this mortall lyff before thend and accomplysshement of ye said .l. yeris, it shall be lefull vnto ye said parson and wardains & to their successours for ye tyme beyng into ye forsaid tenement with thappurtenaunces to entre & distrayn after ye lawe & costum of ye Citie of london, & yff it happ ye said yerly ferme of v marke after eny terme aboue said in which it oweth, to be behynd in part or in all by a monithe vnpaid, yff it be lawfully askid; yat than it shall be leffull vnto ye said parson & wardeins & to their successours for ye tyme beyng, into ye forsaid tenement with ye appurtenaunces to entre & distrayn aftir ye lawe & custom of ye citie of london. And yff it fortune ye sayd yerly ferme of v marke to be behynde in part or in all after eny terme abouesaid in ye which it owght to be paid by oon hole yere vnpaid, and sufficient distresse for ye arrerages of ye said yerly ferme ther can not be fownd, yat than it shall be lefull vnto ye said parson & wardens and to their successours for ye tyme beyng, into ye forsaid tenement with thappurtenaunces holy to re-entre, and ye same as in their former astate to retayn, enioy, & possede, and ye said Andrew, ellyn & elyzabeth & euery of them theroff vtterly to putt owt and amove, this present leese in any wise notwithstandyng. And ye said parson & wardeins & their Successours ye forsaid tenement with thappurtenaunces vnto ye said Andrew, ellyn & elyzabeth & to ye longer liver of them, for ye rent abouesaid & in all maner & form above declaryd, ayenst all maner pepyll shall warant, acquit & defende duryng ye forsaid terme of .l. yeris by this presentes.

Also ye said parson & wardeins couenaunten & [graunten?] yat they or thier successours, IN WITNESSE wheroff as well ye sealys of ye said parson & wardeins as ye sealys of ye forsaid Andrew Evyngar, ellyn his wyff and Elysabethe their doughter, to this Indentures chaungeably been seett.

yeven ye day & yere above wrytyn, Anno xv c vij.

III.

[INVENTORIES.]

[An Inventory of the Church Furniture in A.D. 1431.]

[1] A rem' that William Baker, Pewtrer, & John Hetheman [made] the first day of May, þe ȝere of kynge herry þe vj^e, after þe conquest x^e

ffirst, a cowpe of siluer and gelt, to bere in goddes body, with cristall
Also a cowpe of seluer for goddis body
Also a cowpe of laton & ouergylt
Also v chales of seluer, iiij gilt & j white
Also ij cruettes of seluer
Also iij paxbredes of seluer & gilt
Also ij crossis, on siluer & gelt & anoþer kristall
Also iij sensers of siluer & gilt
Also ij sheppis of seluere
Also a lytill cofir with relekys
Also a cloth of gold cald a fertour, þe champ red
Also anothire fertour of cloth of [2] gold, champ blu
Also iiij stavis of red clothid with damaske
Also a sengil vestyment of white cloth of gold
Also a sengil vestement of blu with sterres
Also a ȝelew vestement with ij toneclys
Also a white vestement of o sewte with briddes & grefons of gold
Also a red vestement of satyn with lyons of gold of o sevte
Also a hole vestement of blak veluet of o sevte
Also a hole vestement of blu veluet with sterres & mones of golde
Also iij blu copes of þe same sevte with sterres & mones
Also a white cope with briddes & grefons of gold
Also a rede cope of selk with lyons of gold
Also a blas cope of veluet

[1] leaf 9.   [2] 'of of' in MS.

Also j ʒelew cope of selk
Also ij grene copes of selk with beres
[1] Also a vestement of o sewte of blu ray with on cope of the same sevte
Also a sengel vestement with a tonecle & a cope of þe same sevte
Also a cope with kynges
Also a olde sengil vestement of grene selk poudrid with floures
Also a olde blu vestement of bord alysaundre with chakerid
Also a sengil vestement of red lyned with grene selk
Also a olde vestement with serkelys lyned [2] with blu tarde
Also a olde vestement of red lyned with ʒelow bokeram
Also a olde vestement of white selk for lente
Also a sengel vestement of white busteyn for lent
Also a olde vestement of red selk lyned with ʒelew, for good friday
Also ij children copes
Also a myter of cloth of gold set with stones
Also v corporas for principall dayes
Also vj seoudaries corporas & a case
Also vij pelewes of selk of diuers colours
Also iij principall towels for þe hye awtere
Also xxj auter clothis of lynnen
Also ij towayles for crosses
Also v smale towayles
Also iij feriall towayles to wype on handes
Also ij sewdarie of lynne cloth enbraudid with gold
Also ij masse bokes and a pistelarie
Also ij grete antyphaners
Also iiij olde smale antyphaners
Also ij legendes & a manwell & a Ordynall
Also iiij grayels & iij sawters & iiij processionares & a marteloge
Also vj candelstykkis of laton more & lasse & a kandelstyk of laton with foure nosis
Also ij olde crosses of laton & ij stanes for þe principall crosses & ij baner clothis
Also a cheste with evydens þat longeth to þe chirche
[3] Also haue in mende of ij chales wheche were broke to þe vse of þe cherche, on to twey sheppis & anoþer to þe princypall coupe with þe cristall
[4] Also a pece of seluer was broke to amend þe fote of þe crosse [3] of seluer

[1] leaf 9, back.   [2] 'lyned lyned' in MS.
[3-3] Scratched out.   [4] leaf 10.

Also a boke of laweis callyd decretallis
Also a stop & a styk of laton

[An Isolated Inventory of the Furniture of a House in 1485.]

[1] ✠ Ihesus.

The which maryn entird at Mighelmas Anno tercio
[R Res .. es . iiij^{ti}?]

Thies goodes after wryten be delyuerd to Maryun Conteryn and to Powle prioures, attorney of Maryn conteryn, marchaunte of venyse, by the handes of Iohn Bedham whan he entyrd into the place in Botolf lane wher nowe one peter Conteryn dwellith, } Anno 1485.

In the Cheffe Chaumbre
a standyng bed, made with estrychborde, with the hed on the same wyse.

In the chambre ouer the parlour
a standyng bed, a fforme, and iij^e barris of yryn for to hyng on corteyns.

Item, a chambre within the same chambre
a standyng bed, corven with estrich borde of beyond see makyng and a fforme.

In the Inner Chaumbre
a standyng bed and a fforme & ij° trestilles.

In another chambre
a bed without a botom.

In the parloure
a [spear?] with ij° leves.

In the Bottrye
iiij schelves.

In the Chambre ouer þe gate
a standyng bed.

In the Chambre ouer þe Kechen
a standyng bedd, a foreme & a stole.

In Antonyes Chambre
a standyng bedd.

[1] MS. B, leaf 24.

In the Chaumbre by þe Sommer parlour
a standyng bedd, a grete, new, standyng almerye with iij levys.

In the chaumbre next Seynt botolphus chirch yard
a standyng bedd.

In the next chaumbre lye
a standyng bedd, also a coumptour that Iohn de pount had covird with grene clothe.

a Coumptour in the chaumbre ouer the well, couerd with grene.

ij° Cowmptoures by antonyes chaumbre couerd with grene.

a Cowmptour by the chaumbre þat peter vatas had couerd with grene.

a newe cowmptour in the highest chaumber ouer the strete, couerd with grene.

In the Kechen
iij schelves, ij dressyng bordes, ij greate fformes, a fforme, and a greate almarye with ij leves.

In the larder house
ij Schelves.

In the house nexte the gardyn
ij schelves and a grete bynn to leye in otes.

In the Stable
a Racke & a mawnger, and it is new planked.

ffor the well
a Bokett with a cheyne of yryn.

Also ther be xxx spryng lockes & keyes.

and ther be xxij stock lockes & keyes.

Also ther be iiij plate lockes for the greate almarye & keyes.

Also v plate lockes & keyes with v boltes, yryn.

Also ther is, for the postern gate, a plate locke with a bolte, yryn, & ij keyes.

Also v plate lockes with v cleket keyes.

Also all the glass wyndowes in the saide place, and in the comptores longyng to the saide place [benethe?] myne, hole and sufficientely amendyd, and made at the commyng in of the saide Powle. And so to leve hem att the goyng owte of the saide Maryn and of his attorney by Couenaunt made bytwene hem & me þe saide I. Bedham.

[An Inventory of the Church Furniture, made in 1496–7.]

[This Inventory was probably made in 1496–7, if we may judge from the date of a transaction in 1492 mentioned at the end, and the fact that our Accounts show that an Inventory was made in 1496–7. Also the mention of the *late* parson, William Wyld, and the name of a donor, Dr. Atclyff, point to this period.]

[1] The Inventorye of the Chyrch goodes.
The Appareyle ffor the hyghe Aulter.

Item, ij° awlter clothes of Russett cloth of golde, of the gyffte of Mr Wylliam Marowe & William & Th. his ij° sonnes by the helpe of Mr John Smarte, grocer.

Item, a corporas caase of the same.

Item, ij° Curtens of Russett sarsynet frengid with sylke.

Item, a Sewte of Rede satyn ffygryd with golde, of the gyffte of the saide Mr Wylliam Marowe and of Iohn Smarte, grocer, conteynyng iij^e Coopes, ij° Cheasybles, ij° Aulbes, ij° Amyttes, ij° stoles, ij° fanons & ij gyrdylles.

Item, a cheasyble of cloth of golde þat Maister Cambryge made, with an Albe & Amyttes, an Albe, stole & fanon; And a gyrdyll of sylke made lyke a call with a corporas caase.

Item, an aulter of whyte damaske with the ffrontel palid with purple clothe of golde and white. And a awlter cloth, dyapre, sewed to the same.

Item, ij Curteynes of white sylke to the same.

Item, an awlter Clothe, Blewe velveut powdird with fflowres of golde and the ffrontell of the same sewte.

Item, a frontell for the schelffe standyng on the alter, of blue sarsenet with bryddes of golde, and ij° blew Curteynes of sylke, ffrenghid.

Item, a peyer Allter Clothes of Grene bawdkyn bothe above & benethe, with ij° Curteynes of grene sarsnet ffrenged with sylke blu, grene, yelou & Rede.

Item, a Sewte of whight clothe of golde, of the gyffte of Iohn Mongeham, ffisshmonger, conteynyng iij^e copes, j cheasible, ij Tonucles, iij^e Albes, iij^e amytes, iij^e stoles, iij^e ffannones & iij girdelles.

Item, ij° Awter clothes of Red cloth of golde and whight, panyd. And ij° curtens of Red sarsynet and whight, panyd & ffr[e]ngid with silke.

[1] MS. B, leaf 25.

An Inventory of the Church Furniture, A.D. 1496-7.

Item, a corporas case with þe one side of clothe of golde of Tysew, al gold, & the oþer syde grene saten barryd with lasis of golde, of the gyffte of Elizabeth gooseweH.

[1] Item, a Sewte of Reede Clothe of lukis Golde, conteynnyng a Coope with a cheasible, ij° tonykles, iij Aulbes, iij^e Amytes, iij^e stolis, iij^e fanonʒ & iij^e gyrdilles, of the gyffte of Wylliam Baker, peautrer.

Item, a Reede vestment, broudred with lyons of golde, of Reede Saten, that is to saye—a cheasible and a tonykle to the same with ij° Awbis, ij° Amytes, ij° stoles, ij° ffanones & ij° girdels, late amended, And a coope therto of reede saten poudird with lyons.

[2] Item, a Coope of white clothe of baudekyn garnyshid with byrdes, grefons and ffloures of golde, prest & dekyn of þe same [nspend?].[2]

Item, a Blewe vestment of velvet, poudyrd with lambes, mones & sterres. The cheasible, þe albe, the Amys, the stole, the fanon & gyrdiH.

Item, a Canapye of blue clothe of baudkyn, with birdes & ffloures in golde.

Item, a Canapye of Rede sylke with grene braunchis & white ffloures poudryd with swannys of golde betwene the braunches.

[3] Item, a vestyment of the gyffte of maister wylliam wylde, late parson of this chirch, conteynyng—a chessyble of blew saten fugerid with syluer, with an albe, an Amys & o gyrdyH.

Item, ij Corperas Casis of Clothe of gold And iiij of nedyH wourke, And vj other casys, of dyuers wourkes.

Item, vj Copes for children, of dyuers sorttes: & viij smale stremers of þe gyfte of Mr Remyngton & Mr RyveH: And oþer square baners.

Item, a Myter for a bysshop at seint Nycholas tyde, garnysshid with syluer & amelyd and perle and Counterfete stone.

Item, ij cheyres of Iron for Rector Coris.

Item, a pyx clothe for the hight auter, of Sipers frenged with gold, with knoppis of golde & sylke of spaynesshe makyng, of the gyft of M^r doctor hatclyff, parson.

Item, a pix clothe of Sipers, ffrenged with grene sylk & Red, with Knoppis syluer & gylt with corners goyng, of Mistres Duklynges gyffte.

Item, iij crosse stavys clothes, gyldyd, with Images of golde.

Item, a Canape for the pyx, of red velwett with iiij Crownys of laton.

---

[1] MS. B, leaf 25, back. This Inventory throughout has each page headed:—
'The Inventorye of the Chyrch goodes.'
[2]–[2] Scratched through.   [3] MS. B, leaf 26.

Item, a Canape for þe pyx, of whigħt Baudekyn lyke clothe of golde.
Item, a deske of laton with a [ff?]akon.
Item, ij standardes of laton.
Item, on the high auter ij gret Candylstykes & iij smaH. And on sent Stephyns Awter ij Candylstykes.
Item, ij Crosse staves, laten, gyldyd.
Item, ij gylt fete for Crossys, and oon Coper & gylt.

[1] The Aulter Clothes.

ffirst, an Awlter clotħ, diaper, hole & sounde, conteynyng in lengtħe iij yardes di., In Breede j eH with iij p^t Blew Rayes at the one ende.

Item, an Awlter Clotħe, diaper, conteynnyng in lengtħe iij yardes di., In Breede j eH with iiij Blew Rayes at euery ende of the saide clotħ.

Item, a clotħe of ffyne diaper, crosse werke, content in lengtħ v yardes quarter, in Breede j eH, & the one ende fasid oute longe.

Item, a clothe, hole, diaper, content in lengthe iiij yardes, in Brede a large yard, gernyschid with blewe at botħe endes.

Item, a clotħe of Crosse diaper, ffyne, content in lengthe ix yerdes and in brede a eH.

Item, an olde Aulter clotħe, diaper, content in lengtħ iij yerdes di. In brede j yerd, merked with iij^e Reyes at euery ende.

Item, another broken pece, diaper, content in lengtħ ij yerdes di., in brede a yerd, merked with ij blew reyes in the myddes.

Item, another aulter clotħ, diaper, content in length iij yardes di., In brede iij quarters & neł, with iij^e blynde Reyes at euery ende.

Item, an olde diaper clotħe of iij [peces?] content in length vij yerdes di., In brede j yard : fuH of holis.

Item, a diaper clotħe, wrack, content in lengtħe iij yardes di., In brede j eH.

Item, an olde diaper clotħ, content in lengtħe iiij yardes & di. o quarter, In brede j yerde.

Item, an olde diaper clotħ with losenghis, content iiij yardes, In Brede o yerde large, with a blew marke on the ende.

Item, an olde diaper clotħe, conteynnyng in lengtħe iiij yardes di., In Brede a large yerd, with iij brede Reyes in the one ende.

[2] Item, a playne clothe, peacid in the myddis, conteynnyng in lengtħe iiij yerdes quarter, In Brede a large yarde, with an Antony Crosse of Rede on the one ende.

---

[1] MS. B, leaf 26, back.   [2] MS. B, leaf 27.

Item, a broken Awlter Clothe, pleyne, content in lengthe iij yardes quarter, In Breede a yard & di. o quarter, with iij blue Reyes in myddes.

[Choir Apparel.]

Item, viij surplyces for the quere of þe whiche ij haue no slevys.
Item, in Rochettes for children vij.
Item, in Albys for chyldren vj, & vj Ameses with parelles & iij Albys and Ameses withowte parelles.

[Miscellaneous.]

Item, ij peyre of old organs.
Item, v grete belles and a sanctus bell, of the which v greate belles the iiij[th] great bell was clere of þe gyfte of Iohn Duklyng, ffysshmonger, as is graved vppon þe bell.
Item, iiij holywatur stopps of laton.
Item, iiij gret quysshons with downe, ij of them with sylke and ij with ffustean.
Item, iij smale Candylstykes of laton for Tapurs.
Item, iiij Candylstykes of laton with braunches for Talough candell.
Item, a gylt Table of the Trynete, for to sett on the high Aulter.
Item, a Coporas Case of Nedyll wourk the bakside purpill velvet, and a ffyne Corporas therin with semys of gold, of the gyfte of Mistres Iulyan Roche.
Item, more of the gyfte of the same Iulyan, a syluer bell parcell gylt.

[1] Towelles.

Item, a ffyene diaper towell, hole, conteynnyng in length vj yardes iij quarters, In Brede di. o ell, with a blewe Raye et eyder ende.
Item, a diaper towell, hole, content in lengthe v yardes o quarter, In Brede di o yard, with vj strakis at euerye ende.
Item, a diaper towell of cross werkes, ffyne & hole, conteynnyng in length x yardes, in Brede iij quarters large.
Item, a ffyne diaper towell, cheker werke, content in lengthe vj yardes di., in Brede di. o yard di. quarter, Chekred at bothe endes with blew & tawnnye.
Item, a diaper towell, hole, content in lengthe viij yardes, in Brede di. o yard.
Item, a diaper towell, Cheker werkes, hole, content in lengthe x yardes, in brede di. o ell, with blewe rayes at eyther ende.

[1] MS. B, leaf 27, back.

34   *An Inventory, imperfect,* A.D. 1523 (?).

Item, a diaper towell, content in lengthe vij yardes iij quarter, in brede di. o yard, with iij white Reyes at eyder ende.

Item, a diaper towell, content in length v yardes, in brede di. o yard, Broudred at bothe endes.

Item, a ffyne diaper towell, content in length iij yardes iij quarters di., in brede iij quarters with iij blue Reyes at the one ende.

Item, a ffyne diaper towell, content in length iiij yardes di., in Brede di. o yerd, broudred at bothe endes.

Item, a diaper towell conteynnyng in length iij yardes di., in brede iij quarters, Reyed at bothe endes.

wrack { Item, an olde diaper towel, conteynnyng in length vij yardes iij quarters, In brede di. ell.
Item, an olde Broken towell, content in length v yardes iij quarters, in brede iij quarters.

Item, a course diaper towell of the gyffte of patryck wolf, late yoman, content in lengthe   and in brede.

[1] Pleyne Towelles.

Item, a pleyne towell content in length iij yardes iij quarters di., In Brede j quarter di.

Item, a pleyne towell, content in length ij yerdes di., In Brede di. yerd.

Item, a towel, content iij yardes di., In Brede o quarter.

Item, a towell, content in length iij yardes, In Brede di. yerd.

Item, a towell, content in length iiij yardes, In Brede di. yerd.

Item, a towell, content

Item, ij Aulter Clothes, canvas, content apece iiij yerdes, In Brede a yard & di. quarter.

Item, ij dyapre Tableclothis for the high Auter, of the gyffte of Mestres Ientyll.

Item, a Towell of the gyfte of Mother Ienet.

Item, a ffyne Ryven Surplis in a lynnyn Bag, of the gyffte of sir Iohn Colyns. [2] this Surples was geven vnto Maister Welliam Weld, parson, be the asentt of the parysh in the yer anno 1492 be the handis of me Ricardo cloos.[2]

[An Inventory, imperfect, of A.D. 1523 (?)].

Five pages of MS. B have clearly been set aside to contain the following Inventory. Little more than one of these pages is, however, occupied by text, the rest remain blank. The date of the

---

[1] MS. B, leaf 28.   [2]–[2] In a different hand.

Inventory may with some degree of certainty be fixed by the fact that the page immediately before the Inventory contains matter of the date 1523, and the back of the last blank page has reference to matters of the year 1524.

[1] The Inuentory of the Chirch Goodes.

Item, an aulter clothe of fyne dyapre with a Cros of Sylke in the Middes and att euer ende, merked in ij places with Emmys, & Crownys ouer the M. & at euery ende v blewe Mylynges, the length þerof } iij elles iij quarters.

Item, a Dyapre aulter cloth, on Marked, of the length } iij elles di.

Item, a playne aulter cloth Merked with sylke, in the Middis our lorde beyng in the sepulcre, in lenthe } iiij elles & quarter.

Item, a dyapre alter clothe, on merked, of þe lengthe of } ij elles di.

Item, a dyapre aulter clothe merked in the myddes with a Cros of Sylke, of the length of } iiij elles quarter.

Item, a Diapre alter clothe Merked in the middis with an M. and at the Ende with k & v, which is in lenth } iiij elles quarter.

Item, a playne alter clothe merked with a Crose of Sylke in the Middis, whiche is in lenthe } iij elles di. & more.

Item, a peced alter clothe with a Seme in the Middis, of } oon ell & di.

Item, a worne alter clothe of dyapre of ij elles long and di. ell broode, } ij elles.

Item, olde Seer dyapur cloth of an   oon ell di.

Item, an Olde Seer dyapur Towell of   iij elles quarter

Item, v dyapur hand Towelles & woon playne Towell.

Item, a holybred clothe of dyapre made doble with a ffrenge at the Ende, merked with Red Sylke with .k. & v.

Item,

Towelles, Dyapre & playne.

Item, a Newe Towell of dyapre branched lyke damaske, of the gyfte of Mestres Roche, merked with W & R, off length } xiij elles, & iij quarters of a yerd brood.

---

[1] MS. B, leaf 89.

36 *An Inventory of the Contents of John Porth's House,* A.D. 1531.

Item, a Dyapre Towell merkyd with whight threde lyke ij Trewlovis, in length xiij elles, in bredith iiij quarters } xiij elles, & in b[r]edith iiij quarters.

Item, a Towell of Dyapre, blewe Mylyd at bothe endis, with an M Crowned of Red sylke merkyd in þe Middes, in lenght } viij elles.

Item, a Towell of Dyapre Towell, merked in the myddes with a crowned M of blake sylke, in lengthe } ij elles iij quarters.

Item, Towell of Dyapre merkyd in the Middes with a Crowned M of blake Sylke, which is in length } v elles.

[1] Item, an aulter clothe of ffyne Dyapre, merked with Reed sylke in ij placis with Ihesus, of the length off } iiij elles.

Item, a Towell of dyapre merked with blake sylke in þe myddis with M Crowned, whiche is in length } ij elles iij quarters.

Item, a playne Towell merked in the myddes with blake sylke with an M Crowned, which is in length } ij elles di.

Item,   playne Surplices for Men, aftir chappell gyse.

Item,   Reveld Surplices for Men.

[AN INVENTORY OF THE CONTENTS OF THE HOUSE OF JOHN PORTH, A.D. 1531 (?).

John Porth was buried in St. Mary's church, in 1525. By his will, made in January, 1524, he directed that the goods at the 'George' at Billingsgate should, at the termination of his lease of that house, be sold, and the proceeds be divided between the poor and in masses to be said in St. Mary's church.]

[2] ✠

here aftor foloythe the Inmytory Iohn port, layt the kynges seruant, as aftor foloythe.

In the halle.

Item, the hyngyng In the halle, 50 yerdes, at ij d the
    yerde. Somme argent . . . . viij s iiij d

[1] MS. B, leaf 89, back.   [2] leaf 725.

An Inventory of the Contents of John Porth's House, A.D. 1531. 37

Item, the Cortyng of the wendo.		iiij d
Item, hallffe a dose Cvshens.	viij s	
Item, a nolde pagent of Ihesus.		iiij d
Item, two bankers of Corse vardours of ix yerdes, at xij d the yerde. Some.	ix s	
Item, viij olde Coshens, at vj d the pese.	iiij s	
Item, two peses of Kentyshe Carpetes.		viij d
Item, a dobell Cownter of damske.	vj s	viij d
Item, a tabull with a payre of foldyng trustylls.	ij s	
Item, iiij Ioyntes scells, at iiij d the pesse. Some.		xvj d
Item, a nolde cobbord.	v s	iiij d
Item, a stakyd fforme.		vj d
Item, two tornyd chares.		iiij d
Item, a lytyll olde oster bord and a pesse of kentes kerpetes.		vj d
Item, a close chare.		x d
Item, a chare of spaynysche makyng.		xvj d
Item, a closse chare of wanskott.		
Item, a hyngyng beme of laten with iiij snosses.	v s	
Item, a payre of andionis and a payre of tonkes with a fyer Raike, with a lityll fyer choffell.		viij d

[1] In the payrlar.

Item, a hangyng of grene say with a bordor of xxxvij yerdes, at ij d the yerde. Some.		
Item, vj paygentes, with a lytyll one.	ij s	viij d
Item, vj coshens of nannt makyng.	iij s	
Item, a Carpet of [? ow]tnold vardors.	iij s	iiij d
Item, a nolde Carpet of Kentesshe make.		viij d
Item, a nolde medell Cowntor.	ij s	
Item, iiij Ioynede formes of wanskot.	iiij s	
Item, two tornede chayres and a [? I]ake.	iiij s	
Item, a Rownde tabull of sypars with a fott.	ij s	
Item, a nolde Rownde tabull with a fott.		xvj d
Item, a Rownde cobbord with a saylyng hause.	viij s	
Item, a hangyng with iiij nosses with a hangyng glase		viij d
Item, a payre of awndorns, cast of yrone.	ij s	
Item, iiij olde bokes and a standyche.		iiij d

[1] leaf 725, back.

38 *An Inventory of the Contents of John Porth's House,* A.D. 1531.

Item, two halbardes and a bell	xx d
Item, two olde polakes	xvj d
Item, two olde sale[thes?] & ij payre of splentes . .	ij s
Item, two bokelers	xvj d
Item, two lytyll tabolles of emaige	iiij d
Item, a payre of olde tabolles, playng	vj d [1]

²✢

In the bottry.

Item, a garnyshe of vessell:—iiij olde chargors, iiij platers, xvj deshes, viij sasers, two potyngars, weyng 152 at iij d ob the lb	xlvij s	x d
Item, two basens, two ewars	iij s	iiij d
Item, v olde basens, gret and small, iij pottyll pottes iij quartes, two peyntes for wyne, iij pottell pottes, two quartes, two peyntes, two halffe peyntes for ayll, ij holly wator stokes, a botell of tenne, weyng all 56 lb, at ij d ob the lb	xj s	viij d
Item, iiij barbors basynges, with broken candelsteks and latten basyns, iiij ewars, weyng 53 lb at ij d the lb	viij s	x d
Item, v small candellstekes		xx d
Item, a nolde cobord, a nolde beme, with other olde lomeber	iij s	iiij d
Item, vj large candelstekes	vj s	
Item, xiiij brase pottes grett and small and a small fyre chaffor, a brasene mortor and a freter chaffor, vij small chaffors with scelles, two lytyll posnettes, weyng all iij c xlij lb, a j d ob the lb . .	xlvij s	iij d
Item, xiij payns grett and small, viij kettelles bound and vnbond, weyng 148 lb, at ij d the lb . . .	xlvj s	viij d
Item, v barbor basyns and a collendar all weyng xiiij lb, at ij d the lb	ij s	iiij d
Item, vj speyttes and a burd spett	ij s	iiij d
Item, a payre of cobe yrons		xij d
Item, a payre of Rakes		xij d
Item, a pot hangar and a pot hoke		iiij d
Item, a drepyng pane and a fyer pane		xij d [3]

In corner of page, 46 s 10 d.   [2] leaf 726.
[3] 9 li 4 s 3 d in corner.

An Inventory of the Contents of John Porth's House, A.D. 1531.

[1]+

Item, a payre of tonges and a fyre shoffell and a fyer forke and a choping knyffe.	ij s
Item, iij treyvettes	iiij d
Item, in lede 40 lb	xvj d
Item, a stone mortor and a skomor	viij d
Item, two bowlles with other olde lomer in the kechyng	xij d

In hes chamber.

Item, the hangyng of the chamber, 50 yedes, at ij d the yerde, Some	viij s iiij d
Item, a siler, payntede, with iij cortens of grene bokerame	vj s viij d
Item, two fether bedes with a bolster, one vij quartes the other viij quartes, Some	xiij s iiij d
Item, a nolde matres	viij d
Item, a payre of wollen blanketes	ij s
Item, a Couereng of vardor on his bede, of xxviij stekes, at viij d the yerde, Some	xviij s viij d
Item, a bed stede, two fett chestes and a stalyd forme	ij s
Item, a nolde coberd with a deske	iiij s
Item, a skawer chest of oke, that the awtor was on	v s iiij d
Item, a nater clothe and a front of whit damaske and Rede velvett frenged with whit and Rede, with a pesse of olde valante	xiij s iiij d [2]

[3]+

Item, a super altare	vj d
Item, two lytyll tabelles of sypars	xx d
Item, a crusyffexe and a emage of owr lady and a paxe	xij d
Item ij crewettes and a pevter candelsteke	viij d
Item, a nator clothe of lennyn	iiij d
Item, a sprewse chestes and two olde skawer chestes	ij s viij d
Item, a shorte standert chest, rownde, and a nother longer chest, rownde, Some	xiij s iiij d
Item, two schepe chestes	xvj d
Item, a nolde closse chere and a Ioynt stolle.	xij d
Item, a payre of small andryons	vj d
Item, a coueryng of vardor, fyne, xxiiij stekes, Some	xxvj s viij

[1] leaf 726, back. [2] 3 li 19 s 8 d in corner. [3] leaf 727.

Item, iij pesses of kentes carpettes in wendo. . . .   iiij d
Item, another couereng of olde emagery worke, xxx
     stekees . . . . xx s[1]

[2]✠
In the chamber ouer the hall.

Item, the hole hangeng . . . . iiij s
Item, a nolde ffether bede and a bolster . . . . . viij s viij d
Item, a nolde seler with a tester, payntyd . . . . ij s
Item, a nolde broken coueryng of tapesey . . . . xvj d
Item, a standyng bede stede with ij sett bankes . . xx d
Item, a nolde presse of wanskott . . . . . . viij s
Item, a tabull and a payre of strestells . . . . ij s
Item, a nolde cowntor and a nold setell . . . . . xvj d
Item, two olde skewre chest . . . . ij s
Item, another skawer couer of wanskott . . . . iiij s
Item, a garde vyanse and a torsyng couer. . . . . xij d
Item, a nolde skawer couer low and a lytyll sprewse
     cheste . . . . ij s
Item, a nolde broken presse . . . .
Item, a pyllo with a Cownter vallans . . . . . ij s viij d[3]

[4]In the lytyll chamber next.

Item, the hangyng in thes chamber, 24 yerdes, at ij d
     the yerde, Some . . . . iiij s
Item, a tester of the bede with a seller . . . . . ij s
Item, a fetherbede with a bolster . . . . x s
Item, a standyng bedestede, a s[ti]s clothe with a forme xvj d
Item, a lytyll torseng couer . . . . ij s
Item, a nalmery, olde, with a deske . . . . . . viij d
Item, a skawer chest . . . . xx d
Item, iij small couers . . . . xij d
Item, a lytyll taboll, foldyng, with one trestell of the
     spaynyardes makyng . . . . iiij s[5]

[6]✠

Item, in the longe standert chest: fyrst a nolde Iakett
     of cremysyn velvett . . . . iiij s

[1] 3 li 10 s 50 s in corner.   [2] leaf 727, back.   [3] 42 s 8 d in corner.
     [4] leaf 728.   [5] 26 s 8 d in corner.   [6] leaf 728, back.

An Inventory of the Contents of John Porth's House, A.D. 1531.

Item, a payr of slevys of cremysng velvet In-broderet with damaske golde . . . . xx s
Item, a payre of sleves of the same velvet . . . . viij s
Item, a lynyng of a Robe of whit sarsenet, two pesses withowt sleffes . . . . xiij s iiij d
Item, a pesse of olde sarsenet, whit. . . . . . . vj d
Item, a Remnant of tawny velvett, moth eyten, Some v s
Item, a quarter and a halffe of cremysyng velvett . . iij s iiij d
Item, a lytyll Ierkyng of cremysyng velvet . . . . xx d
Item, iij schredes of clothe a tessewe . . . . . . vj s viij d
Item, iij lytyll schredes of clothe a sylver . . . . xvj d
Item, x small schredes of tensyn satten . . . . . iij s iiij d
Item, dyuers small schredes of velvet . . . . . . xvj d
Item, a quarter and a halffe of whit satten . . . . xvj d
Item, a quarter Rede a quarter whyt of saten burges . viij d
Item, vj yerdes and a quarter of naro tasco . . . .
Item, xxiiij corsse Romney boge . . . . xij s
Item, a spanyshe skyne, yello . . . . viij d
Item, ij yerdes of lenneg clothe, naro . . . . . . viij d[1]

[2]+

The napry.

Item, taboll clothe of dyapar, content vij yerdes, at vj d the yerd . . . . iij s vj d
Item, a nolde taboll clothe of corsse dyapar, broken . viij d
Item, v olde towelles of dyapar, broken, xxx yerdes, at ij d the yerd . . . . v s
Item, ij olde hengen towelles . . . . iiij d
Item, ij dossen dyapar napkyns . . . . viij s
Item, a corsse dyapar clothe of corse, content ix yerdes ij quarter, at iij d the yerd. . . . . ij s v d
Item, a longe towell of dyapar of xiiij yerdes . . . ij s iiij d
Item, iiij shoortt playne tabul clothes, viij elles, at ij d the ell . . . . xvj d
Item, a tabull clothe of cosse dyamons, content iiij yerdes, at iij d the yerd . . . . xij d
Item, ij towelles of dyapar, content ix yerdes, at ij d the yerde . . . . xviij d
Item, ij olde tabull clothes, broken. . . . . . . iiij d

[1] 4 li 3 s 10 d in corner. [2] leaf 729.

Item, iij shettes of iij breddes, holonde . . . . .   x s
Item, a payre of two bredes and a halffe . . . . .   v s
Item, a beryng shett with a seme . . . .   iiij s
Item, a dossen broken napkyns . . . .   xij d
Item, a payre of shettes of holond of [iij ?] bredes . .   ij s viij d
Item, ij payre of flexen shettes . . . .   iiij s viij d
Item, v payre of shettes, a xvj d the pesse . . . .   vj s viij d
Item, vj pyllobers of holond, Some. . . . . . .   ij s[1]
[2]Item, vj pyllobers of canves . . . .   xiiij d
Item, an olde Rayll of a yerd and[3] half . . . . .   ij s
Item, vij shorttes, olde, at xij d the pesse. . . . .   vij s
Item, vj olde smokes and good . . . .   iiij s

Hes Rayment.

Item, a gowne of tawny chamlett furryd with blake buge . . . .   xxvj s
Item, a nolde gowne of skerlett furryd with blak boge of spayne . . . .   xvj s
Item, a nolde gowne of velvett furryd with blake lame and faced with bugge . . . .   xx s
Item, a gowne of vyolett furred with feches . . . .   xx s
Item, a Rossett olde gowne furred with conny and facede with foxe . . . .   xiij s iiij d
Item, a nolde blake gown furred with olde blake conny   x s
Item, a gowne of pewke with blake sarsnet . . . .   xiij s iiij d
Item, a nolde gowne of pewke lyned with satten of sypars and faced with blake chamlett . . . .   viij s
Item, a gabarden of skayrlett garded with blake velvett   vj s viij d[4]

[5]+

Iakettes.

Item, a Iakett, olde and playne, of blake velvett ffurryd with lame and bugge . . . . . .   xiij s iiij d
Item, a Cott of Tawny chamlett lynede with yello cotton . . . .   v s
Item, a Cott of Russett marbell gardede with velvett .   iiij s
Item, a nolde grene cott Rydyng cotte. . . . . .   xx d
Item, a nolde Iakett of Russett satten furred with Ienettes, pryse. . . . .   vj s viij d

[1] 3 li 2 s 5 d in corner.   [2] leaf 729, back.   [3] MS. and and.
[4] 7. 7. 6 d in corner.   [5] leaf 730.

An Inventory of the Contents of John Porth's House, A.D. 1531. 43

Item, a nold Iaket the ouer part blake velvet, the neder part saten, furyd with lame and boge, whyt	iij s	iiij d
Item, a nolde broken Iaket of blake velvet f[urr]ed with blake lame	ij s	
Item, a nolde Iaket of blake chamlet foryd with blake lame	ij s	
Item, two olde Ierkyns of blake saten, pryse	vj s	viij d
Item, a nolde Iaket of tawne lyned with yello Cotton of chamlet		xvj d [1]

[2] +

Item, a nolde gowne lakyng the [3] . . . . . feryd with brokene ffoxe		xvj d
Item, a doblet of Cremysyng velvett clevyd with tawne velvet	iij s	iiij d
Item, a nolde doblet of Cremysyng Satten, pryse	iiij s	
Item, a nolde doblet of blake satten		viij d
Item, two olde doblet of satten, one whyt the other blake, Some		xx d
Item, two Cottes of ffence, one coueryd with tewke the other with bokeram		xvj s
Item, two armyng doblett and a pare of Sleffes of maylle, pryse		xvj d
Item, a payre of skarlet hosse and a pare of blake, pryse	iiij s	
Item, two olde Caps and two ondercaps		x d
Item, a pello of party sylke [4]		

[5] +

The wyffe[s] Rayment.

Item, a gowne of Tawny chamlett furred with gray	xxxvj s	viij d
Item, a gowne of cremysyn furred with bogge of spayne	xxx s	
Item, a gowne of vyolett furryd with gray	xx s	
Item, a nolde gowne of murre furred with gray	xiij s	iiij d
Item, gowne of vyolet furryd with callybar and mynkes	xxx s	
Item, a nolde gowne of blake furryd with blake sankes	xiij s	iiij d
Item, a nolde gowne of blake furryd with sankes	xx s	
Item, a nolde gowne of blake furryd with old gray	viij s	
Item, a nolde gowne of cremysyn lyned with sarsnett and purfelyd with blake velvet	xxvj s	viij d

[1] 46 s in corner. [2] leaf 730, back.
[3] Damp has rotted away the leaves in part. [4] 33s . 2d in corner.
[5] leaf 731.

Item, a gowne of pewke lyned with t[?]eke purfelyd with tawny velvett	xiij s iiij d
Item, a nolde gown of murrey lyned with bukeram and purfelyd with blake velvett	xiij s iiij d
Item, a kerttell of damaske, the bodys of saten, olde, lynede with yello cotton	x s
Item, a nolde kerttell of satten, broken	ij s viij d
Item, a nolde kerttell of blake chamlett	iij s iiij d
Item, a nolde kerttell of tawny chamlett	iiij s [1]

[2] +

Item, a nolde broken kerttell of tawny chamle[3] . .	xx d
Item, es a yerde of cremysyn clothe, mothe eiton . .	ij s
Item, iij yerdes of whytt cotton.	xij d
Item, ij ol olde furres of kallybar	viij s

Her bonettes.

Item, a bonnett of blak vellvet garnyched with damaske golde	xxvj s viij d
Item, a nolde bonett of blake velvet, worne sore, pryse	iiij s
Item, olde ffrontlettes of dyuers Collors, of velvett, pryse	viij s
Item, iiij parteletes of velvett of[4] tawne and blake two feryd with Cony and two vnefferyde, Some	iiij s
Item, two olde tepettes of sarsenett, worne, pryse . .	xvj d
Item, a kerstenyng towell, broken	ij d [5]

[6] In the garrett ouer the greytt chamber.

Item, iij pesses of olde payntyd hangynges	viij d
Item, a nolde Co[bord?] and a chest, payntyd . . .	xvj d
Item, a bede stede with pyllors	xx d
Item, olde torches, broken	xx d
Item, a nold peyre Clavycordes	viij d
Item, ij pyllos of down couerd with olde broken sarsnett	ij s
Item, vj playne pyllos of down, of dyuers sorttes . .	vj s viij d

In the garrett next the streyt.

Item, in dyuers lomber therfore a sylke [w womon?] .	iij s iiij d

---

[1] 12 . 4 . 8ᵈ in corner. [2] leaf 731, back. [3] Leaf rotted away.
[4] MS. of of. [5] 58ˢ . 10ᵈ in corner. [6] leaf 732.

An Inventory of the Contents of John Porth's House, A.D. 1531. 45

In the chamber ayenst the streyt.

Item, iij perses of olde hangyns	xij d
Item, ij olde fetherbedes wi*th*owt bolsters	viij s
Item, a stondyng bedstede and a payre of blankett*es* of wollen [1]and a norwege[1] coueryng	ij s

In the shope.

Item, ij lode of tawle ? wode	iiij s
Item, in bellett*es*	ij s [2]
Item, in coll*es*	

[3] ✝
In the Countyng howse.

Item, iij Swourd*es* and a hangar & a dager	iiij s	
Item, a prem*er*, prented in p*ar*chement withe ij Claspis of Sylu*er*	iiij s	
Item, a demy portuos, prynted		xij d
Item, a prymm*er* lymmed wi*th* gold and wi*th* Imagery, wretyn hond	viij s	iiij d
Item, an old purse and a pyncase of clothe of gold, price of bothe	ij s	
Item, an Image of o*ur* lady of Mother off perle, price .		iiij d
Item, a payer of smale sylu*er* bedes	iij s	iiij d
Item, a standysshe of Sypres		iiij d
Item, ij Remnaunt*es* of Sarsenet		iiij d
Item, iij olde doblett*es* and Shredys of velwet . . .	viij s	
Item, a lytell button of Course golde		xij d
Item, an olde lytell coue*ry*ng for a lytell Trokell bed .	ij s	
Item, an olde pelyon wi*th* the pelyon clothe of old chamlet		vj d
Item, ij dossen poyntt*es* wi*th* o*th*er [du *or* en?]d*es* of sylk		viij d
Item, xxxvj ell*es* of browne lynnen clothe, the ell iiij d, Su*m*ma	xij s	
Item, o*th*er olde gere founde in the howse		xvj d
Item, an ounce & di. of Corall	ij s	vj d
Item, a Carpett of Ieen makyng	viij s	iiij d [4]

[5] Certen stuff at [the George].

Item, Certen Stuff at the George at byllingesgate, as aperyth by the Testament of Mr porthe [6]

[1—1] Scratched through.   [2] 55s in corner.   [3] leaf 732, back.
[4] 3li in corner.   [5] leaf 733.   [6] xls scratched out.

Sperat dettes.

Item, sir henre wyot, knyght, for his wages	xx s
Item, the prior of Amysbury.	iij^{li} ixs viijd

Chatelles.

Item, for the Recouere [for ?] tho howses at þe stokkes by patent, the Summa of	xxj^{li} xvijs vjd
Item, for the lees of a howse at Byllingesgate . . .	xx s

[1] Desperat dettes.

The Abbot of Bewly	iij . . . . [2]
Item, Mr Copynger	xvj li
Item, the Abbot of Ramsey	v li vjs viijd
Item, the pryour of Tho[w?]erdreth	v li xiijs iiijd
Item, Robert Ionys.	xx s

Dettes that the Testatour oweth.

Item, to the Bere wyffe	xl s
Item, to the wever for wevyng of lynnen clothe . .	v s
Item, for howse Rent	lvs xd

ffynerall Expences.

Item, ffynnerall expences with oþer nesessary charges lxxiij^{li} vjs viijd

Item, the probate of þe Testament with other necessary charges.

[3] +

Playte and Iewells.

Item, a standyng Cope, gelt, with a Couer chassy . . .[2] vpryght and a women In the bodome poys .[2] . . xlj ons, at iijs vjd, Some argent	vij.[2] . .
Item, standyng Cope, playne, with a Couer gelt with a Rosse and a garlent In the bodom, weyng xviij ons, at iijs vjd	iij^{li} iijs
Item, iij goblettes, gelt, with a Couer, and In the cnope a whyt shelde with a grene lyone graven, weyng lxxij ons, at iijs vjd	xij li xijs
Item, a lyte, playne, stondyng cope, gylt, with a Couer, with a broken flower of amell broken in the bodom, weyng	

---

[1] leaf 733, back. [2] Leaf rotted away. [3] leaf 736, back.

An Inventory of the Contents of John Porth's House, A.D. 1531.

Item, iij goblett*es*, p*a*rsell gelt, w*ith* a Co*uer* w*ith* a
Co*l*lombyn In the tope, weyng lvj ons, at iij s
iiij d, Some . . . . ixli vjs viijd

Item, a playne peysse w*ith* a stare and a mane shereng
In the bodom, weyng x ons, at iijs ijd, Some . xxxjs viijd

Item, a pesse, p*a*rsell gelt, w*ith* saynt gregores petty
In the bodome, weyng ix ons, at iijs ijd the ons,
Some argent . . . . xxviijs vjd

Item, two pesses, p*a*rsell gelt, chassyd, w*ith* a Co*uer*,
weyng xxxix ons, at iijs ijd . . . . iiijli xjs xd[1]

[2] +

[3] . . . . . . smalle pesses, p*a*rsell gelt, w*ith* son-
be[am?]es in the bodom, weyng xxiij ons, at iijs
iiijd the ons, Some . . . . iijli xvjs viijd

Item, two Rownde salt*es* w*ith* a Co*uer*, p*a*rsell chassyd,
weyng xlij ons, at iijs iiijd the ons, Some . . vijli

Item, vij spones w*ith* postells, and on gelt[4] spone,
weyng xij ons di., at iijs ijd the ons, Some . . xxxixs vijd

Item, x spowns w*ith* dyomond Cnops, weyng ix ons,
at iijs the ons, Some . . . . xxvijs

Item, two flat massors, one brokene, weyng xvij ons,
at ijs the ons, Some. . . . . xxxiiijs

Item, two medell massors w*ith* olde bonds and bossys,
weyng xiij ons di., at ijs iiijd . . . . . . xxxjs vjd

Item, a flat lytell massor w*ith* owt a bosse, weyng iiij
ons, at ijs the ons, Some . . . . viijs

Item, two skawere saltt*es*, viij skawere wyth the Co*uer*s,
p*a*rsell gelt, weyng xxxij ons, at iijs iiijd the ons,
Some . . . . vli vjs viijd

Item, xiij spons w*ith* the postells, gelt, weyng xxij ons,
at iijs iiijd, Some . . . . iijli xiijs iiijd

Item, two standyng massors w*ith* a brokene Co*uer*, and
two Cnops of masors Co*uer*s, weyng xxviij ons,
at ijs viijd, Some . . . . iijli xiiijs viijd

Item, a naylle pott, p*a*rsell gelt, the co*uer* brokene,
weyng xij ons and a halffe, at iijs iiijd, Some xljs viijd

Item, a lyttell brokene nott w*ith* a Co*uer*, geltte,
weyng xiij ons, at ijs viijd the ons, Some. . . xxxiiijs viijd[5]

[6] Iewells for her body.

Item, a gerdell of Selvar lyned with blake velvett
w*ith* xxxij Rosses, and another gerdell lyned

---

[1] 39 . 17 . 2d in corner.   [2] leaf 737.   [3] Leaf rotted away.
[4] MS. gelt gelt.   [5] 34 . 7 . 9d in corner.   [6] leaf 737, back.

with Cremysyne velvett, weyng bothe the gerdells xix ons, at iij s iiij d, Some .... iij li iij s iiij d

Item, a brodde gerdell of selver with xij stodes of Selvere, weyng xij ons, at iijs iiij d ...... xls

Item, a gerdell of lome worke with a bokell and a pendant the Corsse damaske golde, weyng vij ons, at iijs iiij d .... xxiijs iiij d

Item, a demysent with a chyne and a pommander and a pendantte a treangell of selver and gelt, vj ons, at iijs iiij d, Some .... xxs

Item, two payre of bedes, of selvar geltt, weyng xiij ons, at iijs iiij d, Some .... xliijs iiij d

Item, a payre of Corall bedes gawdyd with gawdys of selvar and geltt and two payre of Iette bedes gawdyde with selver and gelt, weyng x ons, at iijs and iiijd the ons, Some argent ..... xxxiijs iiij d

Item, a demessent and two pare of hokes of selver and gelt, weyng v ons: Some, at iijs iiij d the ons, Some .... xvj s viij d

Item, v grett Rynges of gold, fyne, weyng iij ons and halffe quarter, at xxxvjs the ons, Some .. v li xij s vj d

Item, xv Rynges and two smalle Iem[o?]s and a lyttyll small chyne of golde, weyng ij ons iij quarters, at xxxiijs iiij d, Some .... iiij li xjs viij d[1]

[2] +

...[3] ... broken selvar one onnse iij quarters, at iijs ij d the ons, Some .... vs vj d ob

Item, a lyttell shelde of golde Innamyled with whyt and grene and with iij perlls, weyng a qwarter of a nounce, prasyd at .... viij s[4]

Pledges.[5]

Richard Garlond
{ Item, a Cup with a couer gylt, vpright, chased, of the weight of xv ounces & a quarter
Item, a Maser, Garnysshed with syluer gylt, with a Roose and a garlond of fflowrys in the bottom
Item, a proper Salt, parcelles gylt, viij square, with a gylt knop, weyng x ounces iij quarters
Item, vj sponys with knoppis wrethen & gylt, weyng vj ounces di. & di. a quarter }
delyuered in to þe vestry

[1] 22 4 2d in corner.   [2] leaf 738.   [3] Leaf rotted away.
[4] 13s vd ob in corner.   [5] leaf 739, back.

An Inventory of the Contents of John Porth's House, A.D. 1531.

Iohn Iohnson	Item, more: vj Sponys with woodos gylt, weyng viij ounces & di. Item, vij Sponys with postelys, poyse xij ounces di.
Mistres luke	Item, a Nutt with a couer gylt with a George vppon the couer, weyng xl ounces & di. Item, a whight pares boll, weyng xx ounces
Mistres luke	[1]Item, a lytell Salt, viij square with a couer, parcelles gylt, weyng x ounces. Item, vj sponys with wrethen knoppis, vj ounces di. Item, a lytell fflat maser with a bose, vj ounces. Item, a lytell gylt Cupp with a couer, chased, weyng xv ounces.
Iohn Iohnson	Item, vj Sponys with woodos and vij Sponys with postelys, weyng xxj ounces.[1]
Endyrby paid	Item, a stondyng gylt cup with þe couer and on the knop the barbours armys, weyng xxij ounces. Item, a Goblet, parcell gylt, pounsed, weyng xix ounces. Item, a stondyng Maser with a couer, the knop vj square, weyng xv ounces. All to plege for } v li

[2]Pledges.

Mr Alde[rne]s	Item, a stondyng cup with a couer gylt, pounsed with pescoddes, weyng xxx ounces di. Item, a Salt, Gylt, with the couer with sonn-beamys, weyng xxv ounces; to pledge for } x li Item, a lytell chales with the patent, parcell gylt, weyng vij ounces, the whiche chales was delyuered to Mr Aldernes in þe vestry þe xxviij day of Merche in þe presence of Mr Roche, Iohn Austhorp, Andrewe Evyngar with oþer moo.
William Alderston	Item, a lytell Goblet, weyng v ounces di. Item, a peyer of Course Shetes.
Andrew Evyngar	Item, a Ryng with a dyamond. Item, a Stondyng Cup with a couer gylt, weyng xxiij ounces. Item, a gylt Salt with owte a couer, xiij ounces di.

[1-1] Scratched out.   [2] leaf 740.

MED. REC.   E

Iohnson, baker. paid — Item, a greate Maser with a brode bond and a bose with a lybberdes hed, weyng xj ounces, for } xxviij s

Alys howe — Item, a peyre of bedes of Ieett gaudeyd with syluer, and a Treangle of Syluer & gylt.

Item, iij yerdes of Course Tawney Medley.

Item, an olde gowne of vyolet ffurred with blake lambe.

Item, an olde womans gowne of blewe ffurred with Shankes.

[INVENTORIES OF THE FURNITURE OF THE CHURCH IN 1553.]

[1]These parselles of Napre Insving, latly apertayning to ye seyde Church of Saint Mary at Hill, were delyuered to doctor Crome, Mr bassell & Rycharde Grafton, apointed by ye Kinges maiestes commissioners in yat behalf, ye tenth daye of ffebrvary in the Seventh yere of ye reign of our souerange Lord King Edwarde ye Sixt, in ye presence of Wolstone win, William brafild, William Kelly, Audrian Serle and Edmond Candishe :—

ffirst, delyuered xxxix aubes with lj amices & xij auter clothes, vij of diaper and v of playne cloth.

delyuered xix Svrplices with ij towelles of diaper.

These parselles of plat and ornamenttes Insving, latly appertayning to ye foreseid Church of Saynt Mary at Hill, were delyuered to Stephen Kerton, Cetezen & Allderman of London, Georg Heton and Wylliam Allyn, Commissioners by the Kinges maieste in yat behalf, apointed the therd daye of maye in the Seventh yere of the reign of our Souerangne Lord King Edwarde the Sixt, in the presence of Thomas Cleton

[1] leaf 748.

Inventories of the Furniture of the Church in 1553.

the ellder, Wolston win, William Brafild, William Kelly, Avdrian Serlle, William Steven, Edmond Candisshe, Thomas Shotsham, Iohn Heyns, Harry worland, Wylliam Holstoke, Henry Smith, mercer, Robert Heyes, Artheur malbe, Thomas papworth, Iohn archer, Stephen skidmor, wythe dyvarars other.

[1] ffirst, delyuered a challis of sillver gilt with ye pattin, waing xiiijten oz a half.

& j Crismatory of silluer, waying xv oz.

delyuered ij shippes with ij spones of silluer, parsell gilt, waying xxviij oz.

& ij silluer sensers, parsell gilt, wayng lxxx oz.

delyuered a Cross of silluer gilt with a Cristoll in it bovnd with latten wire, waing xlv oz.

delyuered the silluer of gospell boke, gilt, waing xxxiij oz.

delyuered ij silluer Candelstickes, parsell gilt, waing xlviij oz.

delyuered a pix of Sillver, wayyig viij oz.

delyuered a Canipe Clothe of Red damaske branched withe govld & ij Corporas Cases, one of Red velvett with [bovsaes?] knottes licke gould and ye other of Cloth a govld.

delyuered xj Corperas cases & iij of them Cloth a govld.

delyuered a Svte of Red Clothe of govld & iij Copes of ye same.

delyuered a Svte of blew Clothe of govld & iij Copes of ye same.

delyuered a Svte of whit Cloth of gold & iij Copes of ye same.

delyuered a Svte of Red velvet and iij Copes of ye same.

delyuered a Svte of blew velvet and iij Copes of ye same.

delyuered a Svte of whit velvet & j Cope of ye same.

delyuered a Svte of grene bodkin & a Cope of ye same.

delyuered a Svte of Red bodkin & a Cope of ye same.

delyuered a Svte of blacke velvet & a Cope of ye same.

delyuered a Svte of Red with lyons of gold and a Cope of ye same.

delyuered a Svte of whit damaske and ij Copes of ye same.

delyuered for a preist & a deaken of yeolowe silke.

delyuered ij owld Copes & vj owld Tynacles.

delyuered viij Chilldrens Copes and ij Cross Clothes, one of Red silke and the other of grene.

delyuered a Canipi Cloth of Red bodkin with viij stremars.

delyuered a stayned Cloth yat went about ye Sepultevȝ.

[1] leaf 748, back.

52 *Inventories of the Furniture of the Church in* 1553.

[1]delyuered xv banner clothes & a vestment of gren bodkin.
delyuered for a preist & a deaken of Red and Russet damaske.
delyuered for a preist & a subdeaken of blew bodkin.
delyuered for a preist a vestment of blew with bovnchis of leckes.
delyuered ij vestmenttes, j of gren ye other of blew velvet.
delyuered one owld vestment of sattyn a bridges.
delyuered a vestment of whit bvstine with a Red cros.
delyuered j owld whit vestment of damaske & iiij Copes bodkin with ij Copes of blacke vorsted.
delyuered iiij vestmenttes, one of whit, another of Red, and the other of grene silke.
delyuered ij vestmenttes, one of Red silke the other grine.
delyuered iiij vestmenttes, one of blew bodkin, another of Red bodkin, one of whit cloth, ye other of whit bvstine.
delyuered Cortins of Red & whit Sarcenet.
delyuered whole haninges of Russet Clothe of gold and Covrtins of Russet silke.
delyuered Cortins of blew silke with j ovld cope of blacke welvet.
delyuered one haning, beneth, for ye heigh avter, of whit damask.
delyuered Cortins of whit sarcenet with whole haninges for ye heigh avter, of grine bodkin, & certins of grine silke.
delyuered for Saint Christoffers avter, an haning above, of Cloth a gold, with Cortins of blew silke.
delyuered for St Annes avter, one haning above, of Cloth of gold, with Cortins of Red & whit sarcenet.
delyuered for St Katherins avter one haning beneth, of blacke vellvet & Red satten cortins of Red & whit silke.
delyuered for our ladies avtter, one haning beneith, of whit silke, and Corttyns of the same.
delyuered j other haning beneth, for our ladies avter, of blacke satten.
delyuered ij basons, one of latten & ye other of pevter.
delyuered iiij laten Candellsticckes.
delyuered a bell Cavlled a sacaring bell.

[2]These parselles of ornamenttes, Napre and belles Insving, now apertainning to the seid Church of Sayt Mary at Hill, were delliverid by the said Robert Yovng at the end of this Accompt to stephen Kevald, Churchwardin of the seid parishe Church, saflie to be kept to ye vse of the same Church.

[1] leaf 749. [2] leaf 749, back.

Inventories of the Furniture of the Church in 1553. 53

ffirst, a Challis of Sillver, parsell gilt, with The patten, waing xxx oz.

Item, a Challis of Sillver, gilt, waing with y[e] paten xviij oz.

Item, whole haninges for y[e] heigh avtter, of cloth of govld, Contayned in leinth iij[d] yeardes iij[e] quarters lacking a naile, in bredethe a yeard & iij[e] quarters, with one other haning benethe for the high avter, of blew velvet branched with gold.

Item, a haning benethe for the highe avter, of grine bodkin branched withe govld.

Item, a bvring Clothe a govld & blacke velvet.

Item, a bvring Clothe of blew bodkin branched with gold.

Item, a bvring Clothe of ovld blacke velvet with katherins whelles, & an ovld bvring Cloth for Chilldren withe a Crvcifix in y[e] middest.

Item, xv Cortins ij of grene silke and The rest of payntted Clothes.

Item, x avter, one owld of silke and the rest of paynted Clothes.

Item, a Cope of yeoloe silke, & iij[e] Tinacles, one of Red silke, another of blewe bodkin, and the other of lennen Clothe.

Item, a preist, deaken & svbdeaken of grine bodkin.

Item, iiij Canipi staves with iiij knoppes, gilt, & ij qvoissions, j of grine silke, ye other of nedelworke.

[1]Item, ij gret qvoissians and nine small.

Item, ij basonnes, one latten, the other pevter.

Item, In the vper vestre a gret chist bard with yron.

Item, In the lower vestre iij[e] Small Chistes.

Item, In at y[e] vestre dore a Chist with ij lockes.

Item, In y[e] qvire ij settelles with lockars apece.

Item, before my ladie paiges pew, a chist with ij lockes.

Item, a gret owld Chist bovnd with yron, & ij stovlles.

Item, In our ladies Chappell, a chist with ij lockes.

Item, before y[e] Qvire, a long ssettell with ij lockes.

Item, before y[e] pvllpit, a Chist with one locke.

Item, In y[e] Southe part of the Churche, ij long settelles, In the which we were wont to pvt our torchis.

Item, In the Northe part, a Settell to set apon.

Item, In the Roud loft iij[e] pair of harms with ij paire of spellentes, ij sallettes & ij blacke howbardes.

Item, more in the Roud loft; a long Chist with the fframe of the Sepvllev[r?] in yt.

Item, in the vestre, a Chist with iiij latten Candellstickes & a pixe, & a Crosse ffote of latten.

---

[1] leaf 750.

Item, ij Crvettes of leed & v gret Torchis.
Item, more; iiij staf torchis with iiij short Red torchis.
Item, owld yron, amongest ye which yer is a spit with Cortin Roddes and a sertain of owld leed.
Item, more; a painted Cloth yat did hang before ye Roud.
Item, In one of the settelles in ye sovth part of ye Church, v Torchis, Svm long, som short.
Item, ij fovnt Clothes, j wrovght with Red silk, ye other of gould.
Item, a Canipe Cloth of Red sarcenet sarving Svme tyme for the pixe.
Item, a ffringe with knoppes of silke beloning Svme tyme To a Sacrament Clothe.
Item, ij paire of Organs, ye one gretter yen ye other.
Item, a towell of diaper, in bredeth iij^e quarters of a yeard, in leinthe Ten yeardes.
Item, a Towell of dammaske worke, in bredethe iij^e quarters of a yeard, In leinthe xiij yeardes a half.
Item, an avter Clothe of diaper, in leinthe v yeaddes, in bredeth a yeard a qvarter.
[1] Item, an avter Clothe of diaper, in leinthe v yeardes, in bredeth yeard qvarter a half.
Item, auter Clothe of diaper, in leinth iiij yeardes & better in bredeth a yeard and a qvarter.
Item, xj Svrplices & x aubes, to be mad into Surplices.
Item, in the steple, v gret belles & one Santes bell.
Item, a Mas boke, with ij antiphonars, one greter y^{en} ye other.
Item, a graill, with a littell mas boke.
Item, a gospell boke & x bokes of song to be sovng at mas, in parchement, with v Caroll bokes.
Item, v littell song bokes, in parchement, & v song bokes in paist, with v song bokes to be song at mas, in paist.
Item, a gret boke Cavlled a leigend, which was paid for as here after ffolloithe:—M^r cleton, Thellder, iij s iiij d, Mr Lorimor ij s, M^r brafild ii js iiij d, M^r broke iij s iiij d, Mr Stewen iij s iiij d, & Robert Yong iij s iiij d, and all the rest was paid owt of the Chist in ye Churche of the moni that was Receued at the Commvnion Table, xxj s iiij d—xl s.
Item, ij belles of latten, beloning somtyme to ye Canipe.
Item, a boxe of evidences apertayning to the bell at Towre hill.
deliverid also aqvittaunce in latten being in [print?] for the Subsede of the Church for the Svmma of iijti vj s.

---

[1] leaf 750, back.

Inventories of the Furniture of the Church in 1553. 55

[1] ANO DOMINI 1553.

These parselles of ornamenttes, latlye apertaning to our Churche of Saynt Mari at hill, ar nowe Restorede agayne by the Qvenes maiestes goodnes, for the vse & behovf of ye seid Church, ye xxjth daye of december in the ffirst yere of her maiestes reigne, to the Intent yat god maie be ye more honorably & Reuerenly served; the which ornamenttes were Receued of Arther Stovrton at ye Qvenes wardroppe at westminster, & were deliverid bi the handdes of ye fforeseid Arther Stovrton, by Indenture, vnto Steven Kevald & Thomas shotsham, then being churchwardins of the seid parishe Churche, In the presence of Thomas Lvcas, William stewen, Nicolas Altroppe, Thomas Mvndy, Iohn harison, Thomas bachgate & Robert Young, thes parselles hereafter Insving, yat is to saye:—

ffirst, iij^e Copes of Rede Clothe of gould, the preist, a deaken, & Subdeaken of ye same.

Item, iij^e copes of whit Cloth of gold, the deaken, & Subdeaken of the same.

Item, a Cope of blewe Clothe of gold, the preist, deaken, & Subdeaken of ye same.

Item, for ye highe avter, ij haninges of Clothe of gold Reised with Russet vellet.

Item, a haning for St Christoffers avter, of Clothe a gold Reiseid with wite & grin vellet.

[2] Thes parselles hereafter Insving were geven of our parishners as hereafter Insvithe, yat is to saie:—

Receued, of the gifte of Thomas Cleton, thellder, a Crosse of Copper gilt.

Item, for a preist, a vestment of grine bodkin.

Receued, of the gifte of William Stewens, ij Courttins of whit silke.

Receued, of the gifte of William Brafild, ij paire of Corttins of Red & whit sarcenet.

[Leaves 761–2 *b* form virtually a duplicate of leaves 749 *b*–750 *b*, but the goods were delivered by Robert Young to Stephen Kavoll, and by Kavoll to Thomas Shotsham. After the box of evidence item the list concludes with:—"iij antyphonars, ij grayles, ij hymnolles and ij processyonars," the final acquittance note being omitted. Leaf 763 is virtually a copy of leaves 751 *b*–52.]

[1] leaf 751, back.   [2] leaf 752.

IV.

[THE ROYAL COMMISSIONERS' INQUIRIES RESPECTING CHURCH PLATE, ETC., IN 1552-3.]

[1]The Kynges Maiestes Commission derected by the lord meire and other of our Souerangne lord the kinges Commissionars vnto vs, Edmonde Candishe and Robert Yong, Churchwardins, for the trew sertificathe of all the Churche goodes and Ornamenttes.

We Charge yow, on the King our Soverangne lordes behaf, trewlli and plaineli to sertifie, declare and bring vnto vs ye seid Commissionars, in writing, at our next Sessions here to be hollden the xx[te] daie of this present Ivlli, y[e] wholle trevthe & sertente of all & eueri Tharticles here vnder written:—

1. ffirst, whoe were Churchwardins of your seid paroch in the first yere of the Kinges Maiestes Reign yat nowe is.
2. Itym, what goodes, plate, Ivelles, westmenttes, belles & other ornamenttes, yow or anie other person or persones nowe have or hathe in your possessions beloning & apertaining to your Churche.
3. Itym, to bring fovrth, and delliver vnto vs, the Covnterpayn of the Inventory of your seid Churche goodes, plate, Ivelles and other ornamenttes by the late Churchwardins of your seid paroche, maed and sertified to y[e] officers of the late bovshope of london, or to any other, & in defavte & lacke of souche Inventoris trew & whole [scratched out] transcriptes & Copies of all souche bokes & Reitsters as yow have or kepe in your seid Church, wherin y[e] particvlars of your seid Churche goodes were then sertenli menssioned and expressed.
4. Itym, what part or parsell of your seid Church goodes, plate, Ivelles & other Ornamenttes hathe byn sovld or pvt awaie sence

[1] MS. B, leaf 107, back.

the first yere of y[e] Reign of our souerangne Lorde y[e] king y[a]t now is, & to whome, when, by whome & for what preic y[e] same were pvt awaie, & wher and in whoes handes & keping y[e] monie & other profite therof Coming nowe is or to what vse the same hathe byn ymploied & bestowed & by whome & whoes apoyntment or consent. geven at the Gild hall of the seid Cytte, the xiij[th] daie of Ivlli 1552.

[1] Saint Mary at Hill, in billingesgate warde in London.

The ansever of Edmonde Candishe and Robert Yovng, churchewardins of the parishe Churche of Saint Mary at Hill in London.

To the Right honorable the Lord Maire of the Citte of London & other of our souerangne Lord the kinges maiestes Commissioners assined to take the ssvrwaye & knowledge of all the Churche goodes & ornamenttes within the sayd Citte of London of and apon sertayne articles ssent vnto them by the said Commissionars.

To the ffirst article we, the saide Churche wardins, saye that William broke and Andryan Serle were Churche wardins of owr said parishe Churche In the firste yere of the kinges maiestes Reign y[a]t now is.

To the seconde article we saie that we have in our possession all sovche goodes, plate, westmementes, belles and ornamenttes of the said Churche, as Churche wardins, wherof the particvlars Immediatly Insuethe. [Two Inventories follow, which for all practical purposes are virtually represented by those of 1553 above.]

[2] To the thirde article we say y[a]t we nether have, ne knowe of any Covnterterpayn of any Invetory of our saide Churche goodes deliverid vnto the late bushope of London or to any other, nor have any boke or Reisters In our keping, in our sayd Churche or elswhere, wherin the particvlars of our sayd churche goodes ar menssioned and expressed, to owr knowledge, Save an Inventory of ssouche gooddes, plate, and ornamenttes as we have above menssioned.

To the ffovrthe article we saye y[a]t in the Seconde yere of the kinges maiestes Reign that nowe is, Audryan Serle and Nicolas Austhorpe were churchwardins of owr said Churche, which Searle and Austhorpe deliuerid to hevghe Losse, esquire, the xx[te] daye of marche, in the said Second yere, a Challis of silluer, parsell gilt, waing xij o3, Then beloning to the Late Chantres & stipendary pristes of owr Sayd Churche.

[1] MS. B, leaf 108, back.   [2] MS. B, leaf 110.

Wiche audryan Searle, by whoves conssent we knowe not, soulde In the Seconde yere thes parssells of plate & gooddes Insving Then apartayning to o*u*r said Church, bvt to what vse the mony & proffittes thereof was Imployed & bestowed we knowe not :—

ffirst, to Willi*a*m Tilsworthe, a pix of ssiluer, wainge xlv o$_3$, at ffyve shillinges ffyve pence the ownce, Svm*m*a xijli iijs viijd, & to Thomas Clarke, pevterar, a deske w*ith* other lattin vaying v o. at xixs le o, Svm iiijli xvs.

Svma totalis xvjli xvijs viijd.

But the said Nicolas Austhorpe, then one of y^e Churche wardins of owr Saide Churche, as afore said, by the conssent of the maist anssient of owr Said parisshe Sovlde thes parssels of goodes Inssving then apartayning to o*u*r said Churche :—

ffirst, to Iesper, the basket maker, vij o a halfe of alliblaster, at ijs iiijd le o, Svm*m*a xvjs vjd.

To garret bvrton, the wexe-chandelar, ffyve skore povnd owlde wexe, at fyve pence The povnd, Sum*m*a xljs & viijd.

To Henry bet, a C of owlde yron at vjs, and to William Tvrke, ij Round barres of yron at xvjd.

Svmma totales iijli vijs vjd.

[1] Wiche iijli vijs vjd, was, by the Consent of the mooste avncient of the sayd parishe, layd ovt and p*ai*d by the said Nicolas Austhorpe Towardes the whitting & other necessary Charges apartayning to o*u*r sayd Churche.

Nycolas Austhorpe and Thomas Lvcas were Churche wardins of o*u*r said Churche in the iij^e yere of the kinges maie*st*es Reign That nowe is, & the said Thomas Lvcas then, by the Consent of The said parishene*r*s, Sovlde thes parssels of goodes Insving Then apartayning To the sayd Churche :—

ffirst, to [blank] the gilt of iij^e Images at xijs and to [blank] xiiij^{ten} povnde of pevter at iiijs viijd.

Svm*m*a is xvjs viijd.

Wiche xvjs viijd was Imployede by the said Thomas Lvcas, by the Consent aforesaid, Towardes the necessary Chargis of the said Churche.

Thomas Lvcas & William stewen were Churche wardins of y^e sayd churche in the iiijth yere of the kinges maie*s*ties Reign y*a*t nowe is, and the said Williem stewen Then, by the Conssent of y^e p*a*rishene*r*s aforesaid, Soulde thes p*a*rsels of plate & goodes Insving Then apartayning to owr said Churche :—

ffirst, to [blank] Red, govldsmithe, xij o$_3$ of ssillver, being Claspp*es*

[1] MS. B, leaf 110, back.

of bokes & the plate of a miter, at v s viij d the ownce, Svmma iij li viij s.

a bell of ssillver, waing ix oz a di. at v s the ownce, Svmma xlvij s vj d.

one Challis of Sillver & gilt & a pax parssel gilt waying xxiij[te] oz, at v s xj d the ownce, Svmma vj li xvj s j d.

and to [blank] ij bokes of owld servis, at xlvj[te] shillinges & eight pence, Svmma totales xiiij li xviij s iij d.

Wiche xiiij li xviij s iij d was, by the Sayd william stewen, by the Consent of The mooste avncient of our said parishe, ymployede towardes y[e] payment of ye waiges of sertayne singing men In our Sayd Churche and for ye The Reprayions and other necessary Chargis apertayning to ye same.

[1] Also the Churche Douthe owe vnto Edmond Candisshe ffor diwars necessarye Chargis bovrn & layd owt by hym for the vse of the sayd Churche, as aperethe by his acompt, the Svmma of xlij s.

[2] Sir Georg barne, knight, Lord Mere of the Cytte of London, Nicolas, bovsshe of London, Sir Rogier Chamlle, knight, Chif Ivstis of Yngland, & other, owr seid souerangne lord y[e] kinges Commissioners. To the Church wardins of the parishe Churche of seynt mari at hill within the seid ward & to eueri of them, greting :—

[3] On the king our souerangne lordes behaf, we streittly Charge & Commande yow, yat all excvses & other thinges set apart, ye faille not personalli to apere before vs & other our seid souerang lordes the kinges Commissioners at the Gvild hall of the seid Citte vpon mvndae next Comming, which shal be the xvij[th] daie of this present monethe of Aprell : at one of the Clocke in the after none of y[e] same daie, bring with yow the weri trewe & Ivst sertificathe of all your Church goodes, plate, Ivelles, Ornamenttes & belles of y[e] seid parishe, which y[e] of late or your predissessers maid & presented vnto vs of y[e] same ; then & ther to doe, vnderstond, & accomplishe all & eueri souche thing & thinges as to yow on our seid souerangne Lord the kinges behalf shal be ther declared & emoveved ; faile ye not hereof as ye will ansvere at your perrell. geven at Gvild havll the xv[th] daie of Aprell 1553.

The effect of the kinges maiestes Letters of Commission derected to the Commissioners for the Churche goodes ys :—

[1] MS. B, leaf 111.   [2] MS. B, leaf 107, back.   [3] MS. B, leaf 108.

That all yᵉ lennen of yᵉ Churchis within this Citte of London and Subvrbes of the same, saving yat which shal be necessari for the present vsaiges of the seid Churchis, shovld be deliverid forthwithe to yᵉ vse of yᵉ pooer in the hospitall in Christes Churche in the seid Citte of London vnto the gouerners & ouersears therof.

To yᵉ Cvrat & Church wardins of St. mari at hill.

After our harte Commendacions, thes ar to desire yow to consider the kinges maiestes Letters of Commission lateli derected vnto vs the effect wherof we have sent herewith vnto yow, & will & chardg you, bi vertvs of the same, acording to yᵉ trew mening therof, yat yᵉ will Cavll or Cavse to be Cavlled, with expedicion, a vestre of your parochiners, & then & ther to declare the effect of the seid Letters vnto them, yat the godli pvrpose and intent maie be acomplished acordinglie, & yer yow make or cavse to be made, a trew sertificathe in writting of all yᵉ lennen beloming or in ani wise apertayning to your Church, & the same sertificathe to be brovght by yow or som of yow vnto vs before the xxiiij[th] daie of this present moneth of Ianvari, at the bovsshope of London's hovs within yᵉ seid Citte beside pawlles Churche; & this we bidd yow harteli well to fare, the xxiiij[th] daie Ianvari, in yᵉ Sixt yere of yᵉ Reign of our souerangne lord, King Edward yᵉ Sixt.

Nicolas London, Rowland Hill, Richard Do[. . ?].

V.

[CHURCHWARDENS' ACCOUNTS.]

[.... *Leaves lost* ....]

[A.D. 1420–1.]

[1] Midsomere

Also rec*eued* of sawnder Myles & Nicholas Busshe ffor þe chirche porche	v mark	
Also rec*eued* of þe same saundere anoþ*er* tyme for þe porche	xxxiij s	iiij d
Also rec*eued* on þe Assomcion day for quarterage . .	vj s	vj d
Also rec*eued* for þe beryenge of Willi*a*m Organ . .	x s	
Also rec*eued* for þe beryenge of Emnot hallynge . .	vj s	viij d
Also rec*eued* of Iohn Gretyng for þe same terme . .	ix s	ij d
Also rec*eued* of Willi*a*m Beue*r*age	x s	
Also rec*eued* of Ric*har*d Sowne	xij s	vj d

Mighelmesse

Also rec*eued* for þe beryenge of Eleyne Sany . . .	vj s	viij d
Also rec*eued* on Alhalewyn day in quarterage . . .	vij s	iiij d oƀ
Also rec*eued* of Willi*a*m Beue*r*age for þe same terme .	x s	
Also rec*eued* of Ric*har*d Sowne.	xij s	vj d
Also rec*eued* of Ioħn Gretyng	ix s	ij d

Cristemesse

Also rec*eued* on candelmasse day in quarterage . . .	xj s	iiij d
Also rec*eued* of quite rent of sente Eleyns	xx s	
Also rec*eued* of Willi*a*m Beue*r*age	x s	
Also rec*eued* of Ric*har*d Sowne.	xij s	vj d
Also rec*eued* of Ioħn Gretyng	ix s	ij d

[A.D. 1421–2.]

Anno viij°

Also rec*eued* on Estire day in Candelseluere	x s	j d oƀ
Also rec*eued* for þe beryenge of Ioħn halsangre . .	vj s	viij d

[1] leaf 1.

Also rec*eued* on Whitsonday in quarterage	vj s	ix d
Also rec*eued* of Will*iam* Beue*r*age	x s	
Also rec*eued* of Richard Sowne	xij s	vj d
Also rec*eued* of Ioħn Gretynge	ix s	ij d

Mydsome*r*e

Also rec*eued* on þe Assomcyon day in quarterage . .	v s	x d
Also rec*eued* of Will*iam* Beue*r*age	x s	
Also rec*eued* of Rich*ard* Sowne	xij s	vj d
Also rec*eued* of Ioħn Gretyngee	ix s	ij d

[1] Mighelmesse

Also rec*eued* on Alhalwen day quarterage	vij s	ij d
Also rec*eued* of Will*iam* Beue*r*age	x s	
Also rec*eued* of Rich*ard* Sowne	xij s	vj d
Also rec*eued* of Ioħn Gretynge	ix s	ij d

Cristemasse

Also rec*eued* of þe hous of seint Eleyns	xx s	
Also rec*eued* on Candelmes day in quarterage . . .	vj s	vij d
Also rec*eued* of Will*iam* Beue*r*age	x s	
Also rec*eued* of Rich*ard* Sowne	xij s	vj d
Also rec*eued* of Ioħn Gretyng	ix s	ij d

[A.D. 1422.]
Anno ix°

Also rec*eued* on Estir day for candilseluere	xj s	
Also rec*eued* on Whitsonday quarterage	vj s	x d
Also rec*eued* of Ioħn Bacon for ij yere	vj s	viij d
Also rec*eued* of Will*iam* Beue*r*age	x s	
Also rec*eued* of Rich*ard* Sowne	xij s	vj d
Also rec*eued* of Ioħn Gretyng	ix s	ij d

Mydsome*r*e

Also rec*eued* of sir Ioħn Norffolk for þe swane . . .	xiij s	iij d
Also rec*eued* of Ioħn his man	vj s	vj d
Also rec*eued* of herre Mershe	iiij s	ij d
Also rec*eued* of Will*iam* Beue*r*age	x s	
Also rec*eued* of Rich*ard* Sowne	xij s	vj d
Also rec*eued* of Ioħn Gretynge	ix s	ij d

x ɫi vij s ix d.

[1] leaf 1, back.

[A.D. 142 ?].

[1] also resseued of sertayn men for þe rod lofte

ffyrst of Richard Goslyn	x li
also of Tomas Raynwall	x li
also of Rook	xxs vjs viijd
also of Richard Botelere	xx s
also of harry merch	xx s
also of Tomas wyte	xx s
also of Robert schad	xiij s iiij d
also of Iohan Gladwyn	xiij s iiij d
also of [?]	x s
also of Iohan organ	x s
also of Iohan Baale	x s
also of Robert peny	vj s viij d
also of water hasle	vj s viij d
also of Gretyng	vj s viij d
also of harry clerk	iij s iiij d
also of William archyre	iij s iiij d
also Iohan hacheman	iij s iiij d
also William Bakere	iij s iiij d
also Robert Raff	iij s iiij d
also Robert Rys	iij s iiij d
also Roger ady	xx d

Summa totalis, iiij^{xx} xv li xj s ix d.

[... Leaves lost ....]

[A.D. 1426-7.]

[2] These ben the parcellis of paymentis made be Wilham Gelam and Iohn Gretyng, Wardeyns of the chirche of seint Marie at þe hille, begynnyng at þe feste of Ester the ʒer of þe regne of Kyng herry þe sixte after the conquest v^{te}

ffirst payd for the sepulcre for diuers naylis & wyres & glu	ix d ob
Also payd to Thomas Ioynour for makynge of þe same sepulcre	iiij s

[1] leaf 2. [2] leaf 3.

Churchwardens' Accounts, A.D. 1426-7.

Also payd for a pece of tymbre to þe newe Paschall .	ij s
Also payd for bokeram for penouns & for þe makynge	xxij d
Also payd for betyng & steynynge of þe same penouns	vj s
Also payd for a dysch of peuter for þe Paskall . . .	viij d
Also payd for Pynnes of Iron pynnes [*so in* MS.] for þe same Paskall	iiij d
Also payd for a rolle & ij goiouns of Iron & a rope . .	xiiij d
Also payd to iij carpenters iemoynge þe stallis of þe quere	xx d
Also payd for vj peny nail & v peny nayl	xj d
Also for crochates & iiij Iron pynnes & a staple . . .	xiij d
Also for v ȝerdis and a half of grene bokeram . . .	iij s iij d ob
Also for lengthyng of ij cheynes & vj ȝerdis of gret wyre	xiiij d
Also payd to þe Raker	ij d
Also payd for cariage to a carter	iij d
Also payd for xj pavyng tyle p*ri*s	iij s iiij d
Also for makyng of a peire endento*ur* betwene William Serle, carpenter, & v s for þe rode lofte & þe vndir clerkes chambre	ij s viij d
Also, the day after seint donston, þe xix day of may, ij carpenters with her nonsiens	xvij d
Also for cariage of iij lode tymbre	xij d
Also þe xx day ij carpenters	xvij d
Also þe xxj day iij carpenters	ij s j d
Also þe xxij day ij carpenters	xvij d
Also þe xxiij day ij carpenters	xvij d [1]
[2] Also þe xxiiij day ij carpenters	xvij d
Also þe xxvj day iij carpenters	ij s j d ob
Also for tymbre & estrich borde for gynnes & wyndowes	ij s iiij d ob
Also for caryage of ij lode stone	xj d
Also þe xxvij day iij carpenters	ij s j d ob
Also þe xxviij day iij carpenters	ij s j d ob
Also þe ij [3] day of May iij carpenters	ij s j d ob
Also þe xxxj day iij carpenters	ij s j d ob
Also þe ij day of Iun iij carpenters	ij s j d ob
Also payd to Thomas held for Estrichbord	ij s vj s
Also for iiij munell for wyndowes	v d

[1] Illegible figures in corner of page. [2] leaf 3, back.
[3] 'ij' scratched out.

Churchwardens' Accounts, A.D. 1426-7.

Also þe iij day for iij carpenters	ij s j d ob
Also þe same day for ij cautels of tymber	ij s iiij d
Also þe iiij day iij carpenters	ij s j d ob
Also þe v day iij carpenters	ij s j d ob
Also þe vj day iij carpenters	ij s j d ob
Also þe thorisday in þe Whitson weke at þe reryng of þe same chambre, in bred & ale & ij rybbes beff & oþer costes	xvj d
Also the same day ij masouns to pynne þe same hous takyng with her nonsiens & a laborere	xxij d ob
Also þe same day ij carpenters	xvij d
Also þe same day for a lode lyme & a lode sonde	xix d
Also þe fryday ij masons with her servantis	xxij d ob
Also ij carpenters to amende the stappis	xvij d
Also þe satirday ij carpenters	xvij d
Also þe monday after Trenite sonday ij carpenters	xvij d
Also þe same day payd for m¹ m˟ m¹ tile & þe caryage	xviij s
Also for þe reparacion of Richard dounes hous, a tyler with his servauns ij dayes	ij s iiij d
Also payd for iiij^c hert latthe, pris þe hondrid, vij d	ij s iiij d
Also payd for iij^c hert latthe, short, þe c vj d	xviij d
Also payd for ij^ml traunsum, þe m¹ x d	xx d
Also pay for iij m¹ sprigge, þe m¹ ix d	xxvij d
Also paid for a quartern roff tyle	xv d
Also a buschel tyle pynnes	viij d
	iij li xiij s viij d ob

[1] Also for iiij lode lyme, pris þe lode & ij lode sonde . iij s x d
Also a tewesday ij carpenters	xvij d
Also þe same day a tyler & his seruant	xiiij d
Also þe same day in lyme	xij d
Also in sonde	v d
Also in latthes c hert latthe vij d	vij d
Also payd for v^c rof nayll	v d
Also for v^c sprygge þe same day	iiij d
Also a Wednesday ij carpenters	xvij d [2]
Also þe same day a Tyler & his man	xiiij d
Also a ffryday ij carpenters	xvij d
Also a tyler and his man	xiiij d

[1] leaf 4.   [2] 'corpus christi' in margin.

Also þe same day a dawber and his man		xiiij d
Also for ij^c beche latthe, þe c v d		x d
Also for v^c countre nayl & v^c sprigge & v^c transum .		v d
Also for v lode lombe, þe lode iiij d		xx d
Also for ij lode sonde pris		x d
Also a satirday ij carpenters		xvij d
Also þe same day a dawber & his man		xiiij d
Also on mydsomer eve a dawber and his man . . .		xiiij d
Also for vj dischis cole & xij lb moty		x d
Also for ij lode lomb for teringe of þe chambre . . .		viij d
Also for a lode lyme		xij d
Also payd for a goter betwene þe chirche & þe chambre weyeng a c & xxvj lb	x s	vj d
Also þe first day of Iuyl a pavier and his man to paue in lone lane at þe west dore, v teys	ij s	xj d
Also for a planke to þe goter aboue seyd		xvj d
Also for iiij lode grauell to þe same werk		xvj d
Also paid to Richard Boteler for þe stone to þe same dore	vj s	
Also for a key & a swevyll to þe chirche dore . . .		vij d

Summa, xlix s x d.

[1] Also for a mason to hew þe same dore, vj dayes with nonsiens viij d ob summa	iiij s	iij d
Also payd to sir Iohn Norfolk for halwenge of þe auter clothis		iiij d
Also payd to Thomas Seviere and his felawe to set vndir þe clerkis chamber dore þe o mason a hole woke .	iiij s	iij d
þe toþer mason	ij s	ix d
Also to þe laboreres	ij s	ix d
Also a lode sonde		v d
Also a lode lyme		xij d
Also for cariage of robous.		iiij d ob
Also for a mason & his man a day to make a stayer with iij stappes		xij d ob
Also a carpenter iiij dayes to make þe dore vndir þe clerkes chambre		xxj d
Also for wayneskote		vj d
Also a peire hengis to þe same dore weyenge vj lb & di., pris		xiij d
Also a peire stone hokis, pris		vj d

[1] leaf 4, back.

Churchwardens' Accounts, A.D. 1427-8.

Also for a c silt nayl, pris		xiiij d
Also for a lok and a keye		viij d
Also for Elymesford & his felaw to make þe steyer, al a woke	viij s	vj d
Also paid to more, Tymberman	xv s	vj d
Also for iij^c x peny nayl to þe vyse	ij s	vj d
Also for iiij^c vj peny nayl	ij s	
Also for a pound perchors for ly3t to þe werke men		j d ob
Also payd to Cambregge for nayl		ix d ob
Also payd to Elymesford for a day wages & his mete		x d
Also payd for Elymesfordes table ix dayes, euery day ij d		xviij d
Also for primyng of þe haly water stop		viij d
Also payd for þe stone of sire William Sparke		xxxiij s iiij d
Also payd for certeyne pavynge & mevynge of pewes in the cherche	vij s	ix d
Also for amendyng of bokys	vj s	x d
	v s iij d	
	v li iij s ij d	

[A.D. 1427-8.]

¹ Passhe Anno vj^o

ffirst for beryng owt of donge of þe pardon chirchehawe, to þe raker		ij d
Also for ledyng awey of a cartful of þe same donge		iiij d
Also paid to Richard Mason for þe makyng of a wyndowe in þe abbotis Botery	xx s	viij d
Also for a lode of lyme to þe same werk		xij d
Also payd to þe smyth for a ferment of Iron to the same wyndowe	vj s	viij d
Also payd for leues of þe same wyndowe and for hengis & hokis & nayles		xlv d
Also for ix^c .x. of gret pauyng tyle, þe c v s vj d	xlix s	vj d
Also for ij masons ij dayes for pynnynge of þe new pewes & leyeng of þe same tyle, takyng a man a day viij d ob		xxxiiij d
Also for her servant ij dayes		xj d
Also for oþer ij masons for þe same pauyng a day		xvij d
Also a laborer a day takyng		v d ob
Also payd to þe lauender for wasschyng of diuers clothis		ij d

¹ leaf 5.

Also payd for wasschyng of ij aubis & amys . . .		iij d
Also for beyenge of a gate of stone viij fote of heyghte with inne, boght of William Gemet, Mason, and two fote of thiknes, clene apareled, þe crest iij fote thiknes. Also with þe coynes with inne and withoute as many as be nedful to þe same gate. Also a base vj fote longe and two fote brede ioynynge for þe same gate		xxxv s
Wherof I payd hym in hande	vj s	viij d
Also I payd hym after þo.	xxviij s	iiij d
summa, xxxv s		
Also for cariage of ij lode fro Cambregges key, ladyng & vnladyng		xiiij d
Also for a lode from þe tour wharf, ladynge & vnladynge		viij d
Also a lode of þe same fro baynardes castel, ladyng & vnladyng		vij d
Also for a goter ston for þe same gate		xiiij d
vj li vj s viij d ob		
[1] Also for a carpenter iiij dayes to amende þe pewes þer the olde fonte stode, takyng vj d & his mete a day	ij s	viij d
Also for makyng of iiij polesis of bras & iron werk and lede þat serued for þe vayl	v s	viij d
Also for xxxviij ȝerdis of lyre for þe veyl		xiiij d
Also for soweng & hemmynge of þe same veyl & rynges		xij d
Also for echyng of þe same veil, x elne & di. of lynne cloth, pris the elne viij di. ob	vij s	vij d
Also payd to Richard Boteler for a lode ston for þe corbel of þe rode lofte	vij s	ij d
Also for heweng of þe same corbel	iiij s	iij d
Also a mason & his man iij dayes for settyng vp of þe same corbel	iij s	v d
Also for a lode sond to þe same corbell		v d
Also payd for a lode ston [?] þe bas of þe rode loft .	vj s	ij d
Also for hewyng of þe same stone for a weke . . .	iiij s	iij d
Also for heweng of þe same bas anoþer weke, ij dayes .		xvij d
Also for settyng of þe same ston iij dayes	xxv d ob	
Also for a laborer iij dayes	xvj d ob	
Also for a lode ston for þe dore of þe rode lofte . . .	vj s	ij d
Also for hewynge of þe same dore vj dayes & half . .	iiij s vij d ob	
Also ij masons fror settyng up of þe same dore ij dayes		xxxiiij d

[1] leaf 5, back.

Also for a laborer þe same dayes	xj d
Also for a mason a day to stop vp þe arche	viij d oƀ
Also for a hondred brek to þe same dore	vj d
Also for a laborer to þe same mason	v d oƀ
Also payd for a lode lyme to þe same werk	xij d
Also payd for a lode sonde	v d
Also for a mason pauyng in þe quere for a day & half	xij d oƀ
Also for iij sak lyme to þe same mason	vj d
Also for a laborer to same mason a day	v d oƀ

iij ƚi vij s iij d oƀ

[1] Also for makyng clene þe chirche and þe aley . . . j d
Also for þe caryeng awey . . . . iij d
Also for a plomer on þe vestyarye & on gretynges hous for v ƚb souder, pris þe ƚb vj d . . . . ij s vj d
Also for ij carpenters in gretynges hous a day . . . xvj d
Also for a carpenter half a day in þe sam place . . . iiij d
Also for a pyn of iron for stayenge of þe parclos in þe quere . . . . ij d
Also payd to Appulby for heweng of þe haly water stop . . . . iij s
Also payd for iij baudrikkes to þe bell . . . . . . xxvij d
Also payd to serle for þe rode lofte . . . . xxxvj ƚi
Also payd for iiij garnetes to þe quere with þe nayles . xiij s iiij d
Also paid for a lok to þe same dore with boltes & staples vj s viij d
Also payd to Serle for stalles in þe quere . . . . . xij ƚi
Also payd for garnetes & nayles to þe same stalles . . viij d
Also for ij[c] x peny nayl to þe same werk . . . . . xx d
Also for iiij[c] vj peny nayl to þe same werk . . . . ij s
Also for a c of ij peny nayl . . . . ij d
Also for a quere stole . . . . vij s x d
Also for a parclos betwene þe quere and seint Kateryn chapel . . . . xl s
Also for makyng of a quitance to halsangire . . . ij d
Also payd for a laborer for dyggyng of þe fondemens of þe chirche gate, a day . . . . v d oƀ
Also for ij masons, a day, to make þe fondament . . xvij d oƀ
Also for a laborer þe same day . . . . v d oƀ
Also for iij lode sond . . . . xv d
Also for iij lode lyme . . . . iij s

[1] leaf 6.

Also for a mason al a woke to set vp þe same gate . .	iiij s	iij d
Also for iij masons al a day	ij s	j d ob
Also for a laborer þe same day		v d ob
Also a mason al a day		viij d ob
Also a laborer to make clene þe chirchhawe		v d ob
Also for ledyng awey of iij cartfull robous & donge .		xij d

[A.D. 1428–9.]

[1]PASSHE, ANNO SEPTIMO.

Also for ij carpenters mendyng þe sepulcre a day & more		xij d
Also for viij staplis & iiij haspis & iij d naill . . .		xij d
Also for ij staplis & ij lokes to þe fonte		xij d
Also pay for caryeng of ij lodes donge		viij d
Also payd at hontyngdons tauerne for couenantes of þe rode		xiiij d
Also payd for a patyble to serle	xxxiij s	iiij d
Also payd for iiij Ewangelistes, makyng & keruyng .	xj s	viij d
Also for fecchyng home of þe same crosse . . .		iiij d
Also payd to hoggekyn, peyntour, for þe peyntyng .	iiij mark	
Also for iron werk & nayles for stayeng of þe crosse .	iiij s	j d
Also for ij disches of iron for sensers	ij s	
Also for mendyng of a lok of þe south dore & a keye .		xij d
Also payd to more, tymberman, for tymbre for gretynges hous & for þe piebakers hous	iij s	iij d
Also for serching of þe bell & for a pyn of iron . .		v d
Also paid to gefrey bokeler for makyng of þe chirche wex	x s	v d
Also for a tonne tyght of northerin ston for þe new chirche porche	vij s	viij d
Also for þe caryage & ladyng & vnladyng		ix d
Also payd to a mason for heweing of þe same ston a woke	iiij s	iij d
Also for ij stoms of asscheler lyeng vndir þe same bas		xix d
Also a mason, ij dayes werkyng		xvij d
Also for ij masons half a day to help set it up . . .		viij d
Also for ij irons for stayeng of þe same porche weyeng viij lb & nayles þerto		xvj d

[1] leaf 6, back.

Churchwardens' Accounts, A.D. 1428-9.

Also viij lb lede to lete in þe same irons in to þe wal .	iiij d
Also payd for wrttyng of þe parcell	xx d
Summa, vij lb xl d	
[1] Also payd for ij sholdres of moton at þe settyng vp of þe porche	vj d
Also payd for bred	ij d
Also payd for ij galons ale	iiij d
Also payd for nayll to þe porche celyng	vj d
Also payd for þe none mete on þe morwe of iij carpenters & ij plomers a sholdere & a brist of moton .	iiij d ob
Also for bred	j d
Also for ale	ij d ob
Also for a c lede nayll	viij d
Also on þe morwe whan they helyd þe porche, for a rib of bef	iij d
Also for bred and ale	ij d
Also for a bawdryk to þe meddyll bell	viij d
Also for a c latthes to gretynges hous	vij d
Also payd to Roberd lok for ij dayes & half . . .	xx d
Also for pynnyng of a wall & dawbyng in gretynges hous	ij s
Also for ij sakkes of lyme	vj d
Also for a bord in gretynges hous for a steyer . . .	iiij d ob
Also for beryng of a stone þat hasele 3af to þe chirche	ij d
Also payd to herry mershe for v dossen candell for þe chirche	vij s vj d
Also payd for xxxij potells oyle, pris þe potell vij d .	xviij s viij d
Also for makyng of a pewe in seint kateryns chapell .	vij s j d
Also payd to William Plomer for lede, sowder & nayll	v marces
Also payd to Serle for makyng of þe newe porche . .	x marces
Also payd for a papye	ij s
Also payd for Estrich bord	vj d
Also payd for a carpenter iij dayes	ij s
Also payd for þe ledyng away of a cartfull donge fro þe chirche	vj d
Also payd for pavyng in Eschep at Beveregges hous .	vj s ij d
Also payd for a planke	iiij s iiij d
Also the lauendere for a hole 3ere wasshynge & sowenge	ij s
	xij li xix s xj d

[1] leaf 7.

[A.D. 1429–30.]

¹ Anno viij°

Also payd for a mason heweng þe stop in love lane, xij dayes, takyng a day viij d	viij s	
Also payd for a northrene stone		xvj d
Also payd for þe cariage		ij d
Also payd to Appelby for makyng of þe mortere of þe same stop	iij s	
Also for ij sakkes lyme		iiij d
Also for a lode sonde		v d
Also for makyng of a gate in þe lytell aley	iiij s	vj d
Also payd to John Carpenter for makyng of ij newe gatis	ix s	iiij d
Also for anoþer carpenter to help him ij dayes to hange hem		xvj d
Also for xiij bordys to þe same gatis, summa	vj s	vj d
Also for leggys to þe same ȝatis		xxxiij d
Also for a c blak nayll		vj d
Also for iij ͨ & half white nayll, þe c x d	ij s	xj d
Also for a peire hengys weyeng d ͨ	ix s	iiij d
Also for a peire garnetes for þe weket, weyenge xxij d		xliiij d
Also for þe toþer gate a peire hengis & hokys weyeng xxxij lb	v s	iiij d
Also for a cofyn lok of iron for þe weket, with iij keyes		xl d
Also for ij tilers ij dayes in gretynges hous, takyng þe day viij d ob	ij s	x d
Also for a laborer ij dayes		xj d
Also for v roff tyle		iiij d
Also for iij lb sowdore		xviij d
Also for makyng of ij crossis in a fusteyn vestement		viij d
Also for iij cartfull sond to the chirche		xv d
Also for iij lodes lyme to þe cherche	iij s	
Also for ij sak lyme		iiij d
Also for a c latthes		vij d
Also for m¹ nayll		xiiij d
Also for ij tylers vj dayes, þe day viij d ob	viij s	vj d
Also for a laborer vj dayes, takyng a day v d ob		xxxiij d
Also for cariage of ij lodys robous		viij d
Also for mendynge of þe sepulcre		xvj d
Also for þe lauendere, wasshyng of awbes & surplys	ij s	
	iiij li x s	vj d

¹ leaf 7, back.

Churchwardens' Accounts, A.D. 1429–30.

[1]Also for ij tylers in þe pybakers hous iiij dayes, þe
day viij ob . . . . , v s viij d
Also a laborer iiij dayes, þe day v d ob . . . . , . . xxx d
Also for ij^c latthyes . . . . xiiij d
Also for xx fote Evesbord . . . . v d ob
Also for vij^c tyle to þe same hous, þe c vij d, summa . iiij s j d
Also for m^t & half of rof nayll, pris . . . . . . xxj d
Also for a pekke of tyle pynnes . . . . . . ij d
Also for d^c iij peny nayll . . . . j d ob
Also for d^c iij peny nayll . . . . ij d
Also for vj lb & di. sowder . . . . iij s iiij d
Also ffor ij tylers a woke in þe swan . . . . . viij s vj d
Also for iiij^c hert latthe . . . . ij s viij d
Also for iij^{mt} rof nayll . . . . iij s vj d
Also for ij peny nayll . . . . ij d
Also for ij^{mt} tyle . . . . xj s
Also for tile pynnes . . . . vj d
Also for iij lode sonde . . . . xv d
Also for v lode lyme . . . . v s
Also for ij laboreres . . . . v s v d
Also for a quatern of rof tyle . . . . xij d
Also þe nexte woke a lode sond . . . . v d
Also a lode lyme . . . . xij d
Also m^t latth nayll . . . . xiiij d
Also a c hert latth, set at warbiltons . . . . . viij d
Also for ij tylers v dayes . . . . vij s j d
Also for a laborer v dayes . . . . ij s vj d
Also for noncyens of þe same laborer . . . . . ij d ob
Also for ij pecke tyle pynnes . . . . iiij d
Also for a laborer ij dayes . . . . xj d
        iij li xij s vij d ob

[2]Also a tylere iiij dayes, þe day viij d ob . . . . . ij s x d
Also a laborer iiij dayes, þe day v d ob . . . . . xxij d
Also for ij^c latthes set, at warbiltons . . . . . xvj d
Also ij^{mt} latth nayll . . . . ij s iiij d
Also a lode lyme pris . . . . xij d ob
Also a dawber a day . . . . viij d ob
Also a laborer . . . . v d ob

   [1] leaf 8.   [2] leaf 8, back.

Also a lode lomb	iiij d
Also iij sakkes lyme	vj d
Also payd for þe plomers fyre	iiij d
Also payd for xij ℔ sowder	vj s
Also payd to a laborer for makyng clene of chambres a day	v d
Also a laborer for iij dayes, þe day v d oḃ	xvj d oḃ
Also for ledyng awey of Robys in a lyghtere . . .	xvj d
Also for wasshyng and amendyng of aubes & sarplys . ij s	
Also for wrytyng of þese parcell	xx d

Summa totalis, c ℔ v ℔ xvj s vij d oḃ
c vj ℔ vij s vij d oḃ   xxiiij s v d oḃ

[. . . A.D. 1430–1 lost . . .]
[See p. 26 for Inventory.]

[1] Haue in mende thath in þe yere of kyng [herry] þe sixte, x ȝere, & also þe seconde day of may, delyueryd be Iohan Gretyng to Iohan Hetheman & to Wylliam Baker . . . xviij ℔ xix s in þe boxe.

also a quitavnse for Iohan, so Iohan be William morys ys exemt.

Wylliams [marlbe & þoun?] Ball haþe I Resseywith of [Iohan] hethemann & Wylliams Baker in þe xiij ȝerre of kyng h þe sext, xiij ℔ & ix s & vij d oḃ in þe last day of April.

. . . .
[Accounts for A.D. 1431–76 lost.]
. . . .
[A.D. 1477 and 1479.]

[2] This is thaccompt of Iohn Palmer and Iohn Clerke, Wardens of the Church of Saint Mary atte Hille from the ffest of Saynt Mighell tharchangell In the xvij yere of the Reigne of kynge Edwarde þe iiij[th] Vnto the ffest of Saynt Mighell in the xix[th] yere of the same kyng by ij hoole yere

[3] THe Rentall of Londes & tenementes longyng to diuerse Chawntries [4] & to þe Chyrch [4] founded in the

---

[1] leaf 11.   [2] leaf 12.   [3] leaf 13.
[4–4] In a slightly later hand.

Church of Saynt Mary at Hyll in london renywed atte ffest of Saynt Mighell tharchaungell in the xvij ȝere of the Reygne of Kynge Edwarde the ffourth & ce'

lyuelode belongyng to the Chyrch

[1]IOHN WESTONS CHAUNTRY[1]

In the paressh of Saynt Mary atte hyll
- Harry Williamson, for a tenement . . . iiij li
- William Geffrey, for Rente of a tenement xxxiij s iiij d
- Thomas Raynolde, for Rente of a tenement liij s iiij d
- Sir Iohn Colyns, for Rente of a . . . xx s
- Sir Iohn Mortram, for Rente of a . . . xij s
- Sir Iohn Plummer, for Rente of a . . . ix s
- Iohn Dokelyng, for Rente of a tenement . xx s
- Sir Iohn Philip, for Rente of a . . . . viij s
- Sir Philip Norton, for Rente of a . . . viij s

Iohn Iohnson, Bocher, for a tenement in the paressh of Saynt leonardis in Estchepe . xxvj s viij d

Harry Mersshe, for a tenement and a gardyne atte Towrehill in the paresshe of Saynt Botulphis . . . . xx s

Margarete Powtrell, of quyte Rente goynge owte of a tenement in the paresshe of Saynt Mary atte hylle . . . . . . iij s iiij d

The Wardeyns of the Churche of Saynt Botulphis besides belynesgate, of quite Rente goyng owte of a Tenement longyng to the same Church, sette in the paresshe of . . . . ij s vj d

Summa, xiiij li xvj s ij d.

[2]IOHN CAUSTONS CHAUNTRY

In the parissh of Saint Mary atte hille
- William Blase, for Rent of a tenement iiij li xij s iiij d
- Hew Clerke, for Rent of a tenement . xx s
- Iohn Byrkeby, for Rent of a tenement xx s
- Iohn Modley, for Rent of a tenement. xx s

Iohn Breuster, Tornour, for ij tenementes in the parissh of Andrews[2] in Estchepe . . . . xxxviij s

---

[1-1] Scratched out, and the line above substituted for it.
[2] leaf 13, back.   [3] Andrews *substituted for* leonard.

Churchwardens' Accounts, A.D. 1477–9.

In the parissh of Saynt botulphe withowte algate
- Clement hille, for a tenement . . . viij s
- Iamys Cokke, for ij tenementes . . xvj s viij d
- Iohn Smerte, for a gardyne . . . . iiij s
- Cristan Stevyns, for a gardyne . . . xij s iiij d
- Iohn Motte, Carpinter, for a gardyne . iiij d
- William harrydeson, for ij gardyn [?] . v s iiij d

Iohn ffissh, for a tenement in greschurchehestrete . . . . . . vj li

Summa, xviij li xx d.

[1] TENEMENTES OF THE CHAUNTRY OF RICHARDE GOSSELYNE

In the parissh of Saint leonardes in Vaster lane
- Iohn Dighten, for a tenement . . . . iij li
- lewis   , ffisician, for a tenement xl s
- William Shirburne, Capper, for a tenement xx s
- Alice lovyndon, for a tenement . . . xvj s
- William Cator, Brawderer, for a tenement xviij s
- William levesham, Capper, for a tenement xxvj s viij d
- Williams Busshope, Tailowr . . . . xviij d

Summa, ix li xviij s viij d.

THE CHAUNTRY OF IOHN BEDEHAM

Lewis Lumbarde,   , for a tenement in Saint Botulphez lane in the parissh of saint George . . . . xiij li vj s viij d

THE CHAUNTRY OF WILLIAM CAMBRIDGE

In the parissh of Saint Christofer
- ffor tenementes there for half a yere . iij li
- ffor the same tenement for a hole yere. x li

Summa, xiij li.

Summa of alle the Rente by the said ij yere . . . . cxxv li vj s iiij d

[A.D. 1477–79.]

[2] THis is thaccompt of Iohn Palmer & Iohn Clerke, Wardeyns of the Churche of Saint Mary at Hille besides Belynesgate, in London; ffrom the fest of Mighell tharchaungell in the xvij yere of the Regne of kyng Edward the fourth, vnto the ffest of Saint

---

[1] leaf 14.   [2] leaf 15.

Churchwardens' Accounts, A.D. 1477–9.

Mighell tharchangell in the xix yere of the Regne of the same kyng, that is to say, by ij hole yeris & cetera

ffirst, they be charged with xxix ℔ xij s iiij d of Rentes of the tenementes longyng to the Rentes[1] of Iohn Weston for the said ij yeris, chargyd at xiiij ℔ xvj s ij d by the yere

And with xxxvj ℔ iij s iiij d of Rentes of þe tementes longyng to the tenementes of Iohn Causton for the same ij yere, Chargyd at xviij ℔ xx d by the yere, &c'; And with xix ℔ xvij s iiij d of the Rentes of tenementes longyng to the Chauntry of Richard Gosselyn for the ij yeris aforsayd, Chargid at ix ℔ xviij s viij d by þe yere

And with xxvj ℔ xiij s iiij d of the Rente of a tenement longyng to the chauntry of Iohn Bodeham for ij yere aforsaid, chargid at xiij ℔ vj s viij d by the yere

Item, receyvid of the Rent of a tenement sette in the parissh of Saint Cristofre atte Stokkes, which was sumtyme William Cambridge, for the termes of Midsomer & Mighelmasse A° xviij°, iij ℔, And of the Rent of the same tenement for a yere endid at Mighelmasse, Anno xix^mo, x ℔ . . . . xiij ℔

Summa, cxxv ℔ vj s iiij d.

[2] Increce of Rente
{ Also they charge them selfe with xxiij s iiij d of increse of Rente of a tenement in the parissh of Saint Mary at hille, whiche is chargid among the Rentis of Westens Chauntry, callid the Churche Rentes, at xx s by the yere, now late to Iohn Dokeling for xxxiij s iiij d by the yere, that is, by a yere & iij quarters of a yere, & c'

Summa, xxiij s iiij d.

Bequest { Item, Receyvid of Richard Bliet, of Thurrok in Essex, of his gift to the Churchwerke . vj s viij d

Arrerages
{ Item, Receyvid of Iohn Iohnson, Bocher, of Areragos of his Rente . . . . . xlvj s viij d
Item, of Sir Iohn Mortram, of Arrerages of his Rent . . . . xxiiij s
Item, of William Geffereis wife, of Arrerages of Rente . . . . xx s
And of Iamys Cokke, wever, of Arrerages of his Rent. . . . . xx s ij d

Summa, v ℔ xvij s vj d.
Summa of this side, vij ℔ x d.

---

[1] 'Chauntry' scratched out.   [2] leaf 15, back.

¹Casuell Receytis.

ffor the beme light, Receyved in the said ij yeris	xlij s	
ffor the Paschall tapir in the same yeres	xxv s	iiij d
ffor the wast of ij tapres at Caustons obite		iiij d
ffor the wast of ij tapres at Iohn Bedhams obite		iiij d
ffor the wast of ij tapris at Richarde Gosselyns obite		iiij d
ffor the wast of ij tapris at William Cambridgeȝ obite		iiij d
ffor an empty hoggishede, solde to William proyne		vj d
ffor an olde Gravestone, solde to	vj s	viij d
ffor ij Busshell sande, solde		ij d
Item, Receyvid of Thomas Crullis wife, for Ryngynge of the grete Belle for hir husbonde	iij s	iiij d
ffor Buryyng of Thomas Crulle in the Church	xiij s	iiij d
ffor Buryyng of Sir Thomas Wilkynson, preste, in the Churche	xiij s	iiij d
Receyvid of of William Prune for Buryyng of his sonne in the Churche	xiij s	iiij d
And for the buryyng of a straunge manne in the Churche yarde	iij s	iiij d
Item, Receyved of Iohn Iacob for the obseruaunce in the Churche for a Spaynarde þat was slayne	v s	

Summa, vj li vij s viij d.

²Parcellis Receyved for Buryyng of Corses in the pardon Churchyarde

ffor buryyng of Crullis doghtir	ij s
ffor harry Clerkes, of gifte	ij s
ffor William Blasis Childe	ij s
ffor Iohn Smyth	ij s
ffor the kerchife-launders doghtir	ij s
ffor Dokelyngis manne	ij s
ffor huntis wife	ij s
ffor Cecile Crulle	ij s
ffor John Clerkis doghtir	iiij s
ffor John Bakers doghtir	ij s

Summa, xxij s.
Summa of alle the Charge, cxxxix li xvj s xd.

¹ leaf 16.   ² leaf 16, back.

Payementes and expenses vpon Westons lyvelode

Quite Rentis	ffirst, paid to thabbot of Waltham, of a quite Rent of xxxviij s yerely goyng owte of a tenement that was sumtyme Iohn Westons, sette in the parish of	lxxvj s
	To Myghell harryes, wardeyne of the churche of Saynt george in puddyng lane, of a quite Rent of xx s yerely goyng owte of a tenement sette in the parisshe of Saynt Mary atte hille, for ij yere atte Michelmasse, A° xix°	xl s
	To the priowre of cristchurche withyn Algate of london, of a quite Rent of iij s yerely goynge owte of a tenement sette in the same parisshe of Saint Mary, for ij yere endid at Estir, A° xix^{mo}, by ij Acquitaunce₃	vj s
	To the same priowre, of a quite Rente of v s yerely goyng owte of tenementes sette in the parissh of Saint Botulphis withowte Algate which was Iohn Westons, endyd at Crystmasse, for ij yere, A° xix^{mo} of the sayd kynge	v s

Summa, vj li xij s.

Prestes wages	Item, paid to Sir Iohn Philippe for kepyng of the morow masse, for euery quarter of a yere v s, by þe same ij yers	xl s
	Item, paid to Sir Iohn Colyns, in Augmentacion of his wagis, at viij s iiij d by the quarter, by the space of the same ij yere	iij li vj s viij d

Summa, v li vj s viij d.

Summa, xj li xviij s viij d.

Vacacion	[2] And allowaunce of Rente of a tenement sette in the parisshe of Saint Mary atte hille, in the holdyng of harry Williamson, chargid in the Rentall at iiij li by the yere, stondyng voyd by all the furst yere	iiij li
Obites	Item, paid for thobite of Iohn Weston, holde ij tyme₃ within the tyme of this accompt, for eythir tyme iij s iiij d	vj s viij d
	Item, for the obite of Sir Iohn Bradmere, which gave to the Churche a nywe Chalice weyng [ ], for either yere iij s iiij d	vj s viij d

[1] leaf 17.   [2] leaf 17, back.

Paid to Iohn Modley, for servyng the quere for þe termeȝ of Mydsomer & Mighelmasse, A° xviij°, for eythir quarter, vj s viij d } xiij s   iiij d

To the same Iohn, for his wagis, servyng in the quere from Mighelmasse, A° xviij, vnto Midsomer, A° xix°, for euery quarter, vj s viij d—xx s; And from Midsomer vnto Mighelmasse next suyng, seruyng as a paressh Clerke, for his wages, xiij s iiij d } xxxiij s iiij d

To the parissh preste, to Remembre in the pulpite the sowle of [Richard] Bliot, which gave to the Churche workis vj s viij d } ij d

Item, paid to William paris, for beryng of the grete boke to Sir William palmers Chambre, to write anothir boke by that } iiij d

Item, paid to William paris & the Clerke for ther mete one good ffryday } ij d

Summa, vij li viij d.

¹Expenses for the Churche.

Item, paid to a vestment-maker for the mendyng of the Blak Copes, & of all othir Copeȝ that were fawty, by xiiij daies, takyng by the day ix d. Summa, } x s   vj d

ffor Rede Silke xij d,
Rebende of diuerse colowris iiij s,
for velvet ix d,
ffor bokeram for lynyng, iiij s, } ix s   ix d

To Rafe Smyth, for mendyng of a chayne to a boke in the quere, ij d,
ffor makyng of a bawdryk and a nywe bokyll to the lytill belle, viij d, } x d

ffor a Rope to the same belle, ij d,
ffor viij fathom of Rope for the myddill belle, ix d,
ffor wasshyng of awter-clothis, awbis, amyseȝ, & towellis, xij d, } ij s

ffor scowryng of the Standardis candilstikkis, & the Rode loft, by the space of ij yere } iij s   viij d

¹ leaf 18.

Churchwardens' Accounts, A.D. 1477–9.

Item, for vj doseyne lb of talow Candill, spent in dyvine seruise doon in the said Church withyn the tyme of this accompt, and in wacchyng the Churche } vj s   v d

To William proyne, for xviij galons oyle spent in lampis in the Churche } xvj s

ffor scowryng, amendyng & gyldyng of a crosse . . .   v s

To William paris, for naylis, & amendyng of certeyne pywis in the Churche, x d,
ffor a key to the vestry dore beneth, iij d,
ffor ij smale keys to a lytill Chest in the vestry, vj d,
ffor a nywe key, and mendyng of a lok to the stepull dore, iiij d,
ffor leddir and clapsis to an Antiphoner, viij d, } ij s   vij d

ffor the mendyng of a surplice, v d,
ffor amendyng of the pavement in the Churche, ij d,
Paid to William paris, for takyng downe of the Crosse apon the Stepull, ij d, } ix d

ffor wasshyng and sawyng of Iohn Modleys surplise   ij d

Summa, lvij s viij d.

[1] Item, payd for birche at Midsomer, viij d,
Item, paid for box and palme on palme sonday, xij d,
ffor Colis one Estir evyne, x d,
Item, for Garlondis one Corpus Christi day, x d,
To v men to bere the Torchis, ix d,
ffor Rose-garlondis and wodrove-garlondis on Saynt Barnebes day, xj d,
To Sir Iohn henley, for syngyng tho daies, viij d,
To iiij Childre of Saynt Magnus, for syngynge, iiij d,
To Water plesaunce, for playing at the organs, vj d,
ffor expensis of the said prestis and Clerkis in brede, ale, and wyne, at the sayd ffestis, and at the ffest of Alhalowys, ij s v d, } viij s xj d

ffor a nywe key to the Chest that the torchis be in. .   iij d

Item, payd to Thomas Goldsmyth for the mendyng of ij pax, and the soket of a siluer candilstike } ij s

Item, for mendynge of the capis of the organs by Mighaell Glocetir } viij d

ffor iij mattis of wikirs, boght for prestis and clerkis .   iiij d

Summa, xij s ij d.

[1] leaf 18, back.

[1] Reparacions

Item, paid for iij m^t Tyle, for every m^t, v s iiij d, xvj s
Item, for c of Rofe tyle, xv d,
To harry Clerke, for viij lodis lyme, and a sak, viij s ij d
ffor iij lood sande, xviij d,
ffor ij loode lome, viij d,
ffor ij hundrith lath, iiij d,
ffor iij pecke of tyle-pynnys, iiij d ob, } xxxj s xj d
ffor ij^c of vj peny nayle, xij d,
ffor v c Sprigge, iij d ob,
ffor a watir payle, iij d,
ffor c of iij peny nayle, iij d,
ffor ij lb & iij quartrons of Sawdour spendyd in the tenement of harry Williamsson & Iohn dokelyng, xxij d,

Item, payd to a tyler & his laborer, wirkyng apon the Church by a day, } xiij d

Item, to a tylere and his man, wurkyng apon Thomas Raynoldis howse by a day, } xiij d

Item, to ij tylers and ij laboreris, wirkyng apon Iohn Williamsons howse and Iohn Dokelyns howse, by ix dais, takyng amonge them by the day ij s ij d, } xix s vj d

ffor a welbokette to harry Williamsons well, and for byndynge of the same, } iij s ij d

To a dawber & his laborere, wirkyng there by iij days, at xiij d by the day, } iij s iij d

ffor caryyng awaye of viij loodis Robissh from the same placis, } x d

ffor voyding of ij Tonne owte of a pryve in harry Williamson howse, } v s iiij d

ffor iiij c hertlath, the c at v d, ... xx d

   Summa
Summa of this side, iij li vij s x d

[2] Item, for a wainscotte ix d, spent in harry Williamsons howse,
paid to Stere for sawyng of iij kervis of the same, iij d, } xix d
ffor leggis, iiij d,
ffor c of iij peny nayle, iij d,

[1] leaf 19.   [2] leaf 19, back.

To a Carpynter wirkyng there by ij dais, xvj d, To a Mason and his manne by a day, xiij d,	ij s	v d
To a paviowre, for pavyng of ix teies, afor the tenement of Iohn Modley and hywe Clerke, for euery teis, vij d, ffor iij lodis gravell, xij d,	vj s	iij d
Item, paid to William paris for wacchyng in the Churche in tyme of makyng of the Vestry, by xvj nyghtis, xvj d, ffor a quarter of Colis, v d, ffor brede and ale boght of the wife of the Belle, xvj d, spendid there	iij s	j d
Item, paid to a Carpinter to make a shoppe dore to thomas Reynoldis howse, And for naylis, xij d, And for a key to the same, iij d,		xv d
Item, for iij lood of lyme spent to make vp the Sande that was left of the Stuffe that was purveyd for makyng of the vestry,	iij s	
ffor makyng of a payre endentowres betwene the Churchwardeyns and mille, for the lese of his howse	ij s	vj d
Item, to masse, Scryvenere, for ouerseyng the olde endentures of the same howse,		viij d

Summa, xx s ix d.

[1]Payementes of the tenementes of the Chauntry of Iohn Causton:—

Quite Rente
In money paid to the Wardeins of london Bridge, of quite Rente of xiij sii ij d yerely goyng owte of a tenement in Gresschurche strete that John ffisshe holdith for ij yere endyd atte ffest of Estir in the xix yere of the kynge aforsayde	xxvj s	viij d
Item, to William Inkyrssale and Thomas broke, wardeins of the ffraternitie of owre lady & saynt Thomas of Cantirbury of Salue, Regina ffounded in the church of Saint Magne in london, of a quite Rente of vj s yerely goyng owte of the same tenement, for ij yere endyd at Midsomer, in the said xix yere of þe kynge.	xij s	

[1] leaf 20.

Churchwardens' Accounts, A.D. 1477–9.

Prestis wagis { And to Sir philippe Norton, prest, Syngyng for the Sowle of Iohn Causton, for his wagis for ij yere endid at Mighelmasse in the said xix yere of the kyng, at vj li xiij s iiij d by the yere, } xiij li vj s viij d

Obites { Item, payd for the obite of the said Iohn Caustons for ij yere, } vij s viij d

To hew Clerke and to Robert Clerke, for money diew to them for the dirige of Iohn Cawston, } x d

And in allowans of Rente of a tenement þat hywe Clerke helde for xx s by the yere, standyng void by the terme of Estir, Midsomer, and Mighelmasse, Anno xix^{no} } xv s

And allowaunce of Rente of a tenement þat the Clerke of Saynt Dunstons helde, which was in dette to the church in xxv s, And departid from the same tenement and left no distresse for the said Rente, And aftir died in the pestilence, and had noo good to paye. } xxv s

Summa, xvij li xiij s x d.

[1] Reparacions

ffo ij mł tiles spent in reparacion of the tenement of William Blase and of othir tenementes, x s viij d,
ffor c lath, v d,
ffor c of iiij peny naile, iiij d,
ffor c of v peny nayle, v d,
ffor a pekke of tyle pynnys, j d ob,
ffor a lood lyme, xij d,
ffor a lood Sande, vj d,
ffor a lood loome, iiij d,
ffor iij quarters Sprygge nayle, iij d ob
ffor a lok and a key to Crystian Stevyns gardyne, ix d, and for naylis, } xiiij s x d

Paid to a tyler and his laborer, wirkyng there by iiij dais, takyng both by the day, xiij d—iiij s iiij d,
To a dawber and his laborer, wirkyng in the tenement of Iohn Brewster, tornour, in Estchepe, by a day, xiij d, And in the tenementes of Iames Cok & Clement, ij dais ij s ij d, } vij s vij d

[1] leaf 20, back.

Churchwardens' Accounts, A.D. 1477–9.

Item, for iij loode of pavyng graveH, xij d,
To a paviowre for pavyng of ix teis of pament, for euery teis, vij d—iiij s j d, } v s j d

ffor a post, a plate, and a tresteH hede, to sette vndir the byndyng Ioiste in John Breusters howse, xiiij d,
for ij pecis for Steir shides, vj d,
ffor xxv foote of Elmyn borde, for steppes and standardis for the same steyre, vj d,
ffor vj quarters for the walle, and brydgis for þe stayere, xij d,
To ij Carpinters wirkyng there by ij dais, ij s viij d,
Item, for the mendyng of a lok, and for a nywe key to hew Clerkes howse, iij d,
ffor Reparacions done in the tenement þat Iohn ffishe holdith, } vj s j d

ffor a mł tyle, v s vj d,
ffor a lood & iiij Sakke lyme, xx d,
Item, for iiij Rofe tyles, iiij d,
spent in Reparacion of John ffisshe3 howse in Gresschurch strete, } vij s vj d

To a tyler and his laborere, wirkyng there by iiij dais, at xiij d by the day, } iiij s iiij d

To a Carpynter, for his labour, a principaH post & a watir borde, } xx d

ffor iiij ℔ di.[1] of Sowdour, ij s iiij d,
ffor a key to William Blases shoppe dore, iij d,
ffor cariage of a mł, and a lood of Sande, from fforster lane to greschurch strete, vj d,
ffor Cariage of v lood of Robishe from fforster lane and Estchepe, x d, } iij s x d

Summa, l s xj d.

[2]**P**ayementis and expensis done apon the tenementes longyng to the Chauntry of Richarde Gosselyn :—

Quit Rent { To the prioresse of Kilborne, of a quite Rente of vj d yerely goyng owte of the tenement in ffaster lane, for ij yere endid at the ffest of Saynt MigheH tharchaungeH in the xix yere of the said kynge, } xij d

---
[1] di = dimidium, a half. [2] leaf 21.

Obites	Item, paid for the Costis of the said Richarde Gosselyne₃ obite, holde ij tymes in the tyme of this accompt,	vj s viij d
Vaca-cions	Item, in allowaunce of Rente of a tenement that William Dighton holdith, stondyng void by a yere, for lak of a tenaunte	iij li
	Item, in Rente of a tenement that William Catour, browderere, holdith, standyng void by all the first quarter of this Accompt	iiij s vj d
Prestis wages	Item, paid to Sir Iohn Mounteyne by xij wekis & v dais xxxj s viij d, To Sir Thomas Wilkynson, by a quarter & di, l s, To Sir Thomas , for a quarter, xxxiij s iiij d, To Sir Robert Barette, for v wekes & ij dais, xiij s, And to Sir William lun for vj wekis and a day, xv s iiij d; Prestis syngynge for þe Sowle of the sayd Richarde Gosselyne, withyn the tyme of this accompt,	vij li iij s iiij d
	Item, paid to Sir Thomas Keyle, prest, Singyng for the said Richarde Gosselyne, from Mighemasse A° xix°, vnto viij dais aftir Candilmasse than nexte suyng, by a quarter & di. aftir the tyme of this accompt,	

Summa, xiij li v s vj d.

[1] Reparacions vpon Richard Gosselyns tenementis.

Reparacions. ffor vj m⁺ tiles, for every m⁺, v s iiij d— xxxj s viij d, ffor vj c lathis, for every c, v d—ij s vj d, ffor a quarter of Rofe tile, xvj d, ffor a busshell di. of tile pynnis, ix d, ffor vj lood Sande, iij s, ffor x loode and iiij Sakkis lyme, x s viij d, ffor ij loode of lome, viij d,	l s viij d
ffor xij foot of plancheborde, iiij d, ffor v fote di. of lire borde, ij d, ffor xxxj yardis of Evis borde, xx d,	ij s vij d

[1] leaf 21, back.

ffor quarterborde boght for the phisicians howse, xvj d,
ffor ij quarters, v d oḃ,
ffor a Raftir foot, j d,
ffor a legge, j d oḃ,
ffor a quarter di. of Elmyn borde, vj d,
ffor a quarter of Elme, v d,
ffor ij^c of vj peny nayle, xij d,
ffor a c of v peny nayle, v d,
ffor ij^c of iiij peny nayle, viij d,
ffor iij peny nayle, v d,
ffor lede nayle, j d,
ffor sprigge, xij d, & for Rofe nayle, viij d,
ffor ij hokis, j d,
ffor the Chaunge of a c di. of lede, ij s j d,
ffor x ℔ di. of Sowdre, v s iij d,
ffor a nywe buckette to William Dightons welle, viij d,
ffor ij nywe hopis & byndyng of the same Boket, xiiij d

iij ℔ ix s iiij d

Item, ffor a baste Rope, ij d,
Item, paid to ij tylers & ij laboreres labowryng there by xx dais, takyng both by the day, ij s ij d, Summa, xliij s iiij d,
To a laborere, to cast owte Robissh from the howse, by ij dais, x d,
ffor caryyng awaye of Robisshe, xx d,
ffor caryyng of ij lood of breke, and sum to Cwi..kes hows, iiij d,
ffor brekyng of a chymney in the lytiłł Shope, vj d,
ffor clensyng of the Sege holis, xviij d,
To a Carpynter, by ij dais, xvj d,
To a dawbere and his man, by iiij dais, atte xiij d by the day,—iij s iij d,

Summa, vj ℔ ij s vij d.

[1] Reparacions. Item, paid to a mason, wurkyng to turne the gutter for voydyng of watir in shirbornes kechyne, ij s,
ffor iij c breke, xviij d,
ffor a m^l Tyle spent in the fysicians howse, v s vj d,
ffor ij loodis and vj sackes lyme, iij s,
ffor tyle pynnes, j d,
ffor ij loodis sande, xij d,
To a tyler and his manne, by vij dais, at xiij d by the day, vij s vj d,
To a Carpenter by ij dais, di. xx d,
ffor di. c and viij foote of Elmyn borde, xiiij d,

[1] leaf 22.

ffor naylis, vj d,
for quarter borde, iij d,
ffor legges and hokes, iiij d,
ffor makynge clene of the howse & caryyng away of the dust, viij d,
ffor Caryeng away of iij lood Robissh, x d,   } xxvj s j d

ffor a lood of lome, to ovircast the flore in levishams howse, iiij d,
To a dawber and his man there by a day, xiij d,   } xvij d

    Summa, xxvij s vj d.

[1] Payementes and expensis done apon the tenement that was Iohn Bedehams :—

Prestis wages { ffirst, paid to Sir Iohn plomer, prest of the Chauntry of the said Iohn Bedehams, for his wagis for ij yere, at vj li xiij s iiij d by the yere, } xiij li vj s viij d

Obites { Item, paid for the obite of the said Iohn Bedeham, for eythir yere of this accompt, vj s viij d, } xiij s   iiij d

Bequestis { Item, allowid to the wardens of the said church, of the bequest of the same Iohn, to eythir of them by the yere iij s iiij d for both yeris, } xiij s   iiij d

    Summa, xiiij li xij s iiij d.

Reparacions. Item, paid for iiij^t tyle, xxj s iiii d,
ffor iiij c lathis, xx d,
ffor a m^t cc di. sprigge, vij d ob,
ffor a bussell di. of tyle pynnes, ix d,
ffor v loodis Sande, ij s vj d,
ffor xij lood & ij Sacke lyme, xij s iiij d,   ffor   } xxxix s ij d ob

To ij tylers & ij laborers, wirkyng there xviij di. dais, takynge amonge them by the day, ij s ij d,   } xxxix s vj d

Item, paid ffor di. c & a quartron of pavyng tile, vij d ob,
ffor a quarter of Smale pavyng tyle, v d,
ffor v peny naile, ij^c xd,
ffor a c of iiij peny naile, iiij d,
ffor ij^c of vj peny nayl, xij d,
ffor iiij c iij quarters of quarter borde, xij s ij d ob,
ffor ix quarters of Oke, xvj d,   } xvj s ix d ob

[1] leaf 22, back.

Churchwardens' Accounts, A.D. 1477–9.

To a Carpenter, wirkyng there by v dais, di. iiij s iiij d }
Item, to a Carpenter, to mende the Sege there, vj d, } iiij s x d

  Summa, v ti iiij d.
  Summa, of alle this side, xix ti xiij s viijd d.

[1]Reparacions. ffor a lood lome, iiij d,
ffor Strawe, j d,
ffor a dawber & his laborer, by ij dais, ij s ij d, } ij s   vij d

ffor ij plates of iron and naylis to the gate, xij d,
ffor a Borde to the kechyn, xij d,
ffor naylis to the same, ob, } ij s   o ob

Item, paid to the Skauagers for the pament endited .   viij d

ffor iiij lood of gravell, xvj d,
ffor pavyng xj teis of pament, for euery teis, vij d—
vj s v d, } vij s   ix d

ffor a pek of plastir of paris, for thamendyng of a chymney, } iiij d

ffor caryyng away of Robisshe . . . .   xij d
ffor iij ti of Sawdre there spendid . . . . .   xviij d

ALMES MONEY.

Item, paid to iij poremen of the bequest of Iohn Bedeham, to eueryche of them by the wike, iiij d, that is to wite, from the xxviij daye of Decembre in the xvij yere aforsaid, vnto the vj^te day of ffebruare in the xix yere of the kyng afor named, both dais accompted, that is, by cxj wekes } cxj s

  Summa, vj ti vj s x d ob.

[2]**Payementes** and expenses made for the tenementes longynge to the Chauntry of William Cambryggis & cetera :—

Quite Rente.

ffirste, paid to thabbote of Bermondesey, of a quite Rente of vj s yerely, goyng owte of the same tenementes, for ij yere endid atte Mighelmasse in xix yere of the kynge, } xij s

Prestis Wages.

To Sir Iohn Mortram, preste, Singyng for the said William Cambridgis, for his wagis for a yere and halfe at Mighelmasse in the said xix yere, } x ti

---
[1] leaf 23.   [2] leaf 23, back.

Obites of W. Cambridg.

Item, paid for the Costis of thobite of the sayd William, in the xviij yere of the said kyng, to viij prestis, euerch of them, iiij d — ij s viij d,
To ij clerkes for there labowre and for Ringyng, ij s,
To humfrey heyforde, mayere of london, vj s viij d,
To harry Colette & Iohn Stokker, Sherevis, to eythir of theym, iij s iiij d—vj s viij d,
And to Metford, Swerdeberere, xx d, accordyng to the testament of the said William, for there labourer to see his obseruaunce done,
ffor the wast of ij tapris, iiij d,
ffor brede, xij d,
ffor a kylthirkyn of good ale, ij s,
ffor x Cuppes, iiij d, } xxiij s iiij d

Item, paid for the obite of the said William in the xix yere of the same kynge, to viij prestis, ij s viij d,
To ij Clerkis for there labour and Ringyng, ij s,
To maisteir Gardiner, Mayer, vj s viij d,
To Robert hardynge and to Robert Byfelde, Sherevis, nothyng payd for they came not
To   Metforde, swerdeberer, xx d,
ffor brede, xij d,
ffor a kylthirkyne of ale, ij s ij d,
ffor a woman that drew the ale, ij d,
ffor offryng, j d,
In almes, ij d,
Item, for wast of ij tapris, iiij d, } xvj s xj d

Summa, xij li xij s iij d.

[1] Reparacions.

Item, paid for a lood Sande, vj d,
To the plomer for the mendyng of a Cysterne of lede, vj s,
To a mason for to amende the pament in the kechyn, by ij dais, xvj d,
To a laborer by ij dais, x d,
To a Carpenter by a day, viij d,
ffor ij postes of tymbir to vndirsette the kechyng, xij d,
ffor a quarter of Borde & viij foote, ix d,
ffor playstir of paris, ij d,
And for nailis, iiij d, } xj s vij d

[1] leaf 24.

Item, paid to Richarde Cyryk for Reparacion done in his howse ffor a Rewarde towarde his Costes of the same Reparacions, } v s

Item, for makyng clene of the Sege in Cyrikis howse ij s

Item, paid to hew Clerke and to Robert Clerke for that they lackyd, of thar dueteis of William Cambridgis dirige and obites afor the tyme of this accompt, to eythir of them xij d, } ij s

Summa, xx s vij d.

[1]Item, paid to   Banestre, sergeaunt, for the arrestyng of Crystian Stevyns apon an accion of dette for howse Rente, viij d, ffor entre of the playnt, ij d, ffor withdrawyng of the same, vj d, } xvj d

Item, thay aske allowaunce of money pardoned & forgyven to the same Cristian by the paresshyns, } v s iiij d

Item, paid to Iohn Russell, Clerke, for a quarters wagis, } xij s vj d

Item, paid to Roberte Clerke, for that he lakkyd of his wagis at Mighelmasse A° xix° ij s j d and atte Cristmasse A° xix° iij s iiij d, } v s v d

Item, paid to hewe Clerk that he lackyd in his wagis in the tyme that he was in seruise here, } x s j d

Item, paid to Thomas Warwyk, Clerke, þat he lackyd, of his duetee that shold have be payd by John Smerte, xix d ob, Robert Revell xix d ob, Iohn Braymong xix d ob, and Iohn Palmer xix d ob, } vj s vj d

Also paid to a Clerke that cam [from?] saynt Margaretes, for his wagis, xv s x d, } xv s x d

Summa, lvij s.

[2]Costis of the wex Chaundeler.

Item, paid for nywe wex boght for the vse of the church as in Bemlight tapres, prykettes and Candillis, weyng lxxxxij lb di., prece of euery lb, iiij d ob, xxxiiij s viij d

Item, thay Recceyved in olde wax of Store of the church as in bemlight olde tapris within thies ij yeris ix[xx] xj lb. Summa of the newe wex and of the olde c c iiij[xx] iij lb di. by the Smale c

Paid to Roger Middilton, wex Chaundeler, for makyng of the said nywe wex and olde wex made in tapris for the Bemelight and othir tapris, prickettes and tenebre candill, for euery lb, ob—xj s ix d

[1] leaf 24, back.   [2] leaf 25.

Item, payd to the said Roger, for makyng of the paschall tapre by the said ij yere, eythir yere weyng xxx ℔ ffor euery ℔ j d—v s, and for the wast of the same in ij yere v ℔, for euery ℔ iiij d ob—xxij d ob
Summa, liij s iij d ob.

Potacions

Item, thay aske allowaunce of money spent among the tenauntes in gaderyng of the Rente and ouerseyng reparacions in the said ij yeres x s And for papire boght And spent in makyng of this quayer and othir quaeres made to title ther parcellis apon of payementes and Reparacions iiij d, } x s   iiij d

Summa of this side iij li iij s vij d ob.
Summa of alle payementis and allowaunces cxiij li vij s j d.
And so remayneth xxvj li iiij s ix d.

[1] Item, there Restith in the handis of the tenauntes of thar diew to the Church, whos names folowith &c.

Iohn Iohnson, Cowcher	liij s	iiij d
Iohn Dighton Capper	xlv s	
William Levisham	xxvj s	viij d
William Shirebourne	xv s	
William Breuster	ix s	vj d
Harry Mersshe	v s	
Cobbe, Brewer	vj s	viij d
The Clerke of Saynt Dunstonys	ij li	
Clement atte hille	xij s	
Motte, Carpenter	vj s	
Crystian Stevyns	ij li	
Iames Cokke	xij s	vj d
Iohn Kyrkeby	ij li	

Summa, ix li xj s viij d.

So Remayneth diew to the Churche } xvj li xiij s j d

Receyved per Thomas Breteyn & Iohn Smert, Summa xvj li xiij s j d, that was putte into the Box.

[2] Item, there is diew to the Church for buryyng of Nicholas Vavasere and for his doghtir & for his sonnes childe in the Churche, for euerych of them xiij s iiij d, } xl s

Item, for buryyng of harry vavaseris doghtir in the pardon Churchyarde, } ij s

Item, by Iohn Dokelyng, for buryyng of iij of his childir in the same place, } vj s

Summa, xlviij s.

[1] leaf 25, back.   [2] leaf 26.

[A.D. 1479 & 1481]

This is the accompt of William Mille and Harry Mershe, Wardeyns of the Paresshe churche of Saint Mary atte hille in London, fro the fest of Saynt Mighell tharchaungell in the xix yere of the Reigne of Kynge Edwarde the iiij[the] Vnto the fest of Saynt Mighell in the xxj yere of the Reigne of the same kynge, that is to witte, for ij hoole yere &c.

Arreragis

ffyrst thay charge them selfe with the arrerages of Iohn Palmer and Iohn Clerke, wardeyns of the said Churche for the ij yeris last past, as it apperyth in the foote of ther accompte as in money Remaynyng in the handis of diuerse tenauntis,   ix li   xij s   iiij d

And with money Remaynyng in the handis of diuerse personys, for buryyngis in the church and in the churcheyarde, as it apperyth in the foote of the same accompte,   xlviij s

Summa, xij li iiij d.

Rentis & ffermys.

Item, thay be chargyd with the Rentes longyng to the chauntry of Iohn Westone at xiiij li xvj s ij d by the yere, for ij yere,   xxix li   xij s   iiij d

Also thay be chargyd with the Rentis longyng to the chauntry of Iohn Cawston at xviij li xx d by the yere, Summa for ii yere,   xxxvj li   iij s   iiij d

Also with the Rentis longyng to the Chauntry of Rychard Goslyne at ix li xviij s viij d by the yere, for ij yere,   xix li   xvij s   iiij d

Also with the Rentes of the chauntry of William Cambrygge at x li by the yere, Summa for ij yere,   xx li

Also with the Rentes of the chauntry of Iohn Bedham, atte xiij li vj s viij d by the yere, for ij yere,   xxvj li   xiij s   iiij d

[1] leaf 28.   [2] leaf 28, back.

Also with the Rent*es* of the chauntry of Iohn Nasyng, at ix li iij s iiij d by the yere, that is to say, for the te*r*mys of the annu*n*ciac*i*on of our lady, Midsom*er* & Mighellmasse, Anno Edwardi quarty xxj°,   vj li xvij s vj d

Also with the Rent*es* of the Chauntry of Rose Wrytty*ll*, at vj li xiij s iiij d by the yere. Receyved for a yere an halfe & a quarter,   xj li xiij s iiij d

Su*m*ma total*is* Redd cl li xvij s ij d.

Increse of Rente.

The increse of Rente of the tenement of Iohn Madleys howse, from Mighelmasse A° Edwardi quarti xx°, at xx s by the yere, vnto Mighelmasse A° xxj°, for a hole yere,   vj s viij d

Item, the encrese of Rente of Thom*a*s ffynche Taylo*ur*s howse, at xx s by the yere, for the te*r*mys of Midsom*er* and Mighelmasse Anno xxj°,   iij s iiij d

Su*m*ma, x s.

[1] Dona & legat.

Yiftis and bequestis for the said ij yere, In p*r*imis Receyved of Iohn Crosby, Carpynter, for a trespase done ayenste þe p*a*resshe,   xij d

Item, Receyved of Will*ia*m blase, Barbowre*ȝ* wife, for payntyng of an ymage of owre lady within the same churche,   xx d

Item, Receyved of the churchewardeyns of Alhalowis in lumbarde strete, for hyryng of the churche stuffe,   iiij s viij d

Item, Receyved of Iohn Dey, for payntyng of the same ymage of owre lady, in the same churche,   xxxiij s iiij d

Item, Receyved of Thomas Rowlande in money gyvyn to the church werkes,   xij d

Item, for settyng of a woman into a pywe j d. Item, fownde in the church j d,   ij d

Su*m*ma, xlj s x d.

---

[1] leaf 29.

Bemelyght.

Bemlyght and paschall tapyrs for the same ij yere, as in the boke of parcellis of the same more playnly doth appere,	iiij li	vij s

Summa, iiij li vij s.

Buryyng & knellis.

Inprimis, Receyved of the Buryyng of a Shypman,		xvj d
Item, for the Buryyng of a portyngaler . . .	iij s	iiij d
Item, Receyved of Harry Burgeys of Sowthwolde for buryyng of a man in the Churche, and for the hyre of the Torchis, and for his knelle,		xxvij s

Summa, xxxj s viiij d.
Summa, viij li vj d.

¹Clerkes wages.

Receytis for the clerkes wagis, as it more playnly doth appere by the Boke of Receytis of the same, for ij hole yere,	ix li ij s	ix d

Summa, ix li ij s ix d.
Summa of all thayr Charge } ciiij^{xx} li x s ix d.

her lackyth the Rekenyng of the quyterent of Th. Sayms house, ij° yere	vj s	viij d
Item, the Quyterent of Seynt Botolphus chirch, ij yere	v s	

Allowaunce. Quite Rentis.

Cambrigges. Therof payd to the abbot of Bermondesey, for the quyte Rentes of a tenement in the paresshe of Saynt Christopher, at the stockes, by the yere vj s. Summa for ij yere,	xij s	
Cawstones. Item, payd to the maystres of the Bryggehowse, for the quyte Rente of a tenement lyyng in the paresshe of Saynt leonardes in Estchepe, by the yere, xiij s iiij. Summa for ij yere,	xxvj s	viij d

¹ leaf 29, back.

Westons. Item payd to the wardeyns of the brethirhede of our lady, & Saynt Thomas þe martyr kepte withyn the church of saynt Magnus for the Salue, by the space of ij yere, } xij s

Nasynges. Item payd to the abbot of Waltham for a tenement longyng to Westons Chauntry lyynge in the pareshe of Saynt georges of puddyng lane for þe same space, } lxxvj s

Item, payd to the same abbot for a tenement longyng to Nasynges, by the space of iij quarters, A⁰ xxj⁰, } xvj s vj d

Summa, vij ti iij s ij d.

[1] Item, payd to the priour of Crystes churche for a tenement lyyng in the pareshe of Saynt Mary at hyll, for ij yere, } vj s

Item, to the priowre of the same place for a tenement lyyng in the pareshe of Saynt Botolphis withowte Algate, } x s

Item, to the prioresse of kylbourne for a tenement in fayster lane, for ij yere, } xij d

Item, to the Churchewardeyns of Saynt georges in poddyng lane, for a tenement in the pareshe of Saynt Mary atte hylle, } xl s

Summa, lvij s.

Summa totalis

Vacacions.

In primys, syr Rafis chambyr, voyde by ij quarters, the quarter at ij s iij d. Summa for the halfe yere, } iiij s vj d

Item, the wevers howse atte towre hylle, voyde by a quarter, at xvj s viij d by the yere. Summa, } iiij s ij d

Item, a howse at fayster lane, voyd by iij quarters, At xx s by the yere. Summa, } xv s

Item, harry whetleyseȝ howse at vj s by the yere, voyd by a quarter of a yere, } xx d

Item, Thomas fynches howse at xx s by the yere, voyd by a quartere, } v s

Item, Sawndyr clerkes howse at xx s by the yere, voyd by a quarter, } v s

Summa, xxxv s iiij d.

Summa, iiij ti xij s iiij d.

[1] leaf 30.

¹ Westone.

ffor the obite of Iohn Weston at iij s viij d holdyn by the yere, for ij yere vij s iiij d; for brede and ale to þe prestes and clerkes by the same space. Summa, } viij s

Bedeham.

Item, for the obite of Iohn Bedham, holdyn by ij yere, And in mony yevyn in almys to the poore peple, And in drynkyng amonge prestes and clerkes by the space of this accompt, } xiij s   vj d

Cawston.

Item, for the obite of Iohn Cawston, and in almys yevyn among the pore peple, and in drynkyng among prestes and clerkes for the same ij yere, } vij s   iiij d

Cambrygge.

Item, for the obite of William Cambrigge, And in money yevyn to the poore peple, And for potacions to prestis and clerkes, & for Ryngyng of the bellis, by ij yere, } xv s   iiij d

Item, to the Mayre for ij yere . . . . xiij s   iiij d
Item, to the Sherevis for one yere . . . . vj s   viij d
Item, payd to the Swerde berer for ij yere . . . iij s   iiij d

Goslyne.

Item, payd for the obite of Richarde goslyne, And in almys, And in potacions to prestis and clerkes, by the same space, } vj s   viij d

Syr Io. bradmore.

Item, for the obite of Syr Iohn Bradmore, holdyn by the space of this accompt, } vj s   viij d

Summa, iiij li xd.

² prestes wagis.

Paid to sir Iohn plummer by ij yere . . . . . xiij li vj s viij d
Item, payd to syr philyp Norton per idem tempus. xiij li vj s viiij d
Item, to syr Iohn Martram for ij yere . . . . xiij li vj s viiij d
Item, payd to syr Iohn philypp for iij quarters of a yere, vz aº, c iiijti xxjº. } c s
Item, payd to Sir Thomas Roke for halfe yere, endyd at the ffeste of þe puryficacion of owre lady Anno xxmo, and fro thens vnto owre lady day in lente, Aº xxjº, } iiij li ij s xj d

¹ leaf 30, back.   ² leaf 31.

MED. REC.

Item, to sir Rafe for halfe a yere, A° xxj° . .. . lxvj s viij d

Item, to sir Iohn Dalywagge for iij quarters of a yere, } c s

Item, payd to Syr Richarde Wattisson for a quarter and v wykis, } xlv s x d

Item, payd to syr Richarde Cornysshe for the space of ij wykes, } v s

Item, to Syr William Naghty pakke, for one wyke ij s iiij d

Item, to Syr Iohn Colyns for a quarter of a yere . xxv s

Item, payd for the kypyng of the morow masse, by the space of this accompt, } xl s

Summa, lxiij li vij s ix d.

¹Clerkes wages.

Also payd to Thomas Warwyke, Clere for 1 hole yere, } liij s iiij d

Item, payd to Iohn Modley for kepyng of the churche, when Warwyke wente by þe space of vj wykes, } vj s viij d

Item, to Saundyr, Clerke, for a Rewarde gyvyn to hym for kepyng of the church by the space of viij wykes, } viij s vj d

Item, to the same Sawndyr for iij quarters of a yere, } xl s

Item, payd to Iohn Modley for ij hole yeres, þat is to sey, for vj quarters, euery quarter vj s viij d. Summa for the vj quarters xl s, And for the tithyr ij quarters euery quarter x s. Summa of the ij quarters xx s. Summa totalis, } lx s

Item, payd to Iohn Russell for ij hole ȝere, that is to witte, for v quarters, euery quarter xij s vj d. Summa of the v quarters lx s ij s vj d. And for the tothyr iij quarters, euery quarter xiij s iiij d. Summa of tho iij quarters xl s. Summa for the ij yere, } v li ij s vj d

Summa, xiij li xj s.

¹ leaf 31, back.

[1]Thexpensis of þe Church.

Rolfe smyth. ffyrste payd to Rolfe Smyth for makynge of diuerse stuffe to the Church, as it apperith by a byll of the same, xiij s iiij d,

Item, to the same Rolfe for diuerse thynges nywe made, and mendyd withyn the churche and othyr places, ij s viij d,

Item, for lowsyng of a lokke in the vestiary, j d,

Item, for mendyng of ij lokkes within the churche, iiij d,

Item, for makynge of ij nywe keys, one to the vestry dore, and the to tothyr to the nywe howse in the churche Rente, ix d,

Item, for a nywe lokke to the longe cheste in þe churche, iij d,

Item, for a lokke mendynge for the pardone churchaw gate, for to kepe the Stuffe, ij d. Summa,

xvij s vij d

Wecchyng of þe sepulcre.

Item, payd to the Clerke and paris for mete and drynke, for wechynge of the Sepulcre, with othir bysynes done in the Church at diuerse tymez by the space of this accompt,

xxiij d

A laborer.

Item, payd to Iohn paryse for swepyng of þe churche, & ledynge away of the duste, and mendyng of the wyndowse of the churche, and kepyng clene of the church hawse with othyr diuerse thynges done in the church by the space of this accompte as the boke of purcellis of the same more playnly doth apere. Summa,

vj s iiij d

Reparacions.

Item, for mendyng and dressyng of the awter clothis, Surplisis, towellis, awbis, & amysys with othyr costes and Reparacions done in the church by þe space of þis accompte,

ij s iiij d

Summa, xxviij s ij d.

[2]Item, for Rope and smale Corde for þe church, iij s ix d,

Item, for iij doseyn tukkyng gyrdlis, ij s for the ij yere,

v s ix d

[1] leaf 32. [2] leaf 32, back.

scowryng of þe laton.

Item, for scowryng of the latowne, the grete candylstykkes, and the Rode loft with all othyre smale candylstykkys, per idem tempus, &c. } iiij s vj d

Item, for Colis to the churche, & frankencence, in wechyng of the sepulcre, & at othyre tymeʒ of þe yere by þe same space, } ij s vj d

ffor swete wyne. Item, for brede, wyne, and ale for prestes and clerkes spent in the church apon dedicacions and othyr festyvall days, as the boke of parcellis of the same more playnly doth appere by the tyme of this accompte, } vij s viij d

ffor flaggis & garlondis :
Item, for flagges and garlondis, and pak thredde for þe torchis, apon corpus christi day and apon saynt Barnabeys day & othir days. And for vj men to bere the same torchis, as it more playnly shewith by the boke of parcellis, } iiij s vj d

Item, to a mason for settyng of the hokes of the vestry wyndowys with lede, and for mendyng of othyr thynges in the church, } vj d

Item, for mendyng of the churche lanterne, vj d,
Item, for beryng of iiij torchis, to bury the portyngaler, ij d,
Item, for the caryyng of ij lode gravell, for the procession churcheyarde, iij d, } xj d

ffor makynge of a pywe :
Item, payd to Christofer, Carpynter, for the makynge of a nywe pywe in the churche, as it apperith by a bylle, } xxj s iij d

Item, in expensis and Costis done in fechynge of the chalis. And for rewardis yevyn to the goldsmyth & othirs, as þe boke of parcelis makyth mencion severally, } ij s

for candyll :
Item, payd for viij doseyn lb candyll for the churche, as it aperith &c. by this accompte, } x s

Item, payd for a table & a payr [of] trestellis to stand in the vestry, to ley the Copis apon in festyvall days, } ij s

Item, spent at the Receyvyng of sir Rafe & sir Thomas, prestes, v d,
Item, for a Shovell to the churche, iiij d, } ix d

Summa, iij li ij s vj d.

Churchwardens' Accounts, A.D. 1479-81.

[1]Wex chaundeler:
Item, payd to the wex chaundeler for makyng of all the wex to the churche, by the space of this accompt, &c. } xxij s xj d

Item, for vj loode Robyshe to both churchehawis, xij d,
Item, for haly watyr sprynclys to þe church, iiij d,
Item, for a stone potte to put in oyle, j d ob,
Item, for a bokyll to hange þe clappyr of the lytyll belle, ob,
Item, for nayle to amende the whele of the Sanctus bell, ob,
Item, for papyr spent in makyng of this accompt & for the parcelse of the same, iiij d,
Item, for Bowis and Ivy to the church for ij yere, ij s,
Item, to the cornell Raker for carynge of the Rubbysshe & duste of the churche at diuerse tyme3 xij d,
Item, for evys borde to the lityll howse in the churchyarde, for nayle3 & makyng, iiij d ob,
Item, for c of ij peny nayle, ij d,
Item, for iij peny nayle, j d. Summa, } v s viij d

mendyng of the Crossis:
Item, payd for mendyng of the crosse that is borne abowte euery day, And for mendyng of the mustenaunce crosse, as it apperith in the boke of parcellis of the same, } iij s iiij d

The grete Antiphoner:
Item, payd to a Stacioner for the grete Antyphoner, and for a quayer of clene stuffe sette into the same, & for a Rewarde to the Stacioner, & for berynge of þe same boke, as the boke of parcellis more playnly shewith, } xxij s ij d

the Vestyment makere.
Item, for mendyng of iij Rede copis, the grene cope, & ij blak copis, xvij s j d,
Item, for golde sylke & perle, bokeram & Rebande for the best cope, xiij s,
Item, for mendyng of othyr vestymentes, awbis, chysyblis, copis, & othir diuerse Stuffe boght to the same at diuerse tymes, viij s vij d,
Item, for workemanshyp of the same for the sayd ij yere, xiiij s x d. Summa, } liij s vj d

Item,

Summa.
Summa totalis, v li viij s iij d.
[2]v li viij s v d ob[2]

[1] leaf 33. [2–2] In extreme corner of leaf.

[1] Reparacion of the church.

ffor tyle : ffyrst payd to Iohn Chaundeler of Waltamstow, tyler, and to Knyghte, tyler, and to othyrs, for tyle to þe churche, þat is to say for ix mł, the mł at v s iiij d. Summa, } xlviij s

hertlath :
Item, for ij m{1} & ij c hertlath, the c vj d. Summa, } xj s

Item, for vj mł di. Rofe nayle, the mł at vj d. Summa, vj s   iij d

lyme :
Item, for lyme, to harwarde, lyme man, and to clerke of lyme oste, for vj c a lode, & iiij sackes lyme, as it apery by a byll and by the boke of parcellis of the same more playnly in toto, } xlj s

Item, payd to Rolfe Smyth, for diuerse stuffe of hym boght and made, as it apperith by a byll of the same, } x s

þe glasyer :
Item, to   glasyer, for glasyng and mendyng of the church wyndowis, the vestry wyndowis, with othyr wyndowis longyng to the churche Rente, by the space of this accompte, } xx s   vj d

þe tylers. Item, payd to Rowland, tyler, and his men, and to othyr tylers and thar men for tylyng of the church for the tyme of this accompte, iij łi x s iiij d,
Item, for viij busshell tyle pynnys for þe church & oþer places, iiij s,
Item, for viij loode sande, iiij s,
Item, for caryng away of xij loode Rubyssh, ij s vj d,
Summa, } iiij łi   x d

Iremongers. Item, payd to the iremonger in gresse strete, for diuerse stuffe of hym boght, as it more playnly doth apere by a byll of the same, } xiiij s vij d

Item, payd Iohn Nevell for nayles and othir stuffe boght of hym as the boke of parcelis shewyth, } x s

Item, for Rofe tyle by the same space . . . . .   xvj d

Summa, xij łi iij s vj d.
[2] xj li xix s xj d.[2]

[3] Reparacion of the Steple.

labowrers. ffyrst, for brekfastys of the Carpynters & þe plummers, and in the ernyst penys and potacions at diuerse tymes amonge the workemen, as þe boke of parcellis Shewith, } ij s   vj d

---

[1] leaf 33, back.   [2-2] In extreme corner of leaf.   [3] leaf 34.

Item, to Iohn parysse & Dykson with othyr laborers for brede and ale And for thar labour abowte the steple for to have vp the planckes & þe lode in to þe steple. And for mendyng of the hovell in the steple, and for othyr diuerse labour & attendaunce abowte the same, as it apperith by the parcellis of the same more playnly in the boke. — viij s ij d

Item, payd to a mason for mendyng of the corner of the steple, vj d,
Item, for caryage of viij c borde fro Quenhith to þe church, vj d,
Item, for caryage of ij lode lede for the churche to þe plummers howse, vj d,
Item, for a laddyr to þe steple, x d,
Item, for dowbyll lynyng of the stayre dore into the steple, for borde nayle & workemanshyp of the same, xij d. Summa, — iij s iiij d

Item, to the Kanell Raker for caryyng of the Robyssh of the steple, vj d,
Item, for iiij Raylis to þe steple, iiij d,
Item, for mendyng of the vane of the steple, iiij d. Summa, — x d

Bordeʒ. Item, payde to geffrey Koo for viij c borde, price the c ij s ij d. Summa, — xvij s iiij d

þe Carpynter. Item, payd to Christofer, Carpynter, for takyng downe of the Steple, xx s,
Item, to the same Christofer for tymbyr, and for othyr diuerse stuffe for the steple, and for workmanshypp of the same, as it apperith by a byll of the same, liij s: Summa, — iij li xiij s

Iremonger. Item, for naylis and othir Iren worke for the steple, as it aperith by a byll, xiiij s vij d,
Item, to the same iremonger for othyr diuerse stuffe boght of hym, as it apperith by the boke of parcellis, x s. Summa, — xxiiij s vij d

Summa, vj li ix s ix d.
¹ . . . . .
iiij li xviij . . . ¹

²Reparacion of the lumbardis place and in ffayster lane.

Reparacions of the lumbardys place, and of othyr diuerse tenauntries in ffayster lane.
ffirste, for vj lode lome . . . . iij s

¹⁻¹ In extreme corner of leaf.   ² leaf 34, back.

Item, to a dawber and his man by xvij dais . . .	xviij s	vij d
Item, for iij c lath, the c iiij d. Summa, ...		xij d
Item, for m¹ di. Sprygge nayle, the m¹ vj d. Summa,		ix d
Item, for nayleȝ to the same place		vij d ob
Item, for vj loode Sande, þe loode vj d. Summa, .	iij s	
Item, for xiij loode lyme, price þe lood xiiij d. Summa, ...	xiiij s	ij d
Item, for vij loode breke, þe lode at ij s ij d. Summa,	xv s	ij d
Item, payd to Edmonde halke, mason, and his men, and to burton, mason, and his men, wirkyng within the same place, takyng by the day for the maystyr and his man, ij s ij d. Summa in toto, as it apperyth in the boke of parcelse more playnly,	xxvij s	ix d
Item, payd to Motte, carpynter, for diuerse stuffe boght of hym and for workemanshyp of the same, ...	ix s	iij d
Item, payd to Thomas byrde, carpynter, for xiiij foote tymbyr, price the fote ij d. Summa, ij s iiij d, Item, payd to the same byrde for di. c & xvj fote, quarter borde, ij s, Item, for liiij foote of Elmyn borde, xv d, Item, for iij okyn quarters, ix d. Summa,	vj s	iiij d
Item, payd to Crosby, carpynter, for diuerse stuffe boght of hym, and workemanshyp of the same, and othyr werkemanshyp withyn the same place, as it apperith by a byH,	xxj s	viij d
Item, for caryage of lede to the plummers howse, and for caryage of tymbyr and other stuffe, and for caryage of Robysshe, and ladyng of the carte &c.	ij s	vj d
Item, to ij labowrers within the same place by iiij days, be the day x d. Summa,	iij s	iiij d
Item, for xij fote di. of cane stone for both kychynes, the fote vj d. Summa,	vj s	iij d
Item, for ale and brede spent amonge þe workemen at diuerse tymeȝ, iiij d, Item, for a borde & a quarter pece, viij d, Item, payd to a labowrer by hymselfe, for to make clene the same place by ix days, iij s ix d,	iiij s	ix d
Item, for ij m¹ tyle, prece the m¹ v s iiij d. Summa,	x s	viij d
Item, for a busshell tyle pynnys, price		vj d
Item, to a tyler and his man by iiij days	iiij s	iiij d

Summa, vij li xiij s vij d ob.

[1] Rep*a*racion of Iohnson Bowchers howse, now the howse of Colman bowcher.

ffyrst payd to Knyghte, Tyleman, for ij m¹ tyle, x s viij d,
Item, for dimi bussheli Tyle pynnys, iij d,
Item, for cc hertlath, p*r*ice the c, vj d. S*um*ma xij d,
Item, for a mł Rofnayle, viij d,
Item, for a loode lome, vj d, } xiij s j d

Item, payd for ccc Elmyn borde, p*r*ece le c, ij s iiij d, S*um*ma vij s,
Item, for iij loode lyme, iij s,
Item, for a loode Sande, vj d,
Item, for a quartron Sprygge, j d oƀ,
Item, for nayles to the same howse, vj d. S*um*ma, } xj s id oƀ

Item, payd to a Tyler and his man, by the space of vj dais di. by the day xiij d. S*um*ma vij s ij d oƀ,
Item, payd to a dawber and his man, by the space of ij days, takyng by the day xiij d. S*um*ma, ij s ij d. S*um*ma, } ix s ij d oƀ

Item, payd to Crystofer, carpynter, for tymbyr boght of hym, and for workemanshyp of othyr dyvers workys wroght withyn the same howse at diue*r*se tymes, } iiij s vij d

S*um*ma, xxxviij s.

[2] The t*u*rners howse at saynt Andrews.

ffurst, payd to Burton, Mason, for iij workeme*n* wirkynge and a mendyng of a chymney within the same howse by þe space of a day, ij s,
Item, payd to a laborer by a day, v d,
Item, for ij Sack*es* lyme, iiij d, } ij s ix d

S*um*ma, ij s ix d.

Rep*a*racion of Thomas Raynoldis howse.

Payd to Roberte White for xij load Sande, vj s,
Item, a c di. lyme, x s,
Item, payd to a laborer to make clene the same howse, x d. S*um*ma, } xvj s x d

[1] leaf 35.   [2] leaf 35, back.

Item, payd to Alysaundyr Walis for xvij lood breke, xxxviij s iij d,
Item, payd to Smyth, Mason, for hym and his men for wyrkyng of the same, as it aperith by a byll, xviij s, } lvj s iij d

Item, payd to Nevell the iremonger at the synement of the parysshe for diuerse stuffe boght of hym, as it apperith by a byll of the same schewyd to the paresshe, } xvj s

Item, payd to Crystofer, carpynter, for tymbyr, and for othyr diuerse stuffe boght of hym, and for workemanshyp of the same at diuerse tymeʒ, } xxj s vj d

Item, payd to Crosby, Carpinter, for tymbyr and for othyr diuerse stuffe boght of hym, and for workemanshyp of the same, at the synement of the paresshe, as it more playnly doth apere by a byll shewyd to the paresshe, } iiij li vj s vj d

Summa, ix li xvij s x d.

[1]Reparacion of harry Williams howse.

ffurste, payd to Knyght, tyleman, for ij ml tyle, x s viij d,
Item, for a ml Breke, iiij s vj d,
Item, payd to the kanell Rakere, for caryynge of the Robysshe of the same howse, xij d, } xvj s ij d

Item, payd to a laborer by ij days for to make the place clene, x d,
Item, for a busshell di. tyle pynnys, ix d,
Item, for iij loode Sande, xviij d,
Item, for iij loode lyme, iij s. Summa, } vj s j d

Item, payd to Rowland, tyler, and his ij men & iij workemen, by the space of v days di. by the day iij s iij d. Summa, } xvij s x d ob

Item, payd to Motte, carpynter, for tymbyr and for tymbyr quarters, for to strength and lyne the Cowplis of the same howse, and the kechynne, and for workemanshyppe of the same,
Item, for nayleʒ to the same worke, } vij s viij d

Item, payd to Smyth, mason, and to his men, for worke at diuerse tymeʒ wroght in the same place, } x s

Summa, lvij s ix d ob.

[1] leaf 36.

Churchwardens' Accounts, A.D. 1479-81.

Rep*a*racion of the phesicians howse in ffayste*r* lane.

Payd to Stevyn burton for makyng of a chymney withyn the same howse wit*h* the stuffe of o*u*r owne left of the Rep*a*racio*n* of othy*r* tena*u*ntries agrete, } xiiij s viij d

Item, payd to ij laborers, wirkyng in the same place, and for to make clene the same place, & for clensynge of the gutters at diu*e*rse tyme3, } vij s vij d

Item, for tymbyr, & for settynge vp of the Scaffoldes and takyng downe of the same, and for caryage of the same tymbyr, & the bordis home and owte, iij s vj d, } iij s xj d

Item, for bordis to the chymney, and for naylys to the same, v d,

Su*m*ma xxvj s ij d.
Su*m*ma iiij li iij s xj d ob.

[1]Rep*a*racion of Cryk*es* howse.

ffyrst, for pavyng tyle, & for pavyng of the kechyn, xx s, Ite*m*, for brekyng of the pavyment, iiij d, Item, for pavynge and mendynge of the same pavyment and for Sande, ij s, } xxij s iiij d

Item, for makynge of a key & þe mendyng of a lok, v d, Item, for a nywe key to the Shopp*d*ore, iij d, Item, for a lok & a key to anothyr dore, vj d, Item, for hengis & naylis weynge viij lb di. p*r*ece in toto, iij s vj d, } iiij s viij d

Item, for mendyng of a wyndow, iij d, Item, for a borde to a Stalle, & for workemanshyp, iiij d, Item, for caryyng of a lood Robysshe, ij d, Item, } ix d

Item, payd to Clerke, lyme man, for xij lood lyme, p*r*ece le lood xij d. Su*m*ma xij s, Item, for iiij lood sande, ij s. Su*m*ma, } xiiij s

[1] leaf 36, back.

108   *Churchwardens' Accounts*, A.D. 1479–81.

Item, payd to burton, mason, for hengyng of hokes
into a Selere dore, and for settyng of hokes, henges,
& staplis into a nothyr dore, And for mendyng } ij s   x d
of the wallis & wyndowis & henges of hokys
& henges of the same,

Item, payd to knyght for ij m¹ tyle, xj s,
Item, for a quarter of Rofe tyle, xvj d,
Item, for di. quarter Corner tyle, vij d, } xiiij s xj d
Item, for iiij c hertlath, ij s. Summa,

Item, payd to Rowlonde, tyler, and to his men for
tylyng and poyntyng of the same place, and to
ther laborers, as it more playnly shewyth by a byll } of the same, xxj s vij d,
Item, for ij busshellis of tyle pynnys, xij d,

Item, payd to Christofer, carpynter, for tymbyr
and for workmanshyp of the same, as it aperith in } x s   vj d
the boke of parcellis of the same,

Summa, iiij li xij s vij d.

¹ Reparacion of þe prestes howsis.

ffurste, for a lode lome, vj d,
Item, for lath and nayle, iiij d, } xiij d
Item, for mendynge of a wyndowe, iij d,

Item, payd to a dowber for to dawbe & mend syr } ix d
Thomasis chavmbyr & syr Rafis by a day di,

Item, payd for ij Sakkes lyme, iiij d.
Item, for makyng of an herth in Syr thomas } viij d ob
chambyr, iiij d ob,
Item, to a tyler and his man by ij days there . . ij s   ij d

Summa, iiij s viij d ob.

Reparacion of blasis howse.

Item, for iij lode lome, xviij d,
Item, for a lode sande, vj d, } ij s   ij d
Item, for strawe to þe dawbynge, ij d,

Item, for a m¹ Sprygge, vij d,
Item, for c di. of hertlathe, ix d, } ij s
Item, for iiij Sackes lyme, viij d,

Item, payd to Christofyr, carpynter, for stuffe
boght of hym, and for workemanshyp of the } vj s   iiij d
same, as it aperyth by the parcellis of the same by
a byll,

Summa, x s vj d.
Summa, xv s ij d ob.

¹ leaf 37.

[1] Reparacion of þe seges for the clerkys.

ffor ij Sackes lyme, iiij d,
Item, for c breke, vj d,
Item, payd to a mason and his man by ij days, ij s ij d, } iij s

    Summa, iij s.

Reparacion of ffysshis howse.

ffurst for a lood lyme, xij d,
Item, for a lode sande, vj d,
Item, for a quartron of sprygge, j d ob,
Item, for ij c hartelath, xij d,
Item, for a lode lome, iiij d,
Item, for Rofe nayle, iij d ob,
Item, for othyr naylis, ij d.   Summa, } iij s   v d

Item, to a tyler and his man by iiij days . . . iiij s iiij d

Item, to a dawber and his man by a day . . . xiij d

Item, payd to   , Carpynter, for diuerse stuffe boght of hym, and for workemanshyp of the same, and for naylis as it aperith by a byll, } x s

    Summa, xviij s x d.
    Summa, xxj s x d.

[2] Reparacion of þe Wevers howse.

ffirste, for a lood lyme, xij d,
Item, for a lood sand, iiij d,
Item, for c lath, v d,
Item, for lome, iiij d,
Item, payd to a dawber and his man by a day, xiij d,
Item, to a tyler & his man by ij days, ij s ij d,
Item, for Sprygge nayle, iij d,
Item, payd to a carpynter for diuerse stuffe boght of hym, and for workemanshyp of the same, v s ij d,
Item, for naylis, iiij d, } xj s   j d

   [1] leaf 37, back.   [2] leaf 38.

Oyle for the church.

Item, payd for xxiij galons oyle spende in the churche by the space of this accompt and a poteli of oyle, the galon xij d. Summa, xxiij s vj d, Item, payd for xj galons oyle spende in the church in the tyme of Iohn palmer & Iohn Clerke, churchwardeyns, prece þe galon xij d. Summa totalis, xj s. } xxxiiij s vj d

Summa, xlv s vij d.

[1] Payd to the plummer.

Item, in money payd to Rogere Smalehode, plummer, for lede, Sowdowre, and workemanshyp of the same done and spent apon the church, the stepyli, the tenawntryes, prestis howsis, and apon the gutters of the same, as it apperyth by byllis of parcellis of the same. Summa, } viij li xix s iij d

Summa, viij li xix s iij d.

Almys men.

Item, payd sondayly to iij poore almysmen to pray for the sowle of Iohn Bedham yerely, by the space of this accompte, as it aperyth by the booke of parcellis of the same, &c. } v li iiij s

Summa, v li iiij s.
Summa, xiiij li iij s iij d.

[2] Rewardis & potacions amonge þe tenauntes, & in oþer costes in ouerseyng of þe workys by the same space, &c.

ffirst, yevyn to ther tenauntes at the Receyvyng of the Rentes, and in potacions amonge them, and for owre expensis and costis in waytyng apon the workemen durynge the space of this accompte, } x s v d

Item, in allowaunce to the churchewardeyns for thayr attendaunce apon the churche workes by the yere vj s viij d. Summa for ij hole yere, } xiij s iiij d

[1] leaf 38, back. [2] leaf 39.

Churchwardens' Accounts, A.D. 1479–81.

Vyewers. Item, payd to the vywers for to ouerse
the howse þat dyghton dwellith in, and the ten-
auntryes next the clerkyn well, for to know the
Ryght, ffyrst for ther costes at þe tavyrne for brede
& wyne, vj d,
Item, for a byll of the verdytt hadde owte of the
mayrys courte, viij d,
Item, payd to a sergeaunte for the arrest of our } xj s vj d
tenaunte þat dyd vs wronge, viij d,
Item, for withdrawyng of the Cowrte, iiij d,
Item, payd for the costes of the sergeaunte for his
attendaunce at diuerse tymeȝ for the same arrest,
&c., xij d,
Item, payd for the vywers labour and attendaunce
at diuerse tymeȝ, viij s iiij d,

    Summa, xxxv s iij d.

[1]Item, payd to Maystyr Mandyke and to othyrs for
diuerse expensis done and hadde, as it more playnly } xv s x d
shewith by the parcellis of the same,

Item, for the makyng of this accompt . . . . vj s viij d

Item, payd to Iohn Carpynter for his goodwyll to
be shewyd in the byldyng of the lumbardis place } vj s viij d
in saynt botolfis lane,

    Summa, xxix s ij d.

    Summa of all the allowaunce, clxxli v s vj d ob

    And they owe xj li v s ij d ob

Therof is owynge by diuerse persooneȝ as apperyth }
by the names and summes in the lesse folowynge, } viij li xvij s iiij d

And by the said accomptantis }
clerely to be payd to the church, } vj s x d ob

[2]Olde arrerages, Iohn Dighton, Capper . . . . xlv s

William Sherborne . . . . xv s

  Cobbe, Brewer . . . . vj s viij d

Clemente atte hylle . . . . xij s

Iames Cokke, wever . . . . xij s vj d

Iohn Doklyng for buryyng of iij of his chyldyr in } vj s
þe pardon churchyarde, }

    Summa, iiij li xvij s ij d.

---

[1] leaf 39, back. [2] leaf 40.

Arrere*r* of þe tyme of this Accompte

Iohn Dighton, capper	iij ɫi
William Grene for iij q*uarter*s	vj s
Grene for a quarter Rent	xx d
Nicholas Willi*a*mson, wever, for iij q*uar*ters . .	xiij s vj d

S*um*ma, iiij ɫi xiiij d.

Delyve*r*ed to gabryeɫ lombarde, ow*r*e tenaunte in botoɫ lane, in olde lede, } x^c wegɫite

[1]harry vavaso*ur*, Iohn Baker, } 1483.

[A.D. 1483–5.]

[2]✚ Ihes*u*s.

Thys ys the Rekenyng off harry vavesour and Iohn Baker, late wardens of the Rentes & goodes belongyng to the chyrcɫ of S͞ȝ Marye at hyɫ, ffrome Myghelmas An° 1483, vnto Myghelmas An° 1485. S*um*ma for ij yere.

The Rentaɫ off the chyrcɫ.

Sir Iohn plommer for ij yere Rente, paying yerlye xx s. S*um*ma	xl s
herry Mershe, for the kechen by ij yere, eue*r*y yer vj s viij d. S*um*ma	xiij s iiij d
tow3 hyɫ. herry Mershe, for the howse w*ith* gardens at to*ur* hyɫ, by ij yere. S*um*ma . .	xl s
Syr Iohn Philip, for ij yerys Rente of his Chambre, by yere xij s. S*um*ma	xxiiij s
Syr Willi*a*m Soulby, for ij yere of hys chambre, eue*r*y yere ix s. S*um*ma	xviij s
Syr Iohn lovyer, for ij yer of hys chambre, eue*r*y yere viij s. S*um*ma	xvj s
William haɫ, watirman, for ij yer, paying yerlye xxxiij s iiij d. S*um*ma	iij ɫi vj s viiij d
harry Willi*a*mson, for the house that he ocupied, by yer iiij ɫi. S*um*ma	viij ɫi
Iohn Ducklyng, for the schoppe that he occupied, by yer xvj s viij d. S*um*ma	xxxiij s iiij d

[1] leaf 42. [2] leaf 43.

Churchwardens' Accounts, A.D. 1483–5.

William harman, for the howse above, paying yerlye xvj s viij d. Summa . . . . xxxiij s iiij d

Iohn Colman, Bucher, for hys house, paying yerlye xxvj s viij d. Summa . . . . liij s iiij d

Thomas hunte, draper, for hys house, paying yerlye liij s iiij d. Summa . . . . v ƚi vj s viij d

The Chyrch wardens of seynte Botolphes in Temmistrete, for quitrent . . . . v s

Thomas Seymour, for the quyterent goyng oute of hys house, by ij yere . . . . vj s viij d

Summa totalis, xxx ƚi xvj s iiij d.

The Rentall of Mr William Cambriges.

Rychard Cryke at the Stockes, hauyng all the tenementes yn hys owne handes, paying yerlye x ƚi. } xx ƚi
Summa for ij° yer,

The Rentall of Roose Wrytell.

William Myln, yremonger, hauyng all the tenementes callid the olde Swann, paying yerlye } xiij ƚi vj s viij d
vl ƚi xiij s iiij d. Summa ij° yer,

[1] ƚi s [1]
. . 64 . 3 . .

[2] Ihesus.

The Rentall of Nasynges.

Iohn a Bristowe, for a Chambre occupied ij° yer, paying by yer viij s. Summa, xvj s.

Iohn harris, watirman, for a chambre paying by yer vj s viij d. Summa, xiij s iiij d.

Nicholas Thornley, for a chambre ij° yer, paying by yer viij s. Summa, xvj s.

William Paris, for a chambre ij° yer, paying by yer viij s. Summa, xvj s.

Ysabell Cutler, for a schopp ij° yer, paying by yer vj s viij d. Summa, xiij s iiij d.

Iohn Ionkyns, for a chambre ij° yer, paying by yer viij s. Summa, xvj s.

Iohn harryson, for a chambre ij° yer, paying by yer x s. Summa, xx s.

George olyver, for a chambre ij° yer, paying by yer vj s viij d. Summa, xiij s iiij d.

harry vavesour, a house ij yer and the celer, euery yer xl s. Summa, iiij ƚi.

[1–1] In corner.   [2] leaf 43, back.

MED. REC.

harry vavesour, for a house ij° yer, paying by yer iij ħ iij s iiij d. Summa, vj ħ vj s viij d.

Roberte Baycroffte, for a house ij° yer, paying by yer xiij s iiij d. Summa, xxvj s viij d.

   Summa totalis, xvij ħ xvij s iiij d.

The Rentall off Mr Richard Gosslyn, ffauster lane.

Maister lewes, fecissian, for a house ij yer, paying by yer xl s. Summa, iiij ħ.

large, his wyffe, for a house ij yer, paying euery yer xx s. Summa, xl s.

The housse uppon the steyer off, xviij s o· yer, summa for ij° yer, xxxvj s.

Thomas Exmo, goldsmyth, for a house ij° yer, paying euery yer xlvj s viij d. Summa, iiij li xiij s iiij d.

Iohn Mowce, Clarke, for a house ij° yer, paying euery yer xxvj s viij d. Summa, liij s iiij d.

Alys loffden, for a house ij° yer, paying euery yer xvj s. Summa, xxxij s.

Byschopp, Tayllour, for a house ij° yer, euery yer xviij s. Summa, xxxvj s.

   Summa, xviij ħ x s viij d.

The Rentall of Bedaham.

Gabryell, de vr s ffor the grete lombardes place yn ⎫
Botolph lane, paying yerlye xij ħ vj s viij d, for ⎬ xxvj ħ xiij s iiij d
ij° yer. Summa,   ⎭

[1] ħ   d
63   16 [1]

[2] Ihesus.

The Rentall off Iohn Causton.

Iohn ffyshe, grocer, ffor a house ij° yer, paying yerly vj li. Summa, xij ħ.

Iohn Brewster, tornour, ffor his house ij° yer, euery yer xl s. Summa, iiij ħ.

harry Kello, tayllour, ffor hys house ij° yer, euery yer iiij li xiij s iiij d. Summa, ix ħ vij s viij d.

Alexaunder Worsley, clarke, ffor a house ij° yer, euery yer xx s. Summa, xl s.

Rychard Chelmysho, ffor a house ij° yer, paying euery yer xx s. Summa, xl s.

[1–1] In corner.   [2] leaf 44.

Thomas ffynche and penrethe, ffor a house ij° yer, euery yer xx s. Summa, xl s.

The Bredrede man, ffor a house ij° yer, paying yerly viij s. Summa, xvj s.

The ij wydewys, ffor a house ij° yer, paying yerly viij s. Summa, xvj s.

The wevers wyff, ffor a tenement ij° yer, paying yerly viij s. Summa, xvj s.

Rychard Careden, ffuller, for cobb, a Garden ij° yer, euery yer xiij s. iiij d. Summa, xxvj s viij d.

Iohn Smarte, grocer, for a garden ij° yer, paying yerly iiij s. Summa, viij s.

Mott, Carpenter, for a garden for ij° yer, paying yerly iiij s vj d. Summa, ix s.

Iohn harrys, Gardiner, for ij gardyns, euery off þem ij° yer, paying euery yer iij s for þe oon & ij s viij d for the other. } Summa, xj s iiij d

  Summa totalis, xxxvj li ix s viij d.

  Summa totalis in Renttes, clxiij li xiiij s.

Item, I charge me with the Clarkes wages and Beame ly3te Reseued by us within the tyme off thys acompte. Summa for vij^e quarteres, euerye quarter xxxij s one with another. Summa, } xj li iiij s

Item, I charge me with the pascall money Resseued for ij° yer within the tyme off thys accompte at xij s o yer. Summa, } xxiiij s

   Summa, xij li viij s.

li s d
[1]48 . 17 . 8[1]

[2] Ihesus.

Also I Charche me with such Rerages as y haue Resseyued off them, leffte in harry merschys days, that ys to witt off.

Thomas ffynche, tayllour	xxv s	
Syr William web, prest	ij s iiij d	
Byschop Tayllour	iiij s vj d	
harry Wylliamson, Grocer	xx s	} Summa, iij li xiij s x d
And off Iohn Wade	iiij s	
Elisabeth Cutler	viij s	
Iohn Breuster, Tornour	x s	

  Summa totalis of the hole charge, lxxix li xv s x d.

[1] li s d
  3 18 10 [1]

[1–1] In corner.   [2] leaf 44, back.

[1] Ihesus.

Here followeth the Paymenttes off the same.

ffirst, vacacions off the house that harry Willimson occupied a hole yer . . . . iiij li

Item, vac' off the house that William harman dwellid in o quarter . . . . iiij s ij d

Summa, iiij li iiij s ij d.

Paide for the kepyng off the Obyte off Mr Iohn Bradmer, the xxv day off nouember, for the yere an° xiiij c lxxxiiij^e, to prestes & clerkes, } iij s   iiij d

Item, ffor the kepyng off the obite off Iohn Weston the xix day off Aprell, the space off ij° yere, þat ys to wit yn an° xiiij^c lxxxiiij^e & in a° 1485. } vj s   x d
Summa,

Payd to syr Iohn plommer for hys labur to syng the morowmas, payd yerlye, xx s. Summa for ij° yer, } xl s

Item, payd ffor the wages off Alexaunder Worsleye, for vij quarteres off a yere, within the tyme off thys accompte, euery quarter xiij s iiij d. } iiij li xiij s   iiij d
Summa,

Item, payd to Iohn Russell for hys wages off vij^e quarter, for euery quarter, xiij s iiij d. Summa, } iiij li xiij s   iiij d

Summa, xj li xvj s x d.

Payd to mychaell harrys, chyrchwarden, off S$_3$ Georges beside puddyng lane, for quyte rent off a hole yer at Mighelmas, An° xiiij^c lxxxiiij^e, goyng off the tenementes off Iohn Weston. Summa, } xx s

Item, payd to the Abbott off Waltham for quyt rent goyng owt off the tenementes off Weston for o yer and halfe, fynysched at Ester, An° xiiij c lxxxv, for the yer xxxviij s. Summa for the yer and halfe, } lvij s

Summa, iij li xvij s.

[2] li   s
19 18 [2]

[1] leaf 45.   [2-2] In corner.

[1] Ihe*sus*.

The costes done within the Chyrch.

ffyrst, payde for ij quarters cooles, occupied at ij festes of Ester, within the time of this accompte, xij d,
Item, for palme box, and oblyes for ij° yer, xij d.
Item, for wachyng of the Sepulcre, and in expences of brede & ale to William paris for ij° yer, xij d,
Item, for Byrchene bowes ayenst mydsomer for ij tymes, vj d,
payd to syngers on S₃ Barnabees even yn wyne spent at tavern, and at many other festes of the yer to syngers within the queer, within thys j° yeres, v s,
Item, for a newe holowe key to the Roode loffte dore, price iij d,
Item, for a holowe key to the south dore, xij d,
Item, for mendyng of the orgons, x s,
Item, for mendyng of the dayllye Cross, xij d,
Item, for cariage of xij lodes Rubrysch, the which was leyde out of the chyrch by the good man prewne, vnder Maister pagis wall, ij s,
[2]Item, payd for a prickid song Booke for the chirch,[2]

} xxij s   ix d

Reparacions.

Payd to a dawber for ij days werke in dawbyng within in the house that William harman occupied, euery day, viij d. Summa, xvj d,
Item, to a laborer for ij dayes, x d,
Item, for ij lodes lomb, viij d,
Item, for j c di. saplath, vj d,
Item, for iij quarter of o m^ll spryg, iiij d ob,
Item, for a carpenter for a daye, viij d,
Item, for iiij quarter, viij d,
Item, for borde, ij d,
Item, for naylles, j d,
Item, for a mason for makyng of an herthe in the same house, for a daye, vj d,
Item, that daye to a laborer, iiij d,
Item, for sannde, j d,
Item, for ij sackes lyme, iiij d. Summa totalis,

} vj s vj d ob

Summa totalis off the Chyrch Costes, xxj li vij s iij d ob.

[3]29 s 3 d 3[3]

---
[1] leaf 45, back.   [2–2] Scratched out.   [3–3] In corner.

[1] Ihesus.

The costes of Mr William Caumbriges chauntrye.

ffyrst, payd for a quytrente to the abbot off Barmondsay, goyng oute of the tenementes at the stockes for a hole yer, at myghelmas anno xiiij^c lxxxiiij. Summa, } vj s

Payd for kepyng of Mr Caumbriges Obites ij^o tymes within the yeres of this acompte, to the prestes and clerkes. Summa, } viij s viij d

Item, to ij Mayers of the bequestes of Mr Caumbryges, } xiij s iiij d

Item, to iij Schryves wythin this ij^o yer. . . . xiij s iiij d

Item, to the Swerdeberer, comyng with the Mayer at ij tymes, } iij s iiij d

Summa, xliiij s viij d.

Payd to Sir William Soulby, for hys wages for ij^o yer, euery yer vj li xiij s iiij d. Summa, } xiij li vj s viij d

Summa totalis off Mr Caumbrige, xv li xj s iiij d.

The Costes of Roose Wrytelles Chauntrye.

Payde to Syr Phillip Norton, Syngyng for Roose Writell the space of ij^o yer, euery ȝer vj li xiij s iiij d. Summa, } xiij li vj s viij d

[2] li   s
 28 18 [2]

[3] Ihesus.

The Costes of Nasynges chauntrye.

Vacacion of the house that Richard fflecher late occupied for o quarter . . . . x s

Payd to the abbot of Waltham for quytrente, goyng oute of the tenementes of Nasynges for a yer & di. at xxij s o yer. Summa, } xxxiij s

Payd to a preste to syng for Nasynges the space of ij^o yer, euery yer vj li xiij s iiii d. Summa, } xiij li vj s viij d

Summa, xv li ix s viij d.

---

[1] leaf 46.   [2–2] In corner.   [3] leaf 46, back.

Churchwardens' Accounts, A.D. 1483–5.

Payde to a man werkyng in Barcrofft*es* house, in makyng ther of an herthe, vj d,
Item, to a laborer, iiij d,
Item, for ij° sack*es* lyme & sannde, vj d,
Item, for breke & tyle, iiij d,
Item, for ij° peyer heng*es* & hook*es* to the house next to Iohn Bakers, weying xj ℔ di. price xvij d,
Item, for ij° keyes to the same house, vj d. S*um*ma tot*ali*s, } iij s   vij d

    S*um*ma tot*ali*s, xv ƚi xiij s iij d.

The Cost*es* of Mr Richard Gosslynn.

Vacacion off the house that large, his wyffe, occupied the space of o yer & di. at xx s the yer. S*um*ma, } xxx s

Vacacion of the house uppon the steyer ij° yere yn owre tyme, at xviij s a yer. S*um*ma, } xxxvj s

Vacacion of the house that Thomas Exmo now hath taken, o yer & a q*uar*ter affter, xlvj s viij d o yer. S*um*ma, } lviij s   iiij d

Vacacion of the house that Byschopp Taylo*ur* occupied, a hole yer, } xviij s

Vacacion of the house that Alys loneden hath occupied, o yer and iij quarterys, at xvj s o yer. S*um*ma, } xxviij s

    S*um*ma in vacacions, viij ƚi x s iiij d.

  li   s   d
[1] 24 3 7 [1]

        [2] Ih*esu*s.

Payde to the priores off Kilborn, for quytrent goying oute off the tenement*es* off Maist*er* Gostlynn for o yere yn oure tyme. S*um*ma, } vj d

Payde for the Obite off Mr Rychard gosslynn, kepte the first day off Decembyr, an° xiiij c lxxxiiij, to the prest*es* & clark*es*, & brede, ale, & offeryng. S*um*ma, } iiij s   j d

Payde to a preste for hys salarye, the space of ij° yer, eu*er*y yer, vj ƚi xiij s iiij d. S*um*ma, } xiij ƚi vj s viij d

Payde to a Carpenter werkyng in Maist*er* lewes house, & in the prest*es* house, & in Thomas Exmo house the space off ij days, in makyng of a pent*es* and in mendyng of diuers thynges necessarye, takyng eu*er*y day viij d. S*um*ma, } xvj d

    [1–1] In corner.   [2] leaf 47.

Item, to Iohn Broke for vj c di. & iij fote quarter borde at ij s j d the c. Summa, } xij s vij d

Item, for cariage and wharfage off the same borde, v d.

Item, for iiij quarter, viij d.

Item, for ij c di. iiij penye nayle, x d.

Item, for di. c v d nayle, ij d ob.

Item, for di. a c iij penye nayle, j d ob.

Payde to a tyler for iiij dayes & di. in poyntyng of dyuers houses, at vj d a day. Summa, } ij s iij d

Item, a laborer for iiij dayes & di. xviij d.

Item, for ij lodes & iiij sackes lyme, ij s iiij d.

Item, for ij m¹ tyle, x s iiij d.

Item, for ij⁰ lode sonnde, xij d.

Item, for tyle pynnes, j d.

Payde to a dawber for iij dayes werke in M^r lewes house, and in other tenementes, for euery day, viij d. summa, } ij s

Item, to a laborer for iij dayes, euery day, v d. Summa, } xv d

Item, for di. m^ll sprig, iiij d.

Item, for a c saplath, iiij d.

Item, for a lode lombe, iiij d.

Item, for sannde, ij d.

Item, for pavyng of vj teyse, ij s x d.

Item, for vj lodes gravell, ij s vj d.

Summa totalis, xv li xiiij s viij d.

[1] li s d [1]
15 14 8.

[2] Payde to Iohn draper, laborer, for v dayes & di. in makyng clene off the house that Thomas Exmo hathe taken, euery day iiij d. Summa xxij d.

Item, to Thomas Wycam, laborer, for makyng clene of thes aide house, and the house that the preste hath taken, for vj dayes, ij s.

Item, for a stapull & a haspe to the prestes house, ij d.

[1]–[1] In corner. [2] leaf 47, back.

Item, for a newe key and a lache to the clyket locke, vj d.

Item, ij° newe keyes to the same place, vij d.

Item, for a new spryng to a locke, ij d.

   S*u*mma v s, iij d.

 S*u*mma to*t*alis of Gosslyn, xxiiij ti x s iij d.

   The Paymentes of I. Bedahams chauntrye.

ffyrst, alowed to Gabriell de vrs at euery quarter of hys rente xiij s iiij d yn owre tyme, for vij quarters. S*u*mma,   iiij ti xiij s iiij d

Payde for the Obite of Bedham, kepte twyes, the xxiiij daye off May, at eu*er*y tyme iiij s v d. S*u*mma,   viij s x d

Item, off hys bequeste to the chyrchwardens, for o yer. S*u*mma,   vj s viij d

Item, to iij pore men, of his almes eu*er*y sonday yn þe yer, xij d. S*u*mma off ij° yer, v ti xj s

Item, payde to the preste, Syr Iohn plommer, for hys celarie for ij yer, xiij ti vj s viij d

Item, payde for the oyle for the lampe, expendid the space off oo yer & di. S*u*mma, xviij galons, at xij d the galon. S*u*mma,   xviij s

   S*u*mma to*t*alis, xxiiij ti xvj s vj d.

[1] li s d
25 2 2 [1]

    [2] Ih*es*us.

 The Costes and paymentes of I. Causton chaunterye.

Vacacion att the tenementes at the tourhyll, the space off ij° yer, onelye res*seued* a ffetherbed off the weveres wyff, p*r*ice v s, and so was xliij s

Vacacion of the house that Roger penreth occupied, o yer . . . . xx s

Vacacion of the ij gardens that Iohn harrys, gar- dyner, ocupied, o q*uarter*,   xvij d

Vacacion of the house that Ric*hard* chelmysho now occupieth, di. o yer,   x s

   S*u*mma, iij ti xiiij s v d.

  [1–1] In corner.   [2] leaf 48.

Payde to the Bretherhed of owre ladye, Salue Regina, founded within the chyrch of S3 magnus, for a hole yer, an⁰ xiiij⁰ lxxxiiij at mydsomer, goyng owte of Iohn fischis house. Summa, } vj s

Payde to the Brige house for o quytrent goyng owte of the tenement off I. ff. for the tyme of this accompte, that ys to wit for ij⁰ yer, euery yere xiij s iiij d. Summa, } xxvj s viij d

Payde for the Obite of Iohn Causton, kepte the ij^e dayes of August, twyes within this acompte, spendyng at euery tyme iiij s ij d. Summa, } viij s iiij d

Payde to the preste for his celarye for ij⁰ yer, euery yer vj ħ xiij s iiij d. summa, } xiij ħ vj s viij d

Payde in Reparacions in fischis house for iij newe hopis, and ij⁰ Eris to a Boket, price, } xx d

  Summa totalis, xix ħ iij s ix d.

  Summa totalis payde, cxxxiiij ħ viij s vj d ob.

   Reste due to the chirch, xlv ħ vij s iij d ob.

Wherof ther ys in detters, and moneye delyuerid to William prewne and Iohn halhed as it apperith ffoloyng more pleynlye.

¹ħ s d.
19 3 9¹

² ffyrst delyueryd to them in Redye money by Mr Iohn Redye and Iohn Bakers wyffe Such money as was leffte of beame ly3te monye, clarkes wagis and pascall money to the Summa off } xxxiiij s j d

The names off the detteres that the sayde William Prewne and Iohn halhed Resseyued ffor the Reragis off owre tyme.

ffyrst, off William Myln ffor iij quarteris . . . v ħ
Thomas hunte, ffor di. o yer . . . . xxvj s viij d
Thomas Seymour, ffor quiterent ij⁰ yer . . . . vj s viij d
William harman, ffor o quarter . . . . . . iiij s ij d
William hall, ffor o quarter . . . . viij s iiij d
harry vavesour, ffor ij⁰ yer s' o quarter . . . . ix ħ xvj s viij d

   ^{1—1} In corner.   ² leaf 48, back.

Churchwardens' Accounts, A.D. 1483–5.

Roberd Bercroffte, ffor ij° quarteris	iij s	iiij d
Iohn a Brystow, ffor iij quarteris	vj s	
Iohn harrys, waterman, ffor o quarter		xx d
Syr Iohn phillipp, ffor o quarter	iij s	
Alexaunder Worssley, ffor o quarter	v s	
Thomas Armerer, ffor o quarter	ij s	
Iohn harryson, ffor o quarter	ij s	vj d
William paris, ffor o quarter		xx d
Iohn Ionkyns, ffor o quarter	ij s	
Roger penreth, ffor o quarter	v s	
Iohn Bruster, torner, ffor ij° yere	iiij li	
Gabriell de vrs, ffor o quarter	liij s	iiij d
Richard Crick, vpholster, for o quarter	l s	
Iohn ffysch, grocer, ffor di. o yer	iij li	
Iohn Colman, Bucher	vj s	viij d
Maister lewes, for o yer and di.	iij li	
Thomas Exmo, for iij quarters	xxxv s	
Iohn Mowce, carpenter	xxvj s	viij d

[1]li d
39 5[1]   Summa, xxxvij li vj s iiij d.
         Summa totalis.

[2]Ihesus.

More detters.

Sir William Stodale, preste, for o quarter	v s	
Richard Careden, ffor ij° yer	xxvj s	viij d
Iohn Mott, Carpenter, for ij° yer	ix s	
Iohn harryson, Gardiner	ix s	xj d
Iohn Smarte, for ij° yer	viij s	
The chirchwardens off Sent Botolphes, for ij° yer	v s	

Summa, iij li iij s vij d.

Summa totalis delyuerd to þe wardens William Grene and I. h. xlij li iiij s.

[1–1] In corner.   [2] leaf 49.

Theis be the names off them that I axske alowaunce off that paide no thing in oure dayes.

harry Mershe, ffor o quarter rent off the tour hyll	v s	
Item, ffor ij° yeris rente off the kechyn	xiij s	iiij d
Item, Iohn Ducklyng paide no Rente in owre time ffor the space of ij° yer. Summa,	xxx s	iiij d

Summa totalis due to the chirch, xj s vij d ob.

[1] Ihesus.

The Rentall in the tyme of Iohn halhed & Robert Roucybye.

Seynt Maryhill lane.

Iohn a Bristowe, a chambre by yer,	viij s		
Iohn harris „ [2] „ „	vj s	viij d	
Nicholas Thornlay „ „	viij s		
Wylliam Parys „ „ „	viij s		Nasynges.
Item, a Schopp vnder the chambre by yer,	vj s	viij d	
Iohn Ionkyns, a schopp with a chambre by yer,	x s		
Iohn harryson, a chambre by yer,	x s		
George Olyver „ „ „	vj s	viij d	

The Prestes Aleye.

Syr Iohn Plommer, a house by yer,
Harry Mersche, a kechen by yer,
Syr Iohn Philip, a house by yer,
Syr William Maltbye, ij° chambres by yer,
Syr Iohn lovyer, a chambre by yer,

The chirchyard.

Alysaunder wursley, clarke, a house by yer,
Richard Chelmysho, ioyner „ „
Robart Grapeles, tayllour „ „

[Prices torn away.]

Wylliam Dyckson, grocer, a house by yer,
harry vavesour, diuers tenementes „ „
Robart Barcroffte, waterman, ij° chambres by yer,
Wylliam hall, watirman, a house by yer,
Richard Alenson, tayllour „ „

[1] leaf 51.   [2] Written in full in MS.

Churchwardens' Accounts, A.D. 1483–5.

[1]Iohn causton
The chirch.

In Temmes strete
Roose Wrytell
Sir Th.

harry Kello, tayllour, a house by yer, ... iiij li xij s iiij d
Thomas Seymour, grocer, the Corner house, quytrent by yer,   iiij s iiij d
Thomas hunte, draper, a house by yer, ... iij li vj s viij d
Wylliam Myln, yremonger, by yer, ... vj li xiij s iiij d
The chirchwardens of Seynt Botolphus beside byllynges-gate,   ij s vj d

Summa, xiiij li xv s x d.

Iohn Bedaham.
Gabryell de vrs, ffor the greate lombardis place by yer, } xiij li vj s viij d

Iohn Causton.
Iohn Brewster, Tornor, ij° tenementes by yer. . . . . .   xl s

the chirch.
Thomas Colman, Bocher, & william dye, a house by yer .   xxvj s viij d

Iohn causton.
Iohn ffysche, Grocer, for an house by yer . . . . . . vj li
. . . xxij li xij s . .

. . . Cambrige
. . . he Stokkes.

Robart Crycke, wollmonger, ij° tenementes by yer, } vj li
Iohn Byrlyng, goldsmyth, for a house by yer, } liij s iiij d
William Reynnyssforthe, poyntemaker, for a house by yer, } xxvj s viij d

Summa, x li.

. . . lynn
. . . lane.

Maister lewes, the kynges ffesissyan, a house by yer . . .   xl s
Maistres Browne, wydewe, a house by yer . . . . .   xx s
Item, for the house vppon the steyer by yer . . . .   xiij s iiij d
Thomas Exmo, goldsmyth, a ffayer house by yer, } xlvj s viij d
Iohn Mowce the yonger, capper, a house by yer, } xxvj s viij d
Gloucetter, organ maker, a house by yer . . . . . .   xxvj s
A patynmaker, a hous by yer .   xiij s iiij d

Summa, viij li xvj s.

[1] leaf 51, back.

By the Meneris. Iohn causton.	Iohn Wollmonger, a lytell house by yer	viij s
	The ij° wydewes, a house by yer	viij s
	Ric' a kechen, Bedredman, a house by yer	viij s
	Ric' Garden, ffuller, a garden by yer	xiij s iiij d
	Iohn Smarte, grocer, a garden by yer	iiij s
	Wylliam Boyes, gardyner, a garden by yer	iiij s
	Iohn Harryson wyff, gardyner, a garden by yer . . .	iij s
	Iohn yong, a garden by yer .	ij s viij d
	Summa, lj s	

Tour hiH + Harrye Mersche, paynter, a house by yer   xx s

[1]Ihesus.

The Booke of the clarkes wages.

[that is, the Book of the parishioners' contributions to the Parish Clerk's wages?]

Iohn Crescroffte	j d	Christouer hobye	j d
Iohn Ricard	j d	Iohn a Grene	j d
Nych Roose, taylour	j d	Iohn fformes	j d
Gabriell de vrs	xij d	Reignolde Bull	j d
Iohn harryson	j d	Garard Ionson	j d
harry Mersche	xij d	Iohn Markes	iiij d
Richard Chelmysho	j d	Iohn Clarke	viij d
Iohn a Mylton	viij d	Iohn Smerte	xiiij d
harry vavesour	xiij d	harry Kello	viij d
Richard Cloce	viij d	Th. Wattes	iiij d
William dickson	iiij d	Th. Blake	iiij d
Peter Russell	iiij d	William Graye	xij d
William Geffrey	iiij d	William Duerey	vj d
Maister W. Remyngton	xvj d	Robert Michelson	iiij d
William Cook	ij d	Iohn a downe	iiij d
William hall	ij d	William harman	iiij d
Robart Barcroffte	j d	Robert waldyng	iiij d
Robart Staunsour	iij d	William Remyngton	iiij d
Richard Alenson	viij d	Christian hunte	iiij d
Peter Andrew	vj d	Iohn Ducklyng	xij d
Robert Rivell	xiiij d	Thomas Seymour	viij d
William prene	xij d	Thomas Colyn	vj d
Iohn halhed	viij d	Thomas hunte	viij d

[1] leaf 52.

Churchwardens' Accounts, A.D. 1487–8.

Iohn dewblyn	x d	Richard dockyng	j d
Iohn deraham	viij d	William Maunsfelde	ij d
Robert howtyng	vj d	Iohn hewes	j d
Iohn Townnysend	vj d	Richard westus	j d
Robert Roucybye	vij d	William pratt	j d
Iohane Bremonger	iiij d	Thomas Caley	j d
Nicholas Smythisson	j d	Iohn Bircham	j d
Moder Selbye	j d	Richard welton.	
Iohn Polyver	vj d	Richard Silke.	
Iohn Ionson	vj d	William Silke.	
Wylliam Myln	x d	Th. a bynkes.	
Iohn Nevyle	iiij d	Iohn topladye.	
Iohn Russell	iiij d	Iohn a Bristowe.	
harry Smyth	j d	Th. Baate	
Richard abell	iiij d	Thomas Toddes.	

[... Accounts for A.D. 1485–7 lost ...]
[A.D. 1487–8]

[1] +Ihesus

Here begynneth the Rekenyng of vs, Iohn halhed and Robert Roucyby, ffor o yer, from Mighelmas a° ij° h. vij to Myghelmas a° iij° h. vij.

ffyrst, we charge vs with the monye resseyued of William prene and Iohn halhed, that they leffte Remaynnyng in the Box. Summa, } lj s x d

Also, we charge vs with such detteres as was owyng to the chirch, as yt apperith mor playnly in the ffoote of theyer accompte, Summa, iij li vj s viij d in diuers mennys handes, Of the which Resseyued by vs,

Of Robert Barcroffte, iij s iiij d
Of William Bryan, ffreuterer, v s
Of Iohn harrys, gardyner, xviij d
Of Iohn wolmonger, xij d
Of Richard Chelmysho, iiij s
} Summa resseyued by vs xiiij s x d

in parte of payment of xl s the which he oweth for housrente, that is to wit, in the tyme of harry vavesour o yer di. Summa, xxx s, and in the tyme of William prene & Iohn halhed, for half o yer x s. Summa as is aforesaide, xl s. Iohn a milton, Baker, Sewrete for the saide Richard to paye quarterly iiij s. The ffyrst quarter begon is at Mighelmas last past, & paide by Iohn Milton, Baker, the saide iiij s.

[1] leaf 53.

Also we charge with the Rentall afore rehersid that we haue resseyued within this yer belongyng as wele to the chirch as to the chauntryes.

[1]The Chirch Rentes is   xv li   xj s   vj d
Nasynges Chauntrye   Summa   ix li   viij d
Roose Wrytell   ,,   vj li   xiij s iiij d
Richard Gosslynis   ,,   viij li xvj s
Iohn Causton   ,,   xviij li iiij s iiij d
Iohn Bedaham   ,,   xiij li vj s viij d
Maister William Caimbrige   ,,   x li

                                         xx
                        Summa, iiij.j li xij s vj d.

[2] + Ihesus.

Item, we charge vs with the clarkes wages resseyued at iiij termes of þe yer, that is to wit,

at Cristmas,   xxviij s x d ⎫
Item, at the ffeste of Annuncyacyon,   xxviij s j d ⎪ Summa,
Item, at the ffeste of S₃ Iohn Baptist, xxviij s vj d ⎬ v li xiiij s
Item, at the ffest of S₃ Mychael,   xxix s   iij d⎭   viij d

Item, for the Beame ly3te at þe saide termes, that is to wyt,

At Cristmas,   vj s ij d ⎫
At owr lady day,   v s   vij d ⎪ Summa, xxiij s v d
At Midsommer,   v s   x d   ⎬
And at Mighelmas,   v s   x d   ⎭

Item, we Resseyued at Ester anº xiiijc lxxxvij^e of the howslyng people ffor the pascall. Summa, ⎬ xj s v d

Item, we charge vs with the casueltees Resseyued within þe yer of þis accompte.

ffirst, resseyued of Iohn clark, salter, for þe Beryes of iij childern, ⎬ vj s

Item, we Resseyued for the greate bell rong for hymself . iij s iiij d
Item, for his Beryall in the newe werke . . . . . vj s viij d
Item, we Resseyued of Iohn Milton, Baker, for þe greate bell . . . . iij s iiij d
Item, we Resseyued of Robert waldyng, for a man of caleyes buryed in the greate chirch yard . . . . iij s
Item, we Resseyued of henry vavesour, for a ffrenchman leyde in the new werke . . . . x s
Item, Resseyued of the saide harry for ij taperes brennyng at certen termentes . . . . viij d

---

[1] In margin 'cherch 1 yers.'   [2] leaf 53, back.

Churchwardens' Accounts, A.D. 1487–8.

Item, Resseyued of Iohn polyver, ffor the beryall of a ȝong childe . . . . ij s

Item, Resseyued of Iohn Ionson, for the buryall of Ioane his wif . . . . ij s

Item, Resseyued of the goodwif dewblyn, for þe buriall of her husbond . . . . vj s viij d

Item, for owr parte of the greate bell. Summa . . . . iij s iiij d

Item, Resseyued of peter Andrew, cobler, for þe burial of a childe . . . . ij s

Item, Resseyued of Margarete Bull for þe buriall of a straunge childe . . . . ij s

Item, Resseyued of Alexaunder Worsley for þe buriall of his sonn . . . . xx d
..|∴|..|∴.

[1] + Ihesus

Item, Resseyued of Iohn Townnesend, for a speynerd þat was buryed in the grete chirchyard,   iij s iiij d

Summa Resseyued of Casueltees lvj s.

Item, we charge with xlij s j d ob that we haue resseyued in Torches & werkmanschypp of the lyȝttes of Roger Medilton, wexchaundeler, the which he owed to the chirch in the tyme of w prene & I. halhed,   } Summa, xlij s j d ob

Summa totalis Resseyued, iiij^{xx}xv ij li vj s ix d ob.

[2] Ihesus.

Thies ben the paymentes belongyng to þe chirch.

In primis, vacacyon of Sir William Maltby, a chamber by o quarter. Summa . . . . ij s iij d

Item, that Sir Iohn lovyer paieth nothyng for his chamber. Summa . . . . viij s

Paide ffor the Obyte of Iohn Weston, kepte the xix daye of Aprell in the yer of owre lorde god mł ccccxxxxvj, to prestes, Clarkes, for brede & ale and offeryng. Summa   } iij s   iiij d

Paide for the obyte of maister Iohn Bradmer, kepte the xix day of nouember in þe sayde yer, to prestes, clarkes & oþer   } iij s

[1] leaf 54.   [2] leaf 54, back.

Paide to sir Iohn plommer, for the kepyng of the morowe mass ffor this hole yer from Mighelmas to myghelmas. Summa } xx s

Paide Alexaunder wursley, clarke, for a hole yeres wages at Mighelmas. Summa . . . . . . liij s iiij d

Paide to Iohn Russell, for a yeres wages at Mighelmas. Summa . . . . liij s iiij d

Paide to Michael harrys, warden of the chirch of Sȝ georges in puddyng lane, for o quyterent goyng oute of the tenementes of Iohn Weston ffor a hole ȝer ffynyschid at Mighelmas last past. Summa . . . . xx s

Paide to the Abbot of Waltham for o quyterent goyng owte of the the tenementes of Iohn Weston for a hole yer at Mighelmas past. Summa . . . . xxxviij s

Paide to the priowr of Christ chirch in london, for a quytrent goyng owte of the saide tenementes for a hole yer at Ester last past. Summa . . iij s

Summa, x li iiij s iij d.

[1] Paide to Westwode, smyth, for the makyng of v yryn bolles waying xvj lb, of your owne stuffe, and for tynnyng of the same boltes. Summa } xvj d

Item, to William Stede, ffor viij yardes and o quarter blew bokeram, price the yerde vij d. Summa paide . . . . iiij s viij d

Item, for xj yardes of blue lyes for the saide Corteynes, price . . . . iiij d

Item, for hemmyng and lyryng and settyng on of the Ryngges . . . . viij d

Item, for blue threde and iij dossen laten Rynges, price . . . . viij d ob

Summa, vij s viij d ob

Paide for holme and yve anenst Cristmas, i d.

Item, for naylles for þe schryvyng peawe, ob.

Item, for iij dossen and o halffe talughe candell for the queer & morowmas, price the dossen xv d. Summa, iiij s iiij d ob.

Item, for scowryng of the laten candelstykkys, standardes, branches, and bolles vppon the beame, anenst Ester. Summa, xxiij d.

Item, for a quarter coles ayenst ester, price v d.

Item, for box, palme, fflowres and obleyes occupied on palmesondayes, viij d.

[1] leaf 55.

Item, for wyne spente at the hyghe ffestes of the yer vppon the prestes and clarkes. Summa, iij s iiij d.
Item, to William paris for wachchyng of the sepulcre, for swepyng of the chirch and for meate and drynke, vij d.
Item, for makyng of a keueryng to the ffounte, iij d.
Item, for pynnes for the aulter, ob.
Item, to ij° childern, goyng on processyon on holye thursdaye, ij d.
Item, for ij dossen and o halffe Roose garlondes on seynte Barnabees daye, viij d ob.
Item, for iiij^e laten belles for the canapye on corpus christi daye, iij s iiij d.
Item, for a latyn bell to go with the sacrament, xiiij d.
Item, for byrchen bowes a-yenst mydsomer, iij d.
Item, to w. paris for his labour for a basket to bear in duste, iiij d.
Item, for iij mattes and ij hassockes in Seynte Thomas chapell, price viij d.
Item, for xxxij Corteyn Rynges and hookes to henge the clothe for the newe tabernacle, price xiij d.
Item, for mendyng of the yryn Rodd, xvj d.
Item, for lyne and whippcorde to serve the same clothe, ij d.
    Summa totalis, xx s xj d.
    Summa, xxviij s vij d ob.

[1]Paide to Iohn Russell for ix elles holond clothe to make a surpluse for[2] alisaunder and a Rochett for w. paris, price the ell, vij d. Summa, v s iij d.
Item, for the makyng of the same, ij s.
Item, for mendyng of an olde surplus that Iohn Russell wereth, iiij d.
Item, bowȝte ij° olde surplus, price x s.
Item, for mendyng of a aulbe belongyng to the highe aulter, j d.
Item, for mendyng of the iij^e white Coopes. And of a grene coope of bawdekyn, to Thomas tate, xvj d.
Item, for a dossen tuckyng gyrdilles, x d.
    Summa, xix s x d.

Paide to Thomas fferour, clarke of Seynte Andrews, for mendyng of an olde antyphoner, to peace it, to wryte it and to note yt and also to newe bynde yt, vj s viij d.
Item, to Richard Ryder for mendyng of diuers pynnys & claspis of diuers bookes, iiij d.

---

[1] leaf 55, back.   [2] MS. 'for for.'

Item, for makyng of vj smale tables and for the wrytyng of the names of the ffounnderes of your chauntryes, for perchmyn & for bordes, ix d.

Summa, vij s ix d.

Paide to Roger Midelton, wex chaundeler; first, for xxxv lb wex that was owyng in the last yer, price the lb vij d ob. Summa, xx s v d.

Item, paide for xxxviij lb wex occupied & spent within this yer, price the lb vij d ob. Summa, xxiij s ix d.

Item, we Resseyued of Stoor that was leffte in taperes endes and in Beamelyghte. Summa, iiij^{xx} xviij lb.

Summa of the new wex and olde occupied within this yer is vj^{xx} xvj lb, paide for the makyng of euery lb, ob. Summa, v s viij d.
Paide for the makyng of xxxj lb pascall, at j d lb. Summa, ij s vj d.

Item, for garnyschyng of iiij torches aȝenst corpus christi xvj d.

Item, paide for iiij torches waying lxx lb, at vj d lb. Summa, xxxv s.

Item, for that that we haue paide to hym in monye. Summa, ij s iiij d. [nota?]

Summa, iiij li xj s.

Summa, vj li viij s vij d.

¹ + Ihesus.

REPARACYONS.

Paide to a dawber for stoppyng of an hole in Sir Iohn lovyers chamber, for lath, naylles and werkmanschipp, iij d.

Item, to William paris for mendyng of William halles entre & for bordes & nayle, j d ob.

Item, to christouer kechyn for a werkman o daye in Richard Alenson guttur, viij d.

Item, for a caunte peace for the guttur, iiij d.

Item, ij° long quarteres and a shorte, iij d.

Item, to a tyler and his laborer for a daye & di, xvj d.

Item, to Roger Mott for castyng of j c di. leede for Alenson guttur, xxj d.

Item, to Iohn Russell for naylles, iiij d ob.

Item, for an henge and a hoke sett on the steyer dore where Geffreyes wyff dwellid, iiij d.

Item, for iij wycket keyes to þe entre dorr within the prestes Aleye, price iiij d ob.

¹ leaf 56.

Item, alowed to sir Iohn plommer for the mendyng of his kechen dorr, a wyket keye, price iiij d.
Item, for a keye for the wyket in the newe werke, iij d.
  Summa, vj s iij d ob.

Paide to maistres Breteyn for ij lodes tymber, price x s.
Item, for the sawyng of iij c xv ffoote ffor quarteres, iij s
Item, paid for j c di vj Roffe tyles, iiij s j d.
Item, paide for vj c di planch borde, price þe c ij s ij d and iiij d for the cariage. Summa, xiiij s iiij d.
Item, for iij c quarter borde at ij s iiij d c. Summa, vij s.
Item, for a lode hart lath, xij s.
  Summa totalis, l s iiij d.

Paide to Iohn ducklyng in parte payment of such money as he had leyde out of his purs in the tyme of harry mersch and he wer wardeyns togidder. Summa,   xl s

Item, delyuerd to Alexaunder worsley, clarke, for to Ride to speke with Sir William Palmer ffor the Antiphoner that he hath to wryte. Summa,   vj s   viij d

  Summa, xlvj s viij d.
 Summa totalis of the Chirch Costes xxiij li iiij s ix d.

The Costis of Nasynges Chauntrye.

ffirst, the vacacyon of the house that Iohn harryson occupied o quarter . . . . ij s   vj d
Item, vacacyon of the house that William dyckson dwellit in half o quarter . . . . v s
Paide to the abbot of waltham for quyterent goyng owte of the tenementes of nasynges ffor a hole yer at the ffeste of Seynt mychaell last past. Summa . . . . xxij s
Paide to Sir William Maltbye, prest, syngyng ffor nasynges the space of a hole yere frome the ffest of Seynte Michael vnto the saide ffeste. Summa,   vj li xiij s iiij d
Item, paide vnto hym for his salarye of vij^e wekes affter mighelmas, rebatyng hym for his housrent xxij d ; paide clerlye to hym . . . . xvj s ij d
  Summa, vij li ix s vj d.

[1] leaf 56, back.

Paide to William paris for mendyng of a wyndowe in
the chambre wher Iohn a Bristowe and Nycholas
thornley dwellid . . . .   ij d
  Summa totalis of Nasynges viij li xix s ij d.

The Costes of Iohn Causton Chauntrye.

ffirst, vacacyon of the house that Crapeles now
occupieth, the space of iij quarteres of o yere at
xx s by yer. Summa . . . .   xv s
Item, a garden at tourhill of ij s viij d by yer, voyde
a hole yer . . . .   ij s   viij d
  Summa, xvij s viij d.

[1] Paide to the priour of christchirch in london ffor o
quytrent goyng out of the gardens and tenementes
sett at tourhill beside þe Meneris for a hole yer at
the ffeste of Ester last past. Summa . . . .   v s
Paide to the Bretherhed of owr ladye salue [regina,]
withyn the chirch of Seynte Magnus, ffor o quyterent goyng owte of the house that Iohn ffische,
grocer, now occupieth, for a hole yer at Midsomer
last past. Summa . . . .   vj s
Paide ffor kepyng of the Obyte of Iohn Causton, the
ffirst and second daye of august, to prestes,
clarkes & childern, for brede, ale & offeryng.
Summa . . . .   iij s   ix d
Paid to Sir Iohn Belamye ffor his ffirst quarter at
Cristmas . . . .   xxxvj s viij d
Item, to Sir Iohn Belamye for the seconnd quarter at
Ester . . . .   xxxvj s viij d
And alowed to hym for his chambre in this quarter .   xx d
Item, to Sir Iohn Belamye for half o quarter bytwene
Ester & mydsomer . . . .   xviij s iiij d
Item, to Sir Iohn Belamye for o quarter, fro seynt
peteres day to Michelmas daye, in howsrent and
monye. Summa . . . .   xxxv s x d
  Summa to the preste, vj li ix s ij d.

Kello. Paide to harry kello for that that he leyde oute for brekyng
of the pavement before his dorr, iiij d.
Item, for a hoke to sett on his dorr, j d.
Item, to Christouer, carpenter, for a man werkyng in harry kelloes
schopp in mendyng and makyng new wyndowes the space of iiij
dayes, euery daye, viij d. Summa, ij s viij d.

[1] leaf 57.

Item, for a pewe peace for the stall, ij s.
Item, for iiij ledges di. for the wyndowes, viij d.
Item, for xj ffoote di. Elmyn borde, iij d.
Item, to Iohn Russell for iij c di. iiij peny nayle, xiiij d.
Item, j c v peny nayle, v d.
Item, to westwode, smyth, for ij dossen staples, haspes, henges and boltes, ij s viij d.

Summa, x s iij d.

[1] Paide to Thomas tate ffor mendyng of ij° Cheasibles with the prowres belongyng to Iohn causton chauntrye, iij s iiij d.
Item, for j ell di. holond cloth for ij° Amys, price xv d.
Item, for dying and kalendryng of the iij^e olde corteyns that henge befor in the queer, which serueth for lynyng of þe saide cheasibles, xx d.

Summa totalis, vj s iij d.

Paide for a lock and a keye, & for mendyng of ij lockes & ij keyes to the tenementes at tourhill. Item, for mendyng of ij olde lockes with the keyes for stor, and for settyng on of a locke with a newe staple on the chambre dorr within the ij° widewes, and for makyng of ij° new keyes, for the olde wer broken.

Summa for all, xx d.
Summa of I. causton Chauntrye, viij li xix s ix d.

The Costis of Gooslynn Chauntrye.

ffirst, vacacyons of the house vppon the steyer iij quarter of o yer, x s.
Item, vacacyon of the house that Alis loueden dwelt in a yer, xiij s iiij d.
Item, vacacyon of the house that mychael gloucetter occupied [o?] quarter, iiij s.

Summa, xxvij s iiij d.

Paide to th priores of Kilborn for quytrent of o yer, goyng oute of the tenementes of gosslyn in ffauster lane, at myglemas, } vj d
Paide the last day of nouember, and the fyrst day of december, for the Obyte of Mr Richard Gosslynn, to the prestes and clarkes for brede, ale & offeryng. Summa, iij s iiij d.
Paide to Sir Thomas Marklew from Midsomer to Mighelmas, o quarter, xxxiij s iiij d.
Paide for mendyng of a vestmente of worstede Motleye, xij d.

xxxvij s viij d.

[1] leaf 57, back.

[1] + Ihesus.

Reparacyons of Gosslynn Chauntrye.

ffirst, paide for makyng clene of ij° howses, one that Alis loffden dwelt in, the tother the house vppon the steyer, to ij° laborers for o daye, x d.

Item, for carying of lomber, lathis, bordes, endes and blockes-endes, a lode, iiij d.

Item, for a clyket keye to the Aleye dorr wher the preste dwelt, iij d.

Item, for cariage of iiij lodes Rubrysch, vij d.

Item, paide to Mouce for that that he paide for the Brekyng vp of the pament, iiij d.

Item, to William paris for amendyng of the ffloores in the house vppon the steyer, and for beryng vp of ij° sackes sonde, iij d.

Item, to Thomas wade, mason, for a empereH of ffreestone, quarter vj ffoote di., to a chympney within the house vppon the steyer, price xx d.

Item, to a mason and a laborer for di. o dey and mor, viij d.

Item, to Iames dawber and his laborer for o deye, xiij d.

Item, for a lode lombe, iiij d.

vj s iiij d.

Paide to Rowlond tyler for ij° men workyng on Exmo house frome the ffirst daye of october vnto vj dayes folowyng, euery day, xvj d. Summa . . viij s

Item, to ij° laborers for vj dayes in the same weke, euery day x d. Summa . . . . v s

Item, to a laborer for ij dayes mor in the same . . . x d

Item, to Rowlond for a man workyng in the seconde weke, v dayes. . . . . iij s iiij d

Item, for ij° tylers in the same weke for iiij dayes, euery day xvj d. Summa . . . . v s iiij d

Item, to iiij laborers on the monday in the same weke, xx d.

Item, on tusday ij° laborers, x d.

Item, on Wedynsdaye iij laborers, xv d; on thursday iij laborers, xv d.

Item, on ffrydaye iij laborers, xv d. Summa to þe laborers this weke . . . . vj s iiij d

Item, to Rowlond for ij men werkyng v dayes in the third weke. . . . . vj s viij d

Item, for a tyler werkyng iiij dayes in the same weke ij s viij d

[1] leaf 58.

Item, to iij laborers for v dayes, every day xv d.
Summa . . . . vj s   iij d
Item, to a laborer for ij dayes more in the same weke   x d
Item, to Rowlond for ij° werkman o daye & di., every
day xvj d. Summa . . . . ij s
Item, to ij° laborers for iiij dayes in servyng the tylers,
and makyng clene of the houssis, beryng owte &
castyng oute the Rubrysche . . . . ij s   vj d

   Summa totalis to the tylers, xxviij s.
   Summa totalis to the laborers, xxi s viij d.

   [1] Ihesus.
GOSSLYN.

Paide to Thomas Mondes, yrmonger, for x^e lath at v d ob c. Summa, iiij s vij d.

Item, for v bushelles tyle prynnes, price the busch, vj d. Summa, ij s vj d.

Item, to Iohn Russell for Sprig ix m^l quarter at vj d m^l. Summa, iiij s vij d ob.

Item, for Roffe naylles, ix m^l di. at x d m^l. Summa, vij s xj d.

Item, to harry kny3te of knyghttes hill for viij m^l Tyle at v s vj d m^l. Summa, xliiij s.

Item, to Stevynson, Burcher, for v lodes Saunde, price ij s j d.

Item, to clarkes wyffe for x lodes & iiij sackes lyme, viij s.

And Beside this Ther is spente of your stoor, in lathes, xxiij c.

   Summa, iij li xiij s viij d ob.

Paide to Christouer, carpenter, for a man werkyng iiij dayes di. in Exmo howse in Reysyng & makyng of gutturs & settyng vp of Raffters, every day viij d. Summa, iij s.

Item, for v quarteres for traunsones, x d.
Item, vj quarters di., xiij d.
Item, a pece to bear the Raffters, ij d.
Item, a caunte peace for a ffyllet guttur, vj d.
Item, a caunt peace for a ffillet guttur ouer Alis loueden house, x d.
Item, for xxv yardes lyre borde and eves borde for the gutturs & for furris, ij s j d.

   Summa, viij s vj d.

Item, to Christouer, carpenter, for a man werkyng v dayes di. in Exmo house, & in makyng of the long guttur & settyng vp of Raffters ffeate, and of new Raffters, every day viij d. Summa, iij s viij d.

   [1] leaf 58, back.

Item, for vij ffoote tymber in iij peces for Raffters, xiiij d.
Item, v long quarters, x d.
Item, ij long peces, viij d.
Item, iij quarteres, vj d.
Item, vj quarteres, xij d.
Item, for a caunte pece at the greate gutturs ende, x d.
Item, for v quarters, x d.
Item, for ij° plankes, v d.
Item, for ij eves bordes, ij d.
Item, for vj quarteres, xij d.
Item, for ij° quarters, v d.
Item, for iiij quarteres, viij d.

Summa, xij s ij d.

Item, to Christouer for a man werkyng iiij dayes in Mr lewes house and Maistres Browne, in takyng vp of a guttur ther and mendyng of diuers Raffteres, euery day viij d. Summa, ij s viij d.
Item, for j c di. lyre borde, price iij s iiij d.
Item, for portage & caryage of Raffters, quarteres & borde at diuers tymes, xij d.

Summa, vij s.

Item, to Christouer for a man werkyng iij dayes & di. in the house that olde Mouce hath taken, in translatyng of the steyer and in mendyng of wyndowes and other robbis within the saide house, euery daye viij d.

Summa, ij s iiij d.

Item, for plankes for standardis of the steyer, ix d.
Item, for xlviij ffoote Elmyn borde, xiij d.
Item, for xiij ffoote quarter borde, iiij d ob.
Item, ij long ledges for mendyng of the wyndowes, iiij d.

Summa, ij s vj d ob.

[1] + Ihesus.

Gosslyn.

Paide to Iohn Russell for vj c v peny nayle, price ij s vj d.
Item, for iiij c iiij penye nayle, xvj d.
Item, for ij c di. iij penye nayle, vij d ob.
Item, for viij c vj penye nayle at vj d c. Summa, iiij s.

Summa totalis, viij s v d ob.

[1] leaf 59.

Item, Allowed to Maistres Browne for Rep*ar*acions done by her in carpentrye in makyng of her celer dorr, in mendyng of her steyer and makyng of a Rynnyng dorr bytwene Exmoes well and her. Su*m*ma, xx d.

Paide to Iames dawber ffor werkyng in olde Mowc*es* house and in Mastres Brownes house in wallyng, ffloryng and beame ffillyng. S*um*ma, v dayes at viij d. Su*m*ma, iij s iiij d.

Item, to his laborer for v dayes werke, eu*ery* day v d. S*um*ma, ij s j d.

Item, to Iames dawber for v dayes werk in Exmoes house in beame-ffillyng after the tylers had been there, euery daye viij d. Su*m*ma, iij s iiij d.

Item, to his laborer for v dayes, euerye daye v d. Su*m*ma, ij s j d.

Item, to Stevynson, bucher, for vj lodes lombe, p*rice* ij s.

Item, to hym for cariage of xxij lodes Rubrische owte of ffauster lane, iij s viij d.

Su*m*ma, xvj s vj d.

Paide to Westwode, smyth, for dressyng and mendyng of iij^e olde looke*s* in mowce*s* house, vj d.

Item, a peyer barr hoke*s* with staples to them, waying iiij lb, vj d.

Item, for a peyer henges & hoke*s* to a wyndowe, iiij d.

Item, ij° peyer smale hooke*s* to hang on a wyndowe, ij d.

Item, a peyer garnette*s* with a lytell bolte in ʒong Mowc*es* howc*es*, vj d.

Item, for a newe keye, iij d.

Su*m*ma, ij s iij d.

Paide to Will*ia*m Mott, plommer, for the castyng of vij greate guttur qu*ar*ter*es*, xxviij c di. ix lb leede, paying of eu*er*y c castyng xiiij d. Su*m*ma, xxxiij s ij d.

Item, for the cariage of all the leede in and owte, xij d.

Su*m*ma to*ta*lis of Mr Gosslynn Chauntrye, xiiij li x s ix d ob.

[1] + Ihesus.

The Costis of Maist*er* W. Caumbrig*es* Chauntrye.

Paide to the abbot of Barmondsey for o quyterent goyng owte of the tenement*es* at the stock*es* for a hole yer at Mighelmas last past. Su*m*ma, vj s.

Paide for the Obite of Maist*er* Will*ia*m Caumbrige, kepte the xix day of August, to vj preste*s* and to Iohn Russell, ij s iiij d.

Item, to Saund, clarke, for the dirige & the bell*es*, xij d.

Item, to Milton for spicid Bunnes, xiiij d.

Item, in white Bunnys, xij d.

[1] leaf 59, back.

Item, for a kilderkyn Ale, ij s.
Item, for pearys, ij d.
Item, in wyne, ij d.
Item, to xiij poor men, xiij d.
Item, to Maister herry Colet, mayer, vj s viij d.
Item, to Mr hugh Clopton and to maister percyvale, schryves, vj s viij d.
Item, to the swerdberer, xx d. Summa, xxiij s xj d.
Paide to Sir Iohn philip for o yer wages, ffrome the ffest of Seynte Michaell the archangell vnto the saide ffeste. Summa, vj li xiij s iiij d.
Item, for mendyng of a cheasible of grene bawdekyn browdyrd with ragged staves of golde, vj d.
Item, to Richard Rider for ij claspes sett vppon the massbooke, xvj d.
Summa, vj li xv s ij d.

Paide to Roydon, tyler, for ij deyes werke in mendyng the gable ende, and to his laborer at Cryckes house at the stockes, euerye daye xiij d—ij s ij d.
Item, ij sackes lyme and ij buschelles Sannde, iiij d.
Item, to Rowlond, tyler, for a dayes labour & di. & his laborer, xix d ob.
Item, alowed to Richard Cricke ffor a byll of Reparacions that he had done in the lytell tenemente, the valu of xij s xj d ob. Summa paide, vj s viij d.
Summa, x s ix d ob.
Summa totalis of Mr W. Caumbriges Chauntrye, viij li xv s x d ob.

[1] + Ihesus.

The Costis of Iohn Bedham Chauntrye.

Paide ffor the Obyt of Iohn Bedaham & Beautrice his wif, kepte the xix day of Maye, to prestes, clarkes and to pore ffolkes. Summa, iiij s iij d.
Item, to the chirchwardens for the yer beyng, of Mr bedahams bequest, vj s viij d.
Paide to Sir Iohn Plommer for his salarye of a hole ȝer ffrome Mighelmas to Myghelmas. Summa, vj li xiij s iiij d.
Paide to William prene for iiij galons oyle, iiij s.
Item, to Iohn amassham for iiij galons oyle, iiij s.
Item, to halhed for iiij galons mete oyle, at xvj d o galon, v s iiij d.
Summa totalis in oyle, xij galons. Summa in monye, xiij s iiij d.

[1] leaf 60.

Churchwardens' Accounts, A.D. 1487-8.

Item, to iij^e poore men, that is to wyt, hugħ Iackson, William paris and to William Wylcockes, on euery sonday throwȝe þe yer, xij d. Summa by a hole yer, lij Sondeyes. Summa in money, lij s.

Item, alowed to Gabryeł de vrs of the Rente of the grete tenement of Bedaham, toward the reparacions that Gabryeł hatħ done, euery quarter xiij s iiij d. Summa by a hole yer, liij s iiij d.

Summa to Mr Bedahams Chauntrye, xiij ħ ij s xj d.

[1] + Ihesus.

The Costis of Roose Wrytel Chauntrye.

Paide to Sir Iohn lovyer, syngyng from Mighelmas to Midsomer, that is to wit iij quarter of o yer, euery quarter xxxiij s iiij d. Summa, v li.

Item, allowed to hym his chambre for a hole yer at Myghelmas, viij s.

Item, paide to Mr Robert halhed, syngyng for Roose wryteł the space of vij^e wekes while Sir Iohn lovyer was awaye. Summa, vj s viij d.

Summa of Roose Wrytelles, v ħ xiiij s viij d.

Item, we aske alowaunce of potacions monye geven to your tenauntes in Resseyuyng of the Rentes and charges aforesaide, also in drynkkyng siluer on your werkmen in makyng Reparacions. Summa, x s.

Item, for engrosyng and makyng vp of this accompte, vj s viij d.

Summa, xvj s viij d.

Summa totalis paide, iiij^{xx} iiij li iiij s vij d.

Rest to the chirch, xiij ħ ij s ij d ob. Whereof ther ys in detters handes as yt apperitħ hereafter.

[2] + Harry vavesour, for Richard Chelmysho . . . v s
+ Herry Mersshe, for this yer xxx s.   Resseyued in
   Rekennyng . . . . xxx s.
Nycholas Thornley, waterman . . . . . . iiij s
Iohn harrys, waterman . . . . xx d
h + Richard Alenson, tayllour . . . . . . v ħ plegges
William Miln, yrmonger . . . . iij ħ vj s viij d
                Resseyued xl s
Iohn Byrlyng, goldsmytħ . . . . . . xxvj s viij d
             Resseyued xxvj s viij d
William dye, pastyller . . . . vj s viij d
Richard wodemonger, wyf. . . . . ix d
Iohn harrys, gardyner . . . . xviij d

Summa, xij ħ ij s xj d.

And ther is in monye. Summa, xix s iij d ob.

---

[1] leaf 60, back.   [2] leaf 61.

Churchwardens' Accounts, A.D. 1487–8.

Rerages. +
- [1] Robert Barcroffte . . . . x d pardon
- herry Mersshe . . . . xxvj s viij d pardon[1]
- Richard Chelmysho . . . . vj s
- Iohn harrys, waterman . . . . . . iij s iiij d
- Richard Alenson . . . . . vj s viij d Ressseyued vj s [rest torn off]
- [1] Iohn ducklyng . . . . viij s iiij d[1]

Casueltees
- Mr Robert Ryvel   xiij s iiij d   Resseyued xiij s . . . . [2]
- Thomas hunte   iiij s   Resseyued iij s iiij d . . . . . .
- Thomas Seymour   vj s   Resseyued iiij s by I. deram .
- Iohn deraham   iiij s   Resseyued iiij s by I. derah .
- Richard Cloce   iiij s   Resseyued iiij s by I. deraham
- Mr I. Smerte   xvj s viij d   Resseyued xvj s vij d by. . . .

[3] A Remembraunce that this yer, in march anº 1487, the ffundacyon of the newe yle on the north side of Seynt mary hill chirch was begon, Iohn halhed and Robert Roucyby chirchwardens.

Also Maister William wilde, parson of þe said chirch, yeve an Antiphoner.

Also, Maistres Agnes Breten did do gilte & paynte the tabernacle of owr lady with in þe queer the which cost xxvij li.

Summa of the Remayne in monye, xix s iij d ob.

Resseyued of the detteres:
 ffirst, of W. Miln   iij li vj s viij d
 Resseyued of Richard Alenson v li
 Resseyued of Iohn Birlyng, goldsmyth, xxvj s viij d
    Summa, x li xij s vij d ob

Resseyued of Mr Iohn Smarte for a casuelte, xvj s viij d ⎫
Resseyued of Richard Alenson, taylour, for his promys vj s viij d. ⎬ toward reparacions
        ⎭

Summa totalis that Iohn halhed haue Resseyued of this Rekenyng } xj li xv s xj d ob

Paide to Thomas Colyns in Reparacions of the new werke, xxxiij s iiij d.

Item, to Th. Colynn for a mason for a hole weke, iiij s iij d

Item, to Thomas Colyn for iij lodes Reyegate stone, xvj s
    Summa paide, liij s vij d
   Rest cler to pey in mony, ix li ij s iiij d ob

[1–1] Scratched out. [2] Torn away. [3] leaf 61, back.

Churchwardens' Accounts, A.D. 1487–8.

Paide the xj day of Ianyver, the iiij⁰ yer of kyng herry vj⁰, by vs, Iohn halhed & Robert Roucibye, ix ħ ij s iiij d. In the prese[n]s of Maister William Remyngton, alderman, Robert Rivel, Iohn Smerte, William prene, Harry Mersch and harry vavesour.

[1]
 { harry mersch xxx s : pardon
 harry vavesour v s
h { Nicholas thornley iiij s xij d Resseyued
 Iohn harris, waterman xx d
R { William dye, pastiller vj s viij d
 Richard, wolmonger ix d
 Iohn harrys, gardiner xviij d } Summa, xlix s vij d

[W ?] { Richard Chelmysho vj s
[I ħ] { Iohn harrys iij s iiij d } Rerages

Maister Rivell . . xiij s iiij d
Thomas hunte . . iij s iiij d
Thomas Seymour . iiij s
Iohn deraham . . iiij s
Richard Cloce . . iiij s

All thies above writen be in the charge of Robert Rouciby & of Iohn deraham, chirchwarden [... *torn off.*]

[... Accounts for 1488-9 lost ...]

[1] leaf 62.

[A.D. 1489-90.]

¹Herry Kello } anno xiiij^c lxxxix^e
Thomas Hunt
²lij ti iiij s pardon.
xxxj s iiij d²

³ + Ihesus.

Thies be the names of the dettures leffte the last yer in the tyme of Iohn deraham & herry Kello :—

ffirst, Iohn harrys, watirman .	iijs iiijd	Resseyued iijs iiijd
A. Gardyner, next to Richard a kechen	iiijs iiijd, of old ,,	iiijs iiijd
Richard a kechen	iiijs	,, iiijs
The Breweres Sister	iiijs	,, ,,
Iohn harrys wif, gardyner . .	xviijd	
Thomas Mowce, hewrer . . .	viijs	,, viijs
Iohn Mowce, clarke	vjs viijd	,, vjs viijd
William dye, pastiller . . .	xiijs iiijd	,, xiijs iiijd
Sir Davy, prest	vjs ixd	
Barett, browderer	iijs iiijd	,, iijs iiijd
William Curtyh, patynmaker .	vjs viijd	,, o bras pott in the Revestre

Summa

Roger Midelton, wex chaundler, in wex, xlviij li.

Besides this ther is of olde dettes in the tyme of Robert Rouxby & I. deraham :—

Nycholas Welles	xvj d
Robert Grapeles	xij d
William Wilkynson	xv d
Richard a kechen	iiij d
Alexaunder Worsley	v s
Iohn herrys wif, gardyner	xviij d
William dye, pastiller	xiijs iiij d

All ther was owyng in þe tyme of I. halhed & R. Rouxby :—

Nycholas thornley	iijs
William dye, pastyller.	vjs viijd
Richard, wollmonger	ix d
Iohn Milton + Richard Chelmysho . . .	xxvjs

¹ leaf 63.   ^{2—2} In corner.   ³ leaf 63, back.

Churchwardens' Accounts, A.D. 1489-90.

[1]Ihesus.

This is the Accoumpte of vs, harry Kello and Thomas hunte, wardeynes of the Rentys & goodes belongyng to the chirch of Seynt mary at hyll; charged frome the ffeste of Seynte Mychaell tharchangell an° m᷾ ccccxxxix vnto þe saide ffest of Seynte Michaell an° xiiij c lxxxx^e. That is to wyt, ffor an hole yer.

ffirst, we charge vs with the dettes that we haue Resseyued leffte of the last yer in the tyme of Iohn deraham & herry Kello :—

That is to wit, of Iohn harrys, watirman	iij s	iiij d
Item, of the gardiner next vnto Richard a kechen . .	iiij s	iiij d
Item, of Richard a kechen	iiij s	
Item, of the Brewers Sister	iiij s	
Item, of Iohn Mowce, clark	vj s	viij d
Item, of Thomas Mowce, capper	viij s	
Item, of William dye, pastiller	xiij s	iiij d
Item, of Barett, Browderer	iij s	iiij d
Item, of William Cortyll, a Brass pott: it is in þe Revestre.		

Summa, xlvij s

Item, we charge vs with the Rentalles, as wele the Chirches as the Chauntryes' :—

cherche, 1 yere: ffirst, the chirch Rentes	xv li	xj s	vj d	
Nasynges Chauntrye	ix li		viij d	Summa,
Roose Wrytell	vj li	xiij s	iiij d	lxxxj li
Richard Gosslynn . . . Summa,	viij li	xvj s		xij s vj d
Iohn Causton . . . Summa,	xviij li	iiij s	iiij d	
Iohn Bedaham . . . Summa,	xiij li	vj s	viij d	
Maister William Caumbrige	x li			

Summa lxxxj li xij s vj d.

.... ⁞. :::

[2] + Ihesus.

Item, we charge vs with the clarkes wages Resseyued by iiij^e quarteres of the yer, that is to wyt :—

At the ffest of cristmas	xxx s	v d	⎫
At the ffest of owr lady	xxxiij s	vj d	⎬ Summa, vj li
At the ffest of Midsomer	xxxv s		⎬ xiij s ij d
At the ffest of Seynt Michaell	xxxiiij s	iij d	⎭

[1] leaf 64. [2] leaf 64, back.

MED. REC. L

Item, ffor the Beame lyghte, at the saide termes :—

At Cristmas	v s xj d	
At þe fest of Annunciacion	v s vij d	Summa,
At Midsommer	v s x d	xxij s x d
At Mighelmas	v s vj d	

Item, we charge vs with the monye that we resseyued for the pascall at Ester in the same yer. Summa, xij s vj d.

Item, we charge vs with certeyn Casueltees Resseyued within this saide yer and for certen lyghttes :—

ffirst, Resseyued of Mr horne for ij⁰ taperes at the terment of Sir I. colyns	vj d
Item, of a man that discessid at Billingisgate . . .	xij d
Item, of Thomas Colyns, for a childe lying in þe pardon chirchyard	ij s
Item, of Iohn halhed, for a childe lying ther . . .	ij s
Item, of herry Edmond, for his wiffe	ij s
Item, of Robart Staunsor, for his man.	ij s
Item, of William Overey, for his wif lying in the chirch	xiij s iiij d
Item, of Richard Cloce, ffor a childe	ij s
Item, of Iohn ducklyng, ffor a childe	ij s
Item, of harry vavesour, ffor a childe	
Item, for his wiff Sister lying in the chirch	
Item, of Thomas Andrew, for a childe	ij s
Item, of Mr Iohn smerte, for ij⁰ taperes	iiij d

Summa, xxix s ij d.

Summa totalis of the hole charge iiij xxxiij li xvij s ij d.
93 . 17 . 2

[1] + Ihesus.

Her ffoloweth the discharge.

Quytrentes of the chirch.

ffirst, paide to the parson of Seynt georges & to Robert ffitzherberde, warden of the saide chirch beside pudding lane, for o quytrent goyng out of the tenementes of Iohn Weston for an hole yer at myghelmas last past. Summa, xx s.

Paide to the abbot of Waltham ffor quyterente goyng oute of the tenementes of Iohn Weston for an hole yer past at Mighelmas. Summa, xxxviij s.

[1] leaf 65.

Paide to the priour of christchirch, in london, for quyterente goyng out of tenementes of Iohn Weston ffor an hole yer past at Ester. Summa, iij s.

Obites kepte at þe Chirch costes.

Paide for the kepyng of the obyte of Mr Iohn Bradmer, the xix day of nouember, to þe prestes & clarkes in brede & ale & ffor the offeryng. Summa, iij s iiij d.

Weston. Paide ffor the obyte of Iohn Weston, kepte the xix day of Aprell, to the prestes & clarkes. Summa, iij s ix d.

Paide to Sir Iohn Plommer for kepyng of the morowe masse for an hole yer. Summa, xx s.

[1]iiij li viij s j d.[1]

[2] + Ihesus.

The clarkes wages, with þe costes of ij° childern.

ffirst, paide to William Edmondes, clarke, ffor his yeres wages at Mighelmas last past. Summa . . .	liij s	iiij d
Item, to Alexaunder worsley ffor an hole yeres wages .	xxxiij s	iiij d
paide to Iohn Caumpnel, clarke, for o quarter, cristmas	vij s	
paide to Iohn Browne, clarke, for halff o quarter wages from Midsomer to owre lady day	v s	j d
Item, paide to ij° childern ffor theyr wages of o quarter from Midsomer to Mighelmas, to þem both	iij s	iiij d

The Costes of their ffyndyng.

ffirst, paide for a newe doblet of canvas for Robert, xvj d.
Item, for o peyer hosen, xix d.
Item, for iiij peyer schone, xvj d.
Item, for clowtyng of ij° peyer, iiij d.
Item, for ij° schertes, xv d.
Item, for o capp, x d.
Item, for o yard of black & o yard blanket, xviij d.
Item, for iij quarter of j ell canvas, ij d quarter for o doblet for Robert.
Item, for ij yardes quarter of blue, price vj s.
Item, for iiij yardes di. white ffreese, price ij s iij d.

Summa, xvj s vij d quarter.

[1—1] At foot of page.   [2] leaf 65, back.

Item, spent vppon bynge for ij peyer schone, viij d.
Item, for clowtyng of o peyer, ij d.
Item, for ij schertes, xiiij d.
Item, for o peyer hosen, xx d.
Item, for a capp, ix d.
Item, for o yard black & o yard blanket, xviij d.
Item, for iij quarter of j ell canvas, ij d quarter.
Item, for ij yardes di. quarter blue, v s viij d.
Item, for iiij yardes white ffreese, ij s.
$\qquad$ Summa, xiij s x d quarter.

Item, spent vppon bower at his scole, j d.
Item, paide for þe makyng of o Russet gowne for Robert . . . . viij d
and for ij new gownnes of blu for Robert & bynge, and for the makyng of ij⁰ newe doblettes . . . iij s iiij d
$\qquad$ Summa ⋮⋮⋮ ⁚ ⋮⋮⋮

[1] + Ihesus.

Exspences within the queer & þe chirch.

ffirst, paide ffor ij dossen viij lb candill, price ij s viij d.
Item, for holme & yve anenst Cristmas, j d.
Item, to William paris for swepyng of the chirch, ij d.
Item, for paper, ij d.
Item, to þe clarkes for goode ale, o lb.
Item, for wyne & ale on Candilmas day, iiij d ob.
Item, for palmes, vj d.
Item, for o quarter Cooles, v d.
Item, to the Raker ffor hauyng awaye of the Rubrisch of the chirch, vj d.
Item, for nayllis for þe Sepulcre, j d.
Item, for a poole to swepe the chirch Roffe, price iiij d.
Item, for wachchyng of the sepulcre, to paris, vj d.
Item, for scouryng of all the laten ayenst ester, ij s ij d ob.
Item, to the queer on ester daye, in brede & ale, j d ob.
Item, on Corpus Christi daye for Roose garlandes & for beryng of iiij torches, xij d.
Item, for ale & brede the same daye, ij d ob.

[1] leaf 66.

Item, on Seynt barnabeȝ daye, for Roos garlandes, ffor ale & brede, and to the Clarkes, ij s viij d.
Item, to William paris, ij d.
Item, for byrche at Midsomer, ij d.
Item, for waschyng of the clarkes sirplus, ij d.
Item, for ale & brede on owre lady daye, the assumpcion, iij d.
Item, to þe Ryngers, ij d.
Item, on alhalowen day ffor wyne, ale, & brede for the queer, v d ob.
Item, to ij° childern that went on procession on Seynt barnabeȝ daye & on corpus christi daye, iiij d.
Item, to Mr Iohn Redy ffor rehersyng of the bederoll, viij d.
Item, to sir Iohn tillisley for a key to his almery in the queer, iiij d.
Item, paide for ale & wyne spent on Cristmas daye, newyeres daye, xijth day, and on palmesondey, xj d.
Item, for mendyng of ij° Crewettes, ij d.
Item, for a keye to þe vestrye dorr, & a keye to the sowthe dore, & for a plate to þe same, & o keye for a tyll in þe queer, ij s vj d.

[1] + Ihesus.

The Wex chaundler.

Paide to Roger Medylton for the makyng of the beamelyghte befor the Roode, waying iij quarter xxj ll.
Item, for the makyng of the Rownde taperes, waying xliiij ll.
Item, iiij° torchis waying iij quarter iiij ll.
  Summa, in new wex ij c xiij ll : price of the makyng & all, xlvj s viij d.

Paide in olde wex that remayned in this handes of the last yeres, Summa, xlviij ll.
Item, delyuerd in olde wex this ȝer, Summa, iij quarter xxij ll.
Summa totalis in olde wex, c quarter xiiij ll.
  And ther Remeyneth in the wexchaundeleres handes, in wex, Summa, v ll.

Reparacionȝ of the Chirch Rentes.

Paide to a dawber and his laborer ffor o dayes werk in Richard Chelmyssho house. Summa, xiij d.
Item, for o lode lombe, iiij d.

[1] leaf 66, back.

Item, for mendyng of a locke at William halles, ij d.
Item, for ij c lathes spent in Richard ioynners house, viij d.
Item, for m¹ tyle occupied in diuers places, v s iij d.
paide to a carpenter,

    Summa, vij s vj d.

    ¹ + Ihesus.

Reparacions of certeyn vestymentes and of coopes belongyng to þe queer.

Paide for the makyng of o childes cope, of cloth of golde & the orpharis of blu velveut	xij d
Item, for the makyng of o childes cope, of blu Reye and the orphares of white cloth of golde . . .	xij d
Item, for mendyng of a canapye to bear ouer the sacrament on corpus Christi daye	vj d
Item, for mendyng of a chesible & a decon, of blu baudkyn of ffyne golde, price	xij d
Item, for mendyng of a cope of blew Raye, and the orpharas of grene bawdekyn	vj d
Item, ffor a pece of silke lace for the cheasible, & decon, of blu baudkyng, waying ounce & o quarter, price	xvij d ob
Item, for mendyng of a blew Raye coope, the orpharas purpull and reede sylke chekred	vj d
Item, for makyng of a cope of grene Raye, with an orpharas of chekerd werke, price	xij d
Item, for cere clothe for þe orpharas to þe same cope .	iiij d
Item, for makyng of a cope of grene Raye with an orpharas of blewe raye, price	xij d
Item, for iijᵉ peses of threde laces to þe same ijᵒ copes	xij d
Item, for mendyng of iiijᵉ baner clothes of steyned werke	vj d
Item, for makyng of o coope of blew velveut, the orpharas of rede velveut, price	xvj d
Item, for o pece silke lace, waying j ounce & quarter to the same	xvij d ob
Item, for mendyng of the sonnes in þe orpharas of the same coope and of the sonnys in the bodye . .	xvj d
Item, for Cere clothe to the orpharas, the hode & the moose of the saide coope	viij d

    ¹ leaf 67.

¹ + Ihesus.

Item, for makyng of a cope of blew velveut, poudred with sterres & mones, orphareys of rede velveut .	xvj d
Item, for mendyng of the sterres & mones of the orpharas and bodye of the same cope	xviij d
Item, for a pece silke lace weying o ounce quarter. .	xvij d
Item, for o pece threde lace, price	iiij d
Item, for Cere clothe to the orphareyes of þe same. .	viij d
Item, for blew bokeram to the same copes	iij s
Item, for mendyng of a coope of blu velveut poudred with mones & sterres, orpharised with nedle werke	x d
Item, for mendyng of ij° copes of black velvet orpharised with nedle werke	xvj d

Summa, xxv s.

Summa totalis of the charge of þe chirch, xvj li ij s j d ob.

² + Ihesus.

The Costis & paymentes of Nasinges chauntrye.

Paide to the abbot of Waltham ffor quyterent, goyng oute of the tenementes of nasynges for a hole yer at Mighelmas last past. Summa, xxij s.

Paide to Sir Iohn Tyllysley to syng ffor the saide Iohn Nasyng ffor a hole yer at Mighelmas, vj li xiij s iiij d.

Paide in Reparacions to a carpenter for o dayes werke in mendyng of o steyer at Robert Barcroftes, viij d.

Item, for c vj peny nayle	v d
Item, for c v peny nayle	iiij d
Item, for ij bolttes, iiij plates & ij° staples	v d
Item, for di. c v peny nayle	ij d
Paide to a dawber and his man for ij dayes labour in the clarkes house and other smale tenementes therbye, and for o lode lomb	ij s vj d
Paide ffor makyng of the pament befor Richard abelles dorr, conteynnyng iij^e teysse, price	xxj d
Item, for ij° lodes sannde, price	x d

Summa of Nasynges chauntrye, viij li ij s v d.

... .. :::

¹ leaf 67, back.   ² leaf 68.

[1] + Ihesus.
The Costis of Roose wrytelles chauntrye.

Paide to Sir William Boyes, preste, that syngith for
Roos Wryteɫɫ, for a hole yer at Mighelmas last
past. Summa . . . . vj ɫi xiij s iiij d

The Costes of Richard gosslynn chauntrye.

Paide to the abbes of kylbourne for o quyterent goyng
owte of the tenementes of Richard gosslynn in
ffauster lane, for o yer at Mighelmas last past . vj d

Paide ffor kepyng of the obyte of Mr Richard
gosslynn the ffirst day of december last past.
Summa . . . . iiij s viij d

Paide to Sir william Stokes ffor his salarye synggyng
ffor the saide Mr gosslynn for a hole yer at
Mighelmas last past. Summa . . . . . vj ɫi xiij s iiij d

Item, we aske allowaunce of iij s iiij d of Maistres
Brownes chambre that we er chargyd with more
than we Resseyued, for sche payeth but x s o
yer, and it is sett at xiij s iiij d o yer, so we
lese . . . . iij s iiij d

[2] + Ihesus.
Gosslyn chauntrye.

Paide in Reparacions in maistres Brownes house, to a
dawber & his man ffor o dayes labour . . . . xiij d
Item, for 1 c latħ . . . . [iiij d ?]
Item, for a lode lomb . . . . iiij d
Item, for iiij c latħ naylles, price . . . . iij d
paide to a dawber and his laborer ffor o dayes werke
in maister lewes house . . . . xiij d
Item, for c lathes, hart . . . . vj d
Paide ffor ij armes ffor the whele of the weɫɫ in ffauster
lane . . . . viij d
Item, for plankes to make the brynk of the weɫɫ . . viij d
Item, for a ponchon that the bareɫɫ rynneth in . . . iiij d
Item, for a quarter to steye it withaɫɫ . . . . . ij d
Item, for iij dayes werke & di. of Thomas hochyns . ij s iiij d
Summa [not given].

[1] leaf 68, back.   [2] leaf 69.

paide to Thomas Mondes, yrmonger, ffor nayltes . .		xvij d
paide to a dawber & his man another tyme werkyng in the house of Maistres browne o deye . . .		xiij d
Item, for naylles & lomb		vij d
paide to William Mott, plommer, ffor mendyng of a guttur in maistres brownes house and of another gutter in yong Mowces house, in sowder & all .	ij s	viij d

Summa of Gosslynn chauntry   vj li xv s iiij d

[1] + Ihesus.

The costes of Iohn Causton Chauntrye.

Vacacion of the house that Richard a kechen late occupied, by o quarter at Mighelmas last past .	ij s	
Vacacyon of the house next to Richard a kechen, o quarter	ij s	

Quytrentes.

Paide to the Bretherhede of owre ladye and Seynt Thomas within the chirch of Seynt Magnus, for o quitrent goyng owt of Iohn ffischis house ffor o hole yer at ester last	vj s	
Paide to the maistyrs of the Brigehouse for quytrent goyng out of Iohn ffischis house for a hole yer at Mighelmas last past. Summa	xiij s	iiij d
Paide to the priour of christchirch, in london, for quyterent goyng oute of the tenementes and gardyns beside the menerys at the tourhyll ffor o hole yere at Ester last past. Summa	v s	

[2] + Ihesus.

Causton chauntrye.

Paide for kepyng of the obyte of Iohn causton the ffirst day of august last past, to prestes, clarkes, to the Ryngers, and for brede & ale	iiij s	ij d
Paide to Sir Davy ffor his Salerye to syng for the saide Iohn Causton ffor a hole yere at Mighelmas last past. Summa	vj li xiij s	iiij d
Paide ffor mendyng of a vestyment belongyng to the saide chauntrye		xvj d
Item, for the halowyng of o vestyment		vj d

[1] leaf 69, back.   [2] leaf 70.

Reparacions.

Paide to a carpenter ffor o dayes labour in the Rentes of towrhiH, for mendyng of the garden gate and the garden dorre. Summa	viij d
Item, for naylles	vij d
Item, for mendyng of o locke and for ij newe keyes at towrhyH	x d
paide to Mr smarte for a newe garden dorre	vj d
Paide to a Carpenter werkyng ij⁰ dayes in harry Kello howse in mendyng of dorres & wyndowes . . .	xvj d
Item, for xxxiij ffoote quarter borde, price	xij d
Item, for o quarter and for iiij^e leggis	ix d
payde to William Mott, plommer, ffor	
paide to William paris ffor mendyng of diuers thynges at the gardens at towrhiH	vij d

Summa of caustons chauntrye, viij ti xiij s xj d

.: ::·· :::

[1] + Ihesus.

The costes of Iohn Bedahams chauntrye.

Paide ffor the kepyng of Iohn Bedahams obyte, kepte the xix day of maye last past, to prestes & clarkes in brede & ale and to poore people	vj s	viij d
Paide to Sir Iohn plommer ffor his salery to syng for the saide Iohn bedaham ffor a hole yer at the ffest of Seynt MichaeH tharkangeH last past vj ti	xiij s	iiij d
Paide to vs, the chirchwardens, of the bequest of the saide Iohn bedaham	vj s	viij d
Paide to iij^e pore men of this parisch, that is to wit— to William paris, Reyngnolde BuH and to Richard Sylke, euery sondey, opece, iiij d, þat is xij d. Summa	lij s	
Paide ffor oyle spente in the lampe within the yer of this Accoumpte. Summa, viij galonȝ di. at xij d o g'. Summa	viij s	vj d
paide to gabryeH de vrs towarde the reparacions of the saide grete tenemente in botolph lane, ffor an hole yer past, at Mighelmas. Summa	liij s	iiij d
paide for mendyng of o vestyment of grene bord Alexaunder and for the lace to þe same . . .	x d	

Summa, xiij ti xvj d.

:.. . :·· :..·::

[1] leaf 70, back.

The Costis of Maister Caumbrigez chauntrye.

Paide to the abbot of Bermondsay ffor quytrent goyng out of Maister Cambriges tenementes at the stockes by o hole yer at Mighelmas last past . .	vj s
Paide to Sir Iohn Philip ffor his salerye ffor a hole yer at Mighelmas last past. Summa . . vj li	xiij s iiij d
Paide ffor kepyng of the obyte of Mr William Caumbryge, kepte the xviij dey of August last past, to the prestes, clarkes, to pore ffolkes, in brede & ale. To the Mayer, Mr William White, and to Mr William Capell & to Iohn Broke, schreves, and to the swerdeberer. Summa .	xxviij s iiij d

Reparacions on þe gabyllende at Stockes.

Paide to Christouer, carpenter, for vj quarters of tymber	xij d
Item, for viij c xxxvj ffoote quarter borde spent on the gableende and on pentes & wyndowes, price . .	xxj s iiij d
Item, for ij° ledgis ffor diuers wyndowes	iij d
Item, for viij ffoote di. tymber for o trapp dorr . .	xvij d
Item, for di. c xv ffoote of planche borde of ooke ffor the same dorr, pris	xxj d
Item, to ij° carpenteres, ther werkyng viij dayes & di. at xvj d o daye. Summa	xj s iiij d
Paide to a Smyth ffor o peyer garnettes for the saide seller dorr at stockes, waying xv li di., price . .	ij s vj d
Paide to a dawber and his laborer ffor o dayes werke in Cryckes house and for ij lodes lomb	xxj d

Costes of Mr Caumbriges Chauntrye.

Paide for iiij c di. v penye nayle	
Item, for iiij c di. iiij penye nayle. Summa . . .	ij s viij d
Item, payde to Crycke for naylles spent ther . . .	x d
Item, to Thomas Mondes, yrmonger, for lath & naylles spent ther	xij d

Summa, v li xiij s vj d.

---

[1] leaf 71. [2] leaf 71, back.

Item, we aske allowaunce of potacion monye that we yeve to your tenauntes in Resseyuyng of your Rentes. Summa . . . . v s

Item, for engrosyng and makyng vp of this Accoumpte. Summa Summa . . . . vj s viij d

Summa totalis paide, lxxj li xiij s vij d ob

Rest clere to the chyrch, xxij li iij s vj d ob[1]

∴ ..

[2] + Ihesus.

Whereof ther is in detturs handes

chirch.

+ Syr Davy, prest, ffor his chaumber . . . . . iiij s vj d
William dye, pastiller, for this hole yer xiij s iiij d at Mighelmas.

Nasynges.

[3] William paris, ioynner, for o quarter . . . . . iij s viij d[3]
William Wilkynson, cooke, for di. o yer . v s Resseyued v s
Iohn harrys, watirman, for iij quarter . v s Resseyued iij s iiij d
Galies sonn for o quarter . . . . . . ij s
[3] Richard Abell for o quarter . . . . x s[3]

Causton.

Robert Graples o quarter . . . . . . v s Resseyued v s
The Gardyner next to ffader kechen oweth for di. o yer & iiij d of olde. Summa   iiij s iiij d
The Tayllour next to the garden gate oweth for di. o yer . . . .   iiij s
Iohn harrys wif, gardyner, oweth for o hole yer in owr tyme. Summa . .   iij s

Gosslyn.

Iohn Mowce, clarke, for iij quarter . . xx s
Thomas Mowce, capper, for di. o yer . . viij s
Maistres Browne, wydew, for o yer . . x s Resseyued x s
[3] Barett, browderer, for o quarter . . . xiij s iiij d[3]

[1] In corner of page '71. 13. 7.'
[2] leaf 72.   [3—3] This line scratched out.

Caumbrige.

Byrlynges wif, widew, for o quarter . .	xiij s	iiij d
Summa totalis in detteres of owr tyme . .	iiij li xvij s	vj d
rest clere	xvij li vj s	ob
Item, Resseyued of Iohn amylton . . .	xvj s	
Summa rest	xviij li ij s	ob
harry vavesour oweth for a leystow in the chirch for his sister	xiij s	iiij d
Item, for his childe	ij s	

[1] + Ihesus.

Thies be the detturs that ben owyng of olde:—

Iohn Harris wif, gardyner		xviij d
Sir Davy, prest	vj s	ix d
William turtyll, patynmaker, vj s viij d. Resseyued, a bras pott per li kello.		
Nycholas Welles		xvj d
Robert Graples		xij d
William Wilkenson		xv d
paid. Richard a Kechen		iiij d
William dye, pastiller		xx s
Nycholas Thornley		iij s
Richard Wollmonger		ix d
+ Iohn Milton & Richard Chelmersho xxvj s. Resseyued xvj s : before Resseyued vij s.		

Summa.

Roger Midelton, wexchaundler, oweth in wex [2]iiij ll[2] v li.
[3]Rest in detters handes in the tyme of Iohn halhed & R. Rouxbye, xiiij s vij d. Resseyued, vij s vj d.
Rest Rouxby & Iohn deraham, 1 s j d.

[4] + Ihesus.

Memorandum: that the xx day of Ianuarii, Anno m¹ cccc lxxxx, at the assemble of certeyn of the parisch of seynte Marye at hyll, was agreed, beffore Mr Wylliam wilde, person, & Mr

---

[1] leaf 72, back.   [2–2] Scratched out.   [3] leaf 73.
[4] leaf 73, back.

Remyngton, Alderman, that the saide Mr Remyngton haue grauntid to make a hole arch ⎫
Iohn Smarte, to make a hole arch ⎪
William preue, to make a hole arch or di. one ⎬ All thies persons haue grauntid this.
harry kello, to make [a hole arch?] ⎪
Iohn ducklyng & Sir Iohn plommer, a hole arch ⎭

Iohn halhed haue grauntid xl s, vppon Condycion that all the parysch wyl be contrybutarye to the same, after theyre power, þat maye bere.

Iohn a mylton this yer . . . . xl s
Iohn Mascall this yer . . . . xl s
Robert odiham this yer . . . . xx s
Iohn deraham this yer . . . . xl s

Thomas hunte will geve as Mr Alderman will set hym.

Robert Rouxbye this yer vj s viij d & iij s iiij d o quarter.

Mr William wylde, at his pleasure.

[A.D. 1490-1.]

¹Thomas Hunt ⎫
Iohn Mylton ⎭ Anº 1491.

The names of dettoures leffte vnpaide by herry kello & Thomas hunt, as it apperyth in þe ffoote of theyr Accompt.

²Sir Davy, prest, vj s ix d of olde.²
Wylliam dye, pastiller . . . . xiij s iiij d
Item, of olde . . . . xx s
+ Wylliam wilkenson, cooke, v s. Resseyued v s.
Item, of olde . . . . xv d
Iohn harrys, waterman, v s. Resseyued iij s iiij d, rest xx d.
Galies sonn . . . . ij s
+ Robert Grapeles, v s. Resseyued v s.
The Gardiner next to Richard a kechen . . . . . iiij s iiij d
The tayllour next the garden gate . . . . iiij s
Iohn harris wif, gardyner . . . . iij s
Item, of olde, xviij d.
Iohn Mowce, clarke . . . . xx s
Thomas Mowce, capper . . . . viij s
Maistres Browne, x s. Resseyued x s.
Birlynges wif, xiij s iiij d. Resseyued vj s viij d, rest vj s viij d.
harry vavesour . . . . xv s iiij d
³Iohn Milton & Richard chelmersho, x s.⁴ Resseyued vij s, rest iij s.⁵ Resseyued iij s.⁶
Nycholas welles . . . . xvj d
Robert graples . . . . xij d
Nycholas thornley . . . . iij s
Richard wollmonger . . . . ix d
A Remembraunce of o Brass pott Resseyued of William turtyll, patynmaker, for vj s viij d.

⁷+ Ihesus.

This is the Accoumptes of vs, Thomas hunte and Iohn Milton, wardens of the Rentes and goodes belongyng to the chirche of Seynte maryhill in london, ffor a

---
¹ leaf 74. ²⁻² Scratched out.
³,⁴,⁵,⁶ This is an interesting line, written evidently on three different occasions:—3-4, 4-5, 5-6 as each sum was owing and paid. ⁷ leaf 75.

hole yere, ffrom the ffeste of Seynte Mychaell tharchangell an° domini[1] 1490, vnto þe saide ffeste of Seynte mychaell in the yer of owr lorde 1491.

ffirst, we charge vs with the olde dettes that we haue Resseyued within the yer of this Accoumpte, that is to wyt:—

Of William Wilkynson	v s
Of Iohn harris	iij s iiij d
Of Robert Graples	v s
Of Maistres Browne	x s
Of Iohn Milton & Richard chelmersho	vij s, Item iij s
Of Byrlynges wif	vj s viij d

Summa, xxxvij s.   Summa, xl s.

[2] + Ihesus.

Item, we charge vs with the Rentes belongyng as wele to the chirche as to the chauntryes.

cherche, j yers. The Chirch Rentes, Summa	xv li xj s vj d
Nasynges chauntrye, Summa	ix li viij d
Roose Wrytell, Summa	vj li xiij s iiij d
Richard Gosslynn, Summa	viij li xvj s
Iohn Causton, Summa	xviij li iiij s iiij d
Iohn Bedaham, Summa	xiij li vj s viij d
Mr William Caumbrige	x li

Summa totalis, iiij$\overset{xx}{j}$ li xij s vj d.

Item, we charge vs with the clarkes wages Resseyued by iij quarteres of the yer, þat is to wit:—

At Cristmas	Summa, xxxiij s iiij d
At Anunciacion of owr ladye	Summa, xxxj s vij d
At Midsomer	Summa, xxx s iiij d
At Mighelmas	Summa, xxix s xj d

Summa, vj li v s ij d.

Item, ffor the Beamelighte at the saide termes:—

At Cristmas	Summa, iiij s iij d
At thanunciacion of owr ladye	Summa, iiij s vij d
At Midsomer	Summa, iiij s j d
At Mighelmas	Summa, iiij s

Summa, xvj s xj d.

---

[1] '1489' scratched out.   [2] leaf 75, back.

Churchwardens' Accounts, A.D. 1490-1.

[1] Item, we charge vs with the monye that we Resseyued at ester ffor the pascall in the saide yer. Summa, xiij s viij d ob

Item, we charge vs with certen Casueltees Resseyued within the saide yer for knylles, pyttes and bequestes, & for certen lyʒttes:—

ffirst, of Mr horne for ij° tapers at þe terment of sir Iohn colyn	vj d
Item, for the burying of o portyngaler	iij s
Item, for the pytt & knyll of Sir Iohn philip . . .	v s iiij d
Item, for the knyll of Iames walker, barbour at þe bull	iij s iiij d
Item, of maister Smarte for ij° tapers at þe terment of his wives	iiij d
Item, Resseyued for o lode Rag xvj d, & for iij quarter tyle xiiij d. Summa	ij s vj d
Item, Resseyued of Thomas colyns for berying of o child in the pardon chirchyard. Summa . . .	ij s
Item, Resseyued of Iohn halhed for þe burying of o child	ij s
Item, for the Burying of Mr Rivell in the Revestre .	[Amounts
Item, of the bequest of Mr Revell in his testament, toward the newe werke and þe makyng of þe steple.	not given.]

Summa, xix s.

Summa totalis of this Resseyued of this Accoumpte, lxxxxij li vij s iij d ob.

[2] + Ihesus.

Here ffoloweth the paymentes as wele of that that belongith to the chirch as to þe chauntres . . } Chirch costes.

ffirst, paide to þe parson of Seynt georges & to Robert ffitʒherberd, warden of the saide chirch, for o quyterent goyng [oute] of the tenementes of Iohn weston for o hole yer at Mighelmas last passide. Summa, xx s.

Paide to the abbot of Waltham, for quytrent goyng oute of the tenementes of Iohn weston for o hole yer past at Ester. Summa, xxxviij s.

Paide to the priour of Christchurch, in london, for quytrent goyng oute of the tenementes of Iohn weston for a hole yer at Ester last past. Summa, iij s.

Obittes kepte at the costes of þe chirch.

Paide for the kepyng of the obit of Iohn weston the xix day of Aprell, to the prestes & clarkes. Summa, iij s iij d.

[1] leaf 76.   [2] leaf 77.

Item, for the obyt of Mr Iohn Bradmer, kepte the xix daye of nouember, to the prestes & clarkes. Summa, iij s.

Paide to Sir Iohn plommer ffor the kepyng of the Morowmas for o hole yer at Mighelmas last past, xx s.

Paide to Mr Iohn Redye ffor the Rehersyng of the names [of the] ffounderes of the chauntryes in þe bederoll ffor o hole yer at Mighelmas, xvj d.

Summa, iiij li viij s vij d.

.... v... ┆ ::

[1] + Ihesus.

The Costis of ij° clarkes and of ij° Childern in this yere.

Paide to William Edmondes, clark, ffor o hole yere at the ffest of Seynt Mychaell last passid & endid. Summa . . . . liij s   iiij d

Paide to Alexander wursley ffor o hole yeres wages, ffynyschid at the ffest of Seynt Michaell last past. Summa . . . . xxxiij s   iiij d

The ij° childern.

Paide to Thomas Bynghe, ffor iij quarter of o yer, that is to wit, ffor Cristmas, Ester & mydsomer. Summa . . . . v s

Item, for iij[e] payer schoes ffor the tyme . . . .   xij d

Item, for the makyng of o gowne . . . .   viij d

Paide to Robert ffor the tyme of his Abydyng here almost iij quarter. Summa . . . . . . iiij s vj d

Item, for iij payer schoes ffor hym . . . .   xv d

Item, for the makyng of o payer hosen . . . . .   iiij d

Item, for his borde, to William hall for xiiij wekes .   vij s

Summa, v li vj s v d.

The Costes in the Queer.

Paide ffor iij dossen talough candell, iij s.

Item, for a lampe, j d.

Item, for holme & yve, ij d.

Item, for palmes, obleyes & flowres for palmesondey, vij d.

Item, for o quarter Coles anenst ester, v d ob.

Item, to paris for bromes & for makyng clene of the gutture*s*, ij d.

Item, for settyng vp of the sepulcre & for nayllis, ij d ob.

Item, for his labour on good ffridey & Ester even, vij d.

[1] leaf 77, back.

Item, for Birch at Midsomer, iiij d.

Item, ffor Roose garlondes, and off wodroffe ffor Corpus Christi day, & to iiij torchberers, & ffor Seynt barnabe daye, ix d ob.

Item, ffor the Scowryng of your laten desk standardes candilstickes, laten bolles and þe Crownes of þe Canape anenst owre lady day, Ester & Cristmas, iiij s.

Summa, x s iiij d ob.

[1] + Ihesus.

Payde for the lynyng and makynge of the newe Canape of velvet that Maistres plommer yave, anenst Ester last passid, ij s ij d.

Item, for the ffrengez therto, xv d.

Item, to hewz clarke ffor the mendyng of the white Copes and of the vestimentes, and for mendyng of the best blu copes ix d.

Item, for o Rope ffor the Sanctus bell vj d, & for the halywater stycke.

Summa, iiij s viij d.

Paide to the prestes and clarkes in drynk at pryncipall ffestes, that is to wyt:—

on christmas day, in brede, ale & wyne, iiij d.

Item, on xij[e] dey, iij d ob.

Item, on palmesondey, vj d.

Item, on holye thursdey, iij d ob.

Item, Corpus Christi dey, v d.

Item, on Seynt barnabez even, iiij d.

Item, on Seynt barnabez daye, in wyne & ale and yoven amonges syngeres, iij s iiij d.

Item, on owr lady day assumpcion, iiij d ob.

Summa, v s x d ob.

Paide ffor mendyng of ij keyes to the sowth dorr of the chirch, ij d.

Item, for bryngyng home of o brass pott, j d.

Item, for makyng of a caussey in the grete chirchyard, & for iij lodes gravell therto occupied, xviij d.

Item, for mendyng of o hole in the wall in [sout?]hend in the chirchyard, of breke, v d.

Summa Summa, iiij s ij d.

Item, that I paide for the makyng of a Rentall and of such detts as Remayned þe last yer. Summa, ij s.

Summa, vj li xj s vj d.

::: ::: :::

[1] leaf 78.

[1] + Ihesus.

Exspences ffor the proffit of the chirch.

Payde ffor botehir, goyng to my lorde of Sarum being in ffletestrete for Sir William Palmer, and in wyne spente on Maister page and other of the parisch, xiij d.

Item, to weston, mercer, for v quayers of the new booke that Sir William palmer wrote. Summa, x s.

Item, spent at the tavern in wyne, iij d.

Paide when Mr alderman with other companye of the parysch went to Mr Richard page, in exspences as Botehir, Meate & drynke & other thinges, xxvj s viij d.

Paide to William Iames, Sompnour, for sompnyng of iij tenauntes that owed monye to the chyrch, x d.

Summa, xxxviij s x d.

Expences in wex & to þe wexchaundler.

Paide to Roger Midilton, wexchaundler, ffor the makyng of the beamelyghte, pascall and of other lyghttes spent in the chyrch within this yer. Summa, x s.

paide to Mr smerte for di. c poleyn wex, xxix s.

Summa, xxxix s.

The Saide Roger oweth to the chirch ij ℔ wex.

[2] + Ihesus.

Reparacions on the Chirch rentes.

Paide to Christouer kechen, carpenter, ffor workmanschip in William hallis howse ffor borde and tymber as it apperith mor pleynlye by a byll. Summa, xxiij s.

Item, to a laborer beyng ther ij° deyes, x d.

Item, to caryng awaye of the Rubrush, xiij d.

Summa, xxiiij s xj d.

Paide to a Carpenter for workyng di. o daye and to a laborer in Sir Iohn philip chaumber, vj d ob.

Item, for xxix ffoote of Borde, viij d.

Item, for di. c naylles, ij d ob.

Summa, xvij d.

---

[1] leaf 78, back. [2] leaf 79.

Paide for reparacions on sir Davy chamber ffor di. m* breke, ij s vj d.
Item, for a lode sonde, vj d.
Item, for ij⁰ lodes lyme, ij s.
Item, a lode lomb, iiij d.
Item, to a tyler and o dawber & a laborer ffor ij dayes werke, iij s.
    Summa, viij s iiij d.
    Summa, v li xij s vj d.[1]

[2] + Ihesus.

The Costis & paymentes of Nasynges chauntry.

Paide to the abbot of Waltham ffor quytrent of a hole yere, goyng out of the tenementes of Iohn nasynges at the ffest of Seynt Mighell last past. Summa, xxij s.

Paide to Sir Iohn Tillisley, prest, to syng for the saide Iohn nasynge ffor a hole yer at Mighelmas. [Summa], vj li xiij s iiij d.

Reparacions.

Paide to a carpenter for workmanschipp halff o dey in bynkes house, iiij d.
Item, for xxiij ffoote of Elmyn borde, vj d.
Item, for di. c v peny nayle, ij d ob.
    Summa, xij d ob.
    Summa totalis, vij li xvj s iiij d.

The Costes and paymentes of Roose Wrytelles chauntre.

Paide to Sir William Boyes, prest, to syng ffor the saide Roose Writell ffor o hole yer at Mighelmas last passid. Summa, vj li xiij s iiij d.

A remembraunce that the charge of her chauntry is but iiij li, and therffor her chauntry and Iohn weston chauntry wolde be kynyte togeder.

[3] + Ihesus.

The charges & costes of Richard gosslyn chauntry.

Paide to the abbes of kylborne ffor o quytrent goyng out of the tenementes of gosslyn in fauster lane ffor a hole yer at Mighelmas last passid. Summa, vj d.

---

[1] 6. 17. 7 in corner.   [2] leaf 79, back.   [3] leaf 80.

Paide ffor kepyng of the obyt of Mr Richard gosslyn the ffyrst day of december last passid. Summa, iij s ij d.

Paide to Sir william Stokes, prest, that syngith for the saide Richard gosslyn for a hole yer at Mighelmas. Summa, vj li xiij s iiij d.

The Reparacionȝ of gosslynn chauntry.

Paide ffor naylles c iiij peny nł iiij d for to amend withall a steyer in Mr lewes house, ffesiscian.

Item, to a mason werkyng in Mr lewes howse, ffesissian—

Item, for lyme, sande & breke. Summa, xvj d.

Item, for makyng clene of house that Mastres Browne dwellith in, xij d.

Item, for the amendyng of a Seage and a brekewall in maister lewes, ffesiscian, house, vij d.

Paide to William Mott, plommer, ffor werkmanschip of certen Sesterns & pipes of leede that was done in ffauster lane the last yer. Summa, vj s, per a byll.

Summa.

Item, we aske allowaunce of Maistreȝ Browneȝ house iij s iiij d, ffor that house was wonte to be lett for xiij s iiij d and nowe it is lett for x s, and we ar chargid aftter the hole rent, which is xiij s iiij d.

Summa, vij li ix s vij d.[1]

Summa, xxj li xix s iij d ob

[2] + Ihesus.

The charge & costes of causton chauntre.

Paide to the Bretherhed of owr lady & Seynt Thomas, ffoundid within the chirch of Seynt Magnus, in london, ffor o quytrent goyng out of Iohn ffishes house, grocer, for a hole yer at Ester last passid. Summa, vj s.

Paide to the Maistirs of the Brigehous, ffor o quyterent goyng out of Iohn ffishis house for a hole yer at Mighelmas last passid. Summa, xiij s iiij d.

Paide to the priour of christchurch, in london, ffor quyterent goyng oute of the tenementes and gardens beside the Meneris at tourhill for a hole yer at Ester last passid. Summa, iij s iiij d.

Paide for the Obyt of Iohn causton, kepte the ffirst day of August last passid. Summa, iij s iiij d.

[1] '12 7' in margin.   [2] leaf 80, back.

Paide to Sir Davye, prest, to syng for the saide Iohn causton an hole yer at Mighelmas last passid, with iij s ix d housrent and aH. Summa, vj ti xvij s j d

Reparacionȝ.

Paide to Robert downyng of Maidstone for iij quarter pale borde, ij s x d.

Item, to Iohn pers for c quarter pale bordes, iij s ix d.

Item, for carying to the boote, vij d.

Item, for the ffreyȝte of þe same pale, xx d.

Item, for cariage to the tourhiH, iiij d.

Item, for wharffage of the same, ob.

Item, for cariage of postes & Reyllis to þe garden, iiij d.

Item, to carpenteres & laborers for vij dayes, iiij s.

Item, to William paris for o day & di. in palyng at the goodman prenes garden, vj d.

Item, for nayllis, ij d.

Item, for makyng clene of the Aleyes, ij d.

Item, to Byrd, carpenter, for stolpes & Reylles, viij s iij d.

Summa, xxij s vij d ob.

Summa, ix ti vij s iiij d ob.

[1] + Ihesus.

The Costes & paymentes of Bedaham chauntrye.

Paide for the obyt of Iohn Behaham, kepte the xix day of Maye last past, as wele to prestes, clarkes, pore peple, as to the chirchwardens. Summa, xiij s iiij d.

Paide to Sir Iohn plommer, prest, to syng for the saide Iohn Bedaham for a hole yer at Mighelmas last passid. Summa, vj ti xij s iiij d.

Paide to iij pore men of this parisch, that is to wit, William paris, Reignold BuH and to Iohn toplady, euery sondey in this yer, xij d. Summa, lij s.

Paide ffor oyle spente in the lampe within the Queer in the tyme of this accoumpte x galonȝ, price the galon xij d [2]and ij d mor in AH.[2] Summa, x s ij d.

Paide to GabrieH de vrs toward the Reparacions of the grete tenemente in Botolph lane for an hole yer at Mighelmas last passid. Summa, liij s iiij d.

Summa, xiij ti ij s ij d.
Summa, xxij ti ix s vj d ob.
• •• ∴ ∷ o

[1] leaf 81.   [2–2] Added later.

[1] + Ihesus.

The Charge and costes of Mr Caumbriges Chauntry.

Paide to the abbot of Barmondsey ffor a quyterent goyng out of Mr Caumbriges tenementes at the stockes, ffor o hole yer at Mighelmas last passid. Summa, vj s.

Paide ffor his obyt, kepte the xviij day of August last passid, to prestes, clarkes, pore ffolkes in brede & ale. To the Mayer Mr I. Mathew and to Mr Coote & Mr pemberton, schryves, and to the Swerdberer. Summa, xxviij s.

Paide to Sir Iohn Stede ffor his wages to syng for Maister Caumbrige o hole [yere] at Mighelmas, vj li xiij s iiij d.

Reparacionȝ.

Paide to paris ffor settyng of stulpis and ledgis & nayllis at Reynyssforth house, v d.

Item, for v c nayllis to halles house, ij s j d.

Item, for a lock & o keye to Cryckes hall dorre, v d.

Item, to Mott, plommer, ffor a cestern of leede and for mendyng of a grete pipe of lede, for sowder & werkmanschypp of the same, xiij s iiij d.

Item, repeyred a chympney in byrlynges house, to a mason & his laborer, o day & di. xv d.

Item, ij° sackes lyme, iiij d.

Summa totalis, xvij s x d.
Summa, ix li v s ij d.

[2] Item, we aske allowaunce of potacion money that we yeve vnto the tenauntes in Resseyuyng of your Rentes, v s.

Item, for engrosyng and makyng vp of this. Accoumpte. Summa, vj s viij d.

Summa totalis paide, lxx li xviij s iij d.
Rest due to the chirch. Summa, xxij li ix s ob.

Whereof ther is owyng this yer in detteres handes :—

Wylliam dye, pastiller	xxvj s viij d
Iohn westus	viij s pleges
Wylliam paris	iij s viij d
+ Thomas Bynkes	xx d
Iohn Neele	iiij s
Richard Abell	xl s
Robert graples	xv s
Iohn huntsfeld	vj s

[1] leaf 81, back. [2] leaf 82.

Thomas Rechford	iiij s	
Courtman	xiij s	iiij d
Villiam harrison wif	iij s	
Iohn Smyth, haberdascher	xx s	
Iohn Mowce, clark	xxvj s	viij d
Thomas Mowce	viij s	
Richard Chelmersho	v s	
The Wardens of Seynt botolphus	ij s	vj d
Robert odiham	iij s	iiij d

Summa in detters, ix li x s x d
Rest in monye, xij li xv s ij d ob.
Item, iij s.
Summa totalis, xij li xviij s ij d ob
for Milton.

[1] + Ihesus.

Thies be olde dettes.

Villiam dye, pastiller	xxxiij s	iiij d
Villiam wilkenson		xv d
Iohn harris, waterman		xx d
Watkyn Galies Sonn	ij s	
The gardiner at tourhill	iiij s	iiij d
The Tayllour next þe gate	iiij s	
Iohn harris wif	iiij s	vj d
Iohn Mowce, clark	xx s	
Thomas Mowce	viij s	
Birlynges wif	vj s	viij d
harry vavesour	xv s	iiij d casueltes
+ Iohn Milton & Richard Chelmersho	iij s	
Nycholas welles		xvj d
Robert graples		xij d
Nycholas thornley	iij s	
Richard wollmonger		ix d

Summa, v li x s ij d.

Mr Iohn Smert promysed that the cloth of golde of Maister marowes schall come to the chirch, afor Mr parson with certen of the parisch the day of makyng of this accompte.

[2] iiij^{xx} xv li xix s viij d

[1] leaf 82, back.   [2] leaf 83, back, at foot.

[A.D. 1491-2.]

¹Iohn Melton } A° xiiijᶜlxxxxij
Rychard Cloos

² ✠

Thys ys the Accoumpte of vs, Ioħn mylton & Rychard close, wardens of the goud*es* & Rent*es* belongyng vnto the cherche of saynt mary at hyħ in london, for an hole yere from myhalmas A° 1491 to myhalmas A° 1492.

ffyrst, we charge vs wyth the ould dett*es* that we haue R*esseyued with*in the yere of oure Accoumpte :—

Item, of wyll*iam* dye, bowchere	iij ħ	
Item, of Ioħn harres, waterman		xx d
Item, of wyll*iam* pares	iij s	viij d
Item, of thomas bynk*es*		xx d
Item, of Ioħn neħ	ij s	
Item, of wyll*iam* Courtman	xiij s	iiij d
Item, of Rychard Abeħ, Grocere	xl s	
Item, of wyll*iam* harysons wyff	ij s	
Item, of Ioħn smyth	v s	
Item, of the wardens of sent botolphus	ij s	vj d
Item, of Rob*er*t odyam, mercere	iij s	iiij d
Item, of thomas mowce, clark	xx s	
Ioħn westhowse, waterman	viij s	
Item, of Rob*er*t Graples	iij s	

Su*m*ma, viij ħ vj s ij d.

³ ✠

Item, we charge vs as wele w*ith* the cherche Rent*es* as w*ith* the Rent*es* belongyng vnto the chauntryes for an hole yere :—

⁴The cherche Rent*es*	xv ħ	vij s	vj d
Nasyng*es* chauntrye	viiij° ħ		viij d
Rose wrettels chauntrye	vj ħ	xiij s	iiij d
Rychard Goustlyns	viij ħ	xij s	viij d

---
¹ leaf 84.
² leaf 85. A very beautiful handwriting now commences.
³ leaf 85, back.
⁴ '1 yers for yᵉ cherche' in margin.

Churchwardens' Accounts, A.D. 1491–2.

Iohn Causton . . . . xviij li iiij s iiij d
Iohn Bedham . . . . xiij li vj s viij d
Maister Wylliam Cambrege . . . . x li
    Summa, iiij^{xx} j li v s ij d.

Item, we charge vs with vij li, the whyche sir Iohn plomer hath lent vnto the paryshe, to be payd every quartere v s tyll the sum of the money be payd, vij li.

Item, we charge vs with the clarkes wages & with the bemlyght in the sayd yere Resayved be iiij quarters of the yere, vj li xj s vij d.

Item, we charge vs with the money that we Resayved at estere for pascall, xij s vij d.

+

Item, we charge vs wyth sertayn Casweltes Resayved within the sayd yere :—

Item, of wylliam Courtman, that he gave vs to Reles hym of a gardyn . . . . vj s viij d
Item, of mastere Iohn, at ij tymes . . . . xiiij d
Item, for buryeng of a portyngale . . . . ij s
Item, of thomas colyns for a powre man . . . . . iij s iiij d
Item, of Robert odyham for buryeng of hys chyld . . ij s
Item, for ould tymbere sould to Robert Graples . . ii s vj d
Item, for buryeng of Wylliam abarow . . . . . ij s
Item, for buryeng of a portyngale . . . . iiij s
Item, for ould tymbere sould for . . . . x d
Item, for ould tymbere sould to Robert Clarke . . . iij s iiij d
Item, for buryeng of maister braymonger . . . xiij s iiij d
    Summa, xlj s ij d.
Summa totalis of the hole charge thys yere
 j c v li xvj s viij d.

+

Here foloweth the payementes as wele of that that belongyth to the cherche as to the chauntres.

ffyrst, payd to Robert fygherberd and godfrey oxen-brege, wardens of the paryshe of sent Georges for a quyt Rent goeng owt of the tenementes of Iohn Weston for a hole yere at myhalmas last passid. Summa . . . . xx s

---

¹ leaf 86.   ² leaf 87.

Payd to the prioure of *Chr*istcherche, in london, for a quytte Rentte goeng owt of the tenement*es* of Ioħn Weston, for a hole yer at estere last passed   iij s

Payd to the abbot of Waltham for a quytte Rent goeng owt of the tenement*es* of Ioħn Weston, for a hole yere at ester . . . . xxxviij s

Obytt*es* kepte at the coust*es* of the cherche.

Payd for kepyng of the obytt of Ioħn Weston the xix day of Apreħ, to prest*es* and clark*es*, iij s vj d.

payd for the obett of m*aister* Ioħn bradmere, kept the xxiij day of novembere Å 1492, ij s x d.

payd to s*ir* Ioħn plomere for kepyng of the morowmas for a hole yere at myhalmas last passed, xx s.

payd to m*aster* Ioħn Redye for the Rehersyng of the namys [of the] fownders of the chauntryes in the bed Rolle, for a hole yer at myhalmas last passed, xvj d.

          S*um*ma, iiij ħi viij s viij d.

[1] + the Coust*es* of the ij clark*es*.

payd to Wyll*ia*m edmund*es*, clarke, for a quartere at crystmas . . . . xiij s iiij d

payd to Everod, the chyld, for the same quarte*re* . . vj s viij d

Item, payd to Saundere worsle for a hole yere wag*es*, fynysshed at the fest of sent mychaeħ last passed   xxxvj s viij d

Item, payd to Rob*er*t debenham, clarke, for iij quarters of a yere, that ys to sey—estere, mydsom*er* and myhalmas . . . . xl s

          S*um*ma, iiij ħi xvj s viij d.

Coust*es* of the quere.

Item, payd for holme & ive on crystmas even, ij d.

Item, for mendyng of the Antyfonere, vj s.

Item, for a quarst of bastard on crystmas day, iij d oħ.

Item, for wyn on xij day at masse, iiij d oħ.

Item, for makyng clene of the gutters in the grete snowe, ij d.

Item, for mendyng of the vestment at sent kateryns awtere, vij d.

Item, to m*aster* weston for iiij quayer*es* of the grete boke, xv s.

Item, for mendyng of the sanctus belle, ij d.

Item, for Scowryng of the laton in the cherche, xx d.

[1] leaf 87, back.

Item, for bovx and flowrys on palme sonday, v d.
Item, for palme the same day, iij d.
Item, for wyn on palme sonday, vj d ob.
Item, for a quartere of colles at ester, vj d.
Item, for wachyng of the sepulcre at estere, x d.
xxvij s ob.

[1] + coustes of the quere.

Item, payd for wyn on holy thursday, iiij d.
Item, for Rosys on corpus Christi day, viij d.
Item, for birche at mydsomer, ij d.
Item, for wyne on sent barnabes even, x d.
Item, for wyne on sent barnabes day, viij d ob.
Item, for iiij dousen garlondes on cherche holyday, xv d.
Item, to bowere & hys companye on sent barnabes day, ij s viij d.
Item, to pye for hys labour the same day, viij d.
Item, for wyne on owre ladye day the Assompcyon, v d.
Item, for Caryeng awey of ij lowde Roboys owt of the cherche, v d.
Item, for a c & di. of v peny nayll for the cherche dore, vj d.
Item, for a sourples for the clarke, bought of sir wylliam, ij s.
Item, for makyng of a new pewe in the cherche, ij s.
Item, for a peyre of henges for the pewe dore, vj d.
Item, to wylliam pares for kepyng & wachyng of the cherche the space of x wekes, viij s.
Item, to Iohn dorham for a sourples, xij s.
Item, for wyne on halowmas day, vj d.
Item, for havyng the Roboys for the cherche end, v d.
Item, for naylles to the quere, iij d.
Item, for vj li of candell, vj d.
Item, to the smyth for a key to a hangyng loke in the Roud loufte, iiij d.
Item, for makyng clene of the cherche, iij s iiij d.
Item, payd to the Rakere, viij d.
Item, for ij peyre of patens for the prestes, vj d.
Item, payd to sir Iohn tyllesle for mendyng of the portos, with othere bokes, xvj d.
Item, payd to Raff Colkes for xxj li of candell, xxj d.
Item, payd to Robert wylles for xij li of candell, xij d.

[1] leaf 88.

Item, payd to wyll*a*m pares for the mendyng of o thyng and othere in the cherche, xij d.
Item, for Restyng of Anes benett, vj d.
<blockquote>ij ƚi v s ij d oƀ.
<blockquote>Su*m*ma totallis of aH the coustes of the quere, iij ƚi xij s iij d.</blockquote></blockquote>

[1]+

Expences for the profyt of the cherche.

Item, payd for oure Rydyng to barnett, in coustes, iij s j d.
Item, for enteryng of the axyon of wyll*ia*m dye, bowchere, x d.
Item, for the iugement of wyll*ia*m dye, bouchere, viij d.
Item, payd to fovx for hys laboure, iiij d.
Item, that I spent on the quest for dye, ij s ix d.
Item, payd for a dyne*r* whan M*a*ster parson w*ith* othere of the p*a*ryshe were w*ith* hym at the sonn, xvij s ix d.
Item, spent whan m*a*ste*r* p*a*rson was at gabryeH w*ith* m*a*ste*r* alderma*n* and m*a*ste*r* plomere, iij s x d.
<blockquote>[Summa], xxix s iij d.</blockquote>

Expences in wex to the wex chaundelere.

Item, payd for di. a c & xv ƚi wex at iij ƚi iij s iiij d c. Su*m*ma, xl s ij d.
Item, payd to Rogere mydelton, wex chaundelere, for the makyng of the beame lyght, pascaH, & the trendeH & othere lyghtes spent in the cherche w*ith*in thys sayd yere, viij s xj d.
<blockquote>Su*m*ma, ij ƚi ix s j d.</blockquote>
The sayd Rogere owet*h* vnto the cherche xij ƚi & a q*ua*rte*r* wex.

Rep*a*racyons of the cherche Rentes.

Item, payd for mendyng of prestes seege, iij d.
Item, for tyelyng of the powre mens howsys, ij s ij d.
Item, to *chris*tefer kechyn for a wyndowe bourd & naylles, & hys man a day in s*i*r wyll*ia*m boyes chambere, xvij d.
Item, a loud lome to the same, iiij d.
Item, for a c lath, v d.
Item, for a q*ua*rtere lath nayll, j d oƀ.
Item, for ij sax lyme, iiij d.
Item, for a dawbere & hys man, xij d.

[1] leaf 88, back.

Item, to a dawbere that brought lome in for the flores, iiij d.
Item, for mendyng of iij doures, ij d.
Item, for mendyng of a wyndow & settyng vp of a new wyndow, ij d.
Item, for naylles to the same, ob.
Summa, vj s ix d.

Vacacyouns of the howse that the goudman mershe ocupyed, by halff a yere, v s.
Summa totalis, xj s ix d.

[1] + Reparacyons of the new howse in the cherche Rentes.

Item, payd for makyng of the fowndacyon of the new howse, to ij masons for vij dayes werke, iij s viij d.
Item, to a labourere for v dayes to the same, xx d.
Item, to a labourere for ij dayes to the same, x d.
Item, for a busshell & di. of tyell pyns, vij d ob.
Item, to a mason for iiij dayes werke to the same, ij s viij d.
Item, to a labourer for the same iiij dayes, xx d.
Item, payd to the tyelere for tyelyng of the same howse, vij s.
Item, payd to a mason for iiij dayes werke and ij mt brek, xiij s.
Item, payd to Wylliam horn for vj dayes werke & hys man, vj s vj d.
Item, for a mason ij dayes in the same howse, xvj d.
Item, to hys labourer for the same ij dayes at v d a day, x d.
Item, for di. a quartere of Roufe tyell, vij d.
Item, for strawe to make mortere with to the dawbere, viij d.
Item, for a tyelere & hys man ij dayes more on the same howse, ij s ij d.
Item, for ij mt brek, viij s viij d.
Item, for iij c breke, to Iohn hamsterlay, xvj d.
Item, to Iohn kellay for viij loude of sand, iij s iiij d.
Item, for dawbyng of the same howse vndere & above, xj s.
Item, for ij c ij loud & iiij sax lyme to the same, xiij s.
Item, payd to Roger smalwod for mendyng & makyng of the gutters in the same howse, xxvj s.
Item, bought of the goudman hawlhed, xxvj c hertlath to the same howse, at v d a c, x s x d.
Item, for ij loud of tyell in to the same howse, iiij s viij d.
Item, payd vnto thomas mundes for xj c & a peny worth of v peny naylle, to the same howse, iij s ix d.

[1] leaf 89.

Item, for ij c & d*i*. of vj d nayle, xij d o℔.
Item, for vij c & d*i*. of iiij d nayle, xxij d o℔.
Item, for di. a c of iij d nayle, j d o℔.
Item, for ij c & ij penyworth of xd nayll, xviij d.
Item, for iij m℔ & a o℔ worth of Roufe nayle, ij s vj d o℔.
Item, for xvj m℔ & a q*uar*tere & a o℔ worth of sprygg, viij s ij d.
Item, for viij c & d*i*. & a penyworth of hartlath, iij s vij d o℔.
Item, payd to *chris*tofere kechyn for makyng of the same howse & for the tymbere therto, viij ℔.
Item, payd to the smyth for barres, lok*es*, and keyes to the same howse, xiij s o℔ q*uar*ter.
Item, payd to s*ir* Iohn plomere for the coust*es* that he dyde in takyng downe of the same howse, xxj d.

   S*um*ma t*o*t*all*is coust*es* of the new howse, xvj ℔ [1]xviij s[1] v d o℔ q*uar*ter.

[2]✝ The coust*es* & payement*es* of naysyng*es* chauntrye.

Item, payd to s*ir* Iohn tyllsle, prest, to syng for the sayd Iohn nasyng for a hole yere at myhalmas last passed, vj ℔ xiij s iiij d.
Payd to the abot of Waltham for a quytte Rent goeng owt of the tenement*es* of Iohn nasyng for a hole yer at the fest of sent mychaell last passed, xxij s.

Rep*ar*acyons.

Item, payd for tyelyng of wyll*ia*m olyvers howse, vj d.
Item, payd for mendyng of Rob*er*t clark*es* howse, ij s ij d.
   [Summa], ij s viij d.
   S*um*ma, vij ℔ xviij s.

The coust*es* & payement*es* of Rose wrettell & Iohn weston chauntrye.

Item, payd vnto s*ir* Robert halle, prest, to syng for the sayd Rose wrettell & Iohn weston for a hole yere at the fest of sent mychaell last passed, vj ℔ xiij s iiij d.

[3] ✝ The coust*es* & payement*es* of Rychard goustlyns chauntrye.

Item, payd to s*ir* wyll*ia*m stok*es*, prest, to syng for the sayd Rychard goustlyn for an hole yer at myhalmas last passed, vj ℔ xiij s iiij d.

[1–1] Scratched out.   [2] leaf 89, back.   [3] leaf 90.

payd to the priores[1] of kelborn for a quytt Rent goeng owt of the tenementes in foster lane for a hole yer at myhalmas, vj d.

payd for the obytt of Richard goustlyn kept the fyrst day of decembere last passed, iiij s ij d.

Reparacyons.

In primis, spent for the Resayveng of money of master lewes, iiij d.

Item, for caryeng of a loud of tyell in to foster lane to master exmes, iiij d.

Item, for ij loud of brabant stonys to the same howse, viij d.

[2]Item, for ij dawbers to master selles howse, ij s ij d.

Item, payd to Thomas horle, mason, for makyng of master exmes kechyn & kanellstone, xxxiij s.

Item, for lath into master lews howse, iiij d.

Item, for makyng clene of the same howse, xij d.

Item, for a mason & hys man ij days ij s ij d, & for a loud of sand & a busshell of plastere, xiij d, into master seelles howse.

Item, for naylles to master exmes howse, ij s v d.

Item, for pavyng of the tenementes, v s vj d.

Item, for iij sax lyme into master selles howse, vj d.

Item, for sand to the same, ij d.

Item, for a c of breke tyell into the same howse, vj d.

Item, for a mason & hys man a day in the same howse, xiij d.

Item, for a gabyll to putt into the wall, vj d.

Item, for a c & di. of brabant stone to master exmes kechyn, xvj s vj d.

Item, payd to Christofere kechyn for gyestes & poustes & xxv foute of tymbur to the kechyn in master exmes howse, iiij s ij d.

Item, for a c & xxv fout of planche bourd & quarters to the same kechyn, iij s vj d.

Item, for ij men iij dayes a pece, iiij s.

Item, for a man ij dayes in master selles howse, xvj d.

iiij li xj d.

Summa totallis, x li xviij s xj d.

[3] The coustes & paymentes of Iohn Caustons chauntrye.

Item, payd vnto sir wylliam boyes, prest, to syng for the sayd Iohn Causton for a hole yere at myhalmas last passed vj li xiij s iiij d.

---

[1] 'abbes' scratched out.   [2] 'Item Item' in MS.   [3] leaf 90, back.

payd to the bretherhed of sent thomas fovnded within the cherche of sent magnus, in london, for a quyte Rente goeng owt of Iohn fysshys howse for a hole yere at Estere, vj s.

payd to the masters of the brege howse for a quytte Rent goeng owt of Iohn fysshys howse for a hole yere at myhalmas, xiij s iiij d.

payd to the priore of chrystcherche, in london, for a quytte Rent goeng owt of the tenementes & gardyns besyde the menores at the towre hyll for a hole yere at estere, v s.

payd for the obytt of Iohn Causton, kept the fyrst day of August, to prestes & clarkes and for Ryngyng, iij s xj d.

Reparacyons.

Item, for lath & naylles at the towre hyll, and for a carte to haue thedere tymbere, ij s viij d.

Item, for dawbyng of the same ij howsys, iiij s xj d.

Item, for a mason & hys man a day in fysshys howse, xiij d.

Item, for mendyng of master fysshys howse, ij s viij d.

Item, payd to Christofere kechyn for ij men iij dayes apece at the towre hyll, iiij s.

[Summa], xv s iiij d.

Vacacyon of the howse that william whetlay late ocupyed, by o quartere, ij s.

[Summa], ij s.

Vacacyon of the howse that Gerold ocupyed, by di. a ȝere, iiij s.

Summa, ix li ij s xj d.

[1] + Coustes spent in the lawe aȝenst the priores of sent Elyns for Iohn Caustons chauntrye.

Item, fyrst payd vnto fovx of the yeld halle for the testament of Iohn causton, iiij d.

Item, to Master wode, seriaunt, iij s iiij d.

Item, to master savll and to master marow, iij s iiij d.

Item, that mylton and I spent to lambeth, iij d ob.

Item, to master wod & master sawll and master marow the xxiij day of novembere, x s.

Item, that was spent there vpon them, xj d.

Item, to Mastere Morden for the same cawse, iij s iiij d.

Item, to mastere [2] morden & to master marow, vj s viij d.

Item, for copyeng owt of the testament, to master marows clarke, iij s iiij d.

[1] leaf 91.   [2] MS. has 'm' mastere.'

Item, payd to Iohn purfote, clarke of the mayres court, for copyeng owt of the testament of Iohn causton, vj s viij d.

Item, spent be m*aste*re plomere & Iohn mylton for goeng to westmest*er* And to my lourd bryant*es*, and also at the kyng*es* hed & at the sent Iones hed, ij s iij d.

Item, to m*aste*r wod, iij s iiij d.

Item, to m*aste*r morden, iij s iiij d.

Item, to my lourd cheff Iuge & to my lourd bryant, xiij s iiij d.

Item, to m*aste*r morden & to m*aste*r marowe, vj s viij d.

Item, spent for oure p*ar*te of the dynere whan my lourd hussy & my lourd bryant was at the cardnall*es* hatt ayenst the p*ri*ores of sent Elyns, xviij s xj d.

Item, for a dyn*er* was mad last for my lourd chefe Iuge & my lourd bryant for on thynge & othere that went therto, iiij s x d.

Item, for a ronlett of malvinseyn gevyn vnto m*aste*r plomere, and for the barell, xij s vij d.

    Su*m*ma, v li iij s v d ob.
    Su*m*ma to*t*all*is*, xiiij li vj s iiij d ob.

[1] + The coust*es* & payement*es* of Iohn bedhams chauntrye.

Item, payd vnto s*ir* Iohn plomere, prest, to syng for the sayd Iohn bedham for an hole yere at myhalmas last passed, vj li xiij s iiij d.

payd for the obytt of Iohn bedham kept the xvj day of may last passed, to prest*es* & clark*es*, powre people & to the cherche wardens, xiij s iiij d.

payd to Gabryell de vrs toward hys Rep*ar*acyons of the grete place in sent botolphus lane, for an hole yere at myhalmas, ij li xij s iiij d.

payd vnto iij powre men of thys p*ar*yshe, that ys to wytte, wyll*ia*m pares, Reynold bull and Iohn toplady, every sonday in the yere xij d, ij li xij s.

payd vnto Iohn dorant for the oyle spent in the lampe wythin the quere in the tyme of thys Accoumpte, x galons and d*i*., price of the galoun xij d, x s vj d.

Item, payd for iij tabull*es* :in a Remembrans of the powre mens charge, v d.

    Su*m*ma to*t*all*is*, xiij li ij s xj d.

[2] + The coust*es* & payement*es* of M*aste*r cambreges chauntrye.

Item, payd vnto s*ir* Iohn lovell, prest, to syng for the sayd M*aste*re cambrege, for an hole yere at myhalmas last passed, vj li xiij s iiij d.

---

[1] leaf 91, back.   [2] leaf 92.

payd to the abbot of barmondsey for a quytte Rente goeng owt of the tenemen*tes* of ma*s*tere cambrege at the stok*kes*, for an hole yere at myhalmas last passed, vj s.

payd for the obett of m*aster* cambrege, kept the xix day of August last passed, to prest*es* & clark*es* & for Ryngyng, iiij s ij d.

Item, to poure folke in bred and ale, vj s ix d o℔.

Item, for ij chesys to the same obytt, xviij d.

Item, payd to the mayre and shereves and to the swerdberer at the same obytt, xv s.

[Summa], xxvij s v d o℔.

Repa*r*acyons.

Item, payd to a mason and hys man ij dayes at the stok*es*, ij s ij d.

Item, for nayll*es* to the same howse, ij d o℔.

Item, payd to *Christ*ofere kechyn for xxxv foute of elmen bourd and quarte & quarters and ledg*es* to the same, xxij d.

Item, for pavyng of the t*e*n*e*ment*es*, iiij s viij d.

Item, to phelyp bornham for v loud of sand, xx d.

Item, for caryage of ij loud ston*es*, vj d.

[Summa], xj s o℔.

S*u*m*m*a to*tallis*, viij ℔ xvij s x d.

[1] +

Item, we aske alowaunce for a quartere Rent that was gevyn vnto wyll*iam* edmond*es* . . . . . . ij s vj d

Item, we aske alowaunce of potacyon money that we geve vnto the tena*untes* in Resseyuyng of ȝowre Rent*es* . . . . v s

Item, for engrocyng and makyng vp of thys accompte vj s viij d

S*u*m*m*a, iiij^{xx} xv ℔.

Summa to*talis* payd, xix s viij d.

Rest due vnto the cherche. S*u*m*m*a, viij⁰ li xvij s.[2]

whereof ther ys owyng thys yere in dettours hand*es* thys p*ar*sell*es* folowyng :—

Io*h*n polyvere for buryeng of m*aster* braymong*er* . . xiij s iiij d

+ wyll*iam* halle . . . . viij s iiij d

wyll*iam* dye . . . . vj s viij d

[3] Robert odyam, mercere . . . . iij s iiij d[3]

---

[1] leaf 92, back.
[2] Several sums scratched out here, and the above substituted.
[3]—[3] Scratched out.

Churchwardens' Accounts, A.D. 1491–2.

Iohn westhowse	iiij s	
+Robert debenham, clarke	ij s	vj d
Thomas bynkes		xx d
Nycholas smythson	x s	
Rychard chelmsho	xv s	
Robert a Graples	x s	
wylliam whetlay	iiij s	
anes benett	xvj d, hew	
hebbes suerte to be payd at Ester.		
+modeer boyes	xij d	

Summa deturs, iij ti xvij s x d.[1]
Rest in money, v ti xix s ij d.[1]

[2] +

Thes ben the ould dettes that have be left vnpayd by the cherche wardens in tymes paste.

Robert a Graples	xij s	
Iohn huntyngfeld	vj s	
Thomas Recheforth	iiij s	
wylliam harsons wyff, gardner	v s	iiij d
Iohn smyth	xv s	
T. Mowce	xxvj s	viij d
Iohn Mowce	xvj s	
+Rychard chelmsho	v s	
wylliam wylkenson		xv d
watken Galleson	ij s	
Iohn hogges wyff	iiij s	vj d
The taylore ther next	iiij s	
+Berlynges wyff	vj s	viij d
+harry vavysere	xv s	iiij d &
the clarkes wages for an oul{{t}} yere	iiij s	iiij d
Nycholas welles		xv d
Nycholas thornle	iij s	

Summa, vj ti viij s j d.

[3] +Ihesus, 1492.

Memorandum: that M^r wylliam wylde, parson, schewed, the xxj day of Ianyver, vnto M^r william Remyngton, Alderman, to M^r

---

[1] These sums substituted for others scratched out.
[2] leaf 93.   [3] leaf 93, back.

Robert plommer, gent, to Iohn smarte, william prewne, Iohn ducklyng, herry kello, Iohn deraham, Iohn Mascall, Richard cloce & to Robert howtyng, That the wyll of sir Iohn Motram, prest of Poulles, þat late decessid, yave his booke callid an Antiphoner vnto þe chirch vnder this condicion. That the chirchwardens, now beyng Richard cloce & Robert howtyng, and theyr successoures chirchwardens, schall paye euery yer vjs viijd for the obyte of þe said I. [Motram], to the ffelowes of holmes coleghe ffoundid within Powllis, duryng the termes of xx yeres. To the perfformyng of the which, All the saide persones above writen in the name of all the paryssh be ffully agreed.

[1] Rychard Cloose }
Robard howtyng } A° ml lxxxxiij
Ihesus.

[A.D. 1492–3.]

[2] Thys ys the Accountte of vs, Rychard Cloose and Robard howtyng, wardens of the goodys and Renttes belongyng vnto the cherch of sayntt mary at hyll in london, for an hole yere from Myhelmas, Anno 1492, to Myhelmas Anno 1493.

ffyrste, we charge vs wyth the olde dettes that we haue Resseuid wythin thys yere of owre Accountte :—

In primys, of mothyr boyis		xij d
Item, of Robard debenam, clarke	ij s	vj d
Item, of Wylliam halle	viij s	iiij d
Item, of Thomas bynckys		xx d
Item, of Masters Byrlynges	vj s	viij d
Item, of The wardenys of sentt botolphus	ij s	vj d
Item, of Robard hodyham	iij s	iiij d
Item, of harry Vaveser ys wyffe, for beryinge of barnardys wyffe and for þe clarke ys wagys of olde		xviij s
Item, of Thomas devardys wyffe for mastyr Remyngton, the whyche we hadde in bryke	v s	vj d

Summa, xlix s vj d.

[3] Item, we charge vs as wele wythe the cherche Renttes as wyth the Renttes belongyng to the chauntres for an hole yere at Myhelmas laste passed.

[4] Item, the cherche Renttes . . . . xv li xv s vj d

[1] leaf 94.   [2] leaf 95.   [3] leaf 95, back.   [4] 'cherche, 1 yere' in margin.

Item, Nasyngys Chauntre . . . . ix li   viij d
Item, Rose Wrytylles Chauntre . . . . . . vj li   xiij s iiij d
Item, Rychard Gosselynys Chauntre . . . viij li   xij s   viij d
Item, Iohn Causton ys Chauntre. . . . . . xviij li iiij s iiij d
Item, Iohn Bedhamys Chauntre . . . . . . xiij li   vj s   viij d
Item, Mastyr Wylliam Cambryge ys Chauntre . x li
    Summa, iiij^{xx} j li xiij s ij d

Item, we Charge vs wythe the Clarke ys wagys and wythe sartayne mony Resseuyd for the bemely3ght in the sayd yere. Ressayuyd be iiij quarters of the yere . . . . ix li x s
Item, we charge vs w[i]th the mony that we Resseuide at estyr for the pascall . . . . xj s xj d ob
[1] Item, we Charge vs wythe sartayne Casseweltes Resseuid wythe in thys sayd yere :—
In primys, of leppam of Colchestyr, for byrying of one of hys men . . . . xij d
Item, of develyn ys wyffe, for berying of Iohn Ionys chylde . . . . xij d
Item, of harry vaveser ys wyffe, for berying of hys sone and one of hys seruaunttes . . . . . . iiij s vj d
Item, of Mastyr brande, for a grave stone . . . . v s
Item, for berying of a man of maldon . . . . . . iij s iiij d
Item, Resseuid of Mastyr Iohn Redy at iij tymys . . xix d
Item, for þe waste of ij tapers for the obett of syr Iohn Bradmere . . . . v d
Item, for berying of Petyr Andrewys wyfe . . . . xiij s iiij d
Item, for berying of a stranger . . . . iij s iiij d
Item, for berying of Thomas huntt ys wyffe and ffor the knylle . . . . xvj s viij d
Item, for berying of hys dowtyr . . . . ij s
Item, of Thomas bate for byrying of a stranger . . . iij s iiij d
Item, for berying of Thomas semere . . . . . . ij s
Item, of Mastyr cloose for berying of hys ij prentys and Thomas baker . . . . iiij s
    Summa, iij li xviij d.
    Summa totalys of þe hole charge thys yere ys iiij^{xx} and xvij li vj s j d ob.

[1] leaf 96.

Churchwardens' Accounts, A.D. 1492-3.

[1]Here ffolowyth The paymenttes as wele of that belongyth to the Cherche as to the Chauntres.

ffyrste, payd to the Abbott of Waltham, for a quyte Rentt goyng owte of the Tenementtes of Iohn Weston, for an hole yere at myhelmas laste passed	xxxviij s
Item, payd to Robard ffyherbard and Godfray oxenbryge, wardens of the parysshe of sentt Gorgys in botolphus lane, in london, for a quite Rentt goyng owte of the tenementt of Iohn Weston, for a hole yere at myhelmas	xx s
Item, payd to the prior of Crychyrch, in london, for a quite Rentt goyng owte of the tenementt of Iohn Weston, for a hole yere at Estyr laste passed . .	iij s

Obbettes kepte at The costys of the cherche.

Item, payd for The kepyng of the obett of Iohn Weston, the xix day of Apryll, to prestys and clarkys	iij s vj d
Item, ffor the obett of Mastyr Iohn bradmere kepte the xxiij day of novembyr	iij s vj d
Item, to syr Iohn Plomere for kepyng of the morowe mas, for a hole yere at myhelmas	xx s
Item, to Mastyr Iohn Redy for þe Reherssyng of the namys of the founders of the chauntres and for þe bede Rowle, for a hole yere at myhelmas . .	xvj d
Item, to syr Iohn Plomer in party of paymentt of the vij li the whych he lentt to the Reparacion of the Newe howsyng in the prestes alye	xx s
Summa, v li ix s iiij d.	

[2]The Costys of the ij Clarkys.

Item, payd to Robart debename, Clarke, for a hole yere ys wagys paste at Myhelmas	iiij li xiij s iiij d
Item, payd to saundyr worsselay for iij quarters of a yere an vj wokys	iij li
Item, payd to Mascall towarde the Reparacion of the Newe Ile	xvj s viij d
Summa, viij li x s.	

[1] leaf 97.   [2] leaf 97, back.

The Costys of the quere.

In prymys, for ix ℔ candyll, ix d.

Item, to parys for swepyng of the cherch and makynd clene of the pewys, ij d.

Item, for wyne one xij^th day, viij d.

Item, to parys, þe xxiij day of Ianyuere, for makyng of a payre of trestylles and for ij quartres for the fete of þe same trestylles, viij d.

Item, for iiij ℔ candyll, iiij d.

Item, to the goodman proyne, þe xxviij day of Ianyuere for xx fadym of small Rope, vj d.

Item, the xxx day of Ianyuere for xvj elles and a halfe of holonde clothe to make ij surples and for to mende the Aubys and othyr thynges in the cherch, pris þe ell vj d. Summa, viij s iiij d.

Item,[1] to mastyr dokelyng for xvij ℔ of Ropys for the belles, xxj d.

Item, for ij quarters and for makyng of anothyr payre of trestylles, vj d.

Item, for a ℔ candyll, j d.

Item, for naylys, j d.

Item, for swepyng of the lytyll cherchyarde, ij d.

Item, to the smyth for mendyng of the sauntys bell, xxij d.

Item, for makyng of a ladyr for þe stepyll and for ij pecys of tymbyr for þe same ladyr, xiiij d.

Item, payd for holme on crystemas euyn, iiij d.

[Summa], xvij s iiij d

[2]Item, payd to ij porters for laying vpe of the tymbyr and for beryng of þe pewys and othyr stuffe into the storeh[ow?]e, vj d.

Item, for iij laborars for berynge owte of þe stonys owte of the cherchyarde and for gravelyng of both cherchyardys for iij dayis & di. iij s x d.

Item, for wyne one owre lady day in lentt, iiij d.

Item, for palme, boxe and flowrys on palmson eve, viij d.

Item, for bromys and naylys, j d.

Item, to a laborar for makyng clene of þe prestys Alye and for gravelyng of the cherchyarde, viij d.

Item, for wyne on palme sonday, viij d.

Item, to Thomas hunttes sone the same day, j d.

Item, for a quartyr of colys on estyr eve, v d.

Item, for dyssplyng Roddys, ij d.

Item, for ij ℔ candyll, ij d.

---

[1] MS. Itcm, Itcm.   [2] leaf 98.

Item, to Kyrstofyr kychyn ys man for sartayne thynges that he made in the cherch, x s.

Item, for naylys, iij d.

Item, for tayntyrhokes and ffor wachyng of the sepulture, xij d.

Item, for skowryng of the latayne, xxj d.

Item, for viij baner stavys, viij d.

Item, to parys for swepyng of the cherchyarde, ij d.

Item, to Robard clarke for makyng of ij surples and ij Rochettes, and ffor othyr thynges that he mendyd, v s.

Item, for havyng aweye of the smale stonys in the cherchyarde, ij d.

Item, to parys for takyng downe of þe supulture, ij d.

Item, to the mason for makyng of the ffuntt, for xv dayis workemanshype, x s.

Item, to hys laborar for v dayis labor, ij s j d.

Item, for fyllyng of the ffuntt with watyr, j d.

Item, for wyne one holy thrusday, vj d.

Item for ffyllyng of the ffuntt with watyr at Whytsontyde, j d.

Item, payd for the swaype of þe cherch dore and for garnattes for the pewys and for a locke and a kaye to the same dore and a kaye to the stayre dore in the vestry and for bateryng of the mason ys irynys, x s.

[Summa], xlix s vj d.

[1]Item, for wyne on corpus crysty day, iiij d.

Item, for garlondes on the same day, iiij d.

Item, for beryng of iiij torchys, viij d.

Item, for Roose garlondys on sentt barnaby ys day, xx d.

Item, for wyne and ale to þe prestys and clarkys the same day, ix d.

Item, for wyne on sentt barnabyis euyn for bowier and hys chylderyn and othyr prestes and clarkys att þe sone, viij d.

Item, to bowier and pye for a Rewarde, iij s iiij d.

Item, to parys for mendyng of the sanctes bell, iiij d.

Item, the Raker, for a hole yere at Myhelmas, viij d.

Item, to Raffe þe porter, for makyng clene of the cherchyarde for ij dayis and a half, xv d.

Item, payd to the porters for beryng of the bras pottes of harry vaveserys into þe vestry, iij d.

Item, to harry marsshe ys man for makyng clene of the porche, ij d.

Item, payd to a clarke, for a Rewarde, þe xxiij day of auguste, that wolde a bene in seruys, viij d.

Item, for wyne at the Tauerne the same tyme, v d.

[1] leaf 98, back.

Churchwardens' Accounts, A.D. 1492-3.

Item, for di. a dayis worke on the cherche Roffe and on the prestes chambrys to a tyler and hys man, vij d.

Item, for di. a c tyle, iij d.

Item, payd for pavyng of iij tese of grownde at the weste ende of the cherch, xviij d.

Item, for a loode of gavell to þe same, iiij d.

Item, for havyng aweye of the Robiis in pardon cherchyarde and for brekyng downe of the walle ouer mastyr Ryvell, iiij d.

Item, to Robard Clarke for mendyng of the iij whyte copys, a chesebyll, ij tvnekylles of the same sute and for mendyng of the Aubis to the same, ij s.

Item, for bromys, j d.

Item, for candyll, j d.

Item, for xv ll of candyll, xv d.

Item, payd to the plomere for a pype of lede for þe ffuntt and for a ll di. of sawdyr to sowdyr þe same pype, xij d.

Item, payd to cyrstofyr kechyn for sartayne thynges dune in the chyrch at dyuers tymys, besyde hys byll, viij s viij d.

[Summa], xxvij s v d.

[1] Item, to the ssmyth for ij garnattes, ix smale Rynges, for tylles, and for a locke and iij kayis and a dyssh of Iryn for the lytyll senser and for othyr thynges that he made, iiij s iiij d.

Item, payd to crystofyr kychyn for sartayne thynges that he made for the cherch as hyt aperyth by his Byll. Summa, iij li xiij s iiij d.

Item, to the skreuener in lombard strete for wrytyng of ij dedys and the bede Rowle and for othyr thynges that he made for the cherch, iij s iiij d.

Item, payd to wylliam Gele for makyng of a pewe and mendyng of the vestry dore be Rychard Close ys tyme and for makyng of ix coffynys and the dore of the almery that we laye owre dedes and Indenturs in. Summa, xiiij s.

Item, for havyng awaye of xij lodys of Robys owte of bothe cherchyardys, iiij s.

Item, to parys for makyng clene of the guttyrs in þe snowe, iiij d, and for swepyng of the chyrch.

Item, payd to Iohn delanavsa for wyne drvnky be mastyr Remyngton and þe parson and mastyr cloose at þe cherches coste, xxj d.

Item, payd for byrche on mydsomer euyn, iiij d.

Item, payd to Thomas Mundys for naylys ffett at dyuers tymys for þe cherche and for the bochers howse in estchepe, v s iij d ob.

[Summa], v li vj s viij d ob.

Summa totalys of þe costes of þe quere and othyr thynges to þe behove of þe cherch, ix li xij s v d ob.

[1] leaf 99.

Expensys in wax to the waxchaundeler.

Item, payd for xvij lb of waxe, pris þe lb, vij d.   Summa, ix s xj d.

Item, payd to Roger Mydylton for strekyng of xiij lb (xx) and xvj of waxe and for dressyng of iiij torchys on corpus crysty day, x s.

Summa, xix s xj d.

Item, the sayd Roger owyth to the cherch iiij lb di. of waxe the whych he Resseuid in endys at crystemas.

[1] Reparacionys of the cherch Rentys.

Item, for a plancke for the bocher ys stalle in estechepe that was bowrght of cyrstofyr kechyn	iij s	iiij d
Item, for lockes, kayis, stapyllys and henges and hokys to þe same howse		xviij d
Item, for iiij (xx) pavyntylys for Wylliam hall hys seler and for pavyng of the same	ij s	

Summa, vj s x d.

Vacacion of the cherch Renttes.

Item, we aske alowans of the vacacion of Mastyr wylliam Combys chambyr, for j quartyr . . .	ij s	vj d
Item, for the vacacion of the lowe chambyr that syr Iamys sannys dwellyd in, for di. a yere . . .	vj s	viij d
Item, for the vacacion of the lytyll howse in estechepe, for di. a yere	xiij s	iiij d

Summa, xxij s vj d.

The Costes and paymentt of nasynges chauntre.

Item, payd to syr Iohn Tyllyslay, preste, to syng for the sayd Iohn Nasyng, for a hole yere at myhelmas laste passed	vj li xiij s iiij d
Item, to the abbott of Waltham, for a quite Rentt goynge owte of þe tenementtes of Iohn Nasyng, for a hole yere at myhelmas	xxij s

Reparacionys.

Item, payd to Wylliam olyuere, for sartayne thynges that he Repayryd in hys howse and for proppyng of the dore	vj s

Summa, viij li xvj d.

---

[1] leaf 99, back.

¹The Costys and paymenttes of Roose Wryttyll and Iohn Weston ys chauntre.

Item, payde to syr Robard hall, preste, to synge for the sayd Iohn Weston and Roose Wryttyll, for a hole yere at myhelmas last passed	vj li xiij s iiij d

The Costys and paymenttes of Rychard Gosselyn ys chauntre.

Item, payd to syr Iamys sannys, preste, to synge for the sayd Rychard Gosselyn, for an hole yer at myhelmas laste passed	vj li xiij s iiij d
Item, payd to þe pryores of Kylborne for a quite Rentt goying owte of the tenementtes in faystyr lane, for a hole yere at myhelmas laste passed .	vj d
Item, payd for the obett of the sayd Rychard gosselyn, kepte þe fyrste day of decembyr last passed	iiij s viij d
+ Item, that the sayd Rychard Gosselyn gave to the cherch wardenys for the tyme beyng be hys bequeste	iij s iiij d ²

Reparacionys.

Item, for a kaye to shaylys wyff for the Alye gate .	iiij d
Item, for mendyng of her chymenay and for tylyng of here how[s]e and stopyng of a hole in þe guttyr	vij d
Item, for a Rope for the well, wayng x lb. . . .	x d
Item, for makyng of a pentes and for naylys and bordys to the same on barettes howse . . .	xxj d

Wacacion.

Wacacion of the howse that exmewe dwellyd in, for on quartyr	xj s viij d

Summa, vij li xiij s viij d.

³The Costys and paymentes of Iohn causton ys chauntre.

Item, payd to Syr Wylliam Boyis, preste, to synge for the sayd Iohn Causton, for a hole yere paste at myhelmas	vj li xiij s iiij d

¹ leaf 100. ² This item feebly crossed out. ³ leaf 100, back.

Item, payd to the bretherede of sentt Thomas, fowndyd wit*h*in the p*a*risshe cherch of sentt Maungn*u*s, in london, for a quite Rentt goyng owte of Io*h*n ffyssih*es* howse, for a hole yere at estyr last passed . . . . vj s

Item, to the mastyrs of the bryge howse, for a quite Rentt goyng owte of Io*h*n ffyssih*es* howse, for an hole yere at myhelmas laste passed . . . . . xiij s iiij d

Item, for the obett of the sayd Io*h*n Causton, kepte the ffyrste day of Auguste, to prest*es* and clarkys and for Ryngynd, and to pore pepyll . . . . iiij s vj d

Rep*a*racionys.

Item, payd for hegyng of the gardyn and ffor polys for the gardyn at þe towre hyll . . . . . . xiij d
Item, for ij kayis . . . . vj d
Item, for pavyng of þe pamentt agenste Rychard chemeshow ys howse and craplas howse and the este ende of the cherche, for viij tese, p*r*is þe tese, vij d. S*um*ma . . . . iiij s viij d
Item, for iij lodys of gavell to þe same . . . . . xij d

vacacionys.

Item, for the vacacion of þe howse þ*at* wyll*i*am wettlay dwellyd in, by iij quarters . . . . . vj s
Item, for the howse thatt Anes benett dwellyd in, by iij quarters . . . . vj s
Item, for the howse þ*at* garolde dwellyd in, by ij quartyr . . . . iiij s
Item, for the vacacion of the garden that Corteman kepte, by a lole yere at myhelmas laste passed . xiij s iiij d
S*um*ma, ix li xiij s ix d.

[1]Costes spent in the lawe aȝenste the pryores of sentt Ellynys for Io*h*n causton ys chauntre.

Item, payde for xxxij galonys of maumsay to Anteny bavyon, the whych was sentt to my lorde bryan and my lorde hussy, p*r*is the gelon, x d. S*um*ma, xxvj s viij d

---
[1] leaf 101.

Item, for ij Runlettes for þe same wyne	ij s	viij d
Item, for beryng of the wyne, to þe ij porters . . .		iiij d
Item, to Mastyr Mardantt, at pollys, the xxj day of Auguste.	v s	
Item, for ale the same tyme		j d
Item, payd to Mastyr close for expensys that spentt at the tempyll		v d
Item, payd for a gose, ij kenyis, and a dosen larkes sentt to my lorde bryan and my lorde hussy to þe bysshope of Elye ys plasse, pris		xxj d
Item, for a potell of Raynysshe wyne and a potell of Rede wyne sentt to them the same tyme . . .		xij d
Item, spentt on the paryssñsonys that wentt thythyr þe same tyme, and that mastyr close spent on mastyr plomer.		vij d

Summa, xxxviij s vj d.

[1]The Costys and pamenttes of Iohn Bedham ys chauntre.

Item, payd to syr Iohn plomer, preste, to synge for the sayd Iohn bedham, for an hole yere at myhelmas laste passed	vj li xiij s	iiij d
Item, payd for the obett of the sayd Iohn bedham, kepte the xvj day of maye laste passed, to prestes and clarkys and pore pepyll, and to þe cherch wardenys	xiij s	iiij d
Item, payd to Gabryell de vrs toward hys Reparacion of the grete plase inc sentt botolles lane, for a hole yere at myhelmas	liij s	iiij d
Item, payd to iij pore men of thys parisshe, that ys to wette:—Wylliam parys, Raynolde bulle and Iohn topelady, euery sonday in þe yere, xij d. Summa.	lij s	
Item, payd to Iohn derham and Rychard kokkes, for oyle spentt in the lampe and for lampys within the quere in thys yere of owre accounpte, vj galonys and a potell of Iohn derham and iij galonys and a potell of Rychard kokkes, pris þe galon, xij d. Summa	x s	j d

Summa, xiij li ij s j d.

[1] leaf 101, back.

[1]The Costys and paymenttes of Mastyr wylliam Cambryge ys chauntre.

Item, payd to Mastyr Wylliam Combys and to syr Wylliam stokys to synge for the sayd mastyr wylliam Cambryge with syr Iohn lovell for an hole yere at myhelmas passed [2]	vjł xiij s iiij d
Item, payd ffor the obctt of þe sayd mastyr wylliam cambryge, kepte the xix day of auguste, to prestes and clarkys and for Ryngyng	iiij s viij d
Item, for brede and ale and chese to þe pore pepyll and to all þe parysshe	viij s viij d
Item, to the mayre and to þe sheryves and to the swerdeberer atte the same obett. [3]Summa	xv s

Summa totalys,[3] xxviij s iiij d.

Reparacionys.

Item, for a tyler and hys man for a dayis labor on þe howsyng at þe stokys	xiij d
Item, for ij sackys lyme	iiij d
Item, for iij quarteronys of tyle	vj d
Item, for naylys, legys and hengys for Rychard Iryke ys howse	xij d

Wacacion.

Item, ffor the wacacion of the howse that Wylliam Raynsford dwellyd in, for iij quarters	xx s

Summa, ix li iiij s vij d.

[4]The Costys and paymenttes of the Reparacion of þe Copyng of the new Ile.

Item, payd to þe masonys for a wekys worke for xxij dayis	xx s	viij d
Item, payd to iij masonys and ij laboras for a wekes wagys	xvj s	
Item, payd to the masonys for iij workemen and iij laborars, for xj dayis for the workemen and xviij dayis the laborars	xiiij s	x d

[1] leaf 102. [2] MS. past passed.
[3—3] Scratched out. [4] leaf 102, back.

Churchwardens' Accounts, A.D. 1492-3.

Item, payd to þe plomer for castyng of xxxiiij c of
  lede quarter ix H̄, at xij d þe c. Summa . . . xxxiiij s
Item, payd to þe plomer for a c xj H̄ of lede, and for
  xvj H̄ of sowdyr, and for naylys for the guttyr at
  þe weste ende off þe cherch . . . . xij s   viij d
Item, payd to Thomas debardys wyfte for xiij m̄l di.
  of bryke, pris þe m̄l iiij s. Summa . . . . . liiij s
Item, to the mason for iiij men and iij laborars for iiij
  dayis. . . . . xv s   viij d
Item, xvj lodys of sande . . . . viij s
Item, xliiij lodys of lyme and iij sackes. Summa, vj c
  xj sakes lyme at vs þe c. Summa . . . . xxxij s
  Summa, x ħi vij s x d.

Item, Resseuid of mastyr smartt, in lede that was
spentt at þe copyng of þe sayd Ile, xxix c and a
quarter, the wyche the cherch owyth̄ for

[1] potacionys.

Item, we aske alowans of potacion mony that we have
  gevyn vnto the tenanttes at þe Resseui[n]g of
  owre mony for owre Renttes . . . . v s
Item, for makyng vppe of thys owre accounpte . . . vj s   viij d
  Summa, xj s viij d.
  Summa totalys of the dyscharge payd within thys
  yere of owre accounte ys iiij$\overset{xx}{}$ xiij ħi xvj s v d ob
  Reste due to the chyrche. Summa iij ħi ix s viij d

Whereof there ys owyng thys yere in dettours handys thes
parcelles folowyng.

Ioħn harris, waterman . . . . iij s iiij d
Wylliam haH, waterman . . . . v s
Iohn westehowse . . . . vj s viij d
Thomas bynckes. . . . . xx d
Ioħn Nele . . . . v s
Nycolas smytheson . . . . x s
Gylys garrolde, gardener . . . . iiij s
harry pebyH, marener . . . . ij s
dyryke Ioħnson, wever . . . . ij s
Mothyr boyis . . . . ij s

[1] leaf 103.

194 *Churchwardens' Accounts*, A.D. 1492–3.

Wylliam harryson ys wyff at myle ende . . . . . iij s
+ Iohn smythe, haburdassher . . . . x s
+ Iohn mowse, clarke . . . . vj s viij d
      Summa, iij li xvj d.

Reste in mony of thys acounte in owre hondys . . . viij s iiij d
Vhereof alowed to Robert howtyng for that that he acoumpted mor than he sholde haue done vs xd; rest ijs vjd.
Paide to Iohn maskall the xij [?] yere anno 1494, ij s vj d, in þe presence [of Mr Alderman & Mr Atclyff ?].

[1] Thes bene the olde dettes that have be lefte vnpayde by the cherch wardenys in tymes paste.

Robard a Crapelas . . . . xxij s
Iohn huntyngfelde . . . . vj s
Thomas Recheforthe . . . . iiij s
Wylliam harryson ys wyffe . . . . vj s viij d
    Resseuid per w. overay ij s. Rest iij s iiij d.
Iohn smythe, haburdasshere . . . . xv s
    [?] ix s j d, rest v s xj d.
Iohn Moswe, clarke . . . . xxvj s viij d
    rest xiij s iiij d.
Thomas Mowse, capper . . . . xvj s
    rest iiij s.
+ Rychard chemshowe . . . . xx s
+ wylliam wylkynson . . . . xv d
+ Wattkyn Galleson . . . . ij s
The taylor ther nextt . . . . iiij s
Nycolas welles, bargeman . . . . xvj d
Nycolas thornle . . . . iij s
    Resseuid ij s per mascall, Rest xij d.
+ Iohn polyuere for berying of mastres bremonger . xiij s iiij d
    Resseuid xiij s iiij d per mascall.

Iohn westehowse . . . . iiij s
wylliam whetelaye . . . . iiij s
Iohn hogges wyffe . . . . iiij s vj d
Annes benett . . . . xvj d
    [2] Rychard Closse } Anno ml cccc lxxxxiij.
    Robert owtyng

---

[1] leaf 103, back.   [2] leaf 104, back.

[A.D. 1493-4.]

¹ Robartt howtyng
Wylliam Overay } Anno mt iiijᶜ lxxxxiiij.

² Thys ys the Accountte of vs, Robartt howtyng and Wylliam Overay, wardens of the goodys and Renttes belongeyng vnto the cherch of sentt mary at hyll in london, for an hole yere, from Myhelmas Anno 1493 to Myhelmas Anno 1494.

ffyrste, we charge vs wythe the olde dettes that we have Resseuid within thys yere of owre accountte.

In primys, Resseuid of Thomas Mowse, Capper . . xij s
Item, of Iohn Mowse, clarke. . . . . xx s
Item, Resseuid of mastyr Remyngton, Alderman, for the tymbyr that was in þe grett chyrchyarde . . xvj s
Item, Resseuid of Iohn smyth, haburdassher . . . x s .
      Summa, lviij s.

Item, we charge vs as welle wythe the chyrch Renttes as wythe the Renttes belongyng to þe chauntres.

Item, the chyrche Renttes . . . . xv ti xv s vj d
Item Nasyngys chauntre . . . . ix ti viij d
Item, Roose Wryttylles chauntre . . . . . vj ti xiij s iiij d
Item, Rychard ys chauntre . . . . . . viij ti xij s viij d
Item, Iohn causton ys chauntre . . . . xviij ti iiij s iiij d
Item, Iohn bedham ys chauntre . . . . xiij ti vj s viij d
Item, Mastyr Wylliam cambryges chauntre . . x ti
      Summa, iiij j̄ ti xiij s ij d.

Item, we charge ws wythe the clarke ys wagys and wythe sartayne mony Resseuid for the bemelyȝght within the sayde yere Resseuid be iiij quarters of the yere. Summa . . . . vj ti vij s x d
      Summa, iiij ti & x ti xix s.

³ Item, we charge vs wythe the mony that we Resseuid at ⁴ estyr ffor the paschall. Summa . . . x s v d
Item, we charge vs wythe sartayne Casseweltes Resseuid wythe in thys sayd yere of owre Accountte.
In primys, Resseuid for beryng of a man of dartemowthe that dyide in Wylliam olyuere ys howse iij s iiij d

---

¹ leaf 105.   ² leaf 106.   ³ leaf 106, back.   ⁴ MS. 'at at.'

Item, of Maskall for berying of a breten	iij s	iiij d
Item, Resseuid of Mastyr Iohn Redy at dyuers tymys		x d
Item, Resseuid of Mastyr smarte for þe waste of ij Tapers for hys wyffe ys mynde		iiij d
Item, for berying of a stranger þat dyid at dannys .		xij d
Item, for the berying of Wylliam graye	xiij s	iiij d
Item, ffor the berying of Iohn Condalles wyffe . . .	xiij s	iiij d
Item, ffor the berying of Thomas Andrewys wyffe . .	ij s	
Item, Resseuid of mastyr smarte in mony the he ffownde in þe chyrch		iiij d
Item, Resseuid of Robartt debenam in mony the he fownd in þe chyrch, with a peny þat Robartt howtyng fownde		v d
Item, Resseuid for þe berying of harry kellowe . . .	xiij s	iiij d
Item, Resseuid for hys knylle	iij s	iiij d

Summa, iij li v s iiij d.

Summa of all þe hoole Chargeys thys yere ys
iiij xx xiiij li iiij s iiij d.

[1] The dyssecharge.

Here ffolowythe The paymenttes as welle of that belongyth to þe chyrch as to þe chauntres.

ffyrste, payd to þe Abbott of Waltham for a quyte Rente goynge [owte] of [2] þe tenementt of Iohn Weston for a hole yere at myhelmas laste passed	xxxviij s
Item, payd to Robartt ffyherbard and Godffraye oxinbryge, wardens of þe parysshe of sentt Gorgys in botolffe lane, in london, for a quite Rentt goyng owte of þe tenementt [3] of Iohn Weston, for a hole yere at myhelmas	xx s
Item, payd to the pryor of crychyrche, in london, for a quite Rentt goyng owte of þe tenementt of Iohn Weston for ij yere at þe viij day of July laste passed. Summa	xvj s

Obbettes kepte at the Costes of the chyrch.

Weston. Item, payd for the kepyng of the obbett of Iohn Weston the xix day of Apryll to prestes and clarkys	iij s viij d

[1] leaf 107, back.   [2] MS. 'of of.'   [3] MS. 'Renementt.'

Item, payd for þe obbett of Mastyr Iohn Badmere,
kepte the xxiij day of novembyr . . . . . iij s vj d
þe fyrste yere, Item, payd to the ffeleshype of holmys
Colege, ffowndyd within powlys, for þe obbett
of syr Iohn Morterame, whyche moste be kepte
at þe coste of the chyrche for þe terme of xx
yerys, every yere to paye to þe sayde feleshype
of holmys Coolege . . . . vj s viij d

Summa, iiij li vij s x d.

[1] The Costys of þe clarkes wagys and the morwe masse.

Item, payd to Robartt debenam, clarke, for a hole yere ys wagys past at myhellmas, iiij li xiij s iiij d.
Item, payd to syr Iohn plomer for kepyng of the morowe masse for a hole yere at myhelmas, xx s.
Item, payd syr Iohn plomer, in party of paymentt of vij li, þe whych he lentt to þe Reparacion of þe newe howyng in the prestys aly, xx s.

Summa, vj li xiij s iiij d.

Costes done in the quere and othyr nessesaryis done in the chyrche.

In primys, for holme, iij d.
Item, to a chylde þat songe a trebyll to helpe the quere in crystmas halydayis, xij d.
Item, for naylys, ob.
Item, for wyne on crystmas daye, iiij d.
Item, spentt at the settyng of þe clarkes wages at þe waterbaylyis, ij d.
Item, for wyne on Candelmas day, v d.
Item, for palme, boxe and flloweys on palme sonday, viij d.
Item, for bred and wyne þe same day, viij d.
Item, payd for skowryng of þe laten Canstykes, ij s.
Item, for a quartyr of Colys, iiij d ob.
Item, for naylys and hokes, j d ob.
Item, payd to parys for a saylyng pece for sentt stevyn ys Autyr, iiij d.
Item, payd to parys and Raynolde butt for watchynge of the sepulture, vj d.

[1] leaf 108.

Item, for brede and wyne on holy thursday, iiij d ob.
Item, for garlondys on Corpus Christi day, iij d.
Item, the same day for brede and wyne to þe prestes & clarkes, vj d.

    Summa, viij s j d.
    Summa, vij ħ xvij d.

[1] Item, payd for beryng of iiij torchys þe same day, viij d.
Item, for Roose garlondys on sentt barnabyis day, ij s j d.
Item, for brede, ale & wyne þe same day, xx d.
Item, payd to bowyer and pye, for a Reward, iij s iiij d.
Item, payd to anothyr synger that cam with them, for a Reward, viij d.
Item, payd for byrche at mydsomer, iiij d.
Item, payd for ij burdens of Russhys for þe newe pewys, iij d.
Item, payd for vndyrpynyng of Mastres Atclyffe ys pewe, vj d.
Item, to parys and Wylliam ellmys for makyng clene of þe same pewe, iiij d.
Item, to parys & anothyr mane for makyng clene of þe chychyarde, and settyng vpe of þe frame owyr þe porch on palmesan eve, vj d.
Item, payd to Wylliam parys for ij hyngys for þe tabyll as ye go in to þe Roode lofte, iiij d.
Item, payd for a matte for þe shrevyng pewe, iij d.
Item, payd to Rychard welles, mason, for vndyrpynnyg of þe newe pewys, and closyng of þe ffuntt, and for makyng vpe of þe Autyr and walle ouer mastyr Ryvelles ys Tombe, for x dayis for hyme and hys laborar, x s x d.
Item, payd to Wylliam horne and hys man for vj dayis labor in makyng of the stepys and levelyng of þe grownde, and pavyng of þe same grownde in sentt stevyn ys chapell, vj s vj d.
Item,[2] payd to þe soffrycan of london for halowyng of sentt stevyn ys autyr, x s iiij d.
Item, for a mł bryke for sentt stevyn ys autyr, and for þe wall ouer mastyr Ryvelles tombe, v s.
Item, payd to the kynges Amener for ffauȝght of Ryngyng off þe belles agenste þe kynge, iiij s x d.
Item, for makyng of the crossys on þe superaltarys, iiij d.
Item, payd for naylys, iiij d.
Item, payd for iiij^{xx} pavyngtylys, xviij d.
Item, spentt att [3] The Cuttyng owte of the westmenttes that mastyr marowe made, viij d.

---

  [1] MS. 'Item Item.'   [2] leaf 108, back.
  [3] leaf 109. At foot of leaf 108, back, is—'summa l s vij d.'

Item, payd to þe women that made þe orforas whane mastyr Remyngton was there with sartayne of the parysshe with hyme, viij d.
Item, payd to mascall for xxviij pavyngtylys, viij d.
Item, payd for iij dosen candyll, iij s.
Item, payd to Russell for naylys, v d.
Item, payd to mastyr parson for halowyng of the westementes, xij d.
Item, payd to Robartt Clarke ffor mendyng of þe westementtes and Copys att dyuers tymys within thys yere, vj s iiij d.
Item, payd to hewe materson, ssmyth, for sartayne thynges done in þe chyrch, and chyrch Renttes as yt aperyth by hys bylles, xvj s ix d.
Item, payd to Constantyne þe carpenter for makyng of all þe new pewys and for closyng in off þe ffovntte, vj li xiij s vij d.
Item, payd for naylys, xiij d.
Item, payd to mastyr smartt for a ffothyr and a halfe of lede that þe chyrch owte hyme, v li xix s.
Item, payd to mastyr Remyngton for a pece of lyne of the sanctes bell, pris xij d.
Item, payd to Thomas mondes for naylys, xix d.
Item, payd to þe Raker for havyng away of þe Rubbis, xij d.
   Summa, xiiij li vj s x d.

Expensys in wax to þe waxe chaundelar.

Item, payd to Roger Mydylton for strekyng of vij^{xx} x lb of waxe, and for makyng of þe pascall, and dressyng of iiij torchys at corpus christi tyde, and for waste of ij tapers at an obbett, x s viij d.
Item, payd to water develyn for quarter of waxe þe xxij day of marche, pris þe lb vj d. Summa, xiiij s.
Item, payd to Iohn derham þe xxix day of marche for quarter waxe, pris xvj s.
   Summa, xxx s.
   Summa, xl s viij d.
   Summa totalis, xvj li vij s v d.[1]

[2] Reparacionys of the chyrch Renttes.

Item, for makyng of a wyndow in syr Thomas Assheborne ys chambyr þe xxiiij day of Ianyuere . .	iij s	vj d
Item, for a loode of sande		vj d
Item, for ij loodys of lome		viij d

[1] In corner iiij^{xx} li vij s ij d. [2] leaf 109, back.

Item, for ij c of Tyle		xvj d
Item, for ij loode of lyme	ij s	
Item, for a workeman and hys laborar for vj dayis labore	vj s	vj d
Item, for a mt of bryke	v s	
Item, payed to Roger plomer for xij lt sowdyr, and for newe lede, and for castyng of owre olde lede that was spentt on þe chyrch Renttes and parte at þe towre hyll	x s	
Item, payd to Syr Iamys sannys for hys lattes and hys glase wyndowys the he lefte behynde hym . .	iiij s	

Wacacion.

Item, we aske alowans of þe vacacion of Syr Thomas Russell ys chambyr, for a quartyr	xx d	
Item, we aske alowans of di. a quartyr Rentt, the whyche we shullde haue hade of Iohn pollay, bocher, for þe lytyll howse [in] estechepe . . .	iij s	iiij d
Summa, xxxviij s vj d.		

[1] The Costes and paymenttes of [2] Nasyng ys Chaunttre.

Item, payd to syr Iohn Tyllyslay, preste, to syng for the sayd Iohn Nasyng, for a hole yere at myhellmas laste passyd	vj li	xiij s	iiij d
Item, payd to The abbote of Walteham for a quite Rentt goyng owte of þe tenementt of Iohn Nasyng, for a hole yere at myhellmas laste passyd . . .		xxij s	

Reparacionys.

Item, payd to Rychard Wellys, mason, for v dayis labore for hymselfe and hys man in wylliam Olyuere ys howse, and barketrofte ys howse . .	v s	v d
Item, payd to þe sayd Rychard Welles for vj dayis, ffor hymselfe and hys laborar in þe same howse .	vj s	vj d
Item, payd for makyng of Robartt debenam, þe clarke, ys wyndowys and for mendyng of hys chymnay	iiij s	ob
Item, for naylys to Robard clarkes wyndowys . . .		vj d

[1] leaf 110.   [2] MS. 'of of.'

The Costys and paymenttes of Rose Wryttyll and Iohn Weston ys chaunttre.

Item, payd To syr Robartt hall, preste, to synge for the sayd Rose Wryttyll and Iohn weston for iij quarters of a yere at mydsomer last passyd . . v li

Summa, xiij li xj s ix d ob.

[1] The Costys and paymenttes of Rychard Gosselyn ys chaunttre.

Item, payd to Syr Iamys sonnys, preste, to synge for the sayd Rychard Gosselyn for iij quarters of a yere at mydsomer laste passyd . . . . . . v li

Item, payd to þe priores of Kylborne for a quite Rentt goyng owte of þe tenementtes in faystyr lane, for a hole yere at myhelmas last passyd . . . . vj d

Item, payd for the obbett of the sayd Rychard gosselyn, kepte þe fyrste day of decembyr laste passyd . iiij s ij d

Reparacionys.

Item, payd for Reparacions done in shayle ys howse, as hyt apperyth by a byll of þe same . . . . v s

Item, for iiij peces of tymbyr to kepe vpe the flore in Iohn ssmythes ys howse, habordassheare . . . ij s iiij d

Item, for ij men workyng a day. . . . . xvj d

Item, for mendyng of Tyrry ys stalle, for bordys, tymbyr and workemanshype . . . . iiij s iiij d

Item, payd in expences whane sartayne of þe paryshe yede to Awew þe smoke holys betwene tyrry and Inger . . . . vj d

Item, payd for a Rope for hys well. . . . . . . viij d

Item, we alowyd Tyrry Toward hys harthe and othyr Reparacionys that he dyde in þe howse. . . . x s

Item, payd for naylys . . . . vj d

vj li ix s vj d.

[2] The Costes and paymenttes of Iohn Causton ys Chaunttre.

Item, payd to syr Wylliam Boyis, preste, to synge for the sayd Iohn Causton, for a hole yere at myhelmas . . . . vj li xiij s iiij d

[1] leaf 110, back.   [2] leaf 111.

Item, payd to the bretherede of owre lady and sentt Thomas fowndyd with in þe parisshe cherche of sentt Mangnus, in london, for a hole yere quite Rentt goyng owte of Iohn ffysshes howse at estyr last passyd . . . . vj s

Item, payd to the mastyrs of þe bryge howse for a quite Rentt goyng owte of Iohn ffysshes howse, for a hole yere at myhelmas laste passyd . . . xiij s iiij d

Item, payd for þe obbett of þe sayd Iohn Causton, kepte þe ffyrste day of Auguste, to prestes, clarkes, pore pepyll, and to þe Ryngers . . . iiij s

Reparacionys.

Item, that we alowyd to ffysshes wyffe a quartyr Rentt for þe glase in hare halle and parler and chapell, and for þe selyng in þe parlar and for þe chapell in here chambyr. Summa . . . . xxx s

towre hyll.

Item, payd in Reparacionys of ij chymneys with othyr thynges done there as yt apperyth by a byll of þe same . . . . lj s ij d
Item, for a lode of thornys and for hegyng of þe gardyn iij s
Item, for vj quarters for a Newe stayre, pris . . . x d
Item, for xx fot of elmyn borde . . . . vj d
Item, for a man workyng ij dayis . . . . xvj d
Item, for vj ffoote di. of tymbyr for ij mantelles . . xiij d
Item, for a mane workyng a daye . . . . viij d
Summa, xij li v s ij d.

[1] The Vacacionys of Causton ys Renttes.

Item, we aske alowans of þe vacacion of þe grett garden at þe towre hyll, for a hole yere at myhelmas . . xiij s iiij d
Item, for the vacacion of mastyr smartes garden, for di. a yere at owre lady day in lentt . . . . . . ij s
Item, for the vacacion of proyne ys garden, for di. a yere at owre lady day in lentt . . . . . xvj d
Summa, xvj s viij d.

[1] leaf 111, back.

Costes spentt in the lawe ayenste þe priores of sentt Elynys for the chauntre of Ioħn Causton.

Item, spentt Goyinge to westemynstyr at dyuers tymys		viij d
Item, payd to mastyr ffenowys sargantt	iij s	iiij d
Item, payd for owre parte of iiij dysshes of mete þat was sentt to my lorde hussy and my lorde bryan	ij s	viij d
Item, payd to mastyr mordavntt and mastyr marowe the xxviij day of Ianyuere	vj s	viij d
Item, payd the same daye for bote hyre to Westmynstyr and othyr expences		viij d
Item, payd for our parte of a messe of mete sentt to[1] my lorde hussy and my lorde bryan on sentt Markes day	ij s	v d
Item, payd for brede and wyne at sentt Ioħn ys hede		ix d
Item, payd to mastyr marow	iij s	iiij d
Item, to hys clarke for settyng of þe bylles to my lorde hussyis		ij d
Item, payd for bote hyre and othyr expences in apryll		xvj d
Item, payd þe ffyrste day of maye to my lorde hussy and my lorde bryang for a Rewarde for owre parte		xx s
Item, payd to hys Clarke		iiij d
Item, payd to mastyr marowe the same day	iij s	iiij d
Item, spentt þe x day of Iuly in bote hyre and othyr expences at Westmynstyr whane we yede to speke with my lorde hussys and my lorde bryan .		vj d[2]

Summa, iij li ij s x d.

[3]The Costes and paymenttes of Ioħn Bedham ys chauntre.

Item, payd to syr Ioħn plomer, prest, to syng for the sayd Ioħn bedham, for an hole yere at myhelmas laste passyd	vj li xiij s iiij d
Item, payd for The obbett of þe sayd Ioħn bedham, kepte þe xvj day of maye last passed, to prestes and clarkys[4] and pore pepyll and to þe chyrch wardenys	xiij s iiij d

---

[1] MS. 'to to.'   [2] '1 li 6 s 2 d' in margin.
[3] leaf 112.   [4] MS. 'clarlys.'

Item, payd to Gabryell de vrs toward hys Reparacion of the grete plase in sentt buttolles lane, for a hole yere at myhelmas laste passyd . . . . . liij s iiij d

Item, payd to iij pore men of thys parysshe, that ys to wete, Wylliam parys, Raynolde bull and Iohn toplady, euery sonday in þe yere, xij d. Summa lij s

Item, payd to Iohn derham, grocer, for x galonys of oyle spentt in the lampe within thys yere of owre accountte, pris þe galon, x d. Summa . . . . viij s iiij d

Summa, xiij li iiij d.

[1]The Costes and paymenttes of Mastyr Wylliam cambryge ys chauntre.

Item, payd to syr Thomas Assheborne, preste, to synge for[2] the sayde mastyr Wylliam Cambryge, for an hole yere at Myhelmas last passyd . . . vj li xiij s iiij d

Item, payd for The obbett of þe sayd mastyr Wylliam Cambryge, kepte þe xix day of auguste, to prestes and Clarkys and for Ryngynge . . . . . . iiij s viiij d

Item, payd for brede, ale, wyne and chese to the pore pepyll and to all þe parysshonys . . . . . viij s viij d

Item, payd to þe mayre and to þe ij sheryves and þe swerde berar at þe same obett . . . . xv s

Summa, xxviij s iiij d.

Reparacion.

Item, payd ffor Reparacion in Irithes howse and in þe othyr tenantryis done at dyuers tymys . . . iij s iij d

Vacacion.

Item, for the vacacione of the howse that Wylliam Raynysford dwellyd in, for j quartyr . . . . vj s viij d

Summa, viij li xj s vij d.

[3]Potacionys.

Item, we aske alowans of potacion mony that we have gevyn vnto þe tenanttes att the Ressevyng of owre mony for our Renttes . . . . v s

Item, for makyng vpe of thys owre accountt . . . vj s viij d

Summa, xj s viij d.

[1] leaf 112, back. [2] MS. 'of.' [3] leaf 113.

S*um*ma of all the dysscharge payd w*ith*in thys yere of owre accounte ys iiij ix̅ ƚi xviij s vij d ob̅.

Reste due to the Chyrc̅h in owre hondys iiij ƚi v s viij d ob̅.

Whereof ther ys owyng thys yere in detters handys Thes p*ar*cellys ffolowyng:—

In p*r*imys, Io*h*n Nele	vij s	iiij d
Io*h*n westehowse	iiij s	
Thomas Bynk*es*		xx d
Io*h*n harrys	iij s	iiij d
Wyll*ia*m halle, waterman	ij s	vj d
harry pebyll, marener	ix s	
Myhell Io*h*nson, wever	iiij s	
Wyll*ia*m haryson ys wyff, gardener	iij s	
Mothyr boyis	ij s	

Summa, xxxvj s x d.

So ther Restyt̅h in mony of thys accountte in owre hondys xlviij s x d ob̅. Wherof is allowed for s*yr* Thomas Ashbo*ur*nes chamber vj s viij d. And so he owith clearly vpon this yeres ende xlij s.

[1] + Ih*esus*.

Paide by me, Will*ia*m overeye, in the presence of Mr Remyngton, Aldreman, & Mr Will*ia*m Atclyffe, Io*h*n dooklyng, Io*h*n Milton, Ric*har*d cloce & Io*h*n deraham. S*um*ma, xlij s ij d ob̅: which was d*elyvere*d to Io*h*n mascalde, w*ith* ij s vj d of the rest of Robert howtyng*es* accoumpte, besyde all the dett*es* that er to be Resse*yuid*.

[2] Robert owty*ng*   } A° m̅ƚ cccc iiij xiiij
Wyll*ia*m overey

[A.D. 1494–5.]

[3] The Counte of Will*ia*m Overey and Io*h*n Mascall
A° m̅ƚ cccc iiij xv*th*

[4] This his the Counte of Io*h*n Mascall from the ffest of Mighelmas A° 1494 to Mighelmas A° 1495.

olde dettes.

Robe*r*t Craples, Tailour	xxij s
Io*h*n hontyngfeld	vj s

---

[1] leaf 113, back, but the word 'Ihesus' is scratched out by the same hand.
[2] leaf 114, back. [3] leaf 115. [4] leaf 115, back.

Churchwardens' Accounts, A.D. 1494–5.

Thomas Ratchefourd	iiij s	
William haryson, Gardener, xj s iiij d. Receued by maschaƚƚ	ij s	
Ioħn Smyth, aburdassher	xv s	
Ioħn Mowse, Clerke, xiij s iiij d. Receued by maschaƚ	iij s	iiij d
+ Thomas Mowse, Capper, iiij s. Receued per maschaƚƚ		
+ Richard Chelmysho, Ioynour	xx s	
william wilkynson		xv d
Watkyn Gale	ij s	
The Tailour next	iiij s	
Nicholas welles		xvj d
+ Nicholas Thorneley iij s. per maschaƚ		
+ Ioħn polyver xiij s iiij d. per maschaƚ		
Ioħn westehous	xiiij s	viij d
William whetley	iiij s	
Ioħn hogges wife	iiij s	vj d
Annes Benett		xvj d
Ioħn harres	vij s	
William halle vij s vj d. Receued per maschaƚ . .	ij s	vj d
Thomas Byngkes	iij s	iiij d
Ioħn Nele	xij s	iiij d
[1] Nicolas Smythson	xv s	
Giles Gerold, Gardener	iiij s	
harry pebiƚƚ, Maryner	xj s	
deryk Ioħnson, wever	vj s	
Moder Boyse	iiij s	
+ Thomas hont for I. Stone for his wife	x s +	

Summa totalis, xj ƚi v s vij d.

Wherof Resseyued of Ioħn polyver	xiij s	iiij d
of Ioħn harres		xx d
of William haryson, Gardener	ij s	
of Nicolas Thorneley	ij s paid xij d	
of Ioħn Mowse, Clerke	iij s	iiij d
of Th. hont, by Wiƚƚ overey	x s	
of William halle, by William Overey	ij s	vj d

Summa, by maschaƚƚ, xxij s iiij d.
Summa, xxxiiij s x d. of old mows iiij s
Summa, 38 s x d.

[1] leaf 116.

[1]The Rentes of the Chauntrey of Iohn Nasyng.

ffirst, Resseyued of William Pares, Joynour, for o yere	xiiij s	viij d
of Iohn harres, for o yere	vj s	viij d
of William halle, waterman, for o yere	x s	
of Richard Close, for o yere	xl s	
of Robert Barcrofte, for o yere	xiij s	iiij d
of Iohn Neell, for o yere	viij s	
of Iohn westehous, for o yere	viij s	
of William hemmes, for o yere	x s	
of William Olyver, for o yere . . . . . . iij li	iij s	iiij d
of Thomas Byngkes, for o yere	vj s	viij d

Summa totalis, ix li viij d.

Payementes of The same Rent.

Item, paide to Sir Iohn Telsey, for o yere . .	vj li	xiij s	iiij d
Item, paide to the abbot of Waltham for j quytrent of the same tenement, for o yere		xxij s	

Reparacions of william olyver hous.

Item, for Breke, iij s vj d.
Item, for j lode Sande, vj d.
Item, for ij lode & ij Sakes lyme, ij s ij d.
Item, for mason and his labourer, eche of them ij dayes, ij s ij d.
Item, for mendyng of the Colehous ouer the Sedche, xij d.

Summa, ix s iiij d.
Summa, paide viij li iiij s viij d.
Rest of this Chauntre, xvj s.[2]

[3]The Rentes of the chauntrey of Iohn Cawston.

ffirst Resseyued of hugh Browne, grocer, for o yere	vj li
of Edward pykman, Tourner, for o yere	xl s
of Robert dephenham, Clerk, ffor o yere	xx s
of Richard Chelmysho, Ioynour, for o yere . . .	xx s
of Iohn wason, mason, for o yere	xx s
of harry Kelongh, Tailour, for o yere	iiij li xiij s iiij d
of william harford, for o yere	viij s
of peter Barboure, for o yere	viij s
of Robert Kenby, for o yere	viij s

[1] leaf 116, back. [2] '16 s' at foot of page. [3] leaf 117.

of Will*am* Arondell, gardener, for o yere . . . . xij s
of M*aister* Benedek, for his garden, for o yere . . . iiij s
of I. ffuller, at Crychirche, for j gardey*n*, for o yere . iiij s
of Robert Thomson, for j gardey*n*, for o yere . . . iiij s
of Will*am* harryson wife, for j gardeyn, for o yere . iij s
    Su*m*ma to*talis*, xviij li iiij s iiij d.

Payeme*n*t*s* of the same tene*ment*.

Ite*m*, paide to Sir Will*am* Boyse, for o yere . . vj li xiij s iiij d
Ite*m*, paide to the pryour of Crystechirch for j quyte-
 rent at Towre hille . . . . v s
Ite*m*, paide to the m*aister* of the Breggehous for
 j quyterent of hugh Browne hous . . . . . xiij s iiij d
Ite*m*, paide to the m*aister* of owre lady Bretheod of
 sc*n*t magno*us* for hugh Browne hous . . . . vj s
Ite*m*, paide for j obet for Ioh̄n Cawston . . . . . iiij s x d
Ite*m*, paide for makyng of indenture for hugh Browne
 ho*us*. . . . . xij d
Ite*m*, paide to hugh Browne for Repa*r*acions done by
 hym in dyue*r*se plases of his hous . . . . . xxx s
Ite*m*, for di. yere vacacio*n* of william Arondell
 gardeyn. . . . . vj s
[1] Ite*m*, I aske for o q*uar*ter vacacion of Robe*r*t depen-
 ha*m* hous for Cryst*m*as q*u*arter . . . . . . v s
Ite*m*, for iij q*u*arter of the Rent bated by the yere,
 vj s viij d. Su*m*ma. . . . . v s

Repa*r*acions.

Ite*m*, paide for makyng of the entre of the Northeside to Crystovere
 kechyn, for xvij fote Ieist*es* of ij Ing*es* di., ij s x d.
Item, xiij gret plang*es*, vj s vj d.
Item, cxij fote burde to crosse the ffflower, iij s.
Item, ij c spayneshe naile, x d.
Item, iij c vj d naile, xv d.
Item, for the pentese, ij q*uar*ter, iiij d.
Item, di. c xxij fote q*uar*ter bourde, ij s j d.
Item, iij yerd*es* evesbourde, iij d.
Item, j man iij day*es*, ij s.
Item, for nales to Robert Clerk hous, ij d.
    Su*m*ma, xix s iij d.

[1] leaf 117, back.

Rep*a*racions of harry kelough hous.

It*em*, paide to Symond, dawber, for vij dayes, iiij s viij d.
It*em*, for his labourer vij dayes, ij s xj d.
It*em*, for v lode lome, xx d.
It*em*, for iij c hartlathe, xviij d.
It*em*, for I Giles and his man ij dayes, ij s ij d.
It*em*, ij lode lyme, ij s.
It*em*, for c di. tile, ix d.
It*em*, for spryng & Rofenale, ix d.
It*em*, for j plang for the kechyn & Nailes, vij d.
    Su*mm*a, xvij s.
   Su*mm*a paide, xij li v s.
   Rest of this Chaunterey, v li xix s iiij d.
   Mascall owyth ix d.

[1] The Rent of the Chaunterey of Ric*har*d Gosselyn.

ffirst, R*esseyued of* Ric*hard* Tery, Goldsmythe, for o
 yere . . . . xlvj s viij
of Willi*am* Sayles, Goldsmyth, for o yere . . . . xl s
of Iohn Smyth, Aburdassher, for o yere . . . . . xx s
of Moder Browne, for o yere . . . . x s
of Davy Pawnter, goldsmyth, for o yere . . . . xiij s iiij d
of Iohn Mowse, Capper, for o yere . . . . xxvj s viij d
of Thomas Mowse, Capper, for o yere . . . . . xvj s
  Su*mm*a tot*alis*, viij li xij s viij d.

Payement*es* of the same tene*ment*.

[2] Item, paide to Sir Iohn Matwarde and his felow, for
 o yere . . . . v li xj s iiij d
Item, paid for the Morowmasse kepyng, for o yere. . xix s [2]
Item, paid for j obet for Ric*har*d Gosselyn, the first of
 decembyr . . . . iij s xj d
Item, paide to the pryoresse of kelbourne for j quyterent in ffast*er* lane, for o yere . . . . vj d
Item, for vacacions of davy pantour hous for Crystemas q*u*arter and di. oure lady q*u*arter. Summa v s

---

[1] leaf 118.   [2] 'nota' in margin.

MED. REC.   P

Reparacions.

Item, payede for makyng of j pentese in William Sailes hous		xv d
Item, for ffermyng of j Sedche in Tery hous, vj ton .	xv s	viij d
Item, paide to Symond & his labourer for v dayes . .	v s	v d
Item, ij lode lome & j lode Sand		xiiij d
Item, iij c Saplath		xij d
Item, m ł di. spryng		ix d
Item, j lode lyme, pris xij d. Summa	ij s	ix d
Item, for ij c iiij fote bourde and ij quarter	v s	j d
Item, for j man ij dayes		xvj d
Item, iij c di. v peny Naile		xiiij d
Item, for j Rope for the welle, viij ℔		viij d
Item, paide more for Reparacions of Mowse howse tilyng. Summa	iij s	viij d
Summa paide, viij ƚi xvij s xj d.		
Rest to me, v s iij d.[1]		

[2] The Rentes of William Cambrigge Chaunterey.

ffirst, Resseyued of Robert Cryk, for o yere	vj ƚi	
of Ales Berlynges, for o yere	liij s	iiij d
of Markeret dowsyng, for o yere	xxvj s	viij d
Summa totalis, x ƚi.		

Payementes of the same.

Item, paide to Sir Thomas Asshebourne, for o yere	vj ƚi xiij s	iiij d
Item, paide to hym for his Chamber	vj s	viij d
Item, paide to the abbot of Barmesey for j quyterent of the seide Tenement, for o yere	vj s	
Item, paide for j obbet for Maister Cambrig, the xviij day of August, to the preestes and Clarkes . . .	iiij s	
Item, paide to the Mayer, Maister Chawrey, and to Nicholas Allbyn and warner, Shreves, and the Swer[d]berer. Summa	xv s	
Item, for brede, ale, wyne, peres and Chese	x s	ix d
Item, for vacacions of Mighelmas quarter of Margaret dowsyng	vj s	viij d

[1] '21 d' at foot.   [2] leaf 118, back.

Reparacions.

Ite*m*, paide for mendyng of wendows in the Alle of Ales Berlyng hous.
Ite*m*, j lo[n ?]g q*uarter*, iij d.
Ite*m*, xiij fote of q*uarter* Bourde & ij ledges di., viij d.
Ite*m*, for iij dayes Carpen*ter*, ij s.
        Su*m*ma, ij s xj d.
        Su*m*ma paide, ix li v s iiij d.
Rest of this C[h]aunterey, xiiij s viij d.

[1] Rent*es of* Rose wretell Chaunterey.

Resseyued of Iohn halhed, Grocer, for o yere. Su*m*ma vj li xiij s iiij d

Payement*es* of the same.

Ite*m*, paide to Sir Iohn Kelby, for o yere. Su*m*ma vj li xiij s iiij d
    Rest no thyng.
              Rest no thyng.

Rent*es* of Iohn Bedha*ms* Chauntery.

Resseyued of Gaberell vrse, for o yere. Su*m*ma . xiij li vj s viij d

Payement*es* of the same.

Ite*m*, paide to Sir Iohn Plomer, for o yere. Su*m*ma vj li xiij s iiij d
Ite*m*, paide for j obbet the xvj day of May, to preest*es* and Clerk*es* & pore pepell, and to the Chirch wardens . . . . xiij s iiij d
Ite*m*, paide to Reynold Bolle, Willi*am* pares, Iohn Topelady, for o yere, eu*er*y sonday xij d. Su*m*ma lij s
Ite*m*, paide to Gaberell for j lowans of Rep*a*racions . liij s iiij d
Ite*m*, paide for x galons oyle for the lampe, at x d. Su*m*ma . . . . viij s iiij d
      Su*m*ma tot*alis* paide, xiij li iiij d.
Rest of this Chaunterey, vj s iiij d.

[2] Clerke wag*es* Resseyued this yere.

ffirst Resseyued by o yere. Su*m*ma . . . . . . v li x s v d

              Beme light.

Resseyued by o yere. Su*m*ma . . . . xviij s ij d
Resseyued for the pasquall at Est*er*. Su*m*ma . . . xj s

---

[1] leaf 119.   [2] leaf 119, back.

Caswaltes.

ffirst, Resseyued of maister horne		vj d
of Iohn Doklyng, for j gravestone	vj s	viij d
of Iohn hewes, for pavyng of the Chirche		iiij d
of Iohn Condale, for pavyng of his wife grave . . .		xij d
of Annes Kelow, for j grave Stone	xx s	
of Iohn Smart, for his Beryng	xxiij s	iiij d
of William Mawnfeld, for his Beryng	ij s	
of Thomas Colyns, for his Child	ij s	
of Th. Colens, that he ffownde in the chirch . . .		ij d
of Iohn mascall, for my ffader	ij s	
of harry Mershe, for the gret Belle for his wife . . .	iij s	iiij d
of Iohn Crescrofte, for his Beryng	ij s	

3^{li} 3^s 4^d

Summa totalis, Resseyued of the iij parsels, x li ij s xj d

[1] Payementes of the Same.

Item, payde to Robert depenham, Clerk, for o yere. Summa . . . . iiij li	xiij s	iiij d
Item, paide to William hemes for iij quarter wages by his hous	vij s	vj d
Item, paide to hym for Crystemas quarter	iij s	iiij d
Item, paide to Roger Medelton for the Pasquall . .	ij s	vj d
Item, paide for iiij Torches at Corpus Crysty dressyng		xvj d
Item, paide for strekyng of vij vj lb iij quarter wex at ob the lb. Summa	vj s	j d
Item, paide for xliij lb new wex at vj d ob. Summa .	xxiij s	iij d ob
Item, bought iij olde Torches weyng xl lb	xiij s	iiij d

Summa, paide vij li x s viij d ob.

Rest lij s ij d ob.

[2] The Chirche Rentes Resseyued.

ffirst, Resseyued of Sir Iohn Plomer, for o yere . . .	xvj s	
of Sir Iohn watwoode, for o yere	vj s	viij d
of Sir William Boyse, for o yere	v s	
of Sir Iohn Kelby, for o yere	vj s	viij d
of Sir Iohn Telsey, for o yere	xij s	
of Sir Thomas Asshebourne, for o yere	x s	
of Sir Thomas Russell, for o yere	vj s	viij d

[1] leaf 120.   [2] leaf 120, back.

Churchwardens' Accounts, A.D. 1494–5.

[1]*of* harry Mershe for j howse at Tower hille, for o yere . . xx s
of Willi*a*m halle, waterman, for o yere . . . . . xxxiij s iiij d
of Thomas Colens, for o yere . . . . . . v li
of Thomas hont, for o yere . . . . iij li vj s viij d
of Io*h*n p*a*rtriche, Bocher, for o yere . . . . . xxvj s viij d
of The wardens of Sent Bothols, for o yere . . . . ij s vj d
of Robert hodyh*a*m, Mercer, for o yere . . . . . iij s iiij d
    Su*m*ma to*talis* Resse*yued* xv li xv s vj d.

Payementes *of* the Same.
Vacasyons.

Item, for Sir Thomas Russell Chamber, for iij q*uarter*   v s
of Sir Io*h*n watwood, for di. q*uarter* . . . . . .   x d
    Su*m*ma, v s x d.

[2]Obbettes.

ij yere. Item, paide for obbet for sir Io*h*n Morterh*a*m
   the xxiij day of dec. by sir Io*h*n Sowetheworth . vj s viij d
Item, for j obbet for Io*h*n weston the xix day of
   Aprell . . . . iij s vj d
the last yere. Item, for j obbet for sir Io*h*n Bradmere
   the xxiij day of Nou. and this his the last yere . iij s v d
    Su*m*ma, xiij s vij d.

Quyterent.

Item, paide to the pryour of Cryschirche . . . . . iij s
Item, paide to the wardens of Sent Georges in
   bothol lane for Thomas Colens hous. Su*m*ma . xx s
Item, paide to the abbot of Waltham for Iohn Weston xxxviij s
Item, paide to Master Io*h*n for Bede Rolle . . . ij s
Item, paide to Sir Io*h*n Plomer for mony owyng hym xx s
    Su*m*ma, iiij li iij s.

Rep*a*racions.

Item, paide to Sir Io*h*n Telsey for his Chamb*er* . . iij s iiij d
Item, paide to Thomas Colens hans for castyng of the
   leede in the gotter . . . . iiij s iiij d
Item, for Tiler and his man j day di., eche of them .   xvj d
Item, for j Carpent*er* ij dayes, xvj d. Item, for q*uarter*
   bourde, eves bourdes and nailes, iij s v d. Su*m*ma iiij s ix d

---

[1] '+Nota tower hyll' in margin.   [2] leaf 121.

Item, for Tile pynnes and Tile and lathe and Naile	ij s	iij d
Item, for makyng of and indenture of Iohn partriche hous		viij d

Summa, xvj s viij d.

¹Payementes for the Chirche.

ffirst, for holme & Ive at Crystmas, and wyne		vij d
Item, for Caryage of serteyn Tonnes of baleste yevan by Maister alderman, & for Baskettes. Summa		vij d
Item, for wyne at Candelmas to the preestes		vj d
Item, to the Raker for j yere		viij d
Item, for Caryage of Robesshe from the parsenache		iij d
Item, for pavyng of the chirche by xvj dayes di. at viij d. Summa		xj s
Item, to j laborar xix dayes at v d. summa	vij s	xj d
Item, to Iohn Mason for ij dayes & his labourer ij dayes, ij s ij d; and for pavyng of the entre & j lode gravell, xxj d. summa	iij s	xj d
Item, for j bason & iiij peyer Crewettes for the Awters	iij s	vj d
Item, to Richard Close for j bokskynne	iij s	iiij d
Item, to the plomer for iij c di. lb leed for the Northe dorre	xviij s	vj d
Item, for ix lode lyme & v Sakkes	ix s	
Item, for xj c di. pavyngtile	xv s	
Item, for vj hopes for the Chirche barels		iiij d
Item, for caryage of Robbeshe at the Chirche dorre		vj d
Item, for ij gret leders for the clapers & makyng of the wele	v s	ij d
Item, for j Rope for the ffirst belle		vj d
Item, for palme and wyne on palmesonday		xij d ob
Item, for j quarter Coles at Ester, v d	Summa ix d ob	
Item, for the sepulker nailes ob		
Item, for watchyng of the Sepulker, iiij d		
Item, for storyng of the bemelight & canstikes	ij s	j d
Item, for vecitasion of the Bisshop at Sent Magnous		iiij d
Item, for mendyng of j pew, to pares		ij d
Item, for Rose garlandes, ij s	viij d	iij d
Item, for ale, wyne, xix d		
Item, to Boweyer and ffranses in Sent barneby day, iiij s viij d		

¹ leaf 121, back.

Churchwardens' Accounts, A.D. 1494–5.

[1]Item, to Robert Clerke for mendyng of vessementes . ij s viij d
    Summa, iiij li xvj s vij d.

[2]Item, for Birche at Medsomer . . . . iiij d
Item, for makyng of j ole in the chirche for voyde water ij d
Item, for j Rope, to doklyng . . . . xiij d
Item, for ix elles holond, and makyng of Maister Iohn serplese . . . . viij s ix d
Item, to William Iele for makyng of j Tabull ouer Maister plomer . . . . xiiij d
Item, for hokes of Iren for the Crosse ouer Maister Ryvell Tome[3] . . . . iiij d
Item, for ij pikes for Iudas crosse ij d, & ij hokes & stapuls for the Chirche dorre, ij d. Summa . . iiij d
Item, for j key for the Iuell Chest . . . . . . iij d
Item, for j key & mendyng of the lok next the clerk hous . . . . iiij d
Item, for nailyng & storyng of the beme, & for j bourde onder hit on Maister Smart his Tome. Summa . xiij d
Item, for Makyng of the Spere at Sent Thomas Awter ij d
Item, for Cottyng of the iiij chestes for the preestes . ij s v d ob
Item, for j water potte . . . . j d
Item, for ij alywater sprynges . . . . ij d
Item, for iiij dossyn Candell . . . . iiij s
Item, to Crystover Kechyn for makyng of the pewes for the pore pepull, and j pew at the Northe dorre, and ij benches, and the[4] pewes in Sent steven Chapell with diuerse thyng moe. Summa li s viij d
Item, for nailes for the Chirch, to Th Mondes . . . iij s x d
Item, paide to heklyng for pewes in sent stevyn Chapell . . . . iiij li vj s viij d
Item, for Nailes and hynchis for the pewes . . . . ij s ix d
Item, for vnderpynnyng of the pewes . . . . . . iiij d
    Summa, viij li v s xj d ob.

[5]Item, we aske alowans of potacions mony that the tennauns hath of vs at the Resseyuyng of Rent . v s
Item, for makyng of oure acounte . . . . . . vj s viij d
    Summa, xj s viij d.

    Summa totalis paide of this vij parcels, summa xix li xiij s iij d ob.

    Rest to me iij li xvij s ix d ob of this parcell.

---

[1] 'nota' in margin.   [2] leaf 122.   [3] Mr. Revell's tomb.
[4] MS. 'the the.'   [5] leaf 122, back.

Theise be the parcels of tennantes that I haue Resseyued byfore wreten.

ffirst, Resseyued of the Rentes of Iohn Nasyng. Summa	ix li	viij d
Of the Rentes of Iohn Cawston. Summa . .	xviij li	iiij s iiij d
Of the Rentes of Richard Gosselyn. Summa .	viij li	xij s viij d
Of the Rentes of William Cambrigge. Summa	x li	
Of the Rentes of Rose wretell. Summa . .	vj li	xiij s iiij d
Of the Rentes of Iohn Bedham. Summa . .	xiij li	vj s viij d
Of the Clarkes wages, Bemelight, pasquall & Caswaltes. Summa	x li	ij s xj d
Of the Chirche Rentes. Summa	xv li	xv s vj d

Summa, iiij^{xx} xj li xvj s j d.

Item, Resseyued of olde dette before wreten.
Summa, xxij s iiij d.

Summa totalis Resseyued this yere,
iiij^{xx} xij li xviij s v d.

[1] Theise be payementes of the saide acounte before wrenten.

ffirst, paide for the[1] Chauntre of Iohn Nasyng	viij li	iiij s	viij d
Item, for Iohn Cawston Chauntre	xij li	v s	ix d
Item, for Richard Gosselen Chauntre . . .	viij li	xvij s	xj d
Item, for William Cambrig Chauntre. . .	ix li	v s	iiij d
Item, for Rose wretell Chauntre	vj li	xiij s	iiij d
Item, for Iohn Bedham Chauntre	xiij li		iiij d
Item, for the Clarke wagis with other parcels more. Summa	vij li	x s	viij d ob
Item, for the Chirche of diuerse parcels asse hit showeth before	xix li	xiij s	iij d ob

Summa totalis paide in this yere, iiij^{xx}v li xj s iiij d.
Rest dew to the Chirche in owre handes, vij li vij s j d.
Item, xxviij s viij d ob.
Summa totalis, viij li xv s ix d ob.
Item, ther Remaynneth in Mr Remyngton handes, xlviij s viij d.

[2] Wylliam overey } A° m^t cccc iiij^{xx} xv.
Iohn Maschall

---

[1] leaf 123.   [2] leaf 124, back.

VI.

[Churchwardens' Accounts and Memoranda.

The preceding pages supply the text of MS. A. ($\frac{1239}{1}$) in full till the year 1495. After that year the system of accounts as given in the MS. becomes very largely a repetition of items already set down. To avoid such a continual reiteration in this edition, the plan adopted from this date, 1495, has been to supply, as before, the complete frame of the yearly records, but to print only such items of the accounts and other matter as are of distinct value. In other words, the aim has been to exclude such matter as would bury the gist of the history beneath a mass of text consisting almost wholly of matter printed continually in the earlier pages. Certain sections, however, as, for instance, the income of the church from casual sources, have been printed in full at all times.

The omission of any matter is shown by the presence of asterisks * * * , or its presence in the MS. is stated between square brackets.]

[A.D. 1495–6.]

[1] Iohn Maschall ⎫
    Iohn Russell ⎭ A° m^t cccc iiij^{xx} xvj°.

[2] Here begynneth the Accounte of Iohn Russell, beyng chirchwardeyn with Iohn Maschall fro the fest of Myʒelmasse A° m^t cccc° lxxxxv, vnto Mychelmasse A 1496 et A° regis xj°.

[The Accounts of the Chantries.]

[3] Clerkes wages & Bemeliʒth þis yer.

ffrist, Receued be o hole yere of gaderyng of quarterage
    be quarter of þis yer. Summa . . . . . . v li ix s

---

[1] leaf 125.   [2] leaf 125, back.   [3] leaf 128, back.

Item, Receuyd of the Bemely3th this yere, byside them
that wold not pay syn the ly3th was take down,
and besyde them þat be owyng of this yer . . xviij s
  Summa, vj li vij s.

Casualtes this yer.

Item, Receued of Master horn the last day of Ianuar,
for the wast of ij tapers that brend at sir Iohn
Colyns obbite. Summa . . . .   vj d
Item, Receued the Secund day of may for Beryng of
William Bedelles child in the pardon chyrchyerd.
Summa . . . .   ij s
Item, Receued at ester for the paschall money. Summa xj s x d
Item, Receued the ffrist day of September for the
beryng of Robard Wileis dou3ters child in the
pardon chirchyerd, and for wast of iiij torches
that brend at masse, iiij d þe pec. summa . . iij s iiij d
Item, Receued the xxij day of decembyr of the good-
wiff proun for brekyng of the ground within þe
chirch for her hosbondes pitte . . . . xiij s iiij d
  Summa, xxxj s.
  Summa totalis, vij li xviij s.

[1] Paymentes of same.

ffrist, payd to Robard depbenham, pariche clerk, for o
yeris wagis ful past at Mi3elmasse last was.
Summa . . . . iiij li xiij s iiij d
Item, payd to William helmes for ij quarteres wages
after x s be yer. Summa . . . . v s
Item, payd to Richard abell for ij quarteres wages be
his hows rent, wiche is viij s be yer, that is, ij s
for a quarter. Summa . . . . iiij s
  Summa, v li ij s iiij d.

[Wax Reckoning.

Church Rents.

Reparations.

Vacations.

Obits.

[1] leaf 129.

Quitrents.
Payments for the Church.]

* * * * *

[1]Item, payd for a claspe of yryn & settyng on of a bolt on the neþere ende of the gret wiket vnder the parsonage, and for mendyng of the lokke of the lytiłł wyket	vj d
Item, payd to the rakar for havyng away of rychis and[2] rubycħ; of remevyng of the pewes when the chyrcħ was broke down iiij d, and Richard abełł & elmes for beryng owt, ij d	vj d
Item, payd for a prus bast that the laborer fette of me, pris	v d

* * * * *

Item, payd to thomas austeyns wiff for waschyng of ałł the towelles, auter clothis & schetes of þe chyircħe		xj d
Item, payd for new slevyng of vj awbis & for parelyng of iij		xv d
Item, payd for vj ellys lokerams to the slevys of þe avbis, at v d ełł	ij s	vj d
Item, payd for makyng of a Rochet of an old avbe for Richard abełł		ij d
Item, payd to the laborer of þe masons for makyng of a pentyse ouer the rodeloft, & for iij d nayle therto		iiij d
Item, payd for wyne to the quere on owre lady day .		iiij d
Item, payd for ij paxis bowȝt of Ioħn lumbard for the auters		iiij d

* * * * *

[3]Item, payd to the carpynter for makyng & dressyng vp of the mennys pewys in seynt Katerys chapełł & in the body of the chyrcħ, and closyng of the litil chyr[ch]yerd by the abbotes kechen, & settyng vp of the parclos of the qwere, & makyng of a base vnder tabernałe, for viij days worke & di. at vij d	v s	
Item, payd for v d nayle, iiij d nayle & iij d to same worke	iij s	iiij d
Item, payd to bułł the mason & his felow & his		

---

[1] leaf 130, back. [2] MS. 'and and.' [3] leaf 131.

laborer j day in makyng of the base of breke vnder the tabernale	xix d

* * * * *

Item, payd to Symon dawber for whittyng of the chyrch, v days	iij s

* * * * *

Item, payd to ij dawberes for makyng of the skaffold afore þe tabernacle xij d, & for x d nayle & vj d nayle therto. d. Summa	xiiij d
Item, payd to the kervar that sett vp the ymage & the worke of the tabernacle.	v s j d
Item, payd for spryg braket, ij d nayle, iij d nayle & v d nayle to same.	v d
Item, payd for ij clampys of yryn, j tynnyd, þat hold the tabernale	vj d
Item, payd for xij ti led to yete the clampys in the wall	vj d

* * * * *

[1] Item, payd for di. c bundells reed to close þe wyndows above, & þe fecchyng	viij d
Item, payd for roddes & lathis to bynd þe red j d, and for makyng, viij d. Summa	ix d
Item, payd for skowryng of the gret candilstykkes ageyn cristmasse	viij d
Item, payd to the raker, his iij quarter wages, vj d, & for havyng awey of rotyn mattes and other Robbych ageyn cristmasse	viij d
Item, payd to thomas Mundys, chyrchwarden of seynt botolfes, wyche he stoppyth in his hondes in party payment that is owyng hym for nayll, the quitrent that belongyth to owre chyrch. Summa	ij s vj d

* * * * *

Item, payd to the smyth for makyng schortter of the corteyn rodd above the tabernacle iiij d, and for newe lyne to draw þe cloþe.	vj d

* * * * *

[The two Allowances for Potation Money and Writing the Accounts. The Rehearsal and List of Debts.]

[1] leaf 131, back.

[A.D. 1496–7.

Iohn Russell } Wardens.]
Thomas Colyns

* * * *

[The Accounts of the Chantries.]
¹ ✛ Ihesus.

Clarkes wagys and biemlyʒgthe.

ffurst, receuud for the hoole yere, qwarterly gaderyd .
           Summa v ɫ vj s iiij d

Item, Receuud for the biemliʒht this yere bysydes þem þat wold nott paye or the lyʒht ware sett vpe and them þat be owyng . . . . Summa xviij s iiij d

    Summa, vj ɫ iiij s viij d.

This bene the yefftes and byqwestes receiuid by me in this yere.

ffirst, of mastir William Wylde, parson of thys parishe, receiuid on Cristmas Evyn to the chirche warkes & odir benefyttes . . . . . Summa iij ɫ

Item, of mastres petyt by the handes of mastir Duklyng
            Summa iij s iiij d

Item, of Bedylles wyff at ij tymes for ij of hur geestes .
            Summa viij d

Item, of William Grays bequest by the handes of mastir parson . . . . Summa xl s

Item, of Iohn Bampton for the byquest of his Sustir .
            Summa x s

Item, of Thomas Rivelles byquest by the handes of his executurs . . . . Summa liij s iiij d

Item, of Mathewe huntes wyffes byquest by hur executors . . . . Summa xl s

Item, of Sir Iohn plommer of gaderyng on hokmondaye . . . . Summa xxvij s viij d

Item, Receuud the laste yere by the wymen xx s, & by the men vj s viij d . . . . Summa xxvj s viij d

Item, of Iohn Maschall for a rest of mony left in his handes when he was chirchwardeygne . Summa xv s viij d

    Summa, xiij ɫ xvij s iiij d.

¹ leaf 139.

¹ Casweltes in thys yere.

ffirst, Receuud of Sir Iohn horne for the waste of ij tapers the laste daye of Ianiuer, that brennyd at Sir Iohn Colyns Obytt. Summa		vj d
Item, of Margett proyne, by the handes of mastir Iohn, for the grett bell at hyr husbondes knyell, in mony. Summa	iij s	iiij d
Item, receuud for roton tymbyr & lathe in the howse in Estchepe. Summa		ij d
Item, receuud of M^r pagename for his mannes burying in þe pardon chirchyard	ij s	
Item, of M^r ffabyan, alderman, for m^l tyle. Summa	v s	
Item, Receuud for the pytt & the knyll of William Overay. Summa	xvj s	viij d
Item, Receuud of Iohn Newton for xvij c tyll & a quarter of roffe tyle	ix s	ix d
Item, Receuud of Mr Duklyng, of Merget proyne, & of the goodwyff overaye for the leying of iij gravestones. Summa	ij s	viij d
Item, of Mr Iohn, of the yeft of a Ieyntilwomanne. Summa		ij d
Item, Receuud of Mr Atklyff for the waste of iiij toorches at the Crystenyng of his chylde. Summa		viij d
Item, Receuud for the pytt & the knyll of thomas Ryvell	xvj s	viij d
Item, Receuud for the pytt & the knyell of Mathew huntes wyff	xvj s	viij d
Item, Receuud of Iohn Maskall for j loode of oolde lome. Summa		v d
Item, Receuud of Andrew Evyngare for the burying of his chyld in the pardon chirchard. Summa	ij s	
Item, Receuud of Iohn Maskall for the burying of his chyld in the pardon chirchard. Summa	ij s	
Item, for a gravestoone sold to the executors of thomas Ryvell. Summa	vj s	viij d
Item, Receuud at Estir for the paschall monye. Summa	xij s	ix d
Item, of Mr Duklyng for the pytt & knyell of his wyff. Summa	xvj s	viij d
Item, of William harman for the pytt of his wyff. Summa	xiij s	iiij d
Item, of Robert Odyham for his wyffes pytt	xiij s	iiij d

¹ leaf 139, back.

Item, of diuerse katches & boottes for Robushe to[1] the chirche þat was leyed on the Romlande. Summa		xiiij d
Item, Sparyd of the xx s qwytrent of the Rose for the ayde. Summa		vj d
Item, Receuud of Robert owtyng for serten old tymbir with oon new Raftir		iiij s viij d
Item, Receuud of Iohn halheed for a dorre with a loke & a keye þat longyd to Seint Stephen chapell with serten old tymbyr		v s
Item, Receuud of Iohn Mylton for iij c tyll. Summa		xviij d
Item, Receuud of William Turke for ij peces tymbir of ix foot longe & iiij quarters		xij d
Item, Receuud at Estir for the waste of iiij tapers brennyng abowte þe sepulture, whiche tapers ware of the yeft of William Proyne. Summa		iij s ix d
[2]Item, Receuud of Iohn Russell for a m¹ tyll. Summa	v s	
Item, of Iohn Mylton for a pece of tymbyr. Summa		vj d
Item, Receuud of Iohn Russell þat he Receuud of Mowse for old dettes. Summa		x s
Item, Receuud of Iohn Russell for the qwytrent of Seint botols, þat shuld hafe ben paid to hym by thomas Mondes in his yeres acompt. Summa		ij s vj d
Summa totalis of Casueltʒ, xxij li xiiij s iiij d.		

Paymentes of the Same.

ffirst, paid to Robart debname, parishe clarke, for a yerys wages fful. Summa		iiij li xiij s iiij d
Item, to Richard Abell for a yer wages by hys howse rent. Summa, viij s. Item, iiij s vj d in mony at xviij d a quarter, which is for iij quarters wages from Cristemas vnto Mihelmas last paste, bysydes the Rente of his howse, which was grauntid to hym at the last acompt. Summa		xij s vj d
Summa, v li v s x d.		

Olde dettes paid by me which ware owyng afore my tyme.

*   *   *   *   *

[Wax Reckoning, Church Rents, Payments for the Church Rents.]

---

[1] 'of' scratched out.   [2] leaf 140.

[1]Ihesus.

Costes for the Remevyng of the Roode lofte.

ffurst, paid to the master workeman for iij dayes labour		xxj d
Item, iij karvers, to euery of þem for iij days labour. Summa	ij s	
Item, to pegrym, laborer, the same iij dayes		xv d
Item, to Iohn Redmanne, karver, for ij dayes labour on seint Kateryns yle		xiij d
Item, to pegrym for vj days labour to helpe hym & othyr alsoo	ij s	vj d
Item, for lyme & sande & bryeke	iij s	iiij d
Item, to Richard lorymer for v dayes vndirpynyng	iij s	viij d
Item, to pegrym & an odyr laborer, euery of them iij dayes. Summa	ij s	vj d
Item, to a karver for ij days warke and for nayles		xiiij d
Item, to a carpynter for a grett Iowe piece tymbyr, & for halfe a dayes labour to the karver	ij s	iiij d
Item, to the same karvare for iij dayes labour & a halfe		xxiij d
Item, paid to Iohn Russell for a waynskott & for sawyng of iiij karfe		x d
Item, to Iohn Redman for v dayes workemanshipe	ij s	vj d
Item, to the Smythe for iij Stays and a litill Sterope and a forth Riʒht dogge of Iryn for the Roode-lofte, weyng l ħ, pres	v s	x d
Item, for viij broddes & a brase for þe paschall candill		vj d
Summa totalis, xxxiiij s ij d.		

Costes paid for peyntyng of the Roode, with karvyng and odir costes alsoo.

ffurst, paid at the Note takyng of the Endentour of comnandes		ij d
Item, to Sir Iohn plomer for makyng of the fy[u?]gyrres of þe Roode		xx d
Item, to the karvare for makyng of iij dyadems, & of oon of the Evangelystes, & for mendyng the Roode, the Crosse, þe Mary & Iohn, þe Crown of thorn, with all odyr fawtes. Summa	x s	
Item, paid to vndirwood for payntyng & gyldyng of the Roode, the Crosse, Mary & Iohn, the iiij		

[1] leaf 142.

Evangelistes & iij dyadems; with the ij nobilles
that I owe to hym in monye. Summa ... vł
  Summa, vł xjs xd.

Memorandum: that I Receuud of Iohn halhed for the
burying of Mr Richard hakeneye and Alyce his
wyff. Summa . . . . vijs viijd

Paid for lyme, sande, & for the masons huyr & his
laborer, makyng ayeyn of their tombe, the xx day
of marche, the yer of oure lord god m⁴ cccc lxxxxvj,
& for þeir dyrge & masse & masse peny & for
drynkyng, to the prestes and to the parishons, &
for al maner of charges. Summa, Summa . . . vijs viiijd

[Vacations of Church Rents; Obits, Quitrents.]

[1] Paymentes for the chirche.

 * * * * *

Item, for bryngyng of the new cowcher from M^r
parson & spent at wyne . . . . iiijd ob

 * * * * *

Item, for colys to brenne in the vestrye . . . . ob

 * * * * *

Item, to William Elmys for scowryng of a braunche
of v . . . . jd

 * * * * *

Item, xij foot of borde, elmyn, to knyel on In the pews iiijd
Item, spent at halheedes at a brekfast, & for bred &
ale sent to the vestrye, makyng the Inventorye of
the chirche goodes . . . . xjd
Item, to a carpyntare for mendyng of a pewe þat Mas-
kalles wyff & Overays wyf sat yn . . . . . iiijd ob

 * * * * *

[2] Paid for a dosseyn tukkyng gyrdilles for the prestes,
to halheedes wyff . . . . ixd
Item, for ij foote of free stoon for the yes of the tabir-
nakiłł . . . . vijd
Item, to a mason & hys laborer for iiij dayes warke
levelyng of the gravestoones, & for skaffoldyng of
the tabenacle, & for dressyng of the Iryn to beyre
the hope of Iryn. Summa . . . . iijs iiijd

---

[1] leaf 142, back.   [2] leaf 143.

Item, for mendy*n*g & rowndy*n*g of the seid hope, & for ij yryns sett in the free stoon to beyre the seid hope, weyng xiiij ℔. Summa . . . . ij s

* * * * *

Item, to harry me*r*shes ser*u*ant for mendyng & howsy*n*g of our lady of pyte . . . . xvj d

* * * * *

[1] Paid to cornelis Smythe for makyng of the Iryn at the hye awter that beryth the canapye. Summa viij s viij d

Item, to harry me*r*she for peyntyng & gyldyng of the same . . . . ij s

* * * * *

[2] Item, to the Stacyener for setty*n*g of all the new feest*es* in to the book*es* that lakkyd them and in to the masse book*es*, & for mendy*n*g, pynny*n*g, claspy*n*g of them. Summa . . . . . . xxxiij s iiij d

* * * * *

Item, for mendyng of Curteygnes, albes, Surpeleys, & for Sope to washe them w*ith*, towell*es* and awter clothes also. Summa . . . . x d

Item, to the stacyonar for a reward to set the new feest*es* in the organ book*es*, & for byndy*n*g and dressing of them also. Summa . . . . . . ij s

* * * * *

[The two Allowances respectively for potacion money to the tenants and for writing these accounts.

The brief Rehearsal of receipts and payments.]

[3] Rest dewe to the Chirche of all this p*ar*sell*es*, xiij ℔ ix s ij d o℔.

Of the which som the seid thomas Colyns hath paid in mony xiij ℔ vj s viij d, & the seid p*ar*ishons have grauntid to hym as for the Rest of the seid acompt, which is ij s vj d o℔, shall be leeful to hym to levy it at his owen charge & vse, & he to re[. . ysse?] it to his ow*e*n p*ro*fytt &c ; yef he can gett itt.

[4] + Ih*esus*.

Wherof ther ys owyng thys yere in dettors hand*es* and in plegg*es* theys p*ar*cell*es* foloyng :—

+ Sir Willi*a*m Combys, prest, ow*ith* iij s. Receuud a pledge.
+ Robert Barcrofft ow*ith* . . . . xvj d

---

[1] leaf 143, back. [2] leaf 144. [3] leaf 144, back. [4] leaf 145.

+Iohn Neele ow*ith*. Summa	ij s	
Iohn Smyth, habyrdasher	iij s	iiij d
Iohn a leyton, plege		
frauncen de boye*s*	iij s	iiij d

This aco*m*mpt, made the xxx day of decembir, in the p*re*sence of Mast*er* Willi*a*m Remygton, aldirman; Iohn Milton, Bakar; Thomas hunt, drap*er*; Iohn derham, grocer; Robert howty*n*g, ffishmong*er*; Gylbart gentill, drap*er*; Iohn halhed, grocer; Thomas watt*es*, drap*er* and chirchwardeygne, w*ith* thomas Colyns, chirchewardeygne; the whic*h* thomas colyn*s* hath reqwyred to have a lesse in the howsses at þe Roose for xx[ti] yere, payn*g* by yere v li at iiij termes vsuall. Also to Repeyre & to pave the kechyne and to farme the Siege and to Repeyre the well; which lesse is grauntyd by the seid p*er*sons w*ith* Mr Iohn Redye, p*a*rishe pr*e*ste, as þe p*a*rsons deputie, beyn*g* pr*e*sent. And Iohn Russell, Skynnar, also, &c.

Item. Thomas hunt, drap*er*, shal hafe a lesse of his housse for xx[ti] yer, payn*g* iij l̄ vj s viij d, kepy*n*g all maner of rep*a*racions w*ith* p*r*incipall*es*, and other on hys owen propyr cost*es* dury*n*g the seyd teerme. And yef it happyn the Seid howse to dekeye or fall down in the seid yer*es*; þan it is agreyd & co*n*cludid by the seid p*a*rishon*s* þer beyn*g* pr*e*sent, & by his owen agreement, alsoo to byld it newe of his owen propir cost*es*; at the lattyr ende of hys termes to leeve þe house tenaunt lyke as it was att hys entery*n*g, or in bett*er* caase, &c.

[1] Thies ben the old Dett*es* that hathe ben lefft onpaid by þe chirchwardeyns in tymes past.

Robard Crapleys, tayllour . . . . Su*m*ma, xxij s

* * * * *

[A.D. 1497-8.

Thomas Colyns } Wardens
Thomas Wattes

The Accounts of the Chantries.]

[2] Clark*es* wag*es* and beame ly3hte and paschall.

ffyrst, receuud for the holl yere, qwart*er*ly gaderyd fore the Clark*es* wagys. Su*m*ma . . . . v li xiij d
Item, Receuud for the beamely3lit thys yere bysyd*es* them þat be owyng. Su*m*ma . . . . . . xviij s viij d
Item, at Estir Receuud for paschall monye. Su*m*ma . xj s viij d

Su*m*ma, vj li xj s v d.

---

[1] leaf 145, back.   [2] leaf 151.

The chirch Rentes bysydes the chauntryes.

* * * * *

[1] Casuelties In this yere.

ffirst, Receuud of Iohn Maschall for viij c house-tyll, pris	iiij s	
Item, of Iohn Mongeam for viij Rooffe tylles. Summa		vij d
Item, of Iohn Russell for vij old Raftyrs. Summa .	ij s	iiij d
Item, Receuud of dyuerse of the parishons toward the settyng vpe of the Roode. Summa	vj s	vj d
Item, of the gaderyng of the wymen at hokmondaye. Summa	xiiij s	viij d
Item, Receuud of the men that gaderyd on the tewsdaye. Summa	v s	viij d
Item, Receuud of Ielyan Welles for hyr husbondes grave. Summa	xiij s	iiij d
Item, of hir alsoo for a gravestoon for hym. Summa	v s	
Item, of Iohn MonIame for the pytt of hys chyld in þe pardon chirchard	ij s	
Item, of Robert Owtyng for old tymbyr. Summa .		viij d
Item, for serten balast sold at Romelond by halhed. Summa		vj d
Item, for William bedylles pytt in the pardon chirchard	ij s	
Summa, lvij s iij d.		

[Payments to Parish Clerk, etc.]

[2] Payd to Robart Debnam, parishe clark, for a yeres wagys full. Summa	iiij li	xiij s iiij d
Item, to Richard Abell, for hys wagys, þe Rent of hys hows by yer viij s. Item, in mony bysydes for the hole yer vj s. Summa	xiiij s	
Summa, v li vij s iiij d.		

* * * * *

[Obits, Quitrents, Wax Reckoning, Reparation of Church Rents.]

[3] Ihesus.

Costes made for Settyng vp of the Roode.

ffirst, paid for cariage of borde from Suthwarke for the Skaffold . . . . Summa,		iiij d

---

[1] leaf 151, back. [2] leaf 152. [3] leaf 153.

Churchwardens' Accounts, A.D. 1497–8.

Item, for xv foot of bord, & for sawyng of the same for the pilars of the marye & Iohn, & for the mortes of the Crosse . . . . Summa, ij s ix d

Item, to Iohn Codbeen, carpynter, & hys feloe, the oon for vj days labour, & the odyr for iiij dayes labour. Summa, x days, euery daye viij d . . vj s viij d

Item, for an c of Six peny nayll spent abowt it. Summa, vj d

Item, to bakar, mason, for a days labour settyng vp of the Steyebare . . . . Summa, viij d

Item, to vndirwod, peynter, for a Reward more þan his counant . . . . vj s viij d

Item, paid to Richard garrett, Smythe, for xxiiij lb new Iryn to lenkith the Steybare of the Roode þat goeth from wall to wall, & for mendyng of it alsoo, at j d ob the lb . . . . . . Summa, iij s

Item, for iiij Stayes of new Iryn, weyng xx lb, at j d ob þe lb . . . . Summa, ij s vj d

Item, for grett broddys, weyng ij lb . . . Summa, iij d

Item, for iij gret square stapylles for the Roode. Summa, ij d

Item, for broddes for marye & Iohn . . . Summa, j d

Item, for the long bolt of Iryn comyng down from the Roofe, & for Stapilles & Spekynges to fastyn it to the Roode, weng xliiij lb, at j d ob the lb. Summa, v s vj d

Item, for ij hookes for the lentyn cloth byfor the Roode . . . . Summa, ij d

Item, to hew materson, Smyth, for clampys, naylles & hokes that þe Roode hangith bye . . Summa, viij d

Item, to ij portars for havyng down of the Skaffold, leyng vp the tymbir & makyng holles in the chirchard to avoyd the water . . . . Summa, iiij d

Summa, xxx s iij d.

[1] Paymentes for the chirche.

ffirst paid for holme & Iuye . . . . . . Summa, v d

Item, to Mastir Iohn Redye, parishe prest, for þe beydroll . . . . ij s

Item, to a yong man for a Reward Syngyng in the qwere the halydays in Cristenmas for the sted of Sir Iohn Vpthenns . . . . Summa, vj d

* * * * *

Item, to Richard Abell for goyng to Strattford vnto

[1] leaf 153, back.

M︎ʳ pa*r*son, for to desyre hym to come to the
Avdyt of the last Accmpt . . . . . *Summa*,   iiij d

* * * * *

It*em*, for mendy*n*g of diue*r*se coope*s*, vestemente*s* &
Soyng on of the appareylle*s* when thei came
wasshyng to the clarke . . . . . . *Summa*,   xij d

* * * * *

Ite*m*, for iij Rybbe*s* of bief to the wyves on hokmonday, & for ale & bred for them that gaderyd
Summa,   xvj d

Item, for mendyng of the tabernacle clothe . *Summa*,   vj d

* * * * *

Item, for x elle*s* of nor*m*and clothe bouȝht of Ioħn
Russeɫɫ for Surplesse . . . . . . *Summa*, v s   ij d

Item, for maky*n*g of ij Surplesse & a Rochet of the
same clothe. . . . . *Summa*,   xx d

* * * * *

Ite*m*, for bred, ale, wyne Spent on Strangers Syngars
& theer chyldren on the Evyn & day of Seint
Barnabe . . . . *Summa*, ij s   j d oᵇ

[1]Item, paid [for] bred, ale & a Rybbe of bieff Spent at
the Casteɫɫ in fisħ strett on dyue*r*se of the
p*a*rishons at the visitac*i*on of the bishope of
london in Seint Magnys chirche . . . *Summa*,   viij d

* * * * *

Item, for mendy*n*g of the fyre panne in the chirche,
& for iij ɫɫ d*i*. of new yryn to the Same. *Summa*,   v d

Item, for a new keye to se*r* Ioħn Bardeneys chest, for
Mastres bonyfantes, priest, to occupie the vestemente*s*. . . . . *Summa*,   iiij d

* * * * *

[The two Allowances.
The brief Rehearsal of Receipts and Expences, Rest dew to the Church, etc.]

[2]Item, Rece*uu*d of the bequest of Mʳ Robert Ryveɫɫ, the xv day
of Ianyver an*n*o 1498, by Th. Colyns & Thomas Watte*s*, xx ɫi.,
the vħicħ xx ɫi is in the hande*s* of Th. Watte*s* & herry Edmond
the day & yer afrosayde.

[1] leaf 154.   [2] leaf 155.

Item, ther is solde to Thomas Wattes a bras pot, pris vj s, which is in the bagg with tresory.

* * * * *

[1] + Ihesus 1498.

This acompt, maade the xv day of Ianiuer, anno 1498, in the presence of Mastir William Wyld, parson of the seid chirche, Mr William Remyngton, Aldirman, Mr Atlyff, Iohn Duklyng, thomas hunt, Iohn Milton, Iohn Derham, Robert Owtyng, Iohn halhed, Thomas Colyns, Iohn Maschall, William Smart, thomas Wattes, draper, & harry Edmondes, Salter, the seid thomas Wattes and harry Edmondes beyng chirchwardeygnes for the yer foloyng; it is agreed and concluded by thes seid parishons afore reheercyd, that from hensforth the chirchwardeygnes and the clarke shall take of eueryche knyell with the great bell vj s viij d, þat is, to eyther of them xl d.[2]

[3] Also, moreouer, it is concludid, for the knyell with the second bell, Ryngyng no moor but the Space of an houre, the seid clarke shall taake for it xij d; & yef it be Ronge the Space of halfe a daye he shall taake for it xl d. oonly to hymself.

[4] Also for the lytyll bell, to the clark for a man viij d, and for a child iiij d.

[5] Alsoo to the clarke for a pytt in the chirche ij s.; also for a pytt in the pardon chirchard for a manne viij d. and for a chyld iiij d.; and soo in lykewyȝe in the grett chirchard also.

[A.D. 1498–9.

Thomas Wattys } Wardens.
Harry Edmonde }

Chantry Accounts.

Church Rents.

Quitrents.]

[6] Clarkes wagys, Beame lyȝht & paskall.

ffyrst, Receuud for the hole yer qwarter gaderyd for
the clarkes wages . . . . v li vj s iiij d
Item, Receyuyd for the beame lyȝht thys yer.
Summa . . . . xx s
Item, Receuud at Estir for paschall monye. Summa x s viij d
Summa, vj li xvij s.

[1] leaf 155, back.   [2] 'A knyell with the gret bell' in margin.
[3] 'The ij^{de} bell' in margin.   [4] 'The lytill bell' in margin.
[5] 'The Stent of graves' in margin.   [6] leaf 163, back.

Casuelties yn thys yere.

ffyrst, Receuud of Iohn Maskall for serten tymbyr that bylongyd to the chirche. Summa ...	iiij s
Item, of thomas wattes for a pece of old tymbyr ..	iiij d
Item, of master Duklyng for burying of hys child in the pardon chirchard. Summa	ij s
Item, for burying of a man of ceswell from Will olyuers	xx d
Item, for the burying of a Straunger from Richard Clossys. Summa	iij s
Item, for burying of a man of garneseye. Summa .	xvj d
Item, for the burying of William Bedylles child in the pardon chirchard. Summa	ij s
Item, for the burying of thomas Colyns chyld in þe pardon chirchard	ij s
Item, Receuud of mastir Iohn Redy for di. c of quarter-bord	xij d
Item, Receuud of harry Edmond for xxx[ti] foote of planchebord	viij d
Item, Receuud of the wyves yn the parish yn mony gaderyd on hokemonday. Summa	xiiij s vj d
Item, of the men yn the parishe gaderyd on the tewsday	vj s
Item, of Iohane Remyngton for the burying of hyr husbond in the chirche. Summa	xiij s iiij d
Item, Receuud of mastres Nonnelaye, for an old bedsted. Summa	ix d

Summa, lij s vij d.
Summa totalis Resseyvyd, xxv li ix s j d.

[Obits.]
[1]Paymentes to the Clarkes & Sexton.

paid to Robert Debnam, parish clarke, for hys yerys wages. Summa	iiij li xij s iiij d
Item, to William Raynesford, conduct, which was huryd from shroftyd to lammas. Summa ...	xxij s
Item, for a reward to hym by þe commavndement of Mr Aldirman	iij s iiij d
Item, to Richard Abell for hys wagys, þe Rent of his	

[1] leaf 164.

hows by yer, viij s. Item, in mony bysydes for
the hole yere, vj s. Summa . . . . xiiij s
  Summa, vj ℔ xij s viij d.

[1] The Reknyng of the wax spent in the chirche.

ffyrst, paid for d*i*. c wex . . . . . . Summa   xxvj s
Item, for a quarter vij ℔ & a quarter of wax at xlviij s
 the c . . . . Summa   xv s   ij d
Item, deliuerid to the waxchaunde Robert Bale, yn
 old wax of þe beamely3ht weyng d*i*. c xxiij ℔
 iij quarter. Item, in tapers endes weyng xviij ℔
 d*i*. Summa of the wey3ht of the wax bothe
 newe & olde to hym deliuerid viiij ix ℔ d*i*.;
 wherof Receuud of hym ayeyn for þe roodloft
 and yn tapers spent afore our lady in þe qwyere
 & for Mr cambryge ly3ht in Seint Stephens chapeH
 & afore Seint thomas and afore þe Roode for
 mastres Nonneleye viij v ℔ d*i*., paying for strik-
 yng of euery ℔ to hym ob. . . . . Summa   vj s   x d
So remaynyth still in hys hondes xxiiij ℔ of wax
 in a Stoke.
Item, paid to hym for makyng of the paschaH. Summa   ij s   vij d
Item, for garnyshyng of viij toorches on corpus cristi
 day . . . . Summa   ij s   viij d
  Summa paid for wax & for strykyng   liij s   iij d

Reparacions off the chirche rentes.

*   *   *   *   *

Paymentes for the chirche.

*   *   *   *   *

[2] Paid to Iħon Bentley, carpynter, for viij days labour
 makyng of the deske in the vestrye to the bookes
 & mendyng of dyuerse odur thinges in the
 chirche . . . . Summa   v s   iiij d

*   *   *   *   *

Item, to Symond vauesor for helpyng of the qwiere
 aH the halydays of Crystmas . . . Summa   iij s   iiij d

*   *   *   *   *

Item, for mendyng of the monstyr for the Sacrament .   xvj d

[1] leaf 164, back.   [2] leaf 165.

Item, for the wachyng of the Sepulchre & the chirche, to iiij men	xij d
Item, for bred & ale to them that watchyd . Summa	vj d
Item, for small corde for the Crosse Cloth . Summa	ij d
Item, for a lampe & for tentyr hookes to the Sepulcre	j d ob
Item, to Richard Ioyner for mendyng of ij baner-polles	iiij d
Item, ij Rybbes of bieff & for bred & ale to the wyvys yn the parish that gaderyd on hokmondaye .... Summa	xiiij d
Item, for wyne & ale to the Syngars on holy thursday	vj d
Item, for makyng of yryns for the Curteygnes at the hyȝhe alter	vij d

* * * * *

[1] Item, paid to gowge & to Iohn Nutte & to dyuerse other Syngars and theyr childryn on Seint Barnabes daye .... Summa	iiij s	vj d
Item, for vj elles lynyn clothe for to mende the Cloth afore the Roode ...... Summa	ij s	vj d
Item, to harry mershe for peyntyng of the same clothe .... Summa	iiij s	
Item, for new bokeram & for soyng of the same clothe		vj d ob
Item, for a cheyn & iij stapulles for bookes in the chancell		iiij d

* * * * *

Item, for goldyn Ryband, green sylk & blake, mendyng of the Coopes & westymentes . . Summa	v d
Item, to the Clarke for hys labour mendyng of them .... Summa	iij d
Item, Spent on the official at iij tymes when serten of the parishens ware with hym for the chavntryes	xij d

* * * * *

Item, Spent at the Son apon M[r] aldirman & odir of the parish on the Sonday next aftir Seint Mathews day	vij d

* * * * *

Item, for a peyre of garnettes to the longe pewe . .	iiij d
Item, for makyng of a tabyll for the beyd Roll . . .	ij d

* * * * *

Item, for a new shovyll for the chyrche	iiij d

[1] leaf 165, back.

Item, to ij laborars, every of them for iij days labor . ij s
Item, for a new whielbarowe . . . . . Summa   xij d

* * * * *

[1] Item, for a Crewet to Roose Wrytelles chawntrye . iiij d

* * * * *

Item, to the Rakar for the chirche by the hole yere . viij d

* * * * *

[The two Allowances.
The Rehearsal.]

[A.D. 1499–1500.
Harry Edmond } Wardens.
William Smart
Chantry Accounts.
Church Rents.
Quitrents.]

[2] Clarkes wages, Beme lyght & pascall lygth.

ffyrst, Receyuyd off the hole yere quarterly Gaderyd
 ffor the Clarkes wages. Summa . . . . . v li viij s
Item, Receiuid of þe beme lygth this yere. Summa . xx s ij d
Item, Receiuid at Ester, ffor pascall mony. Summa . xj s ob
  Summa, vj li xix s ij d ob.

[3] Casuelles in this yere.

ffyrst, Receyuyd off the wyffes in this parysh in mony
 Gaderyd on hok monday. Summa . . . . . xv s ix d ob
Item, off men in the parysh Gaderyd on the tvysday.
 Summa . . . . vj s xj d ob
Item, of Edward pekman, taylor, be the handes of
 Iohn Betman, draper, off olde dett that wasse
 dew to þe Cherche, & delyuerd his plegges . . xl s
Item, off Robert hotyng ffor the pytte off his Chyld
 in the pardon Chercheyard. Summa . . . . ij s
Item, ffor the Beryyng off þe man off orford in the
 Grett Chercheyard. Summa . . . . ij s

---

[1] leaf 166. [2] leaf 176. [3] leaf 176, back.

Item, off Th. Cayes, waterman, be the handes off Iohn Mongham, Bequethed to the cherche be the Seyd Th. Summa	vj s	viij d
Item, off William halles wyffe ffor her husbondes pytt in þe Cherche	xiij s	iiij d
Item, off the goodwyff Mascall ffor þe knell of þe gret bell di. a day	vj s	viij d
Item, ffor þe pytt off her hosbond in þe Cherche. Summa	xiij s	iiij d
Item, ffor the makyng off his graue. Summa . . .	ij s	
Item, off the goodwyff mascall ffor the pytt of her sone stephene in the pardon Cherche yard	ij s	
Item, of Iohn halhed ffor the grett bell ffor Masteres Bons ffor di. a day. Summa	iij s	iiij d
Item, off Iohn Condall ffor the pytt & knell off his mayde		xvj d
Item, off William halles wyff ffor þe pytt & knell off her mayde		xvj d
Item, off Iohn Mongham ffor a stranger that was Beryd in the Grett Cherche yard. Summa . .		xij d
Item, off Iohn halhed for a stranger that was beryd in the Grett Cherche yard, ffor the Grownde. Summa		xx d
Item, off Rauff Cokkes wyffe, ffor þe pytt of her hosbond in þe pardon Cherche yard	ij s	
Item, Th. Caunterbery, ffor a olde Chest þat was in the store house		xiiij d
Item, off Rych. Chelmysford of olde dett that was dew sethen the tyme off Iohn Mylton beyng Cherche wardeyne. Summa	xx s	
[1] Item, of Robert debnam, Clarke, be the handes off his wyff of his bequest	vj s	viij d
Item, of Iohn derham, grocer, ffor þe pytt off Iohn gybson in þe pardon yard	ij s	
Item, of Robert hotyng, ffor þe pyt of his Chyld in þe pardon Cherche yard	ij s	
Item, of William Reuell, ffor the pytt off his chy[l]d in the pardon Cherche yarde. Summa . . .	ij s	
Item, off Maister doklyng ffor his wyffes pytt in the Cherche	xiij s	iiij d
Item, ffor the knell off the grett bell ffor di. a day . .	vj s	viij d
Item, ffor the makyng off the pytt	ij s	

[1] leaf 177.

Churchwardens' Accounts, A.D. 1499–1500.

Item, off Maister Iohn ffor sir Adame3 pytt in the pardon Cherche yard . . . . ij s
Item, ffor the knell off the medyll bell ffor di. a day . ij s   iiij d
Item, ffor the wast off ij torches þat longith to þe hey aulter . . . .   xij d
Item, off Iohn halhed ffor the medyll bell ffor his mayd ffor di. a day . . . . iij s   iiij d
Item, ffor her pytt in the pardon Cherche yard . . ij s
Item, ffor the lytyll bell ffor his Sone ffor an owre .   iiij d
Item, ffor his Sone3 pytt in the pardon Cherche yard ij s
Item, ffor the lytyll bell ffor a owre ffor his Chylde .   iiij d
Item, Receuud off Maister Iohn ffor the bequest off William hall to the Cherche. Summa . . . iij s   iiij d
Summa, ix li xiiij s xj d

[Obits.]

[1] Paymentes to the Sexteyne & Clarke.

ffyrst, payd to Robert debnam, Clarke, ffor his yeres wages . . . . iiij li xiij s iiij d
Item, to Rych Abell ffor his wages, the Rent off his house Be yere, viij s. Item, in mony beSydes, vj s. Summa . . . .   xiiij s
Item, payd to lennard, that was heryd be my masteres off the parysh, hauyng ffor Euery halyday vj d when that he Comyth, & payd to hym with þe concepsion of oure lady day tyll Crestmase euen, euery halyday, vj d. summa . . . . ij s
Summa, v li ix s iiij d.

[Wax Reckoning.]

[2] Reparasions off the Chercherentes.

* * * * *

Item, ffor ij new keye3 ffor the pyxt box . . . . .   vj d
Item, ffor a new key to the store house dore . . .   iij d
Item, ffor the mendyng of iij lokkes ffor the iij quyre dores . . . .   vj d

* * * * *

[3] Paymentes ffor the Cherche.

* * * * *

[1] leaf 177, back. [2] leaf 178, back. [3] leaf 179.

Item, ffor wrytyng off the Bedrow		iiij d

* * * * *

Item, to Iohn nott & to his Company Syngers on seynt barnabeys day	v s	iiij d
Item, ffor a Rope ffor the Grett bell weyng x lb . .		x d
Item, ffor caryag and warffage off ij lodes stone ffrom wolkey		vij d
Item, to Iohn wulffe ffor gyldyng and Slueryng off the olde Crosse staffe	v s	
Item, to Robert Clarke ffor mendyng dyuers albys, Surplyces and aulter clothes, wasshyn, & ffor the settyng on off a parell off the Same		xvij d
Item, ffor Byrche at mydsomer		iiij d
Item, ffor a Crosse staff makyng		iij d

* * * * *

[1] Item, ffor Ryngyng off Iohn mascalles knell . . .		vj d
Item, ffor the makyng off his pytt		iiij d
Item, payd at Selere, in the presens off Master Alderman Iohn doklyng, Thomas hunt, Iohn mylton and othere dyuers off the parysh at the Chesyng off the new Clarke		vj d
Item, ffor a Rope ffor the lytyll Sawnse bell . . .		iiij d
Item, ffor Bred, ale and wyne on alhalowne day . .		vij d

* * * * *

Item, payd to Master doklyng ffor Costes spent to the Abbott off Waltham at the abbottes in	iij s	
Item, payd in Costes spent when Master doklyng, Th. hunt, Robert hotyng, Th. Colynez at there Rydyng to Waltham to speke with the Abbott ffor the kechen	viij s	vij d

* * * * *

Item, to Margeret Sotton ffor the makyng off vj Rochettes ffor Chelderne to were in the quyre . . .		xij d

* * * * *

[The two Allowances.
The Rehearsal.]

[2] Nota. Rekened the xviij day of Ianuarii, Anno 150[1], in the presence of My lorde the mayer Vylliam Remyngton and Mr William Wylde, parson, and Maister William Atclyff and other of

[1] leaf 179, back. [2] leaf 180, back.

the parysche as I. ducklyng, I. Milton, I deraham, Robert howtyng, & other moo. And ther is mony brow3t in, xxij ƚi xvj s j d.

Item, Thomas colyns chargid hym with 1s that he Receuyd. And xxx s iiij d is in pledgis in lynnyn clothe, the which is paid by William smert.

Summa totalis, xxvj ƚi xv s v d. And William smert hath the pledges.

[1] Rest due, xxiiij ƚi vj s v d.

The which xxvj ƚi xvj s v d is delyuerd the same day to Thomas Colyns vppon the Rekenyng of expences vppon the Masons werkmanschipp, & ffor stones for the Steple whiche was browghte in Rekenyng by the saide Thomas colyns and harry Edmond, whereof thay chargid them selff with lvij ƚi xix s xj d. And paide by them as it apperith in their Rekenyng lxix ƚi iiij s ix d ob. And so ther was owyng to them in Surplysage xj ƚi iiij s x d ob. Therffore thay Resseyuyd the xxvj ƚi xvj s v d, of the which due to them xj ƚi iiij s x d ob. So Remaynneth in Thomas Colen his handes xv ƚi xj s vj d ob, to be bestowed in tyme to com vppon the werkes of the steple.

Also it is remembred that Sir Iohn plommer brow3te in a Rekennyng that ther was owyng vnto hym for Reparacions done in his howse, clerly Rekened, xiij s ij d, which Gylberd gentyle schaH paye and dyscharge in his Accoumpte.

Also William Smerte asketh allowaunce of Robert dempnahams howse which is Rekened at xx s, and it is but xvj s viij d, the allowaunce is iij s iiij d, which William smert hath atteyned it in his owne handes.

The Rest cler is xxiiij ƚi iij s j d.

Memorandum. Resseyuyd be me, Thomas Colyns, of Wylliam smart xxiiij ƚi iijs jd, Beside 1s that I Resseyuyd of William Smerte in the ffyrst accoumpte, and chargid mye self with aH, and paide in mye Rekenyng þat I laied owte to the mason3 ffor stone and other thynges necessary, as it apperith more playnly in myne Acoumpte, vhereof allowed to Thomas colens in surplisage that he layed owte of his purs xj ƚi iiijs x d ob. So he hath in his handes to bestowe vppon the werkes of the steple xij ƚi xviij s ij d ob.

[A.D. 1500–1.]

Wylliam Smart } Wardens
Gylbert GentyH

[Chantry Accounts.]

* * * * *

[1] leaf 181.

¹ffirst, paid to donyng, gong fermere, the xxx day of Ianier for fermyng of a sege in george gysborow the clarkes chamber wherin was v tone at ij s the tone. . . . . Summa   x s

Item, to Rychard, seruaunte with Iohn Wolff, for watchyng with theyme to se the tomys wele fylyd . . . . Summa   iiij d

*   *   *   *   *

[Church Rents.
Payments, Quitrents and Reparations of the same.]
Paymentes for the church.

*   *   *   *   *

²Item, for a lampe in the quere. Summa . . . .   j d

Item, for iiij fathwme of lyne for the vyse of þe lampe. Summa . . . .   j d

*   *   *   *   *

³Item, to Iohn how, organmaker, for mendyng & makyng of new bellows for the organs . Summa   xv s

*   *   *   *   *

⁴Item, to bull the Sexten for a Surples with slevys.
Summa   ij s

*   *   *   *   *

Item, spent on Master Iohn, Thomas Wattes, Thomas hunt, Iohn derhame, when we aperyd afor the comyssary at Seynt Manguls . . . . Summa   iiij d

[From MS. B. [leaf 62]

Memorandum: in thys yere above wretyn was the ende of the sowthyle of owre Church takyn in wher sum tyme was the abbott of Walthams kechyn: to begynne at Ester & ffro that tyme fforward the parych bene bownde to paye to Waltham, yerly ffor euermore, x s, ffor a quytrent ffor Ever.

A less explicit reference is also found in MS. A.]

*   *   *   *   *

⁵Item, to Maister Iohn for hallowyng of iiij Awbys.
Summa   iiij d

---

¹ leaf 184, back.   ² leaf 188, back.   ³ leaf 189.
⁴ leaf 189, back.   ⁵ leaf 190.

Item, for settyng vp of the old pewys in the medyll
yle, to a carbenter iij days iij men, & ij days & a
halfe ij men . . . . Summa   viij s

* * * * *

Item, to bull the Sexten & Watson for mendyng of
the bawdrykes & clappers of the iij belles.

* * * * *

[1] Caswelltes in this yere.

ffirst, Receyvyd of M*aister* Smart for morter that ley
in churcheyerd . . . . Summa   xx d
Item, of the goodman Derhame for the beqwest of his
ser*u*aunt Iohn gybson, the xvij day of Ianeu*er*
Summa   vj s   viij d
Item, of s*i*r Iohn plom*er* for the grett bell half a day
Ryngyng for his moder . . . . Su*m*ma   iij s   iiij d
Item, for a peyr of Awngell wyng*es* & iij dyodyms
sold . . . . Summa   xiiij d
Item, of the goodwyff of the Swane at byllyng*es*gate
for the berying of her husband in the p*ar*don
churchyerd . . . . Summa   ij s   iiij d
Item, of the goodman howtyng for the berying of his
chyld in the p*ar*don churchyerd . . . Summa   ij s   iiij d
Item, of the goodman collyns for the berying of his
dowghter in the churche . . . . . Summa   xiij s   iiij d
Item, of a part of bull the Sextens dewte of the said
alice collyns Ryng & here pyte . . . Su*m*ma   ij s   viij d
Item, for brekyng of the grownd in the gret churchyerd for a chyld of vj yere old þat dyed at
harmams . . . . Su*m*ma   vj d
Item, of Robert howtyng for the berying of crompe
that dyed wi*th*in M*aster* Duklyng['s] xiij s iiij d,
and for the gret bell Ryngyng half a day iij s
iiij d. Summ*a* . . . .   xvj s   viij d
Item, of Iohn Collyns for the berying of his wyff in
the churche . . . .   xiij s   iiij d

Su*m*ma to*t*all*is*, iij li iiij s.

* * * * *

[2] Clarkes wages, beame lyʒt, & pascal lyʒt.

ffirst, Receyvyd for a hole yere, q*u*artely gaderyd, of
the clarkes wages. Summa . . . . v li iij s   v d

[1] leaf 190, back.   [2] leaf 191.

Item, Resseyvyd of the bemely3t this yerde. Summa xvj s viij d
Item, Resseyvyd at Estur for pascall money. Summa xij s iiij d
   Summa totallis, vj li xij s v d.

Paymentes to the clarkes & Sexten.

ffirst, paid to George gysborowe, paryshe clarke, for
 iij quarteres of a yere wages . . . Summa iij li vj s viij d
Item, to lenard, conducte, for xij days in crystmas
 syngyng & playing at the organs . . Summa iiij s
Item, to Iohn bull, Sexten, for a quarter wages
           Summa x s
Item, Wylliam Wyld for his Reward frome Whyt-
 sontyd to Myghelmas for Syngyng in the qwere
           Summa vj s viij d
Item, to harry fysher, clarke, on Seynt Andrews evyn,
 for vij wekkes seruice . . . . . . Summa xij s viij d
   Summa totallis, v li.
   Rest cler herof xxxij s v d.

*   *   *   *   *

[Obits.
Wax Reckoning.
Allowances.
Rehearsal.]

[A.D. 1501–2.
Gylebert Gentyll }
Iohn Awthorpe } Wardens.]

[1] Ihesus, maria : Amen.

[Chantry Accounts, Church Rents and Payments
and Reparations of same.]
Paymentes ffor the Church.

*   *   *   *   *

[2] Item, payd to Iohn bull & Thomas Watson, ffor
mendyng of pewys in þe church, ych of them ij
days . . . . Summa   xvj d

*   *   *   *   *

[1] leaf 195.   [2] leaf 201.

Item, ffor grete pynnes to the awters . . . Summa	j d
Item, ffor a halywater sprynkkell of laton . Summa	x d
Item, ffor paper Ryall to pryck songes in ffor the qwere . . . . Summa	vij d
Item, ffor brede, wyne & ale to þe syngeres on twelfdaye . . . . Summa	vj d

*　　　*　　　*　　　*　　　*

Item, ffor mendyng of the pax to þe hye Awlter. Summa	ij d

*　　　*　　　*　　　*　　　*

Item, ffor makyng of pewdors & settyng on of garnettes . . . . Summa	vj d
Item, ffor payntyng of the Crosstaffe ffor lent Summa	iiij d
Item, ffor makyng of a lectorne in the Roodlofte & mendyng of deskys in the qwere . . Summa	xij d
Item, ffor mendyng of the best Antyphoners Cuveryng the whych the Rattes had hurte . Summa	xij d

*　　　*　　　*　　　*　　　*

Item, to Iohn bull ffor skowryng of the Egull of laton & the branchys & candelstykkes in the church Summa	ij s	
Item, ffor a shode shovyll to ocupye in the Church Summa		iiij d
Item, ffor bromys to make clene the Church. Summa		ij d

*　　　*　　　*　　　*　　　*

Item, mendyng of the branch beffore ower lady in the qwere & nosyng of þe Candelstykes ffor morowmasse . . . . Summa	xij d

*　　　*　　　*　　　*　　　*

[1]Item, payd for a bedstede in Syr Iohn howelles Chamber . . . . Summa	ij s	iiij d

*　　　*　　　*　　　*　　　*

Item, ffor mendyng of the lokke of the wekytt goyng in to the pardon Churchyerd . . . . Summa	ij d
Item, ffor mendyng of the lokke & makyng of a stapull to the bolt of the gret churchyerd dorre. Summa	vj d

*　　　*　　　*　　　*　　　*

[1] leaf 201, back.

Item, spent at Wylliam Olyueres vppon Mysteres
Nonyley with Maister Alderman & dyueres of
the parych to have hyr grant of mony toward
þe byldyng of the Sowth yle
Item, ffor x elles brussell Clothe to make iiij Awbys
with ther Amys ffor chyldorn . . . Summa iiij s ij d

* * * * *

¹Item, ffor pavyng of vj teys beffore the hye Awter.
                                    Summa iij s

* * * * *

Item, ffor a rope to the Sans bell . . . . Summa iij d
Item, ffor mendyng of the pyxte, & makyng and gyldyng of sen Iohn be the crusyfyx of the same
pyxt. . . . . Summa iij s vj d

* * * * *

Item, payd to Thomas Colyns ffor hys horshyer whan
he went to maydston ffor to bynde Mawnde the
mason to perfforme hys Covenantes. . Summa xx d
Item, ffor makyng of the oblygacion whych mawnde
is bownde in to perfforme his Covenantes. Summa iiij d
Item, to Wylliam Wylde ffor Copying of the yndenters
of Covenantes, the whych copy was delyuerd to
Maister Vartu . . . . Summa iiij d

* * * * *

Item, ffor mendyng of the skonsys in the qwere. Summa iij d

* * * * *

² Casweltyes in this yere.

ffyrst, resseyvyd of harman's wyffe for parte of the
beqwest of hyr husbond . . . . . Summa xx s
Item, in mony that women gaderd on hokmondaye.
                                    Summa xxiij s
Item, that men gaderd on hoktewysdaye . Summa vj s
Item, of Mysteres Nonyley toward the Sowth yle.
                                    Summa v li ij s iiij d
Item, in mony that was gaderd on sent barnabys day,
& lampes & oyle ffor the branch payd ffor. Summa v s
Item, of Mayster Atclyffe ffor the berying of Mayster
leynthorpe. . . . . Summa xiij s iiij d
Item, ffor hys knyll . . . . Summa iij s iiij d

¹ leaf 202.   ² leaf 202, back.

Item, resseyuyd of Martyn of Whytstabyll ffor the berying of hopkyns son of Whytstabyll in the Gret churchyerd . . . . Summa   iij s

Item, ffor the berying of Stephyn Sandersons Chyld in the pardon churchyerd . . . . . Summa   ij s

Item, ffor the pytt of harry baxster in the pardon churchyerd . . . . Summa   ij s

Item, ffor Robert Ryvelles chyld in the pardon churchyerd . . . . Summa   ij s

Item, ffor gyrscroftes wyffe in the pardon churchyerd. Summa   ij s

Item, ffor Andrew Evyngers chyld in þe pardon churchyerd . . . . Summa   ij s

Item, resseyvyd of Rychard close ffor the pyttes of hys broder & hys Chyld . . . . . . Summa   iiij s

Item, resseyvyd of Iohn dereham ffor berying of iij chyldyrn . . . . Summa   vj s

Item, resseyvyd of Robert howtyng ffor the pytt of hys dowter . . . . Summa   ij s

Item, resseyvyd of Iohn ffox ffor the berying of hys wyffe . . . . Summa   ij s

Item, of me, Iohn Awthorpe, ffor the berying of iij of myn owne Chyldyrn . . . . . . Summa   vj s

Item, resseyuyd of Mayster duklyng ffor the stone the whych lyth vppon davy Cromp hys Coffyn. Summa   vj s   viij d

Summa totallis, x li xij s viij d.

payd hereoff to Mawnde in parte of payment of þe wyndows. Summa . . . .   v li

Item, payd to Mayster vartu. Summa . . . . .   xx s
rest of thyes Casweltes, iiij li xij s viij d.

[1] Ihesus.

Clarkys wagys, bemelyght & paskallyght.

ffyrst, Resseyvyd ffor a holl yere, quarterly gaderd, ffor the Clarkes wagys. Summa . . . . . .   v li ij s

Item, Resseyvyd of the bemelyȝht ffor thys yere. Summa . . . .   xvj s

Item, Resseyvyd at Ester ffor paskall mony. Summa   xij s   vj d
Summa totallis, vj li x s vj d.

[1] leaf 203.

Paymentes to the Clarke & Sextyn.

ffyrst, payd to Iohn law, parych clarke, ffor iij quar-
    teres of a yere wagys. Summa . . . . . . iij li x s
Item, to Iohn bull ffor a holl yere wages. Summa . xl s
Item, to Wylliam Wylde ffor a reward in helpyng of
    the quere at Ester & Whytsontyde. Summa . iij s iiij d
        Summa totallis, v li xiij s iiij d.
        rest Clere of thys, xvij s ij d.

[Obits.
Wax Reckoning.
Allowances.
Rehearsal.]

[1]Memorandum: that it is agreed byffor Mr William Wylde, parson, Mr William Remyngton, Aldreman, with all other of the paroschens affore, That Sir Iohn plommers bell schall serve ffor all poor people of this parysche, And for none other, paying j d for the Ryngyng. And it schall be Iugid by the said Sir Iohn plommer, he that desireth the bell whether that he be a poor man or not: And after his descese by the advyse of the Senyoures of the parysche.

Item, it is aggreed byffor maister william wylde and Mr William Remyngton, Aldreman, and afore all the paroschens, That whereas Iohn Ducklyng hath leyed owte of his purs ffor the chyrche werkes Summa x li, it is grauntid by the saide parson and paroschens to paye to the saide Iohn Ducklyng x li at the next Accoumpte, which shal be in the yer of owr lorde god m^{li} cccc iij^e.

Thies bene the dettes that ben oweng of this yer.

Resseyuyd by andrew evynger, Thomas ledale, ffysch-
    monger, for the bequest of William harman . . xx s
Vylliam Smerte, grocer, for the clarkes wages & beame-
    ly3te o yer . . . . iiij s iiij d

[A.D. 1502–3.
Iohn Awthorpe } Wardens.]
Andrew Evyngar

[Chantry Accounts, Church Rents, Payments and Reparations of same.]

[1] leaf 204, back.

Paymentes ffor the Chyrch.

* * * * *

[1]Payd for ij lampe glassis . . . . Som   ij d

* * * * *

Payd for bromys for the Chirche . . . .   iij d

* * * * *

Payd to vj pore men for beryng & holdyng of vj torchis in faenchirche street whan quene Elsab3 was karyid to Westmynster . . . .   xij d

[2]Payd for cortyn Rynges for the Chirche . . pris   ij d

Payd for a basket for holy brede . . . .   ij d

Payd for ryngyng of our bellys whan the kyng came from baynardes castell to powelles . . . . .   iij d

* * * * *

Payd to a fovnder for the makyng Clene & skoryng of the gret Candylstickes & alle the smale candylstickes, and for mendyng of them . . . . . ij s   iiij d

* * * * *

Payd to the Clerke & sexteyn & to watson ffor mete & drynke, from godfrydaye to Estyr eve at nyght   x d

* * * * *

Payd to a skryvener for the makyng of ij payr of Indenturs & ij oblygacions for hickelyng, for the performyng of our newe yle . . . . ij s

* * * * *

Payd to Iohn bull and watson for wachyng of our chirche whilys the chirche stoed opyn, eche of them vj ny3thtes, iiij d euery ny3ght . . . . iiij s

Payd for Rydyng to shoram ffor to see tymbir, for hyryng of iiij horse & horse mete and mannys mete . . . . Som vj s   vij d

* * * * *

Payd ffor wyne that was sent to Master parson to stratford with dyvers of our paryshe . . . .   xij d

* * * * *

[3]Payd to iiij men for beryng of iiij torchis on corpus christi daye . . . .   iiij d

* * * * *

---

[1] leaf 213.   [2] leaf 213, back.   [3] leaf 214.

Payd for v ellys of lynyn Clothe to make ij rochettes
for the quere, & for the makyng of them . . . ij s vj d

* * * * *

Payd for the makyng of a oblygacion with a payre of
desesans for Wylliam husse, grocer . . . . . vj d

Payd for a c of ij d nayl for the brygge of the vestrye
guttyr . . . . ij d

* * * * *

[1]Payd for ij lytyll lockes for the font . . . . . . iij d

Payd for a pike that was sent to my lord Abbot of
Waltham to Abbottes Inne . . . . ij s viij d

Payd for di. a turbutt . . . . xx d

Payd to a sarvant of my lorde Abbotes of Waltham
ffor a reward for bryngyng of venson . . . . xx d

Payd for the bakyng of the same venson and peper to
the same . . . . xxj d

* * * * *

Payd to hickelyng, for the wyndyng vp of the hye
Awtyr stoen hier . . . . v s

Payd to katermole, mason, for vnderpynnyng of the
same avtyr and for the leying of the steppys, for
v dayes . . . . ij s vj d

Payd to a harde hewer for iij dayes for the same, vij d
a daye . . . . xxj d

Payd to lodyan, for v dayes labor . . . . . . xx d

Payd to Iohn Carpenter & his man, for makyng of the
havelpase before the hye Awtyr . . . . . . vj d

* * * * *

[2]Casuelles Receytes.

Resseyvyd for the byryng of a shipman in the gret
chircheyarde . . . . xvj d

Resseyvyd for the ryngyng of our bellys for Mr ly of
Croydon . . . . iij s iiij d

Resseyvyd for the byryng of a Childe owt of bosse
alye . . . . xvj d

Resseyvyd in monye that was gadyrd on hockmondaye xv s v d ob

Resseyvyd de Mr Atclyff for brekyng of the grovnde
in seynt Kateryns Chapell for Iulyan his dowghter xiij s iiij d

Resseyvyd de Thomas hont for brekyng of grovnde
within the Chirche for his dowghter . . . xiij s iiij d

[1] leaf 214, back.   [2] leaf 215.

Churchwardens' Accounts, A.D. 1502-3.

Resseyvyd de Thomas hont for brekyng of grovnde in pardon Chyrcheyarde for a son of his . . . . ij s

Resseyvyd de ledalles wyff for the bequest of wylliam harman . . . . xx s

Resseyvyd de mastresse Noneley for brekyng of grownde for a sarvant of hers in pardon chirche yard . . ij s

Resseyvyd de Mr Iohn for berying of a pore man owt of drynkmylkes howse . . . . ij s

Resseyvyd de Robert Ryvell for brekyng of grovnde in pardon chirche yarde for a Childe of his . . . ij s

Resseyvyd de Stephyn Savndyrson and of Iohn povnde, eche of them a Childe, byryid, bothe in oon pitt iij s

Resseyvyd de Mr Remyngton for brekyng of grovnde in seynt stephyns Chapell for Mastresse Kellowe xiij s iiij d

Resseyvyd de Mr Smart for brekyng of grovnde in pardon chiche yard for ij childryn . . . . . iiij s

Resseyvyd de Mr Iohn for brekyng of grovnde in seynt kateryns Chapell for Mastresse Atclyff . xiij s iiij d

Resseyvyd de Mr Smart for brekyng of grovnde for his wyff in seynt kateryns Chapell . . . . . xiij s iiij d

Somma, vj li iij s j d ob.

[1]Clerkes wages, Beme lyght & Paskall lyght.

R' for the hole yere, quarterly gaderd, ffor the clerkes wages . . . . v li iij s

R' for the beme lyght in this yere. Somma . . . xv s viij d

R' at Estyr for paskall mony. Somma . . . . . xij s

Somma, vj li x s viij d.

Paymentes to the Clerke & Sextyn.

Payd to Iohn lawe, paryshe Clarke, for his yerys wages . . . . Som iiij li xiij s iiij d

Payd to Iohn Bull, sextyn, for his hole yerys wages
Som xl s

Somma, vj li xiij s iiij d.

Soe the paymentes excedes the Receytes ij s viij d.

[Obits.
Wax Reckoning.
Allowances.
Rehearsal.]

* * * * *

[1] leaf 215, back.

[A.D. 1503-4.

Iohn Mongeham ⎫ Wardens.]
Andrew Evyngar ⎭

[Chantry Accounts and Church Rents, Payments and Reparations of the same. The Chantries now pay a small subsidy to the King: Nasing's Chantry pays 4s. 6d.]

The paymentes for the Cherche.

* * * * *

[1] Payd for nayllys to mend the flooyr of the Roodloft — ij d

* * * * *

Payd for box at the hallovyng of þe Cherche to vasche þe Avttyres . . . . — j d

Payd for a skop and a gret laddyll . . . . . . — ij d ob

Payd for bred, ale & vyn at the halloyng of the Cherche . . . . — vij d

Payd to the svffrycan's man for the barrellys & tvbbys — iiij d

Payd for xij ellys of bryssell to mak Cressomes for the ballys . . . . — v s

* * * * *

spent at the abbottes in at the ettyng of a bok þat my lord Abbot of valttom gavf to the parysche . . — xx d

* * * * *

Payd for iij ellys and quarter of Normandy Canvas to mak larger the lenttyn Clothe for the hey avttyr . — xvij d ob

Payd to vovllf for the staynyng of the sam Clothe . — iij s iiij d

* * * * *

Payd for settyng of the Corttens heyyr to the hey Avttyr . . . . — iij d

* * * * *

Payd to a marbler for settyng in of iiij emagys . . . — iij s iiij d

* * * * *

spent appon seyr Iohn Nell & deyv[er]s of þe parysche at hys fyrst Cvmyng and the godes peny gyfyn hym . . . . — v d

* * * * *

[1] leaf 224, back.

[The New Pulpit.]

[1]Payd to Iohn bvH for hys labyr for makkyng þe pvlppet	ix s	viij d
Payd to hys man for xiij dayys vark to the sam . .	iiij s	iiij d
Payd for Nayllys to the sam pvlppet		ij d
Payd for savyng of stvff to the sam		vj d
Payd to a massyn for settyng in þe yerns in to the pellyr		v d
Payd for v ħ yeryn to the sam at j d oƀ þe ħ . . .		vij d oƀ
Payd for a peyyer of garnettes to the sam		vij d
Payd to the jovyner that kyt the lynttelles for þe sam pollpet		xij d
Payd for ij gyrddyllys for the prestes avbbys . . .		j d
Payd for a Cord for the Clovthe afor the Rood and for the savns beH		iiij d

* * * * *

Payd for ij Reddys to lythe Canddyllys vythe . . .		ij d
Payd for skovrryng of the lattyn ageynst Estyr . .		xx d
Payd to a govlldsmythe for makkyng a senssers foott .	ij s	viij d
Payd for a novns & di. and di. quarter of sylvyr to þe sam	v s	iiij d

* * * * *

Payd for a hasp and a stappyH for seynt Catterns ChappeH dor		iiij d
Payd for a gogyn to the savns beH		ij d

* * * * *

[2]Payd to Phellyp, Carppyntter, for makkyng the mens pevys	xxvj s	viij d

* * * * *

spent appon the mendyng ovyr the styer of the Rood-loft		iij d
Payd for a lok, ij keyys, a stappyH set in vythe led & a Ryng to þe Rodlovft dor		xx d

* * * * *

Memorandum: that Iohn Blas gavf to seynt [Ianes ?] avttyr the sylk to mak of a gospler, and the parysche to pay the makkyng, for the vyche I payd as hyt apperrythe by a byH	x s	viij d oƀ

* * * * *

---

[1] leaf 225.   [2] leaf 225, back.

spe*n*t at the havyng in of the ston for the steppyll vynddovs in to the Cherche & for þe stovyng of them	j d
P*a*yd to syr Reychard, the morromas prest, for a godd*es* peny	ij d

*   *   *   *   *

P*a*yd for Nayllys to mend vythe the gret pev . . .	j d
P*a*yd to a jovyner, for makkyng the p*a*rclos of the Rodlvft and the Crestys and for the sellyng vndyr Nethe	xxvj s viij d
[1] P*a*yd for Nayllys to the sam vark	iiij d
P*a*yd to a massyn and hys man, ij dayys & d*i*. to vndyrpyn the pevys in sey*n*t Cattyrns Chappell .	ij s viij d

*   *   *   *   *

P*a*yd for the tynny*n*g of a peyyer of garnett*es* for the gret dor ovt of the Chappell in to þe qvyer . .	ij d

*   *   *   *   *

P*a*yd to the glassyng of þe gret vyndd[ow] vythe þe Trenyte in the sovthe yell	xxv s iiij d

*   *   *   *   *

P*a*yd to Phellyp, Carpyntter, for the makky*n*g of the Nev vemens pevys	iiij li
P*a*yd to hym mor for the Remevyng and setty*n*g vp the ovlld vemens pevys	xx s
P*a*yd for Nev stvf to the sam pevys	xij d
P*a*yd for oovlld bordd*es* to flovyr þe sam pevys. . .	xij d

*   *   *   *   *

P*a*yd to a Boy þ*a*t hovlp to ber Rvbbys in to þe Cherche	ij d

*   *   *   *   *

[2] P*a*yd for a stay bar of yerryn to stay the Nev pevys in to þe vavtt	ij d

*   *   *   *   *

P*a*yd for a C of Reed for the vynddovs	x d
P*a*yd for thred and for Reddyng of þe vynddovs . .	v d
P*a*yd for iij lood iij sakk*es* lym to set þe fvnt, and vnddy*r*py*nn*y*n*g the Nev pevys and the oovlld in the sovthe yell	ij s vj d

*   *   *   *   *

---

[1] leaf 226.   [2] leaf 226, back.

[1] The Casvell Resseyttes.

Receuud de andrev Evyrryngger at his ACvnt makkyng	lix s ix d ob
Receuud de Wylliam Revell for brekkyng grvnd for hys chylld in the pardon Cherche yerd. . . .	ij s
Receuud de Thomas Baat for Brekkyng grvnd for hys vyf in seynt Cattyrns Chappell	xiij s iiij d
Receuud for the Berryyng of a povr voman, for brekkyng Grvnd in the gret Cherche yerd	xj d
Receuud de harry Edmonddes for Brekkyng Grvnd for hys vyf in the pardon Cherche yerd	ij s
Receuud de Iohn bvll for ovlld tymbyr	xij d
Receuud [de] Iohn of vappyng for a vhelbarrov. . .	x d
Receuud appon hokmonday, gaddyrd by the vyffys¦ .	xx s iij d
Receuud de mastyr atclyf for brekkyng grvnd for hys avllmys man in the pardon Cherche yerd . . .	ij s
Receuud de Thomas vattes for brekkyng grvnd in the Cherche for Thomas hvnt	xiij s iiij d
Receuud de Iohn Collyns for brekkyng grvnd for hys Chylld in þe pardon Cherche yerd	ij s
Receuud [de] Myltton for brekkyng grvnd for hys vyf in the Cherche	xiij s iiij d
Receuud de [2] mastyr Iohn for brekkyng grvnd in the Cherche for Thomas Collyns	xiij s iiij d
Receuud for iij lood of ston for þe pament afor þe lovmbarddes plas	iij s iiij d
Receuud de Iohn havlhed for Brekkyng grvnd in the pardon Cherche yerd for Iohn foox	ij s
Receuud de Mastres Nors for a chylld berryd in þe gret Cherche yerd	iiij d

Summa totallis, vij li ix s ix d ob.

[3] The Clarkkys vagys, bemlythe & pascavll lythe.

Receuud for the holl yer, qvarttyrly gaddyrd, for þe Clarkkes vagys	v li iiij s ix d
Receuud for the bemlythe thys yer gaddyrd	xj s ij d
Receuud for the pavscavll lythe	xiiij s

Summa totallis, vj li ix s xj d.

[1] leaf 227. [2] MS. 'the.'
[3] leaf 227, back.

Paymenttes to the Clark and Sextten.

Payd to Iohn lav, parysche Clark, for hys yers vagys iiij li xiij s iiij d
Payd to Iohn boll, sextten, for hys yers vagys . . . xl s
    Summa totallis, vj li xiij s iiij d.
Soo the paymenttes Exseyddys the Resseyttes thys yer, iij s v d.

[Obits.
Wax Reckoning.
Allowances.
Rehearsal.]

* * * * *

[1] Item, that was payede to Mawndye, mason, for the steple wyndow3 . . . . vj li
 Rest clere to the chirch, vij li ij s viij d, by Iohn Mongeham, warden.

Item, Iohn Mongeham most paye xiij s iiij d. Summa totalis, vij li xvj s, accoumptid the xxj day of Ianyver, anno 1504.

Payde by me, Iohn Mongeham, þe viij daye of feverer, Anno 1504, to Master Iohn wyngger, allderman, for money dew to hym for leed, as it aperythe more playnely in the boke of the chyrche byldyng in þe plomer parselles, summa vij li xvj s 728.

[A.D. 1504–5.

William Ryvell ⎫
Iohn Mongeham ⎭ Wardens.]

[Chantry Accounts, Church Rents, Payments and Reparations of the same.]

[2] The paymenttes for the Chyrche.

payde for mendyng a sylver Canstyke, to a goldesmythe . . . . viij d

* * * * *

payde for ij borden Rysches for þe strewyng of þe new pewes . . . . iij d

* * * * *

---

[1] leaf 228, back.   [2] leaf 236, back.

Churchwardens' Accounts, A.D. 1504–5.

payde & spentt vpon Master Monke, wex-chandeler,
when he browghte Master Wyllde bequest on
Crystmas even, Anno 1504 . . . .   iij d

payde for a chollve to pare the Chyrche . . . , . .   iiij d

* * * * *

payde to Ioyner for takeyng downe & settyng vp of
Master allderman pew, and for makyng of new
pew in sentt stevens Chapell . . . .   x s

* * * * *

payde for a wayneskott, and for selyng of þe bake syde
of sentt Anne awter & for sawyng of þe same, &
for workemanschyp . . . .   xviij d

* * * * *

payde for vj elles worsteed for ij blake Cooppes . .   xviij s

payde for xxvj garters for the same, & for make of þe
same ij Cooppes . . . .   x s

* * * * *

payde to a mason for Clensyng of þe sowthermvst arche
of þe stepyll, & for stoppeyng of þe Crase in þe
west wyndow . . . .   xx d

* * * * *

payde to Ioyner for þe makyng of a new Chest to putt
torches & for iren worke of þe same . . . . .   vj s

payde to Cornelys smythe for hangeyng of þe sakeryng
beell, & for þe iren work vnder þe branche byfore
þe rode . . . .   ij s

payde for a quer of paper ryall to wryte in the halowyng of the chyrche with other dyuerse thyngges
wreten by þe goodman hallehede, and sett in to þe
grete boke belongyng vnto the Chyrche. . . .   vj d

payde and spentt vpon the goodman hallehede whan he
wrete hyt . . . .   j d ob

payde to synod, glasyer, for glasyng of iij Cleer story
wyndows with glasse that Thomas wattes gave to
the Chyrche . . . .   x s

* * * * *

[1]payde for wyer & for mendyng of þe laympe in þe
queer & for bromes . . . .   j d ob

* * * * *

payde for ij beem dyschus belongyng to þe Rode lyghte   iij s

* * * * *

[1] leaf 237.

payde to þe Raker for his yeres wagges . . . . . viij d
payde for Crewettes for þe morow Masse prest . . . vij d
payde for iiij yerdes heer for þe hye Awter . . . . xviij d
payde for naylles for þe sepullcre, and spentt in þe Chyrche . . . . ij d oƀ
payde to a strange Clerk for syngyng in þe queer in ester weke . . . . xij d
payde to gylys, attorney, in yelde halle, for þe Copy of þe Constytycyons of offeryngges, & to hys Clerke for þe wrytyng of þe same . . . . iiij s viij d

* * * * *

payde for bote hyer at iij tymes goyng [to] Westmester to speke with þe executours of Mastres baron; Iohn Awthorpe & I, Iohn Mongeham & I . . iiij d oƀ

* * * * *

[1] payde to þe boke bynder at ledon halle, for Coveryng, byndyng & pesyng of iiij Antyfyners, a Masse boke, a manewell, a legentt in ij foloms & iij graylys . . . . xlvj s viij d

* * * * *

payde to synod, westmentt maker, for blake vellvett for to mende Master Cambryge Armes in þe Rede Coppes, & to a breyderer to mende þe orfores of þe same, with other vestmenttes . . . . iiij s ij d

* * * * *

payde for a parchementt skyn & for settyng in of the paper in þe olde boke of þe Chyrche wardens Acowntt . . . . viij d
payde to a glasyer for mendyng of vij wyndows on þe northe syde of þe Chyrche with ij Cler story wyndows . . . . x s

* * * * *

payde to hew Maderson, smythe, for v pentows hokes weyyng xix ℔ di., þe ℔ j d oƀ, & for mendyng of lok of þe vestry dore, & mendyng of the prevy, schottyng of þe same, for makyng of a new key to þe vestry Door . . . . vij s vj d

* * * * *

payde for bryngyng of borde & polys from kyngston . ij s viij d
payde for haveyng vp to þe Chyrche from þe water syde . . . . vij d

* * * * *

[1] leaf 237, back.

Churchwardens' Accounts, A.D. 1504–5.

[1]payde for ij lodys lyme when sentt kateryne chapell
was paved . . . .   xviij d

*   *   *   *   *

payde to the goodwyff huntt for makeyng of iiij awbes   xij d

*   *   *   *   *

The Casewall Reseyttes.

Resseyvyd of Master monke, wexchandeler, a standyng
Cooppe, of the bequest of Master Wylliam Wyllde,
late parson of sentt Mary at hyll, weyyng xxxij
vnces, the vnce iij s vj d. summa . . . .   v li xij s

Resseyvyd of Thomas Wattes, draper, of hys gyffte to
þe chyrche . . . .   xx s

Resseyvyd vpon hookmondaye of þe wyffes getheryng .   xxxiij s iiij d

Resseyvyd vpon hooktwesdaye of þe mens getheryng .   viij s   iiij d

Resseyvyd of thomas Merten towerd þe reparacyon of
hys howse . . . .   liij s   iiij d

Resseyvyd of Water Develyn towerd þe makeyng of a
pentows over hys fathers tombe . . . . .   ij s   viij d

Resseyvyd of Rychard drynkemylke for hys beryyng
[in] þe chyrche . . . .   xij s   iiij d

Resseyvyd of Mylltons [fr?]uer towerd the beoldyng of
þe Chyrche . . . .   xij d ob

Resseyvyd for a allder pole . . . .   viij d

Resseyvyd of þe good wyff huntt for her Chylldes beryyng in þe pardon Chyrche yerde . . . . .   ij s

Summa, xij li xvj d ob.

[2]Ihesus.

Paymenttes for Chyrche of þe Casewall Reseyttes.

payde to Wylliam Ryvell for that he payde for þe
Chyrche at þe byldeyng of the sowthe Ile, as it
aperythe in hys Acownt in that same boke . .   lvij s ij d ob

payde to Robert Mawndy, Mason, for xxxj nowelles,
þe pese ix d . . . .   xxiij s iij d

payde to Robert Mawndy for vj̄ fote water tabyll, þe
fote vij d ob . . . .   iij li xv s

payde to Robert Mawndy for j^c fote Coyne Ascheler .   xiij s iiij d

*   *   *   *   *

[1] leaf 238.   [2] leaf 238, back.

MED. REC.   S

[1] The Clerkke*s* waages, bem lyghte & passecalle.

Receuud for a hole yere, quarterly getherd, for the Clerkes wages	v li xj s	ix d
Receuud for a hole yere for þe bemlyghte	xij s	iij d
Receuud at Estur for the passecallyghte	xj s	v d

Summa, vj li xv s v d.

Paymentte*s* to þe Clerke & sexten.

Paid to Iohn law, parysche Clerke, for hys yere*s* wages	iiij li xiij s	iiij d
Paid to Iohn bolle, sexten, for hys yere*s* wages . . .	xl s	

Summa, vj li xiij s iiij d.

[Obits.

Wax Reckoning.

Allowances.

Rehearsal.

Part of the Will of Thomas Ryvell, grocer;

see p. 18.]

[A.D. 1505–6.

Stevyn Sanderson } Wardens.
William Revelle

The Chantry Accounts.

Rents of the Church.

Quitrents and Payments.

Payments for the Church.]

[2] The crarkys wag*es*, the beme lethe & the passecalle lethe.

Receuud off the clarkys wage*s* for a holl yere .	v li	v s
Receuud off the beme lethe for the holl yere .	xiij s	ij d
Receuud at ester for the pascall	xij s	

Summa, vj li x s ij d.

---

[1] leaf 239. [2] leaf 252.

[Payments.]

payd to Iħon lowne, perrys clarke, for a hoħ yer   iiij ħ xiij s iiij d
payd to Ihon boħe for hys wages for a hoħ yer .   xl s
Summa, vj ħ xiij s iiij d.

[Obits and allowance respecting the clerk's wages.]

[1] Ihesu.

The Casewettes Resayttes.

Receuud off Mestres halhede for the beryng off her hosband in the cherche	xiij s iiij d
Receuud off Wylliam potter, Mestres wattys sarvant, berred in the cherche	xiij s iiij d
Receuud off Master smartt, for the bequeste of Ihon medener hys sarvande	vj s viij d
Receuud be the getteryng off the women on ocke monday & also be the gettryng off the men off ocke teusday	xxvj s viij d
Receuud for a stranger preste yat was berryd in the cherche	xiij s iiij d
Receuud off the gude wyffes althorppe for the gyttryng off sentt bernebys day	xj d oƀ
Receuud yat I Receuud off vylliam Revyħ for v polles	xx d
Receuud off Mestres halhede for her mayd in pardon cherch yerd	ij s
Receuud off gudman edmondes for ij cheldryn in pardon cherch yerd	iiij s
Receuud off Robert hardyng for hys vyffe & hys cheld in pardon cherch[yerd]	iiij s
Receuud off stevyn Sanderson for a cheld in pardon cherch yerd	ij s
Receuud off a strange man belongyn to Master hosse, berryd in the cherche	x s viij d
Receuud off the bayle off bornewode for hys lede in the grett cherche yerde	xx d
[2] Receuud off Mestres hottyng for the beryng [of] hyr hosband in the cherche	xiij s iiij d
Receuud off her for ij off hyr cheldryn in pardon cherche yerd	iiij s
Receuud off her for the bequeste off Master hottyng towuerd the steppyħ beldyng . . . . vj ħ [?]	xiij s iiij d

[1] leaf 253.   [2] leaf 253, back.

260   *Churchwardens' Accounts*, A.D. 1506-7.

Receuud off ser Rycherd brycer for a vacason tyme in hys sarvys	iij s	iiij d
Receuud off Iamys monggoray for a cheld in pardon cher[ch] yerd	ij s	
Receuud off gude everyngger for ij chelder in pardon cher yerd	iiij s	
Receuud off gudeman halthorppe for a chelde in pardon cher yerd	ij s	
Receuud off Master Alderman ffor the beryng off bodylliȝ wyffes dowter beryng in þe pardon Cherche yarde	ij s	
Receuud off Master Al[d]eman ffor the beryng of brytton in the gret Cherch yarde		xij d

Summa, xiij li v s iij d ob.

[Wax Reckoning.
Two Allowances.
Rehearsal, etc.]

[1]Memorandum: yat ye yer of our lord god 15[?] it was determed, at Androw evenger accomptes, yat wer steven sanderson [*illegible*] we ye worshipfull of the parish than being present haith acquited hym for yat was for ye debt off thomas baat in the tyme steven was church warden. And so it was concluded yat I, William hatteclyff, person of sent maris at hyll, shuld thus acquiet hym by this my hand wryten.   per me, William hatteclyff.

[A.D. 1506-7.

Stevyn Saunderson }
Harry Edmonds   } Wardens.

Chantry Accounts.
Church Rents and Payments.]

*   *   *   *   *

[2]payd to Master rychard, pariche prest, for the bedroll . . . .   ij s

*   *   *   *   *

[3]Item, payd for makyng of j surplus for boll the sexten   xij d

*   *   *   *   *

[1] leaf 255.   [2] leaf 264.   [3] leaf 265.

Item, payd for makyng of ij keyes for the tresory
chest in the vestry . . . .   vj d
Item, payd for mendyng of a key for the churchyard
dore next love lane . . . .   iiij d

* * * * *

[1] the clerkes wagys & the beme lyte and the paskall lyte.

R' off the clerkes wagys for an hole yere . . .   v li xix s viij d
R' of the bemlyte for an hole yere . . . . .   xiij s iiij d
R' at estyr for the paskall lyte . . . . . .   xj s ij d
summa, vij li iiij s ij d.

[Payments.]

Item, payd to Iohn law, pariche clerke, for an
hole yere . . . .   iiij li xiij s iiij d
Item, payd to Iohn bull, sexten, for j quarteres
wages . . . .   x s
summa, v li iij s iiij d.

So there Remayneth of the Clerkes wages, beme
lyght and paskall more then the paymenttes   xl s x d

[Obits.]
[2] the casewell reseyttes.

R' off Wylliam ffrances for the det of Iohn blise . .   xx s
R' of Iohn petyte by the handes of stevyn sawndyrson   iij li
R' of robard dawson the he gave to the reparacions of
the hows that annes bedyll dwellyd in . . . .   xl s
R' of Iamys mongombre for the beryell of hys chyld .   ij s
R' of master remyngton, alderman, for the beryell of
my lady hys wyff in sent katerines chapell by þe
awter . . . .   xiij s iiij d
R' of Iohn Mowngham that he gave to the churche .   xx s
R' of sir thomas ascheborne þat he gave to the church   vj s viij d
R' of stevyn sawndyrson of hys gadyryng in þe church   xxxvj s iij ob
R' of Iohn doronttes wyff for the beryell of [her]
hewsbond . . . .   vj s viij d
R' of thomas wattes wyff for the beryell of hyr
howsbud in sent katerines chapell . . . . .   xiij s iiij d

[1] leaf 266.   [2] leaf 266, back.

R' of stevyn sawnderson for the beryell of a stranger . xij d
R' of master grene, costomer, by þe handes of Iamys
   mongombȝ . . . . x li
   Summa totallis, xx li xix s iij d ob.

[1] caswell paymenttes.

payd to Wylliam revell for xlij charder colys . . vj li xix s x d

* * * * *

[Wax Reckoning, Allowances, Rehearsal.]

[2] So Rest Cler of thys Acowntt made the xx daye
of Ianyuer Anno 1507 in the presens of
Master Alldernes, Master Smertt, Iohn
Russell, Iohn Awthorpe, Iohn mongham . ix li viij s iij d

besyde that Iohn banaster, draper, oweth Cler to
the Cherche at thys Acowntt for howse
Rentt . . . . iij li viij s iiij d

[3] Memorandum; that I, harry Edmondes, haue
delyuerd to Iohn Russell, now new chosyn
chyrchwarden, þe sum aforeseyd In the
presens of Master Smert, Stevyn saunderson,
William Roche, William Ryvell & mo othyr,
þe xx 10 Ianuar Anno 1507 . . . . . ix li viij s iij d

[A.D. 1507–8.

Iohn Russell   } Wardens.
Harry Edmonds }

Chantry Accounts.

Church Rents.

Payments.]

[4] The Casualtes thys yere.

Fyrst, We Charge vs with sertayn money delyuerd be the handes
of Stevyn sawnnderson & harry Edmondes vnto harry Edmondes &
Iohn Russell, of all suche proffettes, Revenewes, Arrerages, beqwestes,
Casualtes or eny othere avangtages Commyng to the seyd Cherche in
thys yere past, as hereaftyre folowyth.

Also we haue Resseyuyd of the Supploragiis of
the last yere . . . . ix li viij s iiij d

---

[1] leaf 267.   [2] leaf 268.   [3] leaf 268, back.   [4] leaf 278, back.

Churchwardens' Accounts, A.D. 1507–8.

Receyuyd of the gyft of Master Iohn Redy & Master Rychard the paryche prest for there dewte of the bede Rowll be them gevyn to the Cherche. . . . . ij s

Receyuyd of Iohn Banester for the Arerages of the Corner hows at stokkes, persell of the lyvelod of Maister Cambryge Renttes, the xx day of Aprill, A° m⁴ v c viij, whiche schuld a be payd the yere before vnto harry Edmondes in hys Tyme, that ys to say, mydsomer and myghelmasse. . . . . iij li

And now we have Receyuyd be Arbytrymentt of Maister Aldernesse, Wylliam Smert, Raff Tomson and gylbard gentyll. summa . . . . lj s   viij d

Rec' the viij day of may, of Iamys mongombres wyffe, for her husbandes beryall in the pardon Chyrche yerd, and for the wast of ij Torchys, masse and dyrege. Summa . . . . ij s   viij d

Ress' of Iohn mongham for the beryall of hys dowter wythyn the Cherche . . . . xiij s   iiij d

Rec' of hym for the beryall of hys other dowghter in the pardon Chyrche yerde. summa . . . . ij s

Rec' of Maister Aldernesse for the beryall of hys ij dowghteres in the pardon Cherche yerd and for the wast of ij torchys, to euery Chyld viij d. summa . . . . v s   iiij d

Rec' of Wylliam smert for the beryall of hys doughter wytheyn sentt stevyns Chapell . . . . . . xiij s   iiij d

Rec' of Wylliam pykeryng for the beryall of hys Chyld yn the pardon Cherche yerd . . . . ij s

Rec' of Wylliam Ryvell for the beryall of hys sonn yn pardon Chyrche yerd . . . . ij s

Rec' of Mestres bowghe for the beryall of herre seruantt . . . . ij s

Rec' of water dovlyn for the beryall of hys mothyre . ij s

Rec' of mestres Axe of the quest of Thomas hunt . . vj s   viij d

Rec' of Wylliam husse be an oblygacion of mestres noneley for xxxij wekes, euery sonday xij d. summa . . . . xxxij s

Rec' of the gaderyng of men & women on hop monday and Tewsday. summa . . . . xxx s

Summa, xvij li xv s iiij d.

[Payments for the Church.]

* * * * *

[1] Item, payde for makyng ij gret keys to the west dore yn the lytyll Chyrche yerd. summa . .   viij d

* * * * *

Item, payde for beryng of viij torchys on Corpus Christi day abowt the parysche . . . . . .   viij d

* * * * *

[2] Item, payd for byrchen bowys agayn mydsomer . .   iiij d

Item, payd for brede, wyne and ale on Relyke sonday for the qwere . . . .   iiij d

Item, payd the xxj day of Iulii to Nychollas bettnam, Mason, of ottam yn Kentt, yn party of paymentt of the batylmentt of the south syde of the Chyrche. summa . . . .   iij li

* * * * *

Item, payd for v bell popys for the bell Ropys . . .   xv d

* * * * *

Item, payd to a Carpynter for v days to make the pewys in the west end of the Chyrche and mendyng of other pewe dores. summa . . . . .   iij s iiij d

* * * * *

Item, payd to a fowndere, of lothbery, for makyng & sowdryng of ij branchys, one before owr lady in the qwere, and anothere before the salutacion of owre ady yn seynt katryns Chappell . . . .   xx d

* * * * *

Item, payd att thomas battes for brede & ale spent vppon Certeyn of the parysche when they had Chosyn a new Chyrche warden . . . . . .   ij d ob

Item, payd for iiij dosen Cotton Candell for all thys yere for the qwere and for morowe masse, at xv d the dosen. summa . . . .   v s

* * * * *

[3] Item, payd to Iohn Balame & to anothere porter for leyng vpp the tymber & makyng Clene the Chyrcheyerd & swepyng the wyndows agayn Crystmasse. Summa . . . .   iiij d

Item, payd to the Rakere for C[arege?] of all swepyng of þe Chyrche þis yere . . . .   viij d

* * * * *

---

[1] leaf 279.   [2] leaf 279, back.   [3] leaf 280.

[1] Receites of klerkes wages, beme lyght and paschall money.

Ress' thys yere of the Gaderyng of the klerkes wages	vj li	
Rec' thys yere of the Bemelyght	xiij s	iiij d
Rec' thys yere of the paschall money	xj s	viij d

Summa, vij li v s.

Paymentes of same.

Item, payd to Iohn lawe, paryche Clerke, for a hole yeres wages	iiij li xiij s	iiij d
Item, payd to harry hunt, sexten, for half a yeres wages	xx s	

Summa of this paymentes, v li xiij s iiij d.
Rest Clere of same, xxxj s viiij d.

[Wax Reckoning.
Allowances.
Rehearsal.
Debts to the Church.]

[2] Memorandum: Thomas Byrtte, lyme burner, oweth to sentt mary hyll Chyrche the xij day of Ianuarre, Anno mi v c vij, as ytt aperyth by Wylliam Ryvelles boke, for Colys bowght and delyuerd hym by the parysse. Summa   v li   x s   iiij d

Wherof hath be Resseyvyd yn lyme be me, Iohn Russell, thys yere vnto the Reparacions of all the lyvelod aforseyd, iij C di. at v s the C. summa . . . .   xvij s   vj d

*   *   *   *   *

[A.D. 1508–9.

William Roche } Wardens.
Iohn Russell

Chantry Accounts.
Church Rents.
Quytt Rentes and obyttes of same.]

---

[1] leaf 280, back.   [2] leaf 281, back.

Paymentes and Reparaciones of the same chirch & Rentes.

* * * * *

[1]Item, payd for beryng of iiij torchis when þe kyng was beryd . . . . ƭi s viij d

* * * * *

Item, for ij oblygacions betwixtt [billisdo ?] & þe paryshe for the grett belle . . . . . ƭi s viij d

* * * * *

Item, payd to viij men for beryng of viij torchis on corpus criste day . . . . ƭi s viij d

* * * * *

Item, payd to the clarkes that song ij Evynsonges and on mes . . . . ƭi vs d

Item, for a long poll þat longeth to the cloth of our lady of somsyon [Assumption] . . . ƭi s vj d

* * * * *

Item, for watter for the funt on Wytson yeuyn . ƭi s j d

Item, for mendyng of a syluer candylstecke with vyse . . . . ƭi s viij d

Item, payd to seuyn men that Rong the bellis when the kynges grace whent to Westmyster to be crownnyd . . . . ƭi js ij d

* * * * *

[2]Item, for a new surpelis for the parysh prist, cloth and makyng . . . . ƭi v s iiij d

Item, payd for that was spent at the settyng of ij torchis at Westmystir, geuyn be my ladys grase . . . . ƭi s x d

Item, paid for Ryngyng of sir Iohn plomer is knyll . . . . ƭi s viij d

Item, payd to a man that pleyd apon the organs on owre lady day of Somcion . . . . . ƭi js d

* * * * *

Item, for skonchis ij quartters and a planke & a benche in the pew next to the polpitt . . ƭi s xj d

* * * * *

Item, payd for the mendyng of the vyse of the syluer crose . . . . ƭi s vj d

---

[1] leaf 294.   [2] leaf 294, back.

Item, for mendyng of a key, and bellos of the grett organs . . . . li s v d

Item, payd for makyng of v pewis in ther [houhe?] wech was afore in iiij pewis, for nayllis vij d, for [ponshos?] viij d, ij carpyndars v days apece vj s viij d . . . . li vij s xj d

Item, paid vnto Rechard sons wyf for washyng of the sypers cloth and settyng on the garneshe that belongth to the pyx . . . . li s iiij d

* * * * *

[1] Item, payd to retayn master grenne for cownsell how to take a axcion for cutyng of owr iij bellis . . . . li j s viij d

* * * * *

Item, payd for a peyre of henges weyng iiij li & di. for þe Egill, with nayllis that cost . . li s ix d

Item, for makyng clenne of the same howse . . li s ij d

* * * * *

[2] The Casewell Resetes this yere.

ffyrst, R' of Iohn reseH of the surplesag of the last yere of his acowynte þat Remaneyd in hes handes . . . . li xix s ij d

R' of Master smarte for the Brekyng of the growynd in the churche for Mr Iohn Rodey li xiij s iiij d

Item, R' more, for the knyH for the said prest, of Mr Dokelynges Belle . . . . li vj s viij d

R' of hary hychekoke at ij tymes for þe Beqwest of Thomae Collenes . . . . ix li xix s viij d

R' of Mr smartt & Mestres hawlehed for the bequest of Mr Iohn Rodedy . . . . . iiij li s d

R' for the BeryaH of a prest that dyed at abottes In, in the chercheyerd . . . . . . li ij s d

R' of Iohn Pettett for the BeryaH of WylBam ReveH xiij s iiij d the pytte, vj s viij d the knylle, iij s iiij d the ston, x þat he gaffe to our Baytyllmente. summa . . . . . . j li xiij s iiij d

R' for the pytt wher as goodeman doklynge lythe R' be his lyfe . . . . li xiij s iiij d

R' for the knyH & pytte of Branke Twatte . . li xvj s viij d

R' for the knyH of the grett Belle for sir Iohn plomer, of his Executoures . . . . . li vj s viij d

[1] leaf 295. [2] leaf 296, back.

R' of my laydy the kynges grandam to our churche
xx s, wherof the [smoner ?] hayd viij d, Rest   li   xix s   iiij d
R' of Brankewattes wife that hyre husband be-
qwest to our churche   li   vj s   viij d
R' of Robard Revell for þe pyte of his doyghter   li   ij s   d
R' that Master darby promyseyd for Master parson
towarde the paveynge of our churche . . .   li   x s   d
   o Summa totallis, xxj li viij s x d o.

[1] Paymentes of the said casewalltes.

* * * * *

[2] Clarkes wages, Beme lyȝt & paskall lyght.

R' this yere of the gadyryng of þe clarkes wagges   vj li j s   vj d
R' this yer for the beme lyȝt   li   xv s   j d
R' this yere for the pasecall money   li   xj s   vj d
   Summa, vij li viij s j d.

Paymentes of the same.

fyrst, paid to Iohn lowe, the clark, for his yeres
wages xxiij s iiij d euery quarter . . . .   iiij li xiij s iiij d
Item, paid to william wylld, sexten, for his wages
this yere . . . .   ij li   s   d
   Summa, vj li xiij s iiij d.

And so ther Restes clere that is Resseyuyd more
then is paid, xiiij s ix d.

[Wax Reckoning.
Allowances.
Rehearsal.]

* * * * *

[3] Memorandum : this is Iohn Alltropes hande, wrytyn by hym for the dyschcarge of the said William Roche in presence of the forsaid persones.

[A.D. 1509–10.

Iohn Condall } Wardens.
William Roche

---

[1] leaf 297. [2] leaf 297, back. [3] leaf 299.

Chantry Accounts.
Church Rents.
Quitrents and Obits.
Payments and Reparations.]

* * * * *

[1] Paid to sir William Bryse for a Reward for kepyng the orgons for the hole yere, besidis his salary . x s

* * * * *

Paid for a Cruet for the Morowe Masse . . . . . iiij d

* * * * *

[2] Paid for disseplynyng Roddis & nayles for þe sepulcre . . . . ij d
Paid for a whele Barowe . . . . xiiij d

* * * * *

Paid for a lok to the prestes Ale gate with vj keys . viij d

* * * * *

[3] Paid for brede and ale for the parisshons þat helpid to labor for Nicholas Betnaham when he was taken to the Kynges wourkes at ij tymes . . . ij d ob

* * * * *

Paid for bote hire to Grenewych for Iohn Althorpe and Nicholas Betnaham to speke with M^r hatclyff . . . . v d
Paid to the Mayrys yeman for settyng of the wardens of the Masons before the Mayre . . . . . . iiij d
Paid to a Coper for hopyng of the Tobbys and þe Barelles that longith to the Chirche . . . . . xvj d
Paid for fettyng the Geyn from þe Carpenters . . . j d
Paid for Beryng of the sond in to the chirchyerd ij d
Paid for vj lode of Sonde, the lode vj d. Summa . iij s
Paid for a key for the Chirche box . . . . . . iij d

* * * * *

Paid for my Costes for me & my horse to Kyngeston, for to by bourde and lathe . . . . x d

* * * * *

Paid on Seint Barnabes day for garlondes & yerbis . xiiij d ob

---

[1] leaf 306, back. [2] leaf 307.
[3] leaf 307, back.

Paid þat day for Brede, wyne & ale for þe syngers of the Kynges chapell & for þe Clarkes of þis towne	xv d
Paid for ij galons wyne, gevyn to the syngers of the Kynges chapell at Mr Sidboroughts at dyner . .	xvj d
Paid to the Clarkes of this Citie for theyre Rewarde .	v s
Paid for ffreight of a lode Coynes from Maydstone .	xij d

* * * * *

[1] Paid for Nayles and Mendyng of a Benche in the quere	j d
Paid for a Soper, to Mr Kyght and Mr Sidborowgh, for the Arbetryng betwene the parissh and Bullisdon for þe belles:—for Motton, a shulder iij d; Conys v d; iiij chekyns vj d; a Capon xx d; brede, ale, wyne and Beer xxj d. Summa totallis	iiij s vij d

* * * * *

Paid for mendyng of the fourme in the quere . . .	ij d

* * * * *

Paid to Alis Smale for wasshyng of the lynnen for a yer	iij s iiij d
Paid to Alis Smale for settyng on of the parelles on the Albys and for mendyng of Surplysys & Albis	xij d

* * * * *

[2] Payd for mendyng of sir Iohn Nelis chales . . .	ij d

* * * * *

Paid for iij plattes with nosis for þe skonsis	ij d
Paid for ij hand canstickes	j d

* * * * *

The sute for the belles.

Paid for entryng the playnt & for þe Arest of William Smyth	x d
for entryng of þe Attourney & for his fees	xiiij d
for makyng of our plee & leyng in þerof	vj d
paid to þe Iooge	iiij d
to Master stevyns for councell	xx d
for my dyner & Thomas Mondens, And þe man þat hew the belles & oþer mo	vj d
Whan the mater was pletid to an yssue, paid . . .	iiij d

---

[1] leaf 308. [2] leaf 308, back.

for ij somons, paid to the se*r*geaunt . . . . . . iiij s
Whan the mater was put in dayng at þe salutacion . ij d
for an oblygacion at þat tyme . . . . vj d
Summa   x s

*   *   *   *   *

[1]The Casuell Receytes.

Ress' of s*ir* Thomas of Gravisend and of harry herd for the olde Rode and mary and Iohn þat stode in the chirch . . . . xx s

Ress' of Mays wyffe of Seint Me*r*gret patens, of gyfte   vj s   v:ij d

Ress' of the surplusage of the last yeris Acownte of Will*ia*m Roche, in money . . . . xv s

Ress' of Will*ia*m Roche for halffe a guttu*r* p*ar*table betwene the chirche Rentt*es* and the Chaundeler in seint me*r*gret patens . . . . vj s

Ress' of the gadryng of hokmonday and Tewisday . . xxxij s vj d

Ress' of Iohn Markham at his comyng to his howse . xx s

Ress' of a straunge prest þat dyed at the freer, for his beryall in the p*ar*don chirche yerde . . . . iiij s

Ress' of Will*ia*m Browne, Chaundeler, for the beryall of his wyffe in þe chirche yerde . . . . . . ij s

Ress' of Thomas duklyng for the beryall of his childe and for ij Torches . . . . ij s   iiij d

Ress' of Iohn Wall for ij Bras pott*es* weyng xlij ll, at ij d ob the ll. Sum*m*a . . . . viij s ix d

Ress' of Will*ia*m pykeryng for the beryall of his wyfe   xiij s iiij d
Sum*m*a, vj li x s vij d.

[2]Resseit*es* of clarkis wag*es*, pascall money and Beme lyght.

Ress' this yere of the Gadryng of the clerk*es* wag*es*   vj li xiij s iiij d
Ress' of the pascall money this yere . . . . . . xij s
Ress' of the Bemelight this yere . . . . xiij s iiij d
Sum*m*a, vij li xviij s viij d.

Paymentt*es* of þe same.

Paid to Iohn lawe, p*a*risshe clerke, for his yeris wag*es*, eue*r*y quater xxiij s iiij d. Sum*m*a . . iiij li xiij s iiij d

---

[1] leaf 309.   [2] leaf 309, back.

Paid to lawrence Swayne for his wages for kepyng the Orgons for iij quarters, euery quarter x s. Summa . . . . xxx s
Paid to William Sexten for his wages for a yere . . xl s
Summa, viij ḷi iij s iiij d.

So the paymenttes exsediṭh the Resseittes iiij s viij d.

[Wax Reckoning.
Allowances.
Rehearsal.]

[1] Rekenyd this A Cowntt the xx day of Ienuary, Anno 1510, in the presence of Mr William hatclyff, Mr Robert Aldernes, William Smert, Ioḥn Russeḻḻ, William Roche, Ioḥn Moungeham, Ioḥn Althourpe, Thomas Dukkelyng, withe other. And brought in the same day be the hondis of Ioḥn Condaḻḻ in golde in Noblys . . . . xxj ḷi
The whiche is in the Chirche box.

* * * * *

[A.D. 1510–11.
Thomas Duklyng ⎫ Wardens.
Iohn Condall   ⎭

Chantry Accounts.
Rents of the Church.
Quitrents and Payments of the same.
Payments.]

* * * * *

[2] Paid for ix elles of lynnen clothe for awterclothes, at vj d oḅ the eḻḻ. Summa . . . . iiij s x d oḅ
Paid for markyng and makyng of them . . . . . iiij d
Paid for xxviij elles of lynnen clothe for iiij surplyses, for euery surples vij elles, þe eḻḻ vj d oḅ. Summa . xv s ij d
Paid to Margret Sutton for makyng of them . . . iiij s
Paid for lv elles lynnen clothe for xj Albis, and for vj elles for Amesis, the eḻḻ vj d oḅ. Summa . . . xxiij s oḅ

---

[1] leaf 311.   [2] leaf 319, back.

Churchwardens' Accounts, A.D. 1510–11.

Paid for makyng of xj Albis, vj Amesis & for ij dosseyn Tapis	ij s vj d
Paid for halowyng of xj Albis, the Amyses and iij Awterclothes	ij s vj d
Paid for makyng of v olde Albis, v Amyses & iiij surplises for children	xij d
[1] Paid for makyng of iiij Awterclothes and vij Towelles, whiche wer made of the olde albis	viij d
Paid for mendyng of xij grete Albis, and for settyng on of the parelles	xij d
Paid to Alis Smale for wasshing of þe chi[r]che lynnen for a hole yer	iij s iiij d
Paid more to her for wasshing of M*r* Suttons Corperassis, and for parelyng of his Albes	iiij d
Paid for mendyng of M*r* Cambriges holywatur stoppe of laton	viij d
Paid to the skryvener for makyng of þe Indentures betwixt William Smyth, bell fownder, and the parissh, that tyme Arbytrators M*r* Robyns and M*r* Ientyll, & for wyne	xvij d ob
Paid for Reves labur & his Brekefast for comyng from ludgate to Algate to here þe iiij[th] bell in Tewne	vj d ob

*   *   *   *   *

[2] Paid for a hynge for þe gate on þe west side of the chirch	ij d
Paid for makyng of ij keys for the Chirche box . .	viij d
Paid for a handyll of Iron to the same box	iiij d
Paid for a key to the Est gate in the North chirchyerd	iij d
Paid for makyng of Iren wourke to the Table by þe founte	xij d
Paid for shotyng of a Rodde of Iron for þe grete canope	j d
Paid for Mendyng the key of Seint Annys chapell dore	ij d

*   *   *   *   *

Paid for mendyng of a curten Rodde for M*r* Suttons Alter	j d

*   *   *   *   *

Paid [for] brede & drynke on good friday at dyner and at nyght iij d, And on Estur Eve for dyner and at nyght v d. Summa	viij d

*   *   *   *   *

[1] leaf 320.   [2] leaf 320, back.

[The Bells.]

Paid for wyne & peres at skrasis howse at Algate for Mr Ientyll, Mr Russell, Iohn Althorpe, Iohn Condall & the clarkes of Seynt Antonys to go and see wheþer Smythes bell wer Tewneabill or nat .		viij d
Paid for brede & drynk to hym þat strake þe belles .		ij d
Paid for strekyng of þe iij belles to þe grownde . . .	ij s	
[1] Paid for a C of smale Ropis for to streke the belles .	x s	
Paid for Drynke to the porters þat holpe to stryke þe belles		ij d
Paid for the Cariage of ij belles to the ffownders . .	ij s	
Paid for to vj porters to helpe them on the slede . .		vj d
Paid for brede, ale and wyne at þe fest of transfiguracion		iiij d
Paid for brede, ale and wyne on allhalou day in the vestry		vj d
Paid for xl ll of rope for the belles, at jd quarter the ll. Summa	iiij s	ij d
Paid for wyne, at the salutacion, at the bargeyne makyng for the frame of the belles		vij d
Paid for the oblygacion makyng for þat bargeyne . .		iiij d
Paid for the goddis peny in honde	xl s	
Paid to the Carpenter for his full bargayne	v li	
Paid to William howtyng for a waynskot		xiiij d
Paid for sawyng of þat waynskot for the bell whelis .		vj d
Paid for Naylys for whelis of the belles		j d
Paid for iiij square bolsters of Iron for þe grete belles, weyng vj ll & di.		xiij d
Paid for Mendyng of xij kayes for the belles . . .		ij d
Paid for makyng for boltes of Iron for your sowith bell		x d
Paid for iiij bokylles for the bawdrykes of the belles .		viij d
Paid for dressing of v stayes for þe bell whelis . . .		x d
Paid for kays for the stapulles of a bell		j d
Paid for j c grete Naylys for the belles		x d
Paid for xij wegis of Iron for the gogeons of þe belles		vj d
Paid for dressing of þe harnes for the belles		vj d
Paid for v Casis of Iron for the wyndowys of þe upper story in the chi[r]che, the case xx d. Summa .	viij s	iiij d

---

[1] leaf 321.

Churchwardens' Accounts, A.D. 1510–11.

Paid to Iohn Eylewyke, smyth, for makyng of a kay & Remevyng & settyng on of the lock on the chest with Torchis	iiij d
Paid to a laborer to cary the stuffe owte of the parsonage into the charnell howse, for a day . . .	iiij d
Paid for a bawdryke for the first bell, and for mend[y]ng of the olde bawdrykes	xiij d ob

* * * * *

[1]Paid for settyng of the hoke þat the Table hangith on by the ffownte	iiij d

* * * * *

Paid for Mr Kytis & Mr Cornysh dyner in Mr Aldremans place:—for a pyke xxij d, for a Iowle of fressh samon xxij d, for iij playse xij d, oysters j d, brede, ale, wyne & perys xix d. Summa . . .	vj s iiij d
Paid for a pyke ij s viij d, for ij Solys iiij d, for halff a syde salt fyssh iiij d, for Rochis iiij d, oysters j d, for buttur j d, for a pye of quinsis vj d, for brede, ale, wyne, erbys & a side of lynge & flownders, nottes, ffyre & sawce ij s vj d; for the Cokes labur for dressing this dyner at Mr Sudborowys for Mr Kyte and harry prenttes of the kynges chapell iiij d. Summa	vij s j d
Paid to William Smyth, fownder, for j C di. xvj lb of newe metall to þe iiijth bell, the c xxvj s viij d. Summa	xliij s viij d
[2]Paid to William Smyth, fownder, for makyng the scripture aboughte the bell	xiij s iiij d
Paid for mendyng & garnysshyng of iij bell clapers .	v s x d
Paid to Coulverton, Belfownder, for ij C xiiij lb of Newe metall for the grete bell, after xxviij s the C. Summa	lix s vj d
Paid to Bullisdon, in Bates howse in the presens of Mr Smart for the Rest of the grete bell, in money .	xxix s iiij d
Paid for mendyng & garnysshing of þe grete bell claper	ij s iiij d
Paid for ij New Bawdrykes for the belles	xij d
Paid for Drynke at the havyng vpp of the belles . .	j d
Paid for Naylys for the whelys	ij d
Paid to a Mason for makyng the wyndowys in the steple by the belles, and for stoppyng of the holys at the crosse beamys endes & other plasis in the steple, for ij days & di. wourkyng	xx d

* * * * *

[1] leaf 321, back.   [2] leaf 322.

[1] The Casuell Receytis.

Ress' of the Gadryng of hokmonday by the wemen .	xxj s	j d
Ress' of the Gadryng on Tewysday by Iohn Condall & me	v s	iiij d
Ress' of Goodwyn for the Beryall of an Armyte . .	ij s	
Ress' of a portingale þat was killed in the shipp at Billingesgate		xx d
Ress' of money taken for a Rusty harnes þat was sold	iij s	
Ress' of William wylde for v Candylstyckes . . .		xx d
Ress' of Iohn hutton for the Buryall of his son . .	ij s	
Ress' of Iohn a lathham for his wyffis broder, for buriall		xij d
Ress' of Mr Aylemer for Mr Remyngtons buriall within þe Chirche.	xiij s	iiij d
Ress' more of hym for the knyll vj s viij d, of the which :—paid to Symonde lorymer ij s for the Copy of Mastur Remyngtons wyll, and to William wilde for the Ryngyng of the knyll iij s iiij d	vj s	viij d
Ress' of Iohn Condall in Ernest of Trappis howse . .	vj s	viij d

Summa of thes parcelles, iij li iiij s v d.

[2] Resseites of clarkes wages, pascall money & Beme light.

Ress' this yere of the Gadryng of the Clarkes wagis	vj li x s	iiij d
Ress' of the pascall money this yere	xiij s	

Summa, vij li iij s iiij d.

Paymentis of the same.

Paid to William wilde for his wagis this yere . . .	iiij li
Paid to lawrence Swayne for his wages this yere . .	xl s

Summa, vj li.

So Restith þat þe of this Resseites more þane þe paymentes as aperith aboue. Summa, xxiij s iiij d.

[Wax Reckoning.
Allowances.
Rehearsal.]

[1] leaf 323.   [2] leaf 323, back.

[A.D. 1511–12.

Iohn Woulffe } Wardens.
Thomas Duklyng

Chantry Accounts.
Church Rents.
Quitrents and Payments.
Payments for the Church.]

* * * * *

[1] paid to sir Robert for Candell to sey his matens in the mornynges	iij d
paid for hopys abought the crosse in the grete chirch-yard, & for Naylys to the same crosse	iiij d
paid to Alys Smale for wasshyng of the chirch lynnen for a quarter endyd at our lady day	x d

* * * * *

paid for ij long quarters to kepe the bell Ropis from the wall of the steple	xj d
[2] paid to Iohn Smyth, besydes the gyfte of good Masturs & Mestresis, for the whyte lymyng of the chirche: Summa þat I paid to hym . . .	xv s

* * * * *

paid to Robert Trappis for the chonnge of a Chales & for the overweight of syluer	xiij s iiij d

* * * * *

paid for brede, ale & wyne for þe quere on trinyte sonday	vj d
paid for mendyng of the ladder for þe pulpett . . .	iiij d

* * * * *

paid to broodes wyffe, the Raker, for Midsomer quarter	ij d
paid to Alys smale for wasshyng for þat quarter . .	x d

* * * * *

[3] paid for Drynk for the quere on Relyk sonday . .	iiij d
paid the Suffregan for haloyng of a Chales, iiij Corporassis & iiij vestementtes	iij s viij d
paid for ij Crewettes for sir Mores	viij d

* * * * *

---

[1] leaf 335.   [2] leaf 335, back.
[3] leaf 336.

paid to þe smyth for mendyng of þe lok & þe spryng of þe sowthe chirch dore		iiij d
paid for shevys of Brasse to hange þe lampe & þe pascall, the on peyre cost xij d, the oþer peire viij d. Summa		xx d
paid for iiij polys, the pece j d ob		vj d
paid for Iron warke for þe polys, to bullok		xij d

* * * * *

paid to Alys Smale for wasshyng of the chirche lynnen for a quarter endyd at Mighelmas		x d

* * * * *

[1]paid for a grete hoke for the Rope of þe lampe . .		ij d
paid to sir Iohn Tyllysley, for a Reward for his bokys	iij s	iiij d
paid for mendyng of þe lytell orgons in þe quere . .		vj d
paid to Alys smale for a Reward, at þe comandamentt of Mr Aldreman, Mr Ientyll for her labur besides her quarterage		xvj d

* * * * *

paid for a stok locke to þe chirch yerde dore next the parsonage, with ij keys	ij s	vj d

* * * * *

Item, paid to þe goodman Mershe for di. a day . . .		iiij d
paid for iij days, for his Apprenttes		xij d

* * * * *

paid for a lok & a key, [&] a peyr garnettes for a chest in the quere to ley in old wax		xij d

* * * * *

costes of þe spirituall courte.

paid in the spirituall courte for the Recouere of þe dewtyes of Seint Anne, ayenst Iohn Semper:—

first þe citacion		xvj d
paid for the execucion of þe same		xiiij d
paid for the sertificath vppon the same execucion . .		xiiij d
paid to the proctor in the courte		viij d
paid for makyng of the interogatorys	ij s	
paid for the Actes in the courte		iiij d
paid for the salares of the proctors	iij s	iiij d

[1] leaf 336, back.

paid for wryting of the terogatores	iij s	iiij d
paid for brede & ale, Mr Russell & Mr Ientyll present	ij d ob	

* * * * *

[1] Paid for xvj lb of New lede for the hoke of the vyse dore in the Rood lofte . . . . x d

* * * * *

paid for a Rope for sanctus bell . . . . v d

* * * * *

[2] Resseittes of clarkes wages, pascall money & Beme light.

Ress' this yere of the Gadryng of the Clerkes wages	vij li	iij s
Ress' this yere of the pascall money	xiij s	iiij d

Summa of thes parcelles vij li xvj s iiij d.

Paymenttes of the same.

Paid to Richard Alee, Clerke, for his wages for iij qarters of a yere & a halffe, after vj li þe yere. Summa . . . . v li v s

Paid to William Wylde for his wages this yere for the sextenship, & for halff a quarter of the clerkes wages that he seruyd aftir Mighelmas befor þe clerk cam in seruyce. Summa . . . . . . xlv s

Paid to lawrence Swayne for his wages for halff a yere endid at our lady day. Summa . . . . . . xx s

Summa of þes parcelles viij li x s.

So the paymenttes excedith þe parcelles of the Resseyttes xiij s viij d.

[3] The Casuell Receytis.

Ress' of the Gadryng of hokmonday by the wemen	xx s	
Ress' of the Gadryng on Tewysday	iiij s	
Ress' for a grete laton pot weyng xxxvj lb, the lb ij d ob. Summa	vij s	vj d
Ress', more, for a flat chafur withe a bayle of Iron, an hangyng laver with a cheyne of Iron, a gret olde pan with a bond & ij eres, of Iron, weyng all xxxvij lb, the lb ij d ob. Summa	vij s viij d ob	
Ress' for a chafyng dyssh, price	xvj d	

[1] leaf 337. [2] leaf 337, back. [3] leaf 338.

Ress' of Mr Aldyrnes the viij day of May A° 1512 of the money whiche he hath in custody for the chirche behoff, as shall apere by a byll of my hond, the su*m*ma of . . . . x li

Ress' of Thomas Duklyng for the Rest of his ACompte of the Chirchwardenship . . . . . . iij li xix vij d

Su*m*ma of þes p*a*rcelles xvj li j d ob.

[Wax Reckoning.
Allowances.
Rehearsal.]

[A.D. 1512–13.

Thomas Marten } Wardens.]
Iohn Woulfe

'The quitrentt*es* goyng fourth of the chauntris & chirchrentt*es*.'

* * * * *

[Chantry Accounts.
Church Rents.
Quitrents and Payments.
Payments for the Church.]

* * * * *

[1]Paid to s*ir* Iohn Tyllysley for a Rewarde for his bok*es* . . . . iij s iiij d

* * * * *

Paid to Alys smale for wasshing the lynnen for a yere iiij s

* * * * *

Paid for settyng on of parell*es* on dyu*er*s albys & mendyng of them, to Alys Smale . . . . v d

* * * * *

Paid to a Carpent*er* & his man for a day for Takyng downe of the lampe howse & for makyng of a pentt*es* ou*er* on of the glasse wyndowys on þe north syde . . . . xvj d

* * * * *

[1] leaf 349, back.

Churchwardens' Accounts, A.D. 1512–13.

Paid for settyng of the polyes for the pascall and for Reysyng of a ladder & for Nayles	xvj d
paid to a laborer for Caryeng of Rubbysshe owte of the Chircheyerd and for makyng clene of bothe the Chircheyerdes, for iij days labur	xij d

* * * * *

paid for skowryng of the Chirche laton and for mendyng of the basen for the lamp	ij s	v d
paid for Ryngyng of Mestres Noneleys knyll . . .		vj d
[1] paid to sir Robert for kepyng of the Morowe Masse for iij quarters at myghelmas for a Reward aboue his chauntry	xv s	

* * * * *

paid for nayles for the Sepulcre	j d
paid for a Carpenter to set up the Sepulcre	iiij d

* * * * *

paid to a condukte for the Estur halydays, for lak of the Clarkes absence, for to play at orgons . . .	ij s	iiij d
paid for Bred & dry[n]ke at Batys for Mr Russell, Mr Ientyll, Mr Sydborowe for ij tymes at the hiryng of the clerke Robert Claver		iij d ob

* * * * *

paid for mendyng of the pix clothe þat Mestres Duklyng gave to the high Awter	ij d
paid for wryghting of the counturpane of the clerkys Indenture for the charge of the Revestry . . .	vj d
paid for Nayles for the halpace in the chirche for the belles—first ij c v peny nayle, j c vj peny nayle, ij c iij peny, ij c ij peny nayle, & ob for Nayles for þe garnettes on the vyse dore in the steple by the Bellffray	xx d ob

* * * * *

[2] paid for Mendyng of a lok for þe vyce dore & for ij keys for the same lok	vj d
paid for a square bolt at the lower dore of the vyse & for mendyng of a peyre garnettes & a square staple	v d

* * * * *

paid for mendyng of all the bell clapers, for makyng þe bottes of them newe	vj s iiij d

* * * * *

[1] leaf 350.   [2] leaf 350, back.

paid for Cariage of Tymbre for þe pewys in seint Iohn Chappell	ij d

* * * * *

[1] paid for a Mason & his man for pavyng within Seint Iohns chappell & withowte, And for v trayes of morter	vij d

* * * * *

paid for makyng of iij Mennys pewys, for the popeys & other stuff	xx s

* * * * *

paid for vndyrpynnyng of the Menys pewys And the wonenys pewys, & for pavyng of Iohn lawys grave, & for lyme & sonde, & his labur & his Manys	xx d

* * * * *

[2] Item, paid for x elles of holand clothe for a surplys for Mr Doctor, the ell x d. Summa	viij s iiij d
paid for makyng of the same surplis, to woodkokes wyffe	xx d

* * * * *

paid for the arest of Iohn Banaster	viij d
paid for entryng of the Attorney	ij d

* * * * *

paid for palme the Attorney in þe Mayres courte . .	xij d

* * * * *

[3] Resseittes of the Clarkys wages, pascalmoney & Bemelight.

Ress' this yere of the Gadryng of the Clarkes wagis	vj li xvij s vij d
Ress' this yere of the pascall money	xvj s j d ob
Summa of thes parcelles	viij li xiij s viij d ob

Paymentis of the same.

paid to Iohn davy, clerke, and Robert Claver, clerke, for euery of them for di. a yeres wagys iij li. Summa	vj li

---

[1] leaf 351.   [2] leaf 351, back.
[3] leaf 352.

paid to William Wylde for his wages this yere for
    sextenship . . . .   xl s
        Summa of thes ij parcelles viij li.
    So the Resseites is more than paymentes xiij s viij d ob.

¹The casuell Reseitis.

Ress' for the Buryall of Richard pownde in þe pardon chirchyerd	ij s	
Ress' for the knyll of Mestres Nonelay	vj s	viij d
Ress' for the Brekyng of the Grownde for hyre . .	xiij s	iiij d
Ress' of the Gadryng of the Maydens on seint Barnabes day	vj s	viij d
Ress' of Robert Ryvell for the Buryall of his ij children	iiij s	
Ress' of Thomas Duklyng for þe Buryall of his dowghter	ij s	
Ress' of Thomas Powre for the buryall of his wyffe and his wyffes systur in the pardon Chirch yerd	iiij s	
Ress' of Mr Russell for the buryall of Margery . . .	ij s	
Ress' of Stephyn Sawnderson for the buryall of his ij Children in the pardon chirche yerd	iiij s	
Ress' of Mr Mongeham for þe buryall of a childe . .	ij s	
Ress' of Thomas Baate for the buryall of his son . .	ij s	
Ress' of Robert hardyng for the buryall off a Sowdear	ij s	
Ress' of Mr Roche for the buryall of his son . . .	xiij s	iiij d
Ress' for the grownde for a Maryner þat dyed at Master Smerttes key		iiij d
Ress' for the grownde for a Sowdear þat dyed at Byllingesgate		xj d
Ress' for the Buryall of Iohn lawe, Clarke	xiij s	iiij d
Ress' of drynkmylk for the bequest of his wyffe . .	vj s	viij d
Ress' of Thomas powre for the wast of vj torches for dyrige and masse at þe buryall of his wyff . . .	iij s	
Ress' of the Bretherhed of Seint Christofurs towardes the makyng of the pewys in seint Iohn chapell .	vj s	viij d
Ress' of Iohn Woulffe for the Rest of his Acownte of the chirchewardenshipp . . . . iij li	iiij s	v d ob

Summa of thes parcelles vij li xix s iiij d ob.

Ress' of the wardens of Seint Annys brethehod . . xiij s vj d ob

Summa totallis viij li xij s xj d.

---
¹ leaf 352, back.

[Wax Reckoning.
Allowances.
Rehearsal.]

¹Dettes dew to the chirch at this day of A cownpte.

* * * * *

Ress' | Item, more, the is owyng be watur develyn for the buryall of his sistur in þe pardon chircheyerde . . . . ijs
per gentyll

* * * * *

[Sums mostly due for clerk's wages.]

* * * * *

²Memorandum: the Restith in the hondes of William hewys and Thomas Monden for gadryng of the Almys in the chyrche which shall be reserwed toward beryalles of pure pepull and oyer dedes of charite.

Memorandum: yt is concluded to Ress' the Indenture of Mestres halhed for the byldyng of Robert Ryvell howse; and so to sewe Mʳ Russell by the lettur of Attorney of Mestres halhed. Post.

* * * * *

Item, the Restith in Mʳ Russelles hondes the gret key of the vestry dore. Post.

* * * * *

Item, to make saale of the howsold stuff in the vestry. Post.

Item, to make inquire for certayn tyle.

³It is deteremend that they shall go in hand with the byldyng of the chyrche at merche next.

Memorandum: that Jnᵒ allthrorpe & stevyn sandyrson hath promyseyd to take the charge, & kepe reknynge to pay, all such warkmen as shall make the Battyllment of our church of Breke or ston or led as shal be thorte best & detarmemenyd by Mʳ alldyrman & the parysheynge; & Master parson to aȝyst thame with hes good dylygense & wysedeme for to the best that he can for þe same; & Thomas Monders choseynyn by the said paryshe to waytte apon the said stevyn & allthrorpe in ther absence & at ther comandemente for the fortherence of the same.

Item, it is determinat by all vs, beyng present att ye Accomptes, yat ye old churchwardeyn shall delyuer all ye ornamentes & jowelles

¹ leaf 354, back.   ² leaf 355.   ³ leaf 355, back.

of ye church to ye new wardeyn, and to mak yerof indentoures within viij days aftour yis accompt.

Item, it is ordynat, yat ij prestes shal have bote one chalece and ornamentes, on chest & ij kaeys, so yat yei goo to mase one aftour anoyer, and so ye quere may be ye better keped. And yei to have honest ornamentes assigned to yem by the church wardeyns, and all yer old, vnable to be song in, to be delyuerd to ye said wardens to put to oyer vse.

Item, it is agreed that william wild shal have yerly for gedderyng ye church rentes and writtyng of ye bookes, and for ye ingrossing vpe of ye compte xiij s iiij d.

[1] Memorandum: that the wyll of Iohn mongeam wille be Regesetyred in the bowke of wylles for the welle of our chyrch yf the fyshemongeres do not performe the said wyll.

* * * * *

Memorandum: that Master docter, master parson, hath in his handes vj li that Mestres yngelby gave toward a nawter cloth for the hye awter; & more, he hath vj s viij d of Mestres dockelyne; and besyd þat he hath x s of Mestres Ientyll. summa all vj li xvj s viij d . . . . .

* * * * *

[A.D. 1513–14.

Gilbart Ientyll }
Thomas Marten } Wardens.

Quitrents of Chantries and Church Rents.

Chantry Accounts.

Church Rents.

Quitrents and Payments.

Payments for the Church.]

[2] Item, paid for a Crewet lyd for sir Iohn Tyllysley .   j d

* * * * *

paid at the Taverne at stockes for wyne to the vewars þat vewed the Costes of seid howse that Banaster made. . . . .   ij d

paid for makyng of ij Rowles of þe clerkes wages . .   viij d

* * * * *

[1] leaf 356.   [2] leaf 365, back.

paid for smale lyne for the vayle for þe Roode . . .   ij d

* * * * *

[1] paid for Coueryng newe & mendyng off xv bokes grete and Smale, & for x Newe bosys for þe Newe Antefoner, & for clapsis and Burdons . . . .   viij s

* * * * *

[2] Resseittes of the Clarkis wages, pascalmoney & Bemeliġht.

Ress' this yere of the Gadryng of þe Clarkes wages in the parisshe . . . .   viij li vs ij d
Ress' of the pascall money this yere . . . . . .   xj s   iij d
   Summa of þes parcelles, viij li xvj s v d.

Paymenttes of the same.

Paid to Iohn Snowe, Clerke, for his wages for a hole yere . . . .   vj li
Paid to William Wylde for his wages this yere for sextenshipp . . . .   xl s
   Summa of thes ij parcelles, viij li.
Rest þat þe Resseit is more than the paymentes, xvj s v d.

[3] The Casuell Resseittes.

Ress' of watur develyn for the buryall of his Sistur in the pardon chirche yerd . . . .   iiij s
Ress' of William howtyng for the buryall of his Childe in the pardon Chirche yerde . . . .   ij s
Ress' of Robert hardyng for the buryall of his Childe in the pardon Chirche yerde . . . .   ij s
Ress' of Thomas Marten that Restid of his ACompte, in Money . . . .   v li   xix d
Ress' of Mother Gunter for her entryng into her howse, þat she gave to þe chirche . . . .   xx d
Ress' for the grownde of the buriall of Mr harbys man . . . .   viij d
Ress' of my lady of Clarkenwell for parte of clensing of a sege in ffaster lane . . . .   xvj s
Ress' by þe womens gadryng on hokmonday xvj s viij d: And by the mens gadryng on hok Tewysday . . . .   xxij s viij d

---

[1] leaf 366. [2] leaf 369. [3] leaf 369, back.

Churchwardens' Accounts, A.D. 1513–14.

Ress' for the grounde of the buryall of a prest þat dyed at billingisgate	viij d
Ress' for þe buriall of William [?]entyll	ij s
Ress' for þe buriall of lawrence bonvice seruant . .	ij s
Ress' of Iohn Mongeham as aperith in the fote of þe Acompte of Thomas Marten, the summa of vij li ij s ix d, with vj s viij d whiche Remayned in þe hondes of Iohn Russell by þe gyfte of Thomas Duklyng	vij li ij s ix d
Ress' of Mr Aldernes, þe xx day of May, to pay the mason, of the money þat he had in kepyng. of the chyrche, of þe sum of xxj li; payd. . . .	iiij li
[1] Ress' for the buryall of Iohn dawsons child owte of the ffrere	ij s
Ress' for the grownde of the buriall of a Maryner þat dyed at Mr Smertes key	xij d
Ress' for the buriall of Iohn Mongeham in the Sowthe Ile in the chirche	xiij s iiij d
Ress' for his knyll with þe grete bell	vj s viij d
Ress' for þe buriall of Mr Wrenys clerke	ij s
Ress' for þe buriall of Iamys Ingylby	xiij s iiij d
Ress' for his knyll with þe grete bell	vj s viij d
Ress' for the bequest of Iamys Ingylby	vj s viij d
Ress' of Iohn Warner for old Tymbre	vj s viij d
Ress' for the buriall of a pore maryner	vj d
Ress' for the buriall of Thomas hachis wyffe . . .	ij s
Ress' of the buryall of Thomas Merten	xiij s iiij d
Ress' for þe buryall of Thomas Mondens chyld . . .	ij s
Ress' for þe buryall of Iohn Awsthorpps child in þe pardon chirche yerde	ij s
Ress' of þe wyffe of Robert heyward for the Rest of halffe a yeres Rent dew in the tyme of Thomas Merten	xlvj s viij d
Ress' of Andrewe Evyngare for clerkes wages dewe in þe tyme of Iohn Condall iiij s iiij d. And in the tyme of Thomas Duklyng ij s ij d. Summa . .	vj s vj d
Ress' of Christofur Goswell for Clerkes wages dewe in þe tyme of Iohn Woulff	ix d
[2] Ress' of William Awdewyn for Clerkes wages dewe in the tyme of Iohn Woulffe	xxj d
Ress' of Iohn Austhorp by the bequest off Mestres Noneley, for a yerly obett to be kept the Space of	

[1] leaf 370.   [2] leaf 370, back.

xx yeres, the summa of x ℔, of the whiche paid this yere for dirige, Masse, wex, belles, to pore people acordyng to her will. Summa x s. Rest x ℔

Summa, x ℔ xxj d.

Summa of the Casuell Resseittes this yere, xxxv ℔ xj s x d.

[Wax Reckoning.
Allowances.
Rehearsal.]

[1] *Memorandum*: this accompte, alloved the xxix[th] day of Ianuary, ye yer of our lord a thussand v[th] hundirth and xiiij[th], In the presence of the person, William hatteclyff, Master Robert houldernes, Alderman, Master William [... ich ....], Master Sudbury, Iohn Althrope, Steven Sandersson, Iohn woulff, Iohn tetforde. and so Resteith xxv ℔ ij s viij d, which ys deliuerd to ye said Iohn althrope ye said day, he being church warded.

per me, William Hatteclyff.

[2] *Memorandum*: that ther ys owynge to warner, the mayson, iij ℔ for the sowth ylle the [vyse to be yndeyd?] & more x[?]s for the Rest of xxiiij ℔ for the mydyll ylle; for his dewty was xxiiij ℔ for the said ylle, & Master Ientyll payd hym but xxij ℔. Rest dewe to the said mayson when he hath don his bargane, v ℔, for the ij Cawses aforesayd.

Memorandum: þat I, Iohn Warnar, fremason, hathe receuud of Master Awthorpe, cherchewarden of sent mary at hyll, in full payment of the makyng & fynyschyng of þe battyllmenttes, of ij bargeyns as ys afore specyfyde. Summa, v ℔.

per me, Iohn Warner.

ffor an Obit to be kepte for the sowle of Mergret Noneley the xvj day of Merche.

Memorandum: the ffirst day of Merche in the yere of our lorde god m[l] v c xiij, and in þe v[the] yere of the Rayng of kyng henry the viij. In the presence of Mr William hatclyff, doctor & parson of þe chirche of Seint Mary at hill, Mr Robert Aldernes, Aldreman, William Smert, henre Edmondes, Andrewe Evynger, Stevyn Sawnderson, Iohn Condall, Thomas Duklyng, Iohn Woulff, with other moo of the same parisshe; Witnessith, that Iohn Austhorpe

---
[1] leaf 372.
[2] leaf 372, back. This Memorandum and that following both scratched through. The latter is written in a different hand to the former.

of London, grocer, hath delyuered vnto Thomas Marten and Gilbert
Ientyll, Chirchewardens of the seid chyrche of Seint Mary at hill,
the Summa of x li st. vndir this fourme ffoloyng : that is to sey, the
seyd chirchewardens aboue wretyn and theyre sucsessours chirchewardens [1] of the seid chirche, shall doo & kepe or cause to be done
or kept the xvj day of Merche, a dyrige be note on the even, And þe
next day ffoloyng a masse be note, yerely for to be kepte for þe
space and Tyme of xx^{ti} yeres then next Ensuyng after the date
afore wretyn. That is to [be] seyd for the sowlys of Mergret
Noneley, William proyne & Richard Noneley her husbandes,
William and Mergret her Chyldren, & for the sowlys of her ffather
& mother. And that þe seyd chirchewardens shall spend at the
seid yerely obit the summa of x s st. in this wyse & vnder this
fourme foloyng : that is to sey, to prestes & Clerkes for dyrige &
Masse, þe masse peny & drynkyng as is vsed to be geven at suche
oþer diriges & massis kept & done with þe masse peny for þe sowles
of the ffounders of the Chauntryes in the same chyrche, and for wex
& Ryngyng of all the belles at þe same dyrige & Masse as the
custume ys. This dirige & Masse thus duly & yerely kept by the
seid chirchewardens, The seid Margret Noneley willythe & gevithe
to þe seid chirchewardens for the tyme beyng, to euery of them xij d
for theyre labur in the same ; fferthermore, þe seid Margret willithe
that when the charges affore Rehersed & the chirchewardens be
paid, that then þe Resedewe of þe seid yerely x s þat is left onspent
& not paid, shal be devided & distrubyted be þe seid Chirchewardens
to euery powre howsold in þe seid parisshe of Seint Mary at hill
iiij d, as fer as it will extend.

[A.D. 1514–15.

Iohn Austhorp \} Wardens.
Gilbert Ientyll

Quitrents of Chantries and Church Rents.
Chantry Accounts.
Church Rents.
Quitrents and Payments.
Payments for the Church.]

[1] leaf 373.

[1]Paid for Cariage of ij lode of stuff, Newe & olde, to the potters howse & for the pale at Moþer gunters .... vj d

* * * * *

Paid for the Obit of Mestres Noneley the xvj day of Merche, to the prestes, clerkes, for wex & to pore people, Masse peny, Ryngyng & drynkkyng for þat Dyrige . . . . x s

* * * * *

[2]paid for a Reward to þe Clerkes & þe children at Masse & at bothe Evynsonges . . . . v s

* * * * *

[3]paid for makyng of ij poleys of Iron for þe lanterne . xvj d

* * * * *

[4]Resseittes of þe clarkes wages, pascal money & Bemeligℏt.

Ress' þis yere of the Gadryng of þe clarkes wages viijℏ iijs xd [..?..]
Ress' of the pascaℏ money this yere . . . . . . xiij s
Summa, viijℏ xvj s x d.

Paymentes of the same.

Paid to Ioℏn Snowe, Clerk, for a yeres wages . . . vjℏ
Paid to Nicholus Gladwyn, condukte, for di. a quarters wages betwene our lady day & midsomer x s
Paid to Ioℏn Sprever, Conducte, from Midsomer to Cristemas. Summa xxvj wekes, þe weke ij s. Summa . . . . lij s
Paid to William Wylde, Sexten, for his wages for a hole yere . . . . xl s
Summa of þes iiij parcelles xjℏ ij s.
So the paymenttes excedith the Resseites xlv s ij d.

[5]The Casuell Resseittes.

Memorandum: Ress' of Mr Ientyℏ in money, as aperith in the ffoote of his Acompte . . xxvℏ ij s viij d
Ress' of the Gadryng of the wemen on hok monday. Summa . . . . xiiij s viij d
Ress' of the Gadryng of the Men on hok Tewysday . iiij s v d

[1] leaf 382, back.   [2] leaf 383.   [3] leaf 384.
[4] leaf 386.   [5] leaf 386, back.

Churchwardens' Accounts, A.D. 1514–15.

Ress' for the Buryall of Mestres Ientyll	xiij s	iiij d
Ress' for her knyll with þe grete bell	vj s	viij d
Ress' for the Buryall of Christofur Goswell . . .	xiij s	iiij d
Ress' for the Buryall of þe goodwyff Edmond . . .	xiij s	iiij d
Ress' for the Buryall of þe Goodwyff Condall . . .	xiij s	iiij d

Ress' of Mr Doctor of the good charytie of certen wemen in þe parisshe whiche they gave towardes the awtercloth of whight & Red clothe of gold & the courtens for þe same of whight & Red sarsenet, þat is to sey :—of Inglebys wyff vj li, and of oþer dyuers the summa of iij li x s.

Summa Ress'	ix li	x s
Ress' for the Buryall of a child of William howtynges in þe pardon chirchyerde	ij s	
Ress' for the Buryall of Thomas Mondens ij doughters in þe pardon Chirchyerd	iiij s	
Ress' of Robert Hardyng for ij^c howse tyle		xvj d
Ress' for þe Buryall of a prest from Nixsons, in the grete chircheyerd		viij d
Ress' for þe Buryall of a Breton		xij d
Ress' for þe Buryall of Mawde Ryvell	ij s	
Ress' for the Buryall of Mother Ienet	ij s	
Ress' for the Buryall of William Vaughan	ij s	
Ress' for the Buryall of harry wilshere	ij s	
[1] Ress' for Buryall of Ruxbis wyff	ij s	
Ress' for the Buryall of Drynkmylkes wyff	ij s	
Ress' for the Buryall of William Bromfeldes wyff in the pardon chircheyerd	ij s	

Summa totallis of the Casueltes xxxix li xiiij s ix d.

[Wax Reckoning.
Allowances.
Rehearsal, etc.]

* * * * *

[2] *Memorandum*: that the iij keys of the Chy[r]ch mony Box ben delyuerd—on key to Master doctor Atclyffe, & another keye to Master Aldernes, Alderman, & the iij^{de} keye to Andrew evyngger, Chyrchwarden.

* * * * *

[1] leaf 387.   [2] leaf 391.

[A.D. 1515–16 *lost.*]

[A.D. 1516–17.

Robert Ryvell
William Hewys } Wardens.[1]
Stephyn Saunderson

Quitrents and Payments of Chantries and Church Rents.

Chantry Accounts.

Church Rents.

Quitrents and Payments.

Payments for the Church.]

* * * * *

[2] paid for a Newe lok & ij staplis & a key to *sir* Iohn Wallers chambre dore . . . . x d

paid to hym for his Bedsted in that chambre, and for a Newe lamp glasse . . . . v d

* * * * *

[3] paid to þe vestement maker for mendyng and dressyng of v cheseblys of the chauntrys, and for parelyng of the Albys and Ameses for the Children . . . . iiij s

* * * * *

paid [for] brede, mete & drynk, & for wachyng of the sepulcre good fryday tyll Estur day . . . . . xv d

* * * * *

paid for makyng clene of the Rectors stolys . . . . ij d

* * * * *

[4] paid for brede and ale fett into the chirche to Mr Doctor and the p*a*risshens for the besynes that they had wit*h* M^r chirche of Seint Saviours . . iiij d

* * * * *

paid for mendyng of the Bawdryk*es*, to Iohn Snowe . x d

* * * * *

---

[1] A third warden appears this year because William Hewys died during his term of office. See note of his burial under Casual Receipts.
[2] leaf 401.   [3] leaf 401, back.   [4] leaf 402, back.

Churchwardens' Accounts, A.D. 1516–17.

paid for a key to þe dore of the Medyll quere . . . iiij d

* * * * *

paid for a peyre garnettes for the levys of the high
   alter before the Images . . . . iiij d
paid to Mr Doctor for goyng to lambith to serche for
   Mr Prewnys Testament . . . . ij s iiij d

* * * * *

[1] The Clerkis wagis, the Beame light & pascall money.

Ress' this yere of the gadryng of the Clerkes wages vj li xij s viij d
Ress' of the pascall Money this yere . . . . . xij s iij d ob
   Summa of thes ij parcelles viij li iiij s xj d ob.

Paymenttis of the same.

Paid to Iohn Snowe, Clerke, for on hole yeres wagis . vj li
Paid to William, Sexten, for his hole yeres wagis . . xl s
Paid to Iohn Sprever, Condukt, for iij Monthes wages,
   þat is to say from Mighelmas to Christemas Eve
   xxiiij s, and paid hym more for on hole yeres wages
   endyd att the fest of Christemas. Summa lij
   wekes, euery weke ij s. Summa v li iiij s. Summa vj li viij s
   Summa of thes paymenttes xiiij li viij s.
   So the paymenttes excedith the receytis vj li iij s ob.

[2] The Casuell Reseittes.

Ress' for the Buryall of William Affoo in the pardon
   chirchyerd . . . . ij s
Ress' of Iohn Barbour of Seint Iohns, for the Buryall
   of a Mayde that cam from Seint Margret patens,
   the whiche is buryed in the chirche. Summa . xiij s iiij d
Ress' of Mestres Thorney for ij yeres that she was
   behynd off the clerkes wages in the Tyme of Iohn
   Austhorp and Andrew Evynger. Summa . . v s viij d
Ress' of the wyff of William Affoo for the buryall of
   her seruaunt in the grete chirchyerd . . . . viij d
Ress' for the Buryall of William Bromefeldes wyff in
   the pardon Chirchyerd. summa . . . . . ij s
Ress' for the hyre of ij Torches at þe buryall of
   William hus . . . . viij d
Ress' of Iohn Wall for his entrans in the howse þat
   Merkam had . . . . xx s

[1] leaf 404.   [2] leaf 404, back.

Ress' for the Buryall of William hewys in the chirch ... xiij s iiij d
Ress' for the Buryall of William Browne in the pardon Chirchyerde . . . . ij s
Ress' for the Buryall of a Maryner of Brykylsee . . xij d
Summa of the Casuelles this yere iij li viij d.

[Wax Reckoning.
Allowances.
Rehearsal.]

[1]*Memorandum*: at the day of this said Acompte aboue wretyn, Ress' of William Meryall, of Neyland, Clothear, by Stephyn Saunderson & Robert Ryvell, Chirchewardens of the chirche of Seint Mary at hill, & in the presence of Iohn Austhorp, Grocer, for the bequest of William Prewne & Mergrett his wyff, the summa of xx li, whiche xx li was put in the box of the Chirch by Mr Doctor hatclyff and the said Chirchewardens aboue wretyn.

Also, at the said day aboue wretyn, there was put in the seid box of the Chirch a byll of Band, selyd & subscrybed by the seid William Meryall, of the summa of xj li, to be paid at Mighelmas Anno m¹ v c xviij, & in the xth yere of kyng henre the viijth; xj li.

Item, Mestres Bough oweth for Clerkes wages for iij quarter in þe tyme of Stephyn Saunderson. Summa . . . . iij s vj d
Item, henre Edmondes oweth for clerkes wages at þis tyme for ij quarters . . . . ij s ij d
Item, Iohn Sempare oweth for clerkes wages at þis tyme for a quarter . . . . ix d
Item, Thomas Monden oweth for clerkes wages at þis tyme for ij quarters . . . . xvj d
Item, William howtyng oweth for clerkes wages at þis tyme for a quarter . . . . viij d
Item, Markhams wyff oweth for clerkes wages at þis tyme for a quarter . . . . viij d
Item, Robert Stokes oweth for clerkes wages at þis tyme for ij quarters . . . . viij d
Item, Robert Staunce oweth for clerkes wages at þis tyme for a quarter . . . . iij d
Bryan Wilson oweth for clerkes wages at þis tyme for iij quarters . . . . xv d

[1] leaf 406, back.

[A.D. 1517–18.

Robert Ryvell } Wardens.
Stephen Saunderson

The accounts for this year are in two sections, the first [1] 'from the fest of Seint Mighell tharcangell, in the yere of our lord god m¹ v c xvij vnto the ffest of Seint Iohn Baptyst in Anno m¹ v c xviij.']

[2] Obettes to be kept bi the Chirchwardens.

First, the xvj day of March a diryge to be kept for Margret Nonelay, and at this Diryge to be spent for prestes, Clerkes, pore people, wax, belles, brede and drynke the summa of xs, And the chirchewardens to haue euery of them for theyr labur in this xij d.

Item, the xix day of Apryll a Diryge to be kept for Iohn Weston, And at this Dyrige the parson to haue by the wyll the summa of xx d.

Item, the xvj day of Maii a Diryge to be kept for Iohn Bedham, and at þis diryge to be spent for prestes, Clerkes, powre people, brede and drynke vj s viij d; And euery of the chirchwardens to haue iij s iiij d. Summa vj s viij d.

Item, the last day of Iulii, a Diryge to be kept for Iohn Cawston, and att this Diryge the parson to haue, yff he be there present, by þe wyll iij s iiij d, the Mʳ Clerke to haue xij d, the vndyr clerke to haue by þe wyll vj d.

Item, the xix day of August, a diryge to be kept for William Cambrige, & at þat Diryge the Mayre of london to haue vj s viij d, And euery of þe shrevys iij s iiij d, And the Swerdberer xx d. And more to be spent at this diryge for prestes, Clerkes, brede & drynk vj s viij d, And to þe powre people vj s viij d.

Item, the xxix day of Novembre, a Diryge to be kept for Richard Gosselyn.

[3] Quitrentes paid owte of þe Chauntres & þe chirch.

*   *   *   *   *

[Chantry Accounts.
Church Rents.
Quitrents and Payments.]

*   *   *   *   *

[1] leaf 410 (so in MS.).   [2] leaf 409 (so in MS.).   [3] leaf 409, back.

[1]paid for makyng of the Rowle for the Clerk*es* wag*es*,
in p*ar*chement . . . . vj d

paid the second day of Ianuarii for goyng to ffulham
to my lorde of london with Mr Doctor and other
off the p*ar*isshe to haue tolleracion of Nasyng*es*
chauntry, for ffisshe bougħt & money Gevyn, &
for bote hyre þat day . . . . x s

paid to the chaunselers s*er*uaunt at powlys when the
goodwyff hewys was called befor the chaunseler
for the chirch money wit*h*holdyng . . . . xx d

paid to Mr Chaunselers s*er*uaunt for makyng and
selyng of the wryting of the Tolleracion, yn money xiiij s iiij d

paid for brekefast for Ioħn Austhorp and Meryeɫ at
the Ressyt of the xx ɫi for Mestres Noneley . . xij d

*　　*　　*　　*　　*

paid to watur ffounes for Snoffers of plate for to put
owte the tapurs . . . . v d

*　　*　　*　　*　　*

paid to Mr Grene for his labur goyng to towre hyɫ for
his cownseɫ in case ayenst thabbott for the way
before þe bak dore of þe potters howse . . . . iij s iiij d

*　　*　　*　　*　　*

paid for a great holywatur stopp weyng xiiij ɫ and
di., the ɫ vj d. And to her s*er*uaunt for his
labur for bryngyng home . . . . vij s iiij d

paid for ij holy watur sprynkell*es* . . . . ij d
paid to henre Chylde, Raker, for a hole yer*es* wages . xvj d
paid for an xviij threde lyne for the lyteɫ beɫ . . . ix d
paid for a wayneskot for the Sepulcre. . . . . . x d
paid for a Newe bourde and nayles for the sepulcre . iiij d
paid for ij quarters of Colys for the ffyre, to be
halowed . . . . xj d

*　　*　　*　　*　　*

[2] The Clerk*es* wag*es* and Bemeligħt.

Ress' this yere of the gadryng of the Clerk*es* wagis iiij ɫi iij s ij d
Ress' of the pascall money this yere . . . . . xj s viij d
　　S*um*ma of thes ij parcell*es* iiij ɫi xiiij s x d.

[1] leaf 413.　　　[2] leaf 414.

Paymenttes of the same.

Paid to Iohn Snowe, Clerke, for his wages for iij quarters of a yere.	iiij li x s
Paid to William Wylde for his wages for iij quarters of a yere	xxx s

Summa of thes ij parcelles vj li.

Summa that thes charges excedyth the Resseyttes xxv s ij d.

Item, I ax alowaunce for potacyon money for hallff a yere, ij s vj d.

So the paymenttes is more then the Resseyttes xviij s xj d.

Paid by me, Iohn Woulff, vnto Robert Ryvell in the presens of Mr Austhorp the sum afore wretyn as it was past by his acompt	xviij s xj d
More payd to hym at that tyme for ij m^t breke, whiche was spent in þe newe byldyng	viij s viij d

[The same year.

Obit List.

Quitrent List.]

[1] Here foloith the Acompte of Robert Ryvell and Iohn Woulff, chirchwardens with Stephyn Sawndyrson, of the chirche of Seint Mary att hill, from the [fest] of Seint Mighell tharcangell in the yere off our lord god m¹ v c xvij vnto the fest of Mighelmas Anno m¹ v c xviij.

*   *   *   *   *

[Chantry Accounts.

Church Rents.

Quitrents and Payments.]

*   *   *   *   *

[2] paid to Thabbot of Waltham for quytrent goyng forth of Iohn Westons londys xxxviij s : And for quytrent goyng fourth of the Sowthe Ile of the chirche of Mary at hill x s. Summa	xlviij s

*   *   *   *   *

paid to Mestres Edyth Segemond for halff a yere endyd at Mighelmas Anno 1518, as aperith by a writyng seallyd	l s

*   *   *   *   *

[1] leaf 418. The front leaf of the Accounts (416) has the names of Stephen Saunderson and Iohn Woulff on it.   [2] leaf 422.

[1]paid for brede and drynke at the parsonage at syttyng vppon þe Avdytt for the newe byldyng, to Mr Aldreman & þe parisshens . . . Summa   viij d

* * * * *

paid to Iohn Snowe for mendyng of the Bawdrykes þis yere, and for a lb of Candell & for bromes .   xviij d

* * * * *

[2]The Clarkis wagis and the Bemelight.

Ress' by Robert Ryvell this yere of the clerkes wages, as aperith by his Acompt, the summa   iiij li iij s ij d
Ress' by hym this yere of the pascall money & bemelight . . . .   xj s viij d
Ress' by me, Iohn Woulff, of the clerkes wages this yere . . . .   iiij li iiij s iiij d
Summa of thes parcelles viij li xix s ij d.

Paymenttes of the same.

Paid by Robert Ryvell to Iohn Snowe, clerke, for iij quarters wages . . . .   iiij li x s
Paid by Robert Ryvell to William Wylde for iij quarters wages . . . .   xxx s
Paid by me, Iohn Woulff, to Iohn Snowe for a quarters wages . . . .   xxx s
Paid by me, Iohn Woulff, to Wylliam Wylde for a quarters wages . . . .   x s

Summa of thes paymenttes viij li.
Rest of this wages xix s ij d

[3]The Casuell Resseyttes.

Ress' of sir Iohn Borughbrig for his part of a tapur at Estur . . . .   iiij d
Ress' of Iohn potter for Edmond ffaryngtons graue in the pardon chircheyerde . . . .   ij s iiij d
Ress' of Robert hardyng for his childes graue in the pardon chirchyerd . . . .   ij s
Ress' of Mestres Russell for þe buryall of her mayd in þat chirchyerd . . . .   ij s
Ress' of Mr Doctor for the olde pulpet þat stode in the chirch . . . .   v s

---

[1] leaf 422, back.   [2] leaf 423.   [3] leaf 424.

Churchwardens' Accounts, A.D. 1517–18.

Ress' for the buryall of a straunger in þe greate chircheyard.		viij d
Ress' for the buryall of Iohn Billyntons wyffe in þe pardon chircheyerd		ij s
Ress' for the buryall of Mr William hatclyff in Seint Katheryns quere	xiij s	iiij d
Ress' for the buryall of Thomas Barley in the Medyll Ile	xiij s	iiij d
Ress' of Mr Aldernes by the hondes of Mr Doctor for stuff that he had of the chirches	iiij s	vj d
Ress' of Robert Ryvell for olde Tymber þat he had of the chirch	ix s	xj d
Ress' for the buryall of Richard Richardes in þe pardon chircheyerd		ij s
Ress' of Thomas Clayton for that Remayned in his hondes of the byldyng of Nasynges Renttes next baattes howse	xj s	iij d
Ress' of Stephyn Sawnderson for that Remayned in his hondes for the same Renttes Bildyng	xiij s	xj d
Summa of thes parcelles iiij li ij s vij d.		

[Wax Reckoning.

Allowances.

Rehearsal.]

*   *   *   *   *

[1] Item, the said parson [Dr Atcliff] hathe Ress' to pay to the said Smert the rest of harmans money. Summa xxvij s vij d.

Item, more, the said parson hathe Ress' owte of the Almes box for to pay to the said Smart xxx s ix d.

Item, the said parson thathe Ress' of Iohn Coveney for to pay to the said Smart xxx s vj d.

Summa xij li vj d; wherof the said William hatclyff, parson, hathe paid to William Roche for to pay to Thomas Smart, Carpenter, the summa of xj li as aperith on his Indentur.

Item, paid to Mr Doctor hatclyff, as aperith vppon an oblygacion to hym dew and for alowaunce of xij d [.. ? ..] money whiche wer not [god?], the sum of xx s vj d.

Memorandum: þat Iohn stookes, pewterer, doith awght vnto ye church, anno 1518 for money gayderd ffor the powr peple, the Summa off vij s [.... ? ....]

---

[1] leaf 426, back.

[A.D. 1518–19.

Iohn Woulff } Wardens.
Thomas Clayton

Obit List.
Quitrent List.
Chantry Accounts.
Church Rents.
Quitrents and Payments.]

* * * * *

[1] paid to Mestres Sygemond for money that she lent to þe chirche, to be paid at ij fest, þat is, our lady day & Mighelmas. Summa . . . . v li

paid for a basket for the dust of the chirche . . . j d ob

* * * * *

paid for papur for this boke & the Rentall boke . . ij d

* * * * *

paid to William Bankes for ij days copyng of the stone wall at the Est end of the greate chircheyerde and plastryng of the walles of the same howses. Summa . . . . xvj d

* * * * *

paid for dyggyng and Rakyng and makyng clene of þe greate chircheyerd, and ffyllyng vpp of Mr Roches howse, to Kyng the porter and Sawndyr henre childes man . . . . ij s viij d

paid for settyng of hey seed, to a porter . . . . . ij d

paid for makyng of a Ryng and mendyng of the lok of þe cofer in þe quere . . . . iij d

* * * * *

paid for Nayles for the clampis for the baners, and þe henges of the pewe dores & the Irons . . . ij d

paid to Iohn fight Iohn for makyng of the parclosse abought the crosse in the greate chirchyerd :—

first iiij quarters of bourde . . . . xx d

paid for iiij quarters, the pece ij d. Summa . . viij d

paid to hym for nayles for the Same . . . . . iiij d

---

[1] leaf 433, back. The Accounts now and for several years following are very beautifully written, apparently in the same handwriting as regards the main body of the Accounts for each year.

Churchwardens' Accounts, A.D. 1518-19.

paid to hym for a pece for the fframe þat stondith on þe lede for palme sonday	viij d
paid to hym for iij days labur & for settyng on of clampis in the chirch & wourkyng in the chirchyerd	ij s
paid to Sutton, ffounder, for ij holywatur stoppis ; þat he had in metall xxxiiij lb, the lb ij d. Summa v s viij d, And in money iij s iiij d. Summa	ix s
[1] paid to benet, Mason, & his seruaunt for a day & di. for makyng & mendyng with copyng of the north wall in the greate chirchyerd. Summa	xx d

* * * * *

paid to a smyth for hokes & staplis for the iiij Angelles on þe sepulcre and a clape of Iron on the Rood lofte	vj d
paid to the Smyth for iij clampis of Iron for the pewys before the pulpet, and for nayles . . .	x d

* * * * *

paid for watur on shrofthursday & on Estur Even for þe fount.	j d

* * * * *

paid for a quytaunce made to Iohn Austhorp and William Meryell for the dyscharge of the goodes of William proyne and Margrett Noneley which was bequested to þe chirch of Seint Mary at hill	iiij d
paid for ther brekefast at þe last Resseyte of þat money	iiij d
paid to Smart, Carpenter, the ixth day of Maii, for the howse in the North chircheyerd	xl s

* * * * *

paid for ledder thonges for the stavys of the canape for þe sacrament	j d
paid for beryng of viij torches on corpus christi day which was this yere Midsomer Eve, the torche j d. Summa	viij d
paid for a step of stone at þe sowth dore next þe parsonage	xij d

* * * * *

[2] paid to a Mason & his laborer for ij days labor to make Redy the place for Mr Russelles Tabernacle, þe day xiij d. Summa	ij s	ij d

* * * * *

[1] leaf 434.   [2] leaf 434, back.

Churchwardens' Accounts, A.D. 1518–19.

paid for makyng of a fote of glas in the upper store in the Middyll Ile . . . . iiij d

* * * * *

paid to Baleham for makyng clene of þe lytell chirchyerd . . . . j d
paid to the Carvar and paynters for a Reward for bryngyng home þe Tabernacle of þe trinite þat Mr Russell gave . . . . xx s

* * * * *

paid for a bourde for the shop of partrych, bocher . . v s iiij d
paid for pavyng before the stall & for gravell & stone   xvj d
paid to Mr Doctor for a clampe of Iron of vj lb to the Est chirch gate next þe parsonage, price . .   vij d
paid to Weston, carpenter, for his labur in pullyng vp the Tabernacle & for oþer labur þat he dyd at ij tymes . . . .   viij d

* * * * *

[1] paid for Brede, wyne and ale set at high festes in the chirche this yere for the quere, of the whiche Ress' of Mr Doctor iiij s. Rest . . . . . . j s   v d
paid to Iohn Smyth for makyng of Irons for the Baners stavys in the chirche . . . . . . ij s
paid more to a Smythe for a Newe key for þe chest next Seint Katheryn & for ij hokes for our lady & for a barr of iron for the bell whele . . . .   ix d

* * * * *

[2] The Clarkis wagis and the Bemelight.

Ress' this yere of the Gadryng of the clarkes wagis . . . . viij li xiij s
Ress' of the pascall money this yere . . . . . . xiij s iij d ob
    Summa of thes parcelles, ix li vj s ij d ob.

Paymenttes of the same.

Paid to Iohn Snowe, Clerke, for a hole yeris wagis . vj li
Paid to William wylde, Sexten, for his hole yeris wagis . . . . xl s
Paid to Robert Redknap, Condukt, for his tyme beyng . . . . xxvj s viij d
    Summa of thes paymenttes ix li vj s viij d.
    The paymenttes excedith þe Resseittes v d ob.

---

[1] leaf 435.   [2] leaf 435, back.

Casuell Resseittes this yere.

Ress' for the Buryall of William huskham	ij s	
Ress' for the Buryall of Alis Clark	ij s	
Ress' for the Buryall of a straunger from the gonn .		xij d
Ress' for the Buryall of Mr Thorney and for his knyll	xx s	
Ress' of Iohn Coveney for the hauyng of þe yeres in his howse	xl s	
Ress' of Sutton, fownder, for xxxiiij lb of metall for ij holywatur stoppis, the lb ij d. Summa . . .	v s	viij d

Summa of the Casuelles, iij li x s viij d.

[Wax Reckoning.

Allowances.

Rehearsal.]

* * * * *

[1] *Memorandum* . . . . vj s ij d that was gadred of dyuers persons for the helpyng of the wages of Robert Redknap, condukte. . . .

* * * * *

[2] Articles foloyng for the Chirche.

[3] ffirst, that the chirchwardens shall pay for the chest and that it may be in the Revestry for Chesiblis & Tonecles.

[3] Item, that euery prest shall syng with his ffounders vestementtes. And ther chestes to be at þe awturs Ende next where they syng.

Item, yff ser Thomas Asshbourne will kepe his Chambre, that then he shall haue none of our prestes to ocupy his chambre wherby that our chambris to stond vacant.

[3] Item, that the howsold stuff þat is in the Revestry shal be sold and the money therof to come to þe chirch box.

Item, as towchyng the tabernacles, trymmers, is that a wourkman shall se them & he to shew his best advice in it.

[3] Item, that Mestres Mongeham shal be spoken vnto by Iohn Austhorp, Andrew Evynger, with the ij Chirchwardens, for such money as is in her hondes þat it may come to þe vse of þe chirch.

[3] Item, þat the gutters in the North Chirche yerd may be conveyed in the best maner by wourkmen owte of þe chirchyerde.

Item, that the Clerke & Sexten Swepe the chirche and to Cast watur in the Swepyng of it.

[1] leaf 437. [2] leaf 437, back. [3] This item is scratched out.

Item, that the Clerke in his owne person Reuerently shall distribute the holy wax Candyll.

Item, that the Clarke or the Sexten sett the greate holy wature stop at the quere dore that the holy wature may be made beffore Matens begynnyth.

[1] Item, that the money of the Almes box be made Acompt of.

Item, that the Tabernacle þat Mr Russell gaue shal be Regestrid in the chirch bokes.

Item, that the lokkes, kayes, glasse and latesses of the New bildynges shal be Regestred in the chirch bokes.

Item, that þe chest wherin the wrytinges lyeth in the Revestry shal be locked & shitt.

[A.D. 1519–20.

Robert Game } Wardens.
Thomas Clayton

Obit List.

Quitrent List.

Chantry Accounts.

Church Rents.

Quitrents and Payments.]

* * * * *

[2] Item, paid for a planke for the stepp at the west dore of þe greate chirchyerd . . . . iiij s

* * * * *

Item, paid for Trymmyng of the courten of our ladys tabernacle and for vij Rynges for the same Tabernacle . . . . viij d

Item, paid for a quarter for the skaffold ouer þe porch ayenst palmesonday and for a carpenters labur to mend the same skaffold . . . . vij d

* * * * *

Item, paid to a carpenter for Trymmyng of the peyse of the pyx . . . . iiij d

Item, paid for iij lb lede for the peyse of the same pyx and for iiij lb of lede for to make fast the hoke of the branche of þe Trynite . . . . Summa   v d quarter

---

[1] This item is scratched out.   [2] leaf 444, back.

Churchwardens' Accounts, A.D. 1519-20.

Item, for the hoke that berith the braunche of þe Trynite	iij d
Item, paid for a hoke for the lyne of the pascall . .	ob

* * * * * *

Item, paid for a braunche of iij fflowres that stondith before the Trynyte, weyng xv lb & di., the lb v d. Summa	vj s v d ob
Item, paid for drynke at the takyng downe of the sepulcre	j d

* * * * * *

[1] Item, paid for iij dossen Garlondis on Corpus Christi day for the procession	xv d
Item, paid for ij dossen of Grene Garlondis for that procession	ij d
Item, paid for ij Garlondis for Mr Doctor and the parissh prest	iij d
Item, paid for iij Garlondis for the iij Crossis, euery of them [[2]]. Summa	viij d
Item, paid for ij Newe Torches weyng xxxiij lb, the lb iij d. Summa	viij s iij d
Item, paid for a Braunche of laton before the Tabernacle of our lady Assumpcion, weyng xxxij lb, the lb v d. Summa	xiij s iiij d
Item, paid for mendyng of the crosse of Berall . . .	ij d

* * * * *

Item, paid on Seint Barnebes Eve for drynk for þe clerkes at Evensong	v d

* * * * *

Item, paid for brede, ale and wyne for the clerkes & þe children at Masse	xij d ob

* * * * *

Item, paid for Bryngyng of the Orgons from Seint Andrewys to our chirche ayenst Seint Barnabes Eve	ij d
Item, paid to the Clerkes þat were at Matens, Masse & both Evensonges	v s

* * * * *

Item, paid for the beryng home of the Orgons to Seint Andrewys	iij d
Item, paid to the clerke for mendyng of the Bawdrykes	xvj d

[1] leaf 445.   [2] Sum scratched out.

Item, paid to Gymbold the Ioyner for a chest for the vestmenttes	xiij s	iiij d
Item, paid to Baleham for makyng clene the vestry		ij d
Item, paid for parelyng of vj albis		vj d
Item, for mendyng of the lytell orgons in the quere		vj d
Item, for mendyng of v clappers of the belles	v s	
Item, paid to the Raker for his hole yeris wagis for the chirche		xvj d
Item, paid for mendyng of the lok on þe lytell chirchyerde dore		iij d
Item, paid for a Newe albe for the blake vestment	ij s	viij d

* * * * *

Item, paid to Mr Doctor for Newe cloth for ij Amesys		xiiij d
Item, paid for iij Gyrdellis for the Albis		iij d
Item, paid for a reward gevyng to þe Bisshoppis seruaunt at the halowyng of the vestementtis		xij d

* * * * *

[1]Item, paid for makyng of v trestilles in the vpper vestry . . . . vj d

* * * * *

Item, paid for brede, ale and wyne this yere for the quere, of the whiche Ress' of Mr Doctor þe Summa of ij s viij d. Rest paid . . . . iij s vj d

* * * * *

Item, paid for makyng of the greate bell claper þat was broken	iij s	iiij d
Item, paid for beryng of it to the Smythes & home ayene		ij d

* * * * *

Item, paid to Iohn Woulff for clensing & fresshing our ladys tabernacle . . . . v li

[2] Casuell Resseittis.

Ress' for the Buryall of Iohn Condall this yere in the chirche	xiijs	iiij d
Ress' of Iohn Goodwyns wyffe towarddes the braunche of the Trinite	iijs	viij d
Ress' of the ffounder for xj li of metall at þe chongyng of þat braunch, þe li ij d ob. Summa	ij s	iij d ob

---

[1] leaf 445, back.   [2] leaf 446.

Ress' of the ffounder for xv ℔ of metall at the chonge of the braunche before the Tabernacle of our lady Assumpcion, the ℔ iij d. Summa . . iij s ix d
Ress' for the buryall of Thomas ffurgons wyffe in þe pardon chirchyerd . . . . ij s
Ress' for the buryall of a Breton in the Greate chircheyerd . . . . xij d
Ress' of the goodwyff Burnegyll for the buryall of hir childe in the pardon chirchyerd . . . . . ij s
Ress' of sir Iohn Tyllisley for an olde chest. . . . viij d
Ress' of a pewtrer for xiiij ℔ of olde pewtur, the ℔ ij d ob. Summa . . . . ij s xj d
Ress' of hym more for xlvij ℔ di. of olde laton, the ℔ ij d. Summa . . . . vij s xj d
Ress' more of hym for xxix ℔ of olde potbras, the ℔ j d ob. Summa . . . . iij s vij d ob
Ress' for the Buryall of a yoman of the Gard þat dyed at þe Swan . . . . ij s
Ress' for the wast of iij Torches for the same man . vj d
Ress' of Mestres Mongeham of þe goodys of Thomas Austen towardis þe ffreshing of the tabernacle of our lady Assumpcion . . . . vj ℔
Ress' of the goodwyff condall for þe buriall of her brother . . . . xvj d

* * * * *

Summa of this casuwelles, viij ℔ vij s.

Clerkis wagis & Bemeligth.

Ress' of the Clerkis wagis this yere a[s] aperith by the Rowle . . . . viij ℔ ij s xj d
Ress' for pascall money & Bemelight this yere . . xj s ix d ob.
Summa of thes Resseittis viij ℔ xiiij s viij d ob.

Paymenttis.

Item, paid to Iohn Snowe, Clerke, for a hole yeris wagis . . . . vj ℔
Item, paid to William Wylde, Sexten, for his yeris wagis . . . . xl s
Rest of the clerkes wagis & the beme light xiiij s viij d ob.

[Wax Reckoning.
Rehearsal.]
Articles foloing.

* * * * *

[1] Item, Thomas Clayton is contentyd to pay for the Monyelles of his bay wyndowe whiche he had of the chirche as it shal be Iugged by Woulston Wyn, Carpenter.[3]

* * * * *

[2] Item, that the blake vestmenttes of blake velwett be Regestrid in the boke of the gyfte of William Vagham.

* * * * *

Ress' iij ti

[3] Item, that Robert Game oweth of the xix ti xij s j d in his acompt before wretyn, iij ti: to be brought in on sonday the thyrd day of ffebruarii next foloyng after the date of þis his acompt. Ress' the thirday of ffebruary of Robert Game the sum of iij ti above wretyn.

} iij ti

* * * * *

[4] Memorandum: that it be Regestryd in the greate boke that Iohn Austhorp, sector to Mestres Noneley, hathe geveyn of his porcyon of the goodes whiche wer in his hondes of her goodes of þe se[id arers?] the summa of xx ti for a table to þe high auter, whiche money was Ress' at the byldyng of the new howses in seint mary hill lane, whiche money was paid by phillip heyward of colchester, whiche table to be provided for of þe money of þe chirche box whan the chirche is clere owte of dett.

* * * * *

[5] Memorandum: that the Ivdas of the pascall, þat is to sey the Tymbre that the wax of þe pascall is drevyn vppon, weyeth vij lb di.

* * * * *

[A.D. 1520–1.

Robert Game } Wardens.]
Iohn Potter

---

[1] leaf 448, back.   [2] leaf 449.   [3] This section is scratched out.
[4] leaf 449, back.   [5] leaf 450.

[Obit List.
Quitrent List.
Chantry Accounts.
Church Rents.
Quitrents and Payments.]

[1]Item, paid to Mestres Segesmond for money that she lent to þe churcħ . . . . v li

* * * * *

Item, paid to Mr Alen for the Bede Rowle of the Churcħ . . . . ij s

* * * * *

[2]Item, paid to sir Joħn Borugħbrig by the Comaundement of the Masturs of the parisshe for his labur on the holydays from Christemas to candilmas . vj s viij d

* * * * *

Item, paid for a days labur of a carpenter for makyng of the same dore and mendyng of the almeres & mendyng of ye Iudassis in þe Roode lofte . . . viij d

* * * * *

[3]Item, paid for mendyng of the syluer holy-watur sprynkyll and sowdryng of the same and for Syluer to the same . . . . iiij d

Item, paid for Garlondis on Corpus cristi day for þe Crossis and þe quere . . . . v d oƀ

Item, paid for beryng of viij torches that day, to viij men . . . . viij d

Item, paid for iiij dosen Garlondis withe Roosis and lavender for the Clerkys and the quere, and for iij Garlondis for the Crossis and ij Garlondis for Mastur Doctor and Mastur Alen . . . . . . ij s ix d

[4]Item, Spent vppon the kynges chappell for theyre dyner that day xx s, of the whicħ I ask alowaunce of . . . . xiij s iiij d

* * * * *

[5]Item, paid for latessing of the iiij wyndowys in the Steple next to the bellis, for euery wyndowe ix

---

[1] leaf 457. [2] leaf 457, back. [3] leaf 458.
[4] In margin—"Abated of this xiij s iiij d the sum of iij s iiij d, so was alowed x s." [5] leaf 458, back.

yerdis and a halff of lattes. Su*m*ma xxxviij yerdis,
the yerd ij d oƀ. Su*m*ma p*ai*d . . . . . . viij s

* * * * *

Item, p*ai*d to John Balaham for ij days, to make clene
the Steple ayenst the halowyng of the bellis . . viij d

Item, p*ai*d for ij burdens of Russhis to strawe vnder
the bellis . . . . iij d

* * * * *

Item, p*ai*d for mendyng of the lok on þe wyket in þe
p*ar*don chircħyard . . . . iij d

* * * * *

Item, p*ai*d for Ryngyng of Mr Ientille*s* knyll w*ith* þe
great bell . . . . vj d

Item, p*ai*d for Ryngyng of a knyll for Mr Roches
ser*u*aunt for vj owre*s* . . . . vj d

* * * * *

[1]Item, p*ai*d [for] Ringing of the pelis at Mastur
Ientillis Buryeng . . . . x d

Item, p*ai*d for Ryngyng of the pelis at Mr Rochis
ser*u*aunttes buryeng . . . . x d

Item, p*ai*d for makyng of the pit for Mr Rochis
ser*u*aunt . . . . iiij d

Item, p*ai*d for pavyng of Mastur Rochis ser*u*aunttes
grave . . . . viij d

Item, p*ai*d for the Ryngyng of Mr Doctors knyll . . vj d

Item, p*ai*d for Ryngyng of the pelis at Dirige and
Masse . . . . x d

Vestmentte*s* and Copis.

Item, p*ai*d for a vnce of venes golde iij s viij d & for
an ounce & di. of Ryband xv d. Su*m*ma . . . iiij s xj d

Item, p*ai*d for halff an ounce of yelowe sylke for þe
copis . . . . vj d

Item, p*ai*d for halff an ounce of yelowe threde . . . iij d

Item, p*ai*d for Saffron and flowre and blake sylke . . xij d

Item, p*ai*d to Rich*ar*d peirson, browderer, the first day
of Iunnii, for viij days & a halff wourke in
mendyng of vestymentte*s* & Copis, for eu*er*y day
viij d. Su*m*ma . . . . v s viij d

Item, to Willi*a*m the Browderer, for v days wourke, þe
day vj d. Su*m*ma . . . . ij s vj d

[1] leaf 459.

Item, for ij yerdis & a halff of Bukram, the yerde vj d.
Su*m*ma . . . . xv d
Item, *paid* for an ou*n*ʒ of yelowe thr[e]de and blewe
threde . . . . ij d
Item, *paid* for iij q*uarte*rs of Reband vij d oƀ; and for
whight threde j d. S*u*mma . . . . . . viij d oƀ
Item, *paid* for threde of dyue*r*s colowris . . . . . iij d oƀ
Item, *paid* for Cadas Reband and blake Reband for
the courtens of Mastur Camb[r]iges alter an for
yelowe threde . . . . ij d
Item, *paid* for vj yerdis of blewe Bokeram, the yerd
vj d. S*u*mma. . . . . iij s
Item, *paid* for tawney threde for the vestymen*tte*s . . j d
Item, *paid* to Ric*hard* peirson for xvj days wourke, þe
day viij. S*u*mma . . . . x s viij d

* * * * *

Item, *paid* for Takyng downe of the bridge that was
made owte of the *pa*rsonage into the chirche
ledis . . . . iij d

* * * * *

[1] Item, *paid* for lix ℔ of Newe metall in the Sanct*us*
beℓℓ whicħ was more than the olde bell did way,
for eue*r*y ℔ iiij d. S*u*mma . . . . xix s viij d

* * * * *

[2] Casuell Resceitis.

Rec' for the knyll of the greate bell for Mastur
Ientyll . . . . vj s viij d
Rec' for his buryall in the Churche . . . . . . xiij s iiij d
Rec' for the buryall of vstums se*r*uaunt in þe *pa*rdon
chirchyard . . . . ij s
Rec' for the buryall of Mr Roches se*r*uant in þe churcħ xiij s iiij d
Rec' for his Knyℓℓ of the iiij[th] beℓℓ . . . . . . v s
Rec' for his pitt in the Churche . . . . iij s iiij d
Rec' for the pelis at that dirige and Masse . . . . xx d
Rec' for the knyll of Robert Gamys se*r*uaunt . . . viij d
Rec' for his g*r*aue in the Greate churchyerde . . . iiij d
Rec' for the knyℓℓ of Mr Doctou*r* hatclyff . . . . vj s viij d
Rec' for the pelis at Dirige and Masse . . . . . xx d
Rec' of Will*ia*m Alderston for his entraunce in þe howse vj s viij d

---

[1] leaf 459, back.   [2] leaf 460, back.

312   *Churchwardens' Accounts*, A.D. 1520–1.

Rec' of Stephyn Saunderson in pardon chirchyerd . ij s
Rec' for his knyħ of the second bell . . . . . . viij d
Rec' for the buryall of Robert Austhorp in þe pardon
    chirchyerd . . . . ij s
       Summa of the Casuelles, iij ħ vj s.

[1] Clarkis wagis and Bemelight.

Rec' of the Clarkis wagis this yere, as aperith by þe
    Rowle . . . . vij ħ xvj s j d
Rec' for pascaħ money and Bemeligħt . . . . . xij s   j d oƀ
       Summa of thes parcelles viij ħ viij s ij d oƀ.

Paymenttis.

Item, paid to Ioħn Snowe, Clerk, for a hole yeris wagis vj ħ
Item, paid to William Wylde, Sexten, for his yeres
    wages . . . . xl s
       Summa of the paymenttes, viij ħ.
      Rest of the Clarkes wages and the money
        of the Bemeligħt, viij s ij d oƀ.

[Wax Reckoning.
Allowances.
Rehearsal.

    The new rector now introduces the custom of appending signatures to the year's accounts.]

[2] Memorandum : the xiij day of ffebruarii, in the yere of our lord god m v xxj, (1 c ti) and in the xiij yere of the Rayng of King henre the viij^th, this Acompt, made by me, Ioħn Potter, in the presence of Mr Alen, Curat of the Chirch, Mr Robert Aldernes, William Roche, Ioħn Austhorp, Andrew Evyngar, Ioħn Woulff, Thomas Clayton, Robert Game and Ioħn Waħ, with other moo; and at this day there was brougħt, in money, by me, the said Ioħn Potter, by this Acompt, Summa, the whicħ money at this day was put in þe church box, of the whicħ box the keys remayne in the hondis of Mr Alen, Mr Aldernes, and Ioħn Potter, to euery of them a key.   xviij li xs ij d

      [1] leaf 461.   [2] leaf 463.

Per me, Iohannem alanum, curatum ecclesie diue marie at hyH.
Per me, Robert Aldurnes.
Per me, Wylliam Roche.
Per me, Iohannem Austhorpe.
Per me, Andrew Evyngar.
Per me, Iohn Wolf.
     [A mark, see facsimile.]
Per me, Robard Game.
Per me, Iohnannem Walle.

[A.D. 1521–2.

Iohn Wall } Wardens.
Iohn Potter

Obit List.

Quitrent List.

Chantry Accounts.

Church Rents.

Quitrents and Payments.]

 * * * * *

[1]Item, paid for iiij Geistes that lyeth vndir the halpace of the Orgons . . . .   xvj d

 * * * * *

Item, paid for a bukkeH for the bawdryk of the same beH and for a clapper for a sacryng bell and a brase of iron for the sacryng bell that was whight tynned . . . .   iiij d

Item, paid for settyng in of xxiij newe quarrelles in the wyndowe of the Trynyte whiche was blown downe with the wynde . . . .   xx d

Item, paid for skowryng and newe byndyng of the same glasse . . . .   viij d

 * * * * *

Item, paid to the Glaseer for mendyng of iij holys in the wyndow of Seint Iohn on the northe syde [of] the chirche . . . .   vj d

Item, paid for Obb[l]ees, flowris and palme for palme sonday . . . .

[1] leaf 471.

Item, paid for makyng clene of bothe the chirchyardys	ij d	

* * * * *

[1] Item, paid for Nayles occupyed on palmes sonday in þe greate chirchyard		ob
Item, paid for watur on Mawndy thursday and Estur Eve		j d
Item, paid for a pryksonge boke of kyryes, Allelyas and Sequences whiche was boughte of Iohn Darlyngton the conducte	iiii s	iiij d
Iohn Darlyngton, the conducte	iiij s	iiij d
Item, paid for halowyng of a Corporas		iiij d

* * * * *

Item, paid for new bandyng and stichyng of iij su[r]plyses		x d

* * * * *

[2] Item, paid to the Orgonmaker for the Orgons in money besidis that was gaderid, and for bryngyng home of the same orgons	x s	viij d
Item, paid to the Orgonmaker as aperith by Indenture for the ouersight of the orgons for certen yeris, yerely to haue		xij d

* * * * *

[3] Casuell Resceytis.

Rec' of Stephyn Saunderson for the buriall of his Childe & his cosen in the pardon Chircheyarde .	iiij s	
Rec' for the buryall of a pore man in the greate chirchyerde		viij d
Rec' of William Burngyll for the buryall of his childe	ij s	
Rec' of Iohn Austhorp for the buryall of his doughter	ij s	
Rec' of Stephyn Saunderson for the buryall of his doughter	ij s	
Rec' of Stephyn Saunderson for the buryall of his wyff in Seint Stephyns Chappell	xiij s	iiij d
Rec' for the knyll, with the Greate bell, for her buryall	vj s	viij d
Rec' of Thomas power for the buryall of his sonn . .	ij s	
Rec' of Thomas Mondens mother for her buryall . .	ij s	
Rec' of Mestres Roche for the buryall of her brother in þe chirch	xiij s	iiij d

[1] leaf 471, back.   [2] leaf 472.   [3] leaf 472, back.

Rec' for the buryall of Robert Ryvelles son in þe pardon chirchyerd . . . . ij s
Rec' for the buriall of Iohn Goodwyn in the Chirche . xiij s iiij d
Rec' for the buriall of þe wyff of the chekur in þe pardon chirchyerd . . . . ij s
Rec' for the buriall of a pore Sowdear owte of harrysons house . . . . iiij d
    Summa of the Casuelles this yere, iij li v s viij d.

[1]Clarkis wagis and Bemelight.

Rec' of the Clerkis wages this yere as aperith by þe Rowle . . . . vij li xiiij s xj d
Rec' for pascall money and bemelight this yere . . . xij s
    Summa of thes parcelles, viij li vj s xj d.

Paymenttis.

Item, paid to Roger Mason, Clerk, for his wagis for a hole yere . . . . vij li
Item, paid to William Wylde for his hole yere seruice xxxv s
Item, paid to Iohn Darlyngton, conducte, for his wagis from palme sonday to mydsomer the Summa of . xvj s viij d
Item, paid to the same Iohn Darlyngton for his quarter wages at Mighelmas . . . . xx s
Item, paid to Thomas Smyth, Sexten, for his hole yeres wagis . . . . iij li vj s viij d
    Summa of theis paymenttes, xiij li xviij s iiij d.
So the chargis is more then the Receptis, v li xj s v d.

[Wax Reckoning.
Allowances.
Rehearsal.]

[2]Memorandum: the xxviij day of Ienyuer, Anno 1522, Remayneyth in goodewife walles handes xiij s, which was gadyryd on hope monday.[3]

Also, Thomas dockelynge oweth ij s iiij d, which he promyseyd towardes the organes.

  *   *   *   *   *   *

[1] leaf 473.   [2] leaf 475, back.
[3] This Memorandum is scratched out.

Memorandum: þat Thomas Clayton hathe Rec' of the wyff of Iohn wall as is aboue wretyn, by the hond of Mr Roche, the Summa of xiij s.

Memorandum: the xxvj day of Ienyver, Anno m^l v^c xxiij^t that Io[hn— ?].

[A.D. 1522–3.

Robert Avery } Wardens.
Iohn Wall

Chantry Accounts.

Church Rents.

Quitrents and Payments.]

* * * * *

[1] Item, paid for brede, Drynk and ffire at þe Newe sessing of þe clarkes bill . . . .   vj d ob

* * * * *

[2] Item, paid for Newe Revyng of a Surples & a newe band . . . .   iiij d

* * * * *

[3] Item, paid to Iohn Woulff for payntyng of the blake altercloth and the ffronte of the same belongyng to Seint Stephens alter withe the wavys of gold. Summa . . . .   ij s

Item, on Seint Barnabis day for v dossen of Roose garlondis for the crossis and for the queer. Summa . . . .   ij s   iiij d

Item, for a galon of gascon wyne sent to Iohn Edyalles to the kynges chappell for theyre dyner . . .   xij d

Item, paid to Griffith for a Reward for hym and his children . . . .   xx d

Item, paid to Roger Mason for childrens dyner at his howse . . . .   xx d

Item, paid on Seint Barnabis day, at the Sonn Taverne, after Evynsong, for Drynke for the kynges chappell and for the Clerkis of the Towne, the Summa of . . . .   xxj d

* * * * *

Item, paid to Richard hynde for laboryng on the

---

[1] leaf 482, back.   [2] leaf 483.   [3] leaf 483, back.

Church and for Carriage of Bourdis and hay that[1] was vndir the ledis of the chirche, and for swepyng of all the chirche ledis	v d

* * * * *

Item, paid to ser Richard Ellys, the Morowe Mas preist, for candell to sey his seruyce for kepyng the Mas	iiij d

* * * * *

[2] Item, paid to the Orgonmaker for the ouersight of the Orgons þis yere	xij d
Item, paid for wood to the plomer for sowdryng of ij gratis in the steple and for sowdryng the ledis on the North Ile	ij d

* * * * *

Item, paid for iij ℔ of Sowder for the same gratis and for the Sowthe Ile, the ℔ v d. Summa . .	xv d

* * * * *

Item, paid for a Deske with a fote that stondith at þe Orgons	xij d

* * * * *

Item, paid for ledgeing of the Orgons benethe by the grounde	iiij d

* * * * *

Item, paid for a key for a chest in the vpper vestry that the lynnen clothis lyeth in	iij d

* * * * *

Item, paid for makyng of ij Rochettes for children .	iij d

* * * * *

Item, paid for Sowdryng of the fote of a senser and for mendyng the fote of a chales	iiij d

* * * * *

Item, paid for iij lamp Glassis for the Churche . . .	ij d

* * * * *

[3] Casuell Resceitis this yere.

Rec' for the Buryall of Iohn Colens in the Chirche .	xiij s	iiij d
Rec' for the Buryall of William holyngwourthis childe	ij s	
Rec' for the Buryall of a Straunger in the great chirch-yerd		xij d

---

[1] MS. 'thas.'   [2] leaf 484.   [3] leaf 485.

Churchwardens' Accounts, A.D. 1522-3.

Rec' of the wyffe of Iohn Colens for gravestone for her husband	v s	
Rec' of Thomas Duklyng for the Buryall of his Childe	ij s	
Rec' for Breke sold owte of þe howse that partrich holdith	iij s	viij d
Rec' for the Buryall of a straunger in the greate chirch-yerd		viij d
Rec' for the Buryall of a childe of Stephyn Saundersons	ij s	
Rec' for the Buryall of a preist in þe pardon chirche-yerd	ij s	
Rec' for the Buryall of Robert hikman in Seint Anns chappell	xiij s	iiij d
Rec' for the Buryall of Roger Chaloners childe	ij s	
Rec' of the Masturs of the parissh for money gadred of þe almes	xviij s	j d ob

Summa of thes Receites iij li v s j d ob.

Paymenttis.

Item, paid of the Almes money, for xxv quarters of Colys for þe poure people . . . . xj s v d ob

So the Receites is more then the paymenttes, liij s viij d.

[1] Clarkys wagis and Beamelight.

Rec' for Clerkis wagis this yere as apperith by the Rowle	ix li	xvij d
Rec' for pascall Money and Bemelight this yere	xiij s	iiij d

Summa Rec' ix li xiiij s ix d.

Paymenttis.

Item, paid to Roger Mason, Clerke, for his wages for a hole yere	vij li	xx d
Item, paid to William Wylde for his wages for a hole yere	xx s	
Item, paid to Thomas Smyth, Sexten, for his hole yere wages	iij li vj s	viij d

Summa of theis paymenttes xj li viij s iiij d.

So the charges is more then the Receites, xxxiij s vij d.

[1] leaf 485, back.

[Wax Reckoning.
Allowances.
Rehearsal.]

[1]Memorandum: the xxiij day of Ienuary in the yere of our lord god m^l v^c xxiij^{ti}, and in the xvth yere of the Rayng of kyng henre the viijth, hit was aGreed, and be a Vestry Ordeyned by thes persons ffoloyng. That is to say, the woursshipfull Mr Alen percy, parson of the Churche of Seint Mary at hill, Mr Robert Aldernes, William Roche, Iohn Russell, Iohn Austhorp, Andrew Evyngar, Thomas Duklyng, Iohn Woulff, Thomas Clayton, Robert Ryvell, Robert Game, Iohn Potter, Iohn Wall, Robert Averey, and Iohn Ideall, with other moo, for the Buryall of every person, Man, woman or childe. And as here aftir ffoloyth :—

First, for every person, Man, woman or Childe that shal be Buryed in any of the ij chapelles of Seint Stephyn and Seint Katheryn shall pay for the grounde of theire buryall in any of the said chappelles	xiij s iiij d
Item, yf any Man, woman or Childe that shal be Buryed withowte the quere dore of any of the said Chappelles of Seint Stephyn and Seint Katheryn vnto the west side of the Ile goyng South and North shall pay for theire buryall in that place	x s
Item, yff any Man, woman or Childe that shal be Buryed in the church from the Cros Ile to the west ende of the churche shall pay for the grounde of theire Buryall there in þat place . .	vj s viij d

For the Clarkis Dutie.

Item, it is Condesendid & agreed by the said persons aboue Rehersid, that the Mr Clerk shall haue for the Grownde brekyng in any of the said Chappelles for any Buryall for Man, woman or Childe	iij s iiij d
Item, it is by the said persons aboue Named agreed that the said Clarke shall haue for the Buryall of every Man, woman or childe from the quere doris vnto the west side of the Ile goyng South and North, for brekyng the Grounde in þat place	ii s vj d

[1] leaf 487, back.

Item, it is agreed by the persons aboue Named that the Clerke shall haue for makyng a pitt or buryall place from the Cros Ile to the west ende of the Churche, for Man, woman or Childe . .   xx d

[1]Memorandum: that at the day of the Acompte of this Queyre, that Iohn Ideall is Suretie for the Summa of iij s iiij d, the whiche Thomas Duklyng promysed to the Byeng of the payer of Newe Orgons . . . .   iij s   iiij d

* * * * *

Thomas Harman.

Memorandum: that of xlix li xix d in money brought in by henre Edmond of london, salter, which was left in the custody of the Church of Seint Mary at hill for the behoffe of Thomas Harman the Sonn of William Harman; That there was paid in þe said Church of Seint Mary at hill, & delyuered þe ix[th] day of ffebruarii anno m[l] v[c] xxij & in þe xiiij[th] yere of kyng henre þe viij[th], vnto the said Thomas Harman & henre Edmond in þe presence of þes persons—M[r] William Alen, Curat; William Roche, Iohn Austhorp, Stephyn Saunderson, Thomas Duklyng, Iohn Woulff and Iohn Wall, in money, the summa of   xx li

* * * * *

[2]Memorandum: that hit is agreed and condecendid that there shal be[3] this yere veuers and ouerseers for the Renttes of the chirch and of the chauntr[e]s thes persons foloyng, that is to say, Iohn Austhorp & Iohn Woulff, for all such reparacions as shal be done this yere in any place belongyng to the chirch.

[A.D. 1523–4.

Iohn Edyall } Wardens.
Robert Averey

Obit List.

Quitrent List.

A Memorandum.

Chantry Accounts.

[1] leaf 488.   [2] leaf 489.   [3] MS. 'shalle.'

Church Rents.
Payments.]

* * * * *

[1]paid to Iohn Northfolke for a Rewarde for kepyng the quere and the Orgons all the xij^c days in Cristemas . . . . vj s viij d

* * * * *

paid for iiij ymners and a processione*r*, noted, for þe clerke*s* in þe quere . . . . vj s viij d

* * * * *

[2]paid for makyng clene of a chambre in the Abbotte*s* yn for to be a skole howse for Northfolke*s* children and for hauyng away of Strawe and Rubbussh owte of that howse, the Su*m*ma of . . . . . vj d

paid for Russhis for that Chambre for Strawyng . . iij d

* * * * *

paid for Ryngyng of M*es*tres portte*s* knyll w*ith* the Greate bell . . . . vj d

* * * * *

paid for makyng of xij Surplices ffor men, the pece vj d. Su*m*ma . . . . vj s

paid for makyng of xij Surplice*s* for Children, þe pece v d. Su*m*ma[3] . . . . v s

paid for makyng of iij^c Children Surplice*s*, of the which Surplices Mr Clayton gaue the clothe of them; pa*i*d for makyng . . . . xv d

paid for iiij holywatur sprynklys for the churche . . vj d

paid to s*ir* Ric*har*d Ellys for candell for syngyng þe ffirst mas . . . . ij d

* * * * *

paid for makyng clene of both þe chirchyerdes ayenst þat day [palm sonday] . . . . iij d

paid to Mr Austhorp of the Obbet of M*es*tres Noneley x s

paid for brede and Drynke spent vppon the Orgon maker and other of the p*a*risshe in the tyme of the Amendyng of the Orgons . . . . . . xj d

---

[1] leaf 497.   [2] leaf 497, back.
[3] Forty-eight 'ell*es*' of linen cloth and twenty-six of 'Brode' cloth for Surplices bought separately.

MED. REC.   Y

Churchwardens' Accounts, A.D. 1523–4.

paid to the Orgon maker by þe mynde of M^r person for mendyng the Orgons	iij s iiij d

*****

paid for the Costes of William Smyth, Condukte, for settyng a childe at Waltham	xij d

*****

paid to Iohn Woulff for Shauyng & payntyng of iiij Baner Stavis, the which Stavys wer gevyn by Robert Ryvell	iiij s

*****

[1] paid for Garlondis for the Crossis and the quere and for other Straungers that did bere Copis on corpus cristi day	xxj d
paid for beryng of viij Torches that day with þe Sacrament	viij d

*****

paid to Northfolke and his compeny & þe children when that M^r parson gave to them a playng weke to make mery	iij s iiij d

*****

paid for Milke and Rattisbane for the Rattes in the chirch	j d ob
paid for bromys for the chirch & Grece for the belles	iij d
paid to the Ryngers on our lady day for Ryngyng	viij d
paid for a basket for the Chirch for the Duste	ij d

*****

paid for vj ℔ of Rope for the lamp, the ℔ j d quarter. Summa	vij d ob

*****

paid for ij yerdys of wykur matt for þe childrens fete	xvj d
paid for vj Round Mattes of wykers for the Clerkes	xv d
to a ffounder for mendyng the Branche in the Roodelofte and for makyng of ij Newe Armes for þat branch, of viij ℔. Summa [2]	iiij s v d

*****

[3] paid to Antony Syluer for vj dossen & di. of candell for the chirch	vj s vj d

*****

[1] leaf 498.   [2] '2 . 6' inserted between lines.
[3] leaf 498, back.

paid for ij yards and a halfe of Grene bukram for ȳ same — ij d
paid for ij yerdes of Sylke rebande for the same cope —
paid for brede and drynke in that tyme — ij d
paid for ȳ parson abbott to say psalm by the will —
paid to vj preistes and ij clarkes at that obbet — iij s iiij d
paid for the oȳ pany brede and drynke at ȳ dyrge — vij d
paid for Garlondes for ȳ crosses & ȳ quere on Ascencion day — vij d
paid for Garlondes for ȳ crosse & ȳ quere on Corpus Christi day —
paid for Garlondes for the crosses and the quere and for other
 Strangers that did bere copes on corpus Christi day — iiij d
paid for beryng of viij torches that day to ȳ Sacrament — viij d
paid for ryngyng of the knyll for John Wall at ȳ greate bell — vj d
paid for Bysshe for the churche at mydsom' — iij d
paid to Northfolke and his copeny & ȳ children when that
 ȳ parson gave to them a pleyng cake to make mery — iiij d
paid for making clene of a chambre in the preistes ale and
 cariage a way of duste & for their labor in meate & drinke — viij d
paid for a newe baudryke for the ffyrst bell — viij d
paid for ayzle and ranshane for the uvalt in the churche — ij s ob
paid for bromys for the church & quere for the feste — iij d
paid to the ryngers on o' lady day for ryngyng — vj d
paid for a basket for the church for the duste — ij d
paid for ij lode of tyle in the Storehouse — ob
paid for a quartron of russe tyle — iiij d
paid for vj lb of rope for the lamp thatt is j ȳ d q' viij — vij d q'
paid for bromes for the church — ij d
paid for ij yerdys of hyre matt for ȳ children sete — iiij d
paid for vj pound matts of wykers for the clerke — vj d
paid to a Sowder for mendyng the braunche in the bodalofte
 and for making of ij newe armes for ȳ braunch of bras — iiij s
paid for a lode of broke in the Storehouse — ij s iij d
paid to a mason & his man for a day for mendyng of a
 chemeney in John Coveneys house — ij s
paid for a lode stone occupyed in the preistes ale — vj d
paid to Thomas a Lee glasyer for mendyng of all the
 wyndowes in the body of the church & only in the belfrey — v s
paid to a mason & his labores for a day for mending of ȳ
 chemeneys in Katheryn lacsons house at Stone hill — xvij d

Sum of these payments — xlvij s vj d

A Page of the Accounts. (MS. $\frac{1239}{1}$ leaf 498, A.D. 1524. Reduced in size.)

Churchwardens' Accounts, A.D. 1523-4.

paid for xv fote of Boourde occupied in M*es*tres Rochis Maydens pewe for benches and other thyng*es*		v d
paid for Reysyng of Mr Roches pewe and for a Newe dore to the same pewe and for Stuff and wourkmanship of the same	ij s	iiij d
paid for wourkmanship of Mr Roches Maydens pewe and for Settyng vpp of a pewe in Seint Annys chappell		iiij d

*   *   *   *   *

paid for a peyre of Garnatt*es* for Mr Roches pewe dore		iiij d
paid for a long Deske for the quere	iij s	

*   *   *   *   *

paid to the Raker for his yer*es* wag*es* for the chirc͡h .		xvj d
paid to Balaham, lamerton and Adam, that was graunted to them for blowyng the Orgons and tendyng to the chirc͡h eu*er*y sonday, to haue ij d, that is to say, from the xth day of Septembre vnto the xviij day of Decembre. Su*m*ma xv Sondays, eu*er*y sonday ij d. Su*m*ma	ij s	vj d
paid for Brede, Ale and wyne for the queer at dyu*er*s hig͡ht festis in the yere and for the Kyng*es* chappell xiij s x d; of the whiche Rec*eued* of M^r p*ar*son vj s xj d, And so Restit͡h to the chirches cost	vj s	xj d

*   *   *   *   *

paid for mendyng of the Dayly Cros & Burnysshing therof	ij s

*   *   *   *   *

¹Casuell Receptis this yere.

Rec*eued* for the Buryall of a Straunger in þe Greate chirc͡hyerd		viij d
Rec*eued* for the Buryall of Mr Roches soon in the Chirc͡h	·vj s	viij d
Rec*eued* for the Buryall of Symond vavasours Doughter in þe p*ar*don chirchyerd	ij s	
Rec*eued* for the Buryall of M*es*tres port in Seint Stephins chappell & þe knyll	xx s	
Rec*eued* for the Buryall of Stephyn Saunderson in Seint Stephyns chapell	xiij s	iiij d

¹ leaf 499.

Rec*eued* for the Buryall of Iohn Wall in the chirch & for his knyll	xiij s	iiij d
Rec*eued* for the Buryall of a Man owte of the ffreor at Billingesgate	ij s	
Rec*eued* for the Buryall of Iohn Austhorp in þe p*ar*don chirchyerd	ij s	
Rec*eued* for the Buryall of Iohn Birdes childe in the p*ar*don chirchyerd	ij s	
Rec*eued* for the Buryall of Robert Austhorpis childe in the p*ar*don chirchyerd	ij s	
Rec*eued* for the Buryall of Rich*ar*d Staun*er* in the body of the chirch	vj s	viij d
Rec*eued* for the Buryall of Roger Chaloners childe in the p*ar*don chirchyerd	ij s	
Rec*eued* for thatt was Gadred by þe wyffis on hok-monday	xij s iiij d ob	
Receued of Mˣ Roche of the v li that he lentt to the chirche as apperith in the last ende of þe Acompte afore wretyn. Su*m*ma	ij s	v d

Su*m*ma of theis Recept*is* iiij li vij s v d ob.

[1] Clerkys wagis and Beamelight.

Rec*eued* for Clerkys wagis this yere as Apperith by the Rowle	viij li xiiij s	iiij d
Rec*eued* for pascall money and Beamlight this yere .	xij s	

Su*m*ma, ix li vj s iiij d.

Paymenttis.

paid to Roger Mason, Clerk, for his wagis for a hole yere	vij li vj s	viij d
paid to Thomas, Sexten, for halff a yer*es* wag*es* ended at o*ur* lady day	xxxiij s	iiij d
paid to Augustyn, Sexte*n*, for di. a yer*es* wag*es* ended at o*ur* lady day	xxvj s	viij d
paid to Iohn Northfolke, co*n*dukt, for iij qu*ar*t*er*s wag*es* besidis Mˣ p*ar*sons wag*es*	xxx s	
paid to Will*ia*m Wylde for his wag*es* for a hole yere .	xx s [2]	

Su*m*ma, xij li xvj s viij d.

So the charg*es* is more then the Recept*es* iij li x s iiij d.

---

[1] leaf 499, back.   [2] 12-16-8 in margin.

[Wax Reckoning.
Allowances.
Rehearsal, etc.]

* * * * *

[1]paid, more, to William Wylde for wryting of a New
Inventory . . . . iij s   vij d

* * * * *

[2]Memorandum: the xiij day of ffebruarii Anno m¹ ccccc xxiiij[ts], and in the xvj yere of the Rayng of kyng henre the viij[th], that there is owyng vnto Thomas harman by the chirch of seint Mary at hill, the Summa off viij li x s, to be paid at the ffest of puryficacion of our lady in the yere of our lord god m¹ ccccc xxv. And then and at that day the said Thomas and the Church of Seint Mary at hill shal be clere content & paid of all summaes of Money the whiche [the] said Thomas had in the custody of the chirch before this day.

Memorandum: in the yere of our lord god m¹ v[c] xxiiij[ts], And in the xvj yere of kyng henry the viij[th], that Richard Broke, Thomas Dod, Iohn Good and Richard Tompson, wardens of the ffraternyte or Guylde of Seint Christofur holden and kepte in the Church of Seint Mary at hill, by Byllingesgate in london, made ther Acompte before the Right woursshipfull M[r] percy, parson of the said Chirch and oþer the worsshipfull of the parisshe. And where hit Apperid by ther Acompt brought, that their Receptes þat they had Receued this yere mounte to þe Summa of v li xvj s viij d ob. Whereof they payd, as Apperid by certen parcelles, for dyuers charge þis yere the Summa of iiij li xviij s iij d ob. And so ther Restith by this A-Compte & all charges paid, þe summa of xviij s v d.

And so
There R[em]ayneth in ther box with the Rest of this Acompte and with that money that was in ther box before this Acompt Summa iij li viij s.

[A.D. 1524–5.

Alexaunder Hilton } Wardens.[3]
Thomas Vstum

Obit list.

Quitrents.

---

[1] leaf 501.   [2] leaf 501, back.
[3] Thomas Vstum serves again next year. The explanation of his serving for two years successively is to be found in the fact that a John Edyall served apparently as warden for part of 1524-5. His name is scratched out, and that of Thomas Vstum substituted more than once in the accounts for 1524-5.

A note of money to be paid.
Chantry Accounts.
Church Rents.]

* * * * *

[1]Rec*eued* of Ioħn Northfolke for a chambre for a skole . . . . vj s viij d

* * * * *

[2] Paymenttis.

paid for mendyng of a Chales, iiij d. And for Rattesbane, iiij d. Summa viij d.

paid for beryng of viij Torches on corp*us christ*i day, viij d.

paid for Rose Garlondis that day for the procession, xvj d.

paid to iij men that did bere the iij Crossis, iij d.

paid for the ffilling of the holywatur stopis for ij qu*arte*rs, iiij d.

paid for Glouys at Estur for the chirchwarden & þe clerk, vj d.

ffor þe Romelond.

paid to Mr Norwych, se*r*geaunt, and Mr Densell of lyncolles in, for comyng to þe Guyld hall for the besynes of þe Romeland, xiij s iiij d.

paid to them the xix day of Iunii, at the Guyld hall, for the besynes of the Romelande at this tyme, x s.

paid for ffysshe for theire dyne*r*, and for brede, wyne and ale, iij s iiij d.

paid to Mr Densell for makyng & drawyng owte our plee, iiij s.

paid for bote hire to Westmynste*r* for dyue*r*s of the p*a*risshens & our expensis of our Man of lawe for coste*s* there, xxiij d oƀ.

p*ai*d to a clerk for the wrytyng of our plee, xiiij d.

* * * * *

paid for v processioners for the chirch, the pece, xiij d. Su*m*ma, v s v d.

paid to s*i*r Ioħn Tyllisley for a Tabull of þe ordryng of þe queer, viij d.

paid for makyng of a bourde for the same Table, iiij d.

paid to Thomas Ripton for helpyng the clerk eu*er*y other weke to kepe the morwe mas for that qu*arte*r, ij s vj d.

* * * * *

---

[1] leaf 508.   [2] leaf 508, back.

paid for a great kay for the Sowth dore of the chirche and for ij kays for the wykket next to the parsonage and for ij keys for the Spryng of the Sowthe dore and for the bolt to Seint Stephynns chappell dore. Summa of all iij s.

paid for a Mattok, x d, and for a quarte of lampe oyle, iiij d. Summa xiiij d.

paid for Splisyng of v bell Ropis, v d.

paid for mendyng of a baudryk, iiij d, and for bromys, iij d oƀ. Summa vij d oƀ.

paid to Iohn Tilers wyff for drynk fett to the chirch for þe Ringers & þe clarkes at dyuers tymes at hight ffestes, xij d.

paid for ij long dexkes that be in the queer, vj s.

paid for a quarter that was for the fframe ouer þe North dore of the chirche, þat is for þe profettes on palmesonday, & workmanship, iij d.

paid for a pece of a ponchon for the benche in the queer, j d.

[1] paid to Thabbot of Waltham cros for Iohn Westons londis, xxxviij s, and for the Sowth Ile of the Chirche of Seint Mary at hill, x s. Summa xlviij s.

* * * * *

paid to Iohn Northfolke & the conductes & the Children in þe playng weke aftur christemas for to Sport them, iij s iiij d.

paid to Iohn how, orgon maker, for a yere to tende þe orgons, xij d.

paid for that was spent vppon Tyll Colman and other off the kynges chappell kepyng seruice in the chirche, xviij d.

paid for Nayles to Amend the belles whelis ayenst Mr Russelles dirige, j d.

paid for Ryngyng of Iohn Tylers knyll & Mr Russelles knyll, vij d.

paid to the Ryngers þat dyd Ringe at Mr Russelles dirige & Mas, xiiij d.

paid for Remeving the stone and Mr Russelles pit, x d.

* * * * *

paid for Ryngyng of the belles at the Trivmphe for the takyng of the ffrench kyng and by the comaundement of the Mayer, viij d.

* * * * *

paid for the leyng of the stone on Mr Russelles grave, viij d.

* * * * *

paid for Obleis, fflowres & palmys & bromys ayenst palmesonday, xj d.

* * * * *

[1] leaf 509.

paid for ale spent at the hiryng of a preist, vj d.

* * * * *

[1] paid for mendyng of Mestres Russelles maydes pewe, iiij d.

* * * * *

paid for a Baskett for holy brede, iij d.

* * * * *

paid to Mr Baker for his Councell for the londe lyeng at the stokkes of Mr porttes. Summa, iij s iiij d.

paid to þe Orgon maker for mendyng the orgons Accordyng to the Mynde of Mr Northfolke and at his devyse, ij s.

* * * * *

paid for the pavyng of Mastur porthis graue, viij d.

paid for that was spent vppon Mr Gyles of the chappell for beyng at our lady Mas ij days, vj d.

paid for x dosen of Cotton Candell for the chirche, x s.

paid to the iij Almesmen, to euery of þem ij d, for theyre weke when they do blowe the orgons when þer weke comyth, viij s viij d.

paid for wasshyng of the Chirch lynnen this yere, xiij s iiij d.

* * * * *

paid for brede, ale and wyne for the queer and for other strangers comyng therto at dyuers high ffestis in the yere xiij s ix d, of the whiche Receued of Mr parson . Rest to þe chirch, vj s x d ob.

paid for Drynk[2] for the clerkes at þe kepyng of Mas of Recordare, iiij d.

* * * * *

paid for a shopp borde in partriches shopp in Estchepe, vj s viij d.

paid to Thomas harman, by an obligacion, and for the last payment of all his money þat was in þe chirch of Seint Mary at hill, viij li x s.

* * * * *

paid to Bright for Ridyng to the Moore to Mr parson for to Speke to my lord Cardenall for þe takyng of þe children, iiij s iiij d.

[3] Casuell Receptis this yere.

Receued for the knyll of Iohn Tyler with the iij^{de} bell for oon owre, xvj d.

Receued at the Maryage of chappell, the waturberer, vj d.

Receued for the Buryall of Mr Russell in Seint stephyns chappell, xiij s iiij d.

---

[1] leaf 509, back.   [2] MS. 'Dryng.'   [3] leaf 510.

Receued for his knyll with the greate bell, vj s viij d.
Receued for the pelys for Diryge and Mas, xx d.
Receued for the Grounde & makyng þe pitt in þe chappell, iij s iiij d.
Receued at the chirchyng of Richard Stauners wyff, ij d.
Receued for the pelys at Stephyn Saundersons dirige & Mas, xx d.
Receued for the Buryall of Roger Chaloners childe in þe pardon chirchyerd, ij s.
Receued for the Buryall of Burnynghilles childe in þe pardon chirchyerd, ij s.
Receued, more, for dyuers other casueltyes as shall apere by a byll, xviij s j d ob.
Receued for the Buryall of Raphe Welysme in þe chirche, vj s viij d.
Receued for his knyll with the Greate bell for halff a day, vj s viij d.
Receued for the knyll and for the buryall of M^r port in þe chapell, xx s.

Summa, iij li iiij s j d ob.

[1] Clarkis wagis and Beamelight.

Receued for Clerkes wagis this yere as apperith by the Rowle, vij li xv s ij d.
Receued for pascall money and Beamelight this yere, xij s.

Summa, viij li vij s ij d.

Paymenttis.

paid to Roger Mason for a quarters wagis ended at Christemas, xxxvj s viij d.
paid to Iohn Northfolke, conducte, for his yeres wages of þe parissh, xl s.
paid to Morres, the base, for vj wekes, after xx noblys þe yere. Summa, xvj s viij d.
paid to Austen, þe Sexten, for iij quarters wages ended at Midsomer, xl s.
paid to þe same Austen for kepyng þe seruyce in þe clarkes absence, ij s vj d.
paid to a Conducte helpyng the queer for the xij days, iij s vj d.
paid to William Wylde for his yeres wages ended at Mighelmas, xx s.
paid to the Clerk of Seint Barthilmewys, þat shuld a bene clerk, whiche was graunted hym by the consent of the parisshe, iiij s iiij d.
paid to William Milward for þat he serued in this chirche. Summa, liij s iiij d.

[1] leaf 510, back.

paid to Thomas lawson, Clerk, for di. a yere ended at Mighelmas, iij ħ iij s.

paid to Thomas Ripton, Sexten, for a quarter ended at Migħelmas, xiij s iiij d.

Summa, xiiij ħ xiij s v d.

And so

The charge is more then the Receptes, vj ħ vj s iij d.

[Wax Reckoning.
Allowances.
Rehearsal.]

[1] Memorandum: that hit is Iugged at the day of this Acompt by them that wer there present, that theys parcelles hereafter foloyng shal be discownted owte of the summys aboue wretyn & as aperitħ hereafter:—

ffirst, ytt is, that for the beryng of the crosses on corpus christi day that hit shal not be paid because hit shal not be no presedent, whicħ is, iij d.

Item, more, for that was paid at Estur for ij peyre of gloves for the chirchewardens, the Summa of vj d, whicħ shal not be for no presedent hereafter, vj d.

Item, more, for that which ys Reconyd in this A-count And should be put to the Reconyng of Mr Porthis besynes, þat was paid to Mr Baker, iij s iiij d.

*   *   *   *   *

[2] Memorandum: the iij^{de} day of Merche, Anno 1525, and in the xvij yere of the Rayng of kyng henre the viijth; paid by me, Alexaunder hilton, to lawles wyffe, waxchaundeler, for xxix ħ of wax whiche was MisRekonyd in the byħ of her Acount as aperitħ by a byll nowe brought. Summa in money, xxiiij s xj d.

Item, there was abated in her hole byħ for euery ħ of New wax þat was owyng to her, j d in euery ħ. Summa, iiij s x d.

And so

she hathe in money, clere, xx s j d.

And so

There Restith in money clere to the chirch of this Acounpt, xj ħ vj s vij d.

Item, Reseued more of Elysaundyr hyllton & Thomas husecam, for M^r porth beqwest to this church; pute it in to the chirch chist in presence of xij persones of the parishe, xx s.

Summa put in to the boxe, xij ħ vj s vij d.

[1] leaf 512.   [2] leaf 513.

With xij ti vj s vij d, ys put in to porthes chyste towardes that was borowed of his money the iiij day of feuerell, Anno 1526.

[A.D. 1525–6.

Thomas Vstum \
William Burnynghill / Wardens.

Obit list.

Quitrents.

Chantry Accounts.

Church Rents.]

[1] Paymenttes of the Same.

* * * * *

paid for a Rede for the chirche, ij d.

* * * * *

paid for wasshyng of the pix cloth ouer the alter, iiij d.

paid to Bright, the Conducte, for goyng to Dartforth to speke for the Clark that shuld be with us, xvj d.

* * * * *

paid for openyng and mendyng of the lock of the money cofur within the plate chest in þe vpper vestry, ij d.

paid for makyng clene of the Great chirchyerd & for Carryage of Rubbysshe, ij s.

paid for mendyng of Mastur Alens Surplis, j d.

paid for palme, fflowris and Cakys on palme sonday, ix d.

paid to a plasterer & his laborer for whight lymyng of Seint Katheryns chappell and for lyme, ij s ij d.

paid for a holowe key to the vpper vestry dore, iiij d.

* * * * *

[2] paid for a Man that cam from Dertforth that shulde a be the clarke & gevyn to hym by a vestry, xij d.

paid for Drynke for dyuers of the parisshe at the hyring of Thomas the Sexten, ij d.

paid to Thomas Rippyngton for ij wekes aftur our lady day ij s viij d; And to Richard Broke for iij wekes in the absence of a Sexten, graunted by vestry, iiij s. Summa, vj s viij d.

[1] leaf 520, back.   [2] leaf 521.

paid for mendyng of the trynite wyndowe of the Sowthe[1] side of the church, iij s viij d.

paid at Alderstons for that was spent vppon þe Clerke that shuld a come from Allhalous, iiij d oᵬ.

* * * * *

paid at the hyryng of Skott the Clerk, iiij d.

* * * * *

paid for ffreight of Bourdis and plankes for the Chirch owte of Essex to london, vj s viij d.

paid for ij Carttes to carry the same plankes and Bourdis from the wharff to the chirchyerd, iij s.

[2]paid to iiij laborers for to helpe to lade them and for the leyng of them in the Chirchyerd, ij s.

paid to a Mason, for a day, to mende þe steple batilment, viij d.

paid for that was spent in the parsonage with Mastur parson and dyuers of the parisshens þe xv day of August, x d.

* * * * *

paid for that was spent for dyuers of the parisshe at the goyng to Westmynster to speke with Mr parson, ix d oᵬ.

paid at the Tylers at the hyryng of the clerk, and for dyuers of the parisshe there beyng present, iij d.

paid for Ryngyng of None, Curfew and day pele and Courfewe & other pelis on our lady day the Assumpcion, xij d.

* * * * *

paid for makyng of a ffyre shovill for the vestry, x d.

* * * * *

paid for hay to lay vnder the lede of the chirche, v d.

paid to ij laborers for to help the plankes to þe chirch, ij d.

paid for lede nayle for the chirch, iiij s.

paid for ij porters to helpe to lade þe lede for the chirch, iiij d.

* * * * *

paid at Towre hill when the howse of the bell was bought, j d oᵬ.

[3]Paid to Mr Baker for his counsayle in the byeng of þe bell, iiij s vj d.

paid for [a] kay to the Storehowse Dore in þe preistes Ale, ij d.

paid for a kay for the Chircheyard gate next Iamys hubbardis howse, & a stay of Iron & ij staples, vij d.

* * * * *

paid for a lytell key for þe chest in the queer, iij d.

* * * * *

[1] MS. 'Sowthe Sowthe.' [2] leaf 521, back. [3] leaf 522.

paid for a pewtur pott for watur for the preistes, xiiij d.
paid at the Sonn at the counte of the plomer, v d.

* * * * *

[1] paid for that was spent at Iohn Tylers for dyuers of the parisshe at the Comonyng with William þat shuld a be clerk, ij d ob.

* * * * *

paid for vj skonses for the queer, viij d.
paid to the beedmen for blowyng of the Orgons, for euery weke ij d. Summa, viij s viij d.

* * * * *

paid for Cariage of a lode & di. of Rubbysshe from Mr porttes howse, the lode iij d. Summa, iiij d ob.

* * * * *

[2] paid for ij lamp glassis for the chirche, ij d.

* * * * *

Item, I ax alowaunce for þe chambre þat is the skole, vj s viij d.

* * * * *

paid for a grate of New lede for the chirche, poyse ij ℔, delyuered in olde lede ij ℔, paid þe castyng, ob.

[3] Casuell Receptis this yere.

Receued for the buryall of Alys wall in the chirche, vj s viij d.
Receued for a knyll with the Greate bell for Robert laurence, vj s viij d.
Receued of Casuelties taken by the Sexten, iij s v d ob.
Receued for the buryall of Mestres Aldernes in the chappell, xiij s iiij d.
Receued for the knyll withe the greate bell for her, vj s viij d.
Receued for the buryall of Austens wyff in þe pardon chirchyerd, ij s.
Receued for the buryall of peryes wyff in þe pardon chirchyerd, ij s.
Receued of Iohn potter for the buryall of his son, ij s.
Receued for the buryall of Robert Austhorpis child, ij s.
Receued for the buryall of a Man of Suffolke, ij s.
Receued for the buryall of William Awdewyns chylde, ij s.
Summa, xlviij s ix d ob.

[4] The Clarkis wages & Beamelight.

Receued for Clarkes wages this yere as aperith by the Rowle, viij li xiij s.

[1] leaf 522, back. [2] leaf 523.
[3] leaf 524. [4] leaf 524, back.

Receued for pascall money this yere and beamelight, xij s.
Summa, ix li v s.

Paymenttis.

paid to Thomas lawson for a quarter ended at Cristemas, xxx s.
paid to Iohn Northfolke, conducte, for his wages of þe parisshe, xl s.
paid to William Chambre for a quarter ended at our lady day, xj s viij d.
paid to Iohn Elyard for iij quarters wages ended at Mighelmas, iiij li x s.
paid to Richard Gowge for di. a quarter & vij days ended at Midsomer, aftir viij li the yere, xxiij s j d; more payd to hym for a quarters wages ended at Mighelmas, aftir viij li, payd xl s. Summa, iij li iij s j d.
paid to Thomas Rippyngton, Sexten, for halff a yeres wages and doyng the Clarkes dutye, whiche was graunted hym by the parisshe. Summa, xxxv s x d.
paid to Thomas Monde, Sexten, for halff a quarter and x days wages ended at Midsomer, aftir v merc þe yere, x s ij d; paid more for a quarter ended at Mighelmas xvj s viij d. Summa, xxvj s x d.
paid to William Wylde for a yeres wages ended at Mighelmas, xx s.
Summa, xv li xvij s v d.

And so
The charges is more [then] the Recepttes vj li xij s v d.

[Wax Reckoning.

Allowances.

Rehearsal.]

[Work on the Two Aisles.]

[1] +

Memorandum: that this yere, Anno 1526, was spent apon the ij ylles, in tymbyer, borde, lede & warkmanshipe, as it aperyth by this lytell qware herevnto anexeyd, which amount the holle charge besyd all afore writyn this artykell, lj li ij d; which was borowyd forth of porthes chyste, as doth apere by a bowke in the said chyste how that porthes money doth com in & allso paid forth.

Werof ys paid to porthes cheste by hyllton['s a-]count xij li vj s vij d, and by the fotte of thys acount of husecam x li xiij d, amount both, xxij li vij s viij d: and so the chu[r]che ys in dette at this day to porthes chyste xxviij li xij s vj d.

[1] leaf 526, back.

Churchwardens' Accounts, A.D. 1525-6.

[1] +

+ the fyrste day of nove*m*byer, An*n*o M^1 v^c xxvj^t. here folowth the weyght of all the lede delyu*er*d vnto Will*i*am Rogeres, plom*er*, that was hayde of the north & sowthe ylle of the church of sante marry at hill, in london.

Delyu*er*d by husecam, game & Revell :—

C			C		
vij	——	——	xij	q*uarteres*	xiiij ℔
vij	——	xxiiij ℔	xij	q*uarteres*	——
vij	——	——	xiij	——	vij
vij	j q*uarter*	——	x	ij q*uarteres*	vij
vij	——	x	xv	q*uarter*	xiiij
vj	——	iiij	vj	q*uarter*	xj
vj	iij q*uarteres*		vj	——	——
vj	——	xiij	vj	iij q*uarteres*	——
xj	iij q*uarteres*	xiiij	iiij	ij q*uarteres*	iiij
xiiij	j q*uarter*	xiiij	vj	iij q*uarteres*	xxiiij
lxxx^c–ij q*uarteres* xxiiij ℔			lxxxxiiij^c————xxv		

[2] +

C			C		
vij	iij q*uarteres*	——	ix	ij q*uarteres*	——
iiij	q*uarter*	xxj	ix	iij q*uarteres*	xiiij
v	——	——	vij	——	xiiij
xiiij	——	xiiij	vij	——	——
viij	ij q*uarteres*	——	vij	iij q*uarteres*	——
vij	ij q*uarteres*	——	ix	ij q*uarteres*	——
xj	iij q*uarteres*	——	ix	——	vij
viij	ij q*uarteres*	——	viij	——	xxj
vij	ij q*uarteres*	——	vj	——	——
ix	——	——	vj	——	——
lxxxiiij^c————vij ℔			lxxx^c		

C		
vj	——	——
v	ij q*uarteres*	——
ij	iij q*uarteres*	——
xiiij^c j q*uarter*		

The w*hich* xliij p*ar*selle*s* amount xxxv m^t iij^c q*uarter* & ys old lede.

[1] leaf 527, back, the first leaf of the 'little quire,' which consists of eight leaves, all a little smaller than the ordinary leaves of the MS.
[2] leaf 528.

Churchwardens' Accounts, A.D. 1525-6.

[1] +

here folowth all such newe lede as ys reseued for the forsaide church of the sayd William Rogeres, plomer :—

C			C		
xv	iij quarteres	vij ħ	xvj	j quarter	——
xvij	ij quarteres	——	xv	j quarter	——
xvj	ij quarteres	vij	vij	iij quarteres	vij
xiiij	iij quarteres	——	xv	iij quarteres	——
xviij	iij quarteres	vij	xiij	iij quarteres	——
xiiij	——	xiiij	xvij	iij quarteres	xiiij
xiiij	— quarter	vij	xix	j quarter	——
xiij	iij quarteres	xiiij	xvj	ij quarteres	xiiij
xv	——	vij	xv	iij quarteres	xxj
xiiij	iij quarteres	x ħ	xvj	j quarter	
clv c	ij quarteres	xvij ħ	cliiij c	iij quarteres	——

	[2] C			
17 –021.	xvij		——	xxj ħ
	xiiij		——	xiiij
	xvij		ij quarteres	xiiij
	xvj		j quarter	xiiij
	xj		ij quarteres	xiiij
	xiij		iij quarteres	xiiij
	viij		——	xiiij
	iiij		——	xiiij
	ij		——	xiiij
	iij		j quarter	xxvj
	cviij c		ij quarteres	xix ħ

Summa, xlj m^t ix c viij ħ, and ys newe lede.

	419	0	8
	353	1	0

Reste 65 c 3 quarteres 8 ħ more Reseued then delyuerd lxv c iij quarteres viij ħ.

[3] And so the forsaid church of Sante mayry at hyll owyth vnto the said William Rogeres for castynge of xlij M^l. ix^c. vj ħ. at xiij d the c, which amount xxij ɫi xiiij s.

Item, more, for that the said William Rogeres that he delyuerd more newe lede then[4] he hathe Reseued old lede, lxv c iij quarteres vj ħ, after v ħ for the fother, which ys, the fother, xix c and a hallfe ; amount in money, xvj ɫi xvij s j d.

---

[1] leaf 528, back.   [2] leaf 529.   [3] leaf 529, back.
[4] MS. 'then then.'

Churchwardens' Accounts, A.D. 1525–6.

Item, for sowdyr xxxj lb di., at v d the lb, amount, xiij s j d.
Item, more, for caryage of all the forsaid lede, of old led, with workmanshipe & laynge, vij s x d.

Summa, xl li xij s.

[1]here folowth the charges of the carpenter wynes bill for the carpentershype of the said ij ylles, with stepell, penteses & all his bezynes abowte the said ij ylles :—

ffyrste ffor Rydeynge to the wodes to chose the tymbyr for the church, ij days, xvj d.

  Item, for costes of ij sawyers to go to the said wode &[2] home ayane, xvj d.

  Item, for vij days & a hallfe on the north syd of the churche, for wyn, v s.

  Item, for his servant vij days & a hallfe, v s.

  Item, vij days & a hallfe for his boye, ij s vj d.

[Summa] xv s ij d.

[3]Item, more, for that wyn was on the sowthe ylle, for his sellfe ix days. amount, vj s.

Item, for his servante vj days, iiij s.

Item, for his boye, ix days, iij s.

Item, for a day for wyn whan he mayde the paylle in the church yerd, viij d.

Item, for hys[4] chylld the said day, iiij d.

Item, for iiij days for his servant apon the rofe & stepill, ij s viij d.

Item, more for his Rewarde beyng from his howce, wife & chilldyren, & labour to sett forth the sawyeres warke & to hellpe the tymbyer to the pyttes. amount, viij s viij d.

Summa, xxv s iiij d.

[5]Summa totallis that the carpenter wystowe hayd, xl s vj d.

[6]here folowth such charges as William Roche layd owte for tymbyr for the [corent?] & borde for the forsaid ij ylles :—

ffyrst, ffor sawyng of plankes, to cleston, sawyer, & his fellowe, tyll sonday the x of Iune, for xiiij days at xiiij d euery day, xvj s iiij d.

  Item, more, paid to Edemonde towzy & his felowe sawyeres, for vij days tyll the x day of Iune, at xiiij d the day, viij s ij d.

  Item, more, paid to ballard the owner of the wode, for xj lodes tymbyr for þe said plankes & bord, at iij s the lod, xxxiij s.

  Item, more, for the hewyng of the said tymbyer above that ballard pris, ij s, to haue the chose of all the holl wod, ij s.

---

[1] leaf 530, back.   [2] MS. '& &.'   [3] leaf 531.
[4] MS. 'his hys.'   [5] leaf 531, back.   [6] leaf 532.

Item, more, paid to cleston & his[1] fellow sawyeres, for iiij days, at xiiij d þe day, iiij s viij d.

[Summa] iij ƚi iiij s ij d.

[2] +

Item, more, paid to fayry & his fellowe for sawyng x days at xiiij d the day. amo*u*nt, xj s viij d.

Item, more, paid to towzy & his fellowe, for ix days sawyng at xiiij d the day. *a*mount, x s vj d.

Item, more, for caryage in xij carrt*es* the said xj lod*es* tymbyr, in plank*es* & bord*es*, from the wode to the wat*er*syd, x mylles, at ij s viij d eu*er*y carrtte, xxxij s.

Item, more, to cleston & his fellowe for sawynge vj days at xiiij d the day. amo*u*nt, vij s.

Item, more, paid for makyng of sawe pytt*es*, xvj d.

[Summa] iij ƚi ij s vj d.

S*u*mma [of] the charge of the tymbyr,[3] plank*es* & bord, vj ƚi vj s viij d.

[4] Memorandum: that the forsaid plom*er* haid for newe lede & castynge of newe & old led, wi*th* sowdyr & warkemanshipe as aperyth afore, xl ƚi xij s.

Item, wyn the carpenter hayd, as it aperythe afore declareyd, ij ƚi vj d.

Item, more, payd by Willi*a*m Roche for tymbyr, sawyng, caryage of plank*es* [&] bord for the said ij ylles as afore aperyth, vj ƚi vj s viij d.

Item, more, payde to Robarde game, that hath for the churche as aperyth by his acounte of it, j ƚi xv s viij d.

Item, there was paid, by the hand*es* of claton', w*h*ich ys p[a]id hy*m* agayne, for ij sawyeres that sawyd in the churche yerd, ƚi v s iiij.

[Summa] lj ƚi s ij d.

[A.D. 1526–7.

William Burnynghill }
Roger Chaloner } Wardens.

Obit list.

Quitrent list.

Chantry Accounts.

Church Rents.]

---

[1] MS. '& his & his.' [2] leaf 532, back.
[3] MS. 'tylbyr.' [4] leaf 533, back.

[1]Paymenttes of the same.

* * * * *

Item, paid for a pece of Sandwych lyne for the chirch		iiij d
Item, paid for a Bawdryk for the first bell of the v belles		xvj d

* * * * *

Item, paid to Mr Alen for the Beedrowle of þe chauntries	ij s	
Item, paid to the Orgon maker for a yere for his attendaunce		xij d
Item, paid for mendyng of þe olde Sensor & for siluer þat went to hit	iiij s	
Item, paid at the salutacion at the hiryng of petur þe clarke		vj d ob
Item, paid to hym by commandment of þe vestry for a goddis peny		iiij d

* * * * *

[2]Item, spent on the parisshens at the hiryng of ij preistes		vj d
Item, paid for Smale Rope for þe sanctus bell, þe lamp & þe Orgons		xv d ob
Item, paid for bryngyng Downe & Beryng vppe of the sanctus bell		ij d
Item, paid for garlondis and Rosis & lavender on corpus christi day	ij s	v d

* * * * *

Item, spent vppon Straungers that dyd Syng at our lady Mas		xij d
Item, paid for a henge for a pewe dore in the Churche		ij d
Item, paid to Mr Northfolke for mendyng of dyuers bokis	vj s	viij d
Item, paid for keyes and lockys ffor the ffount		viij d

* * * * *

[3]Item, paid to Thomas Mundy, Sexten, for Bromys for þe church		j d
Item, paid for small lyne for the curten of the Trynyte		ij d
Item, paid at the hyryng of sir humfrey for drynke to þe parisshens		v d
Item, paid for a Shodshovill for the Church		iiij d

[1] leaf 543, back.   [2] leaf 544.   [3] leaf 544, back.

Item, paid for the Celyng of sir Iohn Neelles chambre .... viij d
Item, paid to the Canell Raker for the church for a hole yere .... xvj d
Item, paid to Trappis for mendyng of the ij greate Sensours and for Syluer that wentt to them. Summa .... iiij s x d

* * * * *

Item, for ij lampe glassis ffor the church .... ij d
Item, paid for a key to the Steple dore .... iij d
Item, paid for a garnet to a chest in the chappell .... iiij d
Item, paid for iij bolltes for the Sanctus bell .... iij d
Item, for a clekett key to the preistes Ale gate .... iiij d
Item, paid for vj holywatur Sprynklys .... xij d
Item, paid at the hyring of sir Iohn the Morowe mas preist .... vj d
Item, paid to the Beedmen for Blowyng of the Orgons for lij wekys, the weke ij d. Summa .... viij s viij d

* * * * *

Item, for puttyng of Cordys to the Tabernacle of þe Trynyte .... iiij d
Item, alowed to a carpenter for goyng abought with Mr Roche & the Chirchwarden for the chirches besynes for di. a day .... iiij d
Item, a C of threpeny nayle for þe whele of þe Saunctus bell .... ij d
[1] Item, for mendyng of the Stokke of the Saunctus bell .... iiij d
Item, for the stuff and makyng of a doble deske in the queer .... v s
Item, paid for [a] Bedsted for the preistes chamber þat kepith þe first mas .... xiiij d
Item, paid for chongyng of ij C[r]vwettes for the high Alter .... iiij d

* * * * *

Item, I aske alowans of vacacion for a quarter, of the chambre þat sir petur Raughton kept before his deth .... xx d

* * * * *

Item, I aske for vacacion for a yere of Northfolkes skole .... vj s viij d

* * * * *

[1] leaf 545.

[1] Receptis bi Casuelties this yere.

Rec' of the Gadryng of the wyffis on hok Monday . .	xx s
Rec' for the Buryall of Iohn Coveney in þe pardon chirchyerd	ij s
Rec' of the Orgon Maker for þe olde portatyffis in þe quere	xxvj s viij d
Rec' of Iohn partrich, Butcher, for his Newe lees . .	xl s

Summa, iiij li viij s viij d.

[2] The Clarkis wages and Beamelight.

Rec' of the Clarkes wages this yere as Apperith by the Rowle	viij li xix s viij d
Rec' for pascall money and Beamelight this yere .	xiij s iiij d ob

Summa, ix li xiij s ob.

Paymenttis.

paid to Richard Goge, Clerk, for halff a yere ended at our lady day	iij li vj s viij d
paid to petur purvoche, Clerk, for di. a yere ended at Mighelmas	iij li vj s viij d
paid to Iohn Northfolke, Conducte, for his wages of þe parissh	xl s
paid to Thomas Mondy, Sexten, for his wages for a yere	iij li vj s viij d
paid to Richard Goge for x wekis seruys after our lady day	xxx s ix d
paid to William Wylde for a yeres seruys at Mighelmas	xx s
paid to Iohn Catur for a quarter and v wekys wages, with vj s & viij d that was geven hym by a vestry. Summa payd	iij li x d
paid to Iohn Wright, Conducte, for a quarter wages ended at Mighelmas, Rebatyng viij days. Summa paid	xxxvj s vj d

Summa, xix li viij s j d.[3]

And so

The charges is more then the Receptes, ix li xv s ob.

---

[1] leaf 545, back.   [2] leaf 546.
[3] '19 . 8 . 1' in margin.

[Wax Reckoning.
Two Allowances.
Rehearsal.]

[1] Memorandum: that the xth day of ffebruarii, anno Domini 1527, the xix[th] yer of the Reign of our soueraign lord kyng henry the viij[th]; at the accompt givin vp by William burnynghill & Roger Chaloner, church wardens of Seint Mary at hill; it was condicendid & agreyd by the Right worshipfull Mr Alen percy, parson of the same church, Mr William Roche, Iohn wolf, Thomas Clayton, Robert Game, Robert Revell, Alexaunder hilton, Iohn Potter, Iohn Idiall, Thomas Huston and others of the said parish, that Iames Hubert, at his humble peticion and request made the[n?]; the aboue namyd parson & parisheners for dyuers costes & charges by hym done of & vpon the house which he now dwellith in as by a bill of parcelles by hym exibitid vnto the said parson & parisheners conteynyng the svm of viij li xix s x d; shuld haue & enioy, first the some & iiij li v s due by hym vnto the said churche for rent of the same house of tyme passid & endid at our lady day the Annunciacion next ensuyng the date aboue wretten: and ouer that, of their good & charitable disposicion, in consideracion of his pouertie, haue grauntid vnto the same Iames Hubert, twoo yeres Rent clere from the said ffeast of our Lady day next commyng; fforsene & prouidid alweis that the same Iames shall in all thinges kepe & maynteign all the glasse & other neccessarys, as windowis & other thinges conteynid in his said bill, & at the end of his lease shall not amoue nor put away eny parte of therof, but leue theym to the mer disposicion of the said parson & parisheners & to their successours for euer, and that this graunt & ben[e?]volence shall not be president to none other tenaunt belongyng to the said church for no like matter in eny suche case at eny tyme here aftur.

[A.D. 1527–8.

Antony Elderton } Wardens.
Roger Chaloner

Chantry Accounts.
Church Rents.]

Paymentes concernyng the Church.

* * * * *

[2] paid to Mr Curate for the bedrolles for a yer . . . ij s

---

[1] leaf 548. [2] leaf 556, back.

Churchwardens' Accounts, A.D. 1527–8.

paid for Mending of a pane in oon of the sowth windowse	xij d
paid for the drinking of the Sessours of the clerkes wages	vj d
paid for a key to oon of the chamber durres in the prestes aley	iiij d

* * * * *

paid the last day of ffebruarii for a grett ion to hang the veill of the chauncell ageinst lent	xij d
paid for mending of the same veill & for curten ringes	xij d
paid the vjth day of Merche, at the hiring of balthazar the clerk, at the son tavern	viij d
paid for an eln of fyne lynnyn cloth to amend the sepulture cloth wherat it was eiton with rattes	xij d
paid to a bedmaker for mending & Sowing the same	xij d
paid to M^r wolf for payntyng & renewing the Images in the same cloth	v s

* * * * *

paid for drying of the Sipers for the sacrament against ester	iiij d
[1] Paid to Chapple for filling the holy water stokes for a yer	viij d
paid for ij quarter of Colis for hallowing of the font at estur	xiij d

* * * * *

paid for water on Monday thursday & ester evin spent in the church	ij d

* * * * *

paid for mending of an Iron in the Rode loft, & for a key for the charnell house dur	vj d
paid for a crokid Iron to pike torchis withall	iij d
paid for mending of a snach in the morrow mas prestes chist	ij d

* * * * *

paid to Balaham for blowing of the organs for a yer	viij s viij d

* * * * *

[2] paid vnto a goldsmyth for burnishing of the best cros, & for iiij siluer pinnes for the same, & for saving of the amell	iij s iiij d

---

[1] leaf 557.   [2] leaf 557, back.

paid to Mr Wolf for painting of the crucifix of the same	xij d
paid vnto Hugh Welshe, goldsmyth, for mending & dressing of the berrall cross & for making of an new boss for the same, with iiij onȝ siluer put to the same & for gilding þerof	xxxiiij s vj d
paid vnto an other goldsmyth, a kynsman of the Sexten, for mending of dyuers thinges in the vestre, as sensours, shippis, & gilding & for burnishing of Senssur, candilstikes, basons & other thinges as may apere by the particulers. Summa	xiij s vj d
paid for a hillett & a plate & spikinges for the Southe churchdur	v d

* * * * *

[1]Paide for ix c of lathe, spent at the bell at Tour Hill	iij s xj d ob

* * * * *

paid for brede, ale & wyne for the quere & for other straungers at dyuers high feistes in the yere past, xiiij s, wherof Mr parson most pay the oon half & the church þe other half	vij s
Paid at the Son tavern for the drinking of Mr Colmas with others of the kinges chappte that had songen in the churche	ix d
paid for the making of Iohn Austhrop is grave, & for laying of the ston ageyn	iij s iiij d

* * * * *

+ paid for a pekerell givin to the chaunceler of london for alowing of our tolleracion for Maister Nasing	ij s viij d

* * * * *

I aske allowance for di. a yeres rent of the house at sign of the bell at Tour Hill remayning in sute in guylhall	xx s

* * * * *

[The two Allowances.]

* * * * *

[2]Casuell Receptes this yere.

Receivide for the place of buriall of Iohn Awsthrop in the Middle Ile & for his knyll & graviston. Summa	xx s

[1] leaf 558.   [2] leaf 559.

Receivide for the buriall place of Alex*aunder* Hilton &
for his kny⊬ . . . .   xx s
Receivide of Thomas Hustom for his place of buriage .   vj s viij d
Receivide for his *graviston* and for his kny⊬ . . .   xiij s iiij d
Receivide of the same for his bequest to sent Stephins
chap⊬e . . . .   xx d
Receivide of Thomas Duckling for ij of his children
buridd in the p*ar*don churchyerd . . . . .   iiij s
Receivide of Willi*a*m Holingworthes moder in the
said churchyerd . . . .   ij s
Receivide of Symond vavass*ur* for his buria⊬ ther. .   ij s
Receivide for the buriall of *c*lare, doughte*r* of M^r
Roche, for her place of buriall, for her pitt mak-
ing & other duties . . . .   viij s iiij d
Receivide by the hand*es* of Willi*a*m Wild for the
buriall of Mergaret Roche & for her kny⊬ & other
duties. Su*m*ma . . . .   xv s
Su*m*ma, iiij ⊬i xiij s.

[1] Clerkis wagis & Beame Lyght.

Receivide for the clerk*es* wag*es* this yer as apperit⊬
by the Ro⊬ of gathering . . . .   viij ⊬i x s v d
Receivide for pascall money and beame Light this yer   xv s j d
Su*m*ma, ix ⊬i v s vj d.

Payment*es*.

Paide to Petre p*ur*voc⊬e, p*ar*is⊬ clerke, for a q*uarter*
wag*es* endid at C⊬ristmas. Su*m*ma. . . . .   xxxiij s iiij d
Paid to Balta3ar, clerke, for his wag*es*, oon q*uarter* &
x wek*es*, from o*ur* lady day in lent till his goyng
to Ipiswich, afte*r* xx nob⊬es a yer. Su*m*ma . .   lix s ij d
Paid to Io⊬n Norff., co*n*duct, for his yer*es* reward. .   xl s
Paid to Gose, conduct, for his wag*es* of iij quarte*rs* &
x wek*es*, afte*r* viij ⊬ a yer. Su*m*ma . . . . .   vij ⊬i x s x d
paid to Thomas Monday, Sexten, for a ho⊬ yer*es*
wag*es* . . . .   iij ⊬i vj s viij d
paid the goodman wild for yer*es* reward for keping
the quer . . . .   xx s
paid to Andrew Alen, conducte, for keping the quer
[fro*m* ?] candilmas to o*ur* lady day in lent . . .   x s

[1] leaf 559, back.

Paide to a singingman of Sent Anthis by the hand*es*
of Mr Norff. for keping of *our* lady mas in thab-
scence of gose & the clerke whan they wer takin
to Ipiswich . . . .   iij s   iiij d

S*um*ma, xix li iij s iiij d.
and so
The charge is mor then ·
the Recepte, ix li xvij s iiij d.

[Wax Reckoning.]
[1] Cer*ten* Receit*es* concer*n*yng Mr Porte.

Recevide of *cer*ten house₃ whiche he had by leash of
the *mer*cers, lying as well in brigstrete as in the
old Riall, for oon yer*es* Rent endid at Mighelmas,
wherof detayned in my hand*es* for his bequest
vj s viij d . . . .   ix li vj s viij d

R*ece*vide of the bruers wif at the pewt*re* pott ageynst
Seint Andrewis vn*der*shaft, for a nott & a boll
of Silu*er*, *par*cell gilt, that ley to pledg for the
som of . . . .   iiij li

S*um*ma, xiij li vj s viij d.

Paymentes.

Paide to the Rent gatherer of the m*er*cery for the
Rent of the said house₃ for oon holl yer endid at
Mighelmas. S*um*ma . . . .   vij li

*pa*id to s*i*r Rauf yong, chauntry p*r*est, for j di. yer*es*
wag*es* endid at Midsomer & for keping the quer .   iiij li

paid to s*i*r Thomas hall for wag*es* the space of vj
wek*es*, after viij li a yer. amo*un*t . . . . .   xviij s vj d

Paid to s*i*r pattrik Manfild for his wag*es* from the
tyme that gose & the clerk went awey, to Mighelmas . . . .   x s

Paid for the Obiit of Mr Port to Mr Curate & vj
prest*es*, iiij conduct*es*, & the sexten, for the masse
peny & bred & ale spent vpon the quer at
aldertons. S*um*ma . . . .   vj s

Item, mor, for the bequest as is aforsaid . . . . .   vj s   viij d

S*um*ma, xiij li ix d.

[Rehearsal, etc.]

[1] leaf 560, back.

[A.D. 1528–9.

Antony Elderton } Wardens.[1]
Iohn Byrd

Chantry Accounts, Church Rents.]

Paymentes concernyng the churche.

* * * * *

[2] Paide to the Smythe at the Rode for the makyng of keys and for lockes in the quer and other chestes   vj s   ix d

Paide to [Mastur][3] hilton, prest, for iij quarters, for kepyng daily seruyce in the quer, by the commaundment of the parishe . . . . xij s

Paide for ij poles for the Sacrament and for the amendyng of the same . . . . iij s   x d

Paide for a pully for the sacrament and for a roppe to the same . . . . xij d

* * * * *

[4] Paide to Richard hourdman, for the rent of a house that the parishe oughte to the Chamber of London, at billyngesgate . . . . xlv s   viij d

* * * * *

Paide, the xxviij[th] day of Iune, for dyuerse money laid out by the commaundement of the parishe for Sampe . . . . xij s

* * * * *

Paide to Balam for blouyng of the organs for a hole yere   viij s   viij d

* * * * *

[5] I aske allowaunce for a quarter Rent of a house at the Syne of the bell at Tour hille: And was for the tyme that the kyng caused Salte peter to be made in the said house . . . . x s

* * * * *

[The Two Allowances.]

[6] Casuell Receptes this yere.

Re[cei]vide for the buriall of an olde woman that decessed within Thomas Mundy, the Sexten

---

[1] The names of the wardens on the outside leaves of the year's accounts at this period do not always accord with those in the headings of the Accounts.
[2] leaf 572.   [3] MS. has 'Maistres.'
[4] leaf 572, back.   [5] leaf 574.   [6] leaf 575.

house, And for the knyll of the iij^{de} bell, And for hir buriall in the pardon churche yarde. Summa . . . . v s   iiij d

Receivide for the pellis at Maister saunderson dirge .   xx d

Receivide of the buriall of Thomas Gilman wiff, in the pardon churche yarde buried . . . . . . ij s

Receivide for hir knyll & ryngg at dirg & mase . .   xx d

Receivide for the buriall place of Thomas duckelyn . xvj s viij d

Receivide for the buriall place of William Wayward childe, in the churche buried . . . . iij s iiij d

Receivide of Maister Cleyton for the buriall place of ffather broke . . . . iij s iiij d

    Summa, xxxiiij s.

[1]Clerkes Wages & Beame Lyght.

Receivide for the clerkes wages this yere as appereth by the Roull of gatherynges . . . . viij li vj s viij d

Receivide for pascall money and beame light this yere xiij s viij d

    Summa, ix li iiij d.

Paymentes.

Paide to Mighell Grene, parishe clerke, for ij quarters endid at Cristmas . . . . iij li vj s viij d

Paide to William patten, clerke, for a hole yere endid at Cristmas . . . . viij li

Paide to Iohn Norffloke, conducke, for a hole yere reward . . . . liij s iiij d

Paide to Thomas Mundy, sexten, for his hole yere wages . . . . iij li vj s viij d

Paide to the goodman Wilde for this yere rewarde for the kepyng of the quer . . . . xx s

    Summa, xviij li vj s viij d.

The charge is mor then the receptes, ix li vj s iiij d.

[Wax Reckoning.
Porth Receipts and Payments.
Rehearsal.]

[1] leaf 575, back.

[A.D. 1529–30.

Antony Elderton } Wardens.
Iohn Bird

A Note.
Obit List.
Quitrent List.
Chantry Accounts (with Porth).
Church Rents.]

[1]Paymenttes of the same.

Paid to M_r Channon, Curate, for the Beed-Rowle for a yere	ij s	iiij d
paid to the orgon maker for his ffee at Crystemas . .		xij d
paid for blowyng of the Orgons in the Christemas holydays when Balaham was Syke		iiij d
* * * * *		
paid for a Rope for the bellowys of the Orgons . . .		ob
paid for makyng of a forme & a Deske for the skole .		xvj d
* * * * *		
paid [for] the entryng of an Accion & þe Arest of Iohn Carpenter for howse Rent in þe Ryall . .		x d
* * * * *		
paid to a Somoner for Somenyng of M_r hiltons, preist		ij d
paid to a Dawber & his laborer for a days wourke in the Chambre that Edmond hath for skole howse		xiij d
* * * * *		
paid for xxxj elles of whited normandy Canvas for albys for the Church, the ell vj d. Summa . .	xv s	vj d
paid for ix elles of holand clothe for a Surplys for the parisshe preist, the ell viij d ob. Summa . .	vj s	iiij d ob
* * * * *		
[2]paid for Brede and Drynk att the hyryng off Sir Symond þe Base that cam from Seint Antonys .		iiij d
paid for a boke of playnsong of the offices off Ihesus Mas and our ladys Massis, for the Children . .	ij s	ij d
* * * * *		

[1] leaf 585, back.   [2] leaf 586.

paid for wasshyng of vij Corporassis for þe church	vij d

* * * * *

paid for Carryage of Rubbissh owte of bothe the Churche yerdes ayenst palmesonday		ij d

* * * * *

paid for wasshyng & Starchyng of þe pix clothe		ij d
paid for the makyng of ij Surplices for the Curate	ij s	viij d
paid for makyng of vj Albys & vj Amyttes	iij s	

* * * * *

paid for iiij Tapurs for the Sepulcre more then was gadred of the parisshens	xiij d

* * * * *

[1] paid to Trowlop at Towrehill for quytrent of þe bell	xij d

* * * * *

paid for the Costes of Mr Roche, Iohn Byrd and Mr Rochis seruaunt, and for theire iij hors for Rydyng to Norwych to M^r parson to knowe his mynde for the payng of the Conductes wages	xxij s	iiij d
paid for ij lampreys for M^r parson		xx d

* * * * *

paid for makyng clene of the Guttur in the Chambre þat is the Skole howse for þe Children	ij d

* * * * *

paid to Mighell grene for a quayre of papur Ryall for þe prykked song boke and for mowth glewe	vij d

* * * * *

[2] paid for Ryngyng on our lady day, Assumpcion	iiij d
paid for a Newe kay to the west dore of þe church	iij d
paid to Mighell Grene for Mendyng of þe Antefoners that lye in the quere that [were] torn & brokon	xvj d
payd for lyne for bothe the Clothes of bothe the greate Tabernaclys at the high alter	vj d

* * * * *

paid for mendyng of the Say Curtens in þe quere		ij d
paid for xv elles & a quarter of lokeram for Surplisys for the children, the ell vj d. Summa	vij s	vij d ob
paid to William patten for makyng of vj Surplisis		xviij d
paid for a Bawdryk for the Sanctus bell		ij d

[1] leaf 586, back.   [2] leaf 587.

Churchwardens' Accounts, A.D. 1529–30.

paid to a Scryvener for goyng with Mr parson into Buttolphe lane for to a made an Inventory . .   iiij d

paid to humfrey Barnys for di. C of iiij peny nayle, di. C of iij peny nayll for the deske in the church and other nessesarys in the churche . .   iij d

*   *   *   *   *

paid for mendyng of a deske in the quere . . . .   iiij d

[1] Paid to a Dawber and his laborer, for euery of them a day and a halff Mendyng, Dawbyng and whityng of the entre by the north Chirchyerd . . . .   xix d ob

*   *   *   *   *

paid for mendyng of a Cheyre in the Churche . . .   vj d

*   *   *   *   *

paid for leyng of a gravestone In the Sowth Ile . .   ij s

paid for mendyng of the glas wyndowys in the Churche and the Chappelles þat were brokon .   v s

paid for mendyng of a Senser . . . .   iiij d

paid to baleham for a yere blowyng the Orgons, for euery weke ij d. Summa . . . .   viij s viij d

*   *   *   *   *

paid for wyne for our lady alter[2] Mas for the hole yere, þat is to say, for iiij galons of Malmesey v s iiij d, and for ij quartes of Redwyne v d. Summa . . . .   v s · ix d

*   *   *   *   *

paid for mendyng of a pewe in the churche . . . .   vj d

paid for a fforme fo[r] the Skole howse . . . . .   x d

*   *   *   *   *

Item, I aske allowaunce for sir Symond gyldyr for di. a yeres Rent of his chamber grauntted by the parisshe. . . . .   iij s iiij d

*   *   *   *   *

[3] Item, I aske alowaunce for þe skole howse . . . .   vj s viij d

[The Two Allowances.]

*   *   *   *   *

paid to Iohn Northfolke for prykkyd song bokes, of the whiche v of them be with Antemys and v with Massis . . . .

*   *   *   *   *

---

[1] leaf 587, back.   [2] 'alter' scratched out.   [3] leaf 588.

[1] The Clarkis Wages & Beame light.

Rec' of the Clarkes wages this yer as apperith by the Rowle of the Gatheryng	viij li iiij s viij d
Rec' for pascall money and beame light this yere	xj s x d

Summa, viij li xvj s vj d.

Paymenttis.

paid to Mighell Grene, Clark, for his yeres wages	vj li xiij s iiij d
paid to Wylliam patten, Conducte, for a yeres wages	viij li
paid to Iohn Northfor, Conducte, for his wages of the parisshe, and for that M^r parson paith hym, for a quarter endyd at Cristemas . .	1 s
paid to Thomas Monden, Sexten, for a yeres wages	iij li vj s viij d
paid to William Wylde for a yeres wages . . .	xx s
paid to George Moore for iij quarters endyd at Mighelmas	vj li
paid to Edmond Matryvers, conducte, for iij quarters wages	vij li x s
paid to Donston Chechelly, conducte, for a quarter wages	xxxiij s iiij d

Summa, xxxvj li xiij s iiij d.
And so
The Charge is more then the Receptes, xxvij li xvj s x d.

[2] Casuell Receptes this yere.

Rec' for the Buryall of Thomas Stauner	ij s
Rec' for the Buryall of Iohn vstum	ij s
Rec' for the Buryall of Iohn Burnynghill . . .	ij s
Rec' for the Buryall of Iohn lambys childe . . .	ij s
Rec' for the Buryall of a childe of Iohn Todardes . .	ij s

Summa, x s.

[Wax Reckoning. Rehearsal.]

[3] Memorandum: ther was delyuered to the handes of Thomas goodneston, in the vestry, by Richard Bradford, of the revenews of the Romeland for a yere & a di. Summa, xxv s.

---

[1] leaf 588, back.   [2] leaf 589.   [3] leaf 589, back.

Churchwardens' Accounts, A.D. 1530-31.

Memorandum: to arrest ffold for di. a yeres rent vnpaid for his house in fforster lane & for dyuers thinges spoillid out of our said house contrary to the Custom of the Cittie.

[1] iij⁰ die ffebruarii, anno Domini 1530.

Memorandum: that I, Alane persy, parson of Sancte Mare hyll, aw to the churche aforesaide at the dayet of this Aconte xvj li, and at our laydes daye next I shal owe viij li, whiche ij somys shall mayke me in dew dett vnto the saide chirche þ[is?] daye expired in the sum of xxiiij li, which I knowlege me to aw the church wardens & the parrisens of the sayme; at al tymes hauyng a halfe yere warnyng, at all tymes.

* * * * *

[2] 1 Memorandum: to make serche wher the will of Mr Port is becommyn; whether it be in the handes of hiltons wif or in the handes [of] the wif of Thomas Hustom [3] by cause we may sue the detters of port.[3]

2 Also to Remembre to speke with William Awdr . . . concernyng the lettyng of Romeland.

3 Item, to speke with the detters of port whiche haue plegges lying in the churche either to ffeche theym out or elles to prays the pleges & make money.

4 Also to speke with Crowcher [to?] suche money as he ought to paye.

[A.D. 1530-31.

Iohn Bird } Wardens.
Thomas Goodneston

Obit List.

Quitrent List.

Chantry Accounts with Porth's.

Church Rents.]

Paymenttes.

[4] paid to the Orgon maker for a ffee euery yere . . . . . xij d

* * * * *

paid for Mendyng of Sensurs of Syluer . . . . xij d
paid for papur to Edmond and for pryckyng therof . . . vj d

* * * * *

---

[1] leaf 590, back. [2] leaf 591, back.
[3]—[3] Scratched out. [4] leaf 601.

MED. REC.

paid for settyng on of viij parelles vppon viij Albys .	viij d

* * * * *

paid to a porter for beryng of stresse from þe bell at towre hill	ij d

* * * * *

paid for papur for the profettes on palme sonday in þer hondes	j d
paid for clothes for the Towre on palmesonday . . .	xij d
paid for heres, Berdis and garmenttes on palme sonday	xij d

* * * * *

Paid to the Smyth for a dogg of Iron for þe Roodloft, wayng viij ℔ and a halff, the ℔ j d ob. Summa .	xij d
[1] Paid for a Sqvyer for the same, weyng iij ℔ & a halff	vj d
paid for ij Stayes for the same, weyng x ℔. Summa .	xx d
paid for iiij Oylettes for the pulpet	iiij d
paid for a Stay for the Same pulpet	ij d
paid for a hoke and a wegge for the same	ij d

* * * * *

paid for leyng of stone in the Middill Ile ouer foxleys Chyld	xx d
paid for pavyng of þe grave of ffoxleis childe . . .	iiij d

* * * * *

paid for wayng of þe plate þat Iohn port shuld haue .	iiij d

* * * * *

[2] paid for Mendyng of a payre of Trestilles þat longyd to þe church	vj d
paid for a plank for þe pulpet by the quere	iiij d
paid for a steppe for the same pulpet	iiij d

* * * * *

paid to them þat blowith Orgons, for lij Sondays, þe weke ij d. Summa	viij s viij d

* * * * *

paid for iij galons & vj pynttes of Malnesey for a yere, for our lady Mas. Summa	iij s ix d

[Many Allowances, etc.]

[1] leaf 601, back. [2] leaf 602.

[1] The Clarkis wages and the Beame light.

Rec' of the Clarkys wages this yere as apperith by the Rowle of the Gatheryng of the same . .	vij li xv s x d
Rec' for pascal money and Beame light this yere . .	xj s vij d ob
Summa, viij li vij s v d ob.	

Paymenttis.

Paid to Edmond Matryver for a yeres wagis	x li
paid to Mighell Grene, Clerk, for a yeres wages .	vj li xiij s iiij d
paid to William Patten, Conducte, for a yeres wages .	viij li
paid to Baltasar, Conducte, for ij quarters & di. & xiiij days	v li vj s viij d
paid to Donnstone Checheley for a quarter at Mighelmas	xl s
paid to Thomas Monden, Sexten, for a yeres wages	iij li vj s viij d
paid to William Wylde for a yeres wages	xx s
Summa of theys paymenttes, xxxvj li vj s viiij d.	

And so
The charges is more then þe Receptes xxvij li xix s ij d ob.

[2] Casuell Recepttis this yere.

Rec' of Mestres ffoxley for the buryall of her ij Children in the Sowth Ile and the north Ile of þe church	xiij s iiij d
Rec' of Robert Ryvell for the buryall of his mayde in the pardon Churchyerde	ij s
Rec' of the Churchwardens of Seint Georges in Botolphe lane for theire part of a partable guttur betwene Mr Burlaces and Nevelles. Summa	iiij s j d ob
Summa of theis parcelles, xix s v d ob.	

[Wax Reckoning.
Rehearsal.]

[The following details respecting the sale of certain articles of the property left by Mr. John Porth belong probably to this year or the next, in both of which Thomas Goodneston held office as warden. The full Inventory is printed at p. 36.]

[1] leaf 603. [2] leaf 603, back.

Sowld that halff dossen spo[nys?] ... ² ...
to Master gam [?] viij onces ... ² ...
at iij s ix d the on[ce?]. Summa xxxiij .. ² ...
wharof payd to Thomas port to ... ² ...
ffull of his dewty [with?] þat he had o[uer?] the
vestre iij s ix d; so Remayns In the chest . ² . . xxix s vij d

Item, that ther whas delywert to Iong port the xxvj In [ffefferyH?] anno 31 ffor the bequeest of Master port:—

ffyrst, a gyltt gobylyt with a kewer way[ng] xxxvj
   onces quarter & di., at iiij s þe once, amount vij ħ v s   vj d
vij sponnes of the postylles way[ng] xij vnces & halff,
   at iij s viij d, amount . . . . xlv s   x d
a masar with a kewer vij vnces di., at ij s vj d, amount xviij s ix d
a Ryng with a ston for . . . . viij s
Item, mor, delywert hem a skarlyt gown, ffore with
   bygge, prys . . . . xvj s
Item, a gown, ffore with ffyttews, prys . . . . xx s
Item, a dobylyt of crymsen Satten, prys . . . . . iiij s
Item, old dobylyt of blake satten, prys . . . . .   viij d
Item, a old Iakyt of blake velvet & damaske . . . iij s   iiij d
Item, a old Iakyt of tawny chambylyt . . . .   xvj d

---

[1] leaf 740, back.   [2] leaf rotted away.

The Medieval Records
of a
London City Church.

Early English Text Society.
Original Series, No. 128.
1905

BERLIN: ASHER & CO., 13, UNTER DEN LINDEN.
NEW YORK: C. SCRIBNER & CO.; LEYPOLDT & HOLT.
PHILADELPHIA: J. B. LIPPINCOTT & CO.

The Medieval Records

of a

London City Church

(St. Mary at Hill)

A.D. 1420–1559.

TRANSCRIBED AND EDITED

With Facsimiles and an Introduction

BY

HENRY LITTLEHALES.

LONDON:
PUBLISHED FOR THE EARLY ENGLISH TEXT SOCIETY
By KEGAN PAUL, TRENCH, TRÜBNER & CO., LIMITED,
DRYDEN HOUSE, 43, GERRARD STREET, SOHO, W.
1905

"In the heart of the city . . . .
Daily the tides of life go ebbing and flowing . . . .
Thousands of aching brains, where theirs no longer are busy,
Thousands of toiling hands, where theirs have ceased from their labours."
Longfellow's *Evangeline*.

To
Alderman Sir Reginald Hanson, Bart.,
M.A., LL.D., ETC.,

THE GENEROUS DONOR OF THE BUST

OF

Geoffrey Chaucer

TO THE GUILDHALL LIBRARY, LONDON,

THESE RECORDS

OF A CITY CHURCH

ARE INSCRIBED

BY

THE EDITOR AND MEMBERS

OF

THE EARLY ENGLISH TEXT SOCIETY.

PREFACE.

THE present volume, with Part I, places before the reader the whole of the earlier, and it is hoped all that is necessary of the later, text of the medieval records of the parish church of St. Mary at Hill, near London Bridge.

The chief aim of the Introduction has been to attempt to bring together under various headings the notes and entries which tell the story of the church life of the parish.

In the text probably the most interesting matter will be found in the 'Payments for the Church,' in the 'Casual Receipts' and in the list of 'payments' almost immediately following the Casual Receipts. The long yearly expenses for the repairs of the house property of the chantries do not present a very inviting aspect to the reader.

To enable the reader to grasp the system of accounts the best plan would perhaps be to begin at p. 217.

It is due to the memory of the many people whose names are recorded here under various circumstances, to state that our text contains many evidences of generosity and piety on the part of those mentioned, and but few instances of the reverse.

According to the custom of the Early English Text Society, the contractions in the MSS. have been expanded in the printed text in *italics*, and words not in the MSS. have been printed within square brackets [ ].

The presence of asterisks * * * indicate where matter present in the MSS. has been omitted in the printed edition.

After the year 1495 the text of MS. A is not printed in its entirety.

The page headings and sums total at the bottom of certain pages after 1495 have been omitted and *no asterisks* inserted, because such would interfere with the continuity of the reading; but these two are the only instances where the omission of text is not clearly indicated.

Where the page only of the MS. is mentioned, the reference is to MS. A, which supplies by far the greater part of our text. Where MS. B has provided any part of the text, that MS. will be found invariably specified as MS. B.

Occasionally, but very rarely, the extracts quoted in the Introduction from the text have been put into modern English.

A volume dealing with the property of St. Mary's, entitled 'The Parish of St. Mary at Hill, its Church Estates and Charities,' was printed by J. Draper of Little Tower Street, E.C., in 1878.

My very grateful thanks are due to Mr. Welch, Librarian of the Corporation Library, to Mr. Kettle, and to Mr. Welch, junior, assistants in that Library. Every possible aid which the genial and kindly courtesy and ample literary knowledge of these gentlemen could place at my disposal has been at all times most freely forthcoming. I am, too, very greatly indebted to Mr. Higgleton and the able and obliging staff of the same library.

To Mr. F. Calder, vestry clerk of St. Mary's, our thanks are especially due for his kind aid in facilitating the publication of these records.

To Mr. Deputy White, of the Court of Common Council, students are much indebted for his efforts in promoting the accessibility of the records of many city churches. It is very largely due to Mr. White that so many valuable documents (St. Mary's records amongst others) have been transferred from the church vestries to the care of the officials of the Corporation Library, where, naturally, a more systematic supervision can be exercised over them, and where, under reasonable restrictions, they are now easily accessible to students.

To Dr. Furnivall, to Dr. Murray of the great Dictionary, and to Rev. Chr. Wordsworth this work is also under various obligations.

H. L.

CONTENTS.

INTRODUCTION.

CHAPTER I.
                                                      PAGE

THE MANUSCRIPTS   xiii

CHAPTER II.
THE STAFF OF THE CHURCH.

    The Parson, p. xvi; Parsonage, p. xvii; Parish Priest, p. xviii; Chantries and Chantry Priests, p. xviii; Morrow-Mass Priest, p. xviii; Parish Clerk, p. xix; Sexton, p. xix; Organist, p. xx; Organ Blowers, p. xx; Churchwardens, p. xxi; Singers of the Royal Chapel, p. xxi; Choristers, p. xxii; Rectors of the Choir, p. xxiv; The Vestry, p. xxiv; Viewers and Overseers, p. xxiv; Sureties, p. xxiv; Raker, p. xxiv; Prophets, p. xxiv; Almsmen, p. xxv; Organ Maker, p. xxv; Laundress, p. xxvi; Bell Ringers, p. xxvi.

    The Bishop, p. xxvi; Suffragan, p. xxvi; Archdeacon, p. xxvi; Chancellor, p. xxvii; Commissary, p. xxvii; The Somoner, p. xxvii.

CHAPTER III.
MISCELLANEOUS NOTES.

    Order and Arrangement of the Accounts, Receipts, and Expenses, p. xxvii; Wills, p. xxix; John Porth, p. xxix; Inventories, p. xxx; Lease of a House, p. xxx; Church as Trustee, p. xxxi; Drinking, p. xxxi; Bills and Accounts, p. xxxii; Dinners, p. xxxii; Shops and Stalls, p. xxxii; Building, p. xxxii; Defaulters, p. xxxiii; Money Lent to the Church by Parishioners, p. xxxiii; Distinguished Personages mentioned, p. xxxiii; The Three Fraternities, p. xxxiv; The School, p. xxxiv; Gifts and Bequests, p. xxxv; Pawning, p. xxxvi; Familiar Places, p. xxxvi; Picturesque Notes, p. xxxviii; Rats in the Church, p. xxxix; Personal Notes, p. xxxix; The Abbot's Kitchen, p. xl; Gong Farmers, p. xl; Dung Boat, p. xli; The Fabric of the Church, p. xli; The Churchyards, p. xli; Romeland, p. xlii;

Professions and Trades, p. xliii; Guild of Salve Regina, p. xliv; London Bridge, p. xliv; Quaint Phrases, p. xliv; Tithes, p. xlv; No Relics, p. xlv; Travelling, p. xlv; Of Articles sold by the Wardens, p. xlv; Miscellaneous Items, p. xlvi; Medieval Weather, p. xlvi; Beam-light, p. xlvii; Home for the Dying (?), p. xlvii; God's Penny, p. xlvii; Obscurities, p. xlvii.

CHAPTER IV.
OF SERVICES, etc.

The Services, p. xlviii; Burials, p. xlix; Collections, p. l; Churching, Wedding, and Christening, p. l; The Provision of the Sacred Elements, p. l; Incense, p. li; Division of the Sexes, p. li; Obits, p. li; Bede-Roll, p. li; The Great Festivals, p. lii; Easter Ceremonies, p. liii; Hallowing or Consecrating, p. liii.

CHAPTER V.
THE FURNITURE OF THE CHURCH liii

CHAPTER VI.
THE REFORMATION lxx

CHAPTER VII.
OUR TEXT COMPARED WITH OTHER CITY CHURCH RECORDS lxxiii
THE NAMES OF PERSONS IN OUR TEXT lxxvi
NOTE ON FURNITURE AT CONSECRATIONS xcv

THE TEXT.
I.
Wills 1

II.
The Lease of a House, A.D. 1507 22

III.
Inventories 26

IV.
The Royal Commissioners' Inquiries respecting church plate, etc., A.D. 1552-3 56

V.
CHURCHWARDENS' ACCOUNTS AND MEMORANDA.
MS. A. Printed in full from A.D. 1420 to A.D. 1495.

Midsummer A.D. 1420 to Easter A.D. 1421 61
Easter A.D. 1421 to Easter A.D. 1422 61

Contents. xi

	PAGE
Easter A.D. 1422 to Midsummer 1422	62
Leaves lost.	
Easter to Easter A.D. 1426–30	63
Leaves lost.	
Michaelmas to Michaelmas A.D. 1477–81	74
Leaves lost.	
Michaelmas to Michaelmas A.D. 1483–85	112
Leaves lost.	
Michaelmas to Michaelmas A.D. 1487–8	127
Leaves lost.	
Michaelmas to Michaelmas A.D. 1489–95	144

VI.
Text from the same MS. (A), but not printed in full.

Michaelmas to Michaelmas A.D. 1495–1515	217
Leaves lost.	
Michaelmas to Michaelmas A.D. 1516–1538	292
Leaves lost.	
Michaelmas to Michaelmas A.D. 1539–1540	381
Leaves lost.	
Michaelmas to Michaelmas A.D. 1547–1548	385
Christmas to Christmas A.D. 1548–1549	388
Michaelmas to Michaelmas A.D. 1549–1552	389
A.D. 1553 and 1554	394
Christmas to Christmas A.D. 1554–1558	398
A.D. 1559	411
Glossarial Index	415

FACSIMILES.

1. A Bird's-Eye View of the Neighbourhood of St. Mary's about A.D. 1550   (*Frontispiece*)
2. One of the many Memoranda of the Churchwardens, A.D. 1492 182
3. The Signatures to a Year's Accounts, A.D. 1521 312
4. A Page of our main text, MS. $\frac{1239}{1}$, A.D. 1523–4 ... 322
5. Map of the Neighbourhood of the Church of St. Mary at Hill   (*At end*)

CHAPTER I.

THE MANUSCRIPTS.

The Manuscripts.—THE Records of St. Mary's are contained in two large volumes of the fifteenth and sixteenth centuries.

Both books have been deposited in the Guildhall Library of the City of London, and are labelled respectively MS. $\frac{1239}{1}$ and MS. $\frac{1239}{2}$.

These volumes contain :—

1. A series of Wills under the provisions of which the parish church held certain properties.
2. A copy of the Lease of a House.
3. A number of Inventories both ecclesiastical and secular.
4. A copy of the documents of the Royal Commissioners' Inquiries respecting the Church valuables at the time of the Reformation and the Replies of the Churchwardens thereto, etc.
5. The Accounts and Memoranda of the Churchwardens for nearly a hundred years.

The question naturally arises—What do these Records tell us? To this the answer may fairly be made that, with certain exceptions, they show us clearly the whole system of medieval life as connected with a common city parish church.

MS. B.

MS. $\frac{1239}{2}$, which we may designate as MS. B, is far the less important, and may therefore be very shortly and at once described. It is a large volume standing about twenty inches high, twelve inches wide, and about three inches in thickness. It is bound in parchment, apparently by the same binder by whom MS. A was rebound, probably about A.D. 1559. The presence of the book (much of it a duplicate of the other) is explained, in a measure, by the following inscription on the first page :—

This Booke was made, And the moste parte therin wryten, by the hande*s* of Iohn halhed, groc*er*, a p*ar*ischen of the p*ar*ysche of Seynte Mary at hyH, on whoes sowle Allmyghttye God haue m*er*cye : Amen, for charyte. }anno 1486

The book contains an abbreviated copy of part of the substance of the larger book, copies of most of the Wills under which the church of St. Mary at Hill held property, Inventories, etc. About half the leaves of this volume are blank, the first 114 and two near the end alone being occupied by text.

The last document in this book is of the year 1577. Possibly this MS. is referred to in 1504–5, p. 255.

MS. A.

MS. $\frac{1230}{1}$, the larger book, which we may call MS. A, is about twelve and a half inches high, ten inches wide, and nearly six inches thick. From this book our main text has been taken.

The Binding.—The book is bound in stout parchment, probably of the middle of the sixteenth century, very possibly about the date inscribed on almost the last leaf, A.D. 1559 on leaf 820.

The Leaves.—All the leaves, 821 in number, are of paper, and nearly all of them are of the same size and substance. The first leaves are missing, and how many are wanting at this place it is impossible now to even guess. With perhaps the exception of the Porth Inventory, the leaves up to the year 1537 are probably in their right order. After this date, the proper sequence of the leaves 696–763 is chronologically a good deal disturbed in the MS. In our text, however, an endeavour has been made to print the accounts throughout in their proper order.

The following table will, it is hoped, exhibit this disorder, and show the proper sequence of the leaves as they should have been bound :—

1. Porth Inventory, etc., printed at p. 36, leaves 724–741 b.
2.   1538–9 lost.
3. Michaelmas 1539 to Michaelmas 1540, leaves 712–723 b.
4.   1540–7 lost.
5.   „   1547 to Michaelmas 1548, „   704–711 b.
6. Christmas 1548 to Christmas 1549, „   699–703 b.
7. Michaelmas 1549 to Michaelmas 1550, „   696–698.
8.   „   1550 to   „   1551, „   742–743 b.
9.   „   1551 to   „   1552, „   745–747 b.
10.   1553   „   758–760 b.
     Inventories „   printed pp. 50–5   „   748–752 b and 761–763 b.
                    „   the two wardens' names „   753.
11.   1554   „   754–757 b.
12. Christmas 1554 to Christmas 1555, „   764–773 b.

It will be noticed that the accounts for the year 1550-1 are remarkably scanty; but both writing and pages present every appearance of completeness.

In the last pre-Reformation year our MS. retains, 1539-40, the expenses for garlands and decorations and bell-ringing for festivals have been inserted for comparison with those of earlier periods.

The Writing.—The writing of this MS. varies very considerably, sometimes being very beautifully inscribed, at other times it is set down with great carelessness. In 1524 the writing and spelling are perhaps at their best (see facsimile, p. 322), in 1506 at their wildest.

The entries have been inserted under the authority and possibly sometimes by the hands of the churchwardens. From the manner in which they are set down, the entries were clearly not inserted at the period of each receipt or payment, but from notes made elsewhere. Probably the main text of the MS. is the work of a succession of professional scribes, see the yearly sum expended for writing the Accounts. But additions in various hands have sometimes been appended at the end of the year. The actual handwriting of more than one person is distinctly specified as being present, pp. 260 and 268.

The meaning of the series of dots placed at the foot on many of the leaves about A.D. 1490 is not clear; they are considered by Mr. Welch to have relation to the money totals.

An interesting circumstance lies in the fact that many pages of the MS. have been headed with the name of 'Ihesus,' a tribute to-day of the simple faith and piety of the individuals by whom such inscriptions were placed.

Period covered.—The earliest entries now remaining commence in 1420, and the last dated page, as has been said, carries the date 1559.

Spelling.—The spelling, as was common in the middle ages, is very uncertain. Several instances occur of the transposition of letters and syllables: 'chollve,' p. 255; 'spalter,' p. 389;—shovel, psalter.

Reference to this MS.—Probably the following note entered in the wardens' accounts in 1504-5 has reference to this MS.: —'payde for a parchementt skyn, & for settyng in of the paper in þe olde boke of þe Chyrche wardens Acowntt—viij d,' p. 256.

CHAPTER II.

THE STAFF OF THE CHURCH.

The Parson.—The word parson is used advisedly, for whenever the word occurs in full in the MSS. it is generally so spelt (see facsimile, p. 322). In our text we constantly find mention of six of the parsons who held the benefice of St. Mary's—Thomas Atherston, William Sparke, and John Horne, William Wild, Dr. William Atcliff, and Alen Percy. Very brief mention is made of the earlier three, and they may be set aside.

William Wild is first mentioned in 1492, p. 34; the last time his name occurs as parson is in 1501-2, p. 246; and as the *late* parson in 1504-5, p. 257. William Wild, as we have noted elsewhere, was a generous benefactor to the church of St. Mary. His gift of a blue satin chasuble, ornamented with silver, is noted with other gifts at p. 31. In 1496-7 he gave on Christmas Eve £3 (a considerable sum at that time) to 'the chirche warkes and odir benefyttes,' p. 221. Parson Wild appears to have been at Stratford in 1497-8, when a messenger was sent—

"for to desyre hym to come to the Avdyt of the last Accmpt," p. 230.

In 1502-3 wine 'was sent to Master parson to stratford,' p. 247.

Dr. Atcliff is first mentioned in 1505-6, p. 260, and the record of the ringing of his funeral knell is set down in 1520-1, p. 311. In 1513-14 Dr. Atcliff had £6 16s. 8d. in hand which had been presented by three ladies, the whole probably to go towards a new altar cloth for the high altar, p. 285. In the preceding year viij s and iiij d was expended for ten ells of holland cloth for the doctor's new surplice, which was then made by 'woodkokes wyffe,' for xx d, p. 282. At p. 31 we have the record of his gift to the church of a beautiful pyx cloth 'with knoppis of golde & sylke of spaynesshe makyng.'

Dr. Atcliff appears to have been staying at Greenwich in 1509-10, p. 269.

Alen Percy is first mentioned in 1522-3, p. 319; he held the benefice until and during the Reformation. It was he who instituted the custom of appending signatures to the conclusion of the year's accounts. He also appears to have paid part of the organist's wages (see below), and also, sometimes, part of the cost of the 'bread, ale and wine,' provided for the refreshment of the choristers 'at

CH. II.]   *Introduction. The Staff of the Church.*   xvii

divers high feasts in the year,' p. 344. The document on p. 353 by which parson Percy acknowledges owing £24 to the church, and expects six months' notice before being required to pay it, is of interest.

About the year 1533 Alen Percy made over by a formal deed a proportion of the tithes due to him, pp. 363, 394. At first sight it would appear that this gift might be intended to meet the substantial debt of £24, but apparently the gift is too large for such to have been the case (£17 1s. 8d. in one year, p. 385), and the length of time over which the gift extends is too great. We have seen, too, that Alen Percy was by no means ungenerous in his dealings with the church, and these tithes are distinctly described as for the 'mayntenaunce of the quire.' They are generally termed the 'parsons dewtye,' p. 363.

Alen Percy signs for the last time in the great book of Accounts in 1556–7.

A reference to Alen Percy's housekeeper occurs on p. 407, and this reference is the more curious that it indicates, with another reference at p. 394, that the parson was not living then in the parsonage:—

> "Item, paid to M^r parsons woman that kepes his house, for a quitterent of the newe house in the northe churcheyarde, for one whoale yeare—iij s iiij d."

It is somewhat singular that none of the three parsons of St. Mary's during the period over which the chief part of our Records extend appears to have been buried in either the church or churchyards of St. Mary.

At p. 67, however, we read of a payment for the 'stone of sire William Sparke.'

The Parsonage.—The parsonage occupied much the same position as it does to-day, namely, immediately south of the church towards the east: 'at þe sowth dore next þe parsonage,' p. 301; 'the Est chirch gate next þe parsonage,' p. 302. A bridge apparently at one time reached from the parsonage on to the roof of the church aisle, p. 311.

Meetings of the parishioners took place sometimes at the parsonage, when bread and drink was supplied them at the cost of the church, p. 298. At times parish business was transacted in the church, and 'bread and ale fetched into the church,' p. 292. It is probable that these meetings took place in the vestry: 'colys to brenne in the vestrye,' p. 225.

MED. REC.   *b*

The Parish Priest.—The parish priests were not the parsons of St. Mary's, but were, as is clearly specified more than once, the parson's deputy—'Mr John Redye, parish priest, as the parsons deputy being present,' p. 227, at the time William Wild being parson. The same distinction also occurs in the Will of Mr. Porth. In 1519–20 many garlands were purchased by the churchwardens for the Corpus Christi procession of that year, and the sum of eightpence was 'paid for two garlands for Mr Doctor and the parish priest,' p. 305.

John Alen was 'Curat of the Chirch' in 1520–1, p. 312. In 1537–8 the parish priest lived in Priests Alley, p. 377. Doctor Hardyman was parish priest in 1557–8.

Chantries and Chantry Priests.—A chantry may perhaps be best described as being the income from a certain property left by testamentary disposition for the purpose of providing for certain devotions to be said for the welfare of specified persons.[1] The Chantry Priest was the priest to whom the income was paid for carrying out these devotions, often at an altar mentioned as that at which the prayers should be said.

Our text tells us much of the chantries—by whom they were founded, of what the property of each consisted, their incomes, services, names of the chantry priests, etc. etc. At p. 303 we find an ordinance 'that every priest shall sing with his founder's vestments, and their chests to be at the altar's end next where they sing.' One chantry priest had a cupboard in the choir, p. 149.

There were seven chantries in St. Mary's church:—Nasing's, Goslyn's, Cambridge's, Rose Writtell's, Bedham's and Causton's. Later, the chantry of Mr. Porth became added to the list.

The Morrow-mass Priest.—The Morrow-mass Priest was he who sang the first mass of the day. In 1493–4 Sir John Plomer was in office, p. 197, and in 1522 Sir Richard Ellys, p. 317. The fee appears commonly to have been xx s a year, but in later years considerably more appears to have been paid, p. 402. It will be noticed that candles were sometimes purchased for the Morrow-mass Priest, and naturally, that mass being the first of the day, pp. 317, 321. The Morrow-mass Priest had a particular chest, probably for his vestments, etc., p. 343.

Morrow masses were sung by some of the chantry priests, pp. 13,

---

[1] Mr. A. F. Leach points out that some chantries were established during the lifetime of their founders.

18. Sir William Rychard and Sir Edmond Toe sang the morrow mass in 1555-6, one for half-a-year, the other for a quarter; no payment is entered for the remaining quarter.

The Parish Clerk.—Our text supplies us with the names and particulars of successive parish clerks, how much each was paid, when each one came into office, and when each died or left. The wages of the clerk are entered in the accounts each year. His fees for burial and for funeral knells are set down at pp. 231, 319. At pp. 303-4 we find in the 'Articles following for the Church,' that the clerk and sexton, when sweeping the church, were ' to cast water in the sweeping of it.' Also that one or the other should set the great holy water stoup at the choir door; that the holy water should be made before the commencement of Matins; also that the clerk, personally, was reverently to distribute the holy wax candle.

The clerk in 1557-8 gathered the parson's tithes, but these tithes were probably those given to the church by Alen Percy.

In 1522-3 one and eight pence was paid to the parish clerk, ' Roger Mason, for childrens dyner at his howse,' p. 316.

Michael Grene in 1531-2 changed places with one of the choristers, William Patten by name. In the years succeeding till 1535-6 we find the change maintained, Grene being a conduct at £8 a year, and Patten being parish clerk at £6 13s. 4d., pp. 359, 371.

[*The Parish Clerks, 1493-1558. The earlier names are too uncertain for insertion.*]

1493-1500.	Robert Debname. (1501. George Gysborowe.)
1501-10.	John Law.
1513-21.	John Snow.
1521-5.	Roger Mason.
1527-8.	Peter Purvoche.
1528-31.	Michael Grene.
1531-9 ?	William Paten.
1547 ?-8.	Thomas Marton.
1548- .	William Mondaye.

The Sexton.—The sexton's office was of inferior dignity to that of the parish clerk. John Law and John Bull, respectively parish clerk and sexton, at the beginning of the sixteenth century, received for their annual wages, the former £4 13s. 4d., the latter 40s. In 1512-13 the then sexton, William Wild, appears to have had the management of collecting the church rents and 'engrossing' the accounts, p. 285. In 1527-8 a relative of the sexton, being a goldsmith, carried out many repairs to the plate of the church, p. 344.

In 1539-40 the sexton was paid twopence—
"for prycking of a song booke," p. 382.

In 1500-1 the then Sexton remitted a part of a fee as a gift to the church, the fee being for the grave and funeral knell, p. 241. These fees were evidently in addition to the sextons' annual wages.

[*The Sextons, 1500-1558. The earlier names are too uncertain for insertion.*]

1500-6.	John Bull.
1507.	Harry Hunt.
1508-21.	William Wyld.
1521-3.	William Wyld and Thomas Smyth.
1523.	William Wyld, Thomas Smyth and Augustyn.
1524.	William Wyld, Thomas Ripton and Augustyn.
1525.	William Wyld, Thomas Ripton and Thomas Monday.
1526.	William Wyld and Thomas Monday.
1527-31.	Thomas Monday.
1531.	Thomas Arrowsmyth.
1532-7 ?	Thomas Hoggeson.
1547-	Thomas Monday.

The Organist.—The names of several organists appear in our text. In 1477-9 Walter Plesaunce was paid sixpence 'for playing at the organs,' p. 81. In 1523-4 we find that John Norfolk was paid for keeping the choir and the organs all the twelve days of Christmas. John Norfolk appears to have been a most energetic official, and for some years after this entry a more or less frequent succession of expenses occur in connexion with the music of the church. It is significant that almost immediately after the first appearance of the name of John Norfolk, a school 'for Norfolk's children' was established, and money was expended for the purchase of twelve surplices for men and twelve for children, p. 321. John Norfolk is frequently referred to in the accounts as a 'conduct,' p. 334.

The organist at times repaired books, probably, however, only those with which he and the choir were concerned, p. 339.

The Organ Blowers.—References to the blowing of the organs appear frequently in our text. Sometimes the almsmen appear to have added to their little incomes in this way. At p. 333 we find that they had been constantly employed as organ blowers, receiving for every week the fee of twopence, which was that commonly paid for this work.

For some years before the Reformation Baleham was the official organ blower, being paid eight shillings and eightpence a year for his exertions. In the 'christemas holydays' of the year 1529 he 'was Syke,' and fourpence had to be expended in addition, p. 349. That it was an additional expense we may see from the entry of Baleham's wages of the usual eight and eightpence on p. 351. There are very clear indications that on Sundays alone was the organ in use, for the fee paid to the blower, the common eight shillings and eightpence, and the calculation of his payment is expressed at p. 364 :—

> "to thomas coldale ffor blowynge of the organs lij Sondais in the yere, ffor euery sonday ij d, viij s viij d."

In later times, however, the organ was in use daily, p. 386. Chaucer students will remember the allusion to the 'merry organ' in church.

The Churchwardens.—The wardens were chosen by the parish, and on such occasions refreshment in the shape of bread and ale was provided, p. 264. It will be noticed, p. 264, that one warden only was chosen. The explanation of this will be found if we look at the sequence of the names of the churchwardens, when we shall see that it was customary for one warden to retire each year: thus each warden held office for two years successively, but not with the same colleague.

The names of the wardens for each year will be found at the commencement of each year's accounts. Apparently no one in the parish was ineligible for selection; many were tradesmen, p. 227.

In 1509-10 one of the churchwardens travelled to Kingston :—

> "Paid for my Costes for me & my horse to Kyngeston, for to by bourde and lathe—x d," p. 269.

Singers of the Royal Chapel.—After 1527 we frequently find payments recorded to those of the king's chapel for singing in the church :—

> "Paid at the Son tavern for the drinking of M[r] Colmas with others of the kinges chapple that had songen in the churche—ix d," p. 344.

In the time of Mary the payment was made to—

"gentyllmen of the qwenes chapell for syngynge a mas here," p. 396.

At p. 270 they were entertained at dinner at Mr. Sidborough's, which place appears to have provided dinners more or less frequently (*see* Dinners).

In default of other evidence we may perhaps conclude that these choristers were attached to one of the royal chapels within the precincts of the Tower.

The Choristers.—The terms 'Clerks' and 'Conducts' in our Records appear to be applied commonly to the men choristers and organists.

In 1523-4 several hymnals and a processional were purchased 'for þe clerkes in þe quere,' p. 321. These two books were those especially used by choristers before the Reformation.

References to 'þe clerkes & þe children at Masse' occur at times, pp. 290, 305. At p. 134 we have the apparently clear distinction drawn of 'prestes, clarkes & childern,' and a reference to surplices for conducts and children occurs at p. 358. At p. 81 we have a reference to wicker mats 'boght for prestis and clerkis,' and at p. 322 the entries :—

"paid for ij yerdys of wykur matt for the childrens fete . xvj d
paid for vj Round Mattes of wykers for the Clerkes . . xv d"

At p. 364 we have the conjunction of "the organ player & yᵉ clarkes."

Occasionally, but very rarely, a priest appears to have been employed as a chorister (?) :—

"Sir Symond þe Base," p. 349.

As to the term 'conduct' we have the following :—

"paid to Iohn Northfolke [the organist] & the conductes & the Children," p. 327.

"to hier a conducte, a base," p. 406.

"paid to a condukte for the Estur halydays, for lak of the Clarkes absence, for to play at orgons," p. 281.

And Norfolk the organist is also described as a conduct at p. 324.

At p. 352 William Patten is mentioned as a 'conducte,' his yeares wages being £8; in the year before, p. 348, he is described as a 'clerke,' but receives the £8 certainly for the same period, and we may suppose for the same labour.

At p. 1 we find mention of the wife of a 'clerk,' and at p. 8 a reference to a John of Gildeford, 'sumtyme Citezein and Clerk.'

There seems to have been an understood system at St. Mary's by which certain parishioners agreed to pay so much towards the maintenance of the 'clerks wages,' p. 126. Not unfrequently these payments, apparently purely voluntarily given, were in very considerable arrears.

The 'Rowle for the Clerkes wages' is at times referred to, and it is probable that these rolls (see the 'Booke' at p. 126) were a yearly record of those people who agreed to pay so much for a year towards the wages of the parish clerk, sexton and choristers. At p. 378 we have a reference to 'the roll to gader the clarkes wages by.' And at p. 385:—

> "Receyuid of the parissheners for the clarkes wages this yere, as particularly doth appere in a Roll made for the gathering and leveying therof."

These 'wages' appear to have been paid by the parishioners to the church funds four times a year—at the feasts of Christmas, the Annunciation, St. John Baptist, and St. Michael, pp. 128, 253.

At p. 294 we have a list of those who were behind with their payments towards 'clerkes wages.'

The money collected for 'Clerks Wages,' 'Paschal' and 'Beamlight' was ordinarily used to pay the wages of the parish clerk, sexton, organist, and choristers, p. 324, etc. etc. The wages of John Norfolk, the organist, were paid partly by the parish, partly by the rector, but this arrangement appears to have been exceptional, p. 324.

Sometimes children from another parish were engaged. Four from the neighbouring church of St. Magnus were paid a penny each for singing in 1477–9, p. 81. In 1493–4 a child singing 'trebyll' received twelvepence 'to help the choir in Christmas holidays,' p. 197.

Morres, the bass, was paid at the rate of twenty nobles a year, p. 329.

The number of men and boys in the choir is not at all clear. The children of the choir, excepting three boys in 1489–90 and 1490–1 and 1491–2, do not appear to have received any regular wages, though in the event of additional boys' voices being procured from the neighbouring church of St. Magnus or elsewhere, then such children, as we have seen, received payment. One of the boy choristers mentioned above appears to have been boarded out, for at

p. 162 we find the record of a payment of vij s 'for his borde, to William Hall for xiiij wekes.'

The fact that two yards of wicker mat were purchased for the 'childrens fete,' and six round mats for the clerkes (see above), seem to point to a customary number of six men choristers and six boys, but the wages paid to the conducts and clerks generally seem to imply the engagement of a smaller number of men. Regarding the boys our Inventory at p. 31 refers to ' vj copes for children.'

On special occasions extra singers were engaged, 'bowere & hys companye,' pp. 173, 399. At p. 232 we see a chorister is hired from 'shroftyd to lammas.'

Rectors of the Choir.—Only two references to these two choirmen are to be found in our Records. At p. 31 we find in the Inventory of 1496–7 :—

"Item, ij cheyres of Iron for Rector Coris";

and at p. 358 the expenditure of iiij s ij d is entered by the wardens as having been 'paid for ij stolys for the Rectours in the quyre, and ij Greyes skynnes.'

The Vestry.—Perhaps the most explicit reference to the body forming the Vestry is that on p. 319, where our text, making reference to an ordinance for burial fees, mentions that 'it was agreed, and by a Vestry ordained, by these persons following,' etc. See too p. 357.

The 'Vestry' is often referred to as having ordered such and such to be done or paid. ' The Seniors of the Parish' are at times alluded to, p. 246; and 'the masters of the parish,' pp. 309, 318. At other times money is formally deposited in the church chest in presence of 'xii persons of the parish,' p. 330. More than once the financial difficulties of a tenant of the church were generously considered by the Vestry, p. 342.

Viewers and Overseers.—Viewers and overseers for the Rents of the church and chantries are at times, though rarely, mentioned, pp. 111, 285, 320.

Sureties.—Parishioners sometimes stood as surety one for the payment due from another; an instance may be seen at p. 320.

The Raker.—The raker was hardly, strictly speaking, an official of the church, but was employed as a sort of scavenger. He was paid annually for some time the sum of eightpence, pp. 235, 256. See, too, p. 219.

The Prophets.—The Prophets were those men whose business it was to act on a stage built temporarily at Easter by the north door of

CH. II.] *Introduction. The Staff of the Church.* XXV

the church. In 1524-5 we read of the purchase of wood 'for the fframe ouer þe North dore of the chirche, þat is for þe profettes on palmesonday,' p. 327. At p. 354 we find mention of 'papur for the profettes on palme sonday in þer hondes;' also of their clothes, wigs and false beards, of which some, probably all, were hired.

At p. 369 reference is made to 'ij skaffoldes,' evidently in connexion with the prophets; and the 'settyng vp of the stage' on p. 379.

Extra seats to view the performance, evidently, from the small sum paid, hired, appear to have been procured one year, 1537-8, when the wardens paid 'for cheires and formes on palme sonday, v d,' p. 379.

At p. 304 'the skaffold ouer þe porch ayenst palmesonday' is mentioned.

Almsmen.—The almsmen, though scarcely on the staff of the church, may be mentioned here. They were three in number. Their origin is to be traced to the Will of John Bedham, where at p. 17 we read:—

> "Item, I woll that the said wardeyns .... pay to iij poure people most nedefull ... dwellyng in the said parissh of seynt Mary atte hill, euery Sonday, wekely, euery yere for euermore, that is to sey, to euery of the same poure people, iiij d."

The entry of such payment in our accounts recurs annually, till the destruction of the fund; with often the names of the recipients. In 1487-8 these names were Hugh Jackson, William Paris, and William Wylcockes.

Sometimes the Almsmen added to their little incomes by blowing the organ. On pp. 328 and 340 we have entries to the effect that they were organ blowers for the whole year.

According to the will of Richard Gosslyn, p. 14, two other 'poure men' or 'poure women' were to have sixpence each, weekly, as alms; but our Records contain no entries of such payments.

The Organ Maker.—Various references to 'the organ maker' are recorded in our pages. In 1524-5, p. 328, the organ maker was paid two shillings for mending the organs according to the instructions given by the organist, the energetic Mr. Norfolk.

The sum of twelvepence was paid yearly to the organ maker for supervision of the organs, p. 314, in addition to expenses incurred for their repair.

The Laundress.—Several laundresses were employed at one time and another to wash the church linen, the most conspicuous being Alis Smale, who for several years washed and mended the linen vestments, p. 270, etc.

The Ringers.—The ringers are occasionally alluded to, as at pp. 149, 327, etc. The following entry is, however, unusual :—

> "paid for Ryngyng of None, curfew and day pele and courfewe & other pelis on our lady day the Assumpcion," p. 332.

The greater dignitaries of the diocese are but very rarely referred to in our text, and the following few extracts virtually exhaust the references to any of them.

The Bishop of London.—This great dignitary is seldom mentioned in our Records. The bishop held a visitation in 1494–5 in the neighbouring church of St. Magnus, p. 214, and again there in 1497–8, p. 230, but such appear to have been the only occasions of episcopal visitation in this neighbourhood. At the latter visitation refreshments appear to have been provided :—

> "Item, paid [for] bred, ale & a Rybbe of bieff Spent at the Castell in fish strett on dyuerse of the parishons at the visitacion of the bishope of london in Seint Magnys chirche. Summa viij d," p. 230.

The servant of the bishop, or suffragan bishop, received in 1519–20, twelvepence at the 'halowyng of the vestementtis,' p. 306.

To these references we may add that of the visit paid by the parson and several parishioners to the bishop at Fulham respecting one of the chantries. Apparently the journey was made by boat, p. 296.

The Bishop Suffragan.—The 'soffrycan of london' was in 1493–4 paid ten shillings and fourpence for hallowing the altar of St. Stephen, p. 198. In 1503–4 the 'svffrycans man' was paid fourpence apparently on the occasion of a consecration or 'hallovyng,' p. 250. In 1493–4 xij d was 'payd to mastyr parson for halowyng of the westementes,' p. 199. In 1555–6 no less than thirteen shillings was expended on—

> "the dynner of the suffrycan yat daye he halowed the altars and other yat did service with hym," p. 403.

A list of the suffragan bishops of London will be found in Hennessy's *Novum Repertorium*, p. 3.

CH. II, III.] *Introduction.* III. *Miscellaneous Notes.* xxvii

The Archdeacon.—This dignitary, like the bishop and bishop suffragan, is also rarely mentioned in our text. Two visitations are alluded to, both very late, at pp. 407, 411.

The Chancellor.—Our text contains but few references to this official, one being 'when the goodwyff hewys was called befor the chaunseler for the chirch money withholdyng,' p. 296. At p. 344 occurs the entry of two shillings and eightpence having been paid—

"for a pekerell givin to the chaunceler of london for alowing of our tolleracion for Maister Nasing."

The Commissary.—Two references only to this functionary occur in our text. The first is not very explicit:—

"Item, spent on Master Iohn, Thomas Wattes, Thomas hunt, Iohn derhame, when we aperyd afor the comyssary at Seynt Manguls," p. 240.

But for whom the commissary was acting, whether for the bishop, bishop suffragan or archdeacon, is not told, nor for what purpose these people came before him.

The second reference is nothing more than a mention of 'the Archedeken of london or to his commyssary,' p. 6.

The Somoner.—The somoner, though very far removed from a dignitary, finds perhaps his best place here as being a particular official of dignitaries. The somoner was a server of summonses and an official of the ecclesiastical courts. On p. 410 he is referred to as 'my Lorde of Londons somner.' This official makes his appearance very rarely in our text. In 1529-30 we find he was paid twopence 'for Somenyng of Mr Hiltons, preist,' p. 349.

More than once the somoner appears to have been paid for bringing small articles to the churchwardens. In 1556-7 he brought the chrismatory at Easter, p. 406.

CHAPTER III.

MISCELLANEOUS NOTES.

Order and Arrangement of the Accounts, Receipts, and Expenses.—The accounts of St. Mary's for the first year or so appear almost too concise, they form perhaps an abstract of accounts now lost. Very shortly, however, the plan becomes ample and settled. Its yearly order and arrangement may, after 1495, be described generally as follows:—

1. The Rents of the property of each chantry and the expenses of each.

2. The Rents of the property of the church, and the expenses of the church, both for its property and the payments for the church proper. These payments for the church proper do not include any salaries to the personal staff, the payments being for *things*, not to officials, that is, as a general rule.

3. The casual Income of the church, namely, the 'Casual Receipts.' This section has been printed in full throughout, till the Reformation period, for its value is very considerable. Here are recorded the amounts of the annual Hock Monday and Tuesday collections of money made by the women and men on these days respectively, and in which undertaking the former were very much the more successful. Hock Monday and Tuesday were those two days after Easter Monday and Tuesday. Sometimes the wardens went to the expense of providing refreshments in the form of bread, beef and ale, for those by whom the collections were made, p. 230. Also under this heading the receipt of money for every burial is recorded, and also the receipt of monies from sources differing very widely one from another. Virtually this section forms a burial register of the medieval parish.

4. The Receipt of the funds for the Clerk's Wages, etc.

5. The Payments out from the same fund. This section has also been printed in full till the Reformation. The payments are those to the *personal staff* of the church—parish clerk, sexton, etc., not for things purchased for use.

6. The expenditure upon the wax for the candles, called the 'Wax Reckoning.'

7. Two 'Allowances,' the one for Potation Money, that is, money expended for drink in connexion with the receipt of rents, the second for the expense of having the year's accounts written out fairly.

8. A 'Brief Rehearsal' of all the Receipts and Expenditure, and a general conclusion, with, after the year 1521, various signatures appended.

9. Finally, at times, such Memoranda as the churchwardens thought advisable to set down.

The Obits (expenses for yearly services for certain people) and Quitrents for various properties find no established order in the Accounts.

The Accounts were kept from Michaelmas to Michaelmas, though at the commencement and at the end of the period of our MS. some divergence from this custom will be noticed.

Of tithes no mention is made excepting in the matter of exceptional circumstances, the churchwardens being in no way concerned with those payments. *See* Tithes.

The Wills.—The nine Wills or parts of Wills given herewith are valuable adjuncts to help us to understand whence the properties of the church and charities were derived, and sometimes indicate very clearly the situation of a particular tenement, p. 3. They also tell us of the different services for which the charities were founded, the way in which people in the Middle Ages made their Wills, how they ordinarily left their property, of what that property consisted, and various other details of interest. Such, for instance, as the bequest of John Mongeham, the London fishmonger, who in 1514 leaves a certain sum toward—

"the Reparacions of the body of the parissh chirch of Seint Clementtes, in Rochestur, where I was boorne," p. 20.

The following references indicate the volume and page of these Wills in Sharpe's 'Calendar of Wills of the Court of Husting, London': Rose Wrytell, 1. 306; John Causton, 1. 672; Richard Gosselyn, 2. 464; William Cambridge, 2. 463; John Weston, 2. 441; John Nasing, 2. 50; John Bedham, 2. 570.

John Porth.—John Porth, who died in October, 1525, left considerable property to the church of St. Mary.

His Will, written in London, January 14, 1524, contains instructions for a copy of that document to be entered in the account-book of the church of St. Mary. But no copy is now present in the Records, and the deed has probably been missing for very many years, for as early as 1530, p. 353, the churchwardens took note of the disappearance of the document. Fortunately there is a copy in the Registers at Somerset House (Porth, leaf 1), and from that the following notes have been taken:—

The testator desires to be buried in the church of St. Mary at Hill, of which he was parishioner, and in the chapel of St. Stephen, at the altar's end, by his late wife Maryon.

He leaves £7 13s. 4d. a year for five years for a priest to sing for his soul and the souls of others mentioned by name, and directs that three shillings and fourpence shall be paid to the poor of the parish every 'halowentyde' for five years.

The goods at 'The George' at Billingsgate (see the Inventory, p.

36) are, at the termination of his lease of that house, to be sold and the proceeds to be divided between the poor and in masses in St. Mary's for the good of the souls of various people whose names are given.

In our text the record of the burial of Mrs. Porth is entered at p. 323, 1523–4, and that of Mr. Porth on p. 329, 1524–5.

The Inventories.—The several Inventories in our text are, most fortunately, both ecclesiastical and secular.

The chief secular Inventory is a very valuable and representative list, telling us clearly what was to be seen in the home of a well-to-do London citizen in the time of Henry VIII. So ample is this Inventory that even the clothing of the master and mistress is carefully set down, even to the fact that some garments were 'moth eaten' and a bonnet of black velvet 'worn sore' (p. 44). It is interesting to note that the house contained a printed and a manuscript copy of the common medieval prayer-book, the Prymer.

The ecclesiastical Inventories tell us what was to be seen in the parish church in the years before the Reformation. These Inventories, though ample, can yet be very largely supplemented in detail from the text of the Churchwardens' Accounts.

The date of the Inventory on p. 30 should be probably some few years later than that assigned to it, for the Rector William Wild was living in 1501–2, p. 246.

The Lease of a House in Thames street.—The text of the lease of the house in Thames street is by no means an uninteresting document. The house is taken virtually by a family of three people— father, mother and daughter, for fifty years from the feast of the Annunciation in 1507, at a yearly rental of five marks. The tenant undertakes during the first year of his holding to wholly rebuild the whole house, and keep it in repair for twenty years. The church, by whom the property is owned and let, undertakes to maintain the house after that date for the thirty years following.

During the lifetime of any one of this family of three, within the fifty years, the arrangement stands. But in the event of the death of all three the property reverts to the church, in which case, on the date of the death of the last, a solemn service shall be sung in the church for the souls of all three, yearly, till the expiration of the last of the fifty years originally agreed on. This deed may be compared with the brief agreement on p. 342.

In our Rent roll at p. 376 it will be seen that the rent after thirty years is still being paid.

The Church as Trustee.—Apparently the church of St. Mary, acting through its officials, was prepared to hold property in Trust for the benefit of parishioners. Such certainly appears to have been the case in 1524, when we find the wardens entering a Memorandum in their accounts to the effect that Thomas Harman had money 'in the custody of the church,' p. 325. 'The last payment of all his money that was in the church' is entered in the accounts for the same or following year, p. 328.

Drinking.—The custom of drinking upon the conclusion of any business appears to have been very common. We read of the expenditure of money for ale at the 'hiryng' of a priest, p. 328; for drink for the clerks at the keeping of Mass of Recordare, p. 328; drink at the hiring of a Sexton, p. 331, etc. etc. At p. 163 we find—Paid to the priests and clerks in drink 'at principall ffestes,' and several festivals are mentioned, but bread is here also included, at any rate for Christmas Day. A good deal of money appears in these accounts to have been spent in refreshments. The 'Item, spent at the tavern in wyne, iij d,' entered in the account under 'Expenses for the profit of the Church,' p. 164, is not devoid of humour. The long-established custom of drink being fetched to the church for the ringers finds mention at p. 327.

In 1510–11 money was expended 'for Drynke at the havyng vpp of the belles,' p. 275. When the organ was tuned in 1532–3 money was expended on the organist "& dyuiers of the Cumpany at ye ale howse," p. 361.

At p. 187 an entry records the drinking of wine by the alderman, the parson, and the churchwarden, 'at þe cherches coste.' And at p. 305 the expense is recorded of 'drynke at the takyng downe of the sepulcre.'

Apparently the ale houses were by no means neglected by their customers on Sundays :—

> "Spent at the Son apon M^r aldirman & odir of the parish on the Sonday next aftir Seint Mathews day," p. 234.

It was not unusual to hire a clerk at the tavern :—

> "paid the vjth day of Merche, at the hiring of balthazar the clerk, at the son tavern," p. 343.

At p. 276 we have the entry referring to—

> "a portingale þat was killed in the shipp at Billingesgate."

Bills and Accounts.—The bills and accounts of various people for work done in connexion with the church are very frequently set out in these Records quite separately. In one case it is probable that the original list of materials still on its 'little quire' is that which is bound up with the Accounts and is printed in this edition at p. 335.

On pp. 147 and 162 we have the expenses for the clothes, boots, 'borde,' etc., of Robert and Thomas Bynge, who were apparently two choir boys in 1489–91. On p. 150 we have the full account for the repair of the vestments in 1489–90; for the reparation of the church steeple in 1479–81, p. 102; the repairing of a shop, p. 107; for a dinner, p. 275; for law costs against a prioress, p. 203; for setting up the Rood, p. 228; for making the new pulpit, p. 251. The carpenter's bill at p. 337 gives the time and payments for himself, his 'servant,' and 'for his boye.'

The wax-chandler's bill in 1524–5 was incorrect; the words at p. 330 are—' was MisRekonyd in the byll of her Acount,' and so a penny for every pound of new wax was 'abated in her hole byll.'

Dinners.—Many medieval dinners are referred to in our pages. One at 'The Cardinals Hat' is mentioned at p. 179, another at 'The Sun' at which the rector and some of the parishioners were present, p. 174. The menu of the dinner probably cooked at Mr. Sudborough's in 1510–11 is given in the bill of costs for the same at p. 275 :—pike, soles, oysters (1d.), butter (1d.), a 'pye of quinsis' (vj d.), bread, ale, wine, etc.

Shops and Stalls.—Both shops and stalls are occasionally alluded to. We may instance the shop at p. 107, and a butcher's stall in Eastcheap at p. 188. The boards and timber of Terry's stall are mentioned at 'p. 201; 'the 'shopp borde in partriches shopp in Estchepe,' p. 328. Sometimes the shop would be let to one man and the dwelling-house over it to another. Such was the case in 1483–5, when John Ducklyng rented a shop at a yearly rental of sixteen shillings and eightpence, and ' William harman for the howse above' paid the same, pp. 112–13.

At p. 139 we find mention of a 'Rynnyng dorr.' Mr. Mylton the baker sold 'spiced Bunnes,' p. 139; Mr. I. Halhed the grocer sold oil, p. 140.

Apparently the floor before a stall was paved, p. 302.

Building.—Perhaps every kind of work connected with the art of building finds mention in our text. These details will be

CH. III.] *Introduction. Miscellaneous Notes.* xxxiii

found set out at length, for the most part, in the earlier pages, where are reproduced the accounts for the repairs of the properties of the Chantries. Particulars connected with the arrangements for the supply of water for certain tenants will be found on p. 370. The tables of materials purchased for the work on the two aisles commence on p. 334. In 1493–4 Sir James Sannys received money as compensation for 'hys glase wyndowys the he lefte behynde hym,' p. 200. The payment to carpenter Wyn, in part by reason of his 'beyng from his howce, wyfe & chilldyren,' is interesting, p. 337. So too the mention of the tiles of the houses, p. 174, 175. The 'whyte lymyng of the chirche' is recorded at p. 277.

Defaulters. — Several people during the long period of our accounts appear to have got into financial difficulties respecting money due to the church. Mr. Ralph Challenger appears on p. 369 to have failed to pay 6s. 8d., which should have been given to an applicant for the post of parish priest. In 1516–17, p. 292, we find a record of the death of one of the churchwardens, evidently during his term of office, and at p. 296 is the brief story of the very considerable unpleasantness caused by the widow refusing to part with the church monies, and how consequently she had to be brought before the ecclesiastical court sitting at St. Paul's. At p. 353 we read of the arrest of Mr. Fold, one of the tenants of the church. Mr. Fold had not only failed to pay the rent for six months for his house in Foster Lane, but had 'spoillid' things 'out of our said house contrary to the Custom of the Cittie.'

A curious instance of the death of a choirman owing money is to be found at p. 405 :—

> the payment of lvj s viij d to John Hobbes for his services in the choir "for one quarters wages endynge at thannunciacion of our Ladye, and borrowed xvj s viij d of the nexte quarter, & dyed."

Money Lent to the Church by Parishioners.—Loans to the church by parishioners were not infrequent: see pp. 197, 300, 309, 324.

Distinguished Personages mentioned.—Our text contains several references to distinguished personages—the ringing of the bells when Henry VII came to St. Paul's, p. 247; the bearing of torches when the same king was buried, p. 266; the ringing of the bells when Henry VIII was crowned at Westminster, p. 266; the funeral procession of the mother of Henry VIII, when six men each held a torch in Fenchurch Street as the royal body passed on its way from the Tower to Westminster, p. 247.

In 1536-7 we have a reference to Henry VIII and Jane Seymour :—

"whan ye kyng & ye quene Rode thorowgh the Citie," p. 373.

On the same page is the entry :—

"ffor Ryngyng of the gret bell vj owres ffor quene Iane, and ffor Ryngyng of ye belles dyuers peles to the same."

Immediately next follows the record of money paid :—

"to ij men ffor beryng of ye copes to powlis [St. Paul's] & home agayn at the byrthe of prynce edward" [Edward VI].

Probably the following entry refers to the once great Cardinal Wolsey :—

"paid to Bright for Riding to the Moore to Mr parson for to Speke to my lord Cardenall for þe takyng of þe children, iiij s iiij d," p. 328.

On p. 406 we have a reference to the 'fyve ringars that ronge the same daye' that Philip and Mary 'cam through london.'

The Three Fraternities.—The Fraternities or Guilds attached to St. Mary's were three in number, and were those respectively of St. Anne, St. Christopher, and St. Katherine. These guilds find little mention in our text. Two torches to each guild were bequeathed in the Will of Mr. Porth, and two more to each under the Will of John Mongeham, p. 20. These guilds appear to have kept their accounts quite separate from those of the church, almost the only recognition by the wardens appearing in 1512-13, when the 'Bretherhed' of St. Christopher gave vj s viij d 'towardes the makyng of the pewys in seint Iohn chapell,' p. 283, and "the wardens of Seint Annys bretherhod" gave xiij s vj d ob for some purpose to the church. Also in 1524, p. 325, when a Memorandum referring to the accounts of St. Christopher is entered apparently for no particular reason, in the accounts of the churchwardens.

The School.—The first reference to a school in our text appears to relate to one in no way connected with the church, though apparently the money was paid for the schooling of a choir boy— 'spent vppon Bower at his scole, j d,' p. 148.

The first reference to a school connected with the church is found at p. 321 (1523-4), when sixpence was paid by the churchwardens for the preparing of a chamber 'to be a skole howse for Norfolkes [the organist] children.' At the same time rushes were

CH. III.] *Introduction. Miscellaneous Notes.* XXXV

strewn on the floor. Apparently this chamber was at times paid for by the organist, p. 326, and at times entered in the accounts as bringing in no income, p. 333.

The furniture for the school appears to have consisted of little more than one or two forms and a desk, pp. 349, 351. No entry of any expenditure for books occurs.

The kindly nature of Dr. Furnivall, always in accord with generous instincts, has summarised well in a brief note to the present writer, the care for the children recorded on pp. 322, 327 :—" How nice it is, that care for the school-children, their playing weeks, the money to sport them and make them merry, the wicker mat for their feet, etc. My heart warms to Mr. Northfolk."

In 1537–8 a chimney was erected in the school-house, p. 377.

Gifts and Bequests to the Church.—Many records of gifts and bequests are found in our text—the velvet canopy for the Sacrament given by Mrs. Plommer, p. 163; the Antiphoner bequeathed by Sir John Mortram (a chantry priest of St. Mary's and a priest of St. Paul's Cathedral), and the conditions of his bequest, p. 181; the chalice given by Sir John Bradmore, p. 79 (the prefix 'Sir' was that commonly applied to a priest in the Middle Ages); the meeting of parishioners on the 20th of January, 1490, when several agreed, some to pay for the building of a whole arch, others to contribute various sums of money, p. 157; the bequest of a valuable cup left by the late rector of St. Mary's, and delivered to the churchwardens by 'Master Monke, wex chandeler,' on Christmas Eve, 1504, pp. 255 and 257. The same rector, William Wild, twenty years earlier had given a large service book to the church, p. 142. In 1487–8 a lady, by name Agnes Breten, had paid £27 (a large sum in those days) to have the tabernacle of the Virgin in the choir painted and gilded, p. 142.

In 1514–15 several ladies of the parish collected money for an altar cloth of white and red cloth of gold, and curtains. One lady, Mrs. Ingleby, brought in £6, and by others an additional £3 10s. was procured, p. 291.

In 1519–20 John Goodwyn's wife gave three shillings and eight-pence 'towarddes the braunche of the Trinite,' p. 306. And in 1521 Thomas Duckling, it is noted, still owes the 'iij s iiij d which he promyseyd towardes the organes,' p. 315.

Sometimes a gift would be marked with the initials of the donor, p. 35.

Small sums are more or less frequently bequeathed by servants, p. 259, etc.

Mrs. Noneley bequeaths money for the rebuilding of the south aisle, p. 244; Mr. Hottyng bequeaths money 'towuerd the steppyll beldyng,' p. 259.

Pawning.—At p. 375 we find the entry :—

"paid to Thomas becwithe vppon a chales—viij ti."

The foregoing appears to indicate that the church would lend money upon security.

And that the church at times pawned articles for its own business is clearly seen by the following :—

"Item, paid to Wylliam burnynghill yat he lent vppon a senser—vij ti vj s," p. 375.

The £1 10s. 4d. in 'pledgis in lynnyn clothe' at p. 239 is not clear, but it will be noticed that one of the churchwardens 'hath the pledges,' retaining them probably as security for money due.

Familiar Streets and Places mentioned.—Many places and churches, more or less familiar to us to-day, are mentioned in these accounts; the position of some of them will be found clearly indicated on the accompanying Map.

St. Magnus's church (rebuilt) is of special interest as regards its situation. It occupies the same position as the former church. London Bridge, however, at its last rebuilding, was moved some thirty or forty yards west, consequently St. Magnus's church no longer now faces directly the main thoroughfare to and from the Bridge. Our Map shows excellently the old and present lines of route from London Bridge.

At p. 164 we read of the hiring of a boat to take one or more of the representatives of St. Mary's to see the bishop of Salisbury then in Fleet Street.

In addition to those places in the immediate neighbourhood of the church, Lothbury, Leadenhall, Love Lane, Fish Street, etc., which naturally find mention, frequently other places, some several miles away, are referred to in these Records :—Stratford, Fulham, Kingston, etc. At times, places still further distant are mentioned, and these, for what reason it is difficult to say, appear to be almost wholly in the western division of Kent. At p. 244 we read of twentypence being expended in horse-hire when a Mr. Colyns went to Maidstone to bind Maunde the mason to perform his covenants. At p. 247 expenses connected with the riding to Shoreham to see timber are set down. At p. 331 we find the record of a man coming from Dartford, having apparently been summoned by the Vestry for the purpose of testing his suitability for service as a Clerk in the church. At p. 264 the wardens' entry of a payment 'to Nychollas Bettnam, mason, of ottam yn Kentt' for work done on the church is recorded. At p. 269 the warden enters the sum of tenpence in the accounts:—" Paid for my Costes for me & my horse to Kyngeston, for to by bourde and lathe."

The following list of Places mentioned in our text will be of interest :—

Aldgate, 273.
Barmondsey, 168.
barnett, 174.
baynardes castel, 68.
Billingesgate, 5.
bos alley, 248, 380.
botolffe lane, 196.
brig strete, 346.
Bryggehowse, 95.
clerkyn well, 111.
dartemowthe, 195.
Dartforth, 331.
Essex, 332.
Estchepe, 4.
faenchirche stret, 247.
fish strett, 230.
ffoster lane, 13.
ffulham, 296.
Grenewych, 269.
Gresschurch strete, 85.
Ipiswich, 345.
kylbourne, 96.
Kyngeston, 256, 269.
lambith, 293.
ledon halle, 256.
lovmbarddes place, 253.
london, 332.
london Brigge, 13, 16.
london Brigge, chapel of, 13.
loue lane, 3.
Luddisdon, 20.
Ludgat, 20, 273.

lumbarde strete, 94.
lyncolles in, 326.
Maidstone, 167, 244, 270.
Meneris, the, 126.
Mepam, 20.
Merchelsee, 20.
Moore (the), 328.
Myle ende, 194.
Neugate, 20.
Norwych, 350.
old Riall, 346.
Olde Swann (houses), 113.
ottam yn Kentt, 264.
pudding lane, 79.
Quenhith, 103.
Rochester, 20, 406.
Romeland, 352, 353.
shoram, 247.
Soper lane, 4.
stokkes, 168, 328.
Strattford, 229, 247.
Suthwarke, 228.
temmystrete, 3.
tour wharf, 68.
Tower gate, 381.
towre hylle, 96.
Vappyng, 253.
Waltham, 172.
Westmynster, 247, 266.
Whytstabyll, 245.
yelde halle, 256.

xxxviii   *Introduction. Miscellaneous Notes.*   [CH. III.

Churches.

Alhalowis, 94.	seint Iohns, 293.
St. Andruis vndershaft, 346.	the Kynges chapell, 270.
St. Antonys, 349.	Saint leonardes, 76.
St. Barthilmewys, 329.	St. Magnus, 230.
Christ Church, 130.	Seint Margret patens, 293.
Saynt Dunston's, 84.	powlys (St. Paul's cathedral), 296.
St. George's in puddyng lane, 96.	Seint Saviours, 292.

Inns.

abbotes Inn, 267, etc. Canon Wordsworth writes:—"A Deed of Agreement between the Abbot of Waltham and the Bp. of London respecting a Chapel in the Abbot's House in the parish of St. Mary Hill will be found in MS. Harl. 6956, p. 74."	the Cardnalles hat, 179.
	the Castell, 230.
	hontyngdons tauerne, 70.
	the pewtre pot, 346.
	the sentt John ys hede, 203.
	the salutacion, 274.
	the shipp, 276.
	Sonn Taverne, 234, 316, 333.
the Bell, 347.	the Swane at byllyngesgat, 241.
the bere, 46.	the Tylers, 332.

Picturesque Notes.—These Records, too, at times place before us interesting little pictures of medieval life. For instance, the picture of the scene during the evening service in St. Mary's church on Christmas Day, when the clergy and choristers, each bearing a little lighted candle, all walked, singing, in procession to a certain tomb, p. 16. The scene at the annual memorial service for John Mongham would not be the less picturesque for the presence of members of the Fishmongers' Company in their livery, p. 21.

The last entry on p. 316 places very clearly before us the scene at the 'Sun' tavern late in the June afternoon in 1522 :—

"Item, paid on Seint Barnabis day, at the Sonn Taverne, after Evynsong, for Drynke for the kynges chappell and for the clerkis of the Towne, the Summa of xxj d."

At p. 6 another little scene is presented to us in which the position of five candles burning at certain times in the old church is depicted. The money for these candles was left by John Causton, who by his Will provides that two tapers shall be "brennyng vpon the Iren Beame afore the ymage of our lady atte high awter on Sondayes & halydaies, and ij tapers brennyng before the Aungelles Salutacion of the ymage of our lady in the body of the said Chirch, euery evenyng at the tyme of syngyng of Salue Regina from the begynnyng to the endyng;" and one taper should burn at the south

CH. III.]   *Introduction. Miscellaneous Notes.*   xxxix

altar of the church between the figures of St. Thomas and St. Nicholas. John Weston (p. 11) provides for "ij torches of wexe to brenne euery Sonday & other holy daies at the high awter of the said Chirch in the masse tyme at the leuacion of the blessed Sacrament & after, as it is the vse." Richard Gosslyn (p. 13) provides for a taper of five pounds weight to burn at the altar of St. Katherine every Sunday and at other festivals 'for euer.' John Mongham, too (p. 19), provides for torches to be "light & Burned at þe sacryng tyme of þe high masse vppon high and doble ffestes." Rose Wrytell provides (p. 2) for a taper to burn before an image of the Virgin by the altar of St. Edmond. John Bedham (p. 17) provides for an oil lamp to burn day and night in the choir before the blessed Sacrament. The scene in the old church must at times have been very solemn and impressive.

At p. 201 an entry of vij d is recorded as having been:—

"payd in expences whane sartayne of þe paryshe yede to Awew þe smoke holys betwene tyrry and Inger."

At p. 332 we have the picture of the presence of various parishioners at 'The Tylers at the hyryng of the clerk.'

The Rats in the Church.—These little creatures appear to have made themselves sufficiently conspicuous, and several efforts were made for the reduction of their number. At p. 243 we find they had paid some attention to the service books. At p. 343 we find that a bedmaker had to be called in to repair the Easter sepulchre cloth, 'wherat it was eiton with rattes.'

At p. 379 is the entry:—

"paid to the rat taker for laying of his bayte—iiij d."

At p. 322:—

"paid for Milke and Rattisbane for the Rattes in the chirch."

Personal Notes.—In several places homely and personal references occur:—'the house that olde Mouce hath taken,' p. 138; 'olde father mondaye,' p. 398, but probably this term was to distinguish him from his son Thomas, the parish clerk; 'old mastres Altroppe,' p. 368; 'another gutter in yong Mowces house,' p. 153; 'that *I* spent on the quest for dye' (Dye was a butcher), p. 174; 'Mothyr boyis ij s,' p. 205; 'I payd hym in hande, vj s viij d,' p. 68; 'such money as he had leyde out of his purs,' p. 133; 'paide vnto hym for his salarye of vij^e wekes affter mighelmas, rebatyng hym for his housrent xxij d; paide clerlye to hym xvj s ij d,' p. 133;

'payd to a sergeaunte for the arrest of our tenaunte þat dyd vs wronge,' p. 111; 'The Gardyner next to ffader kechen oweth for di. o yer,' p. 156; 'The Tayllour next to the garden gate oweth,' p. 156; 'that mylton and I spent to lambeth,' p. 178; 'beffore my dore,' p. 382.

Sad but interesting references are by no means uncommon, such as the pathetic note inserted by one of the churchwardens recording the burial of three 'of myn owne Chyldyrn,' p. 245; the wife of Robert Debenham bringing in the sum of six shillings and eightpence, the bequest of her husband to the church of which for some years he had been parish clerk, p. 236; the desire of John Mongham, fishmonger, that his body should 'be buryed in the southe Ile within the parissh churche of Seint Mary at Hill, directly afore the wyndowe of the vij werkes of mercy,' p. 19; the entry in the accounts of the receipt of money from Master Cloose for burying of his 'ij prentys,' p. 183, etc. etc.

The Abbot's Kitchen.—Not far from where the tower of the present church stands to-day, stood, a good many years before the Reformation, the kitchen of the abbot of Waltham Abbey.

The first entry in connexion with the story is that on p. 238, where we see the record of the expenses of four parishioners, who were evidently deputed to ride to Waltham to 'speke with the Abbott ffor the kechen.'

The next entry, set down in the year following, is very clear:—

> In 1500-1 "was the ende of the sowthyle of owre Church takyn in wher sum tyme was the abbott of Walthams kechyn: to begynne at Ester, & ffro that tyme fforward the parych bene bownde to paye to Waltham, yerly ffor euermore, x s, ffor a quytrent ffor Ever," p. 240.

When the king seized the monasteries and their property, he became also possessed of the quitrent paid for our south aisle, which was consequently paid to him:—

> "Paid to the Kynges Maiesties vse for the South Ile, x s," p. 391.

The Gong Farmers.—The gong was the w. c. Such places would be part of the houses forming the property of the church. The gong farmers would be those by whom the cesspools would be emptied. It was clearly customary for these places, as now, to be emptied at night, and that it should be done thoroughly men were often paid to watch the gong farmers at their work, p. 373:—

> "Item, paid to a man yat watched ye gongffarmers ij nyghtes."

An excellent reference respecting this subject is found at p. 240.

The Dung Boat.—This boat is at times referred to, and we may suppose that it was a vessel to carry away dung, p. 378. At p. 395 reference is made of payment to—

> "whyte, the donge man, for the whoale yeare, xvj d."

The Fabric of the Church.—The church appears to have had no remarkable features. It consisted of a tower and a steeple, with a 'vane,' p. 103, chancel, and rood-screen, transepts (the cross aisle, p. 319), nave, chapels—three, St. Stephens, St. Katherines, which joined the choir, p. 69, and St. Anns—apparently enclosed by screens with doors, pp. 251, 273, 327; also the chapel of St. Christopher, p. 366, the whole being set in two churchyards and surrounded by a wall. A house apparently projected into the north churchyard, p. 301.

The upper vestry is alluded to on p. 306. The 'gret key of the vestry dore' is referred to as being kept by Mr. Russell, p. 284.

The clerestory or walls and windows rising clear above the body of the church, and on which the roof was supported, is referred to on p. 255.

The choir was apparently enclosed and the doors locked, pp. 69, 237, 293.

The interesting story of the end of the south aisle will be found under the heading **The Abbot's Kitchen.** The north aisle was commenced in March 1487. St. Stephens chapel was on the north side of the church, and 'made' in the 15th century by William Cambridge, p. 14.

The altar of St. John the Baptist is mentioned at p. 11.

The roofs were apparently partly of lead, partly of tiles, pp. 102, 373, 399. The floor was partly paved with tiles, pp. 257, 370. There were many gravestones :—

> "for the making of Iohn Austhrop is grave, & for laying of the ston ageyn," p. 344.

In 1503-4 the church was reconsecrated, probably necessitated by the rebuilding of the aisles, p, 250.

The Two Churchyards.—From the various designations given to the two churchyards it might be imagined that there were several. Apparently from the different names there were :—the north, p. 351, south, p. 411, great, p. 163, little, p. 185, green, p. 370, pardon, p. 307, and procession churchyard, p. 100. There is, however, indisputable evidence that there were but two churchyards, for *both* churchyards are more than once referred to :—

"for makyng clene of bothe the Chircheyerdes, for iij days labur—xij d," p. 281.

Though it is usual to have but one yard, naturally that surrounding the fabric,—two yards would easily result where the church reached right across from one side of the site to the other, and thus divided the ground into two sections, one north and one south. Apparently, such was the case with St. Mary's, where there is every reason to believe that the old church, like the present building, had its eastern face in St. Mary Hill and its western in Love Lane.

The north churchyard remains to-day, though probably shorn of much of its proportions, but the south has apparently long since disappeared. Ogilby's map of London, 1677, apparently shows both yards, but marks only the northern as 'churchyard.'

At p. 100 reference is made to 'ij lode gravell for the procession churcheyarde'; and other references, pp. 163, 185, indicate that the paths in the two yards were gravelled. In 1492-3, p. 186, twopence was paid 'for havyng aweye of the smale stonys' in one of the churchyards.

The great churchyard was probably that on the north side of the church, for the 'copyng of the north wall in the greate chirchyerd' is referred to on p. 301. At p. 300 the coping of the stone wall at the east end of the great churchyard is mentioned. A cross enclosed by a paling stood in the great churchyard, p. 300. In 1555 yew was planted in one or both of the churchyards, p. 403.

The 'beryng owt of donge of þe pardon chirchehawe ... a cartful' is a remarkable entry dating 1427-8, p. 67, again p. 71.

The 'pardone churchaw gate' had a lock on it 'for to kepe the Stuffe,' p. 99.

There was a 'lityll howse' in one of the churchyards, p. 101. Judging by the reference to the two churchyards at p. 231, the pardon appears to have been the smaller.

The key of one of the churchyards is mentioned at p. 261.

The Romeland.—The Romeland was a piece of land lying by the river's edge, and apparently more or less rough and waste. In 1496-7 the wardens received fourteenpence for 'Robushe to the chirche þat was leyed on the Romlande,' p. 223. In 1547-8 the wardens 'receyuid of a spanyerd for lying his shipp ther—vij s viij d,' p. 385. The Romeland was the subject of litigation in

CH. III.]   *Introduction. Miscellaneous Notes.*   xliii

1524–5, and at the time of the Reformation such church furniture as was not in keeping with the popular opinion of the period was taken to the Romeland and there destroyed.

At p. 389 occurs the entry—

"Item, payde to ye kynge for Rome land as will apere by quyttances—x li."

Professions and Trades.—These Records contain references to perhaps every profession and trade in medieval times—to priests, churchwardens and their children, organists, parish clerks, sextons, choristers, bishops, 230, abbots, p. 46 ; priors, p. 46 ; lawyers, p. 326 ; mayors, p. 155 ; sheriffs, p. 155 ; scriveners, p. 187 ; sompnours (William James was a sompnour in 1490–1), p. 164 ; grocers, p. 114 ; fishmongers, p. 33 ; bricklayers, p. 377 ; ironmongers, p. 153 ; pie bakers, p. 73 ; lime men, p. 102 ; basket makers, p. 358 ; glaziers, p. 102 ; vestment makers, p. 80 ; plumbers, p. 154 ; smiths, p. 155 ; joiners, 'Gymbold the Ioyner,' p. 306 ; alewives, 'þe wyff of the chekur,' p. 315 ; weavers, p. 205 ; artists, John Woulff, p. 316 ; apprentices, p. 278 ; costomer (officer of the customs), p. 262 ; barmaid, 'a woman that drew the ale, ij d,' p. 90 ; cobblers, 'peter Andrew, cobler,' p. 129 ; painters, p. 229 ; kerchief laundress, p. 78 ; constable, p. 370 ; gong farmers, or cesspool cleaners, p. 373 ; brewers, p. 346 ; tailors, p. 141 ; fullers, p. 126 ; salters, p. 128 ; master workman, p. 224 ; physician, p. 76 ; organ-makers, p. 125 ; carvers, p. 224 ; bellfounders, p. 275 ; founders, p. 307 ; pewterers, p. 299 ; servants, p. 293 ; woolmongers, p. 144 ; knights, p. 46 ; masons, p. 207 ; patynmakers, p. 159 ; cappers, p. 159 ; pastillers, p. 159 ; fruiterers, p. 127 ; sawyers, p. 338 ; poyntemakers, p. 125 ; workmen's boys, p. 337 ; drapers, p. 235 ; embroiderers, p. 144 ; upholsterers, p. 123 ; carpenters, p. 224 ; yeomen of the guard, one of the Yeomen of the Guard who died at the Swan, in Billingsgate, was buried in the churchyard of St. Mary's, p. 307 ; watermen, p. 159 ; wax-chandlers, p. 91 ; almsmen, p. 253 ; stationers, p. 226 ; goldsmiths, p. 209 ; butchers, p. 77 ; haberdashers, p. 194 ; barbers, p. 161 ; cooks, p. 159 ; bargemen, p. 194 ; gardeners, p. 159 ; laundresses (for some years, at the beginning of the sixteenth century, Alys Smale washed the church linen for 3s. 4d. a year) ; sailors, p. 193 ; 'rat takers,' p. 379 ; labourers, p. 137 ; waterbearers, p. 328 ; bedmakers, p. 343 ; tilers, p. 136 ; sporyours, p. 10 ; corders and cordewaners, p. 1 ; bladers, p. 5 ; maydes, p. 236 ; marblers, p. 250 ; bokebynders, p. 379 ; harde hewers, p. 248; paviers, p. 391, etc., all of whom have now long since passed into the great silence.

The Guild of Salve Regina.—This Guild was not in the church of St. Mary at Hill, but in that of St. Magnus close by. The Guild received every year an annual payment of six shillings. The origin of this payment is to be found in the fact that John Causton bequeathed to the church of St. Mary a house in the parish of St. Leonard, which was taxed with this payment.

The rental at the end of the copy of John Causton's Will in MS. B thus refers to the property :—

"The parisshe of Seynte leonardes, Estchepe.

Iohn ffyssche, Grocer, vj li o yer; wherof is paide to the Bretherhed of our lady Salue withyn the chirch of Seynt magnus, by yer, Summa, vj s."

London Bridge.—The property above mentioned was also taxed with another payment, namely, that of thirteen shillings and fourpence to the Masters of the Bridgehouse :—

"Item, to the maisteres of the Bryghehouse by yer, Summa xiij s iiij d."

According to the *Chronicles of London Bridge*, 1827, p. 295, the Masters of the Bridge House were "two Bridge-Masters having certain fees and profits, yearly elected .... and set over the Bridge House, 'to look after the reparations of the Bridge.'" William Cambridge in his Will states that in certain contingencies a bequest made by him for another purpose shall fall in for 'the vse and sustentacion of london Brigge,' p. 16. A similar disposition by John Weston will be noticed at p. 13, where also a reference to a contingent service in the chapel on London Bridge is mentioned. The proximity of London Bridge naturally made the same very familiar to the parishioners of St. Mary's.

Quaint Phrases.—The following extracts have an interest by reason of the quaint manner in which they are expressed :—

"payd ij [meaning 'to'] viij syngynge men," p. 403.

"for a xj [a-leven] monthes," p. 401.

"payd sondayly," that is, each Sunday, p. 110.

"Turne over the Leafe," p. 403.

"Item, paid to a prest that did serue our Cure the sondaye folowinge that sir Iohn mychell dyed, beynge our Curat, and lefte vs desolate," p. 407.

"paid to edmond matrevers ffor his wages j quarter & half endynge at candylmas whan that he went his way," p. 365.

Referring to a sum of £73 3s. 7d. we find on p. 364 the note:—

"Thys money fynyshed vp the 9 howsys byldynge."

On p. 369 is a reference to one—

"that shoulde abyne parishe prest."

On p. 329:

"þat shuld a bene clerk."

"and ther is, in monye, Summa. xix s iij d oḃ," p. 141.

"In Redy monny," p. 357.

"to Ihames sharpulles ffor iij quarteres vj li. Item, for myghelmas quarter, because he was in the Contrey he had no more but xxxiij s x d," p. 371.

Tithes.—The payment 'for Mr parsons Tenth of the benefice,' £3 13s. 4d., p. 406, is the payment due to the King by which a tenth of all benefices, etc., was secured under the Act of 1534. (See *Statutes Revised*, 1888, p. 314.) The value of the benefice in the Valor Ecclesiasticus is given as £36 13s. 4d.

No Relics.—It will be noticed that not a penny is spent on relics of saints, nor, with the exception of a penny for part of a finger of St. Andrew, do we find any such expenses recorded in the accounts of the three other churches examined for comparison with our text.

Travelling.—Travelling from one place to another appears to have been invariably on horseback, p. 174, except in London, where the river offered facilities when a boat would be hired, p. 256. In 1529–30 one of the churchwardens rode with two companions to Norwich to consult the parson about the payment of the choristers, p. 350.

Articles sold by the Churchwardens.—Occasionally we read of the sale by the wardens of articles of very varied nature:—

'to make saale of the howsold stuff in the vestry,' p. 284.

Various goods are mentioned on pp. 232, 241, 271, 276, 279. In many cases articles had probably been given to the church, others were apparently at times accepted in lieu of small sums owing:—

'William turtyll patynmaker, vj s viij d. Resseyued a bras pott per h̄ kello," p. 157.

At p. 231 we see that a brass pot was sold. It is natural to suppose that in some cases some articles would be sold because they had been replaced by newer.

Miscellaneous Items.—Many items of a more or less isolated nature occur in our text. The two widows renting a house by the Minories, p. 126; the extra two shillings paid to Mr. Ballard, the owner of a wood, that those who went to hew the timber might pick where they liked in 'all the holl wod,' p. 337; the payment of £4 by 'the brewers wife at The Pewter Pot against St. Andrews Undershaft,' to get back some silver plate which had been pawned, p. 346; the daily service in the choir (ordered by the parish?), p. 347; the coins specified in these accounts as having been in the hands of the wardens—the penny, p. 94; and the gold noble, p. 272; the clerk of St. Dunstan's who died in poverty of the pestilence, p. 84; how the churchwardens sometimes let out the church goods on hire, p. 94; and occasionally borrowed goods themselves for their own services, p. 305; what was paid for the mending of various articles of plate: two shillings and eightpence 'to a goldsmith for making a censers foot,' p. 251, etc. etc.; the failure of the church authorities to let their houses on Tower Hill, so that during two years they 'only received a featherbed of the weaver's wife, price v s.', p. 121; the burial of the alderman's wife near the altar in a chapel, p. 261; and the funeral knell rung for half-a-day on the great bell for the mother of one of the chantry priests, p. 241. Of costs in the ecclesiastical courts, p. 278; of the mayor's court, p. 111; the gift of a buck to the parish by the abbot of Waltham, and where the gift was eaten, p. 250; of the house 'vppon the steyer,' p. 125; the man who filled the holy water stoups for a year for viij d, p. 343; the carrying of copes to St. Paul's apparently for the clergy of St. Mary's to take part in processions in the cathedral, p. 382; the 'stand of good ale for the maundye,' p. 406; the taking of 'gose & the clerke' to Ipswich, p. 346; the garden palings, p. 167; the tiles of the houses, p. 189; the audit meeting, p. 298; the 'settyng of ij torchis at Westmystir,' probably at the abbey church on behalf of the late king, p. 266; the drinking 'at nyght,' p. 273.

Medieval Weather.—The two references to the weather in the Middle Ages in St. Mary's parish, carry one back somehow very realistically to those times. In 1491–2 there was evidently a heavy fall of snow, 'the grete snowe' it is called, p. 172. In 1521–2 a part of the window of the Trinity 'was blown downe with the wynde,' p. 313.

CH. III.]   *Introduction. Miscellaneous Notes.*   xlvii

The Beam-light.—The light, for the sustentation of which subscriptions were received every year apparently at Christmas, Lady Day, Midsummer and Michaelmas, p. 128, was probably a series of lights on a beam by the great Rood, the Rood beam. In 1495-6 the light was temporarily taken down, during which time certain of the subscribers 'wold not pay,' pp. 218, 221.

A Home for the Dying?—Judging by the fact that the mention of 'the freer' 'at Billingesgate' occurs commonly if not invariably in connexion with the burial of a deceased person who had 'dyed' there, it may be with some certainty considered that the freer was a friary or brotherhood of some kind for the reception of the very sick, pp. 271, 287, 324.

God's Penny.—At times, at the engaging or 'hiring' of an official of the church a nominal sum was paid down as a kind of earnest money. Such a payment appears to have been known as a 'goddes peny,' though not necessarily being of that value, pp. 250, 252. Sometimes a somewhat similar payment was made by an incoming tenant, pp. 271, 286, 293, 311.

Occasionally such a payment was made as so much on account of work to be done, 'the goddis peny in honde,' p. 274.

Obscurities.—The following items appear at present to defy elucidation :—

Item, 'the Clerkis of the Towne,' p. 316.
Item, 'for settyng a childe at Waltham,' p. 322.
Item, 'the wardemote enquest for the churche house,' p. 385.
Item, 'ij maryages for that they were maryed in the newe howsse,' p. 398.
Item, 'for settyng of a woman into a pywe,' p. 94.
Item, 'the dewtyes of Seint Anne,' p. 278.
Item, 'Post,' p. 284.
Item, 'payed to the laystowe,' p. 397.
Item, 'Iohn polyvere for buryeng of master braymonger—xiij s iiij d,' p. 180.
Item, 'paid to the sessyng of the dong bote—vj d,' p. 359.
Item, 'paid ffor the sessyng of the laystall—iiij d,' p. 367.
Item, 'the leystoff,' p. 382.
Item, 'tenebyll weddyns day,' p. 397.

At p. 303 John Coveney receives xl s 'for the hauyng of þe yeres in his howse.' Canon Wordsworth thinks 'yeres' may mean the herse or structure placed at times over a coffin on special occasions.

In support of this suggestion we have the fact that a chalice was at one time in the care of a parishioner:—

'Payed to Mr Malbye ffor keping of the chalice—iiij d,' p. 382.

CHAPTER IV.
OF SERVICES, ETC.

The Services in the Church.—The services sung by the parish officials of St. Mary's church cannot, with one exception, be clearly defined. But those which were carried on in the building by the various chantry priests can be set down with considerable certainty.

Early in the morning the doors of the church would be unlocked. The church would not be open all night, as may be gathered from the statement in 1502-3, that two men were employed to watch 'whilys the chirche stoed opyn' six nights, p. 247. Entering the church on any weekday we should find the morrow-mass priest singing his mass so early, that in winter he would require candles, p. 317. Later on, the six or seven chantry priests would be singing their matins, hours and masses, some at one altar, some at another, pp. 11, 17; the chantry priest of John Bedham sang at St. Katherine's altar immediately after the morrow-mass. Later on, the chantry priests would be singing their evensong and compline; and probably at very varying times, Placebo and Dirige, Commendations, the Seven Penitential Psalms and Litany. At p. 1 we find instructions given for 'an honest Preest to syng dyvyne seruice euery day.'

To what extent the parish services would follow the plan of the chantry services it is difficult to say. But if some parts were omitted others would be added, such as weddings, churchings, and funerals, and also Obits, or memorial services.

A particularly interesting fact respecting the services of St. Mary's is afforded by the two following statements. From these we see that a little service, or part of one, took place in the nave of St. Mary's every afternoon :—

"ij tapers brennyng before the Aungelles Salutacion of the ymage of our lady in the body of the said Chirch every evenyng at the tyme of syngyng of Salue Regina," p. 6.

Our second extract is not only corroborative, but tells us of the burial of William Olneye, a fishmonger, by the foot of this figure. He desired in his Will—

"to be buried before the Salutation of the Blessed Virgin Mary where *Salve* is daily sung in the church of S. Mary atte Hull."—Sharpe's *Husting Wills*, 2. 174.

Burials.—The Memorandum on p. 319, dated 1523, gives very exactly the costs of burial fees due to the church and to the Clerk :—
For a grave in either of the chapels of St. Stephen or St. Katherine, 13*s*. 4*d*. was to be paid to the church, and to the Clerk 3*s*. 4*d*. For burial outside these chapels, 10*s*. was due to the church and 2*s*. 6*d*. to the Clerk. For a grave in the nave of the church, 6*s*. 8*d*. was due to the church and 1*s*. 8*d*. to the Clerk.

The ordinance for 1498-9, p. 231, rules that the Clerk's fee for a grave in the church shall be 2*s*., and for burial in either of the churchyards the Clerk shall be entitled to 8*d*. or 4*d*. for a man or child respectively.

We have seen that there were two churchyards. The 'pardon' churchyard appears to have been the more frequently used for interments during the period of our Records: the church received two shillings for each interment there, and generally eightpence or fourpence for burial in the great churchyard.

Two children were buried in one grave in 1502-3.

Knells were rung sometimes on the great bell, sometimes on the middle bell, sometimes on the little bell; the ringing lasting sometimes half-a-day, sometimes for an hour.

The Memorandum of 1498, p. 231, ordains that for the knell with the great bell, the church and Clerk shall each receive 6*s*. 8*d*. Also that the Clerk shall receive for a knell rung on the second bell 12*d*. if rung for an hour, and 40*d*. if rung for half-a-day. For a knell rung on the little bell—if for a man, the Clerk shall receive 8*d*., and if for a child, 4*d*.

Sir John Plommer's bell was used for the poorer people, and a penny only was charged for its use (p. 246).

Torches were at times hired of the church, and kept burning at funerals—'for the hire of ij torches at the burial of William Hus,' p. 293 ; three torches, p. 307 ; 'for bearing of iiij torches to bury the "portyngaler,"' p. 100 ; and for no less than six at the 'dyrige and masse at þe buryall' of Mrs. Powre, p. 283.

The palls used are mentioned in one of the Inventories (p. 53) : one was of gold and black velvet, another, for children, had a crucifix in the midst. About 1550 a charge appears to have been made for the use of the church palls at funerals, p. 391.

A special feature of the Middle Ages was the payment by the well-to-do for the burial of the very poor. In these accounts the receipt of money by the wardens for such a purpose is by no means very rare. An instance may be given :—

'Item, Resseyued of Margarete Bull for þe buriall of a straunge childe,' p. 129.

In only one instance is the age of a parishioner buried recorded, that of 'a chyld of vj yere old, dyed at harmams,' p. 241.

Parishioners were buried in every part of the church and its chapels, even in the vestry, p. 161.

The grave is commonly termed 'pyt,' p. 366.

An armyte or hermit was buried in 1510-11, p. 276.

Collections.—Our Records do not often refer to the collection of money in the church, but a note on p. 284 tells us that certain alms gathered in the church shall be 'reserved towards burials of poor people and other deeds of charity.' At p. 299 is an entry to the effect that—

"Iohn stookes, pewterer, doith awght vnto ye church, anno 1518, for money gayderd ffor the powr peple";

and on p. 261 we have the entry :—

'R. of stevyn sawndyrson of hys gadyryng in þe church, xxxvj s iij d oḃ.'

At p. 259 we have a reference to the collection of elevenpence halfpenny by Mrs. Althorpe; and at p. 128 the collection of eleven shillings and fivepence at the communion at Easter in 1487. At p. 318 we find a note of coals purchased with alms-money and given to the poor. It is significant that our text contains several entries of the finding of money in the church, probably after the dispersal of the congregations, pp. 94, 196, 212; it is not unreasonable to suppose that the coins were dropped when the owners were making their offerings.

Churching and Wedding and Christening.—Two very remarkable payments are recorded under the Casual Receipts for 1524-5. The first is the receipt of sixpence at a marriage, the second the receipt of twopence at a churching.

The reference to the two marriages at p. 398 is perhaps even more remarkable. At p. 222 is the solitary reference to a christening.

By whom the Sacred Elements were Provided most Uncertain.—Our text does not show us by whom the Bread and Wine for the services were provided in the Middle Ages. The Records refer to

Singing Bread and the Wine for the subordinate Masses, but not for the main services of the church. After the death of Henry VIII, as is well known, the elements were provided at the cost of the congregation. It is, however, significant that once or twice money was expended on obb[l]ees for Palm Sunday, pp. 313, 327.

By whom the Incense was Provided.—The incense, as our text shows, was provided at the cost of the parishioners; but it is a curious fact that the amount paid for can in no way have been sufficient to supply the needs of the church. Possibly much of it was given by individuals.

Division of the Sexes in Church.—Our text shows us clearly that it was not the custom for men and women to sit together during service time in the Middle Ages. Under Pews, Chap. V, we see that there were pews for men and pews for women, and that the husband's pew is not that of the wife. In the accounts of St. Stephen Walbrook the evidence that man and wife sat separately is even more clearly given.

" Master dodmeres pewe & his wiffes pewe," Chap. VII.

Obits.—The obits were annual memorial services for various people by whom money was left to pay for such services :—

"my seid Obett or Annuersary, yerely for euermore, þe same day of the moneth my sowle shall depart from þe body," p. 21.

The service is explained on the same page as consisting of the *Dirige* office in the evening and Mass the next morning.

An obit might be endowed to last for a certain specified time or for ever, pp. 21, 182, 197, 213.

A full list of those for the year 1517–18, showing the money expended at each obit for refreshments, fee to parson, churchwardens, bell-ringers, payments for candles, etc., will be found at p. 295.

Perhaps the most striking of these services was that annually performed on the 18th or 19th of August for the soul of William Cambridge, on which occasion, by his Will, the mayor, two sheriffs, and sword-bearer attended at the church, and were remunerated accordingly. In 1478–9 the sheriffs had 'nothyng payd, for they came not,' p. 90. The medieval description of an Obit will be found in that for Margaret Noneley on p. 288.

The Bede-roll.—The bede-roll was the list of those to be mentioned by name in the pulpit that they might be expressly remembered in the prayers of the parishioners :—

> "Item, ffor wrytyng off the Bedrow, iiij d," p. 238.
>
> "to Mr Iohn Redy ffor rehersyng of the bederoll, viij d," p. 149.

A partial explanation of the Bede-roll is afforded in our text on p. 80:—

> "To the parissh preste, to Remembre in the pulpite the sowle of [Richard] Bliot, whiche gave to the Churche workis vj s viij d—ij d."

Apparently the parish priest commonly read the bede-roll, and received a small honorarium for so doing, pp. 149, 260. In 1507–8 the payment was remitted as a gift to the church by those holding the office, p. 263. The list of names was apparently written on a parchment fixed to a board, pp. 132, 326.

Festivals mentioned.—The 'pryncipall ffestes' are apparently intended to be enumerated on p. 163:

> Christmas Day.
> Twelfth Day.
> Palm Sunday.
> Holy Thursday.
> Corpus Christi.
> St. Barnabas.
> The Assumption.

On these occasions refreshments for the priests and clerks were provided.

'Loo sondaye' is referred to at p. 399; 'Candilmas day' at p. 148; 'palmesan eve,' p. 198; 'Relyke sonday,' p. 264; 'trinyte sonday,' p. 277; 'Shoftyd' and 'lammas,' p. 232; 'ester daye,' p. 148; 'alhalowne day,' p. 238; 'Wytson yeuyn,' p. 266; '**Whyt-sontyd**,' p. 242; 'fest of transfiguracion,' p. 274; 'lent,' p. 343; 'shrofthursday,' p. 301; 'Mawndy thursday,' p, 314; the 'puryficacion,' p. 325; 'Estyr eve,' p. 247; 'ascencion day,' p. 382; 'god frydaye,' p. 247; 'lady day,' p. 237; 'our Ladis even,' p. 399; and 'double feest, prycipall feest & solempne feest' at p. 13.

Dr. Wickham-Legg points out that the 'ij° childern goyng on processyon on holye thursdaye,' p. 131, were probably the boys whipped at the boundaries of the parish.

At Midsummer the church was decorated with boughs of birch; the entry of the cost occurs regularly each year:—

> "payd for byrche at mydsomer, iiij d," p. 198.

On St. Barnabas's Day, June 11th, garlands were often purchased:—

"for Roose garlondys on sentt barnaby ys day, xx d," p. 186.

Garlands were also often purchased for the great Corpus Christi festival:—

"for garlondys on Corpus Christi day, iij d," p. 198.

The garlands, sometimes of Roses and of Lavender, were carried by probably many people, no less than four and even five dozen garlands being sometimes purchased, and probably carried by the rector, parish priest, choristers, and borne on the processional crosses, pp. 309, 316.

Holly and ivy were purchased regularly for Christmas decorations:—

"payd for holme & ive on crystmas even, ij d," p. 172.

Box, palm, and flowers were procured for Palm Sunday:—

"Item, for bovx and flowrys on palme sonday, v d."
"Item, for palme the same day, iij d," p. 173.

Easter Ceremonies.—Very few entries refer to the Easter ceremonies, and naturally, because very little additional expense was incurred. We have—

"paid for ij quarter of Colis for hallowing of the font at estur," pp. 296, 343;

and the constant mention of the watching of the Easter Sepulchre, p. 197.

Hallowing or Consecrating.—At p. 199 we see that the parson sometimes hallowed the articles for the use of the church. Sometimes the ceremony was performed by the parish priest, p. 240. The 'halloyng of the cherche' is mentioned at p. 250.

CHAPTER V.

THE PRE-REFORMATION FURNITURE OF THE CHURCH.[1]

The following pages do not profess to give every reference in the Records to the articles of furniture in St. Mary's church. Where several references occur only those have been mentioned where the use or description of the article is more or less clearly specified.

[1] The whole subject of Church Furniture will be dealt with very amply in a forthcoming volume of *The Antiquary's Books*, by Dr. J. C. Cox and Mr. Harvey.

Alms-box.—p. 304.

Altar leaves.—At p. 293 we find—

"paid for a peyre garnettes for the levys of the high alter before the Images—iiij d."

Apparently these leaves swung to on 'garnettes' or hinges for the protection of the figures or picture within.

Altar hangings.—The various 'haninges' mentioned in the Inventory on pp. 52-3 probably refer to the curtains at the sides of each altar, the curtain hanging above each altar at its back, and that hanging immediately in front of each altar. The curtains of the high altar are mentioned on p. 234. An altar frontal of St. Stephen's chapel was ornamented 'withe the wavys of gold,' p. 316.

Altar stones or slabs.—p. 395.

Aumbries or wall cupboards.—Almery, p. 187.

Banner-staves.—In 1492-3 the wardens paid a penny each for eight banner-staves, p. 186. Banner-poles are mentioned on p. 234.

Banners in Rood-loft.—p. 361.

Banners, Square.—Square banners are mentioned in the Inventory of church goods on p. 31.

Barrels.—Barrels were apparently in use and also tubs at times of consecration, or 'halloyng,' p. 250. The 'Chirche barels' are alluded to on p. 214.

Basins.—Two basins, one of latten, the other pewter, are mentioned in the Inventory of 1553, p. 52.

The use of these basins is perhaps explained by the following extract from a Will of 1456:—

"I begueth ij basins with ij Eures, of Syluer and parcel gilt .... not only for to serue vpon the high autier of the same chirch in high principal festis and other festiual daies, But also to wassh in the handes of godfadres and godmoders at cristenying of childern within the same chirch."—Somerset House Wills, Stokton, 60 b.

Basket for Holy Bread.—p. 247.

Basket for dust.—In 1487-8, p. 131, the wardens record the item:—

"to w. paris for his labour for a basket to bear in duste, iiij d."

Bedstead.—The bedstead was apparently for use somewhere in the church, and probably for the Morrowmas priest, whose duty it would be to say the first mass:—

"[a] Bedsted for the preistes chamber þat kepith þe first mas," p. 340.

CH. V.] *Introd. Pre-Reformation Furniture of the Church.* lv

The 'preistes chamber' would probably be over the porch.

The Bells.—There were six large bells in the church. In the Inventory of 1553, p. 54, we read—

"in the steple v gret belles & one Santes bell,"

and almost the same words occur in the Inventory of 1496–7, p. 33, where, however, it is added that—

"the iiijth great bell was clere of þe gyfte of Iohn Duklyng, ffysshmonger, as is graved vppon þe bell."

The sanctus bell would not be in use for ringing a peal. The five bell-ringers are mentioned at p. 406. The payment to the bell-ringers for their labour is rarely mentioned, p. 350.

On p. 33 a silver bell, most probably the sacring bell, is mentioned, the gift of a Mrs. Julyan Roche. The sacring bell is alluded to by name on p. 52.

On p. 131 the four little bells which tinkled on the canopy borne over the Sacrament at the Corpus Christi procession find mention.

On p. 131 the wardens record the purchase for fourteenpence of—

"a latyn bell to go with the sacrament,"

that is, to be carried before the Sacrament when borne to sick people.

At p. 273 is the record of a payment 'to the skryvener for makyng of þe Indentures betwixt William Smyth, bell founder, and the parissh.' Only the year previously William Smyth had been arrested and the bells had been the subject of a law-suit, p. 270.

At the 'halowyng' of the bells in 1520–1 'two burdens of rushes' were strewn beneath them, possibly for those present to stand on, p. 310. But Canon Wordsworth writes:—"Is it not more probable that they were strewn under the bell to receive the washings of holy water, oil and salt with which the bell was smeared all over?" Cp. Maskell Mon. Rit., i. 186.

In 1511–12 long boards were purchased to keep the bell ropes from fraying against the walls of the steeple, p. 277. At p. 274 we find many details respecting the bells. On pages 273, 274, we read, too, of money being paid a man for his 'labur & his brekefast,' in going from Ludgate to Aldgate 'to here þe iiijth bell in Tewne,' and of expenses for wine and pears at Aldgate when several parishioners went to see if 'Smythes bell were Tewneabill or nat.'

lvi *Introd. Pre-Reformation Furniture of the Church.* [CH. V.

Bell chrisoms are mentioned on p. 250, and grease for the bells on p. 322.

Bench in Choir.—On p. 270 we find a reference to a bench in the choir.

Books for Service.—A sufficient but by no means large number of service books were in use at St. Mary's. There were:—

Antiphoners	page	27.	Manual	page	27.
Breviary (portos)	,,	173.	Martiloge	,,	27.
Epistle book	,,	27.	Mass books	,,	27.
Gospel book	,,	54.	Ordinal	,,	27.
Grayels	,,	27.	Processionals	,,	27.
Hymnals	,,	55.	Psalters	,,	27.
Legendas	,,	27.	Sequence book	,,	314.

The church books were sometimes written in full by a priest, p. 133; sometimes bought of a stationer, p. 101; sometimes words and music added, and the book mended and rebound by a clerk of a neighbouring parish, p. 131. In 1496 a stationer set the new feasts in the books and repaired them generally, p. 226. Sometimes one of the chantry priests repaired the books, p. 173; and sometimes the repairs were executed by layfolk, p. 140; 'mowth glewe' appears to have been used sometimes for the repairs, 350; some of the books had clasps, p. 131; the mass book had two, p. 140. The 'organ books,' p. 226, may have been special volumes containing the music only of the services, but were more likely to have been copies of ordinary service books: we know that the neighbouring church of St. Margaret's in Fish street possessed a breviary for the organ. The 'Caroll books,' p. 54, would probably be books of Carols for Christmas time? The 'Song books,' p. 54, from the fact that some of them are specified to have been used in the mass, were probably parts of ordinary service books specially arranged for singing.

The 'boke of playnsong of the offices off Ihesus Mas and our ladys Massis for the children,' p. 349, would be only a selection from the common service books. Several books were chained in the chancel, p. 234.

In 1504–5 the wardens—

> "payde to þe boke bynder at ledon halle, for coveryng, byndyng & pesyng of iiij Antyfyners, a Masse boke, a manewell, a legentt in ij foloms & iiij graylys xlvj s viij d," p. 256.

The reference to "ye bok yat lith affore ye parishe pryste," p. 373, quite possibly, from the date of the entry, may refer to a copy of the Bible ordered by authority.

CH. V.]   *Introd.   Pre-Reformation Furniture of the Church.*   lvii

The following reference at p. 378 is interesting, though what the contents of the 'square bookes' may have been it is not easy to say :—

> "Paid to sir marke for carolles for cristmas and for v square bookes—iij s iiij d."

The books were sometimes mended by the parish clerk. Michael Green was parish clerk in 1529–30 :—

> "paid to Mighell grene for a quayre of papur Ryall for þe prykked song boke and for mowth gleue," p. 350.

> "paid to Mighell Grene for Mendyng of þe Antefoners that lye in the quere that [were] torn and broken," p. 350.

In 1513–14 the sum of viij s was paid for—

> "Coueryng newe & mendyng off xv bokes grete and Smale, & for x Newe bosys for þe Newe Antefoner, & for clapsis and Burdons," p. 286.

John Norfolk the organist appears in 1529–30 to have prepared some—

> "prykkyd song bokes of the whiche v of them be with Antemys and v with Massis," p. 351.

The cowcher alluded to at p. 225 would be a large service book, one large enough to generally lie or couch, an antiphoner, breviary, or missal probably.

The Gospel book was a beautiful volume with (as was often the case with this service book) substantial silver plates to the cover, p. 393.

Branches.—Branches, apparently of iron or brass-work, were to be found in different parts of the church:—'the braunche of þe Trynite' is mentioned at p. 305; the branch of three flowers at p. 305; 'þe branche byfore þe rode,' p. 255; the branch before a figure of the Virgin in the choir, p. 264; that before the representation of the Salutation in St. Katherine's chapel, p. 264; a 'braunche of v,' p. 225.

Brooms.—These are often mentioned.

Candles, p. 322. Candles of 'talow' for 'dyvine seruise' are mentioned at p. 81.

Candelsticks: the Judas.—The explanation of the 'Iudas' is very clearly given in the accounts :—

> "the Ivdas of the Pascall [candle] þat is to sey, the Tymbre that the wax of þe pascall is drevyn vppon," p. 308.

But several 'Iudassis' are mentioned as in the rood loft on p. 309

Canon Wordsworth considers Judas to have been a generic term for holders or saveralls. See Wordsworth's *Medieval Services*, pp. 168–72.

Candlesticks, hanging.—At p. 358 we read of the purchase of " ij hangyng candylstykes for the quyre, v d."

Candlesticks, hand.—Two 'hand canstickes' are mentioned on p. 270.

Candlesticks, bowls.—p. 163.

Candlesticks, skonses.—On p. 270, " iij plattes with nosis for þe skonsis" are mentioned. Also at p. 333, " vj skonses for the queer."

Before the Reformation there were but few candlesticks on the altars. An Inventory tells us that in 1496 there were—

> "on the high auter ij gret Candylstykes & iij small. And on sent Stephyns awter ij Candylstykes," p. 32.

The 'nosyng' of candlesticks is referred to on p. 243.

Canopies.—The canopy over the Sacrament, placed or borne, to do honour to the Sacrament, took certainly two forms, possibly three.

First, would be the little covering within which the Sacrament in its pyx would be suspended above the altar.

Secondly, would be the more elaborate and ample canopy, supported on staves which would be used in bearing the Sacrament in procession. 'A canapye to bear ouer the Sacrament on corpus christi daye,' p. 150.

The canopy, supported on four staves, is clearly referred to in the following extract:—

> " iiij Canipi staves with iiij Knoppes, gilt," p. 53.

They were apparently supported by leather thongs, such being perhaps attached to the waist of each bearer, p. 301.

Thirdly, it is possible that a substantial projection extended above the Sacrament from the east wall of the church; the following note from p. 226 appears to refer to such :—

> "the Iryn at the hye awter that beryth the canapye."

Canopy Crowns.—Crowns, apparently of latten, or mixture largely of brass, were scoured in 1490–1, p. 163. The Inventory on p. 31 refers to—

> "a Canape for the pyx, of red velwett with iij Crownys of laton."

Censers.—At p. 51 the Inventory of 1553 records the presence

Introd. Pre-Reformation Furniture of the Church.

of two heavy silver censers. There are various other references to these articles in our text.

Chairs.—Two chairs of iron for the rectors of the choir are mentioned in the Inventory on p. 31. At p. 351 the mending of a chair is recorded.

Chalices.—There were several chalices belonging to the church, pages 26, 53, etc.

Chest for Documents.—On p. 27 the Inventory of 1431 records the presence of a "cheste with evydens"; and at p. 304 we read of "þe chest wherin the wrytinges lyeth, in the Revestry."

Chest for Easter Sepulchre.—The Inventory of 1553 mentions—
"Item, more, in the Roud loft; a long Chist with the fframe of the Sepvllev[r?] in yt," p. 53.

The Easter Sepulchre chest was a wooden box into which it was customary at Easter to place the pyx containing the Sacrament.

Chest for Plate.—In 1494-5 the wardens paid threepence for—
"j key for the Iuell Chest," p. 215.

Chest for Torches.—In 1477-9 the wardens paid threepence for—
"a nywe key to the Chest that the torchis be in," p. 81.

Chest, Tresory.—'ij keyes for the tresory chest in the vestry,' p. 261.

Chest for Vestments.—A vestment chest is mentioned on p. 230.

Chest for Wax.—On p. 278 is a reference to—
"a chest in the quere to ley in olde wax."

Chest for Linen.—Mentioned on p. 317.

Chest for Tunicles and Chasubles.—Mentioned on p. 303.

Church Box, p. 273.

Cloth of hair for the High Altar.—A hair-cloth was (commonly?) placed over an altar slab :—
"for iiij yerdes heer for þe hye Awter," p. 256; also p. 394.

Cloths, Altar.—Pages 32 and 35 contain a long list of the altar cloths of St. Mary's. One appears to have been pictorial, several bore the initials of the donor. At p. 272 we see that money was paid for 'markyng' as well as 'makyng' altar cloths, the marking probably consisting of the initials of a donor or some form of decoration.

Cloth, Cross.—The banner hung on the processional cross at Easter and other festivals :—
"small corde for the Crosse Cloth," p. 234.

Cloth for the Easter Sepulchre.—The Inventory on p. 51 refers to this cloth.

Cloth for the Font.—The Inventories mention two font clothes, one of red silk, the other of gold, p. 54.

Cloth for the Holy Bread.—The holy bread was bread distributed in the church, but not that of the Communion. On p. 35 the holy bread cloth is described as having a fringe and marked with 'k' and 'v' in red silk. The letters were probably the initials of the donor.

Cloths, Housling.—With the exception of a reference to "ij sacrament clothes," on p. 369, the housling cloths are not directly mentioned in our Records, but the long 'towelles' noted in the Inventory on p. 33 were probably used as housling cloths, or long cloths suspended before the communicants during the reception of the communion. The following extract perhaps proves such :—

"I bequeth to the said chirch of seint Dunstone a dyapre towell of xv yardis in lenght to serue ther at the housling tyme of the parisshoners there."—Somerset House Wills, Milles, 265 a.

At p. 36 of our text we read of a towel marked with white thread 'lyke ij Trewlovis.'

Cloths for Cross Staves.—In the Inventory of 1496-7 we meet with the item—

"iij crosse stavys clothes, gyldyd, with Images of golde," p. 31.

Possibly these cloths depended from transverse staves hanging from the tops of poles. We read of 'baner clothes of steyned werke,' p. 150.

Cloths, painted.—Painted cloths are mentioned at p. 388.

Cloth for the Pyx.—The pyx cloth was that of the pyx or box containing the holy sacrament. The pyx commonly hung suspended above the high altar : 'the pix cloth ouer the alter,' p. 331. Two of great beauty are described in the Inventory at p. 31.

Cloth before the Rood.—The Inventory of 1553 mentions—

"a painted Cloth yat did hang before ye Roud," p. 54.

Cloths, Tabernacle.—p. 230.

'Clothes of the Tower.'—Such cloths are mentioned at p. 381, and appear to have been in use on Palm Sunday. The context seems to indicate that these cloths formed some part of the scenery in connexion with the stage for the Prophets, but the matter is far from clear.

CH. V.] *Introd. Pre-Reformation Furniture of the Church.* lxi

Coffer, Money.—"The mony cofur within the plate chest in þe vpper vestry," p. 331.

Coffer for relics.—A little coffer for relics is mentioned on p. 26.

Corporas.—A corporas is mentioned in the Inventory on p. 33, and the washing of seven corporases on p. 350.

Corporas Case.—A beautiful corporas case given by Elizabeth Gooswell is mentioned in the Inventory of 1496-7, p. 31.

Cruets.—Cruets for the altars are mentioned on pp. 214, 381; two of silver are referred to at p. 26; and those of the high altar at p. 340.

Crismatories.—A silver crismatory weighing fifteen ounces is mentioned in the Inventory on p. 51. In 1535-6, p. 369, xij d was "paid ffor burnysshyng of the Crysmatory." This little vessel contained the holy oils.

Cross, the Mustenaunce, p. 101.—Dr. Cox suggested the reading monstrance cross. This is clearly right, 'the crose of the monestere,' St. A. Hubbard's MSS., leaf 40.

Cross, the Berrell.—pages 305, 361.

Cross, Processional.—On p. 101 the churchwardens record the expenditure of money—

"for mendyng of the crosse that is borne abowte euery day."

Cross Staves.—Two metal cross staves are mentioned in the Inventory on p. 32.

Crosses on the Super-altars.—On p. 198 the wardens record the payment of fourpence—

"for makyng of the crossys on þe superaltarys."

Curtain rings and hooks.—On p. 131 the wardens record the purchase of—

"xxxij Corteyn Rynges and hookes to henge the clothe for the newe tabernacle."

But many curtains were suspended from rings on iron rods.

Cushions.—Cushions of down, two of them silk and two fustian, are mentioned in the Inventory on p. 33. Probably they supported the mass book on the altar.

Desk.—A desk of laton is mentioned on p. 32; a 'doble deske,' p. 340.

Desks, Choir.—The mending of the desks in the choir is noted on p. 243. A 'longe Deske' was purchased for the choir in 1523-4, p. 323. Also two more the next year, p. 327.

Desk for Books.—In the Vestry, p. 233.

Desk, Organ.—p. 317.

Discipline Rods.—In 1492–3 twopence was paid by the wardens for—

"dyssplyng Roddys," p. 185.

The entry occurs also again at p. 269, but on no other occasion; the demand does not appear to have been excessive.

Dish for the Paschal Candlestick.—In 1426–7 the wardens paid eightpence—

"for a dysch of peuter for þe Paskall," p. 64.

Dishes for Censers.—In 1428–9 the wardens paid two shillings for—

"ij disches of iron for sensers," p. 70.

Dishes for the Rood Light.—Two dishes, "belongyng to the Rode-lyghte," were purchased in 1504–5, p. 255.

Easter Sepulchre.—As has been noticed elsewhere the Easter sepulchre was a wooden box to contain the holy Sacrament at Easter. The nails for it, and the payment to a carpenter to set it up are mentioned on p. 281. At p. 301, 'iiij Angelles,' belonging either to the box or its resting-place, are mentioned.

Figures and Images.—There were various figures in the church of St. Mary. One, of 'Our Lady of Pity,' namely, a figure of the Virgin with the dead Christ on her lap, is mentioned at p. 226. Other images were set up near the choir door, p. 359. Another figure of the Virgin stood in the choir, before which tapers were sometimes kept burning, p. 233. Somewhere on the south side of the church were the figures of St. Thomas Becket and St. Nicholas, p. 6.

Fire-Pan.—Mentioned at p. 230.

Flags.—'ffor flaggis and garlondis,' p. 100.

Font.

Font-Cover.—The making of a cover for the font is recorded on p. 131.

Font, Lock.—Two locks for the font are mentioned on p. 70.

Form, in the Choir.—'The fourme in the quere' is mentioned on p. 270.

Frontal altar shelf.—In the Inventory at p. 30 we read:—

"Item, a frontell for the schelffe standyng on the alter, of blue sarsenet with bryddes of golde" (golden birds).

CH. V.] *Introd. Pre-Reformation Furniture of the Church.* lxiii

And some of the many altar-hangings in our Inventories without doubt refer to frontals.

Glass, painted.—Of the painted glass windows of the church the subjects of only three can be indicated, namely, that of St. John on the north side of the church, p. 313; that of the Seven Works of Mercy, p. 19; and that of the Trinity, p. 252. Both of the latter windows were in the south aisle. In 1525-6 the Trinity window was mended, p. 332.

Some, if not all, of the pieces of glass of the Trinity window were of the well-known lozenge or diamond shape, for on p. 313 we have the entry of money paid:—

"for settyng in of xxiij newe quarrelles in the wyndowe of the Trynyte, whiche was blown downe with the wynde."

Gloves.—The two following extracts are not only unusual, but in conflict to some extent with each other. In the first it will be noticed that the gloves were purchased for a churchwarden and parish clerk:—

"paid for Glouys at Estur for the chirchwarden and þe clerk, vj d," p. 326.

But at the rendering of the accounts for the year the following Memorandum was inserted:—

"Item, more, for that was paid at Estur for ij peyre of gloves for the chirchewardens, the Summa of vj d which shal not be for no presedent hereafter, vj d," p. 330.

Hassocks.—Two hassocks are mentioned on p. 131 as having been purchased for St. Thomas's chapel.

Holy-water stoups.—The vessels containing holy water were apparently of two kinds—stone and metal: that of stone, probably situated at an entrance to the church, is referred to on p. 69:—

"Also payd to Appulby for heweng of þe haly water stop, iij s."

The metal stoups or pots are referred to in the Inventory on p. 33.

Holy water Sprinklers.—The purchase of sprinklers is occasionally recorded in the accounts of the churchwardens, p. 101.

Keys: for the Pyx.—p. 237; roodloft, 117.

Ladle.—'A gret laddyll' apparently in use at consecrations or 'halloyngs,' p. 250.

Lamp and its glasses.—Two "lampe glassis ffor the church," p. 340: 'a lampe with oyle in the quere & high Chauncell . . . to brenne alwey, as wele on Dayes as on nyghtes, before the blessed Sacrament,' p. 17.

Lamp basin.—The 'basen for the lamp' is mentioned at p. 281.

Lantern.—In 1479–81 sixpence was paid for mending " the churche lanterne," p. 100. At p. 290 we have the entry : " Paid for makyng of ij poleys of Iron for þe lanterne—xvj d."

Lectern in Roodloft.—At p. 243 we find money expended—

" ffor makyng of a lectorne in the Roodlofte."

Lectern, Eagle.—At p. 243 the 'skowryng of the Egull of laton' is mentioned.

Leystoff.—At p. 382 we find the entry :—

" Payed for the mendyng of the leystoff—iiij d."

Our Records contain no mention of a bier, neither, apparently, do any of the MSS. of other city churches contain any mention of a pre-Reformation bier. And this is remarkable when we bear in mind the fact that in the Middle Ages the bier was a very important article of church furniture, when, as was commonly the case, the body was merely enshrouded and thus borne to the grave without a coffin.

Is it possible that the leystoff above mentioned was the parish bier?

Mats.—Mats were in use in different parts of the church. One was in the confession pew, p. 198. On p. 81 we read of the expenditure of fourpence—

" for iij mattis of wikirs, boght for prestis and clerkis."

Under the little paragraph dealing with choristers several extracts have been given recording the purchase of mats and matting for choristers to stand on.

Mattock.—p. 327.

Money Box.—The church money box with its three keys in different hands is often mentioned, p. 291.

Monstrance.—The Monstrance or little metal altar cross, in the centre of which the Host was placed for demonstration to the congregation, is occasionally referred to in our accounts. For instance on p. 233 :—

" Item, for mendyng of the monstyr for the Sacrament, xvj d."

Oil pots.—On p. 101 mention is made of " a stone potte to put in oyle," and at p. 358, "ij pottes to fett oyle in, j d." Probably,

CH. V.] *Introd. Pre-Reformation Furniture of the Church.* lxv

Canon Wordsworth thinks, from the Maundy Thursday blessing of oils by the bishop.

The Organs.—There were apparently two organs in St. Mary's, though the term 'pair of organs' is the common medieval designation of one instrument. In our Inventory of 1553 one organ is mentioned as being larger than the other, p. 54; and on p. 278 we meet with a reference to 'the little organs in the choir.' In 1532-3 the organ was tuned, xij d being paid for 'tuenyng of ye pipis,' p. 361. On p. 373 the purchase of 'ij quylles ffor the organs' is recorded.

Padlock.—" a key to a hangyng loke in the Roud loufte," p. 173.

Palls, or Burying Cloths.—Several burying cloths are mentioned in the Inventory on p. 53 :—

" a bvring clothe a govld & blacke velvet."
. . . .
"an ovld bvring Cloth for Chilldren, with a Crvcifix in ye middest."

Patens.—Patens are mentioned on p. 53. The paten was a little circular dish or plate for the priest's bread used in the communion. Canon Wordsworth adds—"The Pyx or ciborium or a chalice was used for taking the hosts to the communicants."

Paxes (for kissing).—Three paxes of silver and gilt are mentioned on p. 26, and the pax for the high altar on p. 359.

The Pews.—It was customary for many years before the Reformation for parishioners to have pews allocated to them, though apparently nothing was then paid for the privilege. Mrs. Maskall and Mrs. Overay sat in a particular pew in 1496, p. 225; another lady, 'Mastres Atclyffe,' in another pew, p. 198; and later on the pews used by various people are more or less frequently alluded to :—The alderman's pew, p. 255; Mrs. Russell's maid's pew, p. 328; Mrs. Roche's maiden's pew, Mr. Roche's pew, etc., p. 323; Mrs. Potter's pew, p. 365. There were special pews for the poor people, p. 215, pews for men, p. 251, and for women, p. 252. One pew, containing a mat, was used for confessions, 'shrevyng,' p. 198; one was known as the 'great pew,' p. 252.

The pews were in various parts of the church,—at the west end, p. 264, next the pulpit, p. 266, in the south aisle, p. 252, in the body of the church, p. 219, at the north door, p. 215, and also in the chapels, pp. 252, 255. They had doors, p. 173, and perhaps were not unlike those of fifty years ago. They were in no sense mere benches, for the distinction between pews and benches is

MED. REC. *e*

drawn clearly on p. 215. The pews had a wooden flooring, p. 252, and sometimes an elm board on which to kneel, p. 225. Rushes were strewn on the floors of the pews, p. 254.

Apparently the division of the sexes was maintained in the city churches before the Reformation. See Division of the Sexes, p. li.

Pickaxe.—p. 361.

Pillows.—Besides cushions the church owned—

"vij pelewes of selk of diuers colours," Inventory of 1431, p. 27. These pillows probably supported the mass book on the altar.

Plates with spikes for candles, p. 270.

Poles.—Iron poles for the lantern are mentioned at p. 290, and a pole belonging to the cloth of a figure of the Assumption is alluded to at p. 266. The 'poles for the Sacrament,' mentioned on p. 347, were probably two of the four sustaining the canopy borne over the Sacrament. The following reference is not particularly clear; possibly the pole had a broom at the end of it:—

"a poole to swepe the chirch Roffe, price iiij d," p. 148.

Portatyffis.—In 1526-7 the wardens—

"Rec' of the Orgon Maker for þe olde portatyffis in þe quere, xxvj s viij d," p. 341.

Canon Wordsworth adds, 'small organs, I suppose moved about like our harmoniums.'

The Pulpit.—In 1503-4 a new pulpit was made. The complete account of its cost will be found at p. 251. The pulpit was of wood, was fixed to one of the pillars of the church, and was approached by a ladder, p. 277.

Pyx.—The Inventories record the presence of several pyxes to contain the sacred wafer:—

"a pix of Sillver, wayyig viij oz," p. 51.

One of the pyxes belonging to St. Mary's was evidently a very beautiful little work of art with a representation of the crucifixion, p. 244.

Pyx pulley, p. 347.—This pulley would be for the rope or cord to run over, to raise and lower the pyx containing the sacred wafer, that pyx being suspended above the high altar.

Pyx Plum.—The plum of lead, p. 304, to act as a counterpoise to the weight of the suspended pyx, p. 407.

Pyx Rope.—p. 347.

Rods.—Reeds or Rods to light the candles with are mentioned on p. 251:—

CH. V.] *Introd. Pre-Reformation Furniture of the Church.* lxvii

"Payd for ij Reddys to lythe Canddyllys vythe."

Rood.—The great Rood, or Crucifix with its attendant figures of Mary and John, will be found fully described in our text at pp. 224, 228. It appears to have been erected 1496–8, the old Rood being sold 1509–10, p. 271.

Rushes (for pews).—See Pews.

Sconces.—'vj skonces for the queer, viij d,' p. 333.

Scoop.—A 'skop' apparently in use at consecration or 'halloyng,' p. 250.

Settles.—There were several settles in the church, and they seem to have been very similar to the ordinary settle of to-day, with the lower part made to form a box or chest. On p. 53 we find that there were two in the choir, each with a locker, another before the choir, and two long ones in the southern part of the church, 'in the which we were wont to pvt our torchis,' that is, the torches were kept in the box under the seat.

Ships.—The ship was a little vessel which contained the incense from which the censer was filled. On p. 197 the pretty term 'saylyng pece' is used. Two silver ships are mentioned on p. 26. The term 'sauce boat' is in common use to-day.

Shovel.—Shovels of apparently three different kinds are mentioned in our accounts: a 'shode shovyll,' p. 243, for the church; a fire shovel for the vestry, p. 332; 'colys to brenne in the vestrye,' p. 225; and a paring shovel, p. 255, which, according to the Dictionary, was used in the churchyard.

Snuffers.—Snuffers to snuff the candles with are mentioned on p. 296.

Soap.—p. 226.

Sockets.—Sockets of iron "in the Rode lofte to set in the baners," p. 361.

Spoons.—The Inventory of 1553 mentions the presence of "ij shippes with ij spones of silluer," p. 51. The spoons were used to spoon out the incense from the ship or incense boat to the censer.

Stalls in choir.—The stalls in the choir of St. Mary's were probably somewhat more elaborate than ordinary seats. They were newly built or repaired in 1427–8, in which year the accounts record the expenditure of £12—

"for stalles in þe quere," p. 69.

Stools.—Two stools are mentioned in the Inventory on p. 53;

a choir stool costing 7s. 10d. on p. 69, and "ij stolys for the Rectours in the quyre" on p. 358.

Streamers.—In the Inventory on p. 31 "viij smale stremers" are mentioned. They apparently belonged to a canopy borne over the Sacrament in procession, for in the Inventory of 1553 mention is made of—

"a canipi cloth of Red bodkin with viij stremars," p. 51.

Tablet for the Bede Roll, p. 234.—Apparently the list of the names of those to be prayed for in church. See Bede Roll, p. 51.

Tablet for the Ordering of the Choir.—p. 326. Apparently a list of directions on a parchment fixed to a board.

Tablet, Font.—At. p. 275 we meet with a reference not easily understood :—

"Paid for settyng of the hoke þat the Table hangith on by the ffownte—iiij d."

At p. 273 is also a reference to the iron work—

"to the Table by þe founte."

Tablet of the Trinity :—

"a gylt Table of the Trynete for to sett on the high Aulter," p. 33.

Table in Vestry :—

"Item, payd for a table & a payr [of] trestellis to stand in the vestry, to ley the copis apon in festyvall days—ij s," p. 100.

Tapers, Round.—Round tapers are mentioned on p. 149.

Torch iron.—'a crokid Iron to pike torchis withall, iij d,' p. 343.

Torches.—Torches are often mentioned. They appear to have been employed on special occasions, and were apparently kept in stock by the wardens and let out to burn at funerals, the hire being so much. See page 366, etc.

Torches, Staff.—Staff torches appear to have been those used at the altar step :—

"iij staf torches of wex to hold at the levacion," p. 361.

In other words, to burn at the elevation of the Sacrament. At p. 364 we find the entry :—

"iiij staff torches ffor the highe awter."

Towels.—St. Mary's appears to have been especially rich in towels. Towels "to wype on handes" are mentioned on p. 27. Pages 33, 34 contain a long list of towels.

Introd. Pre-Reformation Furniture of the Church. lxix

Trestles.—In 1492–3 a pair of trestles were purchased, p. 185, and in 1519–20 five trestles were made, p. 306.

Tubs.—Apparently these tubs were in use at the time of consecration, or 'halloyng,' p. 250. They belonged to the church, p. 269.

Veils for Lent.—The chancel veil for Lent is noticed on p. 343.

Vestments.—An interesting bill for the repair of vestments will be found at p. 150.

> *Albs.*—Several albs are mentioned in the Inventory on p. 31, six for children on p. 33. Altar cloths and towels were at times made out of old albs, p. 273.
>
> *Alb girdles.*—See pp. 31, 251.
>
> *Almuces.*—Almuces, or furry capes for the two rectors of the choir, are probably indicated in the reference to the purchase of 'Greyes skynnes' on p. 358.
>
> *Amices.*—Several amices are mentioned at p. 31.
>
> *Chasubles.*—See p. 31.
>
> *Copes.*—Copes of various designs are described at p. 31; also six for children. On p. 51 eight children's copes are mentioned. Some of the copes, probably all connected with the Cambridge Chantry, were ornamented with the armorial bearings of William Cambridge, p. 256.
>
> *Fanons.*—These articles are mentioned in the Inventory of 1496–7, p. 31.
>
> *Mitre.*—The mitre referred to at pp. 27, 31 was probably that worn by a chorister on St. Nicholas's Day, at which time it was customary in most churches for a child to be arrayed in diminutive episcopal vestments:—
>
>> "a Myter for a bysshop at seint Nicholas tyde," p. 31.
>
> *Rochets.*—Seven rochets for children are mentioned in the Inventory at p. 33; and nearly the same number on p. 238:—
>
>> "Item, to Margeret Sotton ffor the makyng off vj Rochettes ffor Chelderne to were in the quyre, xij d."
>
> *Stoles.*—Stoles are mentioned in the Inventory on p. 31.
>
> *Surplices.*—Surplices are often referred to. On p. 33 the Inventory mentions eight—
>
>> "for the quere, of þe whiche ij haue no slevys."

The surplice was similar to the ample garment in use in the English Church to-day, and was worn by the parson, p. 282;

the parish priest, p. 266; the clerk, p. 173; the Sexton, p. 260; and the choirmen and boys, p. 321. The boy choristers, as has been noted, wore rochets in the choir, p. 238; and albs, 244.

Tunicles.—The Inventories tell us of several tunicles, p. 31.

Waterpot.—At p. 333 a "pewtur pott for watur for the preistes" is noticed.

Wheelbarrow.—The church wheelbarrow is occasionally referred to, as, for instance, at p. 269.

Window for the Sacrament.—p. 406, for lepers?

Wire for the Roodloft.—At p. 370 a wire and two staples for the Roodloft are mentioned.

CHAPTER VI.
CHANGES IN THE CHURCH AT THE REFORMATION.

THE story of the alterations in St. Mary's church consequent on the Reformation is set down very clearly in our text. In the brief reign of Edward very great changes are recorded by the churchwardens. Under Mary a return to the old system takes place, more or less fully, and with the accession of Elizabeth comes the complete downfall and collapse of the old order.

In this little chapter no attempt has been made to deal with the general aspects of the Reformation, the plan adopted having been simply to collect and place before the reader the principal entries of the churchwardens' expenses in carrying out the decrees of authority.

1547–53. Destruction and Alterations.—The first items in our text which disclose the progress of the Reformation are found under the year 1547–8, where at pp. 386, 387, we see certain sums of money set down as having been paid for the removal of various substantial fittings.

Further sums are also paid for investigations concerning the Chantries, for the purchase of psalters 'for the quyer,' and for the painting of certain 'scriptures' on the rood loft.

In the year 1548–9 we meet with the greatest change in these Records, when, the Chantries having fallen to the king, the entries of their income and expenditure disappear wholly from the annual accounts.

In this year, too, we have the important record of the purchase of two copies of the first edition of the new Book of Common Prayer. The churchwardens also sell the gilt of three 'ymages' and two painted cloths, one of which was purchased by the only churchwarden apparently then in office.

The next year's accounts, 1549–50, record the sale of two of the old service books and a chalice, a pax, a silver bell and twelve ounces of silver, this scrap silver 'beyng claspes of bokes and the busshops myter,' pp. 389 and 58–9.

In this year, too, the 'Table' that 'stode vpon the Alter' was sold (the 'Table of the Trynete,' p. 33), and 'laborers' were employed for ' vj dayes for takyng downe the Alters,' p. 391, three shillings and fourpence being received for one of the slabs for use as a grave-stone, p. 390.

In 1551–2 the 'Inventory of our Churche gooddes' was written (see p. 50), and an entry of the purchase of 'bred and wyne' is recorded. An entry also occurs of sixpence being paid—

"vnto a goulde smith for to take the sylluer ffrom a gospell boke & to waye it," p. 393.

1553–8. Reconstruction of the Old System.—In 1553 the accounts furnish very curiously the conflicting particulars of expenses connected with both the new and the old forms of service; the reason being that this year covered both the end of the reign of Edward VI and the commencement of that of Queen Mary.

Respecting the former we have the entry telling of the sale of four pieces of hair cloth from the old altars. Also another entry recording the payment to carpenter Wynne (by whom for so many years the carpentry work had been carried out) for the making of 'a benche yat went Rownd abowt ye comvnyon boorde.' Sixpence too is paid—

"for the sowynge together of the best alter clothes for to laye on the Commvnyon boorde," p. 396.

On the other side, that of the reconstructing of the old system, we find entries recording the purchase of a chrismatory of pewter and apparently of several books of the old services, p. 396.

On p. 395 two peculiarly interesting entries are recorded:—

"payed for nayles to mende the kytchyn when yt was broken downe for the alter stone."

"payed to the plasterer for plasterynge the kytchyn."

The amounts for these two items have perished with part of the leaf, but clearly the 'alter stone' (presumably the slab of the high altar) had been built into the wall of a kitchen possibly as a temporary expedient for its security.

In 1554, and for several years after, the old forms are in great measure restored, and many of the common entries of former years again reappear.

A new 'shyppe' for incense is purchased, which however, like the chrismatory lately referred to, is also of pewter.

An interesting item on p. 397 is that of the payment of one shilling and eightpence 'for puttyng owt of the scrypture in the roode lofte,' which only in 1547–8 had been painted on at a cost of £4.

On the same page is also an entry recording the purchase of two loads of 'lyme to make the altars,' and at p. 407 the record of the 'borrowynge' of a cross, two candlesticks and a censer, all of which were of silver.

1559. Final Destruction of the Old Forms and Reconstitution of the New.—In 1559, pp. 411–12, the last complete pages of our text, record the details of the final collapse of the ancient forms.

The communion table is made, and the great Rood with its figures of Mary and John, the 'sepulcure,' and the altars, are all taken down. An entry recording that five men were called in with 'v doble rafters' to 'helpe tack downe the great auterston,' tells also of one rafter being broken. The fact helps us, in a measure, to picture the scene in the old church. The demolition appears to have been very complete, so much so that money was expended for—

"lyme & sande, and for whiting wher ye awltrs wer," p. 412.

The sum of sixteenpence too was paid—

"to whight ye raker for too carry awaie all ye rubbushe of ye auters yat did ly at ye cherch dore," p. 412.

By rubbish is probably meant the rubble or loose material.

Our notice of these great changes may close with the record of the payment of twelvepence—

"for bringging downe of ye Imagis to rome lond and other thinges to be burnt," p. 412.

Such is a brief outline of the sequence of events in the parish church of St. Mary's as set down at the time of the Reformation by the churchwardens.

The student will find in our text additional details bearing on the history of the period; and the Inquiries of the Commissioners respecting the valuables of the church, etc., printed at p. 56, will also be found worthy of attention.

CHAPTER VII.

OUR TEXT COMPARED WITH OTHER CITY CHURCH RECORDS.

IT is perhaps necessary that the reader should be in a position to contrast, at any rate to some extent, the system prevailing at St. Mary's with that of other city churches.

An examination of other pre-Reformation city church records will show us that the story of the church of St. Mary at Hill as shown by our text is virtually representative of the churches of medieval London. At the Guildhall Library are deposited the pre-Reformation records of three London city churches in addition to those forming the text of this volume, the churches being respectively those of St. Stephen Walbrook, St. Andrew Hubbard, and St. Mary Woolnoth.

The records of these three churches consist of the accounts of the churchwardens alone, and though they follow more or less closely the same plan as that adopted in St. Mary's accounts are very inferior in scope and arrangement.

We may now proceed to give a very brief analysis of these MSS., and attempt to point out such items as appear to be in any way noteworthy.

ST. STEPHEN WALBROOK.

MS. $\frac{593}{1}$.

The accounts were kept and the office of warden held from the feast of the Annunciation in each year to the same feast in the year following, one warden only generally holding office.

This MS. shows us that the distinction between the parson and parish priest was not restricted to the church of St. Mary at Hill. The words are:—

"to speke with M*aster* p*ar*son when the p*ar*ische prest was in the cowntre"

(Section II, leaf 5).

At Section IV, leaf 9, back, we read of a gown and a livery hood being 'pledge to the chirche.'

The Prophets are mentioned (Section V, leaf 2, back), and the frame over the church door on Palm Sunday is referred to at leaf 51 of the accounts of St. Andrew Hubbard.

An "Irryn to put owt the torchys and a nodyr to pyke the torchys," is mentioned in Section V, leaf 3, back.

At Section VI, leaf 4, mention is made of 'Master dodmer*es* pewe & his wiff*es* pewe.'

At Section VII, plates to set candles in the church are mentioned at leaf 6.

Garlands of 'geloffers' are purchased for St. Stephen's Day (Section XIII, leaf 3, back).

St. Andrew Hubbard, Eastcheap.
MS. $\frac{1279}{1}$.

These accounts were kept sometimes from the feast of the Annunciation, sometimes from Easter to Easter or days in April, sometimes from Michaelmas, the two wardens holding office for one, two, and sometimes three years successively. One warden, by name Ralph Clark, appears to have held the office for years.

On St. Andrew's Day, 1456-7, money was gathered 'at þe Churche dure,' 'margaret þe ffruterer standynge' there (leaf 5). The next year money was again similarly gathered, at this time some one 'sittyng at þe Churche dure' (leaf 9).

In 1475 (leaf 32) the following entry occurs, but whether Margaret Kene paid £2 to beg for herself, or whether her receipts on behalf of the church amounted to as much, can only be guessed, but from the roundness of the sum, the former seems the more probable:—'Item, resceyued of Margaret Kene for hir stondyng atte Chirch dore for a hole yere—ij ħ.' In 1489-90 (leaf 57) £2 3s. 8d. was 'Resceyved of almes in the strete.'

In 1459 a reference to the May Day dancing with the Hobby Horse appears:—'Item, To Mayers child for dawnsyng with þe hobye hors—ij d' (leaf 17, back).

In 1467-9 (leaf 22, back) 'Richemondes wyfes pewe' is mentioned; also eightpence was paid 'to a carpenter and to a dawber for makyng of a thing in the north side of the chirche for droppyng[s?] of candell' (leaf 23).

On more than one occasion the wardens record the gift of very secular articles to the church: 'a harnes of Syluyr,' sold for two-shillings and twopence (leaf 14, back); 'an old gown that was geven to the chirche, by vs sold—ij s vj d' (leaf 28).

The wife of the 'Waferer' is mentioned on leaf 28.

On leaf 36 we have a reference to forms in the roodloft; and at leaf 101, back, 'pewys in the Rode lofte,' which point to a considerable number of seats there.

'The Chirchyng pewe' is mentioned at leaf 19, back.

An iron tray to receive the candle-droppings before a figure is mentioned on leaf 36.

And at leaf 80, back (1500-3), it is noted that eightpence was 'paid ffor a pewe makeyng in the loft for the maydyns.'

The 'boxe that the sacrament hangith in' is mentioned on leaf 40, and on the back of the same leaf reference is made to the payment of a man 'while we were Clerkles to bere a torche with the hosell,' this being a particularly interesting reference to the carrying of a light before the sacrament as it was borne to a sick parishioner.

At leaf 35 iij d is paid 'for Amendyng of the pewe for bugges.'

Coals in the upper vestry to dry the copes, evidently after an out-door procession in the rain, cost a penny in 1481-3 (leaf 43).

A curious item occurs on leaf 51, where the payment of twopence is recorded 'for loppyng of the tree in the chirche yarde for caterpillers.' This tree apparently produced a regular income to the church.

A 'canstyke for the orgyns, iiij d,' is entered on leaf 79, back.

At leaf 83 a halfpenny was paid for 'Syngyng bred.'

In 1523 fourpence was paid to a priest 'for playing on the organs the iij^{de} day of octobre' (leaf 117, back). And in the same year (leaf 119) the following very curious entry was inserted :—

"It ys agreyd by ye consent of ye holl parysshe the vj daye of Septembar anno 1545 :—

ffor all ded bodys that shall dye withyn the paryshe that shall be carryed too powlls, y*a*t the cwrat shall have of ye same part y*a*t ys [..?..] syon for hys paynns, for all ayg[g?]s [ages?] y*a*t the sayd Corse shall be, iiij d, and the byrryar wyll have mase & dyrryge to agre withe the sayd cwratt. And the clarke, for a knyll of a howar long and for hys paynns to powlles, viij d; yf he saye anye dyryge or ryng anye peylles to paye hyme as they canne agre. And yt yys allsoo agreyd of the remorse of charyte for thes parteys above naymyd that they shall paye all swche costes as ys ordynaryly payd yn the paryshe and the rest to be payd owt of the churche boxe by ye handes of ye cherche wardenns; y*a*t ys to saye, the ordynarye ys for everye berar of ye bodys ij d, and for everye berar of ye torchys ij d, and for every howslyng bodye for ye pytt & knylle xiiij d, and wnder age all ta paye x d, and thys to be fwllfylled : ytt ys so thowght mevt and determynyd by ye sayd paryshnars y*a*t thys shall ynduar and contynue for ye spayse of wonn holl yere from the daye abovesayd ; ther naymys that was consentyng as followythe.

The St. Mary Woolnoth accounts call for no particular remark.

The records of the church of St. Andrew, Holborn, to which my attention was kindly directed by Dr. Wickham-Legg and Mr. St. John Hope, are still kept at the church. Such, too, is the case with the records of the church of St. Margaret Patens.

The records of the church of St. Michael, Cornhill, have been printed, and edited by Mr. Overall, and fragments of the records of city churches will be found printed in *Archæologia*.

THE NAMES IN OUR TEXT.

THE following numbers indicate the pages of our text which contain one or more references to the individual to whose name they are appended.

By consulting the pages indicated an outline may be obtained of the lives of some of the parishioners of St. Mary's before the Reformation. We may find the position of their homes, the amount of rent paid, the debts owing, the profession or trade of the head of the house, the Christian names of the different members of the family, the date and place of their burial, and many other details of a medieval parishioner's life.

In most cases to follow the various incidents of the life of a parishioner and assign them to the right individual presents little difficulty. When, however, the Christian name is not given, or both Christian and surname are common to more than one person, or the distinctive trade is not mentioned, the difficulty has at times proved too great to permit the page number to be placed to unquestionably the right individual. In such cases the number has been appended to the parishioner to whom it seems the most likely to belong. For instance, about the end of the fifteenth century there were in St. Mary's parish three men of the name of Paris, of whom two enjoyed the name of William. One Paris was a joiner, another a labourer, and another an almsman receiving relief each Sunday. It is perhaps impossible to say definitely to whom the many little jobs of sweeping the church, watching the Easter Sepulchre, etc., etc., should be assigned. Circumstances seem to point to the employment of the almsman, and to him the uncertain page numbers have been appended, possibly erroneously. He is definitely associated with another almsman in employment for the church at p. 197.

Dawson's child, too, may be the little one of John or Robert Dawson, or of neither. Ysabell Cutler and Elizabeth Cutler are probably the same, though entered here separately. Thomas Mondens also is probably Thomas Mondaye, but the evidence is hardly suffi-

CH. VII.]   *Introduction. The Names in our Text.*   lxxvii

cient to justify placing the numbers of both after one name. When the same name occurs after the death of a similarly-named parishioner it is not unreasonable to suppose that the son takes the father's place, but the question of relationship, when not specified, is often very obscure.

The spelling of the names, though sometimes widely differing in the case of the same individual, has not proved a serious difficulty. Axe may appear as Ex, John Law as John Lowne, Vstum as Huscam, Austhorpe as Alltrope, and so on.

With such difficulties the following pages cannot be regarded as in any way a very satisfactory piece of work. A certain number of mistakes cannot but be present. Still, this index has its value. Generally speaking, it is substantially accurate, and in every case it furnishes the whole material to at once establish its accuracy or error, or the impossibility of establishing either.

Two curious names occur, Drynkmylk and William Naghty Pakke. Two other names may be those of Hebrew families, Jacob and Baltazar the clerk. Some names seem curiously appropriate, Antony Elderton the churchwarden, William Remyngton the alderman, Gymbold the joiner, Alice Smale the washerwoman, etc., etc.

It is believed that every reference to each name has been given, as well as those to individuals mentioned only by their profession or trade. The last reference after a name is frequently that of the burial.

Abarow, Wylliam, 171.
Abell, Richard, grocer, 127, 151, 156, 168, 170, 218, 219, 223, 228, 229, 232, 237.
Adam, 323.
Adam, priest, 237.
Ady, Roger, 63.
Affoo, William, his wife, her servant, and his burial, 293.
Alan, Iohn, curate of St. Mary's, 313.
Aldernes, Mrs., 333.
Aldernesse, Robert, alderman, 49, 262, 263, 272, 280, 287, 288, 291, 299, 312, 313, 319.
Alderston, William, 49, 311, 332.
Alee, Richard, clerk, 279.
Alen, Andrew, conducte, 345.

Alen, William, 'curat of the chirch,' parish priest?, 309, 320, 331, 339, 342.
Alenson, Richard, tayllour, 124, 126, 132, 141, 142.
Alfold, Piers, 16.
Allbyn, Nicholas, sheriff, 210.
Alltrope, John. *See* Austhorp.
Allyn, Wylliam, 50.
Alston, Edmond, curatt, 395.
Althorppe, Mrs., 259, 368.
Amassham, John, 140.
Andrew, Peter, cobler, 126, 129; his wife, 183.
Andrew, St., church of, 305.
Andrew, Thomas, 146; his wife's burial, 196.
Andrew Undershaft, St., 346.

Anne, St., 20, etc. brethehod, 283.
Anntell, Richard, priest, 376.
Antony, 28, 29.
Antony, St., 346, 349.
Appulby, 69, 72.
Archer, John, 51.
Archyre, William, 63.
Armerer, Thomas, 123.
Arondell, William, 208.
Arowsmyth, Thomas, sexten, 359.
Assheborne, Thomas, chantry priest, 199, 204, 205, 210, 212, 261, 303.
Astrey, Lady, 3.
Astryge, Mr., 378.
Atclyff, William, 222, 231, 238, 244; his daughter Julyan, 248; his burial, 299.
Atclyff, William, parson, 21, 22, 30, 31, 194?, 205?; his handwriting, 260, 269, 272, 282, 285, 288, 291, 292, 293, 294, 298, 299, 302, 305, 306, 309; his knell and funeral peals at the Dirge and Mass, 310, 311.
Atclyffe, Mr., 253.
Atclyffe, Mrs., 198, 249.
Atherston, Thomas, parson, 11.
Augustyn, sexton, 324, 329.
Austen, Iohn, 381.
Austen, Mrs., 333.
Austen, Thomas, 219, 307.
Austhorp, Iohn, grocer, 242, 245, 246, 256, 262, 268, 269, 272, 274, 284, 287, 288, 289, 293, 294, 296, 297, 301, 303, 308, 312, 313, 314, 319, 320, 321; his burial, 324.
Austhorp, Robert, 312, 324, 333.
Austhorpe, Nicolas, 55, 57, 58, 260, 385, 394.
Austhrop, Iohn, 344.
Avery, Robert, 316, 319, 320, 377.
Awdewyn, William, 287, 333.
Awthrope. *See* Austhorp.
Axe, Mrs., 263.
Axe, Thoms, conducte, 365, 368, 371, 375.
Aylemer, Mr., 276.

Baale, Iohan, 63.
Baate, Th., 127, 183, 253, 264, 275, 283.
Bachgate, Thomas, 55.
Bacon, Iohn, 62.
Baker, Iohn, 78, 112, 119.
Baker, mason, 229.
Baker, Mr., 328, 330, 332.
Baker, Mrs. Iohn, 122.
Baker, Thomas, 183.
Baker, William, pewtrer, 26, 31, 63, 74.
Balame, Iohn, 264, 302, 306, 310, 323; for organ blowing, 343, 347, 349, 351.
Bale, Robert, waxchandler, 233.
Ballard, wood owner, 337.
Baltazar, the clerk, 343, 345, 355.
Bampton, Iohn, his sister's bequest, 221.
Banastre, sergeaunt, 91.
Banester, Iohn, draper, 262, 263; arrested, 282, 285.
Bankes, William, 300.
Barbour, Iohn, 293.
Barboure, Peter, 207.
Bardeney, Iohn, priest, 230.
Barett, embroiderer, 144, 145, 156, 189.
Barley, Thomas, 299.
Barnard, Henry, 9, 182.
Barne, Sir Georg, knight and Lord Mere, 59.
Barnebe, St., his annual festival, 81, etc. etc.
Barnys, Humfrey, 351.
Baron, 256, 379.
Barrette, Robert, priest, 86.
Bassell, Mr., 50.
Bate, Peter, 391.
Bavyon, Antony, 190.
Baycroffte, Roberte, watirman, 114, 119, 123, 124, 126, 127, 142, 151, 200, 207, 226.
Baxster, Harry, 245.
Beckwythe, Thomas, 361, 364, 366, 375.

CH. VII.] *Introduction. The Names in our Text.* lxxix

Bedelles, William, 218, 221; his grave, 228, 232.
Bedham, Beautrice, 140.
Bedham, Iohn, fishmonger, his will, 16, 28, 29; his chantry, 76, etc. etc.
Belamye, Iohn, priest, 134.
Benedek, Mr., 208.
Benet, mason, 301.
Benett, Anes, his arrest, 174, 181, 190, 194, 206.
Bentley, Iohn, carpynter, 233.
Bet, Henry, 58.
Betman, Iohn, draper, 235.
Bettes, Thomas, conduct, 390.
Bettnam, Nychollas, mason, of ottam yn Kentt, 264, 269.
Beuevage, William, 61, 62.
Billynton, Iohn, his wife, 299.
Bircham, Iohn, 127.
Birde, Iohn, 324, 347, 349, 350, 353, 360, 363, 372, 374, 376, 389.
Blakden, Thomas, conduct, 390.
Blake, Th., 126.
Blancke, Thomas, 408, 409, 410.
Blas, Iohn, 251.
Blase, William, 75, 78, 84, 85, 94.
Bliet, Richard, 77, 80.
Blise, Iohn, 261.
Bodylliʒ, his 'wyffes dowter,' 260.
Bodyly, Thomas, 4.
Bokeler, Gefrey, 70.
Bons, Mrs., 236.
Bonvice, Lawrence, 287.
Bonyfantes, priest, 230.
Bornham, Phelyp, 180.
Borughbrig, Iohn, priest, 298, 309.
Botelere, Richard, 63, 66, 68.
Botolph, St., church of, 4, etc. etc.
Bower, choir boy ?, 148.
Bowere, 173, 186, 198, 214.
Bowghe, Mrs., 263, 294.
Boyes, Moder, 181, 182, 193, 205, 206.
Boyes, William, chantry priest, 152, 165, 174, 177, 189, 201, 208, 212.
Boyes, William, gardyner, 126.

Bradfford, Rychard, 352; his wife, 366.
Bradmere, Iohn, 79; his obit, 97, 116, 129, 147, 162, 172, 183, 184, 197; last year of obit, 213.
Brafild, William, 50, 51, 54, 55, 381, 394, 395, 398.
Brande, Mr., 183.
Bremonger, Iohane, 127, 194.
Bremonger, Iohn, 16, 18, 91, 171.
Breten, Agnes, 142.
Breteyn, Thomas, 92; Mrs., 133.
Breuster, Iohn, tornour, 75, 84, 85, 114, 115, 123, 125.
Breuster, William, 92.
Bright, conducte, 328, 331.
Broke, ffather, 348.
Broke, Iohn, 120; sheriff, 155.
Broke, Mr., 54.
Broke, Richard, warden of the Fraternity of St. Christopher, 325, 331.
Broke, Thomas, 83.
Broke, William, 57, 366; his wife, 374, 383.
Bromfeld, William, 291, 293.
Brood, the raker, his wife, 277.
Browne, Hugh, grocer, 207, 208.
Browne, Iohn, clarke, 147.
Browne, Mrs., wydewe, 125, 138, 139, 152, 153, 156, 159, 160, 166, 209.
Browne, William, chandler, 271, 294.
Bryan, William, ffreuterer, 127.
Bryant, Lord, 179, 190, 191, 203.
Brycer, Rychard, priest, 260.
Bryse, William, priest, organist, 269.
Bull, mason, 219.
Bull, Iohn, sexton, 240, 241, 242, 243, 246, 247, 249, 254, 258, 259, 260, 261.
Bull, Iohn, 251, 253.
Bull, Margaret, 129.
Bull, Reignolde, almsman, 126, 154, 167, 179, 191, 197, 204, 211.

Bullisdon, 266, 270, 275.
Bulman, a bedman, 375.
Bunntynge, a priest of St. Magnus, 406.
Burgeys, Harry, 95.
Burlace, Mr., 355.
Burngyll, Mr., 360, 374, 383.
Burnynghill, Iohn, 352.
Bvrnynghill, William, 314, 331, 338, 342, 363, 375.
Burnynghill, the goodwyff, 307, 329.
Burton, mason, 104, 105, 108.
Bvrton, Garret, wexe-chandelar, 58.
Burton, Ieram, 404.
Burton, Stevyn, 107.
Burton, William, 14.
Busshe, Nicholas, 61.
Busshope, William, tailowr, 76, 114, 115, 119.
Byfelde, Robert, sheriff, 90.
Bynge, Thomas, choir boy, 148, 162.
Bynkes, Thomas, 168, 170, 181, 182, 193, 205, 206, 207.
Byrde, Thomas, carpynter, 104, 167.
Byrkeby, Iohn, 75.
Byrlyng, Iohn, goldsmyth, 125, 141, 142; his widow, 157, 159, 160, 168, 169, 181, 182, 210, 211.
Byrtte, Thomas, lyme burner, 265.

Caley, Thomas, 127.
Cambregge, 67, 68.
Cambridge, Alice, 14.
Cambridge, Anne, 14.
Cambridge, Iohane, 14.
Cambridge, Luke, 14.
Cambridge, William, grocer, his will, 14, 30; his chantry, 76, etc. etc.; his arms in the red copes, 256, 273, 311.
Candishe, Edmond, 50, 51, 56, 57, 59, 391, 392, 394, 395, 398.
Capell, William, sheriff, 155.
Careden, Rychard, ffuller, 115, 123, 126.
Carpenter, Iohn, 248, 349.

Carter, his wife, 360.
Caston, curat, 411.
Cator, William, embroiderer, 76, 86
Catur, Iohn, 341.
Caumpnel, Iohn, clarke, 147.
Cauntbrigge, William, ironmonger, 17.
Caunterbery, Th., 236.
Causton, Basill, 5.
Causton, Eve, 5.
Causton, Iohn, mercer, his will, 4; his chantry, 75, etc. etc.
Causton, William, 5.
Cayes, Th., waterman, his bequest to the church, 236.
Centon, Roger, conduct?, 375.
Challenger, Raffe, 369.
Chaloner, Roger, 318, 324, 329, 338, 342, 360, 374, 378, 379.
Chambre, William, 334.
Chamlle, Sir Rogier, knight, Chif Ivstis of Yngland, 59.
Channon, Mr., curate, 349.
Chappell, the waturberer, 328.
Chaundeler, Iohn, tyler, 102.
Chawrey, Mr., mayer, 210.
Chechelly, Donston, conducte, 352, 355, 359, 362.
Chelmysford, Richard, 236.
Chelmysho, Rychard, ioyner, 114, 121, 124, 126, 127, 141, 142, 143, 144, 149, 157, 159, 160, 169, 181, 190, 194, 206, 207.
Chibbourne, Mr., tax collector?, 391.
Chirche, Mr., 292.
Christopher, St., 20, 77; paresshe of, 95; bretherhed, 283; chapel of, 364, 366.
Chylde, Henry, raker, 296, 300.
Clark, Alis, 303.
Clarke, Iohn, salter, 126, 128.
Clarke, Thomas, pevterar, 58.
Clarkenwell, My Lady of, 286.
Claver, Robert, clerke, 281, 282.
Clayton, Thomas, 299, 300, 304, 308, 312, 316, 319, 321, 338, 342, 348,

361, 363, 364, 368, 372, 380, 383, 390, 396, 398, 408.
Clement, 84.
Clement atte hill, 92, 111.
Clement, St., 20.
Clerk, Harry, 63, 78, 82.
Clerke, 102.
Clerke, Hew, 75, 83, 84, 85, 91, 163.
Clerke, Iohn, 74, 76, 78, 93, 110.
Clerke, lyme man, 107.
Clerke, Mr., counsellour, 387, 389.
Clerke, Robert, 84, 91, 171, 176, 186, 187, 199, 200, 208, 215, 238.
Cleston, sawyer, 337, 338.
Cleton, Mr. Thomas, thellder, 54, 55, 392.
Cleton, Mrs., 398.
Cleton, Thomas, 50.
Cloce, Richard, 126, 142, 143, 146, 170, 182, 183, 187, 191, 194, 205, 207, 214, 232, 245.
Cloos, Ricardo, 34.
Clopton, Hugh, sheriff, 140.
Cobbe, brewer, 92, 111.
Codbeem, Iohn, carpynter, 229.
Cokke, Iamys, wever, 76, 77, 84, 92, 111.
Cokkes, Rauff, waxchandler?, 173, 236.
Cokkes, Thomas, 363.
Cokkeshed, Iohn, of Kent, 366.
Coldale, Thomas, organ blower, 362, 364, 371, 379.
Colette, Harry, sheriff, 90; mayer, 140.
Collynes, Vxor, 410, 413.
Collyns, Iohn, ffyshemonger, 22; his wife buried, 241, 253, 317; his wife, his gravestone, 318.
Colman, Iohn, butcher, 105, 113, 123.
Colman, Thomas, butcher, 125.
Colman, Tyll, 327.
Colmas, Mr., 344.
Colyn, Thomas, 126, 142, 146, 161, 171, 212, 213, 221, 226, 227, 230, 231, 232, 238, 239; his daughter buried in the church, 241.

Colyns, Iohn, priest, 34, 75, 79, 98; terment of, 146; again, 161; his obit, 222.
Colyns, Thomas, 244, 253, 267.
Combys, William, chantry priest, 188, 192, 226.
Condall, Iohn, his wife's burial, 196, 212; his mayde buried, 236, 268, 272, 274, 276, 287, 288, 306.
Condall, Mrs., 291.
Condall, Mrs., 307.
Constantyne, carpenter, 199.
Conteryn, Marion, marchaunte of venyse, 28, 29.
Conteryn, Peter, 28.
Cook, William, 126.
Cooke, Iohn, carpyndor, 411.
Coote, Mr., sheriff, 168.
Copynger, Mr., 46, 377.
Cornewales, Iohn, priest, 383.
Cornysh, Mr., 275.
Cornysshe, Richard, priest, 98.
Coulverton, belfownder, 275.
Courtman, William, 169, 170, 171, 190.
Coveney, Iohn, 299, 303, 341.
Crase, Nycholas, conducte, 362.
Crescrofte, Iohn, 126, 212.
Crome, Dr., 50.
Crompe, Davy, 241, 245.
Crosby, Iohn, carpenter, 94, 104, 106.
Crowcher, Iohn, 353, 372, 380, 394.
Crulle, Mrs. Thomas, 78.
Crulle, Thomas, 78.
Crycke, Robart, wollmonger, 125, 155; his hall door, 168, 210.
Cryke, Richard, vpholster, 87, 91, 107, 113, 123, 140.
Curtyll, William, patynmaker, 144, 145.
Cutler, Elizabeth, 115.
Cutler, Ysabell, rent of her shop, 113.

Dalywagge, Iohn, priest, 98.
Danyell, Robert, 377.

Darby, Mr., 268.
Darlyngton, Iohn, conducte, 314, 315.
Davy, chantry priest, 144, 153, 156, 157, 159, 165, 167.
Davy, Iohn, clerke, 282.
Davy, William, conduct?, 390.
Dawber, Iames, or Iames the dawber?, 139.
Dawe, William, 'our base,' 393.
Dawson, Iohn, 287, 374, 379.
Dawson, his child, 366.
Dawson, Robard, 261.
Day, Iohn, conduct, 371, 375, 380, 384.
Debenham, Robert, clarke, 172, 181, 182, 184, 196, 197, 200, 207, 208, 212; parish clerk, 218, 223, 228, 232, 237; his bequest, 236, 239.
Delanavsa, Iohn, 187.
Densell, Mr., of lyncolles in, 326.
Derham, Iohn, grocer, 127, 142, 143, 144, 145, 157, 158, 173, 182, 191, 199, 204, 205, 227, 231, 236, 239, 240, 241, 245.
Devardys, Thomas, 182, 193.
Develyn, Water, 183, 199, 257; burial of his mother, 263, 284; burial of his sister, 286.
Dewblyn, Iohn, 127, 129.
Dewblyn, Mrs., 129.
Dey, Iohn, 16, 18, 94.
Diall, Mr., 359.
Dighton, Iohn, capper, 76, 92, 111, 112.
Dighton, William, 86, 87.
Dockyng, Richard, 127.
Dod, Thomas, warden of the Fraternity of St. Christopher, 325.
Dokelyn, Iohn, 82, 92, 111, 124.
Donyng, gong farmer, 240.
Dorant, Iohn, 179; his burial, 261.
Dorant, Mrs., 261.
Doune, Richard, 65.
Downyng, Robert, 167.
Dowsyng, Markeret, 210.
Draper, Iohn, laborer, 120.

Draper, Thomas, 411, 412, 413.
Drynkemylke, Rychard, 249; his burial in the church, 257, 291.
Drynkmylk, his wife's bequest, 283.
Duerey, William, 126.
Dukkelyng, Mrs. (Ann?), 31, 281, 374. .
Duklyng, Iohn, ffysshmonger, 33, 75, 77; his manne, 78; rent of his shop, 112, 126, 133, 142, 146, 158, 182, 185, 205, 212, 221, 222, 231, 232; his wife buried, 236; 238, 239, 241, 245, 246; his bell used to ring the parish priest's knell, 267; his burial, 267.
Duklyng, Thomas, 271, 272, 277, 280, 283, 287, 288, 315, 318, 319, 320, 345; buriall place, 348.
Dutton, Ffulk, 360.
Dunstan, St., 16, 64.
Dyckson, Wylliam, grocer, 124, 126, 133.
Dye, William, 180.
Dye, William, butcher, 170, 174.
Dye, William, pastyller, 141, 143, 144, 145, 156, 157, 159, 168, 169.
Dykson, laborer, 103.

Edmond, 349, 353.
Edmond, Henry, salter, 22; his wife buried, 146, 230, 231, 232, 235, 239, 253, 259, 260, 262, 263, 288, 294, 320.
Edmond, Mrs., 291.
Edmondes, William, clarke, 147, 162, 172, 180.
Edward I, 1.
Edward II, 1.
Edward IV, 74, 75, 76, etc.
Edward VI, 50, 60, 373.
Edyall, Iohn. *See* Ideall.
Elderton, Antony, 342, 347, 349, 368.
Eleyn, St., 7, etc.
Elizabeth, queen of Henry VII, 247.
Ellys, Richard, the Morowe Mas preist, 317, 321, 376.

CH. VII.]   *Introduction. The Names in our Text.*   lxxxiii

Elmys, William, 198, 225.
Elssame, Wyllyam, conduct?, 409.
Elyard, Iohn, 334.
Elymesford, 67.
Endyrby, 49.
Erkenwald, St., 379.
Everod, the chyld, 172.
Evyngar, Andrew, salter, 22, 23, 24, 25, 49, 222, 245, 246, 250, 253, 260, 287, 288, 291, 293, 303, 312, 313, 319.
Evyngar, Ellyn, 22, 23, 24, 25.
Evyngar, Elysabeth, 22, 23, 24, 25, 376.
Ex, Thoms. *See* Axe.
Exmo, Thomas, goldsmyth, 114, 119, 123, 125, 136, 137, 139, 177, 189.
Eylewyke, Iohn, smyth, 275.

Fayry, sawyer?, 338.
Ffabyan, Mr., alderman, 222.
Ffaryngton, Edmond, 298.
Ffayrstede, William, 1.
Ffelyn, Godfrey, 361.
Ffenowys, Mr., sargantt, 203.
Fferour, Thomas, clarke of Seynte Andrews, 131.
Ffissh, Iohn, grocer, 76, 83, 85, 109, 114, 122, 123, 125, 134, 153, 166, 178, 190, 202, 398?.
Ffitzherberde, Robert, 146, 161, 171, 184, 196.
Fflecher, Richard, 118.
Ffletcher, Merke, priest, 376, 378.
Ffold, arrested, 353.
Fformes, Iohn, 126.
Ffounes, Watur, 296.
Ffox, Richard, conduct?, 384.
Ffox, Robert, conduct?, 380.
Ffoxley, 354, 355.
Ffrances, Wylliam, 261.
Ffranses, 214.
Ffurgons, Thomas, his wife, 307.
Ffynche, Thomas, tailor, 94, 96, 115.
Foox, Iohn, 245, 253.
Fovx, 174, 178.

Francke, Mr., 400, 402.
Frauncen de Boyes, 227.
Frogenolde, Mr., 408.
Fuller, I., 208.
Fysher, Harry, clarke, 242.

Gabryell de Vrs, 114, 121, 123, 125, 126, 141, 154, 167, 179, 191, 204, 211.
Gackes, Mr., 399.
Galleson, Watkyn, 156, 159, 169, 181, 194, 206.
Game, Robert, 304, 308, 311, 312, 313, 319, 335, 338, 342, 356, 363, 368; his burial, 374.
Game, Robert, 377.
Gardiner, Mr., Mayer, 90.
Garlond, Richard, 48.
Garrett, Richard, smyth, 229.
Garrolde, Gylys, gardener, 178, 190, 193, 206.
Geffrey, Mrs. W., 77, 132.
Geffrey, William, 75, 126.
Gele, William, 187, 215.
Gemet, William, mason, 68.
Gentill, Gylbart, draper, 227, 239, 242, 263, 273, 274, 278, 279, 281, 285, 288, 289, 290; his knell, and 'ryngyng of the pelis' at his buryeng, 310; his buryall in the Churche, 311.
Gentyll, Mrs., 285.
Gentyll, William, 287.
George, St., 16, 79.
Gelham, William, 13, 63.
Giles, I., 209.
Gilman, Thomas, his wife, 348.
Gladwyn, Iohan, 63.
Gladwyn, Nicholus, condukte, 290.
Gliatson, Iohn, morrowmas priest, 405.
Glocetir, Michael, organ maker, 81, 125, 135.
Golder, Robert, conduct, 390.
Goldsmyth, Thomas, goldsmith, 81.
Good, Iohn, warden of the Fraternity of St. Christopher, 325.

Goodneston, Thomas, 352, 353, 357, 358.
Goodwyn, 276.
Goodwyn, Iohn, his wife, 306, 315.
Goodwyn, Ione, 376, 383.
Goodwyn, Mrs., her husband buried, 360, 374.
Gooswell, Elizabeth, 31, 374.
Gose, conduct, 345.
Goslyn, Richard, 3; ironmonger, his will, 13, 17, 63; his chantry, 76, etc. etc.
Gosselyn, Beatrice, 13.
Goswell, Christofur, 287, 291.
Gowge, Richard, clerk, 234, 334, 341.
Grafton, Rycharde, 50.
'Grandam,' the kynges, her gift, 268.
Grapeles, Robart, tayllour, 124, 134, 144, 156, 157, 159, 160, 168, 169, 170, 171, 181, 190, 194, 205, 227.
Graye, Wylliam, 126, 196, 221.
Grene, Mr., costomer, 262.
Grene, Mighell, parishe clerke, 348, 350, 352, 355, 359; changes to conduct, 362, 365, 368, 371.
Grene, William, 112, 123.
Grenne, Mr., 267, 296.
Grenwaie, Iohn, 413.
Gretyng, Iohn, 13, 61, 62, 63, 71, 72, 74.
Griffith, 316.
Gunter, Mother, 286, 290.
Gybson, Hewe, curatt, 401.
Gybson, Iohn, a servant, his bequest, 241.
Gyldyr, Symond, priest, 351.
Gyles, Mr., of the chapel royal in the Tower ?, 328.
Gylys, attorney, 256.
Gymbold, ioyner, 306.
Gyrscrofte, 245.
Gysborow, George, clerk, 240; parish clerk, 242.

Hacheman, Iohan, 63.
Hachis, Thomas, 287.

Hackett, Iohn, conduct ?, 384.
Hakeneye, Alyce, wife of Richard Hakeneye, her burial, 225.
Hakeneye, Richard, 225.
Halhed, Iohn, grocer, 3, 4, 122, 124, 126, 127, 129, 140, 142, 143, 144, 146, 157, 158, 161, 175, 211, 223, 225, 227, 231, 236; the bell tolled for his mayde and his children buried, 237, 253; his writing in the great book, 255; his burial, 259.
Halhed, Mrs., burial of her mayd in the churchyard, 259, 267, 284.
Halhed, Robert, priest, 141.
Halis, Christopher, 21.
Halke, Edmonde, mason, 104.
Hall, Thomas, priest, 346.
Hall, William, watirman, 112, 122, 124, 126, 132, 150, 162, 164, 180, 182, 188, 193, 205, 206, 207, 213; his burial, 236; his bequest, 237.
Halle, Robert, chantry priest, 176, 189, 201.
Hallynge, Emnot, 61.
Halsangre, Iohn, 61.
Hamond, Margery, 1.
Hamond, Robert, corder, 1.
Hamond, Thomas, conduct ?, 386.
Hamsterlay, Iohn, 175.
Hanckes, Gyles, conduct, 402, 409.
Harby, Mr., his man, 286.
Hardyman, doctor, parysche pryste, 409.
Hardynge, Robert, sheriff, 90, 259, 283; his child buried, 286, 291, 298.
Harford, William, 207.
Harison, Iohn, 55.
Harman, 299.
Harman, Thomas, son of William Harman, 320, 325, 328.
Harman, William, rent of house over Ducklyng's shop, 113, 116, 117, 122, 126; burial of his wife, 222, 241; his wife, 244; his bequest, 244, 246.

CH. VII.]   *Introduction. The Names in our Text.*   lxxxv

Harris, Iohn, 160, 169, 205, 206, 207.
Harris, Iohn, gardiner, 115, 121, 124?, 127, 141, 144, 156, 157, 159.
Harris, Iohn, watirman, 113, 123, 141, 142, 143, 144, 145, 156, 159, 169, 170, 193.
Harrison, Villiam, his wife, 169, 170, 181, 194, 205, 206, 208.
Harrydeson, William, 76.
Harrys, Mychaell, 79, 116, 130.
Harryson, Iohn, 113, 123, 124, 126, 133.
Harryson, 403.
Hartfforthe, Mrs., 409.
Harwarde, lyme man, 102.
Hasle, Water, 63, 71.
Hatclyff. *See* Atclyffe.
Hayward, Mr., 410.
Held, Thomas, 64.
Hemmes, William, 207, 212, 218, 219.
Henley, Iohn, priest, 81.
Henry VI, 63, 74.
Henry VIII, 312, etc.
Herd, Harry, 271.
Hethe, the singing man, 398.
Hetheman, Iohn, 26, 74.
Heton, Georg, 50.
Hewes, Iohn, 127, 212.
Hewys, Mrs., 296.
Hewys, William, 284, 292, 294.
Heyes, Robert, 51.
Heyforde, Humfrey, mayere of london, 90.
Heyns, Iohn, 51.
Heyward, Phillip, of Colchester, 308.
Heyward, Robert, 287.
Hickelyng, 215, 248.
Hikman, Robert, 318.
Hill, Rowland, 60.
Hille, Clement, 76.
Hilton, Alexaunder, 325, 330, 334, 342; his burial, 345; his wife, 353.

Hilton, Mr., priest, 347; summoned, 349.
Hobbes, Iohn, conduct, 402, 405.
Hobye, Christopher, 126.
Hochyns, Thomas, 152.
Hoggekyn, peyntour, 70.
Hogges, Iohn, his wife, 181, 194, 206.
Hoggeson, Thomas, sexten, 362, 365, 368, 371, 375.
Holderness, Robard, merchaunt haberdasher, 22.
Holstocke, Mr., 394.
Holstoke, William, 51, 404, 405, 408, 410, 413.
Holyngwourth, William, 317, 345.
Hontyngdon, 70.
Hopkyns, of Whytstabyll, 245.
Horle, Thomas, mason, 177.
Horne, Iohn, parson, 14.
Horne, Iohn, priest, 222.
Horne, Mr., 146, 161, 212, 218.
Horne, William, 175, 198.
Hourdman, Richard, 347.
How, Iohn, orgon maker, 240, 327, 369, 395, 407.
Howe, Alys, 50.
Howell, Iohn, priest, 243.
Howorthe, Iohn, 407.
Howtyng, William, 274, 286, 291, 294.
Howtynge, Robard, fishmonger, 22, 127, 182, 194, 195, 196, 205, 223, 227, 228, 231, 235, 236, 238, 239, 241; his daughter buried, 245; his burial in the church, 259; his bequest towards the building of the church steeple, 259.
Hubbard, Iamys, 332.
Hubert, Iames, 342.
Humfrey, priest, 339.
Hunt, Harry, sexten, 265.
Hunt, Mathewe, 221; burial of his wife, 222.
Hunt, Mrs., 78, 257.
Hunt, Thomas, draper, 22, 113, 122, 125, 126, 142, 143, 144, 145, 158,

159, 183, 185, 206, 213, 227, 231, 238, 240, 248, 249; burial, 253; his bequest, 263.
Hunte, Christian, 126.
Huntyngfeld, Iohn, 168, 181, 194, 205.
Husecam, Thomas. *See* Vstum.
Huskham, William, 303.
Husse, Wylliam, grocer, 248, 259, 263, 293.
Hussy, Lord, 179, 190, 191, 203.
Hutton, Iohn, 276.
Hychekoke, Harry, 267.
Hynde, Richard, 316.

Ideall, Iohn, 316, 319, 320, 342; his wife, his burial, 360.
Inger, 201.
Ingylby, Iamys, 287; his wife, 291.
Inkyrssale, William, 83.

Iackson, Hugh, 141.
Iacob, Iohn, 78.
Iames, William, sompnour, 164.
Iane, quene, 373.
Iasper, Frauncis, 405.
Ienet, Mother, 34, 291.
Ientyll. *See* Gentyll.
Ientyll, Mrs., 34; her burial, 291.
Iesper, basket maker, 58.
Ihesus, 112, etc.
Ioegame, Mr., 409.
Iohane of ffreestone, 5.
Iohn, carpynter?, 72, 111.
Iohn, morrowmass priest, 340.
Iohn a Bristowe, 113, 123, 124, 127, 134.
Iohn a Downe, 126.
Iohn a Grene, 126.
Iohn a Leyton, 227; his wife's brother buried, 276.
Iohn a Mylton, baker, 126, 127, 128; for spiced Bunnes, 139, 144, 157, 158, 159, 160, 169, 170, 178, 179, 205, 223, 227, 231, 236, 238, 239, 253, 257.
Iohn de Pount, 29.

Iohn fight Iohn, 300.
Iohn, Mr., 171.
Iohn of Gildeford, citizen and clerk, 8.
Iohn of Langton, 5.
Iohn of Oxenf, 5.
Iohn of Vappyng, 253.
Iohn the Baptist, St., 11; chapel of St. Iohn, 282, 283; window of St. Iohn, 313.
Iohnson, baker, 50.
Iohnson, Dyryke, wever, 193, 206.
Iohnson, Iohn, bocher, 49, 75, 77, 105, 127; his wife, 129.
Iohnson, Iohn, cowcher, 92.
Iohnson, Mrs., her husband buried, 360.
Iohnson, Myhell, wever, 205.
Ionkyns, Iohn, 113, 123, 124.
Ionson, Garard, 126.
Ionys, Iohn, 183.
Ionys, Robert, 46.
Ioye, Henry, curat, 401, 405, 406.
Ioynner, Richard, 150, 234.
Ioynour, Thomas, 63.
Iryke, 192, 204.

Katermole, mason, 248.
Katherine, St., 13; the 'yle,' 224, etc. etc.
Kechen, Christouer, carpynter, 100, 103, 105, 106, 108, 134, 137, 138, 155, 164, 174, 176, 177, 178, 180, 186, 187, 208, 215.
Kelby, Iohn, chantry priest, 211, 212.
Kellay, Iohn, 175.
Kello, Harry, tayllour, 114, 125, 126, 134, 144, 145, 154, 158, 159, 182; his burial, 196; his son?, 207, 209.
Kellow, Annes, 212.
Kellowe, Mrs., buried in St. Stephen's chapel, 249.
Kelly, William, 50, 51, 392.
Kenbey, Robert, 207.
Kerton, Stephen, alderman, 50.

Kevald, Stephen, 52, 55, 393, 394, 395, 396.
Keyle, Thomas, priest, 86.
Knolles, Thomas, 14.
Knyght, Mr., 385.
Knyghte, Harry, tyler, 102, 105, 106, 108, 137.
Kokkes, Rychard, 191.
Koo, Geffrey, 103.
Kyght, Mr., 270, 275.
Kyng, 300.
Kyngeston, William, 16.
Kyrke, 387.
Kyrkeby, Iohn, 92.

Lambys, Iohn, 352.
Lame, Mrs., her dowghter, 408.
Lamerton, 323.
Large, Mrs., 114, 119.
Law, Iohn, parych clarke, 246, 249, 254, 258, 259, 261, 265, 268, 271; his grave, 282; and burial, 283.
Lawle, waxchaundeler, his wyffe, 330.
Lawrence, Robert, 333.
Lawson, Thomas, clerk, 330, 334.
Lawson, William, 21.
Ledale, Thomas, ffyschmonger, 246; his wife, 249.
Lennard, conduct, organist, 237, 242.
Leonard, St., 13; paresshe of, 95.
Leppam, 183.
Leversham, his wife, 400, 408.
Levesham, William, capper, 76, 88, 92.
Lewes, Mr., the kynges ffisissyan, 76, 114, 119, 123, 125, 138, 152, 166, 177.
Leynthorpe, Mr., 244.
Loffden, Alys, 114, 119, 135, 136, 137.
Lok, Roberd, 71.
Lombard, Gabryell, 112.
Lording, Mr., 412.
Lorimor, Mr., 54, 395, 399.
Lorymer, Richard, 224.

Lorymer, Symonde, 276.
Lorymer, Thomas, 376, 380, 392.
Losse, Hevghe, esquire, 57.
Lovell, Iohn, chantry priest, 179, 192.
Lovyer, Iohn, priest, 112, 124, 129, 132, 141.
Lovyndon, Alice, 76.
Lowndes, Mr., 403, 412.
Lucas, Iohn, clerk, 8.
Lucas, Thomas, 55, 58, 385, 388, 389, 392, 394, 395, 411.
Luke, Mrs., 49.
Lumbarde, Iohn, 219.
Lumbarde, Lewis, 76.
Lun, William, priest, 86.
Ly, Mr., of Croydon, the church bells rung for, 248.

Maderson, Hew, smythe, 256.
Magnus, St., church of, 81, etc.
Malbe, Artheur, 51, 382.
Maltby, Thomas, 358, 369, 372, 376.
Maltbye, William, priest, 124, 129, 133.
Man, Nycholas, the basse, 389.
Man, William, conduct?, 390.
Mandyke, Mr., 111.
Manfild, Pattrik, priest, 346.
Mardantt, Mr., 191, 203.
Margaret, St., church of, 91.
Markes, Iohn, 126.
Markham, Iohn, 271, 293; his wife, 294.
Marklew, Thomas, priest, 135.
Marow, Mr., 178, 179, 198.
Marowe, Th., 30.
Marowe, William, 30, 169, 203.
Marowe, William, Junr., 30.
Marten, Thomas, 280, 285, 286; his burial, 287, 289.
Marton, Thomas, 386.
Martyn, of Whytstabyll, 245.
Mary, queen, 398, 406.
Mary, St., constantly occurring.
Mascall, Iohn, 158, 182, 184, 194, 196, 199, 205, 206, 212, 216, 217,

221, 222, 225, 228, 231, 232; his grave, 236; ringing his knell, 238.
Mascall, Mrs., 236.
Mascall, Stephene, 236.
Mason, Iohn, 214.
Mason, Richard, 67.
Mason, Roger, parish clerk, 315, 316, 318, 324, 329.
Materson, Hewe, ssmyth, 199, 229.
Mathew, I., mayer, 168.
Mathewe, Iohn, 367.
Matryvers, Edmond, conducte, 352, 355, 359, 362, 365.
Matwarde, Iohn, priest, 209.
Maude, 2.
Maunsefelde, Mr., 405, 406.
Maunsefelde, William, 127, 212.
Mawnde, Robert, mason, 244, 245, 254, 257.
May, Thomas, conduct, his wife, 271, 390.
Medener, Iohn, a servant, 259.
Mershe, Harry, paynter, 62, 63, 71, 75, 92, 93, 112, 124, 126, 133, 141, 142, 143, 175, 186; for the gret Belle for his wife, 212, 213; his servant, 226, 234, 278.
Merten, Thomas, 257.
Meryall, William, clothear, 294, 296, 301.
Metforde, the city swordbearer, 90.
Michael, St., his festival, 85, etc. etc.
Michelson, Robert, 126.
Middilton, Roger, wexchaundeler, 91, 92, 129, 132, 144, 149, 157, 164, 174, 188, 199, 212.
Mille, William, 83, 93.
Miln, William, ironmonger, 3, 113, 122, 125, 127, 141, 142.
Milward, William, 329.
Modley, Iohn, 75, 80, 81, 83, 94, 98.
Mondaye, Thomas, sexten, 334, 339, 341, 345, 347, 348, 352, 355, 378, 380, 384, 386, 388, 390; olde father mondaye, 398, 402, 405, 407, 409.

Mondaye, William, parishe clarke, 388, 390, 398, 402, 406, 409.
Mondens, Thomas, 270, 284, 287, 291, 294, 314.
Mondes, Thomas, yrmonger, 137, 153, 155, 175, 187, 199, 215; chyrchwarden of seynt botolfes, 220, 223.
Mongeham, Alyse, 21.
Mongeham, Iohn, fishmonger, will of, 19, 30, 228, 236, 250, 254, 256, 261, 262, 263, 272, 283, 285, 287; his burial in the south aisle, 287.
Mongeham, Ione, 21.
Mongeham, William, 21.
Mongeham, Mrs., 303, 307, 366.
Mongombre, Iamys, 260, 261, 262; his wife, his burial, 263.
Monke, Mr., waxchandler, 255, 257.
Monnox, his wife, 390.
Moore, George, 352.
Moore, Thomas, 383, 384.
Morden, Mr., 178, 179.
More, tymberman, 67, 70.
Mores, priest, 277.
Morres, the base, 329.
Morton, Iohn, his wife, 390.
Mortram, Iohn, priest of St. Paul's cathedral and chantry priest of St. Mary's, 75, 77, 86, 89, 97, 182, 197, 213.
Morys, William, 74.
Mott, Roger, 132.
Mott, William, plommer, 139, 153, 154, 166, 168.
Motte, Iohn, carpinter, 76, 92, 104, 106, 115, 123.
Mowce, Iohn, capper, 125, 209.
Mowce, Iohn, carpenter, 123, 136.
Mowce, Iohn, clerk, 114, 144, 145, 156, 159, 169, 181, 194, 195, 206, 209.
Mowce, Thomas, capper, 145, 156, 159, 169, 181, 194, 195.
Mowce, Thomas, clark, 170.
Mowce, Thomas, hewrer, 144.

CH. VII.] *Introduction. The Names in our Text.* lxxxix

Mowce, old, 138, 139; young, 139, 153, 210, 223.
Mvndy, Thomas, 55.
Mychell, Iohn, curat, 405, 407.
Myles, Sawnder, 61.

Naghty Pakk, William, priest, 98.
Nasyng, Iohane, 9.
Nasyng, Iohn, brewer, 9, 18; his chantry, 94, etc. etc.
Neele, Iohn, parson of St. Botolph, 4.
Neele, Iohn, 168.
Neell, Alice, 10.
Neell, Iohn, priest, 340.
Neell, William, 10.
Nele, Iohn, 193, 205, 206, 207, 227.
Nell, Iohn, priest, 250; his chalice mended, 270.
Nell, Iohn, 170.
Nevell, Iohn, 102, 127.
Nevell, Mr., 355.
Nevell, ironmonger, 106.
Newgate, Richard, conducte, 362, 365, 368.
Newton, Iohn, 222.
Nicholas, St., 6, 31.
Nicolas, bishop of London, 59, 60.
Nicollson, Thomas, 392.
Nixsons, 291.
Noneley, Richard, husband of Mergret, 289.
Nonnelaye, Mrs. Mergret (her first husband was William Prewne?), buys an old bedstead, 232, 233; her grant of money, 244; her servant buried, 249, 263; her funeral knell, 281, 283, 287; of her Obit, 288, etc.; her children, William and Mergret, etc., 289, 296, 301, 308.
Norffolk, Iohn, priest, 62, 66.
Nors, Mrs., 253.
North, Mr., brycklear, 412.
Northfolke, Iohn, organist, 321, 322; condukt, 324, 326, 327, 329, 334, 339, 340, 341, 345, 346, 348, 351, 352.

Norton, Philip, priest, 75, 84, 97, 118.
Norwych, Mr., sergeaunt, 326.
Notte, Iohn. *See* Nutte.
Nutte, Iohn, 234, 238.
Nycolson, Robert, 376.

Odiham, Richard, 4.
Odiham, Robert, mercer, 158, 169, 170, 171, 180, 182, 213, 222.
Oklond, Robert, orgon player, 365, 368.
Olyver, George, 113, 124.
Olyver, Wylliam, 176, 188, 195, 200, 207, 232, 244.
Organ, Iohan, 63.
Organ, William, 61.
Osborn, Iohn, 380.
Osborn, Mr., 370, 374.
Overey, William, 146, 195, 205, 206, 216; his burial, 222; his wife, 225.
Oxenbrege, Godfrey, 171, 184, 196.

Page, Richard, 117, 164.
Pagename, Mr., 222.
Palme, the attorney, 282.
Palmer, Iohn, 74, 76, 91, 93, 110.
Palmer, William, priest, 80, 133, 164.
Papworth, Thomas, 51.
Paris, William, almsman, 80, 81, 83, 99, 113, 117, 123, 124, 131, 132, 134, 136, 141, 148, 149, 154, 167, 173, 179, 191, 197, 204, 211.
Paris, William, ioynner, 156, 168, 170, 174, 185, 186, 187, 197, 198, 207.
Paris, Iohn, laborer, 99, 103.
Parkyns, Iohn, priest?, a bass, 405.
Partriche, Iohn, butcher, 213, 214, 302, 341.
Partriche, Ione, 376.
Pasmer, William. *See* Pattysmer.
Patten, William, clerke, 348, 350, 352, 355; now parish clerk, 359, 362; paryshe clerk, 365, 368, 371, 375, 380, 384; his wife, 390.

Pattysmer, William, 392, 398, 400, 401, 402, 404; his burial, 408.
Pawnter, Davy, goldsmyth, 209.
Pebyll, Harry, marener, 193, 205, 206.
Pegrym, laborer, 224.
Peirson, Richard, embroiderer, 310, 311.
Pekman, Edward, taylor, 235.
Pemberton, Mr., sheriff, 168.
Pembroke, Earl of, 4.
Penrethe, Roger, 115, 121, 123.
Peny, Robert, 63.
Percy, Alan, parson, 319, 322, 325, 332, 342, 344, 350, 351, 352, 353, 369, 394, 396, 404, 406, 411.
Percyvale, sheriff, 140.
Pers, Iohn, 167.
Pery, his wife, 333.
Petyt, Mrs., 221.
Petyte, Iohn, 261, 267.
Phellyp, carppyntter, 251, 252.
Philip, Iohn, chantry priest, 75, 79, 97, 112, 123, 124, 140, 155; his burial, 161, 164.
Phillip, Mr., of St. Paul's, 411.
Phillipe, of Spain, 398, 406.
Phyllyppes, Hew, curatt, 395.
Piers atte Lee, 1.
Plesaunce, Water, organist, 81.
Plomer, Mr., 179, 215.
Plomer, Roger, 200.
Plomer, William, 71.
Plommer, Mrs., 163.
Plommer, Robert, 'gent,' 182.
Plummer, Iohn, chantry and morrowmass priest, 75, 88, 97, 112, 116, 121, 124, 130, 133, 140, 147, 154, 158, 162, 167; lends £7, 171, 172, 174, 176, 179, 184, 191, 197, 203, 211, 212, 213, 221, 224, 239; the great bell of the church rings half the day for his mother, 241, 246, 266; his own knell rung on the same great bell, 267.
Pollay, Iohn, bocher, 200.
Polyver, Iohn, 127, 129, 180, 194, 206.

Pomfrett, Antony, 383.
Porth, Iohn, Inventory of his household goods, 36; his grave, 328, 329, 330, 331, 333, 334, 346, 353.
Porth, Iohn, Junior?, 354, 356.
Porth, Mrs., her knell, 321; and burial, 323.
Porth, Thomas, 356.
Potter, Iohn, 298, 308, 312, 313, 319, 333, 342, 363, 366.
Potter, Mrs., 365.
Potter, Wyllliam, Mrs. Wattes's servant, his burial, 259.
Povnde, Iohn, 249.
Power, Thomas, 314.
Powlyver, 382.
Powre, Thomas, his wife and wife's sister buried, 283.
Pownde, Richard, 283.
Powtrell, Margaret, 75.
Pratt, William, 127.
Prenttes, Harry, 275.
Prewne, Mergrett, wife of William Prewne, afterwards Mrs. Nonnelaye?, 222, 294.
Prewne, William, 4, 78, 81, 117, 122, 126, 127, 129, 140, 143, 158, 167, 182, 185, 202; his burial, 218, 223, 289, 293, 294, 301.
Prioures, Powle, attorney, 28, 29.
Pryne. *See* Prewne.
Purfote, Iohn, clarke of the mayres court, 179.
Purvoche, Petur, clerk, 339, 341, 345.
Pye, 173, 186, 198.
Pykeryng, Wylliam, 263; his wife buried, 271.
Pykman, Edward, tourner, 207.
Pyrson, Henry, 366.

Quylt, Iames, 380.

Rafe, priest, 96, 98, 100, 108.
Raff, Robert, 63.
Raffe, the porter, 186.
Rastall, Mr., 402.

Rauf a Beryes, cordewaner, 1.
Raughton, Petur, priest, 340.
Raynesford, William, conduct, 232.
Raynolde, Thomas, 75, 83, 105.
Raynwall, Thomas, 63.
Rechardson, his wife, 267.
Rechford, Thomas, 169, 181, 194, 206.
Red, govldsmithe, 58.
Redknap, Robert, condukt, the 'helpyng' of his wages, 303.
Redmanne, Iohn, karver, 224.
Redye, Iohn, parish priest, 122, 149, 162, 172, 183, 184, 196, 213, 215, 222, 227, 229, 232, 237, 240, 249, 253, 263; his burial and knell, 267; his bequest to the church, 267.
Remyngton, Iohane, 232.
Remyngton, William, alderman, 31, 126, 143, 158, 181, 182, 187, 195, 199, 205, 216, 227, 231; mayor, 238, 244, 246, 249, 261; his burial, 276.
Remyngton, William, 126.
Reuell, William, 236, 253, 254, 257, 258, 259, 262, 263, 265; his burial, 267.
Reve, 273.
Revell, Robert, 91, 126, 142, 143; his burial, 161, 187, 198, 215.
Revell, 335.
Reychard, the morrowmas priest, 252.
Reynnysfforthe, William, poyntemaker, 125, 168, 192, 204.
Rian, Iohn, 376, 377.
Ricard, Iohn, 126.
Richard, the bass, 359.
Richard a kechen, 'bedredman,' 126, 144, 145, 153, 157, 159.
Richard de Tystor, 8.
Richard of Lamehithe, 4.
Richardes, Richard, 299.
Rippyngton, Thomas. *See* Ripton.
Ripton, Thomas, 326; sexten, 330, 331, 334.

Robert, chantry priest, 277; morrowmass priest, 281.
Robert, the choir boy, 147, 148, 162.
Robert of Roo, sporyour, 10.
Robyns, George, priest, 363.
Robyns, Mr., 273.
Roche, Clare, 345.
Roche, Mrs. Iulyan, 33.
Roche, Mr. William, his wife, 35, 262, 265, 268, 271, 272, 283, 299, 300, 310, 311, 312, 313, 316, 319, 320, 323, 324, 337, 338, 340, 342; his servant, 350; alderman, 363; his daughter Iulyan, 366, 376, 380; his son Christoffer, 383.
Roche, Margaret, 345.
Roche, Mrs., 314, 323.
Rocklye, priest, 384.
Rogeres, William, plomer, 335, 336, 370.
Roke, Thomas, priest, 97.
Roo, Thomas, conduct?, 380, 384.
Rook, 63.
Roose, Nich., taylour, 126.
Roper, Iohane, 5.
Roper, Robert, the bladare, 5.
Roucybye, Robert, 124, 127, 142, 143, 144, 157, 158.
Rowland, tyler, 102, 106, 108, 136, 137, 140.
Rowlande, Thomas, 94.
Roydon, tyler, 140.
Russell, Iohn, 127, 131, 132, 135, 137, 138, 139, 199, 217, 221, 223, 224, 228, 230, 262, 265, 267, 272, 274, 279, 281, 283, 284, 287, 301, 302, 304, 319; his knell and burial, 327, 328.
Russell, Iohn, skinner, 22, 227.
Russell, Iohn, clerk, 91, 98, 116, 130.
Russell, Mrs., 298, 328.
Russell, Peter, 126.
Russell, Thomas, priest, 200, 212, 213.
Ruxbi, 291.
Rychard, pariche prest, 260, 263.
Rychard, Iohn Wolff's servant, 240.

Rychard, William, morrowmas prest, 401.
Rychardson, Mr., plummer, 407.
Ryder, Richard, 131, 140.
Rys, Robert, 63.
Ryse, Philipp, organ player, 386.
Ryse, William, organist and conduct?, 386.
Ryvell, Alis, 18.
Ryvell, Iohanne, 18, 19.
Ryvell, Iulyan, 18.
Ryvell, Margery, 18.
Ryvell, Mawde, 291.
Ryvell, Mr., 361, 363.
Ryvell, Robert, 230, 245, 249, 268, 283, 284, 292, 294, 295, 297, 298, 299, 315, 319, 322, 342, 355, 357, 366.
Ryvell, Thomas, grocer, part of will, 18, 31, 221; his burial, 222.

Sampe?, 347.
Sampson, Mrs., 390.
Sanderson, Stephen, 245, 249, 258, 259, 260, 261, 262, 283, 284, 288, 292, 294, 295, 297, 299; his burial, 312.
Sannys, Iames, chantry priest, 188, 189, 200, 201.
Sany, Eleyne, 61.
Savll, Mr., 178.
Saunder, the porter, 359.
Saunders, Mergret, 370.
Saunderson, Stephen, his child, daughter, wife, and cosen buried, 314; another child buried, 318, 320; his burial, 323; his memorial service peals, 329, 348.
Saundyr, the raker's man, 300.
Sawndyr, clerk, 96, 98, 139.
Sayles, William, goldsmyth, 209, 210.
Sayms, Th., 95.
Schad, Robert, 63.
Searle, Audrian, 50, 51, 57, 58, 392, 395.
Segemond, Edyth, 297, 300, 309.

Selbye, Moder, 127.
Selles, Mr., 177.
Semere, Thomas, 183.
Semper, Ffraunces, 390, 392; his wife, 393, 398.
Semper, Iohn, action against, 278, 294.
Serle, William, carpenter, 64, 69, 71.
Serrey, William, 395.
Seviere, Thomas, 66.
Sexten, Iamys, 378.
Seymour, Thomas, grocer, 113, 122; the corner house, 125, 126, 142, 143.
Sharpulles, Ihames, conduct, 371, 375, 380.
Sharpwith, Iames. *See* Sharpulles.
Shaxton, Iohn, conduct, 380.
Shayle, 189, 201.
Shirburne, William, capper, 76, 92, 111.
Shorpyn, Iohn, priest, 390, 392, 393.
Shotsham, Thomas, 51, 55, 392, 396, 397, 398.
Sidboughts, Mr., a caterer?, 270, 275, 281.
Silke, Richard, 127, 154.
Silke, William, 127.
Skidmor, Stephen, 51.
Skott, the clerk, 332.
Skrase, 274,
Skynner, Iohn, conduct?, 380.
Smale, Alis, laundress, 270, 273, 277, 278, 280.
Smalehode, Rogere, plummer, 110, 175.
Smart, Mr., his tomb, 215.
Smart, Thomas, carpenter, 299, 301.
Smarte, Iohn, grocer, 30, 76, 91, 92, 115, 123, 126, 142, 143, 146, 154, 158, 161, 164, 169, 182, 196, 199, 202, 212.
Smartt, Mr., 193, 241, 249, 259, 262, 267, 275, 283, 287, 299, 368.
Smerte, Vylliam, grocer, 231, 235, 239, 246, 263, 272, 288.

Smith, Henry, mercer, 51, 127, 383, 398, 399, 400.
Smyth, Iohn, 277, 302.
Smyth, Iohn, haberdascher, 78, 169, 170, 181, 194, 195, 201, 206, 209, 227.
Smyth, mason, 106.
Smyth, Rafe, 80, 99, 102.
Smyth, Thomas, sexten, 315, 318, 324.
Smyth, William, bell fownder, his arrest, 270, 273, 274, 275, 374.
Smyth, William, condukte, 322.
Smythe?, Cornelys, 255.
Smythisson, Nicholas, 127, 181, 193, 206.
Snodlonde, Thomas, parson of St. Botolphs, 4.
Snow, Christofer, priest, 376; his burial, 383.
Snowe, Iohn, parish clerk, 286, 290, 292, 293, 297, 298, 302, 307, 312.
Somers, Henry, 17.
Sotton, Margeret, 238, 272.
Soulby, William, priest, 112, 118.
Sowetheworthe, Iohn, priest, 213.
Sowne, Richard, 61, 62.
Sparke, William, parson, 13, 67.
Sprever, Iohn, conducte, 290, 293.
Staunce, Robert, 294.
Stauner, Richard, 324.
Stauner, Thomas, 352.
Stauner, Mrs., 329.
Staunsour, Robart, 126, 146.
Stede, Iohn, chantry priest, 168.
Stede, William, 130.
Stephen (of Abyngdon?), 5.
Stephen, St., 14, 223, etc. etc.
Stephen, William, 51, 389; his wife, 390, 391, 392, 394, 395, 396.
Stere, 82.
Stevyns, Cristan, 76, 84, 91, 92.
Stevyns, Mr., 270.
Stevynson, bucher, 137, 139.
Stewen, Mr., William, 54, 55, 58, 59.
Stodale, William, preste, 123.
Stokes, Robert, 294.

Stokes, William, chantry priest, 152, 166, 176, 192.
Stokker, Iohn, sheriff, 90.
Stone, I., 206.
Stookes, Iohn, pewterer, 299.
Story, priest, 390.
Stovrton, Arther, 55.
Sudbury, Mr., 288.
Sutton, Mr., founder, 273, 301, 303.
Swayne, Lawrence, organist, 272, 276, 279.
Syluer, Antony, 322.
Symond, dawber, 209, 210, 220.
Symond of Abyngdon, 5.
Symond of Moordon, 10.
Symond, priest?, the base, 349.
Synod, glasyer, 255.
Synod, westmentt maker, 256.

Tallis, Thomas, conduct?, 375, 380.
Tanner, Robert, the basse, 386, 403, 409.
Tate, Thomas, 131, 135.
Tery, Richard, goldsmythe, 201?, 209, 210.
Tetforde, Iohn, 288.
Th. a Bynkes, 127.
Thomas of Ffreestone, 5.
Thomas of Gravisend, priest, 271.
Thomas of Langton, 4.
Thomas, priest, 100, 108.
Thomas, St., of Canterbury, 6, 83, etc.
Thomson, Robert, 208.
Thorne, Iohn, conduct?, 384.
Thorney, Mr., 303.
Thorney, Mrs., 293.
Thornley, Nicholas, waterman, 113, 124, 134, 141, 143, 144, 157, 159, 169, 181, 194, 206.
Thrower, Iohn, clark, 367.
Tiler, Iohn, 213; his wyff, 327, 328, 333.
Tillisley, Iohn, chantry priest, 149, 151, 165, 173, 176, 188, 200, 207, 212, 213, 278, 280, 285, 307, 326.
Tilsworthe, William, 58.

Todard, Iohn, 352.
Toddes, Thomas, 127.
Toe, Edmond, morrowmas prest, 402.
Tompson, Richard, warden of St. Christopher's Fraternity, 325.
Tomson, Raff, 263.
Topladye, Iohn, almsman, 127, 167, 179, 191, 204, 211.
Towlarge, 366.
Townnysend, Iohn, 127, 129.
Towzy, Edemonde, 337, 338.
Trappis, Robert, 276, 277, 340.
Trowlop, at Towrehill, 350.
Tvrke, William, 58, 223, 408.
Turtyll, William, patynmaker, 157, 159.
Twatte, Branke, 267; his wife, 268.
Twyfford, Leonard, 366.

Vartu, Mr., 244, 245.
Vatas, Peter, 29.
Vncle, Thomas, 401.
Vndirwoode, peynter, 224, 229.
Vaucsor, Symond, 233, 323, 345.
Vaughan, William, 291, 308.
Vavasere, Harry, 92, 112, 113, 114, 122, 124, 126, 127, 128, 141, 143, 146, 157, 159, 169, 181, 182, 183, 186.
Vavasere, Nicholas, 92.
Vavyser, Agnes, 363.
Vpthenns, Iohn, 229.
Vstum, Iohn, 352.
Vstum, Thomas, his servant buried in the church, 311, 325, 330, 331, 334, 335, 342; his burial, 345, 353.

Wade, Iohn, 115.
Wade, Thomas, mason, 136.
Waldyng, Robert, 126, 128.
Walis, Alysaundyr, 106.
Walker, Iames, barbour at the bull, his funeral knell, 161.
Wall, Alys, 333.
Wall, Mrs., 315.

Wall, Iohn, 271, 293, 312, 313, 316, 319, 320, 324.
Wallden, Thomas, conduct?, 384.
Waller, Iohn, priest, 292.
Wallys, Iohn, 395.
Walworth, Iohn, vintner, 10.
Warbilton, 73.
Warner, Iohn, mason, 287, 288.
Warner, Mr., sheriff, 210.
Warwyk, Thomas, clerk, 91, 98.
Wason, Iohn, mason, 207.
Watson, Thomas, 241, 242, 247.
Wattes, Mrs., 261.
Wattes, Thomas, draper, 126, 227, 230, 231, 232, 240, 253; his gift of glass, 255; hys gyffte, 257; his wife's servant, 259; his burial in St. Katherine's chapel, 261.
Wattisson, Richard, priest, 98.
Watwoode, Iohn, priest, 212, 213.
Wayward, William, 348.
Web, William, prest, 115.
Welles, Ielyan, 228.
Welles, Nycholas, bargeman, 144, 157, 159, 169, 181, 194, 206.
Welles, Rychard, mason, 198, 200.
Wellys, Iohn, 14.
Welshe, Hugh, goldsmyth, 344.
Welton, Richard, 127.
Welysme, Raphe, 329.
Westhowse, Iohn, waterman, 168, 170, 181, 193, 194, 205, 206, 207.
Weston, carpenter, 302.
Weston, mercer, 164, 172.
Weston, Iohane, 10.
Weston, Iohn, merchant, his will, 10; his chantry, 75, etc. etc.
Westus, Richard, 127.
Westwode, smyth, 130, 135, 139.
Wharlton, Thomas, conduct, 390.
Whetlay, William, 178, 181, 190, 194, 206.
Whetleysey, Harry, 96.
White, Robert, 105.
White, William, mayer, 155.
Whithed, Olyver, 391.

Whyte, the donge man, 395; raker, 412.
Wileis, Robard, 218.
Wilkynson, Thomas, priest, 78, 86.
Wilkynson, William, cooke, 144, 156, 157, 159, 160, 169, 181, 194, 206.
William, 2.
William, 333.
William, the Browderer, 310.
William (of Abyngdon?), 5.
William of Cawston, 5.
William of Sandwych, 1.
Williams, Harry, 106.
Williamson Harry, grocer, 75, 79, 82, 112, 115, 116.
Williamson, Nicholas, wever, 112.
Wilshere, Harry, 291.
Wilson, Bryan, 294.
Win, Wolstone, carpenter, 50, 51, 308, 337, 338, 357, 359, 365, 366, 367, 369, 372, 373, 376, 377, 383, 395, 411.
Winter, Hugh, cvrat, 393.
Wode, Mr., seriaunt, 178, 179.
Wodemonger, Richard, his wife, 141.
Wollmonger, Iohn, 126, 127.
Wollmonger, Richard, 144, 157, 159, 169.
Wolsey?, Cardinal, 328.
Wolston, Thoms, 374.
Woodkok, his wyffe, 282.
Worland, Harry, 51.
Worsley, Alexaunder, clerk, 114, 116, 123, 124, 129, 130, 131, 133, 144, 147, 162, 172.

Wren, Mr., 287.
Wright, Iohn, conducte, 341.
Wryte, Roger, conduct, 402.
Wrytell, Rose, her will, 1; her chantry, 94, etc. etc.
Wulffe, Iohn, 238, 250, 277, 280, 283, 287, 288, 297, 298, 300, 306, 312, 313, 316, 319, 320, 322, 342, 343, 344.
Wycam, Thomas, laborer, 120.
Wylcockes, William, 141.
Wyld, Wylliam, chorister, 242, 244, 246, 318, 324, 325, 329, 334, 341, 345, 348, 352, 355, 360.
Wylde, William, parson, 4, 16, 18, 30, 31, 34, 142, 157, 158, 181, 221, 231, 238, 246; his bequest, 255. and 257.
Wylld, William, sexten, 268, 272, 276, 279, 283, 285, 286, 290, 293, 297, 298, 302, 307, 312, 315.
Wylles, Robert, 173.
Wyngger, Iohn, allderman, 254.
Wynslat, Richard, conduct, 376, 380, 384.
Wyot, Sir Henry, knyght, 46.
Wystowe, carpenter, 337.
Wyte, Tomas, 63.

Yngelby, Mrs., 285.
Yole, Thomas, conduct?, 380.
Yong, Rauf, chauntry prest, 346.
Yonge, Mr., 404, 409.
Yonn, Iohn, 5, 126.
Yovng, Robert, 52, 54, 55, 56, 57, 392, 394, 396.

NOTE ON THE FURNITURE IN USE AT THE CONSECRATION OF A CHURCH.

Contributed by Prebendary Chris. Wordsworth.

[1]**Thees bee thoo thynges that been necessary for the halowyng of a churche.**
In primis .ij. laarge fattes full of water ooñ within the churche dore, and an other with owte.

[1] *Ex Registro* Ro. Halam, Sarisburiensis Episcopi, A.D. 1408-17; in fine addit. saec. xvi⁰.

and .iiij. laarge treyn̄ Bolles or Basyns and a small ladyl of tree.
Item, .xxiiij. wex candelles, euerych of .i. foote longe or more.
Item, a dyssh full of salt.
and a dyssh full of aysshes fayre syfte.
Item, a quarte of Red Wyne.
and an handfull of ysope.
Item, small wex Roll Candelles. to make .v. crosses vpon the awter.
yf the awter be to halowyng.
and half a pound of Incense.
Item, oon lynnen clothe fayre wasshyn, to make clene the awters, which cloth after shall be brent.
and a clene treyn cop or dysshe.
Item, the church and the chauncell flore most be clene voyded from dextes. and segees. and fayre swoped with a Besom̄. i which floor fro the northe corner of the chauncell to the southe corner of the churche ende throw all the churche, and fro the este corner of the chauncell down̄ to the west corner of the churche. ther most be made in the flore or pament an Andrewes crosse of small sonde of a foote Brede. and an yarde thyck atte leest.
Item, .j. Senser withe. colys.
Item, .ij. Elnes of new lynnen̄ clothe for an Apron for the Busshop̄ and for Brachyals. And also lynnen̄ clothe suffycyent for Aprons for his mynysters.
Item, .j. short fourme.
with a tapete and Quysshynes to knele at.
And a tent withowt the west ende of the church yerd made of Clothe, in whiche the Busshop and his mynysters shall be rayed.
All thees thinges above saide. except sond, been̄ necessary and requysyte aswel in the halowyng of a churche yerd. by hym self. as in the halowyng of a churche and the awter :/ Savyng ouer this. in the halowyng of a churcheyerd, ther most be ordeyned .iiij. laarge crosses of tree of .iij. (?.vi.) foote of heyghe. whiche most stond fastened in the erthe at .iiij. corners of the church yerd.
And .xij. wex tapers to be set vpon̄ euery crosse.
Item, at euery corner of the churche yerd, a fatt with fayre water.

[CHURCHWARDENS' ACCOUNTS
continued.]
[1] + anno 1531.

Th[ese] parselles of plat ffollowyng whas delywrt vnto Wolston Wyn by a vestre ffor that the cherche whas dew vnto hem þe 25 day of marche 1531.

Item, a Saltt, parsell geltt, with a kewer, way[ng] xilij once, at iij s x d	liij s viij d
Item, vj sponnes way[ng] vj onces iij quarters, at iij s x d þe once, amount	xxv s x d oƀ
Item, a masser with a fott, way[ng] xj onces & halff, at iij s iiij d þe once	xxxviij s iiij d
Item, þat ther whas delywrt vnto the sayd wolston wyn In Redy monny :—	
ffyrst	xxvj s vj d
[. . ? . .]	xxiij s
mor delywrt hem by thomas goodnyston In monny .	iiij s
amount aHe, xliij s vj d	

Summa totallis amount, viij ƚi xvj d.

This parselles of plat whas thelywert vnto Thomas goodnyston the xxv day of marche Anno 1531 In party of payment of xviij ƚi v s iij d which that he had layd owt In the Reparacyon of the cherche Rentes, as dothe aper by his boke of aCownt.

Item, a geltt standyng coppe with a kewer, wayng xv onces quarter, at yower prys iiij s vj d the once, amount	iij ƚi viij s vij d oƀ
Item, a Saltt with a kewer, parsell gelt, wayyng x onces iij quarter, at iij s x d the once, amount	xlj s ij d oƀ
	v ƚi ix s x d

owt this v ƚi ix s x d payd to wolston wyn at yower assynmen[t], iiij s. So hawe I, Thomas goodnyston, Receyued by this ij parselles v ƚi v s x d at yower praysment.

[2] Ihesu anno 15 . . [3]

Item, that ther whas Sowld at thomas . . . . [3] . . . .
    trappes by the handes of Robart Rewell & th . . [3] . . . .
    & me, thomas goodnyston, the xxvij day of . . . [3] . . . .

---

[1] leaf 741.   [2] leaf 741, back.   [3] leaf rotted away.
MED. REC.   B B

Item, a gyltt challyes with the patten [?...] .... [1] ...
Item, ij paxes, gyltt, which wayd all with the challys
    xxxvij onces & halff, at iiij s þe once .... vij li . [1] .
Item, mor, Sowld another challes with the parsell
    geltt patten & ij small krewytes & a hally
    water styke, way[ng] all xxiiij onces & halff [2]
    a quarter, at iij s x d the once   amount . iiij li xiiij s iiij d
                                    Summa   xij li iiij s   iiij d

Item, þat the cherche ys dew vnto thomas goodnyston
    of this aCownt . . . . xv s   j d

[A.D. 1531–2.

Thomas Goodneston } Wardens.
Thomas Maltby

Chantry Accounts.

Church Rents.]

Paymentes.

* * * * *

[3] paid to a basket maker for v round mattes for the
    Clarkes to stond vpon . . . .   x d
paid for ij pottes to fett oyle in . . . .   j d

* * * * *

paid for ij hangyng candylstykes for the quyre . . .   v d
paid for ij kayes and a lok, and mendyng of other
    lokkes, and a lok for the torch chest . . . .   xvj d
paid for ij stolys for the Rectours in the quyre, and ij
    Greyes skynnes . . . .   iiij s   ij d

* * * * *

[4] Paid for xx[ti] elles of holland cloth, at vj d ob the
    elle, for surplices, x s x d. And for makyng of
    v surplices ij s vj d for the conductes; and for
    iiij surplices for the childern, x elles at vj d the
    elle, v s. And for makyng the same iiij surplices
    xvj d. Summa . . . .   xix s   viij d

* * * * *

paid for the hyre of the Rayment for the prophetes
    on palmesonday . . . .   xij d

---

[1] leaf rotted away.   [2] MS. '& halff & halff.'
[3] leaf 612, back.   [4] leaf 613.

Churchwardens' Accounts, A.D. 1531–2.

paid for the hire of clothes of Aras for palmesonday .   xvj d

*   *   *   *   *

paid to Saunder the porter, for makyng clene the parissh priest chamber. And to the Raker . .   iij d

*   *   *   *   *

[1] paid to Wolston Wyn for mending the wyndowes of the same hous, And for bordes & iij ℔ sowder, price xv d; and for mendyng Master dialles staff; And for xvj staples to the shope wyndowes . .   ij s   viij d

*   *   *   *   *

[2] paid for a pax for the high Alter . . . .   vj d

*   *   *   *   *

[3] paid to the sessyng of the dong-bote . . . . . .   vj d

paid for ij quayres of papur Rial to mende the pryik-song boke . . . .   xiiij d

paid for settyng vp the ymages abought the quyre dore   iij d

*   *   *   *   *

[Quitrents and Allowances.]
[4] The clarkes wagys and the beame lyght.

Rec' of the clerkes wages this yere as it apperith by the Roll of gaderyng of the same . . .   vj li iiij s j d

Rec' for pascall money and beame light this yere   x s   vj d ob

Summa, vij li xiiij s vij d ob.

Paymentes.

Paid to Edmond Matryver for a yeres wages . .   x li

Paid to Mighell Grene for iij quarters seruice v li, And to Wylliam Paten, nowe being clerk, for oon quarter xxxiij s iiij d. Summa . .   vj li xiij s iiij d

Paid to Wylliam Paten as conducte for iij quarters wages . . . .   vj li

Paid dunstane Chicheley for an hole yeres wages   viij li

Paid to Richard the Baas for ix daies wages that he serued before Mighelmas . . . . .   iij s   iiij d

Paid to the Thomas Arowsmyth, sexten, for a yeres wages . . . .   iij li vj s   viij d

---

[1] leaf 613, back.   [2] leaf 614.   [3] leaf 614, back.   [4] leaf 616.

Paid to Wyll*i*am Wylde for iij q*uarters* wag*es* . . xv s
   S*um*ma of thies paymen*tes*, xxxiiij ł*i* xviij s iiij d.
      And so
  The charg*es* is more then the Recep*tes*,
   xxvij ł*i* iij s viij d oƀ.

¹ Casueᶄ Resteit*es* thys yere.

Rece*yved* of Maistres Ideaᶄ for the buryaᶄ of hir husbond in the church and for a small grave stone	xx^{ti} s
Rece*yved* of ffulk Duttons wife for the buriall of hir husbond in the church	vj s viij d
Rece*yved* of M*aister* Burngyll for the buriaᶄ of his doughter in the p*ar*don church yard	ij s
Rece*yved* of Maistres Goodwyn for the buriall of hir husbond in the church and for the great belle .	xiij s iiij d
Rece*yved* of M*aister* Chalo*ner* for the buriaᶄ of his sonne in the p*ar*don church yarde	ij s
Rece*yved* of Iohn Byrd for the buriaᶄ of his doughter in p*ar*don church yard	ij s
Rece*yved* of C*a*rters wife for the buriaᶄ of hir kynneswoma*n* in the p*ar*don church yard	ij s viij d
Rece*yved* of M*aistres* Ioħnson for the buriaᶄ of hir husband in the church and for the kneᶄ w*ith* the great belle	xiij s iiij d

   S*um*ma of thies p*ar*cell*es*, iij ł*i* ij s.

²[The Wax Reckoning.]
Casueᶄ Paymen*tes*.

paid for Rynging of M*aster* Ideall, M*aster* Goodwyn and M*aster* Ioħnson knylles . . . .   xviij d

[The Rehearsal.]

³M*emorandum*: that this accompt was gyuen vpp the xj day of ffebruary A*n*no 1532, that is to wete, for oon hole [yere] endyd at Mighelmas last past.

   *   *   *   *   *

⁴payd to bayesse for makyng of thes ACountħ vj s viij d.

 [The Accounts appear at this period commonly to have been 'given up' in January or February.]

---

¹ leaf 616, back.   ² leaf 617.   ³ leaf 618, back.   ⁴ leaf 619.

[A.D. 1532–3.

Thomas Beckwythe } Wardens.
Thomas Clayton

Obit List.
Quitrent List.
Chantry Accounts.
Church Rents.]

[1]Paymenttes ffor the Chirche.

* * * * *

Item, more to yͤ organ maker ffor a Reward for tuenyng of yͤ pipis		xij d
Item, spent on hym & dyuiers of the Cumpany at yͤ ale howse		vj d
Item, paid for iij staf torches of wex, to hold at the levacion	ij s	vj d

* * * * *

Item, spent vppon them yat went with me to seynt Kateryns to take a stresse at godffrey ffelyns howse, and the Constable withe other of neyghpers . . . . xij d

* * * * *

Item, ffor makynge of yͤ cokk of yͤ bosse at bylyngesgate and settyng in of the same . . . . . xvj d

* * * * *

Item, paid ffor makyng of a pykaxe ffor the Chirch .		iiij d
Item, ffor mendyng of yͤ berrell crosse yat was brokyn	iij s	iiij d

* * * * *

[2]Item, ffor Ryngyng of yͤ gret bell ffor Master Ryvell vj owres . . . . vj d

* * * * *

Item, ffor a crosse to set in yͤ pardon chircheyard by yͤ pale	j d
Item, ffor nayles to make ffast the yrons in the Rode lofte To set in the baners	j d
Item, ffor mendyng of yͤ lock yat stondith on yͤ almery behynd the vestry dore & makynge of a key to the same	iiij d

[1] leaf 627, back.   [2] leaf 628.

Item, paid ffor a key ffor the steple dore . . . . .   iij d
Item, paid to a smythe ffor a bolt ffor the northe chirchyarde dore and ij kepars and a staple . .   iiij d

* * * * *

Item, paid to thomas coldale ffor blowyng of ye organs ffor lij wekes, that ys to say, ffor euery wek ij d .   viij s viij d
Item, paid ffor iij galons iij quartes & j pynt of malvesey ffor owr lady masse ffor the hole yere .   iij s x d ob

* * * * *

[Reparations upon the Church Rents. Quitrents.]

[1]Clarkes wages and beame light.

Rec' ffor the Clarkes wages this yere as yt apperethe by the Rowle of Gatherynge of the same . . . .   vij li xvij s j d
Rec' ffor ye pascall money & ye beame light this yere . . . .   xij s ij d quarter

    Summa of thes Receytes, viij li ix s iij d quarter.

Paymentes.

ffirst, paid to edmond matrevers ffor his yeres wages . . . .   x li
Item, paid to mychaell gren, Conducte, ffor his yeres wages . . . .   viij li
Item, paid to Wylliam paten, ye Clark, ffor his yeres wages . . . .   vj li xiij s iiij d
Item, to donston checheley, conducte, ffor iij quarters wages . . . .   vj li
Item, to nycholas crase, conducte, ffor di. yere & di. quarteres [wages] . . . .   v li
Item, to Richard newgate, conducte, ffor his yeres wages . . . .   vij li
Item, to thomas hoggeson, sexten, ffor his yeres wages . . . .   iij li vj s viij d

    Summa of thes paymentes, xlvj li.

So the charges amountes ouer and above the Receytes, xxxvij li x s viij d ob quarter.

---

[1] leaf 630.

¹Casuall Receytes this yere.

Rec' of thomas Cokkes ffor the pytt of Agnes vavyser in the pardon Chirche yarde	iij s	iiij d
Rec' ffor her knyll with the gret bell vj owres . . .	vj s	viij d
Item, Rec' ffor ye pyt & knyll ffor master Ryvell . .	xiij s	iiij d
Item, Rec' ffor the stone that lythe over hym . . .	vj s	viij d
Rec' ffor the pytt of sir george Robyns	vj s	viij d

Summa of thes Receytes, xxxvj s viij d.

[Wax Reckoning, in which square tapers are mentioned. Rehearsal.]

²Memorandum: that ther ys lefte in the store howse to the vse of the chirche iij m⁺ ij c di. of newe tyles.

[A.D. 1533–4.

Thomas Clayton } Wardens.
Iohn Potter ·

Obit List.

Quitrents.

Chantry Accounts.]

The Rentis of the Chirche.

*   *   *   *   *

ye parson

³Item, Rec' of the parsons dewtye ffor the Chirche yat he oweth by a byll of his own hond to ye mayntenaunce of the quire . . . . . . ix li xvj s iij d

money borewyd

Item, Borowyd of Master Roche, alderman, the xxv day of Iuyn 1534 In Redy [money?] to helpe to maynteyn the Chirch Rentes . . . . xv li
Item, R' of Wylliam burnynghill ffor ye same purpose v li
Item, R' of Robert Game in money for ye same purpose xxij s
Item, R' of Iohn birde in money for ye same purpose . v li

---

¹ leaf 630, back.   ² leaf 632.   ³ leaf 640.

Item, R' of thoms becwith ffor the same purpose . . x s ij d ob
Item, R' of thomas Clayton ffor the same purpose . . xlviij s
    Summa, xxix li ij d ob.

Thys money fynyshed vp Summa totalis of all thes
 the 9 howsys byldynge Receytes ffor ye chirche this
         yere, lxxiij li iij s vij d ob.

paymentes for the Chirche.

*   *   *   *   *

Item, spent vppon the organ player & ye clarkes ye xvj day of merche . . . .   iiij d

*   *   *   *   *

Item, paid for the prophettes Rayment on palme sondas . . . .   xvj d

*   *   *   *   *

Item, paid ffor ij sackes of Coles at ester . . . . .   xij d

*   *   *   *   *

Item, ffor garlondes for them that bare the Canypde [canopy] . . . .   vj d

*   *   *   *   *

Item, paid ffor beryng of the ij Crosses . . . . .   ij d

*   *   *   *   *

[1] Item, spent at the taverne the ix day of octobre vppon the pristes & clarkes & strange men that Cam to the Salve. . . . .   viij d

Item, paid ffor a boke to writ in the Chirche Reconnyng. . . . .   iiij d

*   *   *   *   *

Item, paid ffor ij bassons of laton ffor the high awter   v s

*   *   *   *   *

Item, paid to thomas coldale ffor blowynge of the organs lij Sondais in the yere, ffor euery sonday ij d   viij s viij d

Item, ffor iij galons & j pottell of malvesey ffor owre lady masse. . . . .   iij s vj d

*   *   *   *   *

Item, paid ffor iiij staff torches ffor the highe awter .   iiij s

*   *   *   *   *

[2] Item, payd ffor pavynge of seynt Christoffers Chappell and other places of the Chirche & stuff & workmanshipe abowt the same . . . . .   ij s

---

[1] leaf 640, back.   [2] leaf 641.

Item, paid to a laborer the vj day of novembre ffor
onlodynge & laying of ij lodys of bryk into the
store howse . . . . ij d

Item, ffor mendynge of a pewe yat Mestres potter
sittith in, to Wolston Wynne . . . . iiij d

*   *   *   *   *

[Expenses for the repair of church property,
also Quitrent list and many Allowances.]

[1]Clarkes Wagis ande Beame ligĥt.

Item, R' of the Clarkes Wages thes yere as yt
apperethe by the Rowle of gatherynge of
the same . . . . viij li xiij s viij d

  Summa of thes Receytes, ix li ij s viij d.

paymentes.

Item, paid to edmond matrevers ffor his wages j
quarter & half, endynge at candylmas whan
that he went his way . . . . iij li xv s

Item, paid to Robert oklond, orgon player, ffor
half quarteres [wages] endynge at owre lady
day annuncyacon . . . . xx s

Item, paid to Robert oklond ffor half yeres wages iiij li x s

Item, paid to Myghchaell gren, Conducte, ffor
his yeres wages . . . . viij li

Item, paid to Richard newgate, conducte, ffor
his yeres wages . . . . viij li

Item, paid to Wylliam paten, paryshe clark, ffor
his hole yeres wages endynge at myghelmas
laste paste . . . . vj li xiij s iiij d

Item, paid to thoms hoggeson, Sexten, ffor his
yeres wages . . . . iij li vj s viij d

Item, paid to thoms Axe, conducte, ffor a Reward
ffor that he dyde seruice in the chirche
affore that he was hyred . . . . vj s viij d

  Summa of thes paymentes, xxxv li xj s viij d.

So the paymentes amountes ouer & aboue the Receytes, xxvj li ix s.

[1] leaf 642, back.

¹Casuall Receytes this yere.

ffirst, Rec' ffor a knyll with the gret bell vj owres ffor Iohn cokkeshed of Kent, which departid at bylinges gate, in merche this yere	vj s	viij d
Item, Rec' ffor a pyt in the chirche for yᵉ same man	vj s	viij d
Item, Rec' of thoms becwithe ffor a ston that lith vppon Robert Ryvell in the body of the Chirche accordynge to her fformar bargayne	vj s	viij d
Item, Rec' ffor a pyt for dawsons child in the pardon chirche yarde		xij d
Item, Rec' ffor a pytt ffor leonard twyfford, the xxij day of aprell, in the pardon chirche yarde iij s iiij d. Item, ffor the hire of iiij torches ffor the same leonard ij s	v s	iiij d
Item, Rec' the xvj day of novembre ffor a pyt in the chirch ffor mastres mongham vj s viij d. Item, for a knyll with yᵉ gret bell vj s viij d	xiij s	iiij d
Item, Rec' of Master Roche, the xj day of Decembre ffor a pytt for Iulyan his dowghter in yᵉ chirche by seynt Christofers chapell	vj s	viij d
Item, Rec' ffor a pyt in the body of yᵉ chirch for henry pyrson vj s viij d. Item, Rec' ffor a knyll with yᵉ gret bell ffor yᵉ same henry vj s viij d	xiij s	iiij d
Item, Rec' of Rychard braddford for a pyt for his wyff In the pardon Chirche yard in Decembre last past	iij s	iiij d
Item, ffor a pyt in yᵉ pardon chirche yard for towlarges child	ij s	
Item, Rec' ffor a pytt in the pardon Chirch yard ffor Wylliam brokes child		xx d

Summa of thes casuall Rec', iij li vj s viij d.

[Wax Reckoning.
Rehearsal.]

[A.D. 1534–5.
Iohn Potter } Wardens.
Wolston Wynne

Obit List.
Chantry Quitrent List.
Chantry Accounts.
Church Rents.]

¹ leaf 643.

[1] Paymentes ffor the Chyrche.

* * * * *

Item, paid to Wolston Wyn ffor makyng of a deske
    in seynt stephyns Chapell . . . .   iij s

* * * * *

[Many expenses for house repairs.]

* * * * *

[2] Item, paid to the seriant ffor warnynge of ye vewars
    that went to see owr londe at the towr hill . .   xij d

* * * * *

Item, paid to Wolston Wynne ffor a quarter of
    planche bord to amend serteyn pewes in the
    chirche and to amend the fflowre in the quyre .   ix d

Item, paid ffor j c of ynglishe v peny nayle . . . .   v d

* * * * *

Item, paid to Iohn mathewe ffor the apparelynge of
    xxvij bokes, gret & small, with lether & claspes .   xxiij s vj d

Item, paid to Iohn thrower, clark, ffor makyng of a
    byll of the mynd of the parysshons . . . . .   viij d

* * * * *

Item, paid ffor the sessyng of the laystall . . . .   iiij d
Item, paid ffor water for the chirche ye hole yere . .   iiij d
Item, paid ffor bromes ffor the chirch ye hole yere . .   iiij d
Item, paid ffor vj queres of paper ffor ye chirch
    besynes . . . .   iiij d

* * * * *

[Quitrents and Allowances.]
[3] Clarkes Wages ande beame light.

Item, Rec' of the clarkes wages this yere as yt
    appereth by ye Rowle off gatherynge off the
    same . . . . viij li xj s vij d

Item, Rec' ffor ye pascall money & beame light .   ix s x d

    Summa of thes Receytes, ix li xvij d.

---

[1] leaf 651, back.   [2] leaf 652.   [3] leaf 653, back.

paymentes.

Item, paid to Robert oklond ffor cristmas
quarter xlv s. Item, to hym ffor owr lady
day quarter and mydsomer quarter iij li x s.
Item, paid to hym the viij day of August
for vj wekes & iij dais, after iiij d q, yᵉ day,
xiij s vij d . . . . vj li viij s vij d

Item, paid to thoms Axe ffor cristmas quarter
xl s. Item, to hym for other iij quarteres,
after ix li yᵉ yer, vj li xv s . . . . . . viij li xv s

Item, paid to Richard newgate, conducte, for his
yeres wages . . . . viij li

Item, paid to Wylliam paten, paryshe clark for
his yeres wages endynge at myghelmas . . vj li xiij s iiij d

Item, paid to thoms hoggesson, sexten, ffor his
hole yeres wages endyng at myghelmas . . iiij li

Item, to mychaell gren ffor a yeres wages . . . viij li

Summa of thes paymentes, xlj li xvj s xj d.
So the paymentes amountes ouer & above yᵉ Receytes,
xxxij li xv s vj d.

[1]Casuall Receytes this yere.

Rec' ffor a pytt in the body of the Chirche ffor old
mastres Altroppe . . . . vj s viij d

Item, Rec' of thomas clayton ffor a pyt in the body of
the Chirche ffor his wyff x s. Item, more ffor a
knyll of vj owres with the gret bell ffor mastres
Clayton vj s viij d . . . . xvj s viij d

Summa of thes Receytes, xxiij s iiij d.

[Wax Reckoning. Rehearsal.]

[2]ffor the parsons dute.

anthony elderton ffor smartes kaye, j yere, xxvj li
xiij s iiij d, at ij s ix d . . . . iij li xij s x d ob

Robert Game, j yere, x li, at ij s ix d, xxvij s
vj d, wherof R' of Robert Game xviij s vj d.
Rest . . . . ix s

Rest to the chirch of this recoveryng iiij li xxij d ob

*   *   *   *   *

[1] leaf 654.   [2] leaf 655.

[1]Thomas malby owe*th* for a holle yere of the Rent granted to the dayly se*r*ves by s*ir* alen pe*r*se for an⁰ 1532 . . . .   xx ti s x d

* * * * *

[2]Memorandum : to Recover of raffe challenger vj s viij d ; & is ffor that he sulde a paid vntylle a man that shoulde abyne parishe prest the w*hich* vj s viij d o*ur* churche warden dyd paye yt ffor chalengor ffor M^r p*a*rsoun . . . .   vj s viij d

[A.D. 1535–6.

Wolston Wynne ⎱ Wardens.
Thomas Malby ⎰

Obit List.

Chantry Quitrents.

Chantry Accounts.

Church Rents.]

[3] Payment*s* for the Chirche.

* * * * *

Item, paid to Iohn Howe, orgyn maker, ffor his ffee .	xij d
Item, paid to hym ffor a pype yat was brokyn . . .	xij d
Item, p*ai*d to hy*m* for me*n*dyng of ye bellows yat wer brokyn	xvj d

* * * * *

Item, ffor Rayment for ye p*r*ophette*s* vppon palme sonday	ij s	v d
Item, ffor ij skaffold*es* *in* ye chirche yard, stuff & workma*n*shipe		xvj d

* * * * *

Item, p*ai*d ffor burnysshyng of the Crysmatory . .   xij d

* * * * *

Item, p*ai*d for ij queres of pape*r* ffor ye chirch Reconnyn*g*es . . . .   iiij d

* * * * *

Item, ffor dressyng of ij sacrament Clothes . . . .   xij d

---

[1] leaf 656, back.   [2] leaf 659, back.   [3] leaf 668.

Item, ffor a wyre ffor the Rode lofte & ij stapylles .	viij d

* * * * *

Item, gevyn to them to drynk yat bere the Coopes [on Corpus Christi day]	vj d

* * * * *

[1] Item, ffor mendynge of the pale abowt yᵉ Crosse in yᵉ gren chirche yarde & stuff & workmanshipe .	vj d

* * * * *

Item, paid ffor iiij pavyng tyles ffor the chirche . .	iij d ob

* * * * *

Item, ffor a staple ffor the scole howse dore	j d

* * * * *

[2] Item, paid to Mʳ osborn ffor a pompe yat lythe to brynge the water owt of yᵉ diche into yᵉ ponde .	v s viij d
Item, for xij ffote of tymber to make the steppes wher the tenauntes ffecche ther water	ij s
Item, to ij men ffor a dais work to mak the stayres and layinge of the pompe	xvj d
Item, to a laborer ffor a dais work to digge yᵉ grownd	v d
Item, spent vppon the Constables of seynt kateryns & serteyn oyer at yᵉ takyng of a stresse at mergret saunders	x d
Item, ffor Caryng of yᵉ same gere ffrom yᵉ towre hyll to the [store or stone?] howse.	v d
Item, to yᵉ bedell of yᵉ broderers ffor nayles & other gere yat he paid for when yᵉ gable end of the howse in ffastar lane was bordyd.	x d
Item, paid ffor viij c di. of borde ffor to wederborde the sowth side of wolston wynnys howse, at ij s viij d	xxij s viij d

* * * * *

Item, paid to Rogers yᵉ plomer ffor a pipe of newe lede ffor yᵉ same howse, poiȝ j c iij quarters, at vj s viij d yᵉ c	xj s viij d
Item, ffor a pipe of newe lede in yᵉ kechyn in the same howse, waying iij quarteres	v s

* * * * *

Item, ffor vij lb of sowder ffor the kechyn pipe . . .	ij s xj d

* * * * *

[1] leaf 668, back.   [2] leaf 669.

Item, ffor a boke to writ in ye chirch Reconnynge . .   iiij d

*   *   *   *   *

Item, paid to thoms coldale ffor blowyng of ye organs lij sondais in ye yer, ffor euery sonday ij d. Summa . . . .   viij s viij d

*   *   *   *   *

Item, for ix elles of cloth for a surpluce for ye parishe prist, at viij d ye ell vj s. Item, for makyng of ye same ij s . . . .   viij s

*   *   *   *   *

[Allowances.]
[1] Clarkes Wagis and Beame Light.

Rec' ffor ye clarkes wages this yere as yt appereth by the Rowle of gatherynge of the same . .   viij li iij s iiij d
Item, Rec' of the pascall money & beame light .   xj s vj d
     Summa of thes Receytes, viij li xiiij s x d.

paymentes.

Item, paid to thoms Axe ffor half a yere endyd at owr lady day, after ix li by the yere iiij li x s. Item, ffor half yeres wages endid at myghelmas iiij li . . . .   viij li x s
Item, to Iohn Day ffor di. quarter endid at cristmas xx s. Item, more to hym ffor half yere & vij wekes endyd the xiij day of Auguste v li xix d. . . . .   vj li xix d
Item, paid to mychaell Gren ffor half a quarter .   xx s
Item, paid to Ihames sharpulles ffor iij quarteres vj li. Item, for myghelmas quarter because he was in the Contrey he had no more but xxxiij s x d. . . . .   vij li xiij s x d
Item, paid to William paten ffor his yeres wages   vj li xiij s iiij d
Item, paid to thoms hogeson ffor his yeres wages   iiij li
     Summa of thes paymentes, xxxiij li xviij s ix d.
     So the paymentes amountes ouer & above ye Receytes, xxv li iij s xj d.

[1] leaf 670, back.

[1] Casuall Receytes.

R' of master clayton ffor the stone that lith vppon
his wyffes grave in the Chirche . . . . . . vj s viij d
       Summa of the Receytes, vj s viij d.

[Wax Reckoning. Rehearsal, etc.]

[2] Memorandum: that William [A . . .?] oweth for the
Romeland in the yer of Anno domini 1535, in
Wolston wyns tyme for oon holl yer . . . . xlvj s viij d

*   *   *   *   *

Memorandum: that Crowcher oweth for the parsons
duetie givin to [the] churche toward mayntenaunce of the dayly serues for oon holl yer, endid
at mighelmas anº 1536. Summa . . . . . xj s

*   *   *   *   *

[A.D. 1536–7.

Thomas Malby } Wardens.
Iohn Bird

Obit List.
Quitrent List.
Chantry Accounts.
Church Rents.]

[3] Paymentes ffor the Chirche.

*   *   *   *   *

Item, ffor ij queres of paper iiij d. Item, ffor a quere
of paper Royall viij d . . . . xij d

*   *   *   *   *

Item, paid for xv elles of brod clothe to make surpluces
ffor the conductes, at vij d yᵉ ell, viij s ix d. Item,
ffor makyng of iiij surpluces ij s . . . . . . x s ix d
Item, paid ffor iij elles di. of brucell cloth to mak a
surpluce, at vij d . . . . ij s [. .?]

*   *   *   *   *

[1] leaf 671.   [2] leaf 672.   [3] leaf 678, back.

Item, paid to a man ffor beryng of yᵉ copes to grace chirche agayn whan yᵉ kyng & yᵉ quene Rode thorowgh the Citie . . . . ij d

* * * * *

Item, paid ffor ij quylles ffor the organs . . . . . iij d

* * * * *

Item, paid to Wolston ffor makyng of yᵉ stages ffor yᵉ prophettes . . . . vj d
Item, paid ffor hiryng of yᵉ Raymentes for the prophettes . . . . ij s

* * * * *

Item, paid yᵉ xx day of aprell to pristes, clarkes, conductes, sexten, brede, drynke & masse peny at yᵉ obbyt of Iohn Weston . . . . vj s   j d

* * * * *

Item, paid to a syngynge man yat was sent ffor to be hyred . . . . xij d

* * * * *

Item, paid ffor iij lb of Rope ffor the organs, at j d yᵉ lb . . . . iiij d ob

* * * * *

Item, paid to a lernyd man ffor serchyng in yᵉ kynges escheker ffor the chauntries longynge to the chirche . . . . xvj d
Item, paid ffor byndyng of yᵉ bok yat lith affore yᵉ parishe pryste . . . . vj s

* * * * *

[1] Item, ffor Ryngyng of the gret bell vj owres ffor quene Iane, and ffor Ryngyng of yᵉ belles dyuers peles to the same . . . . ij s   vj d
Item, paid to ij men ffor beryng of yᵉ copes to powlis, & home agayn at the byrthe of prynce edward . xij d

* * * * *

Item, paid to a tylar for mendyng a serteyn hole in yᵉ chirche . . . . iij d
Item, paid ffor a key for yᵉ west chirche dore . . . iiij d

* * * * *

[2] Item, paid to a man yat watched yᵉ gongffarmers ij nyghtes . . . . viij d

* * * * *

[1] leaf 679.   [2] leaf 679, back.

Item, ffor owr lady masse, wyne to serue yᵉ pryst at yᵉ alter ffor the hole yere . . . . xxj d

quyte Rentes.

* * * * *

[1] Alowaunces.

* * * * *

Item, ffor the wryttyng of the Inventory of yᵉ goodes of yᵉ chirche and all the ornymentes of the same   iij s   iiij d

* * * * *

[2] Casuall Receytes.

Item, Rec' yᵉ xx day of merche ffor a pyt in yᵉ chirche & a knyll with yᵉ gret belle ffor thoms Wolston . . . . xiij s iiij d
Item, Rec' yᵉ xiij day of may ffor a pytt & a knyll ffor Wylliam smythe . . . . xiij s iiij d
Item, Rec' the xvj day of Iulii ffor a pyt & a knyll ffor master game xvj s viij d. Item, Rec' ffor yᵉ ston yat lithe vppon hym xx s . . . . . . xxxvj s viij d
Item, Rec' the xx day of Iulii ffor a pyt in the pardon chirche yarde ffor Wylliam brokes wyff . . . iij s iiij d
Item, Rec' yᵉ xix day of August of Mʳ burnynghill ffor a pyt for his child in yᵉ pardon chirche yarde . ij s
Item, R' of Iohn Dawson for a pyt for his child in yᵉ pardon chirch yard . . . . ij s
Item, R' the xvij day of septembre ffor a knyll withe the gret bell ffor Iohn Dawson vj s viij d. Item, Rec' ffor his pyt in yᵉ pardon chirch yarde iij s iiij d. . . . . x s
Item, Rec' of Master Chalyner ffor a pyt for Mʳˢ goswell within the chirche . . . . vj s viij d
Item, Rec' of mastres goodwyn ffor a pyt ffor her mayd in the pardon chirche yarde . . . . . . ij s
Item, Rec' of master byrde ffor a pyt ffor his child In the pardon chirche yarde . . . . ij s
Item, Rec' of master osborn for a pyt for Anne dukkelyng . . . . iij s iiij d

Summa of thes Receytes, iiij li xiiij s viij d.

[1] leaf 680.   [2] leaf 680, back.

[Wax Reckoning.]
[1] Clarkes Wages and the beame lighte.

Item, Rec' of yͤ parryshons this yere ffor the clarkes
wages as yt apperethe by yͤ Rowle of gaydryng
of yͤ same . . . .   viij li iij s ij d

Item, Rec' ffor yͤ pascall money & yͤ beame ligght yis
yere . . . .   xj s vj d

  Summa of yͤ Rec' for yͤ clarkes wages & yͤ
  pascall money, viij li xiiij s viij d.

paymenttes.

Item, paid to Wylliam paten, paryshe clarke, ffor a
yeres wages . . . .   vj li xiij s iiij d

Item, paid to Ihames sharpulles, conducte, ffor a yeres
wages . . . .   viij li

Item, paid to Iohn day, conducte, ffor iij quarteres
wages . . . .   vj li

Item, paid to thomas tallis ffor half [a] yeres wages .   iiij li

Item, paid to thoms Ex ffor a quarter & ij wekes &
ode dais after cristmas . . . .   xlviij s

Item, paid to Roger Centon ffrom the xiiij day of
ffebruar to owr lady day yͤ annuncyacon, xxvj s
viij d. Item, paid to hym more ffor v wekes &
od dais after mydsomer, xvij s . . . . . .   xliij s viij d

Item, paid to thoms hogeson, sexten, ffor his yeres
wages . . . .   iiij li

  Summa of yͤ paymentes of the clarkes wages,
  xxxiij li v s.

So the paymentes amountes ouer & above the Receytes,
xxiiij li x s iiij d.

[Rehearsal.]

[2] Item, more alowyd for bulman, a bedman, whiche
was voyde viij wekes, at iij d the weke . . . .   ij s

  Summa dewe to the chirche, xviij li vij s viij d ob.

Wherof paid to Thomas becwithe vppon a chales . .   viij li

Item, paid to Wylliam burnynghill yat he lent vppon
a senser . . . .   vij li vj s

---

[1] leaf 681.   [2] leaf 681, back.

Item, paid to thoms malby of old det which was ffor lyme at ye buyldyng of ye howsis at seynt kateryns . . . . xij s

      Rest onpaid dewe to the chirche, xlix s viij d ob.

Item, more Rec' of Robert nycolson ffor the parsons dewtye iij li, & notwithstondyng ye dewty ys iij li xij s x d ob, but ye Masters of ye par[i]she Remyttyd ye Rest for serteyn consyde[r]acons . iij li

      So Rest to ye chirche v li ix s viij d ob, Remaynig in thoms malbis hondes.

[A.D. 1537–8.

Iohn Byrd   } Wardens.
Thomas Lorymer

Obit List.

Quitrent List.

Chantry Accounts.

The following complete list of the Church Rents is given in full because it specifies the localities of the properties, and is needed for comparison with the early rent lists.]

[1] The Rentes of the churche.

Rec' of Ione Goodwyn for a yeris rent	v li	
Rec' of Mastres Evynger for a yere rent . . .	iij li vj s	viij d
Rec' of Wolstane Wyn for a yeris rent	iij li vj s	viij d
Rec' of Ione partriche for a yere rent	xxvj s	viij d
Rec' of Master Roch, Alderman, for a yere rent .	xv s	
Rec' of Iohn Rian for a yere rent	xl s	

The Prestes Aley.

Rec' of the parissh priest for a yeris rent	xij s	
Rec' of sir R[i]chard Anntell for a yere	ix s	
Rec' of sir Christofer Snow for a yere	viij s	
Rec' of sir Iohn baret for a yere	vj s	viij d
Rec' of sir Richard Elys for a yere	vj s	viij d
Rec' of Richard Wynslat for a yere	vj s	viij d
Rec' of sir merke ffletcher for a yere	vj s	viij d
Rec' of the scole hous for a yere	vj s	viij d

[1] leaf 689.

The rentes at toure hill.

Resceyued of Robert Danyell for ix houses at toure hill for oon hole yere rent . . . . xij li xijs

Gardens.

Rec' of Robert Avere for a garden rent for a yere . . iiij s
Rec' of Wolston Wyn for a garden rent for a yere . iiij s
Rec' of Robert Game for quiterent due to the churche iij s iiij d
Rec' of the church of saint botulphe for a quiterent due to the church . . . . ij s vj d
Rec' of Master parsons dutie for the church due by a byll of his oun hand to the church for the mayntenaunce of the quere . . . . xij li xs ixd ob
Rec' of Master Copynger vpon a bill, in partie of payment of a more some, for oon yere . . . . iiij li

Summa of the Resceites for the church landes, the parsons dutie and Copynger, xlviij li xiij s xj d ob.

[1] Paymentes made for the churche.

* * * * *

Priestes Aley.

Paid to a tyler and his laborer for ij daies labour in the parissh priestes chambre . . . . ij s ij d

* * * * *

Paid to a bryklayer for xxj daies work for makyng of a chymney in the scolehous & fetching the fundacon frome the storehous flour vpward . . xiiij s

* * * * *

[2] Ihon Rian['s] hous reparacions.

* * * * *

Paid for j lode of bryk for his well mowthe . . . . xiiij d

* * * * *

The churche.

* * * * *

Paid for xxxvj elles of cloth for vj surplyces for the conductes and iiij for the children, at vij d the elle. Summa . . . . xxj s

* * * * *

[1] leaf 690. [2] leaf 690, back.

Churchwardens' Accounts, A.D. 1537–8.

Paid for mendyng of the dore in pardon churchyerd	x d
Paid to the mayers officer when Master Chaloner and Master Astryge were before the mayre	viij d

* * * * *

Paid toward the makyng of the dong bote for þe chirch	xvj d

* * * * *

[1] Paid for mendyng of the key to the southe church yard dore	ij d

* * * * *

Paid to the smyth for ij claspys of yron to set vp the aulter in our lady chappell		iij d
Paid to sir marke for carolles for cristmas and for v square bookes	iij s	iiij d
Paid for paper for the same songes		xij d
Paid for mendyng of a siluer sencer		iiij d
Paid for mendyng of the lok and key to the scole hous dore		iiij d

* * * * *

Paid for a glas for the lamp	j d

* * * * *

Paid for mendyng of the parissh priest surples . . .	vj d

* * * * *

[2] The vestment maker.

Paid to a vestment maker for xxvij dayes labour, at vij d the day	xv s	ix d
Paid for silke tape	iij s	iiij d
Paid for threde and threde tape	iiij s	j d oƀ
Paid for a hole pece of Rone bokeram	ij s	iiij d
Paid for x yardes of burdeux bokeram, at v d the yarde	iiij s	iiij d oƀ
Paid to Thomas Sexten for makyng of the roll to gader the clarkes wages by		xij d

* * * * *

Paid to Iamys sexten for wasshing the church clothes for a hole yere	xiij s	iiij d

* * * * *

[1] leaf 691.   [2] leaf 691, back.

Churchwardens' Accounts, A.D. 1537–8.

Paid for beryng a cope to polles on saynt Erkenwaldes day . . . . j d
Paid to a bokebynder for new byndyng the boke that lieth before the curate and mendyng certain places theryn . . . . vij s

* * * * *

Paid for hire of the prophetes Rayment . . . . . ij s
Paid for settyng vp of the stage . . . . viij d
Paid for nayles to the same . . . . j d
Paid to the rat taker for laying of his bayte . . . iiij d

* * * * *

[1] Paid for cheires and formes on palme sonday . . . v d

* * * * *

Paid to Thomas Coldale for blowing the organs for a yere, at ij d the weke . . . . viij s viij d

* * * * *

[Allowances.]
[2] Casuell Resceites.

Receyued of Master Barons for his wyfes pyt in saint Thomas chappell . . . . xiij s iiij d
Receyued for a child of Iohn Dawson lying in pardon church yerde . . . . ij s
Receyued of Master chaloner for a kynnes-woman of his lying in pardon church yerde . . . . . iij s iiij d
   Summa, xviij s viij d.

[Wax Reckoning.]
Clerk[es] Wages, & the beame light.

Resceyued of the parisshens this yere of the clarkes wages as it apperith by the Rolle of gaderyng of the same . . . . viij li xiiij s viij d
Item, resceyued for the pascall money and the beame lyght gadred this yere . . . . . xj s ij d
   Summa of the resceites of the clarkes wages & pascall money, ix li v s x d.

[1] leaf 692.   [2] leaf 693.

¹Paymentes.

Paid to William Paten, parissh clerk, for oon yere	vj li xiij s iiij d
Paid to Thomas Talies for half a yere	iiij li
Paid to Richard wynslatt for a quarter	l s
Paid to Iohn dey for a hole yere	viij li
Paid to Iohn Shaxton for iij quarters of a yere	vj li
Paid to Thomas Roo for iij quarters & a moneth wages	vj li xij s iiij d
Paid to Robert ffox for half a year & viij wekes and ij daies wages	iij li ix s iiij d
Paid to Iames Sharpwith for a hole yere	viij li
Paid to Thomas yole for a quarter	xxx s
Paid to Iohn Skynner for iij wekes	vj s viij d
Paid to Thomas Sexten for a quarter wages	xxiij s iiij d

Summa of the paymentes of the clerkes wages, xlviij li v s.

[Rehearsal, etc.]

* * * * *

²And more ress' for a pyt of a priest buried in the church out of bos aley, vj s viij d

* * * * *

³and so the accomptant Iohn brid dothe owe cler v s iij d ob. The whiche he hathe delyuered vnto his fellow, Thomas Lorymer, in the presence of Mr William Roche, alderman, Thomas Clayton . . . . . and other howsemen of the same parishe . . . .

* * * * *

⁴These be the names of suche persounes as be detters parcell of the persons duetie.

Iohn Osborn	vj s vj d
The son tavern	viij s iij d
William Awd[. . . ?]	xvij s x d ob
Iohn Crowcher	xj s
Iames Quylt oweth for the churche	xx d

¹ leaf 693, back.   ² leaf 694.   ³ leaf 694, back.   ⁴ leaf 695.

[A.D. 1538-9 lost.]

[A.D. 1539-40.

Iohn Austen } Wardens.
William Brayfeld

Obits List.

Quitrent List.

Chantry Accounts.

The Rentes off the Churche.]

*   *   *   *   *

The Priestes Alley.

Resseyved for the Scolehowse for a yeres rent . . . vj s viij d

*   *   *   *   *

Paymentes consernyng the Churche.

*   *   *   *   *

Payed to the preist for the bedrowlle for a yere	ij s iiij d

*   *   *   *   *

Payed for hollye & yve	xiiij d

*   *   *   *   *

Payed to Orgaynmaker for mending them on newyeres even ij s, and mor payed hym for hys xij d	iij s
Payed for mending a sholve ij d ob, & mending ij candlestickes j d	iij d ob

*   *   *   *   *

Payed for a booke for the churche	xx d
Payed for iij payer of Cruettes	ij s
Payed for the Clothes of the tower for pallme sondaye	xij d
Payed opynyng the Tower gate iiij d, & caryeng of them iiij d	viij d
Payed for hyring the prophyttes clothes on pallme sondaye	ij s

*   *   *   *   *

Payed ij men for watchyng ye sepullcre ij nyghtes	xvj d

*   *   *   *   *

---

[1] leaf 712.   [2] leaf 717.   [3] leaf 717, back.

Payed for a boote to westmynster & home ageyn	vij d

* * * * *

Payed ffor vj barres of yron to my house, wayng lxj ll, at j d ob the pownnde	vij s vij d ob
Payed for pavyeng of x yerdes beffore my dore	xx d

* * * * *

[1] Payed for bred & drynke for the prophettes on palme sondaye	j d ob

* * * * *

Payed to Mr Mallbe for a cheesse for Mr Powlyver	viij d
Payed ffor garllandes on the Ascencion daye	xj d

* * * * *

Payed for garlandes on corpus crysti daye	ij s

* * * * *

[2] Payed for iiij lattessys in the bellffreye	xij d
Payed for byrche at Mydsomer	vj d
Payed for caryeng the coopes to powles dyuers tyms	ij d

* * * * *

Payed for Rynging the belles on owr ladye daye	xvj d
Payed to Mr Malbye ffor keping of the chalice	iiij d
Payed to a trebyll ffor synging in the quyer	iij s iiij d
Payed for my exspences in the Cownter	xvj d

* * * * *

Payed at the heyryng of a preyst for our drynkyng	iij d
Payed for a quartern of Tyells for the Churche	vij d
Payed ye Orgaynemaker for iiij garnetes & iij Skynes for the bellowes of the Orgaynes	ij s iiij d
Payed for the mending of ij Syllver candlestyckes	xviij d

* * * * *

Payed for the mendyng of the leystoff	iiij d

* * * * *

Payed for ffaggottes & for coolles	iiij d

* * * * *

Payed to the Sexten for prycking of a song booke	ij d
Payed for a plancke ffor Romelande	iiij d
Payed to Powelles wif for keping ssir gravesend	iiij s
Payed for ij hockes & iiij staples for ye ij churchedoores	vj d
[3] Payed ffor a Cheste ffor the vesterye	vj s viij d

* * * * *

[1] leaf 718.   [2] leaf 718, back.   [3] leaf 719.

Payed for a caase for my lorde Mayers Sworde . . .	xij d
Payed to iiij men to bere torches on Corpus *Christi* daye	iiij d

* * * * *

Payed for pallme, box & yve xiiij d, & flow*ere*s & cak*es* iiij d	xviij d

* * * * *

QuytRent*es*.

Payed to [the] kyng*es* graice for a quytRent for Walltham ffor Iohn Weston xxxviij s & ffor Iohn Nassyng xxij s, and for the southe ylle of th[e] Churche x s	iij li x s
Payed to seynct george*s* churche in botulphe lane for quytrent for the house that Ione goodwyn dwellith yn	xx s
Payed to the kynge*s* graice for a quytrent for Iohn Weston	xviij s iiij d
Payed to ss*ir* Iohn cornewal*es* for a q*uy*trent of y*e* bell at tower hill	xij d

Allowa*u*nc*es*.

* * * * *

[1] Cassuall Recept*es*.

Resseyved of M*r* Rooche for his wyff*es* pyt & knell	xiij s	iiij d
Resseyved of M*r* Rooche for *Christ*offer his sones pytt	vj s	viij d
Resse*yved* of M*r* Rooche for his servaunt*es* pytt in y*e* churcheyerd	iij s	iiij d
Resseyved of M*r* Bornegyll for a straung*ers* pyt yn y*e* churche	vj s	viij d
Resseyved of Wollston Wynne for hys wyff*es* pytt	vj s	viij d
Resseyved of M*r* Clayton for his kynssewomans pytt .	vj s	viij d
Resseyved ffor ss*ir* Snowes pytte and his knell . . .	xiij s	iiij d
Resseyved of Will*i*am brooke for chylld*es* pyt in y*e* churcheyerd	ij s	
Resseyved of Thoms Moore .for his brother*es* pyt in y*e* churche	vj s	viij d
Resseyved of harrye smythe for a pytt in y*e* churchyerd	vj s	viij d
Resseyved for Antony pomfrett*es* pytt in the churcheyerd	iij s	iiij d

[1] leaf 719, back.

Resseyved of Thomas moore for the leasse of hys howse . . . . xl s
Resseyved of sir Rocklye in party of payment of a chalice . . . . xiij s iiij d
Summa, vj li viij s viij d.

[Wax Reckoning.]
[1] The Clarkes wayges and Beame lighte.

Resseyved of the paryschens fer the Clarkes wayges this yere, as apperithe by the Rowll of gatheryng of ye same . . . . . viij li xiij s iiij d
Resseyved of the beame lyght & pascuall monye this yere . . . . xiij s iiij d
Summa, ix li vj s viij d.

Paymentes to Clarkes and Conductes.

Payed to Richarde wynsselate for a quarter and iij wekes, after x li the yere . . . . . iij li xij d
Payed to Iohn Daye ffor a hoole yere . . . viij li xiij s iiij d
Payed to William Pattyn for one quart[e]rs wayges . . . . xl s
Payed to Thomas Rowe for a hole yere . . . vj li xiij s iiij d
Payed to Iohn Hacket for a hoole yere . . . vij li vj s viij d
Payed to Richard ffox for di. yere & xvj dayes, after vij li ye yere . . . . iij li xvj s iiij d
Payed to the Sexten for a yere . . . . . . viij li
Payed to Thomas Wallden for iij quarteres and ode dayes . . . . v li xiij s iiij d
Payed to Iohn Thorne for di. yere and x wekes v li xvj s
Summa, lj li.
So the paymentes amowntes to more then ye Receptes xlj li xiij s iiij d.

[Rehearsal, etc.
A.D. 1540–7 lost.]

[1] leaf 720.

[A.D. 1547–8.

Nycholas Awsthorpe } Wardens.
Thomas Lucas

Chantry Accounts.
Church Rents.]

¹ Casuell Receytes.

Receyuid for the pytt and knyll for Mʳ Knyght . .	xx s	
Receyuid for a pytt in the churche yarde for a straunger	iij s	iiij d
Receyuid of the wardemote enquest for the churche house	iij s	iiij d

Summa, xxvj s viij d.

Certen things sold.

*   *   *   *   *

Receytes for Rownd lande.

Receyuid of a spanyerd for lying his shipp ther . .   vij s viij d

*   *   *   *   *

The clarkes wages.

Receyuid of the parissheners for the clarkes wages this yere as particularly doth appere in a Roll made for the gathering and leveying therof . . . .   x li

Summa, pȝ.

Summa, pagine xv li xv s ij d.

² The Parsones money for the maynteynyng of the quyere.

Receyuid of the parisshenours of the parsons duety gyuen by hym for the mayntenaunce of the seruice in the quyer as particulerly dothe appere in a Roll made for the gathering therof this yere . .   xvij li   xx d

Summa, pȝ.

Summa totalis of all the charges and Receittes this yere lxxxv li iiijs xd. Wherof ys paid owt as hereafter folowith, that is to saye,

---

¹ leaf 706, back.   ² leaf 707.

Preestes wages.

* * * * *

¹ Conductes wages.

Item, paid to philipp Ryse, organ player, for one quarter wages ending at Christemas in the yere of our lord god Mˡ.vC xlvij	lv s
Item, paid to Ryse William for a whole yeres wages ending at Mighelmas in the yere of our lord god Mˡ.vC xlviij	viij ƭi x s
Item, paid to Ryse William for playing vpon the orgaynes daily at our lady masse for one quarter of a yere	vj s viij d
Item, paid to Robert Tanner for his whole yeres wages ending at Mighelmas aforesaid	viij ƭi x s
Item, paid to Thomas Marton, parisshe Clarke, for his whole yeres wages ending at Mighelmas aforesaid	vj ƭi xiij s iiij d
Item, paid to Thomas Mundy, the sexton, for his whole yeres wages ending at Mighelmas aforesaid	iiij ƭi
Item, paid to Thomas hamond for iij quarters and ix weekes wages ending at Mighelmas aforesaid . .	vij ƭi x s

Summa, xxxviij ƭi v s.

Almes gyuen and paid to poore men, wekely, on the Sonday.

Item, paid to v poore men for xxx[ti] weekes, paid wekely on the sonday, at ij s euery sonday . .	iij ƭi

Summa, p₃.

Summa, pagine xlj ƭi v s.

² Quit Rentes paid owte.

* * * * *

³ Particuler and necessary paymentes paid for the churche.

* * * * *

Item, for taking downe of the Rode lofte [honses?] .	v s
Item, paid by grete for taking down of the tabernacle ouer the vestry doore, being all stone, and other stone workes in the churche, and for making vppe therof, and for lyme and sande	xiij s iiij d

---

[1] leaf 707, back.   [2] leaf 708.   [3] leaf 708, back.

Churchwardens' Accounts, A.D. 1547–8.

Item, paid for taking downe of the Iron worke in the Churche	xvj d
Item, paid to M{r} Clerke, counsellour, for the view of the churche evidences consernyng the Chauntry landes	xx s
Item, to one [blank] kyrke for writing of the Certificat therof	xxvj s viij d
Item, paid in exspences at dynners and suppers for the said Counsellours, by the space of xij days, at iij s iiij d le day	xl s

* * * * *

[1] Item, to the kinges purcyvaunt for bringing of the kinges Commission for the Chauntry landes	xij d

* * * * *

Item, for vj new sawters in englisshe for the quyer	viij s

* * * * *

Item, for cariage of tymbre for scaffoldes for the Rode loft when yt was paynted	xiiij d

* * * * *

Item, for Ropes to bynde the scafoldes	xvj d

* * * * *

Item, paid for paynting of the Rode lofte with scriptures	iiij li

[Potation expenses for priests and clerks on Christmas, New Year's, Twelfth Day, Candlemas, Holy Thursday, the Annunciation, Whitsunday, Trinity, Corpus Christi, Jesus, the day of the Assumption, Dedication, and All Saints.]

* * * * *

[2] Item, paid for a boke of the prayer for the Scottes	ij d
Item, for a boke called the paraphrases of Erasmus	v s

* * * * *

Item, for wyne and synging brede for our lady masse spent daily for a half yere	xvj d

* * * * *

Item, for Removing of thorgaynes	xx d
Item, paid to kyrke for his paynes taking to speke to the kinges Commissyonours for the poore men	xx d
Item, for iiij songe bokes of te deum in Englisshe	viij d

* * * * *

[1] leaf 709.   [2] leaf 709, back.

[1]Rep*a*racions don vpon the grete ten*em*ent in Butolff lane.

* * * * *

[Several 'Allowaunc*es*.']

* * * * *

[A.D. 1548-9.

Thomas Lucas, Warden.

Christmas to Christmas.]

[2]The Counte of me, Thomas Lucas, of londone, Citizine and ffysshemonger, beynge chirche warden of Saynte Mary Hyłł In ye Thirde yere of ye Raygne of oure Soveraigne lorde Edwarde ye sixt, ent*ery*nge my offyce at Crystmas ye same yere And fynished it at Crystmas next ensuynge.

Here foloweth ye receit*es*.

* * * * *

Item, Receyvede for ye gylt of iij ymag*es* . . . . . xij s

* * * * *

[3]Item, M^r p*ar*sone, a paynted clothe that Remaynede to ye quere conteyninge xx^{ti} yardes & a halff, for ye wh*i*ch he was agrede to paye for Everye yarde iiij d . . . . vj s x d

* * * * *

Item, I, Thomas Lucas, hathe a paynted Clothe contayninge xix yard*es* & iij q*uarteres* . . . . . [*blank*]

[4]Here foloweth ye payment*es*.

* * * * *

Item, paide to Thomas Mondaye, the Sexten, for a yere . . . . iiij ℔

Item, paide to Will*ia*m Mondaye, the p*a*rishe Clarcke, ffor a yere . . . . v ℔ vj s viij d

* * * * *

Item, paide for ij bookes of ye new s*er*vice . . . . vij s vj d

* * * * *

[1] leaf 710. [2] leaf 700. [3] leaf 700, back. [4] leaf 701.

Item, payde to Nycholas Man, y̅e̅ basse, for halffe a yere, after vj ℔ by y̅e̅ yere . . . .   iij ℔

* * * * *

Item, for dryncke at y̅e̅ chirche for vj preincypall dayse, at v d a daye . . . .   ij s   vj d

* * * * *

[1] Item, paide to hym that mendid the new Organse, that was dewe to hym before my tyme . . . .   ij s

Item, bought, iiij spalter Bookes which coste ij s the pece, M̅r̅ Byrde toke me mooney for on of them, so that y̅e̅ iij coste me . . . .   vj s

Item, payde to Clarke, the man of law, ffor the makynge of a draught of wrightinge betwene M̅r̅ parsone & y̅e̅ masters of y̅e̅ parishe for the new howse in the chirche yarde . . . .   xx d

Item, payde for vj ℔ of Candell . . . .   x d ob

* * * * *

Item, payde to y̅e̅ kynge for Rome land as will apere by quyttances . . . .   x ℔

[A.D. 1549–50.

William Steven } Wardens.
Thomas Lucas

Michaelmas to Michaelmas.]

[2] The Charges and Receites.

Receyued for one hole yeris rent for the bell at the towre hill . . . .   xl s

Receyued for bokes sold within the tyme of this accompt . . . .   xlvj s viij d

Receyued for xij ounces of siluer, beyng claspes of bokes and the busshops myter, at v s viij d the oz   iij ℔ viij s

Receyued for a bell of Siluer wayeng ix ounces and half, at v s the oz . . . .   xlvij s vj d

Receyued for a gilt chalis and a pax, weyng xxiij ounces, at v s xj d the oz . . . .   vj ℔ xvj s j d

Receyued of certen of the parishe, as apperith by a bill of particulers, of the gift of master parson .   xv ℔

Receyued of the Clarkes wages, as apperith by a bill of particulers . . . .   x ℔ viij s

---

[1] leaf 701, back.   [2] leaf 696.

Receyued of Monnox wif for hir husbondes pyt . .	vj s	viij d
Receyued of William Patten for hir wifes pyt . . .	vj s	viij d
Receyued of William Stevyn for his wifes pyt and knyll	xiij s	iiij d
[1] Receyued of Mr Cleyton for the pit and knyll for his wif	xvj s	viij d
Receyued for the pytt for the goodwif Sampson . .	vj s	viij d
Receyued of Iohn Morton for his wif pytt	vj s	viij d
Receyued for the beryeng cloth for the good wif Sampson and Mortons wif.	ij s	
Receyued for a table that stode vpon the Alter, sold within the tyme of this Accompt	iiij s	viij d
Receyued for one of the Alter stones that lyeth on the good wif Sampsons pyt	iij s	iiij d
Receyued of ffraunces Semper toward the Costes of the Sute for the house in the Church yarde . . .	v li	

Summa totalis of the receites, l li v s vij d.

[2] The discharge.

Paid to sir Iohn Shorpyn for his hole yeris wages	iij li xiij s	iiij d
Paid to William Mundye for his yeris wages . .	v li vj s	viij d
Paid to William Davy for his yeris wages . . .	vj li	
Paid to William Man for one quarter	xxx s	
Paid to Thomas Wharlton, conduct, for one quarter endid at our lady day	xxx s	
Paid to Thomas Bettes, conduct, for half a yere . .	liij s	iiij d
Paid to Robert Golder, conduct, for half a yere .	iij li vj s	viij d
Paid to Thomas Blakden, conduct, for half a yere .	iij li	
Paid to Thomas May, conduct, for one quarter . .	xx s	
Paid to Thomas Mundy, Sexten, for his yeris wages	iiij li	
Paid to sir Story for syngyng all Crystmas	iij s	iiij d
Paid for wasshing of the church clothes for one hole yere	viij s	
Paid to the raker for one hole yere		xvj d
Paid for holly and Ivie at Crystmas; and a fyer iron		ix d
Paid for bread, ale and wyne in vestre for the quere .		xxij d
Paid to the Organ maker for his fee		xij d
Paid for mending of the new Organs	v s	
Paid for ryngyng of two knyllis, the one for mystris Cleyton and the other for William Stevyns wif .		xx d

[1] leaf 696, back.   [2] leaf 697.

[1] paid for brome and birche this yere . . . . . . x d
paid for mendyng of the litill bell clapper and for makyng of thre bawdrikes for the bellis . . . vij s vj d
paid to laborers for vj dayes for takyng downe the Alters, at vij d a day . . . . iij s vj d
paid for mending of the dore commyng in at seynt Mary hill lane . . . . ij s iiij d
Paid for vj pounde of candell . . . . x d ob
Paid to a pavier for paving of xij yardes of pavement in Love Lane . . . . ij s
Paid for a great lode of gravell . . . . xij d
paid to Lusheby for takyng downe of the high Alter and for pavyng of the quere and church . . . xxij s vj d
Paid to Mr Chibbourne for subsedy due to the kynges Maiestie for the parson . . . . iij li vj s iiij d
Paid to the kynges Maiesties vse for the South ile . x s
        Summa, v li xvj s x d ob.

[2] Costes and Charges spent and layed out for the recovery of the howse in the Chvrch yard.

*   *   *   *   *

[A. D. 1550–1.

Edmund Candish }
William Steven } Wardens]

[3] The accompte of Edmond Candishe, beyng Churchwarden with William Stevyn for one hole yere, that is to say, from Mihelmas in the yere of our lord god a thousand fyve hunderd and fiftie vnto Mihelmas Anno domini M^l. v^c lj.

The receites.

Receyued for one hole yeris rent for the bell at the tower hill . . . . xl s

*   *   *   *   *

Receyued of Peter Bate for his mothers Pytt and for the cloth for lyeng vpon hir . . . . iiij s

*   *   *   *   *

[4] Receyued for the cloth lent for Olyver Whithedes buriall . . . . xij d

*   *   *   *   *

---

[1] leaf 697, back.   [2] leaf 698.   [3] leaf 742.   [4] leaf 742, back.

The Paymentes.

Paid to sir Iohn Shorpyn, priste, for his hole yeris
wages . . . . iij li xiij s iiij d

* * * * *

[1] Paid for a scrow to syng on . . . . ij d
Paid to Pasmer and Shottisham for the laystall . . xvj d

* * * * *

[A conclusion, in a different handwriting, is dated Dec. 7th, 1553. Overleaf, 744, is a similarly dated note.]

[A.D. 1551–2.

Robert Young } Wardens.
Edmund Candish

[2] Here after ffolloyth Thacompt of Robert Yovng, Churchwardyn with Edmond Ca[n]dish of the parish church of Saynt Mary at Hill of London, ffrom the ffeast of Saynt My3hell TharCangell in yᵉ yere of our Lord god M'ccccclj vnto the ffeast of Saynt Mi3ell Tharcangell in the yar of our Lord god 1552, that is to saie, for one whole yere.

The Renttes and Recepttes.

* * * * *

[3] Recevede of ssarttayn of the Parishe towardes the payment of the Cvrattes waiges more than maister parson dothe allove, as hereafter Insvith.

Rec' of Thomas Cleton, Thellder, iij s iiij d; of Thomas Nicollson iij s iiij d; of Thomas Lorimor ij s; of William Kelly ij s; of Andrian Searle ij s; of Thomas Lvcas xx d; of William Stewen iij s iiij d, & of Edmonde candish xx d

Suma to xix s iiij d.

Rec' of ffranceis Semper, for a fyne or Incom for yᵉ mesvaige or tenement set and being in yᵉ north church yeard of yᵉ seid parishe Church of Saynt marie at hill, wherin yᵉ seid ffranceis Nowe Inhabith and dwelleth, ffyve povndes. In consideracion of which ffyve povndes for a fyne or Incom as aforesaid it was condissendyd, concludid & agreid, yᵉ Seven & Tw[e]ntie daie of March, in the Sixt yere of the reign of our souerangne Lord king Edward yᵉ Sixt, by yᵉ most avncienttes of yᵉ said parishe

---

[1] leaf 743.   [2] leaf 745.   [3] leaf 745, back.

Churchwardens' Accounts, A.D. 1551–2.

of Saint mari at hill, yat yᵉ said ffranceis Semper & his wife should have, hovld & Inioie yᵉ fforeseid mesvaig or tenement, ffrom yᵉ feast of yᵉ Annvnciacion of our blessed Ladie yᵉ virgin In the said Sixt yere of yᵉ Reign of our seid Soueraingne Lord king Edward the Sixt vnto the end & terme of Twentie yeres ffrom thence next Insving & ffully to be complet, yellding & paing therfore yerelly to yᵉ Church wardins of yᵉ seid parishe Church of St mari at hill for the tyme being, Thertie shillins of lawfull monie of Ingland at ffowre Termes in yᵉ yere vsvall in yᵉ Citte of London, by even porcions, & yat yᵉ Churchwardins of yᵉ seid parishe Church of St mari at hill for yᵉ time being shovlld kepe & maintain the sied mesvaig or tenement ffrom wind & wether tide dvring all yᵉ seid Terme.

Svma totalis of the Receittes, xxxix ƚi vij s vij d.

[1] Wherof ys payde owt as hereafter Inssvith, yat is to Saye:—

Payde to Sir Iohn Sharping, preist, for one qvarters
   wayges ended at our Lady daye . . . . . xviij s iiij d

*   *   *   *   *

Payd to William Dawe, our base, for his wholle yeares
   wayges . . . . vj ƚi

*   *   *   *   *

[2] Payd for the Conffermacion of yᵉ Indenter for the
   hovses in the northe Churche yeard wherin Mʳ
   parson & ffranceis Semper dwell & for the
   bovsshoppes Sealle to have it Reiesterd in yᵉ
   bousshoppes Court . . . . xj s   viij d

*   *   *   *   *

Payd for bred and drynke on Ester daye in the vestre
   for the Qvyre . . . . vj d

*   *   *   *   *

Payd vnto a goulde smith for to take the sylluer
   ffrom a gospell boke & to waye it . . . . vj d

*   *   *   *   *

Payd to sir hvgh winter, Cvrat, towardes the paiment
   of one quarters waiges in stephen kevaldes time . xxv s

*   *   *   *   *

[3] Payd for bred and wyne the xᵗʰ daye of december . ij d q'
Payd for writing agayne of the Inventory of our
   Churche gooddes by Reason yat yᵉ other was
   Retorned by the kinges Maiestes commissioners   iiij s

---

[1] leaf 746.   [2] leaf 746, back.   [3] leaf 747.

Payd for bred and wyne yᵉ Sonday before Christmas   ij d ob

* * * * *

Payd owt of the sayd Rent to sir Allyn persy, Clarke parson of the sayd Church, for a qvitrent as well for the Seyd hous wherin ffranceis semper dwelleth as for the hovs wherin the Seyd sir Allyn Persy nowe lyeth in the north Church Yeard of yᵉ sayde parishe church . . . . . iij s   iiij d

* * * * *

[1] Iohn Crovcher oweth to the Said Church for The Tyth of his hovs for one whole yere ended at Mihillmas Anno Domini 1552, of yᵉ gift of Mʳ parson . .   xj s

* * * * *

There was delyuered also at the ende of this accompt, ij gret bokes apertayning to the seid Church. And in one of the saide bokes were contayned in, the Accompttes of nycolas Awsthorpe, Thomas Lvcas, William Stewen, Edmonde Candishe, and meny others.

[[2] Inventories, etc., see p. 50.]

[A.D. 1553.

Stephen Kavoll } Wardens.]
Robert Young

[3] Here after ffollowethe The accownte of Stevyn Kavoll, Churchewardon with Robarte yonge, of the parishe of saynt marye at hyll, In the yeare of owre lorde God A 1553.

Receptes.

* * * * *

Rec' of William for iij quarters of a yeare toward the
    Curattes wages . . . . vj li xv s
Rec' of Mʳ holstocke for breakynge the grownd in the
    pardon churchyarde . . . . [ij ?]
Rec' of Mʳ holstocke for the clothe of Saynte Anns . v s
Rec' of Mʳ Brayefelde for an olde Clothe . . . . [4]
Rec' of Mʳ Lucas for iiij peces of heary clothe yat laye
    on the altars . . . . [4]

* * * * *

---

[1] leaf 747, back.   [2] leaf 748.   [3] leaf 758.   [4] leaf perished.

Rec' of dyvers, as appearythe by name, for makynge of the hyghe alter of the sayde churche of saynt Mary hyH, that ys to saye—M{r} lorymar iij s iiij d, M{r} Brayefelde iij s, maste[r] Cerle xx d, master lucas xij d, master Candyshe xij d, maste[r] stevyns iij s, of stevyn kavoH xij d, master wynne xx d, which sum drawethe to . . . . [1]

[Payments.]

[2] Payed to sir edmond Alston, curatt, for one whoale yeare . . . . ix ti vj s viij d

Payed to sir hew phyllyppes for v weekes beynge Curatt . . . . x [1]

* * * * *

Payed to William serrey for ij antyphonars, a grayle, ij hymnolles and to presessyonars . . . v ti

payed to Ihon WaHys for ij antyphonars and a grayle xxv [1]

* * * * *

payed to Iohn howe for y{e} hoale yeare to looke and tvne y{e} organs, bothe payre . . . . . . iij s

payed to Ihon howe for mendynge the great organs & mendynge the beHowes and for mendynge the lytteH organs, as dothe appeare by a byH . . . v s vj d

* * * * *

payed to whyte, the donge man, for the whoale yeare xvj d
payed for the makynge of viij{th} surplyces . . . . ij s [1]

* * * * *

payed to M{r} wynne for a benche yat went Rownd abowt y{e} comvnyon boorde . . . . [1]
payed for nayles to mende the kytchyn when yt was broken downe for the alter stone . . . . . [1]
payed to the plasterer for plasterynge the kytchyn . [1]

* * * * *

[3] payed to the felos that helped vp the stone of the alter . . . . iiij d

* * * * *

[4] payed to M{r} Wynne for ij dayes worke in the churcheyarde, for harry and hys man . . . . iij s
payed to M{r} Wynne for the foote pase before the hyghe alter . . . . xij d

[1] leaf perished.   [2] leaf 759.   [3] leaf 759, back.   [4] leaf 760.

payed to Mr stevyns for xxj ti of Candell . . . . iij s   vj d

* * * * *

payed for a Crismatorye of pewter . . . . ij s   vj d
payed for the sowynge together of the best alter
    clothes for to laye on the Commvnyon boorde   vj d

* * * * *

payed to mr parson for the new howse in the northe
    churchyarde . . . . iij s[1]
payed to the gentyllmen of the qwenes chapell, for
    syngynge a mas here the xj[th] daye of November   xvj d

* * * * *

payed for ij quyres of paper for to prycke song*es* in .   viij d
payed for the byndynge of the same bookes. . . .   viij d

* * * * *

payed for the mendynge of the awter clothe of clothe
    of golde for to serve for to hange vppon the hyghe
    alter . . . .   xij d

* * * * *

payed for the wyne and the bread for the Commvnyon   xij [1]

* * * * *

[2] This Cownte of me, Stevyn Cavoll, churchewardon w*ith* Robart yonge, was alowed by the masters of the p*a*rishe, wherevnto they dyd sett to there hand*es* whose names be Resyted hereafter, y*at* is to saye, Thomas Clayton . . . . . . [etc.] the xvj daye of Ianvary in the yeare of o*ur* lord god A 1554.

[Inventories, see p. 55.]

[A.D. 1554.

Thomas Shotsham }
Stephen Cavoll   } Wardens.]

[3] Here after ffolowethe The Accownt of Thomas shotsham, Churchewarden w*ith* stevyn Cavoll, of the p*a*rishe of saynt mary at hyll, In the yeare of owre lorde god A 1554 and in the fyrst and seconde yeare of the Kynge and qwenes prosperous Raygne.

---

[1] leaf perished.   [2] leaf 760, back.   [3] leaf 754.

Paymente*s*.

* * * * *

Item, payed for makyng of the surplyces and the ammasses	xij d
Item, payed for makyng of the albes	viij d
Item, payed for ij albes for the deakyn and the sub-deakyn	xviij d

* * * * *

Item, payed for a latten senser, Gylte	xxxiij s iiij d

* * * * *

[1] Item, payed to the laystowe and boate for the churche	ij s viij d

* * * * *

Item, payed for iij prosessyonar bookes	vij s
Item, payed for ij loade of lyme to make the altars .	xxj d

* * * * *

Item, payed for a holywater stocke.	v s

* * * * *

[2] Item, payed for mendyng of the Canapye over the hygh alter wherin the sacrament hange*s* and for the sylke	vj s

* * * * *

Item, payed ij iij syngyng men at easter for helpyng the quyer	v s

* * * * *

Item, payed for the paskall and for the lyghtes that was burned of tenebyll weddyns day more then was gathered	ij s ij d
Item, payed for a shyppe of pewter	ij s viij d

* * * * *

Item, payed for puttyng owt of the scrypture in the roode lofte	xx d

* * * * *

[3] The Charges payed To the prest and clarke*s* of the Churche of Saynt Mary at hyll.

* * * * *

[4] Rec' these parselle*s* folowyng by me, Thomas shotsham.

* * * * *

[1] leaf 754, back.　　[2] leaf 755.　　[3] leaf 756.　　[4] leaf 757.

[A.D. 1554–5.

Henry Smith } Wardens.]
William Pattysmer

[1] Thys ys the a Counte of Henry Smythe and William Pattyssmer, wardens, of the rentes and goodes belonginge to the Churche of Saynte Mary at Hyll in London for one hole yere, from the byrthe of our Lorde in anno 1554 Vntyll the Byrthe of our Lorde in anno 1555 in the ffyrste and second of Phillipe and Mary, by the grace of god et c'.

ffyrste, we charge vs withe the recetes of this money as herafter followethe :—

Recevyd of ffrancis Sempar for a yers rent of his howse endid at Michaelmas . . . . xxx s

* * * * *

[2] Recevid this yere amonge the parisshioners for the holle yere for the clarkes wagis . . . . . x li xij s iiij d
Recevid this yere for and towardes the paskalle Lyghte viij s ix d ob

* * * * *

The casualtes for this yere as herafter followethe.

Recevid for ij maryages for that they were maryed in the newe howsse . . . . ij s
Recevid of Misteris Cleton for the knell and pytte . xvj s viij d
Recevid of Mr Candyshe . . . . xij s
[3] Recevid of Master Shotsham . . . . xiij s iiij d
Recevid of master fysshe . . . . [blank]
Recevid of master Brayfylde of the yyfte of master Cleyton . . . . xij s

Somma Totallis of the money Recevid by me, henry Smythe, for the yousse of the Churche iij vj li xiij s x d ob.

The Sellary or Wagis of Pristes and Clerkes servinge and singinge withe in the saide Churche in the tyme of this a Counte, Paid vnto them as herafter followethe :—

* * * * *

paid to olde father mondaye for his yers wagis . . iiij li
paid to William mondaye for his yers wagis . . vj li vj s viij d
paid to hethe the singing man for xxj dayes servys . vij s

---

[1] leaf 765.   [2] leaf 765, back.   [3] leaf 766.

[1] paid to ij singing men to singe in the ester hollydayes
and apon loo sondaye . . . . vj s
paid to certen conductes to singe ensonge apon our
Ladis even. . . . . xx d

* * * * *

[2] Ordynary Charges as ffollowithe.

* * * * *

paid for a boke called the manuell . . . . xx d

* * * * *

paid to a man to bere our copes at a generall prosessyon vj d

* * * * *

paid for palmes . . . . viij d

* * * * *

[3] paid for the paskall lighte . . . . xiiij s viij d
paid for wrightinge a boke for the presentment to the
bisshiope . . . . ij s

* * * * *

paid for a crucyfyxe . . . . vij s

* * * * *

paid for mendinge the leade abowt the churche ruffe xij d

* * * * *

paid for makinge the bisshopes myter withe stuffe and
lace that went to yt . . . . iij s

* * * * *

paid for ij bokes of artyckell . . . . viij d
paid for a boke of salmede . . . . ij s
paid for a boke for saynte Nycolas . . . . viij d

* * * * *

[4] Herafter ffolowethe the money Recevid by me, Henry Smythe, of the masters of the parishe, for and towardes the s[e]wte of our Landes belonginge to our Churche of Saynte Mary at Hyll at severall tymes:—

Recevid of Mr Larymer . . . . xx s

* * * * *

The Dyscharge of the same, as herafter followethe, payde out in Sewte.
Paid to Mr Gackes for framynge of a boke to goo to
our counsell . . . . v s

* * * * *

[1] leaf 766, back.   [2] leaf 767.   [3] leaf 767, back.   [4] leaf 768.

[A.D. 1555–6.

[1] 'from the feast of the nativitie of our Lorde a 1555 vnto the feast of the nativitie of our Lord God Anno domini 1556.'

William Pasmer } Wardens.]
Harry Smythe

The Rentes and Receiptes.

* * * * *

[2] Rec' by me, William Pasmor, of The seasement of the parishe of Saynt Mary Hill towarde the Charges of the Roode, Mary and Iohn, and the patrones of the Churche and the Lyghtes of the Roode lofte, as dothe appere hereafter folowynge by name as I Receyved of them 1556.

* * * * *

[3] Receyved bye me, William Pasmer, Churchewarden of Saynt Mary at hyll, as hereafter folowethe.

Receptes.

Rec' of mistris Leversham for the pytt and the knell
at her husbandes beryall . . . . xiij s iiij d

* * * * *

[4] These parselles folowynge hereafter are the Rerages that was in the tenantes handes at the sute of M^r francke, and Receyved by me, William Pasmer, Churchewarden of the parishe of saynt Mary at hill 1556.

Receyptes.

* * * * *

Rec' of these Tenantes folowynge belongyng to the parishe of saynt Mary at hill lying besydes the Towre and beyng within the parishe of Saynte buttolphe without algate 1556.

Receiptes.

* * * * *

[5] These parselles as folowethe was Rec' by me, William Pasmor, and and lent of the parishonars of saynte Mary at hyll whose name[s] ffolowethe hereafter.

[1] leaf 777.   [2] leaf 778.   [3] leaf 779.   [4] leaf 780.   [5] leaf 781.

Receiptes.

* * * * *

These parselles folowinge Rec' by me, William Pasmer, of the last Consent of all the vestrye as hereafter ffolowetes.

Receiptes.

* * * * *

[1] Hereafter folowethe The Chargis of the Roode, Mary and Iohn, layde owte by me, William Pasmer, Churchewarden of the parishe of Saynte Mary at hill in Anno domini 1556.

Paymentes.

In primis, payed for the Roode, Mary and Iohn, for the saide parishe of Saynt Mary at hill . . .	vij li
Item, payed for the patrones of the said churche as apperethe by a byll	xxvj s viij d
Item, payed for the tabernacle that the patrones standethe in, as dothe appeare by a quittaunce .	v s
Item, payed for xvj bolles of laten for the Roode lofte, and every boll at ij s ij d apece, as apperythe by a quyttance	xxxiiij s viij d
Item, payed to Thomas vncle for payntyng the patrones and Reffreshynge of the tabernacle and for Coloryng the backe syde of the borde of the crosse, as dothe appere by a quittance	xviij s iiij d

Sum, xj li iiij s viij d.

[2] Hereafter ffolowethe paymentes that I, William Pasmer, Churchewarden of the parishe of Saynt Mary at hyll, hathe layde out abowte the affayres of the sayde Churche in many parselles, as hereafter dothe ffollow, Anno domini 1556.

Paymentes.

Payed to sir hewe Gybson, Curatt, for one quarteres wages ended at Candelmas 1555 .	iij li
Payed to sir Henry Ioye, Curat, for a xj [a-leven] monthes ended at Crystmas last past Anno 1556	xj li
Payed to sir William Rychard, morrowmas prest, for halfe a yeare ended at midsomer 1556 .	iiij li xvj s viij d

---

[1] leaf 782. [2] leaf 783.

Payed to sir Edmond Toe, morrowmas prest, for one quarter of a yeare ended at Crystmas anno 1556 . . . . 1 s

Payd to sir Roger Wryte, quondocke, for halfe a quarteres wagis ended at Candelmas Anno 1555 . . . . xvij s vj d

Payed to Gyles hanckes, quondocke, for one whoale yeares wages ended at Cristmas last Anno 1556 . . . . viij li

Payed to Iohn Hobbes, quondocke, for one whoale yeares wages ended at Cristmas last Anno 1556 . . . . viij li

Payed to William Mundye, Clarke, for one whoale yeares wages ended at Cristmas last Anno 1556 . . . . vj li xiij s iiij d

Payed to Thomas Mundye, Sexton, for one whoale yeares wages ended at Cristmas last Anno 1556 . . . . iiij li

Sum, xlviij li xvij s vj d.

[1] Hereafter ffolowethe what hathe ben laid owt by me, William Pasmer, Churchewarden, abowte the sute of the landes at towre hill with Mr francke, in many parselles as hereafter folowethe, A 1556.

paymentes.

Item, payed to Mr Rastall . . . . vj s viij d

   *   *   *   *   *

[2] Item, payed to serten of the Jewry to make them dryncke. . . . . ij s

   *   *   *   *   *

[3] Hereafter ffolowethe payementes by me, William Pasmer, Churchewarden of the parishe of Saynte Mary Hill, layde owte abowte the affayres of The sayde Churche, in many parselles as hereafter dothe followe, Anno 1556.

Payementes.

Item, payed for holye and Ivye at cristmas . . . . ij s

   *   *   *   *   *

Item, payed for syngynge bread . . . . ij d

[1] leaf 784.   [2] leaf 788.   [3] leaf 789.

Item, payed for a great wicker matt & ij small peces .	viij s ij d

* * * * *

Item, payed for an homely booke	xvj d

* * * * *

Item, for boate hyer for the chargis of halowyng the altars.	ij d

* * * * *

Item, for seryng Candell, brome, paper and oyle, and for Coales and also braune	ix d

Turne over the leafe.

[1] Item, payed for the dynner of the suffrycan y*at* daye he halowed the altars and other y*at* did se*r*vice w*ith* hym	xiij s
Item, payde in Claret wyne, sacke and sugar . . .	iij s xj d

* * * * *

Item, for payntynge of the Coffen of the pascall . .	xviij d

* * * * *

[2] Item, payed to tanner for greasyng the bell*es* . . .	ij d

* * * * *

[3] Item, payed for a dynnar of o*u*r ladys daye for all the syngynge men and syngynge children	xx s

Turne over the Leafe.

* * * * *

[4] Item, payed ij [meaning 'to'] viij*b* syngynge men, and for the chylderne of saynte Magn*us* . . .	vj s viij d
Item, payed to harryson for bearynge the crosse . .	iiij d

* * * * *

[5] Item, payed for a Copye of the last visitacion . . .	iiij d

* * * * *

Item, payed for a masse booke	xiij s iiij d
Item, payed for you, to sett in the churcheyard . .	v d

* * * * *

Item, payed for wyne at Mr Lownd*es* for to synge masse, and for the quere vppon festivall dayes .	xxxvij s iiij d

* * * * *

[6] Item, payed for a Rest to performe the masse booke	xx d

* * * * *

[1] leaf 790. [2] leaf 791. [3] leaf 792.
[4] leaf 793. [5] leaf 794. [6] leaf 795.

Item, payed for the iiij stockes for the Roodlofte, and for suche waxe as hathe ben burned in the churche at service tyme, to Ieram Burton . . . xxxviij s

Item, payed for iiij wooden pynnes of the tapers in the Roodelofte. . . . . xij d

* * * * *

Item, payed for mendyng of the bell whele and for the stockes of the roodlofte and for the tapers . ij s vj d

* * * * *

[1] Item, payed for Ryngynge of the knell for my wyves buryall . . . . viij d

* * * * *

[2] per me Alanum Percy.

* * * * *

[A.D. 1556–7.

William Holstocke } Wardens.]
William Pasmer

[3] Hereafter folowethe Thaccompte of William Holstocke, Churche Warden with William Pasmer of the parishe Churche of Saynte Marye at hill in London, from the feast of the nativite of oure Lorde God anno 1556 vnto the feast of the Nativite of our Lorde god Anno 1557.

The Rentes and receiptes.

* * * * *

[4] Rec' towardes the paskall lyght at easter of suche as did receyve of the parisheners . . . xij s viij d iij quarteres

Rec' more at easter of the parishioners for ther iiij offerynge dayes . . . . xlix s vij d

* * * * *

Rec' of Mr yonge for the wast of iiij of the Churche torches at his mans buriall. . . . . xvj d

* * * * *

[5] Hereafter folowethe paimentes that I, William Holstocke, Churchewarden of the parishe of Saynte Mary at Hill, hathe layd oute abowte the affayres of the sayde Churche in many parselles, as hereafter dothe ffollowe, in Anno domini 1557.

[1] leaf 796.   [2] leaf 796, back.   [3] leaf 798.
[4] leaf 798, back.   [5] leaf 799, back.

The Charges of the quere, as hereafter folowethe.

* * * * *

Payed to sir Iohn mychell for one monthe servinge
and beynge Curat and after died . . . . . . x s

* * * * *

Payed to sir Iohn Gliatson, morrowmas priest, for one
quarteres wagis and iij weekes . . . . lix s vj d

Payed to sir Iohn parkyns, a base, for to helpe the
quere when hobbes was dead, and to have viij d
daye everi holy daye and sundayes . . . . . xv s viij d

* * * * *

Payed to Iohn hobbes, quondocke, for one quarters
wages endynge at thannunciacion of our Ladye,
and borrowed xvj s viij d of the nexte quarter &
dyed. . . . . lvj s viij d

* * * * *

[1] Payed to Thomas Mundie for his whoale yeares
wages endynge at Cristmas last . . . . . . iiij li

* * * * *

[2] Hereafter folowethe payementes by me, William Holstocke, Churchewarden of the parishe of Saynt mary at hyll, Layede owte
abowte the affayres of the churche in many parselles, as hereafter dothe followe.

* * * * *

Item, payed for ij bookes for the Churche, named the
homylis and the sacramentes: the Curat, henry
Ioye, beynge commaunded by the ordenari to be
had the ixth of Ianuarii. . . . . iij s

* * * * *

Item, payed for holy and Ivye agaynst Cristmas to
garnishe the Churche . . . . ij s viij d

* * * * *

[3] Item, payed the xxviij^{ti} of Ianuarii To frauncis
Iasper for one whoale yeares quitterent of the
Southe Churcheyarde dewe to the kynge and
quenes highnes at mighelmas last past . . . . x s

* * * * *

Item, payed to M^r maunsefelde for the subsedewe
[subsede dewe?] for our parsons benefice dewe to
the kynge and the Quenes highnes . . . iij li v s

[1] leaf 800.   [2] leaf 800, back.   [3] leaf 801.

MED. REC.   E E

Item, payed more for the quittaunce makynge . . .   iiij d
Item, payed more to M^r maunsefelde for M^r parsons
    Tenth of the benefice . . . .   iij li   xiij s   iiij d

*   *   *   *   *

Item, payed for a clothe mendynge of paynted
    Imagery, and for corde to hange the same clothe
    withall vp before the roode and let it downe, the
    x^th of marche . . . .   iiij d
                   Turne over the Leafe.

*   *   *   *   *

[1] Item, payd the xvij^th daye of aprill for a stand of
    good ale for the maundye . . . .   ij s   viij d
Item, payed the daye before saide to the sompner for
    bryngynge the Crismatori at easter . . . . .   xij d

*   *   *   *   *

Item, paied to a mason the xxvij^ti daye of aprill to
    mend the wyndowe for the sacrament . . . .   xj d
[2] Item, paid to a smythe to make a gynne of Iron for
    the sacrament to runne vp in by the lyne . .   xij d
Item, payde for a lace of sylke for the sacrament . .   v s
Item, payed for another lace of sylke for to plucke
    downe and lett vp the sacramente . . . . .   iij s

*   *   *   *   *

Item, payde to fyve ryngars that ronge the same daye
    that the Kynge and the Quenes hignes cam
    through london; by commaundment of the
    bisshop to rynge . . . .   xx d

*   *   *   *   *

Item, payd for thred to bynd the palmes, box & you .   j d
Item, payd for ij reedes to lyght the sepulture . . .   vj d
Item, for the oyle and crealme bryngyng from the
    bisshop . . . .   j d

*   *   *   *   *

[3] Item, payed to William mundye the xij^th daye of
    maye for his Charges to rochester to hier a con-
    ducte, a base, for our Churche . . . . .   ij s

*   *   *   *   *

Item, payd the iiij^th daye of Iulii to sir Bunntynge,
    one of the prestes of Saynt Magnus, for servyng
    the Cure the satterday and sondaye next ensu-
    ynge after Mr Ioye, Curatt, departed . . .   xvj d

---

[1] leaf 801, back.   [2] leaf 802.   [3] leaf 802, back.

Item, paid to M^r parsons woman that kepes his house
for a quitterent of the newe house in the northe
churcheyarde, for one whoale yeare . . . . . iij s iiij d

* * * * *

Item, payed for borrowynge of a sylver Crosse and ij
Candelstyckes of sylver and a senser of sylver to
occupye of our ladis daye . . . .   viij d

* * * * *

[1] Item, paid to the plummer, Mr Rychardson, for ix ℔
of soulder, at vij d the pownd, v s iij d, and more
for a plum of leade for the sacrament, viij d . . v s xj d

[2] Payed to olde mundy for drynke for the syngyng
men of the quere . . . .   iiij d

* * * * *

Item, paid to Iohn howorthe at iij sondrye tymes for
wyne for the whoale yeare for the ministracion of
the masse, and for the hoselynge wyne and for
the festivall dayes, as dothe appeare . . . . xxxij s x d

* * * * *

Item, paid for syngynge bread at sondry tymes for
one whoale yeare . . . .   xxij d

* * * * *

[3] Item, payed to Iohn howe, organ maker, the xxix^{ti}
daye of november for mendyng of bothe the payre
of organs agaynst the Sumpcion of our Ladye . ij s

* * * * *

Item, paid to Mr Archedeakin of polles for M^r
parsons visitacion which was dewe at myghelmas
last . . . . iij s iiij d

Item, paid for a booke of statutes towchynge our
chauntres . . . .   xij d

* * * * *

Item, paid for a keye for the doore that commythe
owte of Love Lane into the northe churcheyarde   iiij d

* * * * *

[4] Item, paid to a prest that did serue our Cure the
sondaye folowinge that sir Iohn mychell dyed,
beynge our Curat, and lefte vs desolate . . .   viij d

Item, paid for a processionar for to be occupied in
our quere at servis tyme . . . .   xvj d

* * * * *

[1] leaf 803.   [2] leaf 803, back.   [3] leaf 804.   [4] leaf 804, back.

[A.D. 1557-8.

Thomas Blancke } Wardens.]
William Hollestocke

[1] Hereaffter ffolowythe The Acownte of Thomas Blancke, Chowrchewarden with William Hollestocke of the parrysche at saynte mary at hill, frome the feste of the natyvyte of owr Lorde god Anno 1557 vnto the ffeste of the natyvyte of owr Lorde god Anno 1558, as folowyth.

[Rents.]

[2] Resseved of the clarkes waedges for oeen hole yere as yt aperethe by a Rovlle of particullers, the somma of x li viij s x d. And the Reste that is not gathered yt shall appere in the latter ende of this boke, soe that as myttche as I cane Resseve ys   x li viij s x d

* * * * *

Resseved towardes the pascall lyght at ester of the parrysyeners . . . .   xij s iiij d

Resseved More of the parryssiners for ther ffower offerynge dayes the somma of . . . . . .   l s   ij d

* * * * *

[Rents.]
[3][Casual Receipts.]

Ressevid for the knyll of M^r frogenolde & brekyng the grovnde the somma of . . . .   xiij s iiij d

Ressevid for waste of the iiij torches . . . . . .   j s iiij d

Ressevid for the knyll & brekynge the grovnde of owlde M^r tv[i?]ke iij s iiij d. Soe he Rebatid for that the churche dyd owe vnto hym [e3?] x s; so I ressevid bvtte . . . .   iij s iiij d

Ressevid for Mr Clayttons knyll & brekynge of the grovnde the s[.?]s of . . . .   xx s

Ressevid for Mrs Leversshame knyll & brekyng the grovnde the somma of . . . .   xiij s iiij d

Ressevid for Mr Passmors knyll & brekynge the grovnde the Svmma of . . . .   xvj s viij d

Ressevid for yoodwyffe Lames dowghter for brekynge the grovnde in pardon chvrcheyarde . . . .   ij s

---

[1] leaf 805.   [2] leaf 805, back.   [3] leaf 807, back.

Ressevid of M{r} Ioegame for the waste of iiij torches
Svmme of . . . . xvj d

Ressevid of M{rs} hartfforthe for the waste of ij torches
Svmma of . . . . viij d

Ressevid of M{r} yonge for the waste of ij torches
Svmma ys . . . . viij d

    Summa of thys syde Ressevid iij li xij s viij d

[1] Summa totales Ressevid by me Thomas Blanke ffor thys hole yere ys lxvj li xv s xj d.
                    ex'.

[2] Paymentes payd by me Thomas Blancke for this yere after ffolowythe.

The chardges of the quyer.

Payde to doctor hardyman, parysche pryste, for oen hole yeres waedges endynge at chrestemas laste paste . . . . xvj li

Payde to Iylles havkes for oen hole yere endinge at chrestemas . . . . viij li xiij s iiij d

Payde to wyllyam Movndye for his hole yeres wadges with xxvj s viij d for gatherynge the parssons tythes . . . . viij li xiij s iiij d

Payd to thomas Mvndye for his hole yeres waedges the somma of . . . . iiij li

Payde to Tanner, the basse, for oen quarters [wages] frome myhellmase to chrystmas . ij li

Payd to wyllyam Elssame for j quarter and vj wyekes the soms of . . . . xix s vj d

Payd one owr Lady daye to a pryste that dyd synge a basse for vij wyckes, at ij s viij d the wycke . . xviij s viij d

Payde to a syngynge man one palme sondaye . . . xij d

Payd to a syngynge man in the ester holy days . . v s

payd to a syngynge man at whyttsontyde . . . . iij s iiij d

payd to dyvers one owr Lady daye to dryncke . . . xij d

Payd to [blank] the xiiij{t} daye of Ivly yat dyd synge in [illegible] . . . . v s

    Summa payyd to the Cvratt & alle owther synggyng men ffor the hole yere ys xlij li – 0 – ij d.

[1] leaf 808.   [2] leaf 809.

[1] Qvytt Rentes & Svbsedyes and tenthes.

* * * * *

[2] Ovther ordenary chardges & ovthers.

* * * * *

Payd for j ti franckenssons		xij d

* * * * *

[3] Payd for wyne for the mawndy one mvnday thvrsdaye the Svmma of	ix s	viij d

* * * * *

payd for brede at the mavndye	iij s	iiij d
payd the 18' daye Auguste to the clarckes and syngynge men for a [backet?] or Recreassion at M^r haywardes one owr Lady even to macke them to dryncke	v s	vj d
payd for the children of saynte magnus	vj s	viij d
payd for borowenge of ij sylver crosses oen owr Lady daye Summa of		xij d

* * * * *

payd one Relycke sondaye for brede & dryncke . .		ij d

* * * * *

Payd to my Lorde of Londons somner	iij s	

* * * * *

Payd for syngynge brede and owsselynge for one hole yere. Svmma		xx d

* * * * *

[4] Thes parrysshenars woos names dothe ffolowe Are behynde with the parssons dewtye & is dewe To me, thomas blancke, churche warden, for mye yere oenty, beynge in the yere of owr Lorde god 1588.

Wyllyam Holdestocke for oen yere endynge at myhell-mas laste paste	xvj s	vj d

* * * * *

[5] Item, ther is dewe in my yere of the Clarkes wages that I cane no[t?] have, as foloethe.

Vxor Collynes for j hole yere	iiij d

* * * * *

[Three debts.]

[1] leaf 809, back.   [2] leaf 810.   [3] leaf 811.   [4] leaf 814.   [5] leaf 815.

[A.D. 1559.

Thomas Draper, Warden.

The following and concluding pages of the MS. appear to be written in a different hand. One of the pages, 818, is headed 'Paymentes 1559.']

[1] Paymentes.

* * * * *

Payd to yᵉ person for a quyt rent for the cherch house   iij s   iiij d
Payd to mʳ Percy for yᵉ second payment of a subsydy
  & for the parsons tenthe dew to the queenes grace,
  as doth appeare by his quyttauncis . . . . vj li xvij s   vj d

* * * * *

Item, spent vppon caston yᵉ curat at yᵉ salutacyon when
  I hired hym with ij or iij of yᵉ parich with us .   xix d

* * * * *

[2] payd to howe for iiij springes for the regalles . . .   xij d

* * * * *

payd to Iohn Cooke, carpyndor, yᵉ xᵗʰ daie of Iune
  for making of a lythe coffen . . . . . .   viij d
Item, payd for bread for yᵉ communyon yᵉ hole yeare   xxij d
payd to mʳ arsdeakon of poles for mʳ persons visitacyon
  dew at miklemas . . . .   iij s   iiij d
Item, spent vppon mʳ phillip of poles for playing at
  organs on enson yᵉ xvij daie of Iuly, at yᵉ
  salutacion, mʳ lukas & mʳ win being ther . . .   xvj d

* * * * *

Item, payd for cuttyng downe of yᵉ grasse in yᵉ south
  church yeard . . . .   ij d
Item, payd for to prossession bokes in Inglish yᵉ won
  an xx daie of Ianuary . . . .   viij d

* * * * *

[3] Payd for iiij sater bookes . . . .   xij s
Payd for the changing agayne of the sayd bookes .   xij d
Payd for iiij playnsong bookes for the quyer . . .   vj s   viij d

* * * * *

Payd for takyng down yᵉ sepulcure . . . . .   xij d

* * * * *

---

[1] leaf 816.   [2] leaf 816, back.   [3] leaf 817.

Payd for making of ye comunyon table . . . . .   xx d

*   *   *   *   *

Payd for taking downe ye rood, ye mary and the Iohn   xvj d

Payd for the Iniomsons book . . . .   iiij d

*   *   *   *   *

[1] payd vnto v men yat did helpe to tack downe the great auterston and for the lone of v doble rafters and for on that was brooken . . . .   iiij s   ij d

Payd to m^r north, brycklear, and iij labres with hym for v daies to take downe the auters and for poyntyng of the steple aboue rounde abought, and for mending of ye wales betwext the lead and ye glasse, and for lyme & sande and for whiting wher ye awltrs wer . . . .   xvij s

Item, payd to ye visyters at saint Brydes ye Third daie of septembre for ye vse of the person . . .   ix s   iiij d

*   *   *   *   *

[2] Payd for bringging downe of ye Imagis to rome lond and other thinges to be burnt . . . .   xij d

*   *   *   *   *

Payd vnto Mr Lownes for wyne yat was fett [from?] his house for ye comunyon . . . .   vij s

Payd vnto a goyner for mending ye pulpet, & ij Irons for to mend ye deske yat ye curat doth reede vppon . . . .   xiij d

*   *   *   *   *

[3] Payd vnto Lording for wrytyng ye Invitory ffaire, to gyue to ye commissioners ye viijth daie of dissembre . . . .   xvj d

*   *   *   *   *

Payd to whight ye raker for too carry awaie all ye rubbushe of ye auters yat did ly at ye cherch dore . . . .   xvj d

*   *   *   *   *

So I do Rest to the church for thys yere of thys Receytes by me, thomas draper, att ye fott of my acompt xxiij s xj d.

*   *   *   *   *

[4] These be ye names of our parisioners as doth staie ye parsons dewty ffor his tythes which is dewe in my tym, Thomas Draper, then being Cherch wardon :—

---

[1] leaf 817, back.   [2] leaf 818.   [3] leaf 818, back.   [4] leaf 820.

Churchwardens' Accounts, A.D. 1559.

Master holstocke, for on hole yeare Ending at myclemas 1559 . . . . xvj s vj d

* * * * *

The Bellowse maker in prestes Ally oyth for half a yers rent of his house . . . . vj s viij d

* * * * *

[1]These be ye names of them That oyth for ye clarkes wagis in my Tyme, Thomas Draper, being cherch warden:

Vxor Collinges, won yeare . . . . iiij d

* * * * *

Iohn Grenwaie for on quartre . . . . j d

Summa xxj s vj d.

[1] leaf 821.

GLOSSARIAL INDEX.

CORRECTIONS AND ADDITIONS.

Bedsteads, standing of, 417/1, *should read* Bedsteads, standing.
Norwegian covering, 433/1, *should read* Norwich covering.
Oster bord, 433/2. Dr. R. Sharpe suggests, 'Estrich board' for this.
Rone, *adj.* roan, 438/2, *should read* Rone, *adj.* Rouen.
Syyars, 442/2, *should read* Sypars.

Reveld Surplices, *n. p.* probably fringed surplices, 36.
Stakyd fforme, stalyd forme, *n.* forms with barred backs, 37, 39.
Tawle wode, *n.* tall wood. "Tall woode, pacte woode to make byllettes of, *taillee*." (Palsgrave, 279/2.) "The term is still used in Kent." (Halliwell, p. 849.) 45.
Vardors, vardours, *n. p.* verdures; tapestries. (Halliwell, p. 909.) "Tapestry of which foliage or leafage on a large scale, scenery with trees, or the like, is the chief subject." (*Century Dictionary.*) 37.

GLOSSARIAL INDEX.

By JOHN JAMES MUNRO.

Abbess of Kilburn. *See* Prioress of Kilburn.

Abbot of Bermondsey, quit rent to, 89, 95, 139, 155, 168, 180, 210, etc.

Abbot of Waltham, business with, 238 ; gift of buck by, 250 ; pike sent to, 248 ; quit rent to, xl, 116, 133, 146, 161, 176, 188, 207, 240, etc. ; venison sent by, 248.

Abbot's buttery, 67.

Abbots, debt of, 46.

Abbot's house, deed respecting, xxxviii.

Abbot's kitchen, xl, xli, 219, 238, 240.

Abought, *prep.* about, 275.

Accion, *n.* action, 91.

Accounts, churchwardens', xv, xxvii, 61-413 ; appending of signatures to, xvi, 312, 313, *fac.*, 312-313 ; audit of, 230 ; book for, 371 ; changes in, lxx ; engrossing of, xxviii, 141, 156, 168, 180, 193, 204, 285 ; guilds', xxxiv ; order of, xxvii ; wax-chandler's (*see* Wax-chandler).

Admove, *v.* (*for* amove), 8.

Aisles, xli. *See also* South and North Aisles.

Alabaster, 58.

Albs, 30, 31, 33, 50 ; apparelling of, 219, 306, 354 ; girdles for, 251, 306 ; hallowing of, 240 ; making of, 257, 397 ; washing of, 72, 74, etc.

Aldermen of London, 18, 50, 143, 195, etc. ; burial of wife of, 261 ; wine for, xxxi, 187.

Ale, 21, 38, 65, 71, 390.

Ale-drawer, payment to, 90.

Allhallows, 61, 81, etc. ; refreshments in vestry on, 274.

Almarye, Almery, Almerye, *n.*

aumbry ; wall-cupboard, 29, 187, 361.

Almesse, *n.* alms, 9, 14.

Alms, lxxiv, 90, 97, 110, 121, 140, 190, 204, 289, 295, 318, etc. *See also* Chantries.

Alms' box, 299, 304.

Almsmen, xxv, 110, 375 ; organ-blowing by, xx, xxv, 328, 333, 340.

Almuces, lxix.

Altar, liv, lxxii, 6 ; apparel for, 30 ; Cambridge's, 311 ; candlesticks of, 32 ; canopy for, 397 ; curtains of, 234 ; frontals for, 30 ; hair-cloth for, lix, 256, 394 ; hallowing of, xxvi, xcvi, 403 ; hangings of, liv, 52, 53 ; latten basins for, 364 ; leaves of, liv, 293 ; linen cloths for, 27 ; making of, 394, 397 ; paving before, 244 ; pins for, 131 ; Our Lady's, 52 ; securing slab of, lxxi, 395 ; St. Ann's, 52, 255, 394 ; St. Catherine's, xxxix, 52, 172 ; St. Christopher's, 52, 55 ; St. Edmond's, 2 ; St. John the Baptist's, xli, 11 ; St. Stephen's, 32, 316 ; sale of table upon, 390 ; sphere for, 215 ; Sutton's, 273 ; tabernacles at, 350 ; taking down of, 391, 412 ; torches for, 11 ; towels for, 27 ; wax taper on feasts at, 13.

Altar cloths, 30, 32, 34, 35 ; baudekin, 30 ; blue, 30 ; canvas, 34 ; cloth of gold, 396 ; damask, 30 ; hallowing of 66, making and marking of, lix ; painting of, 316 ; presentation of, xxxv ; staining of, 250 ; subscription for, xvi.

Altar stones, 395, 412.

Amell, Amelyd, *n.* enamel, 31, 46, 343.

Glossarial Index.

Amener, *n.* almoner, 198.
Amices, 30, 31, 33, 50, 80, etc.
Ammasses, Amesys, Amys, Amysez, *n. p.* amices, 80, 135, 306, 397.
Ammoeved, *pp.* amoved; dismissed, 8, 12.
Andionis, Awndorns, *n. p.* andirons, 37.
Andirons, 37, 39.
Annunciation, feast of, 22, 128, etc.
Ansever, *n.* answer, 57.
Anssient, *adj.* ancient, 58.
Antempne, *n.* anthem, 16.
Antiphoners (books of antiphons), 27, 54, 101, 286, 395; binding of, 256; clasps for, 81; gift of, xxxv, 142, 182; leather for, 81; making of, 131; mending of, 172; rats gnawing covers of, 243; writing of, 133.
Apery, *v.* appeareth, 102.
Apostle-spoons, 47, 49, 356.
Aprons, bishops' and ministers', xcvi.
Arch, building of, xxxv, 158; stopping of, 69.
Archdeacon of St. Paul's, xxvii, 407, 411; presentation of priest to official of, 6; removal of priest by official of, 8.
Arerages, Arrerages, *n. p.* arrears, 77, 93.
Arms, 38, 45, 53.
Arms, barber's, 49.
Armyte, *n.* hermit, 276.
Arras, hiring of, 359.
Articles, books of, 399. Probably referring to the famous 42 Articles of Religion.
Ascension day, *fac.*, 322, 323, 382, etc.
Ashlar, 70, 257.
Asscheler, *n.* ashlar, 70.
Assigneis, *n. p.* assignees, 10.
Assumption day, 61, 173, 219, etc.
Astat, *n.* estate, 24.
Attorney, 23, 28; payment to, 256, 270, 282.
Auctorite, *n.* authority, 8.
Aumbries, 29, 40, 187, 309, 361.
Avbbys, *n. p.* albs, 251.
Avllmys man, *n.* almsman, 253.
Avter, Awter, Awtor, *n.* altar, 2, 6, 13, 19, 52, etc.
Aw, *v.* owe, 353.

Awew, *v.* aview; survey, 201.
Ayein, *adv.* again, 24.
Ayenst, Aȝenst, *prep.* against, 7, 45, 178.
Ayll, *n.* ale, 38.
Aȝyst, *v.* assist, 284.

Baker, xxxii, 127.
Baldricks. See *under* Bells.
Ballast, 214, 228.
Ballys, *n. p.* bells, 250.
Bankers (cloths or cushions for benches), 37.
Banket, *n.* banquet, 20.
Banner, 31, 361.
Banner-cloths, 27, 150.
Banner-poles, 234.
Banner-sockets, lxvii, 361.
Banner-staves, 186, 302, 322.
Banquet, funeral day, 20.
Barber, 94.
Barbowreȝ, *n.* barber's, 94.
Bard, *pp.* barred, 53.
Bargeman, 194.
Barrels, 214, 250, 269; use of, liv.
Basins, 38; altar, 214; barber's, 38; latten, 38, 52, 53; pewter, 52, 53; use of, liv.
Basket, dust, 131, 300, 322; holy bread, 247, 328.
Basket-maker, 58; payment to, 358.
Bass, hiring of, 349; payments to, 359, 393, 405, 409; wages of, xxiii.
Bastard, *n.* sweet Spanish wine, 172.
Baudekin, 31; blue, 52, 53; green, 51, 55; red, 51; white, 31.
Bawdkyn, *n.* baudekin, 30.
Bayle, *n.* bailiff, 259.
Beads, coral, 48; jet, 48, 50; silver, 45, 48.
Beadsmen. See Almsmen.
Beamlight, xlvii, 78, 95, 128, 146, 160, 171, 195, 216, 221, 233, 245, 265, 279, 298, 315, 334, 355, 379, etc.; taking down of, 218, 221.
Beams, latten, 37.
Bearers of body, payment to, 20.
Bede-roll, li, 21, 149, 162, 172, 184, 213, 229, 263, 309, 339, 342, 349, 381; table for, 234; writing of, 187, 229.
Bedredman, Bredrede man, *n.* bed-ridden-man, 115, 126.

Glossarial Index. 417

Beds, feather, 39, 40.
Bedsteads, 39, 40, 44; bottomless, 28; priest's, 340; sale of, 232; standing of, 28, 29, 40, 45.
Beedmen, *n. p.* beadsmen, almsmen, 333, 340.
Beef, ribs of, 65, 71.
Belfry, 281; lattices in, 382; windows in, *fac.*, 322, 323.
Bell, great (*see* Great bell); little (*see* Little bell); sacring (*see* Sacring bell); sanctus (*see* Sanctus bell).
Bellettes, *n. p.* billets; wood for fuel, 45.
Bell-founder, arrest of, 270, 273; payment to, 275.
Bells, lv, 33, 38, 52, 54; arbitration over, 270, 273; baldricks for, 69, 71, 80, 241, 274, 275, 292, 298, 305; buckle for clapper of, 101; clappers of, 214, 241, 281; chrisoms for, 250; engraving on, 33, 275; grease for, 322, 403; gudgeons for, 251, 274; guards for ropes of, 277; hallowing of, lv, 310; inscriptions on, 33, 275; latten, lv, 54, 131; law action over, lv, 267, 270, 273; ringers of (*see* Ringers); ringing of, xv, xxxiv, 11, 21, 90, 97, 128, 178, 212, 231, 236, 247, 266, 295, 322, 327, etc. (*see also* Knells); ropes of, lv, 80, 185, 238, 244; sacrament canopy, lv, 131; sale of silver, 59, 389; silver and gilt, 33; tune of, lv, 273, 274; tuning and fitting up of, 274, 275; wheels of, 101, 214, 302, 327.
Bellows-maker, 412.
Beloming, *pres. p.* belonging, 60.
Bench in choir, 270.
Beoyldyng, *n.* building, 19.
Bequests, xxxv, xliv, 8, 11, 16, 24, 230, 236, 237, 241, 244, 249, 257, 259, 267, 283, 287, 301, 330, 345, 346, 356, etc.
Bere wyffe = wife at Bear Inn, 46.
Berrell cross, mending of, 344.
Beryenge, *n.* burying, 61.
Beryes, *n. p.* burials, 128.
Besom, *n.* broom, xcvi.
Besynes, *n.* business, 8, 292, 326.
Bible, lvi, 373.

Bielde, *v.* build.
Bill of hand, 294.
Bills, xxxii.
Bin, oat, 29.
Binding of parson and parishioners by deed, 4.
Birch, purchase of, 131, 149, 163, 173, 187, 215, 264, 391, etc.
Bird spit, 38.
Bishop, book for, 399.
Bishop of London, xxvi, 56, 296; house of, 60; visitation by, 214, 230.
Bishop's miter, lxix, 27, 31, 389, 399.
Bishop Suffragan, xxvi; hallowing of altar by, 198, 403; hallowing of vestments by, 306.
Bladare, *n.* blader, 5.
Blake, *adj.* black, 20.
Blankets, 39, 45, 147.
Boards, elm, 85, 87, 104, 105, 135, 138, 165; paling, 167; purchase of, 72, 86, 104, 135, 155, 165, 256, etc.
Boat, payment for carriage by, 256.
Boat-hire, xxxvi, 164, 203, 223, 256, 269, 296, 326, 382, 403.
Bocher, *n.* butcher, 77.
Bodkin, *n.* baudekin, 51, 52, 53.
Bodome, *n.* bottom, 46.
Boge, Bogge, Buge, Bugge, *n.* budge; kind of fur prepared from lambskin, 41–43.
Bokelers, *n. p.* bucklers, 38.
Bokell, Bokyll, *n.* buckle, 49, 80, 101.
Bokeram, *n.* buckram, 27, 64, etc.
Bokys, *n. p.* books, 67.
Bolster, 39, 40
Bolts, 69, 151; iron, 29, 130; tinning of, 130.
Bonnets, 44.
Bookbinder, payment to, 256, 379.
Books, delivery to Royal Commission (1553) of, 56, 394; for counsel, 399; of Laws, 28; old, 37; presentation to Bishop of, 399; writing of, 285, 399. *See also* Articles, Decretals, Injunctions, Rental Book, and under Chantries, Counsel and St. Nicholas. For books of service, *see* Service books.

Glossarial Index.

Book-skin, 214.
Boottes, *n. p.* boats, 223.
Bord Alexander (striped silk), 27, 154.
Bord Alysaundre, *n.* striped silk, 27.
Bordys, *n. p.* boards, 72.
Bose, *n.* boss, 49, 50.
Bossys, *n. p.* bosses, 47.
Bottes, *n. p.* butts, 281.
Bottrye, *n.* buttery, 28.
Bovshope, *n.* bishop, 56.
Bovsshoppes Sealle, *n.* Bishop's seal, 393.
Bowls, xcvi, 39, 163.
Bowȝte, *imp. v.* bought, 131.
Box, purchase of, 117, 130, 173, 185, 197, 383, etc.
Brabant stonys, *n. p.?* 177.
Brachyals, *n. p. brachialia*, loose sleeves, xcvi.
Branch of the Trinity, xxxv, lvii, 304–306.
Branches, xxxv, lvii, 33, 225, 255, 264, 304–307.
Brase, *n.* brace, 224, 313.
Brass pot, sale of, 231, 271.
Brawderer, Breyderer, Browderer, *n.* broiderer, 76, 144, 256, 310.
Bread, 21, 65, 71, etc.
Breakfasts, 102, 225.
Breddes, *n. p.* breadths, 42.
Brede, Breede, *n.* breadth, 32–34.
Brek, Breke, *n.* brick, 69, 318.
Brekyng, *n.* bricking, 87.
Brenne, *v.* burn, 2, 13.
Brennyng, *pres. p.* burning, 6.
Brethern, *n. p.* brethren, 5.
Breton, burial of, 196, 291, 307.
Breviary (portos), lvi, 45, 173.
Brewer, 9, 92, 111.
Brewhouse, bequest of, 8.
Brewing, 1.
Bricks, purchase of, 87, 104, 106, 109, etc.; sale of, 318.
Bridge from parsonage to roof of church aisle, xvii, 311.
Bridgehouse, masters of, xliv; quit-rent to masters of, 95, 122, 153, 166, 178, 190, 202, 208.
Brigge, *n.* bridge, 13.
Brist, *n.* breast, 71.
Brodde, *adj.* broad, 48.
Broddes, *n. p.* spikes, 224, 229.
Broom, purchase of, 391.

Brooms, purchase of, 243, 247, 255, 298, 322, 367.
Brotherhoods, xxxiv; Our Lady's (*see* Guild of Salve Regina); torches for, 20; St. Ann's, 20, 283; St. Christopher's, 20, 283, 325; St. Katherine's, 20.
Broudred, *pp.* broidered, 31, 34.
Bruer, *n.* brewer, 9.
Brussels cloth, 244, 372.
Bruyng, *n.* brewing, 1.
Bryddes, *n. p.* birds, 30.
Bucket, well, 29, 82, 87.
Bucklers, 38.
Buckram, 27, 39, 43, 44, 64, 80, 101, 130, 378.
Building, art of, xxxii.
Buns, spiced, 139.
Buriage, *n.* burial, 345.
Burials, xlix, lxiv, 78, 111, 128, 161, 183, 218, 236, 245, 259, 267, 284, 294, 311; *fac.*, 322–323, 344, 363, 383, 400, etc.; fees for, xlix; provision for, 9, 10, 19; regulations concerning, 319; torches at, xlix. *See also* Leystoff.
Burying cloths. *See* Palls.
Bushel, 65, 78, 88, etc.
Bussell, *n.* bushel, 88.
Busteyn, Bvstine, *n.* bustian; a cotton fabric, 27, 52.
Bustian, 27, 52.
Butcher, 77, 113.
Buttery, 38.
Button, gold, 45.
Bvring clothe, *n.* burying cloth; pall, 53.
Byldyd, *pp.* builded, built, 3.

Caas, *n.* case, 10, 12.
Cakes, 383.
Callybar, *n.* Calabar; fur, probably of squirrel, 43.
Camlet, 45; black, 43; tawny, 42, 43, 356.
Canape, Canypde, *n.* canopy, 32, 364.
Candlemas, 61, 86, etc.; decorations at, 148.
Candles, distribution of, xix, 304; gifts of, xxxviii, xxxix, 2, 6, 11, 13, 15, 16, 19, 20; payments at burials and obits for, 78, 90, 128, 146, 161, 183, etc.; plates for, 270; purchase of, 71, 81 (*see also* Waxchandler and Wax-reckoning);

Glossarial Index. 419

reeds for lighting, lxvii, 251; tallow, 33, 81.
Candlesticks, 38; altar, 32; borrowing of, 407; branched, 33; gift of, 15; hand, 270; hanging, 358; latten, 27, 33, 52, 53; pewter, 39; scouring of, 100, 130, 220; silver, 16, 51, 254. *See also* Prickets and Sconces.
Canell, Cornell, *n.* kennel, gutter, drain, 101, 340.
Cane stone, *n.* Caen stone?, 104.
Canopies, lviii, 51, 53, 150; bells of, 54, 131; baudekin, 31; great Corpus Christi, lviii, 53, 131, 150, 273, 301; iron of, 226; iron rod for great, 273; leather thongs for staves of, lviii, 301; red silk, 31; staves of, 53.
Canopy cloth, 54.
Canopy crowns, lviii, 31, 163.
Canvas, 34, 42; Normandy, 250.
Capon, 270.
Capper, 76, 92, 111, 112, 125.
Caps, 43, 147.
Carols, books of, lvi, 54.
Carpenters, payment to, xxxii, 64, 72, 83, 100, 109, 150, 167, 211, 241, 252, 274, 301, 304, 309, 337; refreshments for, 54.
Carpet, 45; Kentish, 37, 40.
Cart, 104, 178.
Carter, payment to, 64.
Carvers, payment to, 224, 302.
Catallis, *n. p.* chattels, 18.
Caunte peace, *n.* cant piece, inclined piece, 132, etc.
Causey, making of, 163.
Cavlled, *pp.* called, 52.
Celarie, *n.* salary, 121.
Celer, *n.* cellar, 113, 139.
Cellar, rental of, 113.
Censers, 16, 51, 407; filling of, lxvii; foot to, 251; iron dishes for, 70, 187; latten, 397; mending of, 339; pawning of, xxxvi, 375; silver, 26, 51, 353; ships for, lxvii, 16, 26, 27, 197, 397.
Cere cloth, 150, 151.
Certins, *n. p.* curtains, 52.
Chafers, 38, 279.
Chaffor, *n.* chafer, 38.
Chafing dish, 279.
Chain, 64; golden, 48.
Chairs, 37; rectors of choir's iron, xxiv, 31; Spanish, 37; wainscot, 37.
Chales, Challyes, *n.* chalice, 26, 49, 270, 277, 358.
Chalices, 270, 277; gift to church of, xxxv, 79; sale of silver, 59; silver, 26, 27, 51, 53, 57, 59.
Chambers, cleaning of, 74; rental of, 124.
Chambylyt, *n.* camlet, 356.
Chancel, books chained in, 234; oil lamp for, 17.
Chancellor, xxvii, 296, 344.
Chantries, xviii; Bedham's, xviii, 16, 76, 88, 93, 110, 114, 140, 154, 160, 179, 195, 216, 250, 295; book of statutes concerning, 407; Cambridge's, xviii, xliv, 14, 76–78, 89, 113, 125, 139, 155, 157, 179, 192, 216, 250, 263, 295; Causton's, xviii, xliv, 4, 75, 77, 83–85, 95, 114, 121, 134, 156, 166, 177–179, 195, 201–203, 250, 295; counsel concerning, 387; expenses of, 234; founders of, 132, 162; Gosslyn's, xviii, 13, 76, 85–87, 93, 114, 135–137, 152, 165, 176, 195, 209, 250, 295; King's Commission for, 387; knitting together of two, 165, 176; loss of, lxx; Nasing's, xviii, 9, 94, 113, 128, 151, 165, 183, 207, 250, 299, 344, 383; ornaments of, 2; overseers for rent of, xxiv, 320; payment of subsidy to King by, 250; Porth's, xviii, 346; priests of (*see* Chantry Priests); Rose Wrytell's, xviii, 1, 94, 118, 125, 141, 160, 176, 201, 250; searching for records of, 373; vacancy of, 6, 10; Weston's, xviii, xliv, 10, 75, 79, 116, 161, 176, 189, 250, 295, 297, 373, 383.
Chantry priests, business of, xviii, xlviii, 5, 12, 17, 18, 303; chests of, 303; choosing of, 6, 8, 10, 12, 13, 14, 18, 19; morrow-mass sung by, xviii; provision against sinful, 3, 8, 10; sustentation of, 11, 13, 17, 19; vestments of, 303; wages of, 346 (*see also* Priests).
Chapels, burying in, xlix. *See* St. Ann's, St. Christopher's, St. John's, St. Katherine's and St. Thomas' Chapels.
Charche, *v.* charge, 115.

Charder, *n.* chaldron, 262.
Chardg, *v.* charge, 60.
Chargers, 38.
Charnel-house, 275, 343.
Chasubles, 30, 31, 101, 135, etc.; chest for, 303; gift to church of, xvi, 31; mending of, 135.
Chattels, 46.
Cheese, 382.
Chekred, *pp.* chequered, 33.
Chese, *v.* choose, 6.
Cheseblys, Chysyblis, *n. p.* chasubles, 101, 292.
Chest, jewel, 215; plate, 331; Porth's, 331, 334, 356; spruce, 39; standard, 40; torch, 81, 255; treasury, 261; vestment, 81, 230, 275, 358; 303, 317; wax, 278.
Chests, 27, 39, 44, 53, etc.; money (*see under* Church).
Chickens, 270.
Children at Mass, xxii; payments to, 147, 162, 172, 290; school for (*see* School and School-house); vestments for, 33, 273, 292, 377; wicker mats for, 322; wine for, 186.
Chimney, bricking of, 87; making of, 107; mending of, 105, 136, 168, 189, 200, 202; *fac.*, 322–323.
Chirchehawe, Churchaw, *n.* churchyard (*O.E.* haʒa, an enclosure), xlii, 67, 70, 99, 101.
Chist, *n.* chest, 53.
Choir, apparel for, xxxii, lxix, 27, 31, 33, 238, 244, 321, 358, etc.; assistance for, xxiii, xxiv, 81, 173, 197, 232, 233, 246, 256, 346, 397, 399; bass of, 329, 349; children in, xxiii; expenses of, 148, 162, 172, 185, 197; maintenance of, xvii, 363, 377 (*see also* Parson's Duty); payments to (*see* Roll of Clerks' wages *and* Payment to Clerks); Rectors of (*see* Rectors of Choir); refreshments for, xvi, 117, 149, 163, 219, 230, 243, 264, 277, 305, 306, 344; trebles for, 197, 382.

Choir, xli; antiphoners in, 350; chest in, 278, 332; coffer in, 300; curtains in, 135; desks in, 243, 323, 327, 351; double desk in, 340; doors of, 69, 237, 293; floor of, 367; form in, 270; garnets for doors of, 69; hanging candlestick in, 358; images by door of, 359; lamp for, 240, 255; little organ in, 306, 395; locks to doors of, 69, 237, 293; middle, 293; paving of, 69; pulpit by, 354; sconces for, 244, 333; screen in, 69, 219; stalls in, lxvii, 64, 69.

Chollve, *n. for* chovell, shovel, 255.
Chonnge, *n.* change, 277.
Chongyng, *n.* changing, 306.
Choristers, xxii; boarding of, xxiii, 162; books used by, xxii; debt of, xxxiii, 405; clothes for, xxxii; number of, xxiv; wages of, 59; wicker mats for (*see* Wicker mats). *See also* Clerks.

Christening, 1, liv, 222.
Christmas, 61, 91, 185, 402, etc.; carols for, 378; cleaning for, 264; decorations at, liii (*see also* Holly *and* Ivy); evening service at, xxxviii, 16; refreshments at, xxxi.
Church,[1] accounts of, xv, xxviii, 61–

---

[1] A short account of the church and its vestments will be found in Knight's *London*, Vol. v. p. 191. Noorthouck's *London* (1773) gives various interesting particulars (p. 552), together with a useful map of Billingsgate Ward and a small picture of the church. *A New View of London* (1708) gives a more elaborate account of the fabric, organ, officers, etc. (Vol. ii. p. 373). Stow's *Survey of London*, etc., seems to be the source from which many of the old writers drew much of their information. An account of St. Mary at Hill will be found at page 168, Vol. i. book 2 (Strype's edition) of the above work. A map of Billingsgate Ward is given at p. 165. Various particulars are also given in Seymour's *Survey of London* (1735), Vol. i. bk. 2, p. 435, and in Maitland's *History of London* (1756), Vol. ii. bk. 3, p. 1139. Malcolm in his *Londinium Redivivum* (Vol. iv. p. 421) prints a bad version of the first part of the Inventory given at page 30 of these Records. He misreads "Mongeham" as "Yongeham," "blewe" as "black," "fugerid" as "fringed," "Rector Coris" as "Rectes Copes," etc., and omits the last item on our page 31, the

Glossarial Index. 421

413; acting by door of, xxiv (*see also* Palm Sunday *and* Prophets); aisles of, xli (*see also* North aisle *and* South aisle); arms in, 53; banner staves in, 186, 302, 322; barrels of, 214, 250, 269; battlement of, 264, 267, 284, 288; benevolence of, 342; bequests to (*see* Bequests); borrowing by, xxxvi, lxxii, 305, 309, 324, 331, 334, 363; bridge to parsonage from, 311; brotherhoods of (*see* Brotherhoods); burials in,[1] xlix, 9, 10, 19, 78, 218, 225, 232, 241, 253, 261, 271, 293, 306, 314, 317, 319, 324, 348, 368, 374, 383; business conducted in, xvii; candles in, xxxviii (*see also* Candles); casual receipts of, xxviii, 78, 128, 142, etc.; chairs in, 31, 351; changes at Reformation in, lxx, lxxi, lxxii; chapels of, xli (*see also* Chapels); cleaning of, 69, 173; clerestory of, xli, 255, 256; coals for (*see* Coals); collections in, l, 261, 284; debt of, 59, 308, 325 (*see also* Borrowing by Church); debt to, xxxv, 84, 92, 111, 122, 127, 193, 194, 353 (*see also* Debtors *and* Money lent by Church); decorations in, lii, liii, 81, 130, 163, 185, 214, etc. (*see also* Palm, Flowers, Birch, etc.); delivery to King's commissioners of goods of, 50; demolition at Reformation in,[2] lxxii; derivation of properties of, xxix; destruction of furniture of, xliii; division of sexes in, li, lxxiv; donation to works of, 94; dust basket for, 131, 300, 322; east gate of, 302; erection of gate of, 69; evidence belonging to, 27; expenses for profit of, 164, 174; fabric of, xli; fishmongers in livery at, 21; fund for charities of, 284; furniture of, 26, 30, 35, 50; gifts to, xx, xxxv, lii, lv, lxxiv, 14, 30, 34, 35, 54, 55, 77, 78, 79, 80, 94, 126, 142, 145, 146, 158, 161, 182, 214, 221–223, 228, 236, 241, 244, 250, 251, 255, 257, 261, 263, 271, 277, 281, 285, 286, 291, 302, 306–308, 315, 389, 399; gloves for officers of, lxiii, 326, 330; great book of, 255; hallowing of, xcv, 250, 255; hallowing of articles for, liii, 199, 240; hiring of goods of, 94; images in, xxxix, lxii, lxvii, 2, 6, 224, 250, 271, 359, 401 (*see also under* Our Lady);

---

first words of which are exactly the same as those of the following item. Allen in his *History of London* (1828), Vol. iii. p. 113, prints Malcolm's version with its errors, and adds more, giving "Trenne" for "Prewne," "starvs" for "stavys," etc. Allen says, Vol. iii. p. 116: "In Mr. Nichol's *Illustrations of the Manners and Expenses of Ancient Times*, published in 1797, are considerable extracts from the registers of this church (St. Mary at Hill); they relate to the plate, vestments, property, etc., of the parish for a number of years." I have not met with this book. The most valuable publication in this connection would appear to be that mentioned in the Preface to these *Records*, p. viii.

[1] On p. 248 of Riley's *Memorials of London* will be found a Release given by Wm. Olneye to Sir Adam de Burdene, rector of St. Mary at Hill (1362), as one of the executors of Richard de Hakeneye. Hakeneye was sheriff of London in 1321, and both he and his wife were buried in the church. In 1496, however, when workmen were making a foundation within the edifice, the body of Alice Hakenye was accidentally exhumed. (Stow—Strype's edition—quoting Fabian, Vol. i. bk. 2, p. 168, but giving the date as 1497.) Malcolm, in *Londinium Redivivum*, p. 420, says that the exhumation took place during work on the South Aisle. But the South Aisle was not begun until 1500-1 (*Med. Records*, p. 240). The work in question was probably in connection with the Roodloft (p. 224). After remaining above ground some days, the bodies of Hakeneye and his wife were buried together once more, the costs being this time borne by John Halhed. See p. 225 of these Records, where we are told of lime and sand for "makyng ayeyn of their tombe," with the date, mᶜccc lxxxvj.

[2] The order for this demolition may be seen in Elisabeth's book of Injunctions. *See* Injunctions.

MED. REC. F F

inventories of goods of, xxx, 26, 30,[1] 35, 50, 374, 393, 412; jewels of, 284; key and swivel for door of, 66; keys for money-chest of, 269, 273, 291; lamp for, 17; lands of (see Church lands and Romeland); lead for roof of, 332; light at night in, 17; mats in, lxiv; money-chest of, xxiv, 53, 269, 273, 291, 303, 308, 312, 330; money-coffer of, 331; money found in, 94, 196, 212; money in custody of, 320, 328; money lent by, xxxiii, xxxvi, 197, 300, 309, 324, 375; napery of, 50, 52; nave of, xlviii; north door of, 327; oil for (see Oil); oil-pots for, lxiv, 101, 358; ornaments of, 50, 52, 55; painted glass in, lxiii; patroness of, 401; paving of, 67, 81, 214, 268; paving lane at west of, 66; plate of, xx, 51, 53, 56; plate chest of, 331; pledge to, lxxiii; poles in, lxvi; pole to sweep roof of, 148; porch of (see Porch of Church); position of, xlii; precedent in, 330, 342; pre-reformation furniture of, liii; procession in, 16; raker of, xxiv (see also Raker); rats in, xxxix, 243, 322, 343; relic coffer of, 26; reparation of, 19, 59, 102, etc.; restoration under Mary of goods of, 53; roof of, xli, 187, 332, 399; royal commissioners' inquiries, 1552, respecting goods of, 56; sale of goods of, lxx, lxxi, 58, 388–390, 394; services in, xxxviii, xlviii; settles in, lxvii, 53; shovels for, 100, 234, 255; shovels used in, lxvii; south aisle of (see South aisle); south door of, 70, 278, 327, 344; south window of, 332; staff of, xvi; staple and keys for door of, 135; steeple of (see Steeple); storehouse of, 236, 237; fac., 322–323, 363, 365, 370; subsidy of, 54; superfluous linen of, 60; sweeping of, xix, xcvi, 99, 131, 148, 185, 303; sweeping roof of, lxvi; refreshments bought by, xvii, xxxi, xxxii, lii, 21, 71, 80, 81, 83, 90, 92, 97, 100, 111, 117, 140, 148, 163, 164, 179, 186, 190–192, 210, 230, 247, 248, 264, 270, 275, 281, 295, 316, 326, 328, etc.; rents of (see Church rents); transept of (cross aisle), 319, 320; trusteeship of, xxxi; upper storey of, xli, 274; vestments of,[2] lxix (see also Vestments, etc.); washing cloths of (see Laundress; watching in, 81, 83, 173, 234, 247; water for, 367; west door of, 350, 373; west gate of, 273; whiting of, 58, 220, 277; windows of (see Windows); withholding money of, 296; work done for, xxxii.

Churching, 1, 329.
Church lands, 367; lawsuit concerning, 399, 402. See also Romeland.

---

[1] The date assigned to the Inventory of the Church Furniture at p. 30 is open to criticism. The leaves of the MS. (B. 25, etc.) are inscribed at the top right-hand corner with the names of Halhed and Prewne, churchwardens. The correct date of the Inventory would, therefore, in all probability correspond with the date of office of these two men. There is ample evidence, although the accounts for 1485-7 are now, unfortunately, lost, that Halhed and Prewne were wardens in 1485-6, the date which Malcolm prints above the Inventory (Lond. Red. Vol. v. p. 421). Towards the end of our Accounts for 1483-5 (p. 122) will be seen an account of the money delivered by the outgoing wardens to the incoming wardens, Wm. Prewne and John Halhed. On page 123 is the total sum delivered them ("Grene" here should be "Prene"; see Errata)— and notes on pages 127, 129, show that in 1487-8 they had lately given up office. The date, however, is completely settled by the note on p. 4 which speaks of Prewne and Halhed as churchwardens in m^l cccc lxxxvj. The expression "late parson" in connection with William Wild (p. 31) is not clear. Wild was certainly parson still in 1500-1 (p. 238). The note concerning the surplice (p. 34), dated 1492, was evidently a later addition. On the whole it seems fairly certain that the Inventory should be dated 1485-6.

[2] See previous note, on Inventories, above.

Glossarial Index. 423

Church rents, xxviii, xxix, xxxii, xxxiii, 112, 125, 128, 145, 160, 170, 174, 182, 195, 199, 212, 216; book for, 300; complete list of, 376; gathering of, 285; maintenance of, 363; overseers of, xxiv, 111, 285, 320; reparation of, 357.

Churchwardens, xxi; accounts of, xv, xxvii, 61–413; articles sold by, xlv, 232, 236, 253, 257, 259, 271, 276, 279, 298, 306, 307, 318, 357, 358, 389, 390, 394; business of, xxi, lxxiv, 4, 12, 14, 17–19, 20, 22, 52, 55–57, 59–61, 63, 92, 110, 143, 182, 262, 285, 295; choosing of, xxi, 264; extent of office of, xxi; gloves for, 326, 330; notes by, xxviii, 16, 74, 152, 157, 165, 169, 181, 227, 231, 239, 240, 246, 251, 260, 262, 284, 285, 288, 294, 303, 304, 308, 312, 316, 319, 325, 330, 342, 352, 353; payment to, 14, 88, 110, 121, 140, 154, 189, 211, 289, 295.

Churchyard, xlii; caussey in, 163; cross in, xlii, 300; cutting grass in, 411; doors of, 261, 278; door to, 362; entry into, 351; gate in, 273; gravelling of, 185, 186; great (*see* Great churchyard); gutters in, 303; hallowing of, xcvi; houses in, 101, 124, 301, 389, 390, 391, 393, 396; key of, xlii, 261; pale in, 337; pardon (*see* Pardon churchyard); paths in, xlii; procession, xlii, 100; sand in, 269; sawing in, 338; sweeping and cleaning of, 67, 70, 185, 186, 198, 302, 314, 321; walls of, 300, 301; work in, 215, 229; yew planted in, xlii, 403.

Chyne, *n.* chain, 48.

Cistern, 166; mending of, 90.

City, custom of the, 353.

Claret, 403.

Clavicords, 44.

Clerks, xxii; absence of, 329; business of, xlix, lxxv, 21, 133, 303, 304, 319; engaging of, xxxi, xxxvii, xxix, 238, 281, 329, 331, 332, 333, 339, 343; gloves for, 326, 330; house of, 85, 151; privies for, 109; refreshments for (*see* Refreshments bought by church); wicker mats for (*see* Wicker mats); payment to, xxiii, xlix, lxxv, 6, 7, 11, 21, 80, 90, 98, 119, 131, 153-155, 178–180, 197, 214, 238, 247, 266, 289, 295, 305, 364, 373, 397, etc. (*see also* Parish clerk). *See also* Conducts, Parish clerk *and* Choristers.

Clerks' wages, roll of, xxiii, 126, 128, 145, 160, 171, 181-183, 195, 211, 216, 227, 241, 261, 279, 293, 296, 307, 333, 362, 379, 398, etc.; making of roll of, 285, 378.

Cloth, calendering of, 135; crimson, 44; Cypress, 31, 267; green, 29; Normandy, 230; silver, 41; stained, 51.

Clothes, 42, 43.

Clothes of the Tower, lx. *See also under* Prophets.

Cloth of gold, 26, 27, 30, 31, 45, etc.; blue, 51, 55; purple, 30; red, 30, 51; russet, 30, 52; white, 30, 51.

Cloths, altar (*see* Altar cloths); banner, lx, 27, 52, 150; canopy, 54; cross, lix, 51, 234; cross staves, lx, 31; font, 54; golden ornament on, 31; holy-bread, lx, 35; housling, lx; painted, 53, 54, 388; pyx (*see* Pyx cloths); rood, 54; sacrament, lx, 54, 369; sepulcre, lx, 51, 343; tabernacle, 131, 230.

Cnop, Cnope, *n.* knop, knob, 46, 47.

Coalhouse, 207.

Coals, 45; distribution to poor of, l, 318; purchase of, 81, 100, 130, 162, 197, 214, 296, 364.

Coats of fence, 43.

Cobbler, 129.

Cobbord, *n.* cupboard, 37.

Cobe yrons, *n.p.* cobirons, 38.

Coffers. *See* Money coffer of church, *and* Relic coffer of church.

Coffins, 245; making of, 187, 411.

Coins, xlvi.

Colander, 38.

Colis, Colles, Cooles, *n.p.* coals, 45, 81, 117.

Collets, 12, 16.

Collombyn, *n.* columbine, 47.

Collors, *n.p.* colours, 44.

Commissary, xxvii, 6, 240.

Commission, royal. *See* Royal commission.

424   *Glossarial Index.*

Communion, bread and wine for, 396, 411, 412; collection at, 1, 128.
Communion board, bench round, 395; cloths for, 396; making of, 412; money received at, 54.
Complene, *n.* compline, 17.
Conduct, xix, xx; hiring of, 406; meaning of, xxii; payments to, 232, 242, 281, 293, 302, 314, 329, 334, 345, 352, 359, 365, 375, 386, 402, etc.; surplices for, 358, 372; wages of, xxii, 350.
Conny, *n.* fur of rabbit, 42.
Conscience, discharging of, 19.
Constables, 370.
Conys, *n.p.* rabbits, 270.
Cook, 156.
Cooper, payment to, 269.
Cope, Cooppe, Coppe, Cowpe, *n.* cup, 26, 46, 257, 357.
Copes, xlvi, lxix, lxxv, 26, 27, 30, 31, 51, 101, etc.; arms worked on, 256; children's, lxix, 27, 31, 51; drying of, lxxv; gift of, 20; tables and trestles for, 100.
Coral, 45.
Cord, purchase of, 99.
Corder, 1.
Cordewaner *n.* cordwainer; worker in leather, 1.
Coronations, xxxiii.
Corporas, 27, 30, 33, etc.; hallowing of, 314; washing of, 350.
Corporas cases, 30, 31, 33, 51, etc.
Corpus Christi day, xviii, liii, lviii, 81, 100, 131, 149, 173, 186, 305, 309, 322, 330.
Corse, 41, "Corse of a gyrdell—*tissu*" (Palgrave, 209).
Cortins, *n.p.* curtains, 52, 53.
Cosen, *n.* cousin, 314.
Cosse dyamons?, 41.
Cott, *n.* coat, 42.
Cotton, white, 44; yellow, 42, 44.
Coucher, lvii, 225.
Couent, *n.* convent, 4.
Counsel, book for, 309.
Covnterpayn, Counturpane, *n.* counterpart (of a deed), 56, 281.
Counters, 29, 37, 40. "At a later time there appears to have been a piece of ordinary furniture in the hall of a mansion termed a counter, probably from its resemblance to the table properly so called. In the Inventories printed by the Surtees Society, mention frequently occurs of the counter and the counter-cloths; as likewise of 'doble counters, counters of myddell bynde, Flanders counters with their carpets.'—*Wills and Invent.*" (*Promptorium Parv.* p. 98.)
Counting house, 45.
Covering, Norwegian, 45.
Cowplis, *n.p.* couples, rafters of roof; chevrons, 106.
Coynes, *n.p.* coignes, 68.
Crase, *n.* crack, 255.
Cremysyn, *adj.* crimson, 40.
Cressomes, *n.p.* chrisoms, 250.
Crismatories, xxvii, lxi; burnishing of, 369; pewter, 396; silver, 51.
Crochates, *n.* crockets; small ornaments in Gothic architecture, 64.
Cross-aisle (transept), 319, 320.
Crosses, lxi; Berrell, 305, 361; best, 343; borrowing of, 407; copper, 55; crystal, 26; every-day, or processional, 101, 117; fixing of, 70; foot of, 32, 53; gilding of, 81; latten, 27; making of, 70; mending of, 101; monstrance (*see* Monstrance); St. Anthony's, 32; silver, 26, 27, 51; super-altar, 198; use at hallowing of, xcvi.
Cross staves, lxi; cloths for, lx, 31; gilding of, 238; latten, 32.
Crucifixes, 39, 53, 399; painting of, 344.
Cruets, 39, 214; changing of, 340; lead, 54; mending of, 149; purchase of, 278, 381; sale of, 358; silver, 26.
Cunnyng, *n.* ability, 5.
Cupboard, 37, 38, 44.
Cups, 49; enchased, 48, 49; gift of, xxxv, 255, 257; latten, 26; purchase of, 90; silver, 26; standing, 46, 358.
Curate, book that lay before, 379; hiring of, 411; payments to, lxxv, 21, 392-395, 401, 409; reading desk of, 412; surplices for, 351.
Curfew, ringing of, xxvi, 332.
Curtain rings and hooks, 131.
Curtains, 28, 30, 37, 39, 51, 55, 130, etc. (*see also* Hangings); bars

Glossarial Index. 425

for, 28; rods for, 54; suspension of, lxi, 131.
Cushions, lxi, 33, 37, 53.
Cvshens, *n. p.* cushions, 37.
Cypress cloth, 31, 267.

Dagger, 45.
Daily cross, 323.
Damask, 26, 30, 35; gold, 41, 44; red, 51, 52; russet, 52; white, 39.
Daubers, payment to, 66, 73, 109, 132, 151, 174, 209, etc.
Daubing, straw for, 108.
Daughter by name, 24.
Daughter, natural, 22.
Deacon, 51–53, 397.
Debtors, xvii, 142, 156, 168–170, 193, 205, 226, 260, 265, 293, 308, 369, etc.; suing of, 353; surety for, 137, 320. *See also under* Church.
Debts, xvii, 46; bequest of, 18; distraint for, 7; desperate, 46; six months' notice for payment of, xvii. *See also under* Church.
Decretals, book of, 28.
Defaulters, xxxiii.
Defayle, *v.* defail, fail, 7, 12,
Dekyn, *n.* decking, 31.
Delywrt, *pp.* delivered, 357.
Demessent, Demysent, *n.* demiceint, woman's ornamented girdle, 48.
De Profundis, 12.
Desks, xcvi, 40, etc.; book, 233; choir, 243, 323, 327, 340, 351; double, 340; latten, 32; organ, 317.
Dexkes, Dextes, *n. p.* desks, xcvi, 327.
Dey, *v.* die, 19.
Di = L. *dimidium;* one half, 16, 32, *et passim.*
Diaper work, 30, 32–36, 41.
Dinners, bills of, xxxii, 275.
Dirige, *n.* first word of Latin antiphon in office for dead: hence, name for that service, dirge, 6, 11, 15, 17, 21, 84, 139, 225, 283, 310; ringing bells at, 311.
Discipling rods, lxii, 185, 269. "The discipline rods were for use on Good Friday. Sir Thomas More speaks of the lady who wept when she remembered 'that the priest had on Good Friday with the dyspelyng roade beaten her harde vppon her lylye white hands.'" Wickham Legg's *Clerk's Book,* p. 118. Henry Bradshaw Society.
Dishes, 38; censer, 70; paschal, 64; rood light, 255.
Divinity, learning in, 14.
Dog, iron, 224.
Doghtir, *n.* daughter, 78.
Dole, *n.* share, 20.
Dona, *n. p.* gifts (*plur.* L. *donum*), 94.
Donge, *n.* dung, 67, 70.
Door, running, 139.
Dots, meaning of series of, xv.
Doublets, 43, 45; canvas, 147; making of, 148; satin, 356.
Draper, 22, 113, 125, 235.
Dressing boards, 29.
Drinking, xxxi. *See under* Rent and Church.
Dripping-pan, 38.
Dung, clearing of, 67, 70, 82, 87, 210, 227, 292, etc.
Dung-boat, xli, 359, 397 (?), making of, 378.
Durre, *n.* door, 3.
Dust, clearing of, 88, 99, 101, 131, etc.
Dying, home for, xlvii.
Dyssplyng Roddys, *n. p.* discipline rods, 185.
Dyuyne, *adj.* divine, 5.
Dyvarars, *adj.* divers, 51.
Dyvynite, *n.* divinity, 14.

Eagle, latten, 243, 267. *See* Falcon.
Earnest penny, 102.
Easter, 4, 61, 81, 117, 173, etc.; acting at (*see under* Palm Sunday); ceremonies at, liii; coals for, liii, 117, 131, 162, 173; preparations for, 343; sepulchre for (*see* Sepulchre); water for font at, 301.
Easter Eve, dinner on, 273.
Eaves board, 73, 86, 101, 137, etc.
Ecclesiastical Court, proceedings at, xxxiii, 278, 296.
Echyng, *n.* enlarging, 68.
Edward VI, birth of, xxxiv, 373; changes in reign of, lxx, lxxi; commissioners of, 50.
Eiton, Eyten, *pp.* eaten, 41, 44.

Glossarial Index.

Elisabeth of York, funeral of, xxxiii, 247.
Ell, 32, 33, 34, *et passim*.
Elm, purchase of, 85, 87, 104, 105, 135, 138, 165.
Elmyn borde, *n.* elm board, 85, 87, 104, etc.
Elnes, *n. p.* ells, xcvi.
Emmys, *n. p.* M's, 35.
Emperell, *n.* 136.
Enamel, 31, 46; white and green, 49.
England, church of, 14.
Engraving on bell, 33.
Enioie, *v.* enjoy, 24.
Epistle book, 27.
Erasmus, Paraphrases of[1] (1547), 387.
Erbys, *n. p.* herbs, 275.
Ereres, *n. p.* heirs, 20.
Eres, Eris, *n. p.* ears (of a pan and bucket), 122, 279.
Estire, *adj.* Easter, 61.
Estrich borde, *n.* Estrich board; Baltic timber, 64, 71.
Evensong, xlviii, 5, 15–17; tavern expenses after, xxxviii.
Ewers, 38.
Exchequer, King's, 373.
Executors, business of, 3.
Exseyddys, *v.* exceed, 254.

Fadym, *n.* fathom, 185.
Faggots, 382.
Falcon, latten, 32. *See also* Eagle.
Fanons, 30, 31.
Fathom, 80, 185.
Fatte, *n.* fat ; water vessel, xcvi.
Fawty, *adj.* faulty, 80.
Feasts, copes at, 100; donations at, xxiii; double, 13, 15, 19; illuminations for, xxxviii, xxxix; list of, mentioned, lii. (*See also* Ascension day, Corpus Christi, Good Friday, etc.).
Featherbeds, 40, 45, 121.
Febyłł, *adj.* feeble, weak, 23.

Feches, *n. p.* fitchews, 42.
Fecissian, Ffisician, *n.* physician, 76, 114.
Fee simple, estate in, 21.
Fencing coats, 43.
Feretory, 26.
Ferial, *adj.* ordinary, 15, 27.
Fertour, *n.* feretory, 26.
Feuerell, *n.* February, 331.
Ffader, *n.* father, 2.
Ffakon, *n.* falcon; latten falcon to desk, 32.
Ffau3ght, *n.* default, 198.
Ffelawes preestes, *n. p.* fellow priests, 17.
Ffermys, *n. p.* residences, 93.
Fflowre, *n.* floor, 367.
Ffothyr, *n.* fother, 199.
Ffreese, *n.* frieze, 147, 148.
Ffrey3te, *n.* freight, 167.
Ffustean, *n.* fustian, 33.
Fire-fork, 39.
Fire-iron, 390.
Fire-pan, 38, 230.
Fishmonger, 16, 19, 22, 30, 33.
Fishmongers' Fellowship, 20, 285; at church, xxxviii; hall of, 20; lands for, 21; payment to wardens of, 21.
Fitchews, 42, 356.
Flags, purchase of, 100.
Floor, making of, 88, 139; mending of, 367.
Flowers, purchase of, 130, 162, 185, 313, 339, 383, etc.
Flownders, 275.
Fondemens, *n. p.* foundations, 69.
Font, closing in of, 198, 199; cloths of, 54; covering for, 131; fixing of, 252; hallowing of, liii, 343; keys for, 339; lead pipe for, 187; locks, for, 70, 248, 339; making of, 186; old, 68; table by, 273, 275.
Forms, 28; choir, 270; staked, 37; wainscot, 37.
Foryd, *pp.* furred, 43.

---

[1] In 1547 (Edward VI) it was ordered that the Paraphrase of Erasmus "bee read, used, and studied by euery curate and priest," and that it be set up in every parish church, and in 1559 in the Elisabethan Injunctions (*see* Injunctions) it was ordered that the whole Bible in English be obtained together with the Paraphrases of Erasmus also in English, and the same set up in the church in order that the parishioners might read out of service time. The cost of the Paraphrases was to be equally divided between parson and parishioners.

Glossarial Index. 427

Fother (weight for lead of 19½ cwt.), 199, 336.
Founder, payment to, 264.
Fox, 42.
Francis I of France, capture of, 327.
Frankincense, purchase of, 100, 410.
Fraternities. *See* Brotherhoods.
Freer, xlvii, 271, 287, 303, 324.
Freestone, purchase of, 225.
Frenchman, burial of, 128.
Frontals, altar, lxii, 30.
Frontlets, velvet, 44.
Fruiterer, 127.
Fugerid, *pp.* figured? 31.
Fuller, 126.
Funeral, costs of, lxxv. *See also* Burials.
Furniture, inventory of Church (*see under* Church); house, 28.
Furres of kallybar, *n. p.* furs of Calabar; probably furs of squirrels, 44.
Fustian, 33, 72.

Gabardine, 42.
Gable, 177.
Gardener, 126, 127, 156.
Gardens, 29; bequest of, 5, 16, 18; hedging of, 190, 202; rents of, 75, 76, 115, 377.
Garde vyanse, *n.* = F. *garde-viandes*, cupboard, safe, 40.
Garlands, xv, lxxiv, 100, 131, 163, 186, 198, 305, 316, 382, etc.
Garnets, liv, 139, 155, etc.; tinning of, 252.
Garret, 44.
Gate, chamber over, 28; lock to churchyard, 99; making of, 72; postern, 29; stone, 68.
Gaudyd, Gawdyd, *pp.* embellished, 48, 50.
Gaudys, *n. p.* ornaments, 48.
Genets, 42.
Gentlewoman, gift by, 222.
Gere, *n.* gear, 45.
Gernyschid, *pp.* garnished, 32.
Gilt, parcel (part-gilt), 33, 47-49, etc.
Girdles, 30, 31, 48, etc.; silver, 47, 48; tucking, 99, 131.
Glass, 302, 313 (*see also* Windows); hanging, 37; painted, lxiii. *See also* Windows.

Glazier, payment to, 102, 255, 256, 313; *fac.*, 322-323.
Glouys, *n. p.* gloves, 326.
Gloves. *See under* Churchwardens *and* Clerks.
Glue, 63; mouth, 350.
Goblets, 49; gilt, 46; sale of, 356.
Godparents at christening, liv.
God's Body (Sacrament bread), 26.
God's Penny, xlvii, 250, 252, 274, 339.
Gogeons, Goiouns, *n. p.* gudgeons, 274.
Gogyn, *n.* gudgeon, 64.
Gold, ornament of, 30, 31, etc.
Goldsmith, 58, 100, 114, 125, etc.; payment to, 251, 343, 344.
Gong, xl.
Gong-farmer, xl, 240, 373; watching of, xl, 373.
Good Friday, 80; refreshments on, 273; vestment for, 27.
Goose, 191.
Gospel Book, lvii, 54, 393; silver of, 51.
Goter, *n.* gutter, 66.
Gould, Govld, *n.* gold, 51.
Gowns, 42, 43, 50.
Goyner, *n.* joiner, 412.
Graill, *n.* grayel, 54.
Gratis, *n. p.* gratis, gratings, 317.
Gravel, 66, 83, 85, 89, 100, 120, etc.
Graves, cost of special, xlix; digging of, 225, 231, 344; paving of, 310.
Gravestones, xli, 183, 212, 228, 245, 318, 372, 374; altar stone as, lxxi, 390; laying of, 222; sale of, 78, 222.
Graviston, *n.* gravestone, 344.
Grayels (books of choral responses), 27, 45, 54, 55, 395; binding of, 256.
Great bell, lv, 33, 266; clapper of, 306; ringing of, xxxiv, 78, 128, 129, 222, 231, 236, 267, 276, 291, 311, 314, 329, 333, 360, 366, 374.
Great churchyard, xli, xlix; burials in, 253, 293, 299, 311, 317, 383, etc.; cleaning of, 300, 331; cross in, 277; east wall of, 300; north wall of, 301; parclos in, 300; west door of, 304.
Grine, *adj.* green, 52, 53.

Grocer, xxxii, 3, 14, 30, 114, 115, etc.; craft of, 14.
Guilds. See Brotherhoods *and* Salve Regina.
Gutters, 107, 110, 132, 139; fillet, 137; raising of, 137.
Gyestes, *n. p.* joists, 177.
Gyrddyllys, *n. p.* girdles, 251.

Haberdasher, 22, 195, 201.
Hair-cloth, lix, 256, 394.
Halberds, 38, 53.
Hall, 36, 202; door of, 168.
Hallowing, church, xcv; ladle for, lxiii; scoop for, lxvii; tubs for, lxix. *See also* Church, Font, Vestments, etc.
Hally water styke, *n.* holy water stock, 358.
Halpace, *n.* haut pas; raised platform, 281, 313.
Halvendele, *n.* halfendeal, half, moiety, 9.
Halwenge, *n.* hallowing, 66.
Halydaies, *n. p.* holydays, 6.
Handwritings, different, xv.
Hanger, 45.
Hangings, 36, 37, 39, 44, 53, etc.
Haning, *n.* hanging, 52.
Hard hewer, 248.
Harness, sale of old, 276.
Hasps, purchase of, 70, 121, 135.
Hassocks, 131.
Havelpase, *n.* haut pas?, 48.
Hawle, *n.* hall, 23.
Heading with name of Jesus. *See* Jesus.
Hearth, making of, 109, 117, 119; repairs to, 201.
Heary clothe, *n.* hair-cloth, 394.
Heer, *n.* hair, hair-cloth, 256.
Henge, *v.* hang, 131.
Hengen towelles, *n. p.* hanging towels, 41.
Hengis, *n. p.* hinges, 66, 67.
Henry VII, funeral of, 266.
Henry VIII, crowning of, 266; in City, 373.
Her, *poss. pron.* their, 64, 65, 67.
Heres, *n. p.* hairs; *i. e.* wigs, 354.
Hermit, burial of, 1, 276.

Hewrer, *n.* hewer, 144.
Highway, King's, 3, 22; pavement of the King's, 23, 24.
Hillet, *n.*? 344.
Hinges, purchase of, 66, 67, 72, 107, 108.
Hobby Horse, May Day dancing with, lxxiv.
Hock Monday, collections on, xxviii, 221, 228, 232, 235, 248, 257, 263, 276, 290, 341, etc.; refreshments on, xxviii, 230.
Hock Tuesday, collections on, xxviii, 228, 232, 235, 244, 259, 271, 286, etc.
Hode, *n.* hood, 150.
Hogshead, sale of, 78.
Holland cloth, xvi, 42, 131.
Holly, purchase of, 381, 390, 402, 405.
Holm, purchase of, 131, 148, 162, 185, 214, 229, etc.
Holmes College, payment to fellowship of, 182, 197.
Holy bread, lx; basket for, 247, 328; cloth for, lx, 35.
Holydays, illuminations for, 6, 11, 13.
Holy Thursday, 173, 186; children's procession on, lii, 131; singers on, 234.
Holy water sprinklers, 101, 215, 243, 296, 309, 321.
Holywater stocks, 38, 163, 397; sale of, 358.
Holy water stoups, xix, lxiii, 33, 67, 69, 273, 296, 301, 303, 304; filling of, xlvi, 326, 343; hewing of, 69.
Homilies,[1] book of, 403, 405.
Hooks, purchase of, 67, 88, etc.; silver, 48.
Hop Monday, *n.* Hock Monday, 263.
Horse-hire, xxxvi, 174, 244, 247.
Hose, 43, 147, 148, 162.
Hoselynge, *adj.* housling, 407.
Hours canon, 12, 13, 17.
House, building of, 23; description of new, 23; lease of, 46, 83; letting of, xlvi; parts of, 23; pinning of, 65; pointing of, 120; poor

---

[1] It is at these Homilies that Avarice in the play of "Respublica" (1553) is supposed to jeer when he says, "Geate more or I shall geve thee a homlye greetinge."—E. E. T. S., No. XCIV, pp. xxix, 27.

Glossarial Index. 429

men's, 174; rental of, xxxii; rooms of a, 28; taking down of, 176; tiles of, xxxiii. *See also* Tiles.
House upon the stair, 114, 119, 125, 135, 136.
Household goods, inventories of, 28, 36; sale of, 356.
Housekeeper, parson's, xvii, 407.
Housling, lx; donations at, 128.
Hovell, *n.* hutch, 103.
Howbardes, *n. p.* halberds, 53.
Hymnals, xxii, 55, 321, 395.

Iakett, *n.* jacket, 40.
Ieen, *n.* Genoa, 45.
Ieett, *n.* jet, 50.
Ienettes, *n. p.* genets, 42.
Ienyuer, *n.* January, 315.
Ierkyng, *n.* jerkin, 41.
Images (*see under* Church); burning of, lxxii, 412; sale of gilt of, 58; taking down of, 412; taper before, 2.
In-broderet, *pp.* embroidered, 411.
Incense, li.
Indentures, 22; counterpart of, 281; making of, 208, 214, 244, 247.
Inducte, *v.* induct, 6, 7, 10.
Iniomsons, *n. p.* injunctions, 412.
Injunctions, book of,[1] 412.
Inventories, xiii, xxx; church furniture, 26, 30, 35, 50, 374, 393, 412 (*see footnote under* Church); house furniture, 28, 36; making of, 225, 325, 351; Porth's, xiv, 36, 356.
Iooge, *n.* judge, 270.
Ioynour, *n.* joiner, 63.
Ioyntes scells. *See* Errata.
Iron, andirons of, 37; bars of, 28; bolts of, 29; chain of, 29; chairs of, 31; clamps of, 220; pins of, 64, 69, 70; plates of, 89; sale of old, 58; stays of, 70; work of, 23, 70.
Ironmonger, 3, 13, 17, 102, 103.
Irynys, *n. p.* irons, 186.
Iuellis, *n. p.* jewels, 18.
Iunnii, *n.* June, 310.
Iuye, *n.* ivy, 229.
Iuyl, Ivlli, *n.* July, 56, 66.

Ivelles, *n. p.* jewels, 56, 59.
Ivstis, *n.* justice, 59.
Ivy, purchase of, 101, 130, 162, 214, 229, 381, 390, 402, etc.

Jackets, 42, 43, 356.
Jerkins, 41, 43.
Jesus, heading with name of, xv, 18, 28, 112, 116, 119, 124, etc.; pagent of, 37.
Jewels, 18, 46, 47; chest for, 215.
Joiner, 124, 156; payment to, 63, 251, 252, 255.
Joint-stools, 37, 39.
Joist, 85.
Judas, lvii, 308, 309.
Judge, payment to, 270.
Jury, drink for, 402.

Kanell, *n.* kennel, gutter, drain, 106.
Kanellstone, *n.* gutter-stone, 177.
Katches, *n. p.* ketches, 223.
Kechyng, *n.* kitchen, 39.
Kenyis, *n. p.* conies, rabbits, 191.
Kerchief-laundress, 78.
Kettles, 38.
Kerstenyng towel, *n.* Christening towel, 44.
Keruyng, *n.* carving, 70.
Keueryng, *n.* covering, 131.
Kewer, *n.* cover, 356, 357.
Keys, 29, 67, 84; clicket, 29, 136, 340; pyx, 237; wicket, 132, 133.
Kilburn, prioress of. *See* Prioress of Kilburn.
Kilderkin, 21, 90, 140.
King, payment of quitrent to, xl, 383, 389, 391 (*see also* Queen); pursuivant of, 387; (Edward VI); subsidy due to, 391 (*see also* Queen).
King's almoner, 198.
King's Bench, prisoners of, 20.
King's Chapel. *See* Royal Chapel.
King's Commissioners, lxxii, 387, 412; churchwardens before, 59; list of church goods delivered to, 50.
King's exchequer, 373.
King's highway, 3, 22–24.
King's works, 269.

---

[1] "Injunctions given by the Queen's majesty, concerning both the clergy and laity of this realm, published anno Domini M.DLIX," etc.—See Wilkins, *Concilia Magnæ Britanniæ*, vol. iv. 182.

430   *Glossarial Index.*

Kirtles, 44.
Kitchen, 28, 39, Abbot's. *See* Abbot's Kitchen.
Knells, xvi, xlvi, xlix, 95, 196, 222, 236, 244, 267, 283, 321, 333, 373, etc.
Knife, chopping, 39.
Knoppis, *n. p.* knops, knobs, 31, 48.
Kynges grandam, Margaret Countess of Richmond, grandmother of Henry VIII, 268.
Kyryes, *n. p.* kyries, 314.

Labourers, payment to, 66, 69, 82, 87, 90, 106, 117, 138, 149, 164, 192, 200, 209, 214, 235, 275, 288, 301, *fac.*, 322–323; refreshments for, 73.
Labres, *n. p.* labourers, 412.
Lace, silk, 150, 151.
Ladder, 103.
Laddyll, *n.* ladle, 250.
Ladles, lxiii, xcvi, 250.
Lady day, 322, 332.
Ladyl of tree, *n.* ladle of wood, xcvi.
Lammas, 232.
Lamp, basin for, 281; gift of 17; glasses for, 247, 292, 317, 340; oil for, 327; purchase of, 162.
Lands, purchase of, 20.
Lantern, iron poles for, 290; mending of, 100.
Larder, 29.
Larks, 191.
Latch, purchase of, 121.
Laths, beech, 66; purchase of, 65, 73, 82, 84, 88, etc.
Laton, *n.* latten, 26, 27, 28, etc.
Latten, 27, 28, 37, 136, etc.; sale of, 307; scouring of, 148, 163, 172, 186, 251.
Lattes, *n.* lattice, 200, 310.
Laude, *n.* praise, 6, 19.
Lauendere, *n.* laundress, 67, 71.
Laundress, payments to, xxvi, 67, 71, 219, 270, 277, 284, etc.
Laver, *n.* large basin, 279.
Lavender, 339.
Law, xxxii.
Laws, book of, 28.
Lawyer, payment to, 326, 389.
Laystall, *n.* repository for dung, xlvii, 367, 392.
Laystowe, *n.* laystall?, xlvii, 397.

Lead, 39, 71, 332, 335, etc.
Lease, 341; granting of, 227; of tenement in Thames St., 3, 22.
Lecturn, 243.
Ledder, Leddir, *n.* leather, 81, 301.
Lede, Lode, *n.* lead, 39, 103.
Lefull, *adj.* lawful, 7.
Legendas, 27, 54, 256.
Leggys, *n. p.* legs, 72.
Leigend, *n.* legendas, 54.
Leinth, *n.* length 53.
Lenneg cloth, 41.
Lent, 97; veil for, lxix, 343; white vestment for, 27.
Lesse, *n.* lease, 3.
Lethe, *n.* light, 258.
Lette, *n.* let, hindrance, 2.
Lette, *p.p.* excused, 6.
Leuacion, *n.* levation, 11.
Leues, *n. p.* leaves, 67.
Levation of sacrament, 11, 361.
Leystoff, *n.* laystall?, xlvii, lxiv, 382.
Leystow, *n.* grave, 157.
Lighter, 74.
Lights, gifts for, 17, 146, 161. *See also* Candles *and* Beamlight.
Lime-burner, 265.
Lime man, 102, 107.
Lime, purchase of, 65, 69, 71, 73, 83, etc.
Line, purchase of, 131.
Linen cloth, 20, 45, 46, 53; chest for, 317; pledges in, 239; purchase of, 272; use in church-hallowing of, xcvi.
Linen, washing of, xxvi, 270, 273, 328.
Ling, 275.
Lire borde, Lyre borde, *n.* edge board?, 86, 137, 138.
Litany, xlviii.
Little bell, 231, 296.
Locks, 29, 53; clicket, 121; coffin, 72; mending of, 70; plate, 29; purchase of, 67, 69, 71, 84; spring for, 121; stock, 29.
Lockers, 53.
Lode, Lood, *n.* load, 45, 82.
Lokeram, *n.* lockram, a linen cloth, 219, 350.
Lole, *adj.* whole, 190.
Lomb, Lombe, Loome, *n.* loam, 66, 74, 84, etc.
Lome work, *n.* loom work, 48.

Glossarial Index. 431

London, bishop of (*see* Bishop of London); commonalty of city of, 12; suburbs of, 18.
London Bridge, chapel of,[1] 13; Chronicles of, xliv; old and new, xxxvi; provision for repairing, 13; reparations of, xliv, 16; wardens of,[1] 13, 83.
Loo Sunday, 399.
Lord Cardinal (Wolsey?), 328.
Lord Chief Judge, payment to, 179.
Lords of the fee, 1, 2, 5, 9, 12, 13.
Losenghis, *n. p.* lozenges, 32.
Lowsyng, *n.* loosing, 99.
Lukis golde, *n.* Lucchese gold, 31.
Lumber, 38, 39, 44.
Lybberdes hed, *n.* libbard's head, leopard's head, 50.
Lyes, *n. p.* alkalized water, 130.
Lyre, *n.* lear, fringe edging, 68.
Lyryng, *n.* fringing, edging, 130.
Lyte, Lytt, Lyȝtte, *n.* light, 46, 67, 129.

Magnificat, 16.
Maids, collection by, 283.
Malmsey wine, purchase of, 190, 351, 354, 362, 364.
Malvesey, Malvinseyn, *n.* Malmsey wine, 70, 362, 364.
Manger, 29.
Man of Calais, burial of, 128.
Mantles, timber, 202.
Manual, lvi, 27; binding of, 256; purchase of, 399.
Manuscripts, xiii; chronological order in, xiv; period covered by, xv; spelling of, xv; writing and binding of original, xiii, xiv, xv.
Manwell, *n.* manual, 27.
Map, Ogilby's, xlii; reference to Horwood's, xxxvi.
Marbler, payment to, 250.
Margaret, countess of Richmond, gift by, 268.
Mariner, 205, 206; burial of, 95, 248, 287, 294.
Mark, 2, 3, 6, 11, *et passim.*
Marriages, l, 328, 398.
Martiloge, lvi, 27.
Mary and Philip in London, 406.
Mary, changes in the reign of, lxx,

lxxi; restoration of church goods by, 53.
Masar, Maser, Masser, Massor, *n.* mazer, large drinking bowl, 47, 48, 49, 50, 356, 357.
Masons, business with, xxxvi; indenture with, 244; payment to, 65, 72, 100, 109, 117, 136, 166, 192, 219, 229, 251, 275, 282, 301, etc.; refreshment for, 65, 66.
Mass, xxii, 6, 11, 19, 25, 225, 305; songs at, 54; torches at, xxxix, 11.
Mass of Recordare, 328—"Missa Recordare (so called from the introit, 'Remember, O Lord, thy covenant, and say to the destroying angel, Stay now thy hand'), is a votive mass in time of Plague."—Canon Wordsworth.
Mass Books, lvi, 27, 54, 349, 403; binding of, 256; clasps for, 140; little, 54; rest for, 403.
Mass penny, 225, 289, 373. [Money given during the singing of mass by mourners at a funeral.]
Mat, 198; wicker. *See* Wicker mats.
Matins, xlviii, 12, 15; candles at, 277; holy water at, 304.
Matress, 39.
Mattock, 327.
Maundy Thursday, 314, 406, 410.
Mayor of London, li, 12, 13, 15, 18, 56, 59, 327; payment to, 15, 97, 118, 140, 168, 192, 210, 295; swordcase for, 383; yeoman of, 269.
Mayor's court, 111, 179, 282.
May Day, dancing on, lxxiv.
Mazers, 47, 356, etc.
Medieval Life, pictures of, xxxviii.
Medley, *n.* wool yarn fabric, 50.
Menu of dinner, xxxii, 275.
Mercer, 4, 51, 164.
Messuage, Mesvaige, *n.* messuage, manor house, (*O.Fr. mesuage*), 20, 392.
Michaelmas, 4, 61, 79, 80, etc.
Middest, Middis, Myddes, *n.* midst, middle, 32, 35, 53.
Middle aisle, burial in, 290, 344, 354; upper storey of, 302.

---

[1] For Inventories of the articles in the Chapel of London Bridge and the stores of the Wardens, see Riley's *Memorials of London,* pages 261, 263.

Middle bell, 71, 80, 237.
Midsummer, 61, 80, 81, 187, etc.; decorations at, lii, 81, 117, etc.
Mighelmasse, *n.* Michaelmass, 61.
Miter, lxix, 27, 31, etc.; sale of plate of, 59; use of, lxix.
Modeer, *n.* mother, 181.
Monstrance, lxiv, 233; cross of, lxi, 101. "Latin, (*monstrare*). — A vessel of precious metal in which the Blessed Sacrament is carried in solemn procession and exposed on the altar. It is on this account sometimes called an ostensory (*ostensorium*) ... Anciently this form varied; sometimes they were made in the shape of a tower ... or a covered chalice; sometimes in the form of images carrying silver pyxes, in which the sacrament is placed."—(Lee's Glossary.)
Monstyr, *n.* monstrance, 233.
Monyelles, *n. p.* monials, mullions, 308.
Moose, *n.* 150.
Morrow-mass, xviii, xlviii, 13, 18, 79, 116, 147, 172, 209, 281, etc.; assistance at, 326; candles for, 264, 317, 321; cruets for, 256, 269.
Morrow-mass priest, xviii, xlviii; bedstead for, liv, 340; chest for, 343; god's penny for, 252; payment to, 401, 402, 405.
Mortar, 72, 241; straw for, 89, 175.
Mortar, brazen, 38.
Mortere, *n.* mortar, 72.
Mortes, *n.* mortise, 229.
Morwe, *n.* morrow, 71.
Moth, 41, 44.
Moty, *n.* ? 66.
Mowth glewe, *n.* mouth glue, 350.
Munell, *n.* monial, mullion, 64.
Murre, Murrey, *n.* murrey; a dark red colour, 43, 44.
Mutton, 71, 270.
Mynkes, *n.* mink, 44.
Myttche, *adj.* much, 408.

Nails, bell, 274; bell-wheel, 340; black, 72; English, 367; lath, 73, 174; lead, 87; Palm-Sunday scaffold, 314; pew, 215; roof, 65, 73, 105, 109, 137, 176, 209; sepulchre, 214, 281; silt(?), 67; Spanish, 208; sprig, 65, 82, 87, 105, 117, 176, 220; white, 72.
Dr. Murray points out that these *Records* completely explain the term "tenpenny" nail. The price of nails was expressed in their cost per hundred: twopenny nails originally cost twopence per hundred, pp. 69, 73, 101; threepenny nails threepence, 73, 82, 120, 138; fourpenny nails fourpence, 84, 87, 120, 138; fivepenny nails fivepence, 84, 88, 135; sixpenny nails sixpence, 67, 82, 87, 138; and so with tenpenny nails, 67, 69, 72. These prices were retained until 1487-8, p. 138: after that date, however, the price dropped one penny per hundred, but the old designations were still used. Sixpenny nails were sold for fivepence per hundred, 151, 176, 281; fivepenny nails for fourpence, 173, 175, 210, 281; fourpenny nails for threepence, 176, 351; threepenny nails for twopence, 281, 340, 351; threepence was charged for two-hundred twopenny nails, 281; and tenpenny nails appear, on one occasion, to have been bought at eightpence per hundred, p. 176. Entries which apparently signify recurrence to original prices occur at pp. 165, 176, 229, 248.
Nalmery, *n.* aumbry, 40.
Names, ambiguity of, lxxvi; list of, mentioned, lxxvii.
Napkins, 41, 42.
Napre, Napry, *n.* napery, 41, 50, 52.
Nater cloth, Nator cloth, *n.* altar cloth, 39.
Naylis, *n. p.* nails, 63.
Nece, *n.* niece, 1.
Neder, *adj.* nether, 43.
Needlework, 31, 53, 151, etc.
New Year's day, 149.
Neyghpers, *n. p.* neighbours, 361.
Noble, *n.* gold coin, worth 6*s.* 8*d.*, 225.
Noncyens, Nonsiens, *n.* nunchions, 64-66, 73.
None, *n.* noon, 59.

None-mete, *n.* noon-meat, mid-day repast, 71.
Normandy cloth, 230, 349.
North aisle, burial in, 355; coping of, 192; foundation of, 142; reparation of, 184; work on, 334, 335, 337.
Northerin ston, Northrene stone, *n.* northern stone, 70, 72.
Norwegian covering, 45.
Nosses, *n. p.* noses?, hooks, 37.
Notes, personal, xxxix; picturesque, xxxviii.
Nottes, *n.p.* nuts, 275.
Novns, *n.* ounce, 251.
Nowelles, *n. p.* stair-posts, 257.
Nuts, 275.
Nuts (drinking cups), 49, 346.
Nutt, *n.* nut, a drinking cup, made of a large nut-shell mounted, 49.

Oak, 89, 104.
Oats, 29.
Ob, *for* Obolus (*Gr.*), halfpenny, 38, *et passim.*
Obbless, *n. p.* obleys, thin round cakes for Eucharist, li.
Obits, xxviii, li, 5, 9, 13, 17, 25, 78, 84, 88, 91, 97, 129, 147, 161, 184, 213, 287, 321, 346, etc. *See also* Chantries.
Obleys, li, 117, 130, 162, 313, 327.
Odir, *adj.* other, 224.
Offerings, 119, 129, 134, 147, 256.
Oil, 71, 81, 110, 121, 140, 154, 167, 179, 191, 204.
Oil pots, lxiv, 101, 358.
Oke, *n.* oak, 89.
Okyn, *adj.* oaken, 104.
Ons, *n.* ounces, 46, 47, etc.
Oovlld, *adj.* old, 252.
Or, *adv.* ere, 20.
Ordinal (book of ritual), 27.
Orfaras, Orfores, Orphareys, Orpharis, *n.p.* orphreys; rich embroidery, 150, 151, 199, 256.
Organ, lxv, 54; bellows of, 240, 267, 349, 369, 382, 395; blowing of, xx (*see* Organ Blowers); borrowing of, 305; breviary for, lvi; desk at, 317; donation towards new, 315, 320; great, 395; little, lxv, 306, 395; old, 33; played by man of St. Paul's, 411; mending of, xxv, xxxi, 81, 117, 321, 328;

Organs, quills for, 373; rope for, 373; supervision of, xxv, 269, 314, 317; tuning of, lxv, 361; use of, xxi.
Organ Blowers, xx, xxi, 343; almsmen as, 328, 333, 340; payment to, 323, 347, 349, 351, 354, 362, 364, 371, 379; wages of, xxi.
Organ books, lvi, 226.
Organist, xx; at tavern, xxxi; holiday for children of, 322, 327; payment to, 81, 272, 276, 279, 321, 339 (*see also* Conducts); payment to casual, 266; school for children of, 321, 326, 333, 340 (*see* School); wages of, xvi, xxiii.
Organ Maker, xxv, 125; payment to, 314, 317, 322, 327, 339, 349, 353, 361, 369, 381, 390, 407.
Orphrey; rich embroidery, 150, 151, 199, 256.
Oster bord, *n.* oyster board?, 37.
Ounce, 45, 46, *et passim.*
Our Lady, altar of, 52; brotherhood of (*see* Salve Regina); candles before image of, xxxviii, 6; image of, 39, 45; painting of image of, 94; painting of tabernacle of, 142.
Our Lady day, 97, 128, 149, 163, 173; ringing on, 350.
Owre, *n. p.* hours, 310.
Owsselynge, *adj.* housling, 410.
Oyer, *pron.* other, 370.

Pack thread, purchase of, 100.
Padlock, lxv, 173.
Pagents, 35, 37.
Pail, water, 82.
Painted cloth, 54, 234, 406.
Painter, 126; payment to, 70, 229, 302.
Palls, xlix, lxv, 53, 390, 391.
Palm, purchase of, 117, 148, 162, 173, 185, 214, 327, etc.
Palm-Sunday, acting on, xxv; arras for, 359; cakes for, 331; chairs and forms for, 379; decorations on, liii, 81, 130, 313, 327; prophets on (*see* Prophets); scaffold for, xxv, 198, 301, 304, 327, 369, 373, 379.
Pane, *n.* pan, 38.
Paper, purchase of, lvii, 92, 101,

148, 164, 172, 255, 300, 359, 369, 372.
Papye, *n.* Poppy?—the carved finial at the end of a stall, etc., 71.
Paraphrases of Erasmus. *See* Erasmus.
Parcel gilt, *adj.* part gilt, 33, 47–49, 357.
Parchment, xv, 45, 54 ; purchase of, 256.
Parclos, *n.* screen, 69, 252.
Pardon churchyard, xli, xlii, xlix; burials in, 78, 92, 161, 222, 245, 263, 293, 312, 341, 366, 383, etc.; cleaning of, xlii, 187; cross in, 361, 370; door in, 378; pale in, 361, 370; wicket to, 243, 310.
Parelyng, *n.* apparelling, 219, 306. [The apparel of albs was ornamental embroidery.]
Pares boll, *n.* Paris ball, 49.
Parish, bearing torches about, 264; bier of, lxiv (*see* Leystoff); four honest men of, 12, 14; four worthiest and mightiest men of, 6, 7, 9 ; gift to parson by assent of, 34 ; loan to, 171; masters of, xxiv, 318; payment for trespass against, 94; purchase and delivery of coals by, 265; seniors of, xxiv, 58, 246, 392 ; trespass against, 94.
Parish Clerks, business of, xix ; fees for, xix; list of, xix; payments to, 116, 147, 172, 218, 242, 259, 279, 282, 286, 297, 315, 319, 330, 341, 345, 348, 368, 386, 402, 409; wages of, xix.
Parishioners, offerings by, 404, 408; gifts by, 126 (*see also* Gifts to church); lending by, 400 (*see also* Borrowing by church); meetings of, xvii, 298; pardon of arrears of rent by, 91 ; records of individual, lxxvi; refreshments for, xvii, xxvi, 204 (*see also* Refreshments bought by church); vestry of, 60; visiting by boat by, xxvi, 296.
Parish priest, xviii; book that lay before, lvi, 373 ; chamber of, 359 ; deputy to parson, 227; garlands for, 305; gift by, 263; house of, 376; payment to, 80, 229, 260, 409; surplice for, 266, 349, 371.
Parisshens, *n. p.* parishioners, 9, 12, 16, etc.

Parlour, 28, 37, 202 ; summer, 29.
Parson, xvi ; burial of, 311; business of, 6, 10–14, 17–19, 21–25, 199, 230, 260, 284, 285, 325, 328, 351; debt of, xvii, 353; deputy of, xviii, 227 ; garlands for, 305 ; gathering tithes of, 409; gift by, 31; housekeeper of, xvii, 407; indenture between tenant and, 11 ; lampreys for, 350; note by, 353; part-payment for refreshments for choir by, 302, 306, 323, 328; payment of tithes to, xlv; payments to, 6, 7, 11, 21, 199, 295, 299, 306, 394, 396; residence of, xvii, 393, 394; stone of, 67; visited at Norwich, 350; wine sent to, xvi, 247.
Parsonage, xvii, 301; bridge to church from, 311; wicket by, 219, 327.
Parson's Duty, xvii, 363, 368, 372, 376, 377, 380, 385, 410, 412.
Parteletes, *n. p.* partlets, apparel worn by women about chest and neck, 44.
Party silk, *n.* silk of different colours, 43.
Paschal candle, 78, 92, 115, 146, 171, 195, 216, 222, 224, 249, 276, 312, 352, 398, 404, etc.; coffin of, 403; Judas of, lvii, 308, 309; line of, 305 ; making of, 64 ; poles for, 281.
Pastiller, Pastyller, *n.* pastler, pastry maker, 141, 143, 144, 156.
Patens, 49, 51, 53 ; part gilt, 358; use of, lxv.
Patent, Pattin, *n.* paten, 49, 51.
Pathways, gravelled, xlii, 100, 163, 185. *See also* Gravel.
Patten-maker, 125, 144, 157.
Pattens, 173.
Patyble, *n.* cross, 70.
Pavement, breaking of, 134, 136 ; laying of, 66, 71, 83, 85, 89, 120, 151, etc.
Pavia, rejoicings over battle of, 327.
Paving tiles, purchase of, 64, 67, 88, 107, 199, etc.
Paviour, payment to, 66, 83, 85, etc.
Pawning, xxxvi, 346, 375.
Paxbredes, *n. p.* paxes (*osculatoria*), 26.
Paxes, lxv, 26, 39 ; purchase of, 219,

Glossarial Index.   435

359; silver and gilt, 26; sale of, 59, 358.
Payns, *n. p.* pans, 38.
Pearl, 31, 48, 101; mother of, 45.
Pears, purchase of, 140.
Peck, 73, 84.
Pekerell, *n.* pickerel, xxvii, 344.
Pelewes, *n. p.* pillows, 27.
Pelyon, *n.* pillion, 45.
Pendant, 48.
Penons, making of, 64.
Pentes, *n.* pentice, penthouse, 119, 155, 189, 280.
Penthouse, 119, 155, 189, 208, etc.
Pentows, *n.* penthouse, pentice, 256, 257.
Pepper, 248.
Pepyħ, *n.* people, 25.
Perchors, *n. p.* perchers; large wax candles, 67.
Perchmyn, *n.* parchment, 132.
Per idem tempus (L.) = for the same time, x, 97.
Perrell, *n.* peril, 59.
Perrys, *n.* parish, 259.
Personages, distinguished, xxxiii.
Pescoddes, *n. p.* peascods, 49.
Pestilence, death by, 84.
Pevterar, *n.* pewterer, 58.
Pewke, *n.* puke, dark red, 42, 44.
Pews, xxxiv; account of, lxv; allocation of, lxv; Atclyffe's, 198; boards for kneeling in, 225; churching, lxxv; cleaning of, 185; doors of, 173, 243, 264, 300; garnets for, 234; great, 252; lady Page's, 53; maid's, lxxv, 323, 328; making of, 100, 173, 199, 215; mending of, 68, 242; men's, 219, 251, 282; moving of, 67; paving of, 67; pinning of, 67; poor people's, 215; Roche's, 323; rushes for, 198, 254; shriving, 130, 198; women's, 252, 282.
Pewter, 52, 58; sale of, 307.
Pewterer, 26, 31, 58.
Peyntes, *n. p.* pints, 38.
Peyntour, *n.* painter, 70.
Peyse, *n.* weight; plum of pyx, 304.
Philip of Spain (called King), in London, 406.
Phrases, homely, xxxix; quaint, xliv.
Physician, 76, 107, 114; king's, 125.

Pickaxe, 361.
Pie-baker, 70, 73.
Pike, 275.
Pillion, 45.
Pillion cloth, 45.
Pillows, 40; down, 44; silk, 27.
Pillow cases, canvas, 42.
Pin-case, 45.
Pins, tile, 73, 82, 84, 86, 102, 104, 108, 137, 175..
Pipes, lead, 166, 168, 370.
Pistelarie, *n.* Epistle book, 27.
Placebo, 6, 11, 15, 17, 25, etc. "A term to designate the old English vespers for the dead, so called because the antiphon commenced in *placebo*."—(Lee's Glossary.)
Places in text, list of interesting, xxxvi, xxxvii. *See also* Place Index.
Plancheborde, *n.* plank board, 86, 133, 155, etc.
Planges, *n. p.* planks, 208.
Planks, 86, 103, 133, 138, 155, 208, etc.
Plaster, 177.
Plaster of Paris, 89, 90.
Plasterer, payment to, 331.
Plat, *n.* plate, 50.
Plate, 46, 51.
Plate chest, 215, 331.
Platers, *n.* platters, 38.
Plates, candle, 270.
Playing week, 322, 327.
Pledges, 48, 49, 141, 235, 346, 353.
Plomer, *n.* plumber, 69, 71.
Plumbers, 69, 71, 102; business with, 335, 336, 338; fire for, 74; payment to, 71, 90, 110, 139, 153, 154, 166, 168, 187, 193, 200, 214.
Pointmaker, 125.
Points, silk, 45.
Polakes, *n. p.* pole-axes, 38.
Pole-axes, 38.
Poles, lxvi, 148, 347; alder, 257; brass, 68; iron, 68; iron lantern, 290; purchase of, 256.
Poles, Polles, Powles, Powlis, *n.* Pauls (St. Paul's), 373, 379, 382, 407, 411.
Polesis, poles, *n.* 68.
Poleyn wax, *n.* Polish wax?, 164.
Pomander, 48.
Ponchon, *n.* puncheon, cask, 152.
Ponchon, *n.* upright post, 327.

Glossarial Index.

Poor, alms for, 1, 12, 14, 17, 20, 89, 97, 140, 141, 154, 155, 167, 168, 179, 180, 190, 191; 202–204, 211, 289, 290, 295, 386; bell for, 246; burial of, 1, 171, 284, 314; coals for, 1, 318; collection for, 299; church linen for, 60; houses of, 174; pews for, 215; refreshments for, 192; shirts and smocks for, 20.
Poppies, carved finials for stall ends, etc., 71 (?), 264 (?), 282.
Popys, *n. p.* poppies? — carved finials, 264.
Porch of church, building of, 70, 71; cleaning of, 186; donations towards, 61; scaffold over. *See* Palm-Sunday.
Porcyone*?*, *n. p.* portions, 4.
Portatyffis, lxvi, 341.
Porters, 185.
Porth, John, burial of, 329; chest of, 331, 334, 356; disposal of property of, xxx, 356, 357, 358; obit of, xxix; will of, xxix, 45, 353.
Porth, Mistress, burial of, 323.
Portingale, Portyngaler, *n.* Portuguese, xxxi, 95, 276.
Portos, Portuos, *n. p.* breviary, 45, 173.
Portuguese, burial of, 95, 161, 171, 276; killing of, 276; torches at burial of, 100.
Posnettes, *n. p.* small basins, 38.
Post, purchase of, 85.
Postells, *n. p.* apostles, 47.
Posterngate, 29.
Potation expenses, xxviii, 92, 110, 141, 156, 168, 180, 193, 204, 215, 297. *See also* Refreshments bought by church.
Potbras, *n.* pot-brass, 307.
Pots, brass, 38, 145, 157, 159, 163; latten, 279; nail, 47; oil, 101, 358.
Pottle, *n.* measure of two quarts, 71, 110.
Pottle pots, *n. p.* pots holding two quarts, 38.
Pot-hanger, 38.
Pot-hook, 38.
Pounsed, *pp.* pounced, ornamented by punching, 49.
Poustes, *n. p.* posts, 177.

Poynttes, *n. p.* points, 45.
Poyse, *n.* weight, 46, 49, 333.
Prayer-Books, Cranmer's Chertsey (books of new service, 1549), lxx, 388; medieval (Primer), xxx, 45.
Prayer for the Scots, 387.
Precious stones, counterfeit, 31.
Premer, Prymmer, *n.* Primer; medieval prayer-book, 45.
Prentys, *n. p.* apprentices, 183.
Press, wainscot, 40.
Pricked song books, lvii, 117, 243, 314, 350, 351, 353, 359, 382: "Paper to pryk songes in for the churche." — Churchwardens' Accounts of the town of Ludlow (1540, etc.), ed. Thos. Wright, 1869. "Prick-Song. An ancient English name for ornate Plain Song; so called, in all probability, because the vellum leaves on which the MS. music was written were marked with an instrument called a pricket, so as to enable the stave of four lines to be drawn thereupon."—(Lee's Gloss.)
Prickets, 91.
Priest, augmentation of wages of, 79; arrears of, 115; bedstead for, 243, 292; burial of, 78, 380; burial of strange, 259; chamber of, 303; chantry (*see* Chantry priest); chests for, 215; choosing of, 3, 13; girdles for, 225, 251; helping of singers by, 6; hiring of, xxxi, 328, 339, 340, 382; house of, 120; money lent by, 184, 197, 213; morrow-mass (*see* Morrow-mass priest); ornaments for, 285; parish (*see* Parish priest); pattens for, 173; payment to, 86, 88, 97, 116, 121, 133, 140, 151–155, 165–168, 176–180, 200, 207–211, 252, 289, 295, 309, 346, 390, 401, 402, 406; pewter pot for, 333; prescribed services of, 5, 12; presentation to official of Archdeacon of, 6, 10; provision against sinful, 3, 12; refreshments for (*see* Refreshments bought by Church); reparation of house of, 108, 110; summoning of, 349; sustentation of, 1, 3, 6, 15, etc.; vestments of, lxix, 303.

Glossarial Index. 437

Priest's alley, 136, 184, 185; door to, 132.
Printing, 45.
Prior of Amesbury, 46.
Prior of Christchurch, quitrents to, 79, 96, 134, 147, 153, 172, 184, 208, etc.
Prioress of Kilburn, quitrent to, 85, 96, 119, 135, 152, 177, 201, 209.
Prioress of St. Helen's,[1] 4; church at law against, 190, 203.
Prisoners, provision for release of, poor, 20.
Privy, cleaning of, 24, 87, 207, 210, 227, etc.; mending of, 89, 109, 166, 174.
Probate, 46.
Processionals, xxii, 27, 55, 321, 326, 395, 397, 407.
Processions. *See* Corpus Christi, Holy Thursday *and under* Church.
Proctors, payment to, 278.
Professions, list of, mentioned, xliii.
Prophets, xxiv, lxxiii, 327; acting of, xxiv; garments for, xxv, 354, 358, 364, 369, 373, 379, 381; paper for, 354; refreshments for, 382; scaffold for (*see under* Palm Sunday); wigs for, 354.
Prowres, *n.* prioress, 135.
Psalmody, book of (1554–5),[2] 399.
Psalms, 15; penitential, xlviii.
Psalters, 27, 387, 389, 411.
Pulpit, lxvi; by choir, 354; chest before, 53; ladder to, 277; lintels to, 251; mention of Bede-roll, names from, lii, 80, etc.; new, 251; old, 298; oylets for, 354; pew next, 266; pews before, 301; stays for, 354.
Pump, 370.
Purcyvaunt, *n.* pursuivant, 387.
Purfelyd, *pp.* purfled, decorated at edges, 43, 44.
Purification, feast of, 97.
Purse, 45.
Pyllobers, *n. p.* pillow-beres, pillow-cases, 42.

Pyllors, *n. p.* pillars, 44.
Pywe, *n.* pew, 94.
Pywis, *n. p.* pews, 81.
Pyxes, lxvi, 51, 53, 304; canopies for, 31, 32; key for, 237; mending of, 244; plum for, lxvi, 304, 407; position of, lx; pulley for, lxvi, 347; rope for, 347.
Pyx-box, keys for, 237.
Pyx-cloths, lx, 31, 281, 331; gift of, xvi, 31; starching of, 350.

Quarrels, *n. p.* squares (of glass), 313.
Quayer, Qware, *n.* quire, 101, 334.
Queen (Mary), payment of quitrent to, 405 (*see also* King); subsidy due to, 405, 411. *See also* King.
Queen Jane (Jane Seymour), death of, 373.
Queen's Chapel, singers of. *See* Royal Chapel.
Queer, Quere, Qvire, *n.* choir, 16, 17, 33, 53.
Quinsis, *n. p.* quinsy-berries, black currants, xxxii, 275.
Quitrents, xvii, xl, 4, 79, 83, 85, 89, 95, 96, 116, 122, 134, 146, 165, 166, 172, 180, 196, 202, 213, 297, 327, 350, 383, etc.
Quondocke, *n.* conduct, 402, 405.
Quylles, *n. p.* quills, 373.
Quysshynes, Quysshons, Qvoissions, *n. p.* cushions, xcvi, 33, 53.

Rack, stable, 29.
Rafters, 87, 137, 138, 228.
Rag, sale of, 161.
Rails, 167.
Raiment, 42, 43,
Rake, fire, 37, 38.
Raker, xxiv; payment to, 64, 67, 101, 106, 148, 173, 186, 199, 214, 219, 235, 256, 264, 296, 306, 323, 340, 359, 390, 412.
Rat-catcher, payment to, 379.
Rats, ravages by, xxxix, 343. *See also* Rats in church.

---

[1] Priory of the Black Nuns of St. Helens founded by Wm. Basing, dean of St. Paul's in the reign of Henry III. This afterwards became Leathersellers' Hall. A picture of the remains of one of the old crypts is given towards the end of Smith's *Antiquities of London* (1791).

[2] Probably the metrical rendering of the Psalms by Sternhold, Hopkins, etc.

MED. REC. G G

Ratsbane, purchase of, xxxix, 322, 326.
Ray (striped silk), blue; 27, 150.
Rayll, *n.* rail; linen garment for woman's neck, 42.
Rays, *n. p.* stripes, bands, 32–34.
Receipts, order of, xxvii.
Recordare, mass of. *See* Mass of Recordare.
Rector Coris, *n. p.* rectors of the choir, 31.
Rectors of Choir, xxiv, chairs for, 31; stools for, 358. The *Rectores Chori* were the directors of the choir. "In our ancient cathedrals they were often persons of dignity ... They stood at the antiphon-lectern, facing eastwards, bearing staves of office to beat time, and moved, as necessity arose, from that position to their own seats and fald-stools. At Lincoln minster a slab remains in the chancel pavement marked 'Cantate Hic.'"—(Lee's Gloss.) The term *Rector Chori* seems to be one peculiar to the English Church.
Reddys, *n. p.* reeds, 251.
Reeds for lighting, 406.
Reformation, changes in church at, lxx–lxxii; destruction of church furniture at, xliii.
Reitsters, *n. p.* registers, 56.
Relekys, *n. p.* relics, 26.
Relics, xlv, 26.
Relic Sunday, 264, 277, 410. [The Sunday after St. Michael's day.]
Rent, 1–5, 23, etc.; arrears of, 92, 112, 262, 263, 287, 413; arrest for arrears of, xxxiii, 91, 282, 349, 353; decrease of, 166; deduction from salary of, 133; distraint for, 25; drinking at receipt of (*see* Potations); increase of, 94; overseers and viewers for, xxiv, 111, 285, 320; surplus of, 11, 14.
Rental book, 300.
Rent-gatherer, payment to, 346.
Renywed, *pp.* renewed, 75.
Reprayions, *n. p.* reparations, 59.
Requiem, mass of. *See* Mass.
Revell's tomb, repairs at, 198, 215.
Revestiary, burial in, 161; chest for vestments in, 303; chest for writings in, 304.

Revestre, Revestry, *n.* revestiary, 145, 161, 281.
Reyegate stone, *n.* Reigate stone; rag stone, 142.
Ribbon, purchase of, 80, 101, 234.
Riding-coat, 42.
Riding. *See* Horse-hire.
Ringers, xxvi; drink for, xxxi, 327; payment to, 153, 178, 202, 322, 406.
Rings, diamond, 49; gold, 48; jewelled, 356; latten, 130.
Robes, 41.
Robiis, Robous, Roboys, Robys, *n.* rubbish, 66, 70, 72, 74, 173, 187.
Rochets, 33, 131.
Rochis, *n. p.* roaches, 275.
Rod, iron, 131.
Rods, discipline, lxii, 185, 269. *See* Discipline Rods.
Roll of Clerks' Wages. *See* Clerks' Wages.
Romeland, xlii; at law concerning, 326; destruction of church furniture on, xliii; burning images on, lxxii, 412; laying of rubbish on, 223; letting of, 353; payment to king for, xliii, 389; revenues of, 352; Spanish ship on, xlii, 385.
Rone, *adj.* roan, 378.
Ronne, *pp.* run, 7.
Rood, lxvii, 54, 224, 228, 400, 401; branch before, 255; carving and painting of, 224; expenses in connection with new, 224, 228, 229; painted cloth before, 54, 234, 251, 406; sale of, 271; setting up of new, xxxii, 224, 228; staybar of, 229; taking down, 412; veil for, 286.
Rood-light, 255.
Roodloft, lxiv, lxxii, 53, 64, 69, 173, 387; banners in, 361; branch in, 322; corbel of, 68; destruction of scripture in, 397; door of, 68, 251; floor of, 250; hollow key for, 117; iron dog for, 354; Judases in, lvii, 309; latten bowls for, 401; lectern in, 243; lights of, 400, 404; painting of, 387; painting of scriptures in, lxxii, 387; parclos of, 252; receipts for, 63; removing of, 224; scouring of, 80, 100; stair of, 251;

Glossarial Index. 439

table by, 198; winding stair to (?), 279, 281.
Roofs, tiles and lead for. *See* Tiles *and* Lead.
Rope, bast, 87; purchase of, 64, 87, 99, 185.
Roper, 5.
Roses, 173.
Rosse, *n.* rose, 46.
Royal Chapel, singers of, xxi, 270, 275, 309, 316, 323, 327, 344, 396.
Royal Commission (1553), lxxii, 56, 387, 394; delivery of books to, 56, 394.
Rubbish, clearing of, 70, 82, 88, 102, 107, 137, 164, etc.
Runlettes, *n. p.* runlet, rundlet, small barrel, 191.
Rushes, purchase of, xxxiv, lv, 198, 254, 310, 321.

Sack, *n.* Spanish wines, 403.
Sack and sugar, 403.
Sacrament, book of, 405; canopy for, xxxv, 150, 301; cloths for, 369; illumination at, xxxix; latten bell for, 131; light before, lxxv; oil lamp before, 17; poles for, 347; provision of, 1; silk lace for, 406; streamers for canopy of, lxviii, 31, 51; torches for, 11; window for, lxx, 406.
Sacring bell, lv, 52, 313; hanging of, 255.
St. Andrew Hubbard, Eastcheap, records of, lxxiv.
St. Andrew's Day, collection on, lxxiv.
St. Ann's Chapel, xli; burial in, 318; door of, 273.
St. Barnabas day, 1, 131, 173; collection on, 244, 283; decorations on, 316; evensong on, 305; garlands for, liii, 81; procession on, 149.
St. Christopher's Chapel, burial in, 366; paving of, 364.
St. Clement's, Rochester, repair of, 20.
St. Dunstan's day, 64.
St. Erkenwald's day, 379.
St. Gregores petty, x, 47.
St. Helen's priory. *See* Prioress of St. Helen's.
St. John, window of, 313.

St. John Baptist, feast of, 128.
St. John's Chapel, paving of, 282; pews in, 282.
St. Katherine's Chapel, 13, 17, 18; burials in, xlix, 248, 249, 253, 261, 299, 319; paving of, 257; pews in, 71, 252; screen between choir and, 69; whiting of, 331.
St. Magnus, guild in, xliv; position of old, xxxvi.
St. Michael, feast of, 74, 77, 128.
St. Nicholas, book for, 399.
St. Nicholas' Tide, miter for, lxix, 27, 31.
St. Stephen Walbrook, records of, lxxiii.
St. Stephen's Chapel, liv, 14, 316; bequest to, 345; burials in, xlix, 249, 263, 314, 319, 323, 328; desk in, 367; door of, 327; paving of, 198; pews in, 255.
St. Stephen's Day, garlands for, lxxiv.
St. Thomas's Chapel, burial in, 379; mats and hassocks in, 131.
Sak, *n.* sack, 69.
Sallettes, *n. p.* sallets; kind of headpiece, 53.
Salmede, *n.* Psalmody, 399.
Salmon, fresh, 275.
Salter, 22, 128.
Saltpetre, making of, 347.
Salts, *n. p.* salt-cellars, 47, 48, 49, 357.
Salve Regina, 12; guild of, xliv, 83, 96, 122, 134, 153, 166, 178, 190, 202, 208; singing of, xxxviii, xlviii, 5, 6, 364.
Sanctus bell, lv, 33, 54, 311; baldrick for, 350; gudgeon for, 251; line for, 199; mending of, 172, 185, 186, 340; rope for, 163, 244, 279, 339; wheel of, 101.
Sand, 69, 72, 78, 83, etc.
Sandwich line, 339.
Sankes, Shankes, *n. p.* furs from shanks of animals, 43, 50.
Sans bell, Sauntys bell, Savns bell, Sawnse bell, *n.* sanctus bell, 185, 238, 244, 251.
Saplath, 117, 120, etc.
Sarplys, *n. p.* surplices, 74.
Sarsenet, 44, 45; black, 42; blue, 30; green, 30; red, 30, 52; russet, 30; white, 30, 55.

Sasers, *n. p.* saucers, sauce vessels, 38.
Sater, *n.* psalter, 411.
Satin, black, 43 ; blue, 30, 31 ; crimson, 43 ; green, 30, 31 ; red, 30, 31, 52 ; russet, 42 ; white, 41 ; yellow, 30.
Satten of sypars, *n.* satin of Cypress, 42.
Sattyn a bridges, satin de Bruges, 52.
Sawdre, *n.* solder, 89.
Saw pits, 337, 338.
Sawters, *n. p.* psalters, 27, 387.
Sawyers, payments to, 337, 338.
Sawyng, soyng, *n.* sewing, 81, 234.
Say (woollen cloth), 37, 350.
Sayling hause, *n.* ? 37.
Sayling pece, *n.* sailing-piece ; *i. e.* ship for censers, 197.
Scaffold, Easter (*see under* Palm Sunday) ; setting up, 107.
Scavengers, payment to, 89.
Schone, *n. p.* shoon, shoes, 147, 148.
School for Organist's children, xx, xxxiv. *See under* Organist.
School-house, chimney of, xxxv, 377 ; door of, 370 ; furniture for, xxxv, 349, 351 ; gutter in, 350 ; lock for door of, 378 ; position of, 321, 376 ; rent of, 326, 333, 376, 381 ; rushes for floor of, 321 ; vacancy of, 340.
School, money spent at, 148.
Schottyng, *n.* shooting, 256.
Schryves, *n. p.* sheriffs, 140.
Sconces, 266, 270, 333.
Scoop, lxvii, 250.
Scripture, *n.* inscription, 275.
Scrivener, payment to, 187, 247, 273, 351.
Seage, Sedche, Sege, Siege, *n.* privy, 24, 87, 89, 109, 166, 174, 207, etc.
Seer, *adj.* sere, 35.
Segees, *n. p.* seats (Fr. *siége*), xcvi.
Seler, Seller, Siler, *n.* bed canopy, 39, 40.
Selere, *n.* cellar, 108.
Selyng, *n.* ceiling, 202.
Seoudaries, sudaries ?, 27.
Sepulchre, lxii ; angels on, 301 ; chest for, lix, 53 ; cloth of, lx, 51, 343 ; frame of, 53 ; lamp for, 234 ; making of, 63 ; mending of, 70, 72 ; taking down of, 186, 411 ; tapers for, 350 ; wainscot for, 296 ; watching of, 99, 117, 131, 186, 214, 292, 381.
Sepultev3, *n.* sepulchre, 51.
Sequence book, 314.
Sergeaunt, payment to, 91, 111, 203, 271.
Serkelys, *n. p.* circles, 27.
Sertente, *n.* certainty, 56.
Sertificathe, *n.* certificate, 56, 59.
Service books, binding of, 226 ; chaining of, lvi, 80, 234 ; list and account of, lvi ; mending of, lvi, lvii, 67, 131, 226, 286, 359, 367 ; mouth glue for, 350 ; presentation to church of, xxxv ; new, 388 ; sale of, 59, 389 ; sale of clasps of, 58. *See also* Antiphoners, Bible, Carol books, Coucher, Epistle book, Gospel books, Grayels, Homilies, Hymnals, Legendas, Manuals, Mass books, Ordinal, Organ books, Paraphrases of Erasmus, Prayer books, Prayer for Scots, Pricked Song Books, Primer, Processionals, Psalters, Sacrament, Sequence book, Song books, *and* Square books.
Sessing, *n.* assessing, 316.
Sessours, *n. p.* assessors, 343.
Sesterns, *n. p.* cisterns, 166.
Sethen, *adv.* since, 236.
Settles, 40, 53, 54.
Sewdarie, *n.* sudary, 27.
Sextons, xix ; business of, 240, 241, 285, 303, 304, 329, 333, 339, 378, 382 ; engaging of, 331 ; house of, 348 ; kinsman of, 344 ; list of, xx ; payments to, 242, 247, 249, 265, 268, 302, 324, 329, 330, 334, 346, 359, 362, 373, 378, 386, 402, etc. ; status of, xix ; surplice for, 260 ; wages of, xix.
Seymour, Jane, death of, 373 ; in City, 373.
Sheaves, brass, 278.
Sheets, 49 ; flaxen, 42 ; holland, 42.
Shelves, 28–30.
Sheppis, *n. p.* ships, 26, 27.
Sheriffs, absence at obit of, 90 ; church attendance of, li ; payment to, 15, 90, 118, 140, 155, 180, 204, 210, 295, etc.
Shettes, *n. p.* sheets, 42.

Glossarial Index. 441

Shevys, *n. p.* sheaves, 278.
Shides, *n. p.* strips of wood, planks, 85.
Shield, gold, 48.
Ships for censer filling, lxvii, lxxii, 26, 51, 197.
Shirts, 147, 148.
Shodshovill, *n.* shovel shod with iron, 339.
Shoes, clouting of, 147, 148; purchase of, 162.
Sholve, *n.* shovel, 381.
Shops, xxxii, 45; bequest of, 5, 6, 9; key for door of, 85, 107; rental of, xxxii, 3, 112, 124; repairing of, xxxii, 83, 302, 328; windows of, 134, 359.
Shorttes, *n. p.* shirts, 42.
Shovels, lxvii; fire, 37, 39, 332; paring, 255; purchase of, 100, 234; shod, 243, 339.
Shriving pew, mat for, 198.
Shrove Thursday, water for font on, 301.
Shrovetide, 232.
Sick, sacrament for, lxxv.
Silk, 27; black, 36; blue, 30, 52; fringes of, 30, 31; green, 31, 51; red, 31, 35; russet, 52; Spanish, 31; white, 30, 52; yellow, 51.
Silt nails ?, 67.
Silver, 31, 45, 47, etc.; purchase of, 251.
Silver plate, pawning of, xlvi, 346.
Sipers, *n.* Cypress; originally cloth imported from Cypress, 31, 343.
Skawer, Skawere, Skewre, *adj.* square ?, 39, 40.
Skimmer, cook's, 39.
Skin, Spanish, 41.
Skinner, 22.
Skole, *p.* school, 326.
Skomor, *n.* skimmer, 39.
Skop, *n.* scoop, 250.
Skore, *n.* score, 58.
Sleffes, Slevys, *n. p.* sleeves, 33, 41, 43.
Sleeves of mail, 43.
Smith, payment to, 67, 130, 155, 185, 220, 256, 278, 301, 362, etc.
Smokes, *n. p.* smocks, 42.
Snosses, *n. p.* noses ?, hooks, 37.
Snow, clearing of, 187; great, 172.
Snuffers, 296.
Soap, purchase of, 226.

Solder, purchase of, 71–73, 82, 85, etc.
Soldier, burial of, 283, 315.
Solers, *n. p.* sollars, 5, 16, 23.
Sonde, *n.* sand, xcvi, 65, 66.
Sondayly, *adv.* Sundayly; *i. e.* every Sunday, 110.
Song, books of, 54, 314, 340, 351, 359, 387, 396, 411.
Songen, *pp.* sung, 344.
Sonnbeamys, *n. p.* sunbeams, 49.
Soper, *n.* supper, 270.
Souder, Sowdear, Sowder, Sowdore, Sowdowre, *n.* solder, 69, 71, 72, 110, 283, 315.
Souerange, *n.* sovereign, 50.
Soul, service for. *See* Obits.
Sourples, *n.* surplice, 173.
South aisle, building of, xxxvi, xl, xli, 240, 257, 288; burial in, 287, 355; contribution towards, 244; gravestone in, 351; great window in, 252; indentures concerning, 247; payment to king of quitrent for, 391; quitrent for, 240, 297, 327, 391; work on, 334, 335, 337.
Spaniard, burial of, 78, 129; slain, 78.
Spanish silk, 31.
Spear, 28.
Spekynges, *n. p.* spikings, spikes, 229.
Spellentes, Splentes, *n. p.* splints (armour), 38, 53.
Spere, *n.* sphere, 215.
Speynerd, *n.* Spaniard, 129.
Spits, 38, 54.
Splints, 38, 53.
Spones with postells, Sponnes of the postylles, *n. p.* apostle-spoons, 47, 356.
Sponys, *n. p.* spoons, 48, 49.
Spoons, 47–49, 51; apostle, 47, 356; censer filling, lxvii, 51.
Sporyour, *n.* spurrier, 10.
Sprigs, purchase of, 65, 66, 82, 84, etc.
Spruce, 39.
Sprynclys, *n. p.* sprinklers, 101.
Spurrier, 10.
Sqvyer, *n.* square, 373.
Ssvrwaye, *n.* survey, 57.
Stable, 29.
Staff torches. *See under* Torches.

Stage, Easter. *See under* Palm Sunday.
Stairs, making of, 66, 67; mending of, 65; standards for, 85.
Stalls, xxxii, 188, 201, 302, 359; butcher's, xxxii, 188.
Standards, latten, 32.
Standish, 37, 45.
Staples, purchase of, 64, 69, 70, 108, etc.
Stappis, *n. p.* steps, 65.
Stare, *n.* star ?, 47.
Stationer, payment to, 101, 226, etc.
Staves, red, 26.
Stayer, Steyer, *n.* stair, 66, 71.
Steeple, battlement of, 332; bells in, 54; contribution towards building of, xxxvi, 161, 259; cross-beams in, 275; cross on, 81; door to, 81, 103, 340, 362; hovel in, 103; iron work for, 103; ladder for, 185; pointing the, 412; rails to, 103; reparation of, xxxii, 102, 103, 110, 239, 337; stone for windows of, 252, 254; vane of, 133; windows in, 275, 309.
Sterope, *n.* stirrup, 224.
Sterres, *n. p.* stars, 26.
Steynynge, *n.* staining, 64.
Stock, latten, 28.
Stodes, *n. p.* studs, 48.
Stole, *n.* stool, 28.
Stoles, 30, 31.
Stolpes, Stulpis, *n. p.* short posts of wood, 167, 168.
Stolys, *n. p.* stools, privies, 292.
Stone, gutter of, 68; loads of, 64, 68; purchase of, 66; step of, 301.
Stools, 28, 53, 69; for rector of choir, xxiv, lxviii, 358.
Stoor, *n.* store, 132.
Stoppis, *n. p.* stoups, 301, 303.
Store, *n.* story, 302.
Storehouse. *See under* Church.
Stoup, latten, 28.
Stoups. *See* Holy water stoups.
Stovlles, *n. p.* stools, 53.
Strangers, burial of, 78, 129, 262, 299.
Strakis, *n. p.* streaks, 33.
Straw, purchase of, 89, 108.
Streamers, 31, 51.
Street, chamber over, 29.

Streets, mention of familiar, xxxvi. *See also* Place Index.
Strekyng, *n.* striking, 274.
Stresse, *n.* distraint, 370.
Strestells, *n. p.* trestles, 40.
Streyt, *n.* street, 45.
Stycke, *n.* stock, 163.
Subdeacon, 52, 53, 397.
Subsede, *n.* subsidy, 54.
Sudary, 27.
Suerte, *n.* surety, 18.
Suffragan, xxvi, 250; payment to, 277, 403.
Summoner, business of, xxvii; payment to, 349, 406, 410.
Sunday, tavern expenses on, xxxi, 234.
Super altars, 39; crosses on, 198.
Supper, bill of, 270.
Supploragiis, *n. p.* surplusages, 262.
Sureties, xxiv.
Surplices, lxix, 34, 36, 72, 81, etc.; after chapel guise, 36; children's mass, xxii; holland cloth for, xvi, 282; men's plain, 36; purchase of, xx, 321, etc.
Sustern, *n. p.* sisters, 5.
Svm, *pron.* some, 54.
Syyars, Sypres, *n.* Cypress wood, 37, 45.
Swordbearer, Mayor's, 15; payments, 90, 118, 155, 180, 204, 210, etc.
Swords, 45.

Tabernacle of the Virgin, painting of, xxxv, 142.
Tabernacles, 303; cloth of, 131, 230; curtain to, 304; freestone for, 225; making of base under, 219, 220; Russell's, 301, 302, 304; scaffold of, 220, 225; taking down of, 386.
Table, 40; Cypress, 37; folding, 40; font, lxviii, 273, 275; making of, 215; playing, 38.
Tablecloths, 34, 41.
Tablet of the Trinity, 33.
Tailor, 76, 94, 114, 115.
Tallow candles, 33, 81, 130, etc.
Talughe, *n.* tallow, 130.
Tape, silk, 378.
Tapestry, 40, 273.
Tapete, *n.* carpet, xcvi.
Tapis, *n.* tapestry, 273.

Glossarial Index. 443

Tarde, *n.*? 27.
Tasco, *n.*? 41.
Tavern, dinners at, xxxii; expenses at, 70, 83, 111, 117, 164, 186, 203, 230, 234, 285, 316, 361, 364; hiring of clerk at, xxxi, 343.
Tayntyrhokes, *n. p.* tenter hooks, 186.
Te Deum, 387.
Tenancy, terms of, 392.
Tenant, agreement with, 392; arrest of, 111 (*see also under* Rent); benevolence towards poor, 342; contract between landlord and, xxx; generosity of vestry to, xxiv; payment at entrance by, xlvii, 271, 286, 293, 311; water supply for, xxxiii.
Tenebræ candle, 91.
Tenebyll weddyns day, *n.* Teneble-Wednesday, xlvii, 397. "*Mercredy de la semayne peneuse, Mercredy saint.*" Palsgrave.
Tenement, lawsuit over, 344; profits of, 12; rebuilding of, 7; rents of, 75, 76, etc.; reparation of, 2, 7, 12, 103, 110, etc.; vacant, 86, 96, 116, 134, 175, 189, 200, 208, 213, 340, etc.
Tenne, *n.* tin? 38.
Tensyn satin, *n.*? 41.
Tent at church hallowing, xcvi.
Tenter-hooks, 186, 234.
Terogatores, *n. p.* Interrogatories, 279.
Testaments. *See* Wills.
Tester (bed-canopy), 40.
Tewke, 43. "Tewke to make purses of, *trelis*." Palsgrave, subst. f. 69 (from Halliwell).
Tewneabill, *adj.* tunable, 274.
Text, comparison of, lxxiii; handwriting and spelling, etc., of, xv; names mentioned in, lxxvi; obscurities in, xlvii; professions mentioned in, xliii; streets and places mentioned in, xxxvi. *See also* Place Index.
Thaduyse = the advice, 20, 21.
Thellder = the elder, 55.
Thorisday, *n.* Thursday, 65.
Thorns, purchase of, 202,
Thread, blue, 130; tawny, 311; white, 36; yellow, 311.
Throwȝe, *prep.* through, 141.

þerto, *adv.* thereto, 70.
Tile pins, purchase of, 65, 82, 84, 88.
Tilers, payment to, 65, 82, 102, 102, 120, 175, 213, etc.
Tiles, paving, 64, 67, 88; roof, 65, 73, 82, 84, etc.
Timber, carriage of, 64, 282, 332; choosing of, xlvi, 337; inspection of, 247; posts of, 90; purchase of, 64, 104, 108, 133, 337; sale of old, 171; sawing of, 133, 337, 338.
Timberman, 67, 70.
Tinacles, Toneclys, Tynacles, *n. p.* tunicles, 26, 53.
Tippet, sarcenet, 44.
Tithes, xlv, 394; forgotten, 19; gathering of, xix; making over of, xvii; payment of, xxix.
Tithyr, *adj.* other, 98.
Togider, *adv.* together, 1.
Tombs. *See* Graves.
Tongs, 37, 39.
Tonkes, *n. p.* tongs, 37.
Torches, lxviii, 44, 53, 54, 81; bearing of, xxxiii, 100, 186; bequest to guilds of, xxxiv, 20; chest for, 81, 255, 275, 358; garnishing of, 132; iron for, 343; purchase of, 305; staff, lxviii, 54, 361, 364; use at funerals of, xlix. *See also* Burials.
Torseng couer, Torsyng couer, *n.*? 40.
Toþer, *adj.* other, 66.
Towels, lx, lxviii, 27, 33–35, 41, 50, 54, 226, 273.
Trades, list of, mentioned, xliii.
Transept (cross aisle), 319, 320.
Transfiguration, feast of, 274.
Trap door, 155.
Traunsones, *n. p.* transoms, crossbars, 137.
Travelling, means of, xlv; expenses of, 269, etc. *See* Boat-hire, Horse-hire, etc.
Treangell, *n.* triangle, 48.
Trestles, 28, 37, 185, 306; for copes, 100.
Trestle head, purchase of, 85.
Trewlli, *adv.* truly, 56.
Trewlovis, *n. p.* truelove knots, or imitations of the herb or flower *Truelove*, 36. (See p. 22, 'Wright's Chaste Wife,' E.E.T.S., No. 12.)

Treyn bolles, *n. p.* treen bowls, wooden bowls, xcvi.
Treyn cop, *n.* treen cup; wooden cup, xcvi.
Treyvettes, *n. p.* trivets, 39.
Triangle, silver, 48, 50.
Trinity, curtain of, 339; tabernacle of, 301, 302, 304; tablet of, 33; window of, 252, 313.
Trinity Sunday, 65, 277.
Trivets, 39.
Trokell, *n.* truckle, 45.
Truckle-bed, 45.
Tubs, lxix, 250, 269.
Tunicles, 26, 27, 30, 31, 51, etc.; chest for, 303.
Turbot, 248.
Turner, 75, 84, 105, 114, etc.
Twelfth day, 172, 185.
Twyes, *adv.* twice, 121.

Undercaps, 43.
Underclerk, 6, 11; payment to, 295.
Upholsterer, 123.
Upper Vestry, 53, 317, 331; trestles in, 306.

Valante, *n.* valance, 39.
Valor Ecclesiasticus, xlv.
Vane, steeple, 103.
Vardours?, *n. p.* 37.
Vark, *n.* work, 252.
Vavtt, *n.* vault, 252.
Vayle, *n.* veil, 286.
Veil, Lenten, 68, 343; rood, 286.
Velvet, 45; black, 42, 44, 53; blue, 30, 53; crimson, 40, 47; green, 52, 55; purple, 33; red, 39, 51; russet, 55; white, 51, 55.
Vemens, *n. p.* women's, 252.
Venes gold, *n.* Venetian gold, 310.
Venison, cooking of, 248.
Verdytt, *n.* verdict, 111.
Versicle, 16.
Vestments, lxix, 26, 27, 30, 31, etc.; chests for, 81, 230, 303, 306; gift of, 20; hallowing of, xxvi, 153, 199, 273, 277; maker of, 80, 101, repair of, xxxii, 18, 80, 270, etc.
Vestry, xvii, xxiv; chest in, 81, 261, 382; coals for, xvii, 225, etc.; desk in, 233; door of, 81; fire-shovel for, 332; gutter of, 248; lower, 53; making of, 83; upper. *See* Upper Vestry.

Vestyarye, *n.* vestry, 69.
Vintner, 10.
Vnce, *n.* ounce, 310, etc.
Vnefferyde, *pp.* unfurred, 44.
Vyewers, *n. p.* viewers, 111.
Vynter, *n.* vintner, 10.
Vyse dore, *n.* door to winding stair? (Palsgrave, p. 158), 279, 281.

Wacchyng, Wecchyng, *n.* watching, 81, 83, 99.
Wainscot, 37, 40, 66, 82.
Wall, pinning of, 71.
Walling, 139.
Wardroppe, *n.* wardrobe, 55.
Water-baylyis, *n. p.* water-bailiffs, 197.
Waterbearer, 328.
Waterman, 112, 113, 123.
Waterpot, 215; pewter, 333.
Water tabyll, *n.* water-table; projection to throw off water, 257.
Wax, 132, 295; chest for, 278; sale of, 58.
Wax-chandler, xxxii, 58, 91, 101, 129, 132, 144, 157, 174, 188, 199, 233.
Wax reckoning, xxviii.
Wayneskote, *n.* wainscot, 66.
Wayyig, Weyng, *pres. pt.* weighing, 46–48, 51.
Weather, medieval, xlvi.
Weatherboard, 370.
Weaver, 46, 96, 109, 111, 112, etc.
Wedding. *See* Marriage.
Wederborde, *n.* weatherboard, 370.
Weket, *n.* wicket, 72.
Welbokette, *n.* well-bucket, 82.
Well, 29, 82, 152; bricked mouth of, 377; brink of, 152; chamber over, 29; rope for, 201, 210.
Welle, *n.* weal, 285.
Wendo, *n.* window, 37.
Weng, *pres. p.* weighing, 229.
Werkeday, *n.* workday, weekday, 17.
Wharfage, cost of, 120, 167.
Wheel, arms for, 152; bell. *See under* Bells.
Wheelbarrow, purchase of, 235, 269; sale of, 253.
Wheels, Catherine, 53.
Wherthurgh, *adv.* wherethrough, through which, 2.
Whight, *adj.* white, 20.
Whipcord, 131.

Whitsun, 62, 65, 242, 266; *fac.*, 322-323.
Wicker Mats, for priests, clerks, and children, xxii, xxiv, 81, 131 (?), 322, 358, 403.
Wicket, 72; garnets for, 72.
Wife of the Belle = wife at the Bell Inn, 83.
Wikirs, *n. p.* wickers, 81.
Wills, xiv, xxix; Bedham's, 16; book of, 285; calendar of, xxix; Cambridge's, 14; Causton's, 4; copying of, 178, 179; Gosselyn's, 13; Mongeham's, 19, 285; Motram's, 182, 197; Nasyng's, 9; Porth's, xviii, 353; Prewn's, 293; Ryvell's, 18; Weston's, 10; Wrytell's, 1.
Wind, damage by, 313.
Windows, xxxiii, 29, 200; bay, 308; of seven works of mercy, 19; making of, 67, 134, 199, etc.; mending of, 107, 138; mullion for, 64, 308; north, 256, 280; reeding of, 252; sacrament, lxx, 406; steeple, 252; west, 255; wood for, 64. *See also* Clerestory *under* Church *and* Trinity.
Wine, Claret, 403; Gascon, 316; Malmsey, 190, 351, 354, 362; purchase of, xxxi, 100, 131, 172, 185, 190, 197, 198, 219, 225, 230, 247, 250, 270, 316, 351, 387, 403, 407; Rhenish, 191; Sack, 403; Sweet, 100.
Wire, 63, 64, 255, 370; latten, 51.
Wodrove-garlondis, *n. p.* woodruff garlands, 81.
Woke, Wycke, *n.* week, 66, 67, 73, 409.
Woodos, *n. p.* woodwoses (at the handles of spoons instead of apostles); *satyrs*, 49.

Woolmonger, 125, 127, 143.
Workmen, drink for, 102.
Worsted, 52, 135, 255.
Woodruff, purchase of, 81, 163.
Wretyn, *pp.* written, 45.
Writing, payment for, 71, 74.
Wrttyng, *n.* writing, 71.
Wydewys, *n. p.* widows, 115.
Wydue, *n.* widow, 1.

Yard, 32, 54, etc.
Yat, *conj.* that, 60.
Yeaddes, *n. p.* yards, 54.
Yefftes, Yiftis, *n. p.* gifts, 94, 221.
Yei, *pron.* they, 285.
Yeħ, *n.* aisle, 252.
Yen, *conj.* than, 54.
Yeomen of Guard, burial of, 307.
Yer, *adv.* there, 60.
Yerbis, *n. p.* herbs, 269.
Yeres, *n.* herse; a wood or metal frame which originally supported the pall at funerals, xlvii, 303.
Yerns, *n. p.* irons, 251.
Yeryn, *n.* iron, 251.
Yes, *n. p.* eyes, 225.
Yeuyn, *n.* even, 266.
Yeve, *v. (imp.)* gave, 142.
Yeven, Yoven, *pp.* given, 100, 163.
Yle, *n.* aisle, 142.
Ymners, *n. p.* hymnals, 321.
Yower, *pron.* your, 357.
Yremonger, *n.* ironmonger, 3.
Ysope, *n.* hyssop, xcvi.
Yve, *n.* ivy, 130, 148.

ȝaf, *v. (imp.)* gave, 71.
ȝatis, *n. p.* gates, 72.
ȝelew, *adj.* yellow, 26, 27.
ȝer, *n.* year, 63, 140.
ȝerdis, *n. p.* yards, 64, 68.
ȝong, *adj.* young, 129, 139.

ADDITIONAL NOTE.

p. 22. *Andrew Evyngar.* Mr. E. S. Dewick has kindly pointed out that Andrew Evyngar, to whom one of the church properties was leased (p. 22), lies buried with his wife beneath the pavement of a church near the Tower. Mr. Dewick has most kindly forwarded to the editor the number of the *Transactions of the St. Paul's Ecclesiological Society* in which a facsimile of the brass above the grave is reproduced, with a description of the same by Mr. A. Oliver (vol. III. pt. I.). Read in connexion with the terms of the lease in our records, this description is of much interest. We have among our facsimiles the signature of Andrew Evyngar (p. 312).

Mr. Oliver's description is as follows:—

"In the Nave of All Hallows Barking, is the Brass of *Andrew Evyngar,* 1535, it is a Flemish example. It is inlaid in a slab, round which is an incised marginal inscription. The left side of the slab has been destroyed, together with the sentence, and also the evangelistic symbols, of which traces may be seen. The Brass consists of the figures of Evyngar, his wife, son, and daughters, standing under a canopy of pointed arches which spring from side shafts. In the centre on a throne or a chair is placed our Lady of Pity, supported underneath by a corbel. The background is richly diapered. The figures of the personages commemorated stand on a tessellated pavement, and are turned the one towards the other. Scrolls, bearing sentences, issue from the mouths of Evyngar and his wife, and address each of the personages above. That from the man bears the words, 'O filii (sic) dei miserere mei,' and that from the woman, 'O mater dei memento mei.' The figure of Evyngar is dressed in a long, loose gown, with deep full sleeves, under which is worn an under-garment; the feet are in broad-toed shoes. The wife's figure is in a long mantle with long gauntlet cuffs at the wrists; round the waist is a broad ornamented belt, with a large round buckle, from which hangs a rosary, which terminates in a tassel; a large plain hood is worn over the head. The son's dress is similar to that worn by his father, excepting the sleeves, which in this case fit close. The five daughters are placed at the side of the mother in three rows. The two in the front row wear a similar dress, excepting for the belt and rosary, which are omitted, their place being taken by a crossed girdle. Of the other figures only the head-dress, which is similar to that worn by the others, is seen. The arms of the Merchant Adventurers and the Salters Company are placed on either side at the top of the Brass. The Merchants' mark is borne on a shield placed between the feet of the principal figures. At the bottom of the Brass is all that remains of the inscription: '. . . of Andrewe Evyngar cytezen and salter of london and ellyn hys . . .' The words with which the inscription commenced, 'Of your charite pray for the soules,' were doubtless erased to save the Brass from total destruction as 'a monument of superstition.'"

CORRIGENDA AND ERRATA.

Page xxxvii, *erase* Tower gate, 381.
Page lxxxiv, *erase* 123 *after* William Grene.
Page 37, *for* iiij Ioyntes scells *read* iiij Ioyntes stolls
Page 123, *for* William Grene *read* William Prene.

PLACE INDEX.

Abbot's Inn, xxxviii, 238, 248, 250, 267, 321.
Abbot's Kitchen. See Glossarial Index.
Aldgate, lv, 5, 18, 76, 273, 274.
Allhallows, Lombard St., 94, 332.
Amesbury, 46.

Barnards Castle, 68, 247.
Barnet, 174.
Bear Inn, 46.
Bell Inn, 83.
Bell, Tower Hill, 54, 332, 344, 347, 350, 354, 383, 389, 391.
Bermondsey Abbey. See Abbot of Bermondsey, Glossarial Index.
Bewly, Beaulieu, or Bewley, Hants, 46.
Billingsgate, xxix, xxxi, xlvii, 1, 5, 36, 146, 241, 276, 283, 287, 347, 361, 366.
Bishop's Court, the, 393.
Bornewode, 259. ["Read Bernewode = Bernwood forest, round Brill (Cos. Bucks and Oxford). Perhaps, however, it may be Burwood Park, Chertsey."—W. H. Stevenson, M.A., Fellow St. John's Coll., Oxford.]
Boss Alley, 248, 380.
Botolph Lane, 28, 111, 114, 154, 167, 179, 191, 196, 204, 213, 351.
Bridgehouse, the, xliv, 95, 122, 153, 166, 178, 190, 202, 208.
Bridge St., 346.
Brittlesea, 294.
Bull, the, 161.

Calais, 128.
Cambridge's Quay, 68.
Cardinal's Hat Tavern, xxxii, 179.
Castle Tavern, Fish St., 230.
Ceswell, 232. "Chiswell Green, parish of Abbots Langley, Herts, or Sizewell, parish of Leiston, Suffolk?"—W. H. S.
Chantry Lands, 387.

Christchurch, Aldgate. See Prior of Christchurch, Glossarial Index.
Church Rents. See Glossarial Index.
Churchyards. See Glossarial Index.
City of London, xxxiv, 12, 15, 18, etc.
Clerkenwell, 111, 286.
Colchester, 183, 308.
Croydon, 248.

Dartford, 331.
Dartmouth, 195.

Eastcheap, xxxii, xliv, 4, 71, 84, 187, 200, 222, 328.
Ely Place, 191.
Essex, 332.

Fenchurch St., xxxiv, 247.
Fish St., 230.
Fleet St., 164.
Foster Lane, xxxiii, 13, 85, 96, 103, 107, 114, 139, 152, 166, 177, 286, 353, 370.
Freer. See Glossarial Index.
Fulham, xxvi, 296.

George Inn, Billingsgate, xxix, 36, 45.
"Gonn," the, 303.
Gracechurch St., 76, 83, 85, 373.
Gravesend, 271.
Greenwich, xvi, 269.
Guildhall, 178, 256, 326, 344.
Guernsey, 232.

House upon the Stair, 114, 119, 125, 135, 136.
Huntingdon's Tavern, 70.

Ipswich, 345, 346.

Kent, 366.
Kilburn, priory of. See Prioress of Kilburn, Glossarial Index.
King's Chapel. See Royal Chapel, Glossarial Index.

448 Place Index.

King's Exchequer, 373.
King's Head, 179.
Kingston, xxi, 256, 269.
Knights Hill, 137.

Lambeth, 178, 293.
Leadenhall, lvi, 256.
Lincoln's Inn, 326.
Little Alley, 72.
Lombard St., 94, 187.
Lombard's Place, 103, 111, 114, 125, 253.
London Bridge. *See* Glossarial Index.
London Bridge Chapel, 13.
Lothbury, 264.
Love Lane, xlii, 3, 16, 391, 407.
Luddesdon, Kent, 20.
Ludgate, lv, 20, 273.

Maidstone, 167, 244, 270.
Maldon, 183.
Marshalsea, 20.
Mayor's Court, 282.
Mepam, Kent, 20.
Mile End, 194.
Minories, 126, 134, 166, etc.
Moor, the, 328.

Newgate, 20.
Norwich, xlv, 350.

Old Royal, 346, 349.
Old Swan, 113.
Orford, 235.

Parsonage. *See* Glossarial Index.
Parson's house, 407.
Pewter Pot, the, 346.
Places, list of familiar, xxxvi.
Poor men's houses, 174.
Priests Alley, xviii, 132, 136, 184, 185, 269, *fac.*, 322, 332, 340, 343, 376, 413.
Priest's House, 120.
Pudding Lane, 79, 116, 130, etc.

Queenhithe, 103.

Ramsey, 46.
Rochester, xxix, 20, 406.
Romeland, lxxii, 223, 228, 326, 352, 353, 372, 382, 385, 389, 412.
Rose, the, 223, 227.
Royal Chapel. *See* Glossarial Index.

St. Andrew, Holborn, lxxv.
St. Andrew Hubbard, lxi, lxxiii, lxxiv, 4, 75, 105, 131, 305.
St. Andrews Undershaft, 346.
St. Anthonys, 274, 346, 349.
St. Bartholomews, 329.
St. Botolph's Church, 4, 16, 29, 95, 113, 123, 170, 182, 213, 223, 377.
St. Botolph's Lane, 16.
St. Botolph's Parish, 4, 75, 79, 96, 400.
St. Brides, 412.
St. Christopher's Parish, 76.
St. Clement's Church, Rochester, xxix, 20.
St. Dunstan's, 16, 84.
St. Gabriel, Fenchurch Street (gabryett), 174.
St. George's, Pudding Lane, 16, 79, 96, 116, 130, 146, 161, 171, 184, 196, 213, 355, 383.
St. Helen's Priory. *See* Glossarial Index.
St. John's, 293.
St. John's Head, 179, 203.
St. Katherine's, 361, 370, 376.
St. Leonard's, Eastcheap, xliv, 5, 75, 95.
St. Leonard's, Foster Lane, 13, 76.
St. Magnus Church, xxiii, xxvi, xxvii, xxxvi, xliv, 81, 83, 96, 122, 153, 178, 202, 230, 240, 406, 410.
St. Margaret Patens, lxxvi, 10, 271, 293.
St. Mary-at-Hill Church, vii–lxxvii, 1, 5, 9, 10, 14, 16, 19, *et passim*.
St. Mary-at-Hill Parish, xiii, xxv, lii, 1, 4, 9, 21, etc.
St. Mary Hill Lane, 308, 391.
St. Mary Woolnoth, lxxiii.
St. Michael, Cornhill, lxxvi.
St. Pancras, Soper Lane, 4.
St. Paul's, xxxiii–xxxv, 60, 182, 192, 197, 247, 296, 373, 382, 407, 411.
St. Saviour's, 292.
St. Stephen, Walbrook, lxxiii.
Salutation Tavern, 271, 274, 339, 411.
Schoolhouse. *See* Glossarial Index.
Ship Tavern, Billingsgate, xxxi, 276.
Shops, xxxii, 3, 5, 6, 9, 45, 83, 85, 112, 124, 134, 302, 328, 359.
Shoreham, 247.

Smart's Quay, 283, 287.
Somerset House, xxxix, liv, lx.
Soper Lane, 4.
Southwark, 228.
Southwold, 95.
Stalls, xxxii, 188, 201.
Stocks, the, 46, 95, 113, 125, 140, 155, 263, 328; Tavern at, 285.
Stratford, xvi, 229, 247.
Streets, list of familiar, xxxvi.
Suffolk, 333.
Sun Tavern, xxxii, xxxviii, 174, 234, 316, 333, 343, 344, 380.
Swan, Billingsgate, 241, 307.
Swan on the Hope, 3, 113.

Taverns (unnamed), 117, 164, 186, 364.
Temple, 191.

Thames St., 3, 4, 22, 113, 125.
Tho[w?]erdreth, 46. "Tywardreath priory, Cornwall." W.H.S.
Thussocks, Essex, 77.
Tower, xxxiv, 400.
Tower Hill, 18, 75, 112, 121, 135, 154, 167, 190, 202, 208, 213, 296, *fac.*, 322, 367, 370, 377.
Tower Wharf, 68.
Tylers Inn, xxxix, 332.

Waltham, 238.
Waltham Abbey. *See* Abbot of Waltham, Glossarial Index.
Walthamstow, 102.
Wapping, 253.
Westminster, xxxiii, xxxiv, 55, 179, 203, 247, 256, 266, 326, 332, 382.
Whitstable, 245.